DILEMMAS OF POLITICAL CHANGE IN MEXICO

DILEMMAS OF POLITICAL CHANGE IN MEXICO

Edited by
KEVIN J. MIDDLEBROOK

Institute of Latin American Studies
University of London

Center for U.S.–Mexican Studies
University of California, San Diego

First published 2004 by
Institute of Latin American Studies
31 Tavistock Square
London
WC1H 9HA

Copyright © 2004 Institute of Latin American Studies

British Library Cataloguing-in-Publication Data
A British Library CIP record is available.

ISBN 1-900039-45-1 *limp*

Typeset in Garamond by
Koinonia, Bury, Lancashire

Contents

List of Figures and Tables

Figures

Tables

Acknowledgments

This volume examines patterns of political change in contemporary Mexico. All but one of the contributors' essays were presented in draft form at an international conference hosted by the Center for U.S.–Mexican Studies in October 1999; the chapter by David Fitzgerald was added to the collection of essays in 2001. All the papers were subsequently revised and thoroughly updated prior to publication.

The October 1999 conference was one of three such events organized to celebrate the twentieth anniversary of the founding of the Center for U.S.–Mexican Studies at the University of California, San Diego. Each of these conferences focused upon a substantive area that has formed an important part of the Center's research agenda: Mexico–U.S. relations, economic and social policy issues in Mexico, and political change in Mexico. Financial support for these events came from the Center's core grant from the William and Flora Hewlett Foundation.

Debate at the conference was enriched by the participation of Jesús Blancornelas, Kathleen Bruhn, María Amparo Casar, Roxanna DiCarlo, Jorge I. Domínguez, Denise Dresser, Federico Estévez, Julio Labastida Martín del Campo, Soledad Loaeza, Luis Carlos Ugalde, Laurence Whitehead, and Roberto Zamarripa, all of whom graciously served as panel discussants or roundtable participants.

Collaborative books depend heavily upon the commitment and goodwill of the participating authors. Those qualities were especially important in bringing to conclusion a volume of this length. The contributors were exemplary in their dedication to this common effort.

Sandra del Castillo, the Center for U.S.–Mexican Studies' senior editor, had responsibility for the initial copy-editing of most of the essays included in this volume. John Maher, editor at the Institute of Latin American Studies, expertly oversaw final production of the book.

List of Acronyms

ABM	Asociación de Banqueros de México / Mexican Bankers' Association
AC	Alianza Cívica / Civic Alliance
ADESE	Asociación por la Democracia y el Sufragio Efectivo / Association for Democracy and Effective Suffrage
AFL–CIO	American Federation of Labor–Congress of Industrial Organizations
AFORE	Administrador de Fondos para el Retiro / Retirement Fund Administrator
AFSC	American Friends Service Committee
AIFI	Asociación de Intermediarios Financieros Internacionales / Association of International Financial Brokers
ALBAMEX	Alimentos Balanceados de México / Mexican Balanced Foodstuffs
ALCANO	Alianza Campesina del Noroeste / Northwestern Peasant Alliance
AMDH	Academia Mexicana de Derechos Humanos / Mexican Academy of Human Rights
AMIB	Asociación Mexicana de Intermediarios Bursátiles / Mexican Association of Stock Investment Firms
AMIS	Asociación Mexicana de Instituciones de Seguros / Mexican Association of Insurance Institutions
AMUCCS	Asociación Mexicana de Uniones de Crédito del Sector Social / Mexican Association of Social-Sector Credit Unions
ANADEGES	Autonomía, Descentralización y Gestión / Autonomy, Decentralization, and Management
ANAGSA	Aseguradora Nacional Agrícola y Ganadera / National Agricultural and Cattlemen's Insurance Company
ANECPC	Asociación Nacional de Empresas Comercializadoras de Productores del Campo / National Association of Trading Companies for Rural Producers
ANEPC	Acuerdo Nacional para la Elaboración de la Productividad y la Calidad / National Agreement for the Promotion of Productivity and Quality
ANIERM	Asociación Nacional de Importadores y Exportadores de la República Mexicana / National Association of Mexican Importers and Exporters
ANIPA	Asamblea Nacional Indígena Plural sobre Autonomía / Plural Indigenous National Assembly on Autonomy

ANIT   Asociación Nacional de Industriales de la Transformación / National
                Association of Industrial Manufacturers
ANT   Asamblea Nacional de Trabajadores / National Assembly of Workers
APN   agrupación política nacional / national political grouping
ARIC   asociación rural de interés colectivo / collective-interest rural association
ASERCA   Apoyos y Servicios a la Comercialización Agropecuaria / Supports and
                Services for Agricultural and Livestock Marketing
ASSA   Asociación Sindical de Sobrecargos de Aviación / Union of Air
                Stewards
AUDAS   Asociaciones Unidas para el Desarrollo y la Acción Social de Tijuana /
                United Associations for Development and Social Action in Tijuana
BANRURAL   Banco Nacional de Crédito Rural / National Rural Credit Bank
BECC   Border Environment Cooperation Commission
CAADES   Confederación de Asociaciones Agrícolas del Estado de Sinaloa /
                Confederation of Agricultural Associations of Sinaloa
CAM   Confederación Agrarista Mexicana / Mexican Agrarian Confederation
CANACINTRA   Cámara Nacional de la Industria de Transformación / National
                Chamber of Manufacturers
CAP   Congreso Agrario Permanente / Permanent Agrarian Congress
CBCs   Christian base communities
CCC   Central Campesina Cardenista / Cardenista Peasant Union
CCE   Consejo Coordinador Empresarial / Private Sector Coordinating
                Council
CCF   Consejo Coordinador Financiero / Financial Coordinating Council
CCI   Central Campesina Independiente / Independent Peasant
                Confederation
CD   Convergencia por la Democracia / Democratic Convergence
CDN   Colegio de Defensa Nacional / National Defense College
CDP   Comité de Defensa Popular / Committee for Popular Defense
CEMAI   Consejo Empresarial Mexicano para Asuntos Internacionales / Mexican
                Business Council for International Affairs
CEMEFI   Centro Mexicano de Filantropía / Mexican Center for Philanthropy
CEPAL   Comisión Económica para América Latina y el Caribe / Economic
                Commission for Latin America and the Caribbean
CEPCO   Coordinadora Estatal de Productores de Café de Oaxaca / Statewide
                Coordinating Network of Coffee Producers of Oaxaca
CFE   Comisión Federal Electoral / Federal Electoral Commission
CFO   Comité Fronterizo de Obreras / Border Committee of Women Workers
CGT   Confederación General de Trabajadores / General Confederation of
                Workers
CIOAC   Central Independiente de Obreros Agrícolas y Campesinos /
                Independent Confederation of Agricultural Workers and Peasants
CIPM   Coordinadora Intersindical Primero de Mayo / May 1 Inter-Union
                Coordinating Network

CJM	Coalition for Justice in the Maquiladoras
CMHN	Consejo Mexicano de Hombres de Negocios / Mexican Council of Businessmen
CNA	Consejo Nacional Agropecuario / National Agricultural and Livestock Council
CNBV	Comisión Nacional Bancaria y de Valores / National Banking and Securities Commission
CNC	Confederación Nacional Campesina / National Peasants' Confederation
CNDH	Comisión Nacional de Derechos Humanos / National Human Rights Commission
CNG	Confederación Nacional Ganadera / National Cattlemen's Confederation
CNI	Congreso Nacional Indígena / National Indigenous Congress
CNOC	Coordinadora Nacional de Organizaciones Cafetaleras / National Coordinating Network of Coffee Producers' Organizations
CNOP	Confederación Nacional de Organizaciones Populares / National Confederation of Popular Organizations
CNPA	Coordinadora Nacional Plan de Ayala / "Plan de Ayala" National Coordinating Network
CNPH	Confederación Nacional de Productores de Hortalizas / National Confederation of Horticultural Producers
CNPP	Confederación Nacional de la Pequeña Propiedad / National Confederation of Smallholders
CNPR	Confederación Nacional de Proprietarios Rurales / National Confederation of Rural Property Owners
CNSM	Comisión Nacional de los Salarios Mínimos / National Minimum Wage Commission
COAES	Confederación de Agricultores del Estado de Sonora / Confederation of Agricultural Producers of Sonora
COCD	Convergencia de Organizaciones Civiles por la Democracia / Convergence of Civic Organizations for Democracy
COCOPA	Comisión de Concordia y Pacificación / Commission on Concordance and Pacification
CODUC	Coalición de Organizaciones Democráticas Urbanas, Campesinas y Populares / Coalition of Urban, Peasant, and Popular Democratic Organizations
COECE	Coordinadora de Organizaciones Empresariales de Comercio Exterior / Foreign Trade Business Organizations' Coordinating Network
COFIPE	Código Federal de Instituciones y Procedimientos Electorales / Federal Code of Electoral Institutions and Procedures
COM	Casa del Obrero Mundial / House of the World Worker
COMCE	Consejo Mexicano de Comercio Exterior / Mexican Foreign Trade Council

CONACEX   Consejo Nacional de Comercio Exterior / National Council on Foreign
              Trade
CONACYT   Consejo Nacional de Ciencia y Tecnología / National Council of
              Science and Technology
CONAGO   Conferencia Nacional de Gobernadores / National Governors'
              Conference
CONAPO   Consejo Nacional de Población / National Population Council
CONASUPO   Compañía Nacional de Subsistencias Populares / National Basic Foods
              Company
CONCAMIN   Confederación Nacional de Cámaras Industriales / National
              Confederation of Chambers of Industry
CONCANACO   Confederación de Cámaras Nacionales de Comercio / Confederation of
              National Chambers of Commerce
CONSAR   Comisión Nacional del Sistema de Ahorro para el Retiro / National
              Commission on Retirement Savings
CONSUCC   Coordinadora Nacional de Sociedades y Uniones de Campesinos y
              Colonos / National Coordinating Network of Societies and Unions of
              Peasants and Settlers
COPARMEX   Confederación Patronal de la República Mexicana / Mexican
              Employers' Confederation
COR   Confederación Obrera Revolucionaria / Revolutionary Labor
              Confederation
CPSU   Communist Party of the Soviet Union
CRICP   Comisión de Regimen Interno y Concertación Política / Commission
              on Agenda Control and Political Concertation
CROC   Confederación Revolucionaria de Obreros y Campesinos /
              Revolutionary Confederation of Workers and Peasants
CROM   Confederación Regional Obrera Mexicana / Mexican Regional Labor
              Confederation
CT   Congreso del Trabajo / Labor Congress
CTC   Citizens' Trade Campaign
CTM   Confederación de Trabajadores de México / Confederation of Mexican
              Workers
CUT   Central Única de Trabajadores / Unitary Workers' Confederation
CWA   Communications Workers of America
DICONSA   Distribuidora CONASUPO, S.A. / CONASUPO Distributors, Inc.
DS   Democracia Social / Social Democracy
ECLAC   Economic Commission for Latin America and the Caribbean
ENOC   Encuentro Nacional de Organizaciones Civiles / National Encounter of
              Civic Organizations
ERP   Ejército Revolucionario Popular / Popular Revolutionary Army
ESG   Escuela Superior de Guerra / Advanced War College
EZLN   Ejército Zapatista de Liberación Nacional / Zapatista Army of National
              Liberation

FAM	Foro de Apoyo Mutuo / Forum for Mutual Support
FAT	Frente Auténtico del Trabajo / Authentic Labor Front
FDN	Frente Democrático Nacional / National Democratic Front
FENASIB	Federación Nacional de Sindicatos Bancarios / National Federation of Bank Unions
FEPADE	Fiscal Especializado para la Atención de Delitos Electorales / Special Prosecutor for Electoral Crimes
FESEBES	Federación de Sindicatos de Empresas de Bienes y Servicios / Federation of Unions of Goods and Services Enterprises
FFM	Fondo de Fomento Municipal / Municipal Development Fund
FIOB	Frente Indígena Oaxaqueño Binacional / Binational Indigenous Oaxacan Front
FISM	Fondo de Infraestructura Social Municipal / Municipal Social Infrastructure Fund
FLOC	Farm Labor Organizing Committee
FOBAPROA	Fondo Bancario de Protección al Ahorro / Bank Savings Protection Fund
FOCIV	Frente de Organizaciones Civiles / Civic Organizations Front
FOCO	Foro de Organizaciones Civiles de Oaxaca / Oaxaca Forum of Civic Organizations
FORTAMUN	Fondo de Fortalecimiento Municipal / Municipal Strengthening Fund
FPPM	Federación de Partidos del Pueblo Mexicano / Federation of Parties of the Mexican People
FSTSE	Federación de Sindicatos de Trabajadores al Servicio del Estado / Federation of Public Service Workers' Unions
FUNTEC	Fundación para la Innovación y Transferencia de Tecnología para las Pequeñas y Medianas Empresas / Foundation for Innovation and Technology Transfer for Small and Midsize Firms
FZLN	Frente Zapatista de Liberación Nacional / Zapatista Front for National Liberation
GATT	General Agreement on Tariffs and Trade
GDP	gross domestic product
HTA	hometown association
IAF	Inter-American Foundation
IFE	Instituto Federal Electoral / Federal Electoral Institute
ILO	International Labour Office
IMSS	Instituto Mexicano del Seguro Social / Mexican Social Security Institute
INEGI	Instituto Nacional de Estadística, Geografía e Informática / National Institute for Statistics, Geography, and Informatics
INI	Instituto Nacional Indigenista / National Indigenous Institute
INMECAFE	Instituto Mexicano del Café / Mexican Coffee Institute
IPAB	Instituto para la Protección del Ahorro Bancario / Bank Savings Protection Institute

IPN	Instituto Politécnico Nacional / National Polytechnic Institute
ISI	import-substitution industrialization
ISSSTE	Instituto de Seguridad y Servicios Sociales de los Trabajadores del Estado / Social Security Institute for State Workers
LFOPPE	Ley Federal de Organizaciones Políticas y Procesos Electorales / Federal Law on Political Organizations and Electoral Processes
MALDEF	Mexican American Legal Defense and Educational Fund
MNCP	Movimiento Nacional de los Cuatrocientos Pueblos / National Movement of the Four Hundred Peoples
MST	Movimiento Social de los Trabajadores / Workers' Social Movement
NADBank	North American Development Bank
NAFTA	North American Free Trade Agreement
NED	National Endowment for Democracy
NGOs	nongovernmental organizations
OECD	Organisation for Economic Co-operation and Development
OIDHO	Organización India de Derechos Humanos en Oaxaca / Indian Organization for Human Rights in Oaxaca
OMD	Organization of Mexicans for Democracy
PAN	Partido Acción Nacional / National Action Party
PARM	Partido Auténtico de la Revolución Mexicana / Authentic Party of the Mexican Revolution
PAS	Partido Alianza Social / Social Alliance Party
PC	Partido Cardenista / Cardenista Party
PCD	Partido del Centro Democrático / Party of the Democratic Center
PCM	Partido Comunista Mexicano / Mexican Communist Party
PCME	Programa para las Comunidades Mexicanas en el Exterior / Program for Mexican Communities Abroad
PDC	Partido Demócrata Cristiano / Christian Democratic Party
PDM	Partido Demócrata Mexicano / Mexican Democratic Party
PECE	Pacto para la Estabilidad, la Competitividad y el Empleo / Pact for Stability, Competitiveness, and Employment
PEM	Partido Ecologista de México / Ecologist Party of Mexico
PEMEX	Petróleos Mexicanos / Mexican Petroleum Company
PFCRN	Partido del Frente Cardenista de Reconstrucción Nacional / Party of the Cardenista Front for National Reconstruction
PFP	Partido Fuerza Popular / Popular Force Party
PIPSA	Productora e Importadora de Papel, S.A. / Newsprint Producer and Importer, Inc.
PIRE	Programa Inmediato de Reordenación Económica / Immediate Program for Economic Reordering
PLM	Partido Liberal Mexicano / Mexican Liberal Party
PMS	Partido Mexicano Socialista / Mexican Socialist Party
PMT	Partido Mexicano de los Trabajadores / Mexican Workers' Party
PNR	Partido Nacional Revolucionario / Revolutionary National Party

POCM	Partido Obrero Campesino Mexicano / Mexican Worker-Peasant Party
PP	Partido Popular / Popular Party
PPS	Partido Popular Socialista / Socialist Popular Party
PRD	Partido de la Revolución Democrática / Party of the Democratic Revolution
PRI	Partido Revolucionario Institucional / Institutional Revolutionary Party
PRM	Partido de la Revolución Mexicana / Party of the Mexican Revolution
PROCAMPO	Programa de Apoyos Directos al Campo / Direct-Support Program for the Farm Sector
PROCEDE	Programa de Certificación de Derechos Ejidales y Titulación de Solares Urbanos / Program for the Certification of Ejidal Rights and the Titling of Urban Plots
PRODUSSEP	Promoción de Servicios de Salud y Educación Popular / Promoting Health Care and Popular Education
PROGRESA	Programa de Educación, Salud y Alimentación / Program for Education, Health, and Nutrition
PRONASOL	Programa Nacional de Solidaridad / National Solidarity Program
PRS	Partido de la Revolución Socialista / Party of the Socialist Revolution
PRT	Partido Revolucionario de los Trabajadores / Revolutionary Workers' Party
PSD	Partido Social Demócrata / Social Democratic Party
PSE	Pacto de Solidaridad Económica / Economic Solidarity Pact
PSN	Partido de la Sociedad Nacionalista / Party of the Nationalist Society
PST	Partido Socialista de los Trabajadores / Socialist Workers' Party
PSUM	Partido Socialista Unificado de México / Mexican Unified Socialist Party
PT	Partido del Trabajo / Labor Party
PVEM	Partido Verde Ecologista de México / Mexican Ecological Green Party
Red MOCAF	Red Mexicana de Organizaciones Campesinas Forestales / Mexican Network of Peasant Organizations in Forestry
RMALC	Red Mexicana de Acción frente al Libre Comercio / Mexican Action Network Against Free Trade
ROCVER	Red de Organizaciones Civiles de Veracruz / Veracruz Network of Civic Organizations
SAGAR	Secretaría de Agricultura, Ganadería y Desarrollo Rural / Ministry of Agriculture, Livestock, and Rural Development
SAR	Sistema de Ahorro para el Retiro / Retirement Savings System
SARH	Secretaría de Agricultura y Recursos Hidráulicos / Ministry of Agriculture and Water Resources
SECOFI	Secretaría de Comercio y Fomento Industrial / Ministry of Commerce and Industrial Development
SEDESOL	Secretaría de Desarrollo Social / Ministry of Social Development
SER	Servicios al Pueblo Mixe / Services to the Mixe People

SHCP	Secretaría de Hacienda y Crédito Público / Ministry of Finance and Public Credit
SITUAM	Sindicato Independiente de Trabajadores de la Universidad Autónoma Metropolitana / Independent Union of Metropolitan Autonomous University Workers
SME	Sindicato Mexicano de Electricistas / Mexican Electricians' Union
SNTE	Sindicato Nacional de Trabajadores de la Educación / National Education Workers' Union
SNTMMSRM	Sindicato Nacional de Trabajadores Mineros, Metalúrgicos y Similares de la República Mexicana / Mexican Mining and Metalworkers' Union
SNTSS	Sindicato Nacional de Trabajadores del Seguro Social / National Union of Social Security Workers
SPP	Secretaría de Programación y Presupuesto / Ministry of Programming and Budget
SRA	Secretaría de la Reforma Agraria / Ministry of Agrarian Reform
SRE	Secretaría de Relaciones Exteriores / Ministry of Foreign Relations
STFRM	Sindicato de Trabajadores Ferrocarrileros de la República Mexicana / Mexican Railroad Workers' Union
STIMAHCS	Sindicato de Trabajadores de la Industria Metálica, Acero, Hierro, Conexos y Similares / Union of Metal, Steel, and Iron Industry Workers
STPRM	Sindicato de Trabajadores Petroleros de la República Mexicana / Mexican Petroleum Workers' Union
STPS	Secretaría del Trabajo y Previsión Social / Ministry of Labor and Social Welfare
STRM	Sindicato de Telefonistas de la República Mexicana / Mexican Telephone Workers' Union
SUTERM	Sindicato Único de Trabajadores Electricistas de la República Mexicana / General Union of Mexican Electrical Workers
TABAMEX	Tabacos Mexicanos / Mexican Tobacco
TELMEX	Teléfonos de México / Mexican Telephone Company
TEPJF	Tribunal Electoral del Poder Judicial de la Federación / Electoral Tribunal of the Federal Judicial Branch
TFE	Tribunal Federal Electoral / Federal Electoral Tribunal
UAM	Universidad Autónoma Metropolitana / Metropolitan Autonomous University
UAW	United Auto Workers
UCD	Unión Campesina Democrática / Democratic Peasant Union
UCIZONI	Unión de Comunidades Indígenas de la Zona Norte del Istmo / Union of Indigenous Communities of the Northern Isthmus
UE	United Electrical, Radio, and Machine Workers of America
UFW	United Farm Workers
UGOCM	Unión General de Obreros y Campesinos de México / General Union of Mexican Workers and Peasants

UGOCP	Unión General Obrera, Campesina y Popular / General Worker-Peasant-Popular Union
UNAM	Universidad Nacional Autónoma de México / National Autonomous University of Mexico
UNORCA	Unión Nacional de Organizaciones Regionales Campesinas Autónomas / National Union of Autonomous Regional Peasant Organizations
UNPH	Unión Nacional de Productores de Hortalizas / National Union of Horticultural Producers
UNT	Unión Nacional de Trabajadores / National Union of Workers
UNTA	Unión Nacional de Trabajadores Agrícolas / National Farm Workers' Union
UOI	Unidad Obrera Independiente / Independent Worker Unit
USAID	United States Agency for International Development
VERTEBRA	Vertebración Social / Social Linkage
WTO	World Trade Organization

I

Mexico's Democratic Transitions: Dynamics and Prospects

Kevin J. Middlebrook

Vicente Fox Quesada's victory in the July 2000 presidential election marked a historic turning point in Mexico's lengthy process of democratic regime change. From the late 1970s through the mid-1990s, a series of reforms gradually liberalized the country's party and electoral systems. Opposition forces grew considerably in strength over this period, and opposition political parties and nongovernmental organizations together gradually succeeded in establishing more transparent electoral procedures. As a consequence of both institutional changes in the electoral arena and the erosion of the long-ruling Institutional Revolutionary Party's (PRI) bases of mass support, the PRI slowly but continuously lost ground to rivals on both the left and right.[1] In 1989, for example, federal authorities formally recognized an opposition victory in a gubernatorial race (Baja California), and in the 1997 midterm elections the PRI lost its majority in the federal Chamber of Deputies and its control over the government of the Federal District.

In the months preceding the year 2000 general elections, the Federal Electoral Institute (IFE) sought to build public confidence in the electoral process and establish the conditions for equitable competition by, among other measures, ensuring transparency in balloting procedures and constraining government agencies' use of public resources to benefit particular parties and candidates. Nevertheless, until Fox won the presidency, there remained some doubt as to whether changes such as these had been sufficient to permit an opposition party or coalition to break the PRI's enduring control over the federal executive, an event that many observers regarded as the crucial test of electoral democratization in Mexico.[2]

The author gratefully acknowledges very helpful comments and suggestions on an earlier version of this essay from Helga Baitenmann, Jorge I. Domínguez, and Horacio Mackinlay.

1 Mexico's "official" party was founded in 1929 as the Revolutionary National Party (PNR), with the goal of curtailing factional rivalries and political instability by uniting in a single body all "revolutionary" forces emerging from the country's 1910–1920 social revolution. It was restructured as the Party of the Mexican Revolution (PRM) in 1938 on the basis of labor, peasant, military, and "popular" sectors. The military sector was formally eliminated in 1940 and became part of the popular sector after the latter was reorganized in 1943. Further internal reforms were effected in 1946, and the party was renamed the Institutional Revolutionary Party (PRI).

2 In fact, until the late 1990s, few observers contemplated national-level electoral democrati-

The outcome in July 2000 did not make the struggle for electoral democracy a subject of merely historical interest; at state and municipal levels in particular, much remains to be done to ensure that conditions exist for free and fair electoral competition.[3] Nonetheless, the overall focus of debate concerning political change in Mexico quickly shifted to the obstacles to longer-term democratic consolidation. In this sense, Fox's victory brought the country into the mainstream of Latin American democratization processes. The legacies of postrevolutionary authoritarian rule certainly pose special challenges in such areas as the democratic reordering of state-society relations. Yet, in the wake of the year 2000 elections, the reform agenda in Mexico parallels that in many other post-transition countries, where the fundamental goal is to make real the formal conditions of political democracy.[4]

The contributors to this book analyze both the main factors underlying Mexico's long march to electoral democracy and the principal challenges involved in establishing democratic norms and practices in non-electoral arenas. In considering Mexico's political transformation it is most appropriate, therefore, to refer to

---

zation in Mexico. For example, even though their assessment of Mexico's "alternative political futures" came shortly after the near-defeat of the PRI in the 1988 presidential election, Wayne A. Cornelius, Judith Gentleman, and Peter H. Smith (1989: 37–45) foresaw only limited "Indian Congress Party model" electoral liberalization (one of four possible scenarios, including political closure, the "modernization of authoritarianism" via the successful reform of the state-supported ruling party, and "democratization from below" in which massive protest demonstrations and civil disobedience might topple the incumbent regime). In this scenario, opposition parties might win greater representation at state and local levels, but the PRI would retain national power.

Similarly, even so perceptive an analyst as Laurence Whitehead (1994: 340–44) found it difficult to envision a "transition by stealth" in which the gradual liberalization of electoral conditions resulted in a democratic transition. He anticipated that some "strongly destabilizing interregnum" would accompany eventual democratic regime change. And as late as 1995, Ann L. Craig and Wayne A. Cornelius (1995: 250–51) concluded that "competitive, North American-style democracy can no longer be considered the virtually inevitable consequence of the weakening of the PRI-government apparatus ..."

3 As in many other countries, the debate over campaign finance reform continues in Mexico. For examples of continued state-level electoral problems, see Bizberg 2003: 171.

4 There is considerable consensus on the minimum criteria for political democracy, although specific organizational arrangements and political practices vary widely from one country to another. The essential requirements include the guarantee of (usually constitutionally defined) individual rights, including freedoms of expression and association and especially protection against arbitrary state action; frequently scheduled, fairly conducted elections in which all citizens are fully free to participate (universal suffrage) in the selection of representatives who will exercise public authority; and institutionalized procedures to ensure that citizens can through the rule of law hold rulers accountable for their public actions. These requirements are mutually reinforcing. See Dahl 1971: 2–9, and 1982: 10–11; O'Donnell and Schmitter 1986: 7–11; Schmitter and Karl 1991; and Rueschemeyer, Stephens, and Stephens 1992: 10, 43–44. For thoughtful reflections on the limitations of definitions such as this, see Whitehead 2002: 11–26.

democratic transitions – multiple processes that, even though they often intersect and sometimes overlap in significant ways, move at varying speeds and at times respond to different logics. It is also important to emphasize that, although the year 2000 presidential election was a major point of inflection in a longer-term process of democratic regime change, the outcome on July 2, 2000 marked neither the beginning of political democratization in Mexico (important shifts in state-society relations and major institutional reforms preceded it and, indeed, made it possible) nor the end of transitions occurring in both electoral and non-electoral areas.[5] Fox's victory (and the PRI's defeat) may have culminated a process of electoral democratization at the national level, but these events only initiated or accelerated transitions in other spheres.[6]

The essays in this volume address these issues from several different perspectives. The opening chapters analyze the main elements of Mexico's electoral transition, including evolution in the party system as "official" party hegemony gradually gave way to increasingly vigorous multiparty competition, the emergence of autonomous federal electoral institutions, and the different factors motivating voters' decisions at the polls. The contributions in the second section examine the parameters of a new institutional order, including shifts in executive-legislative relations, challenges to judicial performance and the effective rule of law, and the changing character of federal arrangements. In turn, the essays in the third section assess the changes that have occurred as "pillars of the old regime" – trade unions, rural producers' organizations, the business sector, the armed forces, and the mass media – responded to economic and political changes during the 1990s. Finally, the chapters in the concluding section highlight unresolved challenges of rights and representation (the role of civil society, the rights of Mexico's indigenous peoples,

---

5 There is less consensus on this last point than one might expect. For example, Caroline C. Beer (2002: 150) describes Fox's election and peaceful assumption of power as "the final act of Mexico's prolonged transition to democracy."

6 In the enthusiasm generated by Fox's election, this point has sometimes been overlooked. It is especially worth underlining in the Mexican context because postrevolutionary authoritarian rule was highly institutionalized and long enjoyed substantial popular support.

This is the main analytic reason to discuss Mexico's democratic transitions in the plural. However, there are also strong pragmatic reasons to do so given the possibility that the PRI might one day regain the presidency by democratic means. The fact that, even in the wake of its defeat in the 2000 presidential election, the PRI remained the country's most important party in terms of its overall congressional representation and its control of public offices at the state and municipal levels, and the fact that it was still highly competitive in electoral terms, were important political realities. Even more, the possibility that the PRI might eventually retake the highest ground in Mexican politics may influence the expectations of key actors (including, for example, organized labor, big business, and the armed forces) in ways that significantly shape the parameters of broader democratization processes.

Of course, if Mexico is to meet Huntington's (1991: 267–68) strict "two turnovers" test for the consolidation of electoral democracy, then the PRI *must* regain the presidency at some point – and lose it again thereafter.

the political and social impact of cross-border civil society coalitions, and the representation of Mexicans living abroad) that will shape the future character of Mexican democracy.[7]

This introductory chapter establishes the context for the essays that follow by examining three overarching questions. First, what factors led to Mexico's slow but successful transition to electoral democracy? In particular, what contributions did opposition political parties, a more vibrant civil society and the mass media, domestic political and economic crises, and international actors make to this process? Second, given that the country's democratic transition is taking place within the established constitutional order, what challenges of political re-institutionalization are involved in consolidating a more democratic regime? Third, what additional issues of rights and representation face twenty-first-century Mexico? In addressing these issues, this essay engages in a semi-structured dialogue with the broader literature on democratization in Latin America. The goal is to focus a consideration of the Mexican case around topics that facilitate a comparison with other countries and sharpen our understanding of important causal relationships.

The Mexican Road to (Electoral) Democracy

Since the beginning of the wave of democratic political transitions that swept Latin America after the late 1970s, scholars have highlighted the special importance of elections as a means of transiting from authoritarian rule to more democratic forms of governance.[8] There is broad consensus that merely holding elections is insufficient to constitute democracy, but frequently scheduled elections in which all citizens are free to participate (universal suffrage) in the selection of representatives who will exercise public authority is an elemental requirement of it. Elections constitute an important focal point for collective political organization and civic mobilization. They are also a principal means through which citizens can hold rulers accountable for their public actions.

In the Mexican case, the issue was not whether or when elections would be held, but rather the conditions governing electoral competition. Regularly scheduled elections were a central feature of Mexico's highly institutionalized postrevolutionary authoritarian regime. They legitimated the regime by demonstrating a symbolic commitment to popular sovereignty, provided a means of periodically mobilizing public support for government activities and the party system, encouraged elite rotation in office, and offered citizens a limited opportunity to express their demands. In fact, as José Antonio Crespo argues in his chapter in this volume,

---

7 As extensive as this range of topics is, this volume does not examine several important political subjects. For instance, it proved impossible to secure an essay examining the impact of illegal drug trafficking on Mexican politics. Nor does this collection include an analysis of the political influence of the Roman Catholic Church and other religious groups.

8 See, for example, Guillermo O'Donnell and Philippe C. Schmitter's discussion of "founding elections" (1986: 57–64).

elections held under conditions in which the "party of the revolution" predictably won were an essential element in preserving hegemonic party rule.[9] So long as they occurred on schedule and at least one legally registered opposition party participated in them, elections preserved the illusion of political competition and thus helped avoid the domestic and international criticism that would have arisen had the regime truly become a single-party system.[10]

The electoral reforms enacted between 1946 and 1977 obeyed this systemic logic. Because it was essential to sustain opposition parties' participation in an electoral game almost completely dominated by the "official" party, different presidential administrations implemented measures to promote competition and ensure opposition parties minimum representation in the federal Chamber of Deputies. It was this dynamic that accounted for what Crespo (this volume) calls one of the principal paradoxes of the federal electoral legislation adopted during this period: the most progressive reforms occurred when opposition forces were weakest, not when they enjoyed sufficient strength to lobby effectively for electoral liberalization. The initial phases of political opening in Mexico were thus largely elite-driven and controlled from above; the governing political elite reacted to changing sociopolitical conditions, but the regime's high level of institutionalization and its still broad bases of organized mass support insulated it from serious challenge.

In subsequent years, however, the character of the transition process changed markedly. The electoral legislation adopted in 1987, 1990, and 1993 was more regressive in content because the ruling political elite sought to preserve the conditions for PRI dominance (particularly its majority in the federal Chamber of Deputies) against the rising tide of opposition forces.[11] Those forces were still not

---

9 José Antonio Crespo (this volume) and Silvia Gómez Tagle (this volume) broadly agree upon the conditions that sustained Mexico's hegemonic-party system: the federal executive could, via the requirements for party registration, determine how many and which parties competed electorally; government resources were used to sustain and promote the "official" party; the president and the "official" party controlled the institutions that organized elections and certified their results; the "official" party held a majority of seats in the Congress; and strong discipline prevailed within the ruling party. As Jeffrey A. Weldon (this volume) argues, these factors were also crucial to preserving the federal executive's dominance in Mexico's highly presidential system.

10 The PRI faced precisely this prospect in 1976 when the Authentic Party of the Mexican Revolution (PARM) and the Socialist Popular Party (PPS) once again backed the PRI's presidential nominee and internal divisions over the merits of participating in a one-sided electoral contest prevented the National Action Party (PAN) from nominating a candidate. As a result, the PRI faced no registered opposition candidate in the presidential race. (Two unregistered parties, the Mexican Communist Party [PCM] and the Partido Femenino Mexicano [Mexican Feminine Party], fielded "symbolic" candidates in 1976. See Paoli 1978: 63, 68 n1).

11 For example, the federal electoral law enacted in 1987 included a so-called governability clause, which allocated sufficient proportional-representation seats to the largest party (the PRI) to guarantee it an absolute majority in the federal Chamber of Deputies. For details on the 1987, 1990, and 1993 electoral laws, see Crespo (this volume).

strong enough to deprive the governing elite of its control over the pace of political liberalization, but the balance of forces between the regime and the opposition had begun to shift substantially. It tilted even more strongly against the regime during the 1994–1996 period.[12] Indeed, the electoral reform implemented in 1996 marked a real turning point by establishing the conditions for much more transparent electoral processes and the opposition's accelerating political advances.

It was in this context that the autonomy of electoral institutions assumed crucial importance. Government control over the institutions responsible for organizing elections and certifying their results had been a core feature of Mexican electoral politics since the founding of an "official" party in 1929; even the landmark 1977 political reform had not altered this feature of hegemonic-party rule.[13] Yet as Silvia Gómez Tagle observes in her chapter in this book, these institutions were "the indispensable link between democratic rules and democracy in practice." Ensuring the trustworthiness of key electoral institutions was, therefore, a principal challenge in ensuring the transparency and legitimacy of electoral processes – and thus laying the bases for a gradual transition from a hegemonic-party system to truly competitive national politics.

Between 1990 and 1996, the administrations of Carlos Salinas de Gortari (1988–1994) and Ernesto Zedillo Ponce de León (1994–2000) were compelled to enact a series of reforms that gradually gave institutional coherence and autonomy to federal electoral bodies. These measures established the Federal Electoral Institute (IFE) as a permanent organization with its own budget and staff (1990); introduced citizen representatives to the IFE's General Council (1994); and, finally, freed the IFE from direct control by the Ministry of the Interior (Secretaría de Gobernación) by granting it full legal autonomy (1996). At the same time, these laws created and slowly strengthened special institutions responsible for resolving post-electoral disputes.[14] The main challenge facing IFE officials after 1996 was to demonstrate

12 Although the overall course of political change during the 1994–1996 period is well known (and several contributors to this volume comment upon the impact that developments during these years had on political opening in Mexico), there is as yet no detailed study of this crucial period that is based upon interviews with leading figures in the administrations of Carlos Salinas de Gortari (1988–1994) and Ernesto Zedillo Ponce de León (1994–2000).

13 The 1946 federal election law created the Federal Electoral Commission under the jurisdiction of the Ministry of the Interior (Secretaría de Gobernación). However, state governments continued to organize the actual voting process until 1969. The author is grateful to Juan Molinar Horcasitas for clarifying this point.

14 The latest of these institutions, the Electoral Tribunal of the Federal Judicial Branch (TEPJF), was established in 1996.

Gómez Tagle (this volume) traces the evolution of federal electoral institutions in detail. She also provides a summary of legal reforms enacted during the 1990s concerning such matters as funding for political parties and election campaigns. See Eisenstadt 2003: 36–39 on post-electoral conflict and bargaining in the late 1980s and early 1990s.

Gómez Tagle argues that a functioning democracy requires laws and institutions that ensure electoral transparency, the presence of competitive and autonomous political parties,

that their juridical autonomy was meaningful in practice. This they largely did through their competent organization and oversight of the 1997 midterm elections, in which opposition parties for the first time displaced the PRI as the majority bloc in the federal Chamber of Deputies and the Party of the Democratic Revolution (PRD) won control of the Federal District government.[15]

Most analysts would concur that institutional reform was the main battleground on which the struggle for electoral democracy was fought in Mexico during the late 1980s and the 1990s. There is probably less consensus, however, regarding the factors that brought about these changes. Certainly it was not a question of mass actors such as organized labor mobilizing against incumbent elites to bring about democratic regime change "from below." Indeed, viewed in comparative perspective, one of the most striking aspects of the Mexican transition is how durable support from the PRI's traditional constituencies proved to be.[16]

Nor can one easily explain accelerating political opening during this period as a simple consequence of the far-reaching program of market-oriented reforms undertaken by the administrations of Miguel de la Madrid Hurtado (1982–1988) and Carlos Salinas de Gortari. Economic liberalization had multiple, sometimes contradictory, and perhaps still poorly understood political consequences – some of which reinforced rather than undermined authoritarian rule.[17] The unintended consequences of economic reform included new divisions within the political elite (some of which strengthened the party-based political opposition) and increased pluralism in state-society relations as the state's role in economic affairs declined sharply. However, the process of economic restructuring also undermined social structures and organizational networks that had sustained pro-democracy mobilizations in earlier periods. More generally, the main thrust of democratic struggles during the 1990s – the efforts by opposition parties and nongovernmental organizations to ensure transparent, fair elections – proceeded quite autonomously from developments in the economic realm. If anything, it was *resistance* to structural adjustment policies and the market-oriented reform project and the new economic model's *failures* that contributed to the unraveling of Mexico's durable authoritarian regime.

A balanced account of Mexico's transition to electoral democracy must include attention to the growing strength and strategic orientation of opposition political

---

and citizens' confidence in elections as a means of achieving power. For statistical evidence that Mexican citizens' growing confidence in the electoral system during the 1990s had a positive impact upon support for the PAN and the Party of the Democratic Revolution (PRD), and that lack of credibility in the electoral process gradually became less important as a cause of abstention, see the essay by Jorge Buendía in this volume (table 4.3).

15 See Gómez Tagle (this volume) for a discussion of the political controversies surrounding the administrative reorganization of the IFE after 1997.

16 See Middlebrook 1997. The impact of financial crisis and prolonged economic stagnation upon the PRI's traditional mass constituencies is examined below.

17 This discussion draws upon Middlebrook and Zepeda 2003a.

parties, the new dynamics emanating from civil society, important shifts in the political role of the mass media, and the catalytic effects over time of political and economic crises. Although they hold considerable potential to influence Mexican politics in the future, international factors (including the positions assumed by the U.S. government, the indirect influence of Mexican emigrant groups, or the actions of cross-border civil society coalitions) had a less significant impact than domestic elements on regime opening during the 1980s and 1990s.

A close examination of these various factors calls into question the increasingly widely held view that successful electoral democratization at the national level and the PRI's historic defeat in the year 2000 presidential election were inevitable. There were certainly socioeconomic and demographic forces (including urbanization, the declining importance of traditional manufacturing activities, and increasing generational distance from the founding mobilizational moments that gave rise to the postrevolutionary regime) that progressively undercut the PRI's electoral base and produced a nearly continuous erosion of its position in federal elections from the 1960s onward. However, as the following analysis shows, electoral democratization in Mexico owed as much or more to contingent political and economic events.[18]

The Growing Strength of Opposition Parties

Opposition parties had always been present in postrevolutionary Mexican politics, and at times they played important roles either as vehicles for electoral protests against "official" party dominance (as in the case of the Federation of Parties of the Mexican People [FPPM], organized around Miguel Henríquez Guzmán's strong presidential challenge in 1952) or as allies in major sociopolitical conflicts (as in the case of the Mexican Worker-Peasant Party [POCM], the Mexican Communist Party [PCM], and the Popular Party [PP] during national railroad workers' strikes in 1958 and 1959). Nevertheless, especially during the heyday of PRI hegemony in the 1950s and 1960s, these organizations frequently functioned as little more than satellites of the ruling party – recipients of state financial and representational subsidies and available as its political and legislative allies.[19] It was not until after the 1977 political reform liberalized conditions for party registration and electoral competition that new opposition parties – especially those representing forces on the left of the ideological spectrum – began to gain electoral strength, organizational coherence, and political importance.

Because of the nearly all-encompassing character of the PRI–led governing coalition, Mexico's opposition parties did not engage the transition process on the

18 This discussion does not analyze the 2000 election campaign and the ways in which various campaign effects shaped the outcome on July 2. For a detailed assessment of these questions, see Domínguez and Lawson 2003.

19 One telling fact is that the PARM and the PPS, two of the three (with the PAN) most visible opposition parties from the mid–1950s through the early 1970s, failed to nominate their own candidates for the 1958, 1964, 1970, and 1976 presidential elections. Instead, they regularly backed the PRI's nominee.

basis of already identified and mobilized mass constituencies. Both of the opposition parties that were most prominent during the late 1980s and the 1990s did in fact have core constituencies of some long standing – Catholic and urban middle-class groups in the case of the PAN, and former communist and socialist parties in the case of the PRD. For the most part, however, these parties grew in size and assumed their contemporary membership and programmatic profiles in the course of expanding their electoral significance during this period. In fact, this is an important reason why Mexico's electoral transition was so comparatively slow; it involved the gradual erosion of a hegemonic party's bases and the slow accumulation of strength by its main opponents on the left and right. Opposition parties were among the most important actors pushing for liberalized electoral laws and autonomous electoral institutions precisely because more competitive elections permitted them to grow.

Especially from the late 1970s onward, then, opposition parties' strategic actions focused upon electoral competition.[20] This orientation was initially a point of controversy within the Left, with some activists worrying that "electioneering" would dissipate leftist parties' energies and resources and perhaps distract them from longer-term organizational work at the grassroots. However, these concerns were effectively silenced by the surprisingly strong showing of the center-left coalition that Cuauhtémoc Cárdenas led in the 1988 presidential race, the quickening flow of public resources for party activities, and the enhanced credibility that electoral participation gave to some parties' local organizational efforts (Semo 2002: 435–42). In the case of the PAN, in contrast, electoral competition had been the party's main concern since its founding in 1939. Both of the party's principal founders, Manuel Gómez Morin and Efraín González Luna, were strongly committed to electoral participation as a strategy for party building (Lujambio 2001).

Two important consequences flowed from opposition parties' strategic focus upon elections. First, at different times these parties exercised crucial leverage in pushing forward the liberalization of electoral rules and procedures. For example, in the context of the political crisis provoked by the Zapatista Army of National Liberation's (EZLN) armed uprising in the southern state of Chiapas in January 1994, the PRD and the PAN led opposition efforts to extract concessions from the Salinas administration over the rules that would govern the August 1994 general

---

20 See González Casanova 1995: 591–95, 607, for a discussion of opposition parties' emerging consensus in favor of electoral strategies, including inter-party alliances established in the mid–1980s to defend the vote. Among leftist parties, only the Party of the Socialist Revolution (PRS) declined to participate in the 1988 elections (p. 602).

González Casanova notes (pp. 595, 607) that, as opposition parties' commitment to elections grew and elections became more competitive, the government backed away from its historical commitment to promote electoral participation and increasingly relied upon abstention to sustain the PRI's position against its rivals.

elections.[21] These two parties were also the principal interlocutors in negotiations with the Zedillo administration over the terms of the 1996 electoral reform (though, in the end, representatives of both parties voted against the measure when it came up for consideration in the federal Chamber of Deputies).[22]

Second, over time competitive party systems gradually emerged in Mexico at the subnational level.[23] On some occasions, opposition parties cooperated effectively with each other in gubernatorial and other state- or municipal-level elections. For example, coalitions linking the PRD, the Labor Party (PT), and the Mexican Ecological Green Party (PVEM) in Tlaxcala in 1998; the PRD and the PT in Baja California Sur in 1999; the PAN, PRD, and PT in Nayarit in 1999; and the PAN, PRD, PT, and PVEM in Chiapas in 2000 and in Yucatán in 2001, all won gubernatorial elections. The more general pattern, however, was for de facto two-party systems to emerge in different parts of the country, with PAN–PRI rivalries concentrated in electoral districts in northern and central-western states and PRD–PRI competition focused upon districts in southern and central states.[24]

Effective two-party or multiparty competition at state and municipal levels became increasingly common during the 1990s in part because opposition parties were able to create or strengthen links to mobilizing civil society organizations whose demands frequently included electoral transparency.[25] These alliances often provided opposition parties with more durable constituent bases, and in the case of some state-level PRD organizations, they infused opposition politics with a social movement character. More generally, however, this transformation slowly established the basis for more competitive national elections by strengthening opposition party organizations, demonstrating that opposition parties represented a viable alternative to the PRI, and habituating citizens to partisan alternation in power.

The magnitude of this political shift was impressive. Between 1988 and 1999, the PAN and the PRD governed for at least three years 27 of the 30 largest municipalities in the country. Indeed, in 1999 the PAN (33.1 percent) and the PRD (12.3 percent) together governed 45.4 percent of Mexico's population at the municipal

---

21 Loaeza 1999: 424–25. The January 1994 "Pact for Peace, Democracy, and Justice" was signed by seven of the eight registered parties (the PPS declined to join the initiative) and all eight presidential candidates (including the PPS's Marcela Lombardo).

22 However, all the parties then represented in the Chamber of Deputies – the PAN, PRD, PRI, and the Labor Party (PT) – unanimously approved legislation granting full autonomy to the Federal Electoral Institute.

23 Among the catalysts for this change were reforms in 1977 and 1983 that introduced proportional representation in state legislatures and municipal councils.

   It is important to recognize, however, that different parties' organizational strength varies greatly from one state or region to another.

24 Joseph L. Klesner (2003: table 4.2) reports that the proportion of two- or three-party-competitive districts in federal deputy elections increased from 37.7 percent in 1991 to 93.7 percent in 1997.

25 The next section addresses this point in more detail. For examples of PAN alliances with local civic organizations, see Middlebrook 2001; for parallel examples of PRD alliances, see Bruhn 1997.

level, and by the year 2000 approximately 63 percent of the country's total population had experienced opposition municipal government for at least three years (Lujambio 2001: 85–86). Between 1994 and 2000 the opposition also defeated the PRI in gubernatorial elections in seven states (Baja California, Baja California Sur, Guanajuato, Jalisco, Nuevo León, Querétaro, and Tlaxcala) (Lujambio 2001: 86). In federal elections as well, the PRI slowly but continuously lost ground from 1991 onward. Its share of the valid vote in federal elections (for the federal Chamber of Deputies in midterm elections, or for the presidency) fell from 61.4 percent in 1991 to 50.4 percent in 1994, 39.1 percent in 1997, and 36.9 percent in 2000.[26]

New Dynamics in Civil Society

Although the effects were sometimes indirect, the rise of a more dynamic civil society contributed very significantly to political opening in Mexico. Over time, human rights and pro-democracy groups, community-based popular movements, and feminist and environmental organizations assumed increasing public visibility and political importance.[27] This development was only partially related to the emergence of politically independent labor and peasant organizations during the 1970s and the erosion of support for the PRI's "official" sector organizations in the 1980s and 1990s. Rather, it reflected the complex changes occurring in Mexican urban society during these latter two decades and specific societal responses to such catalytic events as the post-1982 debt crisis, the scandalously incompetent government responses to the devastating earthquakes that struck Mexico City in September 1985, and the fraud-ridden 1988 presidential election.[28] Over time, an increasingly dense and mobilized civil society promoted demands for electoral transparency, greater accountability on the part of public officials, and the rule of law.

The Roman Catholic Church played an important role in this process of societal transformation.[29] Alberto J. Olvera (this volume) notes that the church had long represented an exception to the postrevolutionary regime's near monopoly over the public sphere and the organization of society. From the 1960s onward, the church

26 With the exceptions of the 1976 and 1991 midterm elections, the PRI's share of the valid vote in federal Chamber of Deputies elections fell continuously from 1961 to 2000. See Klesner 2003: figure 4.1.

27 Alberto J. Olvera (this volume, tables 13.1–13.3) provides information concerning the number, substantive focus, and geographic distribution of nongovernmental organizations in Mexico in the mid–1990s. For an excellent discussion of the evolution of the Mexican feminist movement and its contributions to democratization, see Lamas 2003.

28 Olvera (this volume) links this shift in part to the process of market-oriented economic restructuring and the Mexican state's de facto retreat from its long-standing social justice commitments. He argues that the Salinas administration's decisions to privatize public enterprises on a large scale and to end land redistribution were two key moments in the erosion of the regime's ideological foundations. See also González Casanova 1995: 598 on this point.

On the impact of civic mobilizations by the 1985 Mexico City earthquake victims' movement, see Tavera-Fenollosa 1998.

29 See Camp 1997 and Aguilar Ascencio 2000.

– in part responding to the doctrinal shifts associated with the Second Vatican Council (1962–1965) – supported the formation of local-level associations focused upon socioeconomic development problems. Despite the church hierarchy's overall conservatism, Jesuits and other religious orders were actively involved in the creation of nongovernmental organizations (NGOs). In particular, Christian base communities devoted to consciousness raising proliferated during the 1970s, and over time they helped open public spaces for popular groups and shaped a new generation of potential social leaders. In some areas, more conservative Catholic groups also constituted part of a network of societal organizations that increasingly questioned the legitimacy of the postrevolutionary political order.[30]

There were two areas in which a more active and politically engaged civil society directly promoted electoral democratization. First, civic organizations were key constituents in the coalitions that opposition parties mobilized at state and municipal levels during elections in the 1980s and 1990s. Specific political traditions and sociocultural orientations varied enormously from one region to another, but parties such as the PAN and the PRD depended heavily upon such groups as the bases for their challenges to PRI dominance. In some instances, regional resentment against political centralism was an important factor behind local civic organizations' support for opposition parties; in other cases, local groups had been alienated by PRI electoral fraud, unpopular federal government decisions, or the especially egregious public conduct of PRI–affiliated government officials. The PAN in particular became the favored vehicle for middle-class groups alienated by economic instability and the government's reluctance to open electoral channels for the expression of societal discontent.

Second, nongovernmental organizations became leading actors in efforts to ensure free and fair elections by organizing national networks of election observers. From their first significant emergence in the 1960s as a confluence of Christian groups and leftist activists disillusioned with political parties, Mexican NGOs had focused principally upon promoting economic and social development at the local level (Aguayo Quezada 1998a). However, the De la Madrid administration's resort to fraud to contain limited opposition electoral gains at state and municipal levels in 1985–1986, and particularly the blatant fraud committed in the 1988 presidential election, galvanized many of these groups into concerted action to ensure electoral transparency.[31]

Thus, the Mexican Academy of Human Rights (AMDH) and other civic organizations established a network of observers to oversee the 1991 midterm federal legislative elections, and for the crucial 1994 presidential election, some four hundred civic

---

30 Olvera (this volume); see also Aguayo Quezada 1998a.
31 Flagrant fraud against the PAN in the 1986 Chihuahua gubernatorial election encouraged the Catholic Church to play a more active role in promoting clean elections – a position which, given the PAN's Catholic identity, was of particular value to it. See Camp 1994: 95–96; Loaeza 1999: 352, 391; and Chand 2001: chap. 4.

groups and NGOs joined forces as the Civic Alliance (AC). This initiative included not only poll watching and the oversight of electoral officials on election day, but also an assessment of media coverage (both news reporting and paid advertising) and campaign spending and a more general effort to inform potential voters of their rights.[32] Such efforts contributed greatly to increased electoral transparency, significantly advanced demands for the effective autonomy of electoral institutions, focused increased international attention upon democracy issues in Mexico during the 1990s, promoted citizen awareness and involvement in public life, and reinforced citizens' commitment to making elections the means for peaceful regime change.

Changes in Government-Media Relations

Greater freedom of expression and increased political diversity in the print and electronic media also played an important role in democratization in Mexico.[33] Chappell H. Lawson's essay in this book explains how government-media relations in Mexico had long been characterized by co-optation, collusion, and censorship. Through a combination of direct controls (government censorship of newspaper and magazine content, administrative sanctions, and control over the distribution of subsidized newsprint supplies), political alliances with media owners, financial inducements (ranging from the highly selective allocation of all-important government advertising funds to outright bribery of newspaper owners and reporters), and the threat – and, all too frequently, the reality – of physical violence, PRI governments ensured generally favorable media coverage and framed the public agenda to suit their interests. Governmental control over broadcast concessions translated into especially strong political dominance over radio and television news coverage. Indeed, the Televisa monopoly's historical alliance with the PRI was a pillar of authoritarian rule from the early 1950s through the mid-1990s.

Yet by the 1990s, both print media and radio and television had experienced major changes in their content and political orientation. Lawson (this volume) argues convincingly that media opening was only partly a consequence of the

---

32 Many thousands of Mexican citizens (joined by some 900 "international visitors," as they were designated by the Mexican government) were involved in observing the 1994 elections. Sergio Aguayo Quezada (1998a: 179) places the number at approximately 20,000; Olvera (this volume) estimates that as many as 40,000 individuals were involved.

Civic Alliance managed to create chapters in 29 of Mexico's 31 states. The organization remained active throughout the 1990s, devoting its energies to state-level electoral observation, civic education, and the coordination of various popular referendums on political and social justice questions. AC also organized an important electoral observation initiative around the 2000 elections, although its efforts were somewhat overshadowed by a now-independent and more vigorous Federal Electoral Institute. For details, see Olvera (this volume).

33 Several early studies of social and political change in developing countries highlighted the relationship between access to information (and, at least implicitly, the role of the mass media) and shifts in political attitudes. For representative works, see Lerner 1958, Deutsch 1961, and Inkeles and Smith 1974.

political liberalization that began in the late 1970s. Political reforms did make it more difficult for government officials to engage in direct censorship and physical violence against dissident journalists. However, Lawson stresses that the growing independence and pluralism of Mexico's media also reflected changes in journalistic norms, especially the gradual diffusion of stronger professional ethics.[34] Equally important over the longer term was the emergence of market competition among different media outlets. This transformation did not always result in higher-quality coverage or programming,[35] nor did it entirely end multiple forms of media vulnerability to government pressures. Yet in the main, the most successful newspapers, magazines, and radio and television networks became more secure in their sources of financing and were therefore far less hesitant to criticize state policies or investigate alleged misconduct by government officials.

These changes had very significant political consequences. Lawson shows that media opening contributed directly to democratization by ending the tradition of selective silence on such highly sensitive topics as government corruption (especially corruption linked to drug trafficking), electoral fraud, and political repression, opening up these previously "closed" subjects to greater scrutiny and debate and discrediting authoritarian institutions and practices. Media opening also had an important impact upon pro-democracy elements in civil society, whose activities were further legitimated by the increased media attention they received. Equally important, the media provided much more balanced coverage (in both amount and tone) of opposition political parties and candidates during election campaigns, a shift that greatly reduced the PRI's traditional electoral advantage. This departure was especially notable where television reporting was concerned, and by the 2000 general elections media coverage was generally quite equitable.

Crises and Political Opening

The preceding overview of the political impact of opposition parties, nongovernmental organizations and other societal actors, and the mass media might suggest that regime liberalization in Mexico was primarily due to incremental sociopolitical change and the "official" party's secular decline (the long-term erosion of the legitimacy it had derived from postrevolutionary mobilizations, generational change and the inevitable disappearance of its founding supporters, and so forth). The fact that opposition forces gradually gained ground over a period of many years – first at the municipal and state levels and then at the federal level, first winning a majority of seats in the federal Chamber of Deputies and then control over the presidency – and the fact that shifts in the balance of political power occurred within the established constitutional order certainly reinforce this view. Indeed, this is very much the message conveyed by a graphic display of the near-

---

34 On this topic, see also Hughes 2003.

35 By the late 1990s, coverage of political scandals had become a journalistic staple, with a very real impact upon the conduct of government officials.

continuous decline in the PRI's share of all valid votes cast in elections for the federal Chamber of Deputies between 1961 and the year 2000.[36]

Yet for all the gradualism of Mexico's electoral transition, one can scarcely over-emphasize the impact of political and economic crises on this process. This subsection considers the nature and consequences of these events.

Political Catalysts of Regime Liberalization

A series of political crises from the late 1960s through the early 1990s played a crucial role in initiating and then driving forward Mexico's slow, uneven liberalization process. These crises were somewhat different in character; some broadly challenged the legitimacy of postrevolutionary authoritarian rule (the 1968 student-popular movement and the 1994 Zapatista rebellion), while others more directly accentuated divisions within the governing elite (the 1986–1988 split within the PRI and the assassination of the PRI's designated presidential candidate in 1994). Taken together, however, these events increased the scale of political opposition and enlarged opposition forces' room for maneuver.

President Gustavo Díaz Ordaz's (1964–1970) violent repression of the 1968 student-popular movement – particularly the Ttatelolco massacre, in which army troops killed or wounded several hundred demonstrators at Tlatelolco Plaza in Mexico City – was a key early catalyst in this regard. The resulting public outcry especially undercut the regime's legitimacy among the urban middle-class groups that constituted the ruling elite's most politically articulate constituency. More-over, the events of 1968 gave rise both to a generation of political leaders committed to democratizing Mexican politics and society and to several new leftist parties that operated outside the officially recognized party system. In this sense, the political reform legislation introduced in 1977 sought to address the legacies of the 1968 crisis by liberalizing electoral rules, augmenting opposition parties' representation in the federal Chamber of Deputies, and expanding these parties' access to the mass media (Middlebrook 1986).

More proximately, the formation of the dissident "Democratic Current" within the Institutional Revolutionary Party in 1986–1987 and the political shocks generated by the 1988 presidential election – particularly the surprising success of the Cárdenas coalition and the extent of government/ruling party fraud during the vote count (and the widely held view that Cuauhtémoc Cárdenas may actually have polled more votes than the PRI's Carlos Salinas de Gortari)[37] – seriously divided the ruling political elite, galvanized a deepening civic commitment to electoral transparency, and demonstrated that victory by the PRI was no longer inevitable. The subsequent founding in 1989 of the Party of the Democratic Revolution,

36 See Klesner 2003: figure 1. Only in 1976 (a presidential election in which the PRI faced no registered opposition candidate) and 1991 did the PRI's share of the valid vote increase in comparison to its performance in the preceding federal election.

37 For an analysis suggesting that Cárdenas may in fact have won more votes than Salinas, see Castañeda 1999: 327–38 ("Apéndice: 6 de julio de 1988").

which linked the 1988 Cárdenas coalition with long-established leftist parties like the PCM, created the first significant leftist opposition to the "official" party since at least the late 1940s.

The events of January-March 1994 further increased pressures for regime opening. The EZLN's armed rebellion in January energized a broad range of socio-political groups opposed both to continued PRI rule and the market-oriented economic reform project implemented after the mid-1980s. The fact that the rebellion coincided precisely with the entering into effect of the North American Free Trade Agreement (NAFTA), whose approval was so crucial to the support Salinas won from both domestic and international economic and political actors, squarely focused national and international attention upon the question of democracy in Mexico. By forcing Salinas to accept some PRD demands for electoral reform in order to ensure stable conditions for the 1994 general elections and a peaceful transfer of power at the end of his presidential term, the Chiapas uprising ended the regressive phase of Mexican electoral reform and helped establish more equitable conditions in federal elections (Crespo, this volume). At virtually the same time, the assassination of PRI presidential candidate Luis Donaldo Colosio in March threw the governing coalition into disarray and sharply undercut any plans that Salinas may have had to exercise behind-the-scenes power through his designated successor.

It is difficult to judge whether, in the absence of prolonged economic stagnation during the 1980s and renewed financial crisis in 1994–1995, the political shocks of the late 1980s and the mid-1990s would have been sufficient to compel the governing elite to accept the additional reforms of electoral rules and institutions that permitted major opposition triumphs in 1997 and 2000. In considering this question, it is important to recall that Mexico's postrevolutionary regime had demonstrated exceptional resilience in the face of serious political challenges from the late 1940s through the 1970s – a point strongly underscored by the very length of a political transition process whose origins can be traced back to at least 1968. It is also worth noting that, in the wake of the 1988 electoral earthquake, Salinas very quickly established a strong personal political position and the PRI recovered much of the electoral ground it had lost (winning 61.4 percent of the valid vote in the 1991 midterm legislative elections). The political crisis provoked in early 1994 by the Chiapas uprising and the Colosio assassination was particularly serious because these unprecedented and destabilizing events occurred in a presidential transition year.[38] But even in these difficult conditions, the PRI managed a persuasive win in the 1994 general elections.[39] The significant concessions embodied in the (still

---

38 There had been no assassination of a mainstream national political leader since 1928, when Álvaro Obregón was shot and killed shortly after his reelection to the presidency.

39 The PRI's presidential candidate, Ernesto Zedillo Ponce de León, won 50.4 percent of the valid vote in an electoral contest generally judged to be clean (it was not significantly marred by electoral fraud) but highly unequal (the PRI held overwhelming advantages in terms of campaign spending and media coverage).

imperfect) 1996 electoral reform came only in the wake of Mexico's devastating 1994–1995 financial crisis, which left the Zedillo administration in a greatly weakened position.[40]

Economic Crises and the Erosion of PRI Hegemony

As in several other Latin American countries, economic crisis played a central role in eroding authoritarian rule in Mexico. The global economic instability produced by petroleum price shocks in the 1970s, coupled with the Latin American debt crisis of the 1980s (the catalyst for which was Mexico's announcement in August 1982 that it could not pay the interest due on its external public debt), accelerated democratic transitions in Argentina, Bolivia, Brazil, Peru, and Uruguay.[41] In Mexico, the erosion of PRI control was sufficiently slow that many observers wondered whether the stresses associated with recurrent economic instability and prolonged stagnation would necessarily have the same effect as they did elsewhere in the region. Indeed, with the restoration of relatively rapid (but short-lived) growth after 1989, the PRI substantially recovered its electoral position in the 1991 midterm and 1994 general elections. But with the devastating 1994–1995 financial crisis, many voters abandoned their previous faith in PRI governments' capacity to manage the economy.

Viewed over the longer term, the 1982 debt crisis and the two decades of (mostly) economic stagnation that it entrained had three major consequences for the PRI–led governing coalition. First, these economic reverses sapped the legitimacy of the established regime. Because the Mexican regime originated in a revolutionary transformation rather than in an inclusive and widely accepted electoral process, for many years public perceptions of its legitimacy depended more upon overall evaluations of governmental performance (and, in the first decades after the 1910–1920 revolution, the fulfillment of a comprehensive revolutionary program) than upon adherence to particular procedural requirements. This performance-based legitimacy suffered greatly during the 1980s, and again after 1994–1995, because persistent economic stagnation called into question the state's capacity to lead the development process.

Second, President José López Portillo's (1976–1982) crisis-induced nationalization of the banking system in September 1982 – the high-water mark of postrevolutionary state economic intervention – produced a dramatic rupture in state-private sector relations. Although there had always been tensions in this relationship, Mexico's postrevolutionary governing pact linked the public and private sectors in an overarching partnership to promote capital accumulation and growth. President Luis Echeverría's (1970–1976) radical rhetoric and redistributive economic policies

---

40 In historical perspective, Zedillo's greatest virtue as president may have been that his political ineptness seemingly prevented him from becoming frustrated by the weakness of his own position. At key moments, therefore, he conducted himself as a democrat. For an assessment of Zedillo's political record, see Hernández Rodríguez 2003

41 Huntington 1991: 51–53, 59; Haggard and Kaufman 1995: chap. 1. See also Remmer 1991 and Gasiorowski 1995.

elicited strong reactions from leading business groups.[42] However, it was the 1982 bank nationalization that sharply increased entrepreneurs' support for, and direct involvement with, the National Action Party. They especially sought to end "economic populism" and promote democratic accountability by creating a check on the discretionary power of the federal government.[43]

Regardless of how compatible leading entrepreneurs may have found the PAN's positions in ideological or programmatic terms, their continued dependence upon government contracts or subsidies (and, therefore, their vulnerability to political sanctions) remained a powerful disincentive to involvement with the party. But the owners of many small and midsize businesses faced far fewer constraints in this regard. In northern Mexico in particular, they joined the PAN in significant numbers, channeled financial resources to the party, and frequently ran as its candidates for state and municipal offices. Several of the PAN's most important figures during the 1980s and 1990s came from private-sector backgrounds (including Vicente Fox in Guanajuato), and entrepreneurs' organizational skills and financial support were key elements in the party's growing electoral success.

Third, prolonged economic stagnation (manifested in reduced real incomes, more limited employment opportunities, and increased poverty and inequality), government budgetary shortfalls, and some of the market-oriented reforms implemented to redress these problems significantly eroded support for the PRI among peasants, workers, and other popular groups. In the countryside, the Salinas administration officially suspended land distribution and largely eliminated a complex system of price supports and production credits, thus reducing the state's economic presence in a way that weakened the PRI's clientelist networks and eroded its traditional bases of rural support.[44] Among urban and industrial workers, the combination of constrained state resources, industrial restructuring at the firm level, and the relentless hostility of technocratic reformers undercut the position of the traditionally dominant, PRI–affiliated Confederation of Mexican Workers (CTM) and encouraged the emergence of alternative, more radical labor groups. The broader consequence of this process was more an overall weakening of the labor movement than an upturn in independent worker organization, but progovernment union leaders' declining control over patronage resources may well have undermined workers' support at the polls for PRI candidates.[45]

42 See Arriola 1988: 31 and Bizberg 2003: 164–65. Arriola notes the impact of Echeverría's radicalism upon the attitudes and actions of Manuel J. Clouthier, the Sinaloa-based businessman who became the PAN's 1988 presidential candidate and who was responsible for recruiting a number of entrepreneurs (including Vicente Fox Quesada) into the party's ranks.

43 On the impact of the bank nationalization upon entrepreneurs' changing political views, see Camp 1989: 136–38; Mizrahi: 1995: 83–85; and Loaeza 1999: 12, 17, 23.

44 Horacio Mackinlay's essay in this volume overviews economic reforms in the Mexican countryside in the 1980s and 1990s. See also Randall 1996 and Pastor and Wise 1998: 63–70.

45 In the 1988 general elections, for example, PRI–affiliated labor leaders conspicuously failed to deliver their members' votes for a party responsible for years of declining real wages and

The combination of deeply rooted popular allegiances to the PRI and a complex network of state controls over worker and peasant organizations made regime decomposition a slow process. Over time, however, the "official" party's affiliated mass organizations proved less and less effective at mobilizing electoral support for the PRI and its candidates, and the simultaneous strengthening of the institutional bases for free and fair elections enabled popular elements to express their economic discontent more freely in the privacy of the polling place.[46] In the year 2000 presidential election, for example, only 49 percent of all union members voted for the PRI's candidate. In fact, Chappell H. Lawson's statistical analysis of voting preferences has shown that (after controlling for demographic factors and other relevant variables) membership in a union increased the likelihood of favoring the PRI by only about 7 percent.[47]

The temporal coincidence of economic crisis and market liberalization makes it difficult in practice to disentangle their effects. However, economic crises and prolonged stagnation were probably more significant in their political consequences than were neoliberal reform and economic opening per se.[48] Market-oriented reforms – particularly the large-scale privatization of state-owned enterprises and substantial cutbacks in government price supports and other economic subsidies – did loosen some of the ties that bound important rural and urban constituencies to the Institutional Revolutionary Party. Yet even among the "official" party's organized mass supporters, these reforms did not have homogeneous effects. For example, despite the serious wage and employment losses suffered by major public-sector unions, the organized labor movement proved much more adept at preserving its array of legal and financial subsidies than did small-scale rural producers. Nor were the reforms wholly negative in their social and economic impact; blue-collar workers may even have benefited relatively more than middle-class groups from declining inflation rates and lower-priced imported consumer goods. What *was*

significant job losses in key industries. See Middlebrook 1995: 293–94.

In the case of the Confederation of Mexican Workers (CTM), these problems were almost certainly aggravated by the growing physical infirmity of its long-time leader, Fidel Velázquez (he died in June 1997 at age 97), and the increasing immobilism of the senior CTM leadership. Velázquez exited the political scene just before opposition parties won control of the federal Chamber of Deputies and the government of the Federal District in August 1997, events that shook the foundations of the political regime he had long defended.

46 Buendía (this volume) provides data concerning the PRI's declining support among lower-income and less-educated social strata between 1991 and 2000. The decline was especially significant after 1994.

47 Author's correspondence with Lawson, September 2002. The author is grateful to Lawson for sharing with him this unpublished analysis of the impact of demographic factors on Mexican voting behavior.

48 For an optimistic view of the anticipated impact of trade liberalization on political opening in Mexico, see Baer 1991; for a similar but after-the-fact view, see Benítez Manaut 2003: 56. Teichman 1997 also stresses the corrosive effects of market-oriented economic reforms on authoritarian political arrangements.

damaging to the PRI's position was the more open Mexican economy's greater vulnerability to financial shocks and the failure of the neoliberal model to generate sustained growth or sufficient employment opportunities in the formal sector.[49]

There are strong indications that problems such as these contributed directly to the erosion of the PRI's electoral support. Jorge Buendía's chapter in this volume shows that in the year 2000, unlike in the past, voters were unwilling to give the PRI credit for the generally positive economic conditions that prevailed at the time. Rather, they feared another devastating economic crisis like those that had accompanied all prior presidential successions since 1976. Even more telling, in the year 2000 Mexican voters perceived the PAN's Vicente Fox to be a more credible manager of the economy than the PRI's Francisco Labastida, and they did so in numbers sufficient to affect the final outcome. This is very strong evidence of the lasting political impact of the 1994–1995 crisis and its lingering effects upon incomes and poverty. It is, furthermore, a compelling reason why an assessment of regime change in Mexico should focus not just on long-term secular causes of PRI electoral decline but also on the particular impact that crises had upon this process.

International Influences upon Political Change in Mexico

Many analysts of Latin American politics might still concur with Guillermo O'Donnell's and Philippe C. Schmitter's summary judgment (1986: 18–19) that domestic actors generally play a predominant role in transitions to democracy. Yet students of democratic regime change in the region have increasingly drawn attention to the ways in which international circumstances shape such processes.[50]

In the case of Mexico, the general transitions literature outlines three ways in which the international context might have influenced domestic developments.[51] First, an external power such as the United States can seek, as a matter of deliberate policy, to overturn authoritarian rule and impose democratic institutions on a country subject to its influence. Second, geographic contiguity to a democracy can have demonstration effects upon both political elites and societal groups in a nondemocratic country, encouraging them to reconfigure domestic political arrangements along parallel lines. One might anticipate that these effects would have been particularly strong in Mexico because of the United States' regionally dominant position and the breadth and depth of economic, social, and cultural interchanges between the two countries. Third, democratizing a country's domestic political institutions may become an implicit (or even explicit) condition for the distribution of regional or international benefits it seeks. For example, historical examples such as Greece, Portugal, and Spain indicate that economic integration

---

49 For an overall assessment of Mexico's new development model and its economic and social impacts, see the essays in Middlebrook and Zepeda 2003b.

50 See, for example, Huntington 1991: 92–98, 102–3; Gasiorowski 1995: 893; Remmer 1996; and Whitehead 1996. For overall assessments of international (especially U.S.) influences on political developments in Mexico over time, see Dresser 1996, Coatsworth 1999, and Covarrubias 2001.

51 This discussion draws upon Huntington 1991, Whitehead 1996, and Schmitter 1996.

with well-institutionalized democracies (in this case, Canada and the United States) can contribute to democratization by providing a broad range of political, economic, and even military forces – pro-democracy and authoritarian alike – with strong symbolic and material incentives to bring national political practices into line with those of a country's future economic partners.

Certainly there is no shortage of examples demonstrating that, from the mid-1980s onward, international considerations did in fact influence the behavior of domestic political actors in Mexico. Among other such instances, in the mid- and late 1980s PAN activists blocked strategic Mexico–U.S. border crossing points, lobbied the U.S. Congress, and protested to the Inter-American Commission on Human Rights as part of their campaign to denounce the PRI regime's resort to electoral fraud; beginning with the 1988 presidential election, both "official" and opposition candidates sought the backing of government, business, academic, and media opinion leaders in the United States, and opposition candidates (though, in deference to the party's long tradition of holding U.S. influence at arm's length, *not* the PRI nominee) regularly campaigned for support from the Mexican emigrant and Mexican American communities in the United States; beginning in the early 1990s with the debate over the North American Free Trade Agreement (NAFTA), a broad range of nongovernmental actors in Mexico sought political, organizational, and financial support from allies in the United States and Canada; after the Chiapas uprising in January 1994, the EZLN repeatedly mobilized international allies to thwart the Mexican government's military and political offensives against it; the Salinas administration acceded to demands for international election observers in order to legitimate the PRI's victory in the 1994 general elections; and Vicente Fox's non-party electoral organization, "Friends of Fox," raised funds in the United States for his 1999–2000 presidential campaign.

On balance, however, external actors were only of indirect or secondary importance in Mexico's gradual process of political opening during the 1980s and 1990s.[52] The potential political effects flowing from geographic contiguity with the United

52 John H. Coatsworth (1999: 152) argues persuasively that, by the late 1990s, there would have been significant external costs if the governing PRI had sought seriously to reverse the process of electoral opening. Yet even so, it seems more likely that the principal obstacle to regressive political steps was internal – especially the growing strength of opposition parties and an increasingly contentious civil society. After all, external actors (particularly U.S. political and economic elites) had shown no great reluctance about accepting Salinas's recipe of economic liberalization combined with continued political control (including electoral legislation explicitly designed to safeguard the PRI's congressional majority, regardless of opposition parties' electoral gains). Given the potential bilateral and international repercussions of Mexico's 1994–1995 financial crisis, it is not implausible to think that U.S. political and economic decision makers would have backed an effort by the Zedillo administration to shore up the PRI's position and forestall further opposition electoral advances if this had been presented as the necessary price to maintain the country's economic stability. The main impediment to this course of action was, however, internal: the weakness of Zedillo's own position vis-à-vis both his own party and a mobilizing political opposition.

States and North American economic integration may have been constrained not only by active opposition from the PRI–led authoritarian regime, but also (paradoxically) by broader nationalist sentiment within Mexico based upon popular resistance to an even greater U.S. presence in domestic affairs.[53] For example, the established regime had for decades sought (generally successfully) to shield domestic politics from external influences.[54] PRI governments drew considerable legitimacy from their defense of Mexican sovereignty against real or potential threats from abroad, and principled opposition to foreign interference in national affairs helped sustain postrevolutionary authoritarian rule (Aguayo Quezada 1998b).

Both governmental and nongovernmental actors in the United States may have been similarly constrained by calculations of strategic interest and the historical legacies of the bilateral relationship. In any event, it was only with the gradual erosion of PRI dominance after the mid-1980s that the international context – especially diverse ties with the United States – became increasingly relevant in internal political and electoral calculations, and most U.S. government agencies and nongovernmental actors did not adopt a pro-democracy agenda in their relations with Mexico until the mid-1990s.[55] This timing in and of itself strongly suggests that domestic factors were more determinative than external ones in advancing Mexican democratization, particularly during the 1980s and early 1990s. There are, however, substantial reasons to believe that the international context will become increasingly important to Mexican politics in the future.[56]

Dilemmas of Change: The Re-institutionalization of Mexican Politics

Electoral democratization in Mexico has formed part of – and has further accelerated – broader processes of sociopolitical change. As noted at the outset of this essay, electoral democratization itself remains incomplete, particularly at state and municipal levels. However, the most fundamental challenges to the consolidation and deepening of Mexican democracy lie elsewhere.[57] Unlike some other Latin American

53 It is also possible that contiguity with an established democracy is a less powerful source of political influence than proximity to one or more *democratizing* countries.

54 One consequence of this policy was the enduring suspicion that the Mexican armed forces had of their U.S. counterparts, despite their doctrinal and material dependence upon the U.S. military. For details, see Roderic Camp's chapter in this volume.

55 Fitzgerald (this volume) offers multiple historical examples of political interactions across the Mexico–U.S. border. See also Knight 1997.

56 The final section of this essay returns to this topic.

57 In this discussion, "consolidation" refers to actors' increasing acceptance of, or habituation to, democratic rules and procedures governing electoral competition, intergovernmental relations, and other areas of public decision making. "Deepening" refers both to the progressive incorporation of broader portions of the population into democratic political processes and to the expansion of democratic practices from electoral to non-electoral spheres.

By distinguishing between "formally institutionalized" and "informally institutionalized" polyarchies, O'Donnell 1999a: 178 usefully cautions against assuming that democratic

countries in the 1980s and 1990s, there is no significant risk of authoritarian regression, at least in the conventional sense of a military-led or -backed overthrow of a still-fragile civilian regime. Rather, the principal dilemmas facing early twenty-first-century Mexico concern how to re-institutionalize the political order so as to deconcentrate political authority, redress the balance of power between the state and society, and ensure the effective guarantee of citizenship rights and the rule of law.[58] The changes required to bring about this deeper democratic transformation range from organizational innovation and legal reforms, to major shifts in the balance and exercise of power within public institutions, to measures designed to expand citizen engagement in the public sphere and ensure the exercise of broadly defined citizenship rights, to the extension of rights and representation to groups previously excluded from meaningful participation in national affairs.

This section examines dilemmas of re-institutionalization in four areas: intergovernmental relations (executive-legislative relations, judicial politics, and relations between the federal government and state and municipal governments), civil-military relations, state-society relations (links between the state and rural producers, urban and industrial workers, and the private sector), and the rights and representation of indigenous peoples and Mexican emigrant communities in the United States. In each case, the discussion focuses upon both the challenges posed by the legacies of postrevolutionary authoritarian rule and the main issues on the democratization agenda.

Intergovernmental Relations

The formation of an "official" party in 1929 and the consolidation of its hegemony in subsequent decades permitted Mexico's postrevolutionary governing elite to centralize political power and concentrate decision-making authority in the federal executive. One key issue on the democratization agenda, therefore, is making real the formal division of constitutional authority between the federal executive, on the one hand, and the Congress, the judiciary, and state and municipal governments, on the other. Deconcentrating authority and altering the balance of political power within public institutions are essential requirements for expanding the scope for political contestation and strengthening the rule of law and citizenship rights.

Executive-Legislative Relations

The federal executive's dominance over the Congress was for six decades a core institutional relationship in Mexican politics.[59] Indeed, in his contribution to this

consolidation (defined in these terms) implies the elimination of informal or particularistic – but perhaps highly institutionalized – patterns of behavior. For further discussion of the dilemmas of consolidation, see Mainwaring, O'Donnell, and Valenzuela 1992; Schmitter 1992; and Linz and Stepan 1996.

58 For a salutary reminder of just how elusive the goal of achieving "full civil freedom" has been in Mexico, see Needler 1961: 308.

59 See Casar 1998 for a summary of the formal division of powers between the executive and legislative branches.

volume, Jeffrey A. Weldon identifies unified government (a situation in which the same party controls both the executive and legislative branches) as one of the key elements that long permitted Mexican presidents to exercise "metaconstitutional" powers substantially exceeding those defined by the 1917 Constitution.[60] In the legislative arena, presidential dominance was manifested both in the executive's important role in preparing the bills that were submitted to Congress and, especially, in the very high success rate that it achieved.[61] From the mid-1930s through the mid-1990s, at least 95 percent (and, at times, 100 percent) of executive-sponsored bills were approved by the federal Chamber of Deputies, almost all of them without amendment either in committee or on the floor of the Chamber.

Yet executive-legislative relations were among the first areas measurably affected by increased political pluralism. Over the course of the late 1980s and early 1990s, gradual political opening had slowly produced a more plural federal Chamber of Deputies. However, the PRI's loss of its majority position in the Chamber in 1997 had a near-immediate effect upon President Zedillo's legislative strategy and record. He submitted much less legislation to the Chamber of Deputies, choosing instead to route important initiatives to the more politically reliable, PRI–controlled Senate. Many of the executive-sponsored bills that were susceptible to amendment (spending and taxation proposals, for instance, but excluding presidential requests for congressional authorization to travel abroad) were substantially modified in committee or on the floor of the Chamber. Indeed, the overall approval rate for executive-sponsored bills was 91.3 percent during the 1997–2000 period, compared to an average of 98.7 percent during the preceding three legislatures (1988–1997) and 98.9 percent during the first half of Zedillo's six-year term. Moreover, the number of bills submitted by deputies themselves increased sharply.[62]

Significant changes also occurred in the internal organization and operating procedures of the Chamber of Deputies itself. As Weldon (this volume) notes, the Congressional Organic Law (Ley Orgánica del Congreso General de los Estados Unidos Mexicanos) adopted in 1979 had not anticipated a situation in which no party held a majority in the Chamber. In fact, the law stipulated that the Chamber's principal internal governing body, the High Commission, could only be formed if one party held an absolute majority of seats, and that its members could only come from the majority party. The unprecedented situation that arose

60 The other conditions for metaconstitutional presidentialism were strong discipline within the majority party and the president's role as de facto head of a centralized party. For a discussion of these conditions and the historical circumstances in which they developed in Mexico, see Weldon (this volume).

61 Weldon (this volume) notes that "between 1928 and 1997, the president had always sponsored at least three-fifths of the bills passed by the Chamber, and during the 1950s this proportion approached 100 percent."

62 These data are drawn from Weldon (this volume), tables 5.4, 5.7. The smaller number of executive-sponsored legislative initiatives, and the character of the bills themselves, still kept President Zedillo's legislative approval rate relatively high during the 1997–2000 period.

following the 1997 elections thus required political compromises among the five parties represented in the Chamber in order to make committee assignments and organize the Chamber's regular business. Moreover, in 1999 the organic law was reformed to adapt Chamber procedures to the realities of multiparty competition and to ensure more efficient and politically balanced internal representation and governance. Other reforms professionalized the lower chamber's Executive Committee and created the position of secretary general to oversee administrative matters in a more politically neutral fashion.[63]

These changes did not prevent a degree of political gridlock in executive-legislative relations once the PRI lost control of the presidency in the year 2000, but many of the Fox administration's initial legislative difficulties were clearly attributable to conjunctural factors.[64] These included: purposeful obstruction by intransigent elements within the PRD and the PRI, who sought to block the "rightist" Fox administration's legislative agenda and thereby prevent the PAN from strengthening its position in the 2003 midterm legislative elections or retaining the presidency in 2006; broad center-left opposition (including a PRI freed from domination by neoliberal technocrats) to tax increases and private sector-oriented economic proposals (including measures that would permit expanded private investment in electrical power generation and in gas and petroleum exploration); and errors committed by the Fox administration itself in the design and pursuit of its legislative agenda, including its decision to invest substantial political capital in policy initiatives that required congressional approval rather than pursuing measures that fell more securely under executive-branch jurisdiction.

Beyond these considerations, however, there remain important institutional obstacles to consolidating more balanced executive-legislative relations over the longer term. The most important of these is the constitutional prohibition (in effect since 1933) against the consecutive re-election of federal deputies and senators to positions in the same chamber.[65] There is considerable agreement among political analysts that the "no re-election" rule hinders the development of a more autonomous and influential legislative branch by limiting legislators' accountability to their constituents and by preventing them from accumulating experience or acquiring substantive expertise in specialized areas.[66] Nevertheless, despite some support for a consti-

---

63 See Weldon (this volume) for details.

64 Weldon (this volume) notes that Fox's legislative approval rate in the Chamber of Deputies fell to under 86 percent through December 2002. This rate was certainly well below the executive branch's historical average, but it was perhaps not so bad given the PAN's minority status in the Chamber.

65 The Constitution's "no re-election" provisions (Article 59) also apply to the president, governors, members of state legislatures, and mayors.

66 See Ugalde 2000 for a more detailed consideration of these issues. Mexican legislators' accountability to their constituents is also constrained by proportional-representation arrangements and internal congressional rules that concentrate power and resources in the hands of party leaders.

tutional reform that would permit consecutive re-election (with term limits) to positions other than the presidency, none of Mexico's major parties made this issue a high priority for legislative action during the first half of the Fox administration.

Judicial Reform and the Rule of Law

As in the case of executive-legislative relations, significant changes affecting the Mexican judiciary occurred even before Fox's electoral victory in July 2000. President Ernesto Zedillo's first major policy initiative was a 1994 constitutional reform that substantially increased the formal authority and political independence of the Supreme Court.[67] Most important, it empowered the Court to interpret the constitutionality of laws and arbitrate conflicts among different branches and levels of government. The measure also introduced selection criteria for justices designed to ensure their nonpartisanship (for example, nominees must be law graduates with at least ten years of professional experience, and they cannot have held a senior political post in the year before their appointment), and it altered appointment procedures so as to increase the judiciary's autonomy vis-à-vis the executive (the president nominates Supreme Court justices to staggered fifteen-year terms, but appointment requires a two-thirds affirmative vote by the federal Senate).[68]

The 1994 reform sought to reverse a long history of judicial subordination to executive power. Nevertheless, as Beatriz Magaloni and Guillermo Zepeda argue in their chapter in this book, many of the changes affecting the Supreme Court have thus far had only a limited impact upon the everyday lives of Mexican citizens.[69] Because the actions of state-level judiciaries (where most civil and criminal cases are heard) are much more relevant in this regard, their essay focuses in detail upon the effectiveness of state-level judicial and law enforcement institutions and the struggle against violent crime.

Establishing the conditions for citizens' security is a crucial test for new democracies (Whitehead 2002: 165–85), and both the severity of the public security problem since the late 1980s and the intensity of citizen concerns about it make this a particularly important issue in Mexico. Yet Magaloni and Zepeda (this volume) demonstrate that Mexican states vary dramatically in terms of their ability to

67 This discussion draws upon the chapter by Beatriz Magaloni and Guillermo Zepeda in this volume and Domingo 2000. Domingo provides an excellent overview of the general issues of judicial independence and accountability.

68 The 1994 constitutional reform also established a Judicial Board (Consejo de la Judicatura) to administer the federal judiciary, including selecting judges and overseeing judicial promotions. See Magaloni and Zepeda (this volume) for details.

69 Magaloni and Zepeda (this volume) note that most of the so-called constitutional actions (the vehicle for Supreme Court review of legislation) brought before the Court during the late 1990s addressed the constitutional interpretation of electoral laws. They also observe that it may be some time yet before Supreme Court actions have a significant impact upon the criteria employed by lower-level courts. However, the Court's rulings against compulsory membership in public-employee unions and chambers of commerce and industry are important exceptions to these generalizations.

investigate, prosecute, and punish crime effectively. The magnitude of the challenge is easily summarized: a mere three percent of criminal suspects are ever brought before a court of law. One important reason for states' poor overall record in combating crime is that most of them fail to devote sufficient resources to this purpose. However, Magaloni and Zepeda also show that most judicial and law enforcement authorities are quite inefficient in their conduct of criminal investigations. In the year 2000, for example, state-level public prosecutors failed to conduct effective investigations into 81.5 percent of reported crimes. Even in the most high-profile cases (murders), the best-performing state (Tabasco) only managed a 31.1 percent conviction rate over the 1996–2000 period.[70]

Magaloni and Zepeda (this volume) conclude that the overall incidence of crime in Mexico during the 1996–2000 period varied with levels of poverty, differences in states' economic performance, and the quality of judicial and law enforcement institutions. Increasing the severity of punishment did not deter criminals, but improving the efficiency of law enforcement operations (that is, carrying out more effective investigations, apprehending more criminals, and convicting them more often) did. The distribution of authority within Mexico's federal system means that, although the national government can help fight crime by allocating more federal funds to this effort or by gathering information on criminal organizations that operate across state boundaries, state-level public prosecutors' offices and judiciaries are the main actors in this area. This is one further example of the way in which developments at state and local levels of government are increasingly important to the overall quality of democracy in Mexico.

Reforms that improve the effectiveness of judicial and law enforcement institutions are vital to establishing firmly the rule of law and overcoming the challenge of "democracy without citizenship" (Pinheiro 1999: 2).[71] However, nongovernmental organizations, mass communications media, and other non-state actors can also play a significant role in this regard by monitoring the performance of judicial and law enforcement personnel and by helping define the agenda for further reforms in this arena. Their contributions may be especially important in the human rights area, where a key issue remains how to strengthen legal due process and protect citizens from arbitrary state action.

The New Federalism

The gradual centralization of political power in the decades after the Mexican revolution produced a federal arrangement whose dynamics were considerably at odds with the formal distribution of governmental responsibilities established by the 1917 Constitution. The president's control over the "official" party provided him with ample leverage over state and municipal government officials, including

---

70 Magaloni and Zepeda (this volume), figure 6.2 and table 6.4.

71 See Domingo and Sieder 2001 for an overview of the multiple changes involved in strengthening the rule of law in Latin America.

the capacity to compel the resignation of governors who lost presidential favor. A federal/state compact on tax collection negotiated in 1947 further reduced local governments' effective authority by permitting the national government, in exchange for limited revenue sharing with state and municipal governments and local officials' access to various forms of political patronage, to levy nearly all taxes.[72] Although recent scholarship has rightly questioned exaggerated accounts of centralism that denied the existence of a vibrant political life at state and local levels (Rubin 1997), central government dominance over state and municipal authorities was a key feature of postrevolutionary authoritarian rule.

Yet Mexico's federal system also provided important venues for the development of vigorous multiparty competition and partisan alternation in government. Indeed, as Alberto Díaz-Cayeros observes in his chapter in this volume, political liberalization and gradual decentralization were overlapping trends from the 1980s onwards. For instance, at the same time that state and municipal elections were emerging as important political battlegrounds, President Miguel de la Madrid implemented a 1983 constitutional reform that strengthened municipalities' financial and administrative autonomy. Similarly, in 1998 the Zedillo administration established a special budgetary item (*ramo 33 aportaciones*) to facilitate federal transfers to local governments for education, health care, and social infrastructure. By the late 1990s, state and municipal governments carried out more than half of all national expenditures (Díaz-Cayeros, this volume).

Yet despite their growing political importance and policy relevance, state and municipal governments remained highly dependent upon federal revenue transfers, making this a priority area for action after the Fox administration took office in December 2000. In seeking to bolster local governments' financial and administrative capacities, President Fox responded not only to local officials' calls for devolution of the resources necessary to satisfy citizens' demands, but also to the substantial experience that the National Action Party (and Fox himself, as governor of Guanajuato between 1995 and 1999) had acquired by governing at state and municipal levels during the 1980s and 1990s and to the PAN's long-held ideological position in favor of strengthening those branches of government in closest contact with individual citizens.[73]

Nevertheless, how to undertake a more general renewal of federalism by designing fiscal and administrative arrangements that better reflect the country's altered political realities is one of the most important policy issues in contemporary Mexico. Díaz-Cayeros (this volume) notes that this challenge is especially acute because of severe regional inequalities and the differential growth prospects that states face in a liberalized economy because of substantial variations in their

---

72 For a discussion of this compact, see the essay by Alberto Díaz-Cayeros in this volume. Díaz-Cayeros estimates that, circa 2000, state and municipal governments collected only five percent of national revenue.

73 For discussions of the PAN's advocacy of strengthened local government, see Lujambio 2001 and Middlebrook 2001.

infrastructure and human capital resources. The fiscal compact in effect since the late 1940s permits the federal government to allocate funds to poorer states in order to compensate them for their greater socioeconomic needs, but richer states have a strong interest in reforming fiscal federalism so as to provide them with greater control over the tax revenues derived from local economic activity. Díaz-Cayeros concludes that, if states and the federal government are to collaborate successfully to increase local autonomy while simultaneously preserving the federal government's capacity to promote the national interest by offering additional support to disadvantaged regions, then "governors and municipal presidents will need to risk losing popularity by increasing local taxation, and the federal government must devolve the authority to levy taxes even at the cost of less efficient tax collection." He cautions, however, that the reality of heightened party competition at the state level and the possibility that rival parties might mobilize divisions between richer and poorer states may seriously complicate efforts to reform Mexico's federal system.

Civil-Military Relations

Civil-military interactions are a fourth important example of the major challenges involved in re-institutionalizing Mexican politics in a more plural, competitive context. Unlike democratic transitions in many other countries during the 1980s and 1990s, there is virtually no risk in Mexico that an elected civilian government will be overthrown by coup d'état. The pattern of civil-military relations established under postrevolutionary authoritarian rule was quite stable, and since the 1940s the armed forces have been firmly under civilian control.[74] The Mexican military has frequently been guilty of major human rights violations,[75] and the military's increasing involvement in drug interdiction and eradication efforts since the late 1970s has produced serious problems of corruption at the highest levels of the armed forces. Yet one positive legacy of Mexico's hegemonic-party regime is that

---

74 Indeed, Roderic Camp (this volume) argues that Mexico has the longest record of military subordination to civilian rule of any Latin American country.

    For more extensive treatments of civil-military relations in Mexico, see Camp 1992 and Serrano 1995.

75 One consequence of political opening in Mexico (and one way in which the Mexican case parallels the experience of other democratizing countries) has been greatly expanded access to documentary information concerning the military's human rights violations and public demands for comprehensive investigations of them. Under pressure from human rights groups, victims' families, and the mass media, the Fox administration opened military and police files compiled from 1950 to 1985. This new information provided evidentiary support for efforts to bring to justice those civilian, military, and police officials responsible for Mexico's "dirty war" against leftist opponents in the late 1960s and early 1970s. The cases under examination included the October 2, 1968 Tlatelolco massacre (in which as many as three hundred student demonstrators were killed), the June 10, 1971 ("Jueves de Corpus") attack by paramilitary groups on demonstrators in Mexico City that left 29 dead, and the approximately 275 people who were "disappeared" while in government custody during the late 1960s and early 1970s. See *San Diego Union-Tribune* 23 June 2002, p. A19.

there is no established tradition of anti-system partisan competition for military support, the dynamic that has frequently contributed to breakdowns of democratic regimes elsewhere in Latin America. Nor do the civilian leaders of Mexico's democratic transition face the politically contentious task of curtailing institutional, policy-making, and budgetary privileges accumulated by the armed forces during a lengthy period of military rule.[76]

There are, however, sources of tension in contemporary civil-military relations. As Roderic Camp argues in his contribution to this volume, the (re)emergence of armed guerrilla groups in the 1990s and the rising levels of violence associated with drug trafficking unsettled the Mexican military. The EZLN rebellion (followed by the appearance of the Popular Revolutionary Army [ERP] and other armed groups) raised particularly serious concerns within the armed forces regarding the effectiveness of their internal organization, technical training, and equipment. These events led the Salinas and Zedillo administrations to expand significantly the military's personnel and budgetary resources. Nevertheless, in the context of growing political and media pluralism, dissident elements within the armed forces increasingly articulated their concerns in public. At the same time, greater freedom of expression in the mass media contributed to more intensive scrutiny of the military's actions, and military involvement in human rights violations led to conflictive relations between the armed forces and communications media, the Roman Catholic Church, and human rights groups.

Over a number of decades the Mexican armed forces maintained a strong public posture of nonpartisanship, a position greatly facilitated by the absence of any significant challenge to PRI rule. For this very reason, however, what is at stake in future years is the military's capacity to operate effectively in a more plural political environment. During the late 1990s the armed forces' leadership undertook several initiatives designed to reduce their insularity, including increasing the number of civilian instructors in advanced-training courses, admitting larger numbers of civilian students to classes at the National Defense College (CDN), and expanding military officers' participation in master's and doctoral programs at civilian educational institutions. At the same time, opposition parties' growing strength in the late 1990s gradually compelled the officer corps to deal with a broader range of partisan forces (Camp, this volume).[77] Nonetheless, it remains to be seen whether more intense multiparty competition might over time create new fissures within the military and undermine the armed forces' institutional cohesion and loyalty. Parties such as the PAN and PRD will also be challenged to develop for the first time national security strategies and ways off dealing with military concerns, especially on such symbolically important and politically sensitive matters as human rights violations by armed forces personnel.

76 For a comparative analysis of these challenges in South American transitions, see Stepan 1988.
77 Serrano reports (1995: 444) that, of the many military officers who held public posts between 1935 and 1987, only one belonged to the opposition. Not until the early 1990s did officers express public sympathy for an opposition party.

State-Society Relations

The pattern of state-society relations defined (and encrusted) in Mexico over a period of eight decades was a core element of the old regime's institutionality and, where the construction of a more democratic political and social order is concerned, perhaps the most problematic aspect of the country's authoritarian legacy. Democratization in this area promises to be an even slower, more complicated process than in the electoral arena, both because the rules of electoral competition constitute a comparatively simpler focus for democratizing initiatives and because changes in state-society relations may have ambiguous political consequences. Moreover, electoral democracy itself may have a more gradual, uneven impact in this area than it has had on, for instance, intergovernmental relations. At a minimum, it is probable that processes of democratic opening and consolidation will continue to follow different logics and proceed at different paces in the electoral and non-electoral spheres.

Whereas political factors such as increased partisan competition and media opening have been the main sources of change in intergovernmental and civil-military relations, economic forces (especially the combination of financial crisis, prolonged economic stagnation, and market-oriented reforms) have been the principal elements producing major shifts in the state's relations with rural producers, urban and industrial workers, and the private sector. Of course, political liberalization was also significant in this regard because, among other things, this process slowly but continuously raised the costs of repression for state elites and permitted some societal organizations to establish somewhat greater autonomy vis-à-vis the state. It is also important to recognize that different combinations of political and economic forces had differential effects upon the state's ties with distinct social groups.[78]

At least in the three instances considered in this volume – the state's links with rural producers, organized labor, and business interests – there has been a roughly U-shaped relationship between the impact upon state-society relations of financial crisis, market-oriented economic reforms, and political opening, on the one hand, and the social status of the actor involved, on the other. That is, these factors have effected the most significant changes in the character of the state's relations with rural producers and with private-sector interests. There have also been substantial shifts in state-labor relations, but patterns in this area at the beginning of the Fox administration more closely paralleled those in place during the PRI's long reign than in the other two cases examined here.

In each of these three examples, there were two broad consequences of economic and political change. First, "state withdrawal" and increasingly competitive electoral contests promoted greater political pluralism both within sectors and in key societal actors' partisan allegiances, even though some older patterns have proved

78 For an initial assessment of the impacts of economic and political liberalization on state-society relations in Mexico, see Cook, Middlebrook, and Molinar 1994.

remarkably resilient and, in some instances (ties between the traditionally state-supported labor movement and the PRI, for example), more competitive electoral politics may actually have reinforced some long-established ties. Second, economic restructuring also promoted institutional innovation within sectors in terms of the different forms of collective organization (and the character of ties between organizations' leaders and members) that emerged to represent different constituencies' interests in a more competitive political and economic environment.

Rural Producers and the State

Market-oriented economic reforms were especially important in substantially redefining relations between rural producers' organizations and the PRI–led regime during the late 1980s and the 1990s. As Horacio Mackinlay shows in his contribution to this volume, both peasants and family farmers had long been embedded in a complex system of state-mediated interest representation based upon, respectively, social-property and private forms of land tenure. Federal regulation of land tenure arrangements (including the promise/threat of land expropriation and distribution under the terms of postrevolutionary agrarian reform legislation), government management of extensive credit and marketing facilities, and the hierarchical organization of rural producers (especially agrarian reform beneficiaries) through "official" party-affiliated associations that reached upward from local ejido leadership bodies to national party structures, all provided governing elites with strong political controls – and, for several decades, a reservoir of real popular support – in the countryside. In some instances, private-sector groups secured from government agencies the right to fulfill important administrative and marketing functions (for example, establishing sanitary and shipping guidelines and granting certificates of origin and export permits), thus cementing their alliance with the regime.

However, the economic reforms introduced during the Salinas administration (particularly the 1992 constitutional and legislative reforms ending land distribution and permitting the privatization of ejido lands, the dismantling or privatization of state-owned firms supporting agricultural production, the reduction or elimination of subsidized credit and production inputs and price supports for agricultural commodities, and sharp cuts in tariff protection for domestic producers) implied dramatic changes in the scale and form of state intervention in rural production. This transformation, coupled with the reorganization of agricultural activities in the context of regional and global economic integration, substantially altered the political and policy-making circumstances facing rural producers.

Sharply reduced state involvement and increased domestic and foreign economic competition challenged the established position of many private-sector rural producers' associations. Rapid market deregulation deprived many of them of their quasi-governmental administrative faculties, causing some producers' associations to disintegrate and others to adopt significantly different strategies to sustain their memberships. In the case of peasant groups, the redefinition of the state's role and shifts in the range and character of government agricultural policies also strongly affected the fates of different organizations, eliminating their intermediary functions and leaving many of them without a clear policy agenda and in organizational disarray. The National Peasants' Confederation (CNC, founded in 1938) – long a mainstay of the rural corporatist system and the "official" party's principal vehicle for mobilizing electoral support in the countryside – initially weathered the winds of neoliberal transformation by using its national political ties to gain privileged access to policy-making councils and acquire the assets of many of those state-owned firms transferred to rural producers' groups. However, the CNC's rote defense of the established regime and its inability to deliver policies to counteract a deepening economic crisis in the countryside eventually left it weakened and discredited.[79]

For the purposes of this analysis, however, the most important consequences of market-oriented economic restructuring in the Mexican countryside occurred in the political sphere. By greatly reducing the regulatory intervention of state officials in ejidos' and agrarian communities' internal affairs, the economic reform process significantly eroded political controls over peasants. As a consequence, the PRI's hitherto reliable "green vote" declined in importance, and rural voters became more available for mobilization by opposition parties.[80] The dimensions of this shift became fully apparent in the year 2000 presidential election when Vicente Fox – a charismatic candidate with a background in rural Guanajuato, a plainspoken and often rough-edged style, casual dress that featured cowboy boots and an oversized belt buckle emblazoned "Fox," and a quarter horse named "2 de julio" (Fox's birthday, and the date of presidential balloting) – won significant rural support.[81]

Thus, what occurred in rural Mexico was gradual change in the political landscape – the implications of which were illuminated at a key electoral moment – rather than a major fracturing of rural producers' organizations and open alliances with opposition parties. In this regard, there are parallels between the character of political change in rural areas and in the urban/industrial labor sector (see below).

---

79 As Mackinlay (this volume) observes, the PRI's loss of the presidency in the year 2000 greatly contributed to divisive internal factionalism within the CNC, which suddenly found itself in an unaccustomed opposition role.

80 Of course, economic changes affecting rural producers' relations with the state interacted with national political developments. Mackinlay (this volume) notes that the PRI's near-loss in the 1988 presidential election eroded regime legitimacy and accelerated some rural organizations' drive for greater autonomy vis-à-vis the state.

81 The PAN more than doubled its support among rural voters between 1991 and the year 2000. See Buendía (this volume, figure 4.2).

Fox's down-to-earth personal manner, which many Mexican voters found highly appealing, was clearly in evidence on election eve. As Fox stood on the balcony of the PAN headquarters building in Mexico City and greeted cheering supporters, someone handed him a bottle of champagne. Fox took a long drink directly from the open bottle, wiped his mouth with the back of his hand, and exclaimed to the admiring crowd, "Tequila is better!" ("¡El tequila está mejor!").

However, this pattern contrasts with developments in state-private sector relations, where some employers' groups and important numbers of entrepreneurs openly embraced opposition parties (especially the PAN) at a much earlier date.

Despite the significance of these developments, political and societal democratization remains a tremendous challenge in rural Mexico. As Mackinlay (this volume) shows, declining state influence and growing political pluralism within producers' associations have permitted rural groups to mobilize much more vigorously against trade opening and other policies that threaten rural livelihoods. However, in many areas local bosses and old-style organizations like the CNC continue to dominate. Nor has the state's reduced regulatory control over ejidos and agrarian communities automatically produced improved opportunities for local-level participation by rural residents.

State-Labor Relations

Changes in Mexico's political economy during the 1980s and 1990s also had major consequences for the organized labor movement and for state-labor relations. The durable (albeit highly unequal) alliance between successive governments and major elements of the organized labor movement was a central pillar of the postrevolutionary authoritarian regime. Participation in the governing coalition permitted many labor organizations to win both significant material benefits for members (including access to government-financed housing, health care, low-cost consumer goods, and a legally mandated share of enterprise profits) and representation in important elective and administrative offices. Yet the combination of state administrative controls on labor participation, selective repression, and many unions' heavy dependence upon state-provided legal, financial, and political subsidies allowed the ruling political elite to define (and redefine) the terms of its alliance with labor. The principal value that labor organizations historically had for Mexico's postrevolutionary political elite was their capacity to constrain workers' economic demands and block worker mobilization during periods of actual or potential economic and political instability.

Over the course of several decades, Mexico's model of import-substituting industrialization helped sustain this alliance by delivering economic growth, employment opportunities, and, especially after the mid-1950s, rising real wages and expanding social welfare benefits that significantly improved many workers' standard of living.[82] However, as Graciela Bensusán amply demonstrates in her chapter in this volume, the shift to a market-led development strategy and extensive industrial restructuring during the 1980s and 1990s significantly reduced the labor movement's overall size, mobilizational capacity, and bargaining power. Government officials

---

82 Because they were protected from import competition, private-sector firms could maintain comfortable profit margins despite rising wages. Active state regulation of economic affairs and an expanding public sector also made it easier for major labor organizations to translate their political importance into social and economic policy gains.

kept wage increases well below the rate of inflation in order to maintain macro-economic stability and improve Mexico's comparative advantage in international economic competition. As a result, wage differences between unionized and non-unionized workers virtually disappeared. Business interests were the principal winners in a process of economic transformation that greatly enhanced their bargaining leverage vis-à-vis both organized labor and the government and produced extensive job losses and sharp cutbacks in contract-based wages and fringe benefits.[83]

However, the impact of these trends upon specific labor organizations varied substantially. Bensusán (this volume) argues persuasively that these differences reflected variations in unions' autonomy vis-à-vis employers and the state, the character of union leadership (especially union leaders' accountability to rank-and-file members), and the extent of union democracy. Thus, traditional elements such as the Confederation of Mexican Workers (CTM, the PRI's labor sector and still Mexico's largest single labor organization) preserved many of their formal prerogatives and successfully avoided modifications of the federal labor code that would have undercut their entrenched position in the workplace, but they found it increasingly difficult to influence government policies, shield their members from employment and wage cuts, or develop innovative responses to the demands posed by new technologies, production processes, and forms of workplace organization. More democratic unions with higher degrees of leadership accountability and operational autonomy (such as the Mexican Telephone Workers' Union, STRM) also faced significant challenges, but they had a comparatively greater capacity to mobilize rank-and-file support to confront the dilemmas posed by technological change and radical industrial restructuring as employers sought to gain additional flexibility in increasingly competitive domestic and international markets. As a consequence, they proved more capable of bargaining effectively with both employers and the government to defend their members' core interests.

Mexico's gradual process of political opening intersected obliquely with these developments. Such factors as the expanding strength of opposition parties, the gradual erosion of hyper-presidentialism after the mid-1990s, and declining government repression all strengthened the position of independent labor organizations and enhanced their autonomy vis-à-vis the state. These changes, coupled with the discredit that the CTM and other government-aligned labor organizations incurred because of their acceptance of privatization and industrial restructuring initiatives, eroded "official" unions' control over their members and produced greater political pluralism within both individual unions and the labor movement as a whole. In 1997 a substantial coalition of more politically independent unions

---

83 Graciela Bensusán (this volume) reports that the inflation-adjusted official minimum wage fell by 74.6 percent between 1982 and 2001, while average real contract-based wages declined by 59.3 percent over the 1982–2000 period. Job losses were particularly severe in sectors with high union density, especially in activities dominated by the powerful national industrial unions that had been the backbone of the Mexican labor movement.

came together as the National Union of Workers (UNT), with the explicit goal of contesting CTM leadership in the labor movement and advocating an alternative development model. For the most part, however, links between labor unions and parties such as the PRD and the PAN remained quite limited.[84] Indeed, the PRI's historic alliance with the CTM and other unions grouped in the Labor Congress (CT) remained largely intact, and the PAN's national victory in the year 2000 may actually have reinforced these ties by increasing the CTM's relative importance to the PRI as a stalwart electoral ally in a much more competitive political environment.

In other areas as well, electoral democratization has thus far exerted only modest pressures for change in the pattern of state-labor relations established during decades of authoritarian rule. Bensusán (this volume) demonstrates that the historical alliance between leading labor organizations and postrevolutionary governments had ceased to protect workers' interests well before the PRI lost control of the federal executive. During the 1990s, new sources of labor power (including international alliances with foreign trade unions and nongovernmental organizations) acquired greater potential importance. Yet it remains to be seen how rapidly and broadly these forces will transform Mexican labor politics.

It was particularly telling in this regard that the CT and the leading employers' organizations dominated negotiations over reform of the federal labor code during 2001 and 2002. In fact, the UNT withdrew from the negotiations when it failed to advance the proposals it considered of vital importance (ending the state's regulatory role in union registration, requiring that union elections be held by secret ballot, ensuring a nonpartisan system of labor justice, and so forth). The legislative proposal for a revised labor code that the PAN and the PRI jointly submitted to Congress in December 2002 included provisions designed to increase transparency in state regulation of labor affairs and promote flexibility in work practices, but it left unchanged key articles that had long underpinned traditional labor unions' organizational presence in the workplace. Overall, then, the prospects for significant democratization of union and workplace affairs remained uncertain despite substantial changes in the political and economic environment in which labor organizations operate.

State-Private Sector Relations
Of the three instances of state-society relations considered in this subsection, ties between the private sector and the state evidenced the most rapid transformation over the course of the 1980s and 1990s. As noted above, the 1982 bank nationalization compelled many private-sector groups to reassess their traditional alliance with state elites, and their search for increased organizational autonomy and their efforts

84 One important exception involved the Authentic Labor Front (FAT), an independent organization with Christian Democratic roots that parlayed its opposition to the North American Free Trade Agreement and its resulting alliances with U.S. and Canadian unions into a much more visible political presence. Several of its affiliates became PRD party-list nominees for the federal Chamber of Deputies.

to constrain the discretionary powers of the presidency were important elements in promoting regime opening. In turn, Mexico's altered economic and political environment during the 1990s opened new avenues of political action to business interests and encouraged the emergence of different forms of private-sector collective organization.

As Matilde Luna notes in her essay in this volume, one of the most important departures involved the institutional context for private-sector political action and forms of economic governance. Compulsory membership in chambers of commerce and industry had since 1936 structured relations between the state and business interests along corporatist lines, and it had laid the bases for such forms of state-business cooperation as the tripartite economic pacts negotiated among government, labor, and business to promote macroeconomic stability between 1987 and 1995. The abolition of compulsory membership in sector organizations in 1996 thus encouraged diversification in the private sector's political alignments and strategies. Equally important in this regard was increasing pluralism in national politics, which significantly expanded the range of potential allies available to the private sector.

Over the course of the 1980s and 1990s, then, business organizations became more actively engaged in public debates over government economic policy.[85] The negotiations over the North American Free Trade Agreement were a high-water mark in this regard, with a wide range of private-sector interests organized in a special consultative body (the Foreign Trade Business Organizations' Coordinating Network, COECE) established to help shape the Mexican government's bargaining positions. At the same time, more traditional, hierarchical business organizations lost credibility and influence in a much more competitive political and economic environment, and more flexible and representative forms of private-sector economic governance (voluntary membership associations, informal networks, and policy communities) gained increasing prominence. These changes may have laid the bases for more effective, policy-specific business lobbying in a more democratic Mexico.

Somewhat ironically, one consequence of these overlapping political, economic, and institutional shifts has been substantially increased conflict within business organizations themselves (rather than with government).[86] This development reflected both the elimination of compulsory sector membership and the differential effects of economic liberalization (especially the privatization of state-owned enterprises and trade opening). Some of these disputes have focused upon the

---

85 As Matilde Luna (this volume) notes, private-sector groups also established liaison commissions and other arrangements designed to influence congressional debates and other kinds of public policies. In addition, business leaders themselves became increasingly active politically as candidates for elective office. Many of these candidates were affiliated with the PAN and the PRI, but in the late 1990s the PRD actively sought to build a network of state-level business roundtables.

86 This discussion draws upon Luna (this volume).

authority of the Private Sector Coordinating Council (CCE, the body that has grouped the largest national business associations), the policies it advocates (particularly the relative importance to be given macroeconomic and micro-economic priorities in national development strategy, the merits of formulating a national industrial policy, and the role that government should play in these areas), and the extent to which it is representative of the private sector as a whole. The new bases for political differentiation within the private sector include divisions between producers and financiers, between large and small firms, between export-oriented companies and those producing primarily for the domestic market, and between firms located in the Mexico City metropolitan area and those in other regions of the country.

Challenges of Rights and Representation

In addition to redefining the balance in state-society relations so as to expand opportunities for participation, consolidating and deepening democracy in Mexico requires expanding citizenship rights and creating new forms of representation in several areas. Among the topics examined in this volume, the rights of indigenous peoples constitute the most pressing example of the unresolved representational challenges facing Mexican democracy.

The chapter by Luis Hernández Navarro and Laura Carlsen recounts that indigenous peoples had struggled for centuries to establish the constitutional and legal conditions for the exercise of political, economic, and cultural autonomy, and in 1992 the Salinas administration modified Article 4 of the 1917 Constitution to recognize formally Mexico's Indian peoples. Nevertheless, it was not until the EZLN–led rebellion broke out in Chiapas that the question of indigenous rights moved to the center of national political debate. In February 1996 the Zedillo administration and the Zapatistas signed the so-called San Andrés Accords on Indigenous Rights and Culture,[87] and the multiparty congressional Commission on Concordance and Pacification (COCOPA) used these agreements as the basis for a formal proposal for constitutional reform. However, the Zedillo administration subsequently rejected the November 1996 COCOPA proposal on the grounds that its provisions threatened national unity by creating special territorial, political, and legal privi-leges for indigenous groups.[88] The result was a prolonged stalemate in negotiations with the EZLN. Not until the newly inaugurated Fox administration addressed the issue did the Mexican Congress actually enact (in May 2001) the required constitutional reforms and the Law on Indigenous Rights and Culture.

---

87 The agreements were named after the town of San Andrés Larráinzar, Chiapas, where the negotiations took place.

88 See the chapter by Luis Hernández Navarro and Laura Carlsen in this volume for a more detailed examination of the political considerations behind the Zedillo administration's stance regarding the COCOPA proposal.

The EZLN, the National Indigenous Congress (CNI), and their political allies denounced the 2001 reform measures as woefully inadequate, and indeed they were not ratified by legislatures in several of the states with the largest indigenous populations. Hernández Navarro and Carlsen (this volume) strongly criticize the legislation for failing to establish the collective political rights – that is, the rights of indigenous *peoples*, not just the rights of individual citizens – outlined in the original San Andrés Accords. Among other things, they argue that the 2001 "counterreform" fails to transfer to indigenous peoples in any meaningful way the faculties and functions (including forms of political representation within the community and the municipality, autonomy of the local justice system, and control over land, natural resources, and administrative affairs) necessary to permit the real self-determination of indigenous peoples. Moreover, it constrained the exercise of indigenous common law and traditional forms of self-government, and it left to the states the question of what forms of autonomy would be granted to indigenous communities. A legal challenge to the 2001 law was rejected by the Supreme Court in September 2002, but, given the issues and the intensity of the political convictions involved, it seemed unlikely that this outcome would end the longer-term struggle over how to recognize in political terms the ethnic and cultural pluralism that characterizes Mexican society.

The political status of Mexican emigrants abroad offers a second important example of a pending representational challenge. In his contribution to this volume, David Fitzgerald notes that in the late 1990s President Ernesto Zedillo embraced a more expansive definition of the Mexican "nation" that included extra-territorial citizens, and he backed a 1996 constitutional amendment that allowed Mexicans to maintain their Mexican nationality even after they become naturalized citizens of another country – thus establishing dual nationality but not dual citizenship.[89] From the outset of his administration, President Vicente Fox also explicitly recognized Mexicans living abroad as part of the national community. There has, moreover, been some discussion of the possibility of creating an extra-territorial electoral district to provide Mexicans abroad with direct representation in the federal Congress. Nevertheless, precisely where the boundary between the national and transnational Mexican communities should be drawn, and the potentially decisive impact upon Mexican elections of several million expatriate voters who may not otherwise participate actively in national life, remain sources of potential controversy. At a purely practical level, overcoming the resistance posed by some segments of the domestic population and passing the legislation necessary to implement the 1996 émigré voting rights provision will require the investment of substantial political capital.

89 Under this constitutional provision, former Mexican nationals can "recover" their Mexican nationality, and first-generation children born to Mexican nationals outside Mexico can also apply for dual nationality. As David Fitzgerald (this volume) notes, "dual nationals have property rights in Mexico and other privileges denied to foreigners, but they do not have the right to vote."

It is paradoxical that, as democratization has advanced and opened up additional issues for public debate, some questions of citizenship rights and representation have become more controversial. For example, just as initial media opening actually provoked an increase in repressive retaliation against dissident editors and reporters, the consideration of such matters as the rights of indigenous peoples has generated greater controversy because of the more politically plural context in which it occurs – the very emergence of which permitted this debate to occur. The resolution of such questions will necessarily involve sustained debate about how to balance Mexico's traditions of collective social and individual political rights, both of which are embedded in the 1917 Constitution and recognized in different laws. The contemporary democratic ethos certainly privileges individual rights and freedoms. However, significant portions of Mexican society support the view (articulated in this volume by Hernández Navarro and Carlsen) that creating the constitutional and political conditions that would permit indigenous peoples to rebuild their communities in the broadest economic and cultural sense requires the "the *different exercise of rights* in order to ensure access to *universal rights*" within a larger community. This is, of course, not only a question of governmental policy or initiative. As the cases of both indigenous and immigrant rights amply illustrate, advancing rights and representation will also depend fundamentally upon the actions taken and spaces created by social actors themselves.[90]

Challenges for Mexican Democracy

This concluding section highlights three issues of particular importance to the future of democracy in Mexico. These are: the impact of severe inequality and poverty upon the inclusiveness of democratic political arrangements and overall public support for democracy; the relationship between political culture and the longer-term strength and character of democracy; and the growing influence of international forces in Mexican politics.

Inequality, Poverty, and Democracy

Many observers have voiced concern about the medium- and long-term effects that socioeconomic inequality and poverty may have upon the quality of democracy in Mexico. This concern reflects the simple but compelling fact that political opening has coincided with a substantial worsening of both problems.[91] Indeed, income inequality grew considerably from the mid-1980s through the year 2000, with the Gini coefficient of total (monetary and non-monetary) income rising from 0.429 in 1984 to 0.481 in the year 2000 (Boltvinik 2003: table 11.3). Similarly, income

---

90 One such example involves the 2,000-member Binational Indigenous Oaxacan Front (FIOB), which has created a vigorous binational movement demanding recognition of the special rights of indigenous peoples. See Fitzgerald (this volume).
91 This discussion draws upon Middlebrook and Zepeda 2003a: 31–35.

poverty rose significantly over the 1981–1989 and 1994–1996 periods, and some studies suggest that the incidence of income poverty was greater in 1998 than in 1968 – with as much as one-fifth of Mexico's total population and two-thirds of the rural population living in extreme poverty.[92] Of course, Mexico has long suffered from serious problems of inequality and poverty, and it is not surprising that the situation worsened during the post-1982 period of deep recession and structural adjustment. However, there is considerable evidence that the central characteristics of Mexico's new economic model – especially macroeconomic policies that depressed real wages and aggregate demand in order to control inflation, relatively modest employment creation in export-oriented sectors, and changes in governmental social welfare policies that reduced public-sector health care and social security benefits – badly aggravated these problems.[93]

Poverty and inequality are no doubt major public policy challenges, but do these problems pose substantial risks to the consolidation and deepening of democracy? Some analysts argue that severe socioeconomic inequality does indeed constitute a significant threat to democratic stability.[94] However, few of them detail how this threat might be manifested. Castañeda, for example, has suggested (1996: 48, 53) that accumulated popular demands and deep-seated frustration with social injustice could produce a social explosion that might overwhelm a recently installed democratic government, although there was no clear-cut instance of this occurring in Latin America during the 1980s and 1990s. There is, nevertheless, evidence indicating a strong inverse relationship between inequality and the public acceptance of democracy.[95] This phenomenon might be manifested as a general disillusionment with politics, abstention from electoral processes, and so forth.

There may also be three further ways in which inequality and poverty might negatively affect democracy in Mexico. First, as O'Donnell (1999a: 205 and 1999b: 306–7) has forcefully argued, these problems challenge a principal underpinning of democracy: the assumption of the basic equality of individuals. Thus, unless government officials undertake vigorous measures to reduce substantially existing socioeconomic differences, the persistence of poverty and inequality may sap the legitimacy of democracy. Moreover, these problems may increase the probability that large sectors of the population will remain vulnerable to political coercion, clientelist domination, and violence of different kinds, thus precluding the

---

92 Boltvinik 2003: 405; Alarcón 2003: 455–58. Boltvinik provides a systematic analysis of the evolution of both income poverty and what he labels "specific poverties" – that is, deprivation in such specific needs as access to publicly provided goods and services (including piped-in water, sewerage, electricity, health care, and social security), free time, and knowledge.

93 Julio Boltvinik (2003: 404) concludes that "greater inequality is intrinsic to Mexico's new economic model."

94 See, for example, Castañeda 1996: 49–50 and 2003: 141; Vilas 1997; and Karl 2000: 155–56. Adam Przeworski et al. (1996: 43) found that "democracy is much more likely to survive in countries where income inequality is declining over time."

95 See Elizondo 2003: figure 1.11, and Karl 2000: 155–56.

development of individual and associational autonomy so crucial to the functioning of a democratic polity.[96]

Second, severe inequality and poverty may substantially constrain the opportunities that poor people have to participate meaningfully in politics, thereby
reducing the inclusiveness and quality of democracy. It is well-established that
differences in socioeconomic status affect individuals' capacity to engage in different forms of political participation, with lower-status individuals frequently lacking
the time or material resources required to exercise effective political influence.[97] Early
in Mexico's postrevolutionary period, the mass organization of workers, peasants,
and other popular groups partially compensated for status disadvantages by
increasing these elements' political leverage. It is somewhat ironic, therefore, that
one consequence of regime opening has been the erosion of mass organizations and
an increased emphasis upon individual political participation – processes that
accentuate the socioeconomic status bias in politics and therefore privilege the
power and influence of upper strata in electoral politics, legislative policy making,
and other public spheres.[98]

Third, poverty and inequality may worsen specific problems that in themselves
constitute threats to democratic governance. One such example is crime. As Magaloni and Zepeda (this volume) document, rising income inequality in developing
countries during the 1990s contributed directly to higher rates of violent crime
such as robbery and murder. By producing a generalized sense of public insecurity, a
high incidence of crime can undermine civic trust and reduce citizens' participation in the community-level activities and social organizations that underpin
representative democracy.

Given the severity of the challenges that poverty and inequality potentially pose
to democratic governance, one must ask whether a newly established democracy is
capable of coping with them. One could argue that the intensity of Mexican voters'
concern about poverty,[99] voters' demonstrated willingness since the 1990s to withdraw their electoral support and thereby sanction parties that fail to meet their
expectations for performance in office, and the correspondingly greater accountability of public officials in a highly competitive electoral environment are all
factors that substantially increase the pressures on government to act effectively in

96 See Fox 1997 for an exploration of these issues in the context of rural Mexico.
97 See Nie and Verba 1975 for a review of the literature on political participation.
      Moreover, to the extent that civil society organizations' efforts to promote broadly defined
    human rights require "… social spaces and fields in which to experiment with different
    lifestyles, and a pluralistic culture open to change…" (Olvera, this volume), extreme social
    inequality denies such spaces to the vast majority of the population.
98 Jorge Correa Sutil (1999: 268–69) reaches similar conclusions regarding the consequences of
    the state's declining socioeconomic activism and the growing prominence of the market in
    Latin America.
99 A national public opinion poll conducted by *Reforma* newspaper in May 2003 found that
    voters were more concerned about poverty than any other major public policy issue.

this area. However, as Castañeda (1996: 57, 59–60) has cautioned, a democratic government's actual capacity to reduce inequalities over time (via such modestly redistributive policies as higher government expenditures on education, health care, housing, and so forth) requires sustained economic growth. And in this regard, Mexico, like other Latin American countries, faces severe constraints in the form of continued capital scarcity and foreign debt obligations – long-term consequences of the debt crisis of the 1980s.

Political Culture and Democracy

One of the longest debates in the study of politics concerns the relationship between political culture and democracy.[100] The central question is whether certain attitudes, beliefs, values, and associated patterns of behavior are more conducive to the construction and practice of political democracy than others. As Huntington (1991: 298) summarizes the matter, "A profoundly anti-democratic culture would impede the spread of democratic norms in society, deny legitimacy to democratic institutions, and thus greatly complicate if not prevent the emergence and effective functioning of those institutions." This issue is especially important for recently established democracies because, as Turner (1995: 212) and other authors have stressed, deep-rooted cultural values change slowly – over generations rather than a few years.

Some researchers have questioned the significance of political culture as an explanatory factor in the success of democracy by stressing the broad variations in attitudes, values, and practices that exist within a national territory (Knight 2001: 225–26). Nevertheless, there remains a widely shared sense that there is an important, if not easily explicated, relationship between pre-existing cultural norms and the legacies of authoritarian rule, on the one hand, and the prospects for democracy in countries like Mexico, on the other.[101]

There is unlikely to be quick closure to the debate about the impact that underlying cultural values have on democratization or the longer-term character of democracy. Even if one accepts the argument that some attitudes, values, and behavioral patterns (interpersonal trust, for instance)[102] are more congruent with democracy than others, and that some cultural traditions historically are more (or less) closely associated with political democracy than others, the internal diversity of all cultures makes it difficult to argue that any particular cultural tradition is (or

100 See Elkins and Simeon 1979, Inglehart 1988, and Lane 1992 for overviews of this debate.
101 For assessments of political values and democracy in Mexico based upon data from a 1998 public opinion survey, see Klesner 2001, Moreno 2001, Power and Clark 2001, and Turner and Elordi 2001.

Political culture is the focus of increasing attention in analyses of Mexico's longer-term democratization process. In 2002, for example, the Federal Electoral Institute sponsored a special seminar on this topic. For representative scholarly works, see Durand Ponte 2002 and Peschard 2003.
102 Power and Clark 2001.

is not) inherently conducive to democracy.[103] In the end, assuming some capacity for change in cultural norms (even if such change only occurs over an extended period of time), the most important matter may be the impact that the practice of political democracy has on citizens' attitudes, beliefs, and values. Comparative political experience powerfully demonstrates that, even though some societies may have weak democratic traditions, individuals in those societies can be molded into practicing democrats.

The challenges for Mexican democrats are quite clear in this regard. First, the strength and quality of democracy in Mexico will depend centrally upon the degree of success that democratic forces have in firmly establishing the rule of law and defining high standards of probity for government officials' public conduct.[104] One key test in this regard will be their ability to define and defend the boundaries between public and private spheres of activity. In some instances, this may require the creation of new institutions capable of ensuring horizontal accountability (O'Donnell 1999a: 185); in other cases, the main challenge may be to improve access to information or otherwise enhance sociopolitical actors' capacity to enforce accountability on the part of those individuals responsible for protecting the public trust.[105] But whatever the particular issue or arena, the guiding goal of such reform efforts should be to end traditions of corruption and impunity and strengthen the effective exercise of citizenship.[106]

Second, both domestic and international allies of democracy should concentrate priority attention on reinforcing the intermediate sociopolitical organizations that can help consolidate and deepen democratic practices over the longer term. One of the paradoxes of Mexico's electoral route to democracy is that the political party-

---

103 Camp (2001: 8) concludes that "...the difficulty in examining the relationship between culture and democratic political beliefs is that culture is so all-encompassing that it is challenging, if not impossible, to determine any causal relationships between specific cultural variables and democratic attitudes."

104 More generally, democratic governments' efficacy in addressing pressing national problems – and thus demonstrating the value of democratic governance – is also important in this regard. However, as Huntington (1991: 262–63) has trenchantly observed, "Democracy does not mean that problems will be solved; it does mean that rulers can be removed; and the essence of democratic behavior is doing the latter because it is impossible to do the former. Disillusionment and the lowered expectations it produces are the foundation of democratic stability. Democracies become consolidated when people learn that democracy is a solution to the problem of tyranny, but not necessarily to anything else."

105 In 2002 the Mexican Congress passed the Federal Law on Transparency and Access to Public Governmental Information (Ley Federal de Transparencia y Acceso a la Información Pública Gubernamental), which was formally implemented in June 2003. This measure substantially increases citizens' access to information concerning government officials' expenses, perfor-mance, and use of public funds in executive-branch agencies. See *La Jornada Virtu@l*, 13 June 2003.

106 Drug trafficking and other forms of organized crime are particularly nefarious problems because they strongly foster violence and corruption.

civil society alliances that were so important in propelling the transition forward (through their insistent demands for, and mobilizations in favor of, electoral transparency) were thrown into some disarray by their own success. As Olvera (this volume) notes, civic actors were particularly successful when their demands concentrated upon party and election issues. But once opposition forces took power, it was often difficult to identify a similar common axis for action.[107] In some ways, therefore, building strong party-civil society linkages has proved more difficult within a democratic context than when a broad array of forces had been allied against authoritarianism.[108]

In considering these questions, it is important to recognize that the National Action Party's political ascendance ushered in a model of politics whose underlying assumptions differ substantially from the practices of the long-ruling Institutional Revolutionary Party. Whereas the PRI has historically been a mass party in which affiliation is based principally upon membership in an affiliated social organization, the PAN is a selective party with stringent procedures for evaluating and approving potential members. Whereas the PRI long operated as a classic political machine that treated public goods and services as patronage resources to be used to attract electoral support and reinforce partisan loyalty, the PAN in government has promoted a model of party-constituency and government-citizen relations that stresses individual autonomy and initiative rather than dependence upon the state. For example, by including on goods distributed through government anti-poverty programs the prominent notice that the item in question was paid for by public funds and was not the contribution of a particular political party, the Fox administration explicitly sought to break with long-established traditions of political patronage and reaffirm citizens' rights to government services irrespective of their partisan affiliations.[109] Policies such as these may not produce an immediate transformation in long-established attitudes toward government and individual rights, but they certainly set important precedents in these areas.

The Internationalization of Mexican Politics

International forces may have been less significant than domestic actors as original promoters of political liberalization in Mexico, but their relative importance will certainly increase in the future. In part this is because a more democratic political

107 In the case of the PRD government in the Federal District after 1997, civic actors sometimes lost experienced leaders who took up governmental positions, found it difficult to criticize an administration in which former nongovernmental leaders were employed, and encountered questions about their perceived autonomy vis-à-vis government (Olvera, this volume).

108 Olvera (this volume) discusses nongovernmental organizations' fitful efforts since the mid-1990s to unite behind a common "citizens' rights" agenda.

109 That the Fox administration took constructive initiatives such as this does not imply that its overall human rights record was above reproach. For critical assessments of the human rights situation in Mexico during the early Fox administration, see America's Watch 2003 and *International Herald-Tribune*, August 26, 2003, p. 6.

order and an increasingly open society are more susceptible to international effects than the comparatively closed *ancien régime* dominated by a hegemonic party that was committed to blocking foreign influences in the name of national sovereignty.[110]

The specific form and consequences of increased international influence upon Mexico's domestic political affairs are, of course, difficult to predict. Nevertheless, some important trends are already evident. For example, Jonathan Fox's chapter in this volume highlights the growing prominence of binational civil society linkages among Mexican and U.S. labor unions and worker rights activists, environmentalists, democracy and human rights activists, trade policy advocacy groups, women's rights activists, and Latino immigrant and civil rights organizations.[111] Although some of these Mexico–U.S. partnerships are of much longer standing, the political debate over the North American Free Trade Agreement was a particularly important catalyst for the formation of many such cross-border alliances. Fox's assessment is that, with the exception of the environmental policy arena, few of these interactions evolved from networks between *national* social and civic organizations to become durable, balanced binational civil society coalitions, or had a clear, independent impact upon the issues they addressed. However, by the end of the 1990s there was evidence of an increasingly dense binational civil society – especially in the Mexico–U.S. border area – with substantially greater mutual awareness, improved understanding, and considerable practical experience in reaching out to potential partners across the border in order to increase leverage over public policy formation and implementation.

Fox (this volume) devotes special attention to binational solidarity initiatives focused upon the EZLN and the conflict in Chiapas because this is often identified as a prime example of the way in which transnational advocacy networks can mobilize international opposition to political repression. Yet Fox makes clear that, contrary to a widespread tendency to assume that cross-border activist mobilization and the expression of intense international concern about the Mexican government's response to the EZLN–led rebellion had a significant impact upon the course of the conflict, the evidence strongly suggests that "international civil society actors engaged in the Chiapas conflict may have been marginal to what has been primarily a nationally determined political process." Nevertheless, he also points out that both the Salinas and the Zedillo administrations curtailed military offensives against the Zapatista rebels in part because of their concern about U.S. government and private-sector reactions to violent civil conflict – with the attending intense media coverage – affecting a NAFTA partner.

---

110 By the same token, the collapse of PRI hegemony and the erosion of hyper-presidentialism have also increased the relative importance of subnational actors (state governors, for example) in Mexican politics.

111 Although focusing primarily upon civil society-to-civil society linkages, Jonathan Fox's chapter in this book also overviews state-to-state interactions and ties between the Mexican and U.S. governments and civil society actors in the other country.

Fitzgerald (this volume) examines a second, parallel form of international influence: the increasingly prominent role of Mexican emigrants and Mexican Americans in Mexican politics. He notes, for example, the rapid expansion after the mid-1980s of the so-called hometown associations (HTAs) that link immigrants in the United States with sending communities in Mexico. These bodies are very important to maintaining migrants' sociocultural ties and identification with their place of origin, and both migrant activists and federal and state government agencies in Mexico have sought to capitalize upon these linkages by using HTAs as vehicles through which to channel migrants' financial support to community-level economic and social development projects.[112] During the late 1980s and the 1990s, hometown associations also became part of the communications network that linked emigrants to political activity in Mexico. In fact, the opposition PRD and the ruling PRI both sought to utilize such groups for partisan advantage, mainly by trying to encourage emigrants to persuade relatives remaining in Mexico to vote in line with their own partisan preferences.[113]

Through these links, migrant activists successfully lobbied for legal recognition of the right to vote from abroad. The PRD embraced this demand following party founder Cuauhtémoc Cárdenas's presidential campaigning among Mexican emigrants in the United States in 1988 and 1994, and the PAN (with perhaps somewhat less enthusiasm) also supported it. As a result, the 1996 electoral reform granted Mexican citizens the right to vote from abroad in presidential elections. However, in 1999 the PRI – apparently fearing that emigrants' votes would predominantly favor opposition parties – used its majority in the Senate to veto legislation that would have implemented this provision (by establishing registration procedures and sufficient polling stations in the United States and other countries) for the year 2000 elections. Fitzgerald (this volume) notes that, as a consequence, most Mexican emigrants did not have valid voter registration cards, and only a comparatively small number of those who were resident in the United States were able to vote in the special polling stations for voters in transit that were established in cities along Mexico's northern border. He thus concludes that Mexican emigrants may have some direct impact upon political developments in Mexico by using the financial leverage of HTA–funded projects to demand greater accountability on the part of state and municipal elected officials, but their real political potential lies in the still-unrealized opportunity to participate in large numbers in Mexican presidential elections.

The heightened prominence of cross-border civil society coalitions and of emigrants' networks reflects closer economic, social, and cultural exchanges between Mexico and the United States. Many of these influences may over time contribute significantly to greater political pluralism and societal democratization in Mexico.

112 By one estimate, circa the year 2000 some 1.5 million Mexican households depended partially or totally upon migrant remittances. See Pacific Council on International Policy 2002.

113 As Fitzgerald (this volume) notes, there is also the distinct possibility that hometown associations provide the links through which Mexicans abroad contribute financially to political parties and campaigns in Mexico, although this would violate federal electoral law.

However, as indicated by the prolonged public controversy over (illegal) foreign financial contributions to Vicente Fox's 2000 presidential campaign,[114] not all the opportunities arising from the increased internationalization of Mexican politics may be benign.

References

Aguayo Quezada, Sergio. 1998a. "Electoral Observation and Democracy in Mexico." In *Electoral Observation and Democratic Transitions in Latin America*, edited by Kevin J. Middlebrook. La Jolla: Center for U.S.–Mexican Studies, University of California, San Diego

——. 1998b. *Myths and (Mis)perceptions: Changing U.S. Elite Visions of Mexico*. La Jolla and Mexico City: Center for U.S.–Mexican Studies, University of California, San Diego / El Colegio de México.

Aguilar Ascencio, Oscar. 2000. "La iglesia católica y la democratización en México." In *La iglesia católica y la política en México de hoy*, edited by José de Jesús Legorreta Zepeda. Mexico City: Universidad Iberoamericana.

Alarcón, Diana. 2003. "Income Distribution and Poverty Alleviation in Mexico: A Comparative Analysis." In *Confronting Development: Assessing Mexico's Economic and Social Policy Challenges*, edited by Kevin J. Middlebrook and Eduardo Zepeda. Stanford, Calif.: Stanford University Press and Center for U.S.–Mexican Studies, University of California, San Diego.

Arriola, Carlos. 1988. "La campaña electoral de Manuel J. Clouthier en Sinaloa, México, 1986," *Foro Internacional* 29 (1): 30–48.

Baer, M. Delal. 1991. "North American Free Trade," *Foreign Affairs* 70 (4): 132–49.

Beer, Caroline C. 2002. "Institutional Change in Mexico: Politics after One-Party Rule," *Latin American Research Review* 37 (3): 149–6

Benítez Manaut, Raúl. 2003. "Security and Governance: The Urgent Need for State Reform." In *Mexico's Politics and Society in Transition*, edited by Joseph S. Tulchin and Andrew D. Selee. Boulder, Colo.: Lynn Rienner Publishers.

Bizberg, Ilán. 2003. "Transition or Restructuring of Society?" In *Mexico's Politics and Society in Transition*, edited by Joseph S. Tulchin and Andrew D. Selee. Boulder, Colo.: Lynne Rienner Publishers.

Boltvinik, Julio. 2003. "Welfare, Inequality, and Poverty in Mexico, 1970–2000." In *Confronting Development: Assessing Mexico's Economic and Social Policy Challenges*, edited by Kevin J. Middlebrook and Eduardo Zepeda. Stanford, Calif.: Stanford University Press and Center for U.S.–Mexican Studies, University of California, San Diego.

Bruhn, Kathleen. 1997. "The Seven-Month Itch? Neoliberal Politics, Popular Movements, and the Left in Mexico." In *The New Politics of Inequality in Latin America: Rethinking Participation and Representation*, edited by Douglas A. Chalmers et al. New York: Oxford University Press.

Camp, Roderic A. 1989. *Entrepreneurs and Politics in Twentieth-Century Mexico*. New York: Oxford University Press.

——. 1992. *Generals in the Palacio: The Military in Modern Mexico*. New York: Oxford University Press.

——. 1994. "The Cross in the Polling Booth: Religion, Politics, and the Laity in Mexico," *Latin*

---

114 See Gómez Tagle (this volume) for a discussion of the "Friends of Fox" campaign funding controversy.

American Research Review 29 (3): 69–100.

———. 1997. *Crossing Swords: Religion and Politics in Mexico.* New York: Oxford University Press.

———. 2001. "Democracy through Latin American Lenses: An Appraisal." In *Citizen Views of Democracy in Latin America*, edited by Roderic Ai Camp. Pittsburgh, Penn.: University of Pittsburgh Press.

Casar, María Amparo. 1998. "Executive-Legislative Relations: The Case of Mexico." Documento de Trabajo no. 84. Mexico City: División de Estudios Políticos, Centro de Investigación y Docencia Económicas.

Castañeda, Jorge G. 1996. "Democracy and Inequality in Latin America: A Tension of the Times." In *Constructing Democratic Governance: Latin America and the Caribbean in the 1990s*, edited by Jorge I. Domínguez and Abraham F. Lowenthal. Baltimore, Md.: Johns Hopkins University Press.

———. 1999. *La herencia: arqueología de la sucesión presidencial en México.* Mexico City: Alfaguara.

———. 2003. "La relación olvidada." *Foreign Affairs en Español* 3 (2): 138–53.

Chand, Vikram K. 2001. *Mexico's Political Awakening.* Notre Dame, Ind.: University of Notre Dame Press.

Coatsworth, John H. 1999. "The United States and Democracy in Mexico." In *The United States and Latin America: The New Agenda*, edited by Victor Bulmer-Thomas and James Dunkerley. London: Institute of Latin American Studies, University of London / David Rockefeller Center for Latin American Studies, Harvard University.

Cook, Maria Lorena, Kevin J. Middlebrook, and Juan Molinar Horcasitas, eds. 1994. *The Politics of Economic Restructuring: State-Society Relations and Regime Change in Mexico.* La Jolla: Center for U.S.–Mexican Studies, University of California, San Diego.

Cornelius, Wayne A., Judith Gentleman, and Peter H. Smith. 1989. "Overview: The Dynamics of Political Change in Mexico." In *Mexico's Alternative Political Futures*, edited by Wayne A. Cornelius, Judith Gentleman, and Peter H. Smith. La Jolla: Center for U.S.–Mexican Studies, University of California, San Diego.

Correa Sutil, Jorge. 1999. "Judicial Reforms in Latin America: Good News for the Under-privileged?" In *The (Un)Rule of Law and the Underprivileged in Latin America*, edited by Juan E. Méndez, Guillermo O'Donnell, and Paulo Sérgio Pinheiro. Notre Dame, Ind.: University of Notre Dame Press.

Covarrubias, Ana. 2001. "El ámbito internacional y el proceso de cambio político en México." In *Caminos a la democracia*, edited by Reynaldo Yunuen Ortega Ortiz. Mexico City: El Colegio de México.

Craig, Ann L., and Wayne A. Cornelius. 1995. "Houses Divided: Parties and Political Reform in Mexico." In *Building Democratic Institutions: Party Systems in Latin America*, edited by Scott Mainwaring and Timothy R. Scully. Stanford, Calif.: Stanford University Press.

Dahl, Robert A. 1971. *Polyarchy: Participation and Opposition.* New Haven, Conn.: Yale University Press.

———. 1982. *Dilemmas of Pluralist Democracy: Autonomy vs. Control.* New Haven, Conn.: Yale University Press.

Deutsch, Karl W. 1961. "Social Mobilization and Political Development," *American Political Science Review* 55 (3): 493–514.

Domingo, Pilar. 2000. "Judicial Independence: The Politics of the Supreme Court in Mexico," *Journal of Latin American Studies* 32 (3): 705–35.

Domingo, Pilar, and Rachel Sieder. 2001. "Conclusions: Promoting the Rule of Law in Latin America." In *The Rule of Law in Latin America: The International Promotion of Judicial Reform*, edited by Pilar Domingo and Rachel Sieder. London: Institute of Latin American Studies, University of London.

Domínguez, Jorge I., and Chappell Lawson, eds. 2003. *Mexico's Pivotal Democratic Election: Campaigns, Votes, and the 2000 Presidential Race.* Stanford, Calif.: Stanford University Press and Center for U.S.–Mexican Studies, University of California, San Diego.

Dresser, Denise. 1996. "Treading Lightly and without a Stick: International Actors and the Promotion of Democracy in Mexico." In *Beyond Sovereignty: Collectively Defending Democracy in the Americas*, edited by Tom Farer. Baltimore, Md.: Johns Hopkins University Press.

Durand Ponte, Víctor Manuel. 2002. *Ciudadanía y cultura política en México, 1993–2002.* Mexico City: Siglo Veintiuno.

Eisenstadt, Todd A. 2003. "Thinking Outside the (Ballot) Box: Informal Electoral Institutions and Mexico's Political Opening," *Latin American Politics and Society* 45 (1): 25–54.

Elizondo, Carlos. 2003. "After the Second of July: Challenges and Opportunities for the Fox Administration." In *Mexico's Politics and Society in Transition*, edited by Joseph S. Tulchin and Andrew D. Selee. Boulder, Colo.: Lynn Rienner Publishers.

Elkins, David J., and Richard E.B. Simeon. 1979. "A Cause in Search of Its Effect, or What Does Political Culture Explain?" *Comparative Politics* 11 (2): 127–45.

Fox, Jonathan. 1997. "The Difficult Transition from Clientelism to Citizenship: Lessons from Mexico." In *The New Politics of Inequality in Latin America: Rethinking Participation and Representation*, edited by Douglas A. Chalmers et al. New York: Oxford University Press.

Gasiorowski, Mark J. 1995. "Economic Crisis and Political Regime Change: An Event History Analysis," *American Political Science Review* 89 (4): 882–97.

González Casanova, Pablo. 1995. "La democracia en México: actualidad y perspectivas." In *La democracia en América Latina: actualidad y perspectivas*, edited by Pablo González Casanova and Marcos Roitman Rosenmann. Mexico City: La Jornada Ediciones / Centro de Investigaciones Interdisciplinarias en Ciencias y Humanidades, Universidad Nacional Autónoma de México.

Haggard, Stephan, and Robert R. Kaufman. 1995. *The Political Economy of Democratic Transitions.* Princeton, N.J.: Princeton University Press.

Hernández Rodríguez, Rogelio. 2003. "Ernesto Zedillo: la presidencia contenida," *Foro Internacional* 43 (1): 39–70

Hughes, Sallie. 2003. "From the Inside Out: How 'Institutional Entrepreneurs' Transformed the Mexican Press." Paper presented at the international congress of the Latin American Studies Association, Dallas, Texas, March.

Human Rights Watch. 2003. "Justice in Jeopardy: Why Mexico's First Real Effort to Address Past Abuses Risks Becoming its Latest." [www.hrw.org/reports/2003/mexico0703].

Huntington, Samuel P. 1991. *The Third Wave: Democratization in the Late Twentieth Century.* Norman: University of Oklahoma Press.

Inglehart, Ronald. 1988. "The Renaissance of Political Culture," *American Political Science Review* 82 (4): 1203–30.

Inkeles, Alex, and David H. Smith. 1974. *Becoming Modern: Individual Change in Six Developing Countries.* Cambridge, Mass.: Harvard University Press.

Karl, Terry Lynn. 2000. "Economic Inequality and Democratic Stability," *Journal of Democracy* 11 (1): 149–56.

Klesner, Joseph L. 2001. "Legacies of Authoritarianism: Political Attitudes in Chile and Mexico." In *Citizen Views of Democracy in Latin America*, edited by Roderic Ai Camp. Pittsburgh, Penn.: University of Pittsburgh Press.

——. 2003. "The Structure of the Mexican Electorate: Social, Attitudinal, and Partisan Bases of Vicente Fox's Victory." In *Mexico's Pivotal Democratic Election: Campaigns, Votes, and the 2000 Presidential Race*, edited by Jorge I. Domínguez and Chappell Lawson. Stanford, Calif.: Stanford University Press and Center for U.S.–Mexican Studies, University of California, San Diego.

Knight, Alan. 1997. "Dealing with the American Political System: An Historical Overview." In *Bridging the Border: Transforming Mexico-U.S. Relations*, edited by Rodolfo O. de la Garza and Jesús Velasco. Lanham, Md.: Rowman and Littlefield.

——. 2001. "Polls, Political Culture, and Democracy: A Heretical Historical Look." In *Citizen Views of Democracy in Latin America*, edited by Roderic Ai Camp. Pittsburgh, Penn.: University of Pittsburgh Press.

Lamas, Marta. 2003. "The Role of Women in the New Mexico." In *Mexico's Politics and Society in Transition*, edited by Joseph S. Tulchin and Andrew D. Selee. Boulder, Colo.: Lynn Rienner Publishers.

Lane, Ruth. 1992. "Political Culture: Residual Category or General Theory?" *Comparative Political Studies* 25 (4): 362–87.

Lerner, Daniel. 1958. *The Passing of Traditional Society: Modernizing the Middle East*. Glencoe, Ill.: The Free Press.

Linz, Juan J., and Alfred Stepan. 1996. *Problems of Democratic Transition and Consolidation: Southern Europe, South America, and Post-Communist Europe*. Baltimore, Md.: Johns Hopkins University Press.

Loaeza, Soledad. 1999. *El Partido Acción Nacional: la larga marcha, 1939–1984; oposición leal y partido de protesta*. Mexico City: Fondo de Cultura Económica.

Lujambio, Alonso. 2001. "Democratization through Federalism? The National Action Party Strategy, 1939–2000." In *Party Politics and the Struggle for Democracy in Mexico: National and State-Level Analyses of the Partido Acción Nacional*, edited by Kevin J. Middlebrook. La Jolla: Center for U.S.–Mexican Studies, University of California, San Diego.

Mainwaring, Scott, Guillermo O'Donnell, and J. Samuel Valenzuela, eds. 1992. *Issues in Democratic Consolidation: The New South American Democracies in Comparative Perspective*. Notre Dame, Ind.: University of Notre Dame Press.

Middlebrook, Kevin J. 1986. "Political Liberalization in an Authoritarian Regime: The Case of Mexico." In *Latin America*. Pt. 2, *Transitions from Authoritarian Rule: Prospects for Democracy*, edited by Guillermo O'Donnell, Philippe C. Schmitter, and Laurence Whitehead. Baltimore, Md.: Johns Hopkins University Press.

——. 1995. *The Paradox of Revolution: Labor, the State, and Authoritarianism in Mexico*. Baltimore, Md.: Johns Hopkins University Press.

——. 1997. "Movimiento obrero y democratización en regimenes posrevolucionarios: las políticas de transición en Nicaragua, Rusia y México," *Foro Internacional* 149 (July–September): 365–407.

——. 2001. "Party Politics and Democratization in Mexico: The Partido Acción Nacional in Comparative Perspective." In *Party Politics and the Struggle for Democracy in Mexico: National and State-Level Analyses of the Partido Acción Nacional*, edited by Kevin J. Middlebrook. La Jolla: Center for U.S.–Mexican Studies, University of California, San Diego.

Middlebrook, Kevin J., and Eduardo Zepeda. 2003a. "On the Political Economy of Mexican Development Policy." In *Confronting Development: Assessing Mexico's Economic and Social Policy Challenges*, edited by Kevin J. Middlebrook and Eduardo Zepeda. Stanford, Calif.: Stanford University Press and Center for U.S.–Mexican Studies, University of California, San Diego.

Middlebrook, Kevin J., and Eduardo Zepeda, eds. 2003b. *Confronting Development: Assessing Mexico's Economic and Social Policy Challenges*. Stanford, Calif.: Stanford University Press and Center for U.S.–Mexican Studies, University of California, San Diego.

Mizrahi, Yemile. 1995. "Entrepreneurs in the Opposition: Modes of Political Participation in Chihuahua." In *Opposition Government in Mexico*, edited by Victoria E. Rodríguez and Peter M. Ward. Albuquerque: University of New Mexico Press.

Moreno, Alejandro. 2001. "Democracy and Mass Belief Systems in Latin America." In *Citizen Views of Democracy in Latin Amesrica*, edited by Roderic Ai Camp. Pittsburgh, Penn.: University of Pittsburgh Press.

Needler, Martin C. 1961. "The Political Development of Mexico," *American Political Science Review* 55 (2): 308–12.

Nie, Norman H., and Sidney Verba. 1975. "Political Participation." In *Nongovernmental Politics*. Vol. 4 of *Handbook of Political Science*, edited by Fred I. Greenstein and Nelson W. Polsby. Reading, Mass.: Addison-Wesley Publishing Company.

O'Donnell, Guillermo. 1999a. *Counterpoints: Selected Essays on Authoritarianism and Democratization*. Notre Dame, Ind.: University of Notre Dame Press.

——. 1999b. "Polyarchies and the (Un)Rule of Law in Latin America: A Partial Conclusion." In *The (Un)Rule of Law and the Underprivileged in Latin America*, edited by Juan E. Méndez, Guillermo O'Donnell, and Paulo Sérgio Pinheiro. Notre Dame, Ind.: University of Notre Dame Press.

O'Donnell, Guillermo, and Philippe C. Schmitter. 1986. *Tentative Conclusions about Uncertain Democracies*. Vol. 4 of *Transitions from Authoritarian Rule: Prospects for Democracy*, edited by Guillermo O'Donnell, Philippe C. Schmitter, and Laurence Whitehead. Baltimore, Md.: Johns Hopkins University Press.

Pacific Council on International Policy. 2002. "Envisioning North American Futures: Transnational Challenges and Opportunities." Mimeo.

Paoli, Francisco J. 1978. "Legislación electoral y proceso político," *Jurídica* (Universidad Iberoamericana), July.

Pastor, Manuel, Jr., and Carol Wise. 1998. "Mexican-Style Neoliberalism: State Policy and Distributional Stress." In *The Post-NAFTA Political Economy: Mexico and the Western Hemisphere*, edited by Carol Wise. University Park: Pennsylvania State University Press.

Peschard, Jacqueline. 2003. "La cultura política mexicana después de la alternancia." Paper presented at the international congress of the Latin American Studies Association, Dallas, Texas, March.

Pinheiro, Paulo Sérgio. 1999. "The Rule of Law and the Underprivileged in Latin America: Introduction." In *The (Un)Rule of Law and the Underprivileged in Latin America*, edited by Juan E. Méndez, Guillermo O'Donnell, and Paulo Sérgio Pinheiro. Notre Dame, Ind.: University of Notre Dame Press.

Power, Timothy J., and Mary A. Clark. 2001. "Does Trust Matter? Interpersonal Trust and Democratic Values in Chile, Costa Rica, and Mexico." In *Citizen Views of Democracy in Latin America*, edited by Roderic Ai Camp. Pittsburgh, Penn.: University of Pittsburgh Press.

Przeworski, Adam, et al. 1996. "What Makes Democracies Endure?" *Journal of Democracy* 7 (1): 39–55.

Randall, Laura, ed. 1996. *Reforming Mexico's Agrarian Reform*. Armonk, N.Y.: M.E. Sharpe.

Remmer, Karen L. 1991. "The Political Impact of Economic Crisis in Latin America in the 1980s," *American Political Science Review* 85 (3): 777–800.

——. 1996. "External Pressures and Domestic Constraints: The Lessons of the Four Case Studies." In *Beyond Sovereignty: Collectively Defending Democracy in the Americas*, edited by Tom Farer. Baltimore, Md.: Johns Hopkins University Press.

Rubin, Jeffrey W. 1997. *Decentering the Regime: Ethnicity, Radicalism, and Democracy in Juchitán, Mexico*. Durham, N.C.: Duke University Press.

Rueschemeyer, Dietrich, Evelyne Huber Stephens, and John D. Stephens. 1992. *Capitalist Development and Democracy*. Chicago, Ill.: University of Chicago Press.

Schmitter, Philippe C. 1992. "The Consolidation of Democracy and Representation of Social Groups," *American Behavioral Scientist* 35 (4/5): 422–49.

———. 1996. "The Influence of the International Context upon the Choice of National Institutions and Policies in Neo-Democracies." In *The International Dimensions of Democratization: Europe and the Americas*, edited by Laurence Whitehead. Oxford: Oxford University Press.

Schmitter, Philippe C., and Terry Lynn Karl. 1991. "What Democracy Is ... and Is Not," *Journal of Democracy* 2 (3): 75–88.

Semo, Enrique. 2002. "La izquierda en la era del neoliberalismo, 1976–2001." In *Crisis, reforma y revolución: México, historias de fin de siglo*, edited by Leticia Reina and Elisa Servín. Mexico City: Editorial Taurus / Consejo Nacional de la Cultura / Instituto Nacional de Antropología e Historia.

Serrano, Mónica. 1995. "The Armed Branch of the State: Civil-Military Relations in Mexico," *Journal of Latin American Studies* 27 (2): 423–48.

Stepan, Alfred. 1988. *Rethinking Military Politics: Brazil and the Southern Cone*. Princeton, N.J.: Princeton University Press.

Tavera-Fenollosa, Ligia. 1998. "Social Movements and Civil Society: The Mexico City 1985 Earthquake Victims' Movement in Mexico City." Ph.D. diss., Yale University.

Teichman, Judith. 1997. "Neoliberalism and the Transformation of Mexican Authoritarianism," *Mexican Studies/Estudios Mexicanos* 13 (1): 121–47.

Turner, Frederick C. 1995. "Reassessing Political Culture." In *Latin America in Comparative Perspective: New Approaches to Methods and Analysis*, edited by Peter H. Smith. Boulder, Colo.: Westview Press.

Turner, Frederick C., and Carlos A. Elordi. 2001. "Mexico and the United States: Two Distinct Political Cultures?" In *Citizen Views of Democracy in Latin America*, edited by Roderic Ai Camp. Pittsburgh, Penn.: University of Pittsburgh Press.

Ugalde, Luis Carlos. 2000. *The Mexican Congress: Old Player, New Power*. Washington, D.C.: Center for Strategic and International Studies.

Vilas, Carlos M. 1997. "Participation, Inequality, and the Whereabouts of Democracy." In *The New Politics of Inequality in Latin America: Rethinking Participation and Representation*, edited by Douglas A. Chalmers et al. New York: Oxford University Press.

Whitehead, Laurence. 1994. "Prospects for a 'Transition' from Authoritarian Rule in Mexico." In *The Politics of Economic Restructuring: State-Society Relations and Regime Change in Mexico*, edited by Maria Lorena Cook, Kevin J. Middlebrook, and Juan Molinar Horcasitas. La Jolla: Center for U.S.–Mexican Studies, University of California, San Diego.

———. 1996. "The International Dimensions of Democratization." In *The International Dimensions of Democratization: Europe and the Americas*, edited by Laurence Whitehead. Oxford: Oxford University Press.

———. 2002. *Democratization: Theory and Experience*. Oxford: Oxford University Press.

PART I
Parties, Elections, and the Mexican Voter

2

Party Competition in Mexico: Evolution and Prospects

José Antonio Crespo

From its birth in 1929 as the Revolutionary National Party (PNR) through its long rule as the Institutional Revolutionary Party (PRI), Mexico's "official" party operated as a true hegemonic party in the sense that, having itself achieved a de facto monopoly over the country's political life, opposition parties were always legally recognized. It would in fact have been extremely difficult for those who came to power after Mexico's 1910–1920 revolution to build a one-party regime such as those constructed in the wake of the Russian or Chinese revolutions because, unlike the Russian Bolsheviks or the Chinese Communists, the banner under which Francisco Madero's supporters initiated the Mexican Revolution was that of political democracy. For this essential reason, completely abandoning a democratic framework would have had high political costs in terms of legitimacy. In addition, proximity to the United States – and the decisive U.S. role in consolidating or undermining Mexican governments in the nineteenth and early twentieth centuries – made it all but indispensable to preserve democratic forms, which were demanded by the U.S. government as a condition for the full recognition of the new revolutionary regime in Mexico.

Because democratic stage-setting required formally competitive elections as well as the presence of legally recognized opposition parties, Mexico's revolutionary elite had no choice but to accept a multiparty political model, although in reality power was heavily concentrated in the "official" party. However, in contrast to the views long held by various political analysts and opposition leaders, the post-revolutionary regime was not a one-party system with a thin democratic veneer. Rather, the hegemonic arrangement generated a peculiar political dynamic that permitted the PRI's domination to last more than seventy years, with institutions and procedures that were more flexible than those of a one-party system. The need to keep opposition parties in the electoral game – precisely so as to avoid falling into the one-party category – led successive governments, little by little, to adopt measures to promote competition and to accept some minor opposition victories. The goal, of course, was to accomplish this delicate balancing act without endangering the ruling party's control over the federal Congress and the presidency.

Translated by Aníbal Yáñez-Chávez and Kevin J. Middlebrook

Despite the constraints upon democratic participation that were inherent in the hegemonic-party model, over time the Mexican party system gradually came to approximate an authentically democratic and competitive regime. This transition fundamentally occurred between 1996 and 1997. In 1996, reforms to the federal election law for the first time clearly granted electoral authorities full autonomy from the government (and from the PRI), so that election results unfavorable to the ruling party could no longer be easily overturned. Then, in the 1997 midterm legislative elections, the PRI in fact failed to win sufficient votes to preserve its traditional absolute majority in the federal Chamber of Deputies. These developments together eliminated the pillars supporting the PRI's long party hegemony, transforming it into a simple majority party between 1997 and 2000. And, following its defeat in the historic July 2000 presidential election, the PRI became an opposition party, embedded in party and electoral dynamics characteristic of fully competitive systems.

The relatively greater flexibility of a hegemonic-party system (compared to that of a one-party system) is what allowed the PRI to avoid for so long a definitive crisis such as that which eventually confronted the Communist Party of the Soviet Union (CPSU) and other one-party systems in Eastern Europe, which ended in their electoral defeat and disappearance. Although the PRI suffered a major electoral crisis in the 1988 presidential contest, this did not result in its demise.[1] Indeed, only three years later, thanks to an apparent economic recovery achieved by President Carlos Salinas de Gortari (1988–1994), the PRI won an enormous 64.0 percent of the total valid vote, 13.6 percentage points more than what it officially received in 1988. It is notable that the PRI's electoral recovery occurred on the same day that a coup d'état was in progress in the Soviet Union – an action which, although it failed, precipitated the dissolution of the CPSU and of the Soviet Union itself. The great difference between the fates of the PRI and the CPSU in 1991 succinctly summarized the hegemonic-party system's greater institutional flexibility and room for maneuver at a time of political-electoral crisis.[2]

The PRI's 71-year reign made it the most durable hegemonic party of the modern era. Moreover, at the turn of the twenty-first century it was still Mexico's largest political party, even if it was forced to operate under different, more fully competitive conditions. If it survives the challenge of adjusting to these new political and electoral conditions, the PRI could become a dominant democratic party, as in Japan or Sweden. However, if it is not able to make the democratic adjustment, it could suffer the same fate as the single parties of Eastern Europe in the face of the democratic onslaught – that is, disintegration (Crespo 1998).

The secret of the PRI's hegemony – what enabled it to maintain both a de facto

---

1 There is, however, still reason to doubt the veracity of the victory by the PRI's candidate, Carlos Salinas de Gortari.

2 Some analysts had long noted that the PRI's relatively greater flexibility would provide it with more room for maneuver. See Huntington 1972, chap. 7.

one-party monopoly, reinforced by comparative institutional flexibility, and a halo of democratic legitimacy – lay essentially in the frequency and content of the electoral legislation that successive governments adopted from 1946 until 1994. The central challenge for the regime (and for its "official" party) was to keep the political opposition involved in the electoral game. It was essential that the opposition neither leave the field nor perish in electoral terms, thereby turning the regime into a single-party system and depriving it of internal and international legitimacy. But at the same time, different governments faced the imperative of preventing that same opposition from uniting or growing strong enough so that it would constitute a real threat to the PRI – in which case the PRI would have ceased being hegemonic and become simply a majority party (Molinar Horcasitas 1991a), as occurred in 1997. Electoral legislation was the main instrument for maintaining this difficult balance. Thus, when the opposition showed signs of disappearing (whether due to weakness or weariness), electoral reforms would offer improved competitive conditions and greater opportunities to gain new political spaces. And vice versa, when the opposition gave dangerous signs of expansion, changes in electoral law would strengthen the PRI's position.

Such a difficult balance could not be maintained indefinitely. The PRI was, however, able to sustain it for a number of years – indeed, for much longer than other hegemonic parties around the world. This chapter reviews how Mexico's electoral legislation changed over time so as to maintain the peculiar and complicated "hegemonic balance" that the PRI was able to preserve masterfully for so long. At the same time, it explores how and why the Mexican regime eventually crossed the threshold of electoral competitiveness leading to an authentic (not just a formal) multiparty system.

The Long Era of "Official" Party Hegemony

In the specialized literature on political parties, there is a category that fits perfectly the party system that existed in Mexico between 1929 (the year in which the "official" party was born) and the late 1990s. This is the category of hegemonic-party system. Party hegemony is understood in this context as the exercise of a virtual political monopoly by a party that nevertheless coexists with legally registered opposition parties.

Hegemonic systems share with one-party regimes the fact that the ruling party is organically linked to the state. The state provides copious, decisively important resources for the preservation of the "official" party (which, precisely for this reason, may be considered a state party). In addition, the hegemonic party remains in power under conditions that are not competitive; it does not vie for power with other parties upon the basis of rules that are fair (under which any of the contestants could win), transparent, and impartial. Giovanni Sartori, a leading specialist on political parties, precisely defines the limits of competition in a hegemonic-party system:

> The hegemonic party does not allow either official competition for power or de facto competition. Other parties are allowed to exist, but as authorized, second-class parties, because they are not allowed to compete with the hegemonic party as antagonists on an equal footing. Not only is there no party alternation in power, but in fact it cannot take place because even the possibility of taking turns in power is inconceivable .... Whatever its politics, its domination cannot be subject to debate (Sartori 1980: 278–79).

In a single-party system, the ruling party's permanence in power lasts as long as the regime itself endures. Because the existence of other parties is constitutionally prohibited, the state party is not obliged to compete electorally against any political formation. Elections under such circumstances tend to be by acclamation – that is, citizens do not have a choice in the election of their rulers (at least, there are no candidates put forward by other parties) and they go to the polls simply to express their supposed acceptance of the regime in power. Moreover, in these contexts there is no authority that oversees those who organize the electoral exercise. Thus there is nothing to guarantee that the results of such elections (which typically have participation rates of 99 percent) reflect faithfully the will of the citizens (Duverger 1996: 284–85).

In contrast, in a hegemonic-party system, the "official" party maintains a democratic format that presupposes the legal existence of opposition parties. In reality, the conditions under which elections are held and under which power is exercised do not correspond to those that prevail in authentic democracies. Nevertheless, the hegemonic party is interested in presenting a democratic façade in order to gain a certain degree of legal-democratic legitimacy without necessarily risking its political monopoly. Elites in a hegemonic-party regime therefore organize elections that are formally similar to those in a democracy, with more than one party participating in the contest so that citizens can presumably choose their rulers. Depending upon the extent of hegemony exercised by the "official" party, power may in fact be shared at some local levels of government. This does not, however, include power sharing at the national level because (by definition) such an arrangement would not be a hegemonic-party system.

Thus the hegemonic party's victory is practically assured in advance of the electoral contest. Party leaders and members know that the essential aspects of power are guaranteed, election after election, as long as the established regime endures. In this regard, the result of elections is similar in hegemonic and one-party systems. Similarly, political elites in both one-party and hegemonic-party systems are not accountable to the electorate for their performance in office; they are neither rewarded (ratified in power) nor punished (removed from power) via electoral processes, as occurs in an authentic party democracy. This is both a cause and a consequence of the fact that alternation between parties is politically and institutionally impossible, even if in the rules that make up a hegemonic-party regime there is theoretically an acceptance of this possibility. These circumstances (along with other features of one-party and hegemonic regimes) translate into impunity for those in office – a typical characteristic of a non-democratic regime, whether it is a monarchy, a military or personal dictatorship, or a monopolistic party system.

Despite these similarities, there are of course significant differences between one-party and hegemonic systems. In the former, the ruling party exercises its monopoly in a more complete and open manner, while in the latter it somewhat dissimulates this monopoly in order to win a degree of democratic legitimacy. A hegemonic party must therefore accept the existence of opposition parties and share some spaces of power with them. It does so in order to convince both outsiders and its own citizens that the regime is indeed essentially democratic, as well as to encourage opposition forces to continue participating in a game that they know ahead of time they will lose. Given the institutional impossibility of their aspiring to head the government, the minor offices that opposition parties are allowed to hold are a kind of consolation prize. Yet even so, the opposition may take advantage of the formally democratic institutional framework to pressure the regime to make a gradual transition toward democracy. In the words of Dieter Nohlen, "Unlike democracies, political power is not at stake under authoritarian systems. But unlike elections in totalitarian systems, the opposition can organize" (Nohlen 1995: 14).

If the opposition were to remove itself from the electoral contest because it thought participation was useless, or if it could no longer participate because of its own political and electoral weakness, the hegemonic-party system would turn into a one-party regime. In many instances, this would not make much of a difference in practice. But in cases such as Mexico, it would have provoked a serious legitimacy crisis and placed in doubt the regime's continuity. In Mexico, the hegemonic system's democratic halo was not a mere cosmetic luxury; it was important for the survival of the postrevolutionary regime.

There were primarily two reasons why democratic legitimacy was important in the PRI–led political order. First, the armed movement (1910) from which the regime emerged had taken political democracy as its banner. Second, recognition of the new regime by the U.S. government – something essential for the consolidation of any government in Mexico – required that at least democratic forms be maintained, even if they served to cover up the fact that power was exercised in an essentially authoritarian manner. Thus a hegemonic party like the PRI, insofar as it tried to avoid becoming a one-party system in order to preserve a certain democratic legitimacy, had to honor democratic rituals. It was obliged to adopt institutions and procedures typical of a democracy, even though in reality these institutions and procedures lost their original function.

In order for this to work, it was necessary to maintain a certain degree of political openness and tolerance toward opponents in terms of political participation, freedom of expression, and distribution of power, even though in some areas it took decades for even a limited pluralism to reach the same levels that can be found in authentically democratic regimes. As a consequence, Mexico's hegemonic-party system not only appeared to be, but actually was, less repressive, more flexible, and more tolerant of dissidents than were totalitarian one-party regimes (whether Nazi, Fascist, or Communist). And although it certainly was not free of repression, censorship, and the persecution of political opponents, it engaged in these abuses to a significantly lesser degree than did the Southern Cone military dictatorships of the 1960s and 1970s (see Duff and McCamant 1976).

The discussion so far has compared hegemonic and single-party systems. However, the hegemonic-party system also has another institutional relative, this one on the democratic side: the dominant-party system. In these regimes, a particular party is able to maintain itself in power for extended periods of time, but it does so under conditions of real electoral competition. In other words, it does not need the illicit support and unfair advantages that monopoly parties receive in order to preserve its grip on the levers of power for a much longer period than is usually the case in most democracies (Huntington 1972: 368).

Focusing only upon formal political structures, it is not always easy to distinguish between a hegemonic and a dominant-party system. In both instances a considerably stronger party coexists with much smaller opposition parties, and entire decades may pass without a change of the party in power (although, in institutional terms, the possibility that this could happen can never be ruled out). There is, however, an important qualitative difference between them: the hegemonic party is solidly grounded upon the terrain of no competition, while the dominant party operates in a competitive environment. A careful comparison of the Japanese or the Indian party system, on the one hand, and the Mexican party system before the late 1990s, on the other, is more than sufficient to reveal the functional differences that place a dominant-party system in the clearly democratic camp and a hegemonic party in the no-competition (authoritarian) sphere (Crespo 1995a, Crespo and Sahni 1998).

Nevertheless, because a hegemonic party must preserve democratic forms that include legally registered opposition parties, it is crucially important to prevent opposition forces' withdrawal from the electoral arena (because the opposition believes it is meaningless to participate) or their disappearance from the electoral landscape (because of their endemic electoral weakness). Hence the pressure to which hegemonic parties are constantly subjected to become increasingly open, to accept more competitive conditions, and gradually to share power with the opposition. These reforms, even if carried out slowly and in a limited way, little by little bring a hegemonic-party system closer to the border that separates it from a dominant-party system (even if many years pass without crossing that line). Of course, this does not guarantee that the outcome of this dynamic will be a democratic dominant party. This is a possibility. But the hegemonic party may also turn back at some point along the way, or it may suffer a defeat and disappear as it attempts to transform itself into a democratic dominant party.

In any event, ruling elites in a hegemonic system typically insist that alternating parties in power is not an indispensable requirement in order to classify the regime as democratic (as, in fact, it is not), and on this basis they demand the same legitimacy enjoyed by truly democratic dominant-party systems (for example, India, Japan, Sweden, and, for many years, Italy) (Pempel 1991). One example of this claim is the statement made in 1990 by President Salinas: "I keep hearing that in Mexico one party has held power for [70] years, but when I think about how long one party has ruled Japan or Italy, I pay less attention to the criticism" (interview in *Newsweek*, December 3, 1990, p. 39).

Despite the enormous differences that distinguish authoritarian hegemony (such as that the PRI exercised in Mexico) from democratic dominance (such as that of dominant parties in Japan, Sweden, and India), there are also similarities between these two party systems that are rather more important than those between hegemonic and one-party systems. In other words, a hegemonic-party system is more than a one-party system masquerading as a democracy, as is often believed. The dynamic of a hegemonic system is significantly different from what is at work in a one-party system, making some of its characteristics similar to those of a dominant-party system. We can therefore pose the hypothesis that a hegemonic-party system has its own traits that simultaneously distinguish it from, and make it similar to, both one-party and dominant-party systems (although obviously for opposite reasons).

This also raises the possibility of characterizing a hegemonic system as a hybrid of one-party and dominant-party systems. The hegemonic party in part has features and dynamics of both single and dominant parties, and even if these are mutually incompatible, they have achieved a peculiar coexistence and complementarity within a hegemonic-party system. For the same reason, party hegemony may be seen as a point midway between its two "relatives" (the one-party system and the democratic dominant-party system). This situation demands the maintenance of a difficult equilibrium, a struggle between two opposed and mutually exclusive dynamics that push the hegemonic party either toward the one-party pole (thus abandoning its relative democratic legitimacy) or toward the dominant-party pole (losing its relative monopoly of power and its guarantee of assured victory) (Crespo 1994). Whether the tendency is for the hegemonic party to move toward the one-party or dominant-party pole depends upon the political conditions it faces at a given time.

In Search of Equilibrium

In order for the hegemonic party to preserve its position, it is equally necessary to prevent opposition parties from deserting or disappearing and to block them for as long as possible from becoming strong or fusing (or allying) themselves in a single party, which might permit them to constitute a real challenge to the undisputed and guaranteed power of the hegemonic party. However, these two strategies clearly run counter to one another. The steps that must be taken to prevent the disappearance of the opposition strengthen it, and, vice versa, the measures that weaken the opposition and prevent it from challenging the hegemonic party could lead to its disappearance. Thus party hegemony demands a balance between these two types of solutions, at least so long as it is possible to avoid both the disappearance of opposition parties (which would make the hegemonic party a one-party system) and their real strengthening (to the point that they could vie for power with the hegemonic party). This dilemma explains the difficulties that many hegemonic parties face in maintaining their peculiar balance, as well as the fact that many of them have failed to preserve their hegemony over a prolonged period of time.

Mexico's PRI was thus exceptional in more than one sense, because it was able to maintain this difficult balance for more than seven consecutive decades.[3] As noted above, the key to its difficult but successful experiment was the ruling elite's able handling of electoral legislation, which for decades served as a fundamental instrument to prevent the disappearance, withdrawal, strengthening, or unification of opposition parties. When there was a danger of their disappearance or withdrawal, the electoral system would be opened up sufficiently to stimulate and provide oxygen to the opposition; when it appeared that opposition forces might become strong or unite, the electoral system was closed off in order to weaken or contain them. Thus the hegemony of the PRI was preserved.

The frequent modifications in Mexican electoral legislation that occurred between 1946 and 1994 can be understood in the context of this overall strategy (Molinar Horcasitas 1991b). Yet these changes were not linear or consistently progressive. Rather, on more than one occasion they represented steps backward. What was, however, unusual in a vigorous authoritarian regime (as the Mexican regime was for several decades) was that the most progressive electoral reforms came about as a result of the regime's own initiative, precisely when the strength or commitment of opposition parties waned. The norm in dictatorial authoritarian or one-party regimes is that ruling elites only accept liberalizing measures when the political opposition gains enough strength to force them to open up to a certain extent. But until dissidents overcome their weakness and mobilize successfully, those in power have no reason to adopt progressive reforms.

This was the context in which Mexico's political opposition long operated. For years the main opposition party was the National Action Party (PAN), which was founded in 1939 with the aim of rescuing the (mainly *maderista*) liberal-democratic legacy of the Mexican Revolution that postrevolutionary generals-as-presidents had placed on hold as they turned their attention to issues of social justice and economic sovereignty. The PAN was the most credible opposition to the PRI because it maintained its autonomy vis-à-vis both the government and the "official"

---

3 Sartori acknowledged the PRI's "feat" in the following terms: "If the Mexican case is evaluated for what it is in and of itself (a hegemonic-party system), it deserves at least two compliments: one for its inventive capacity, and another for the able and successful way in which it has undertaken a difficult experiment" (1980: 285).

party, something that the other two main opposition parties during the 1950s and 1960s – the Socialist Popular Party (PPS) and the Authentic Party of the Mexican Revolution (PARM) – found difficult to do. Indeed, these latter parties quickly became satellites of the PRI. They functioned as electoral "scabs," forcing the PAN to continue participating in electoral contests (against its proclivity to withdraw) and almost invariably casting votes that followed the PRI's line in the various bodies where they were represented. Even more, over time they became habituated to nominating the PRI's presidential candidate as their own candidate – a situation that ended only in 1987 when conditions finally made it advisable to back a common candidate, Cuauhtémoc Cárdenas, in opposition to the ruling party.

It is possible to identify four stages in the development of Mexican electoral legislation that are closely linked to the evolution of party competitiveness from the 1940s through the 1990s: (1) the consolidation of the hegemonic party; (2) limited political opening; (3) regressive reforms; and (4) democratic opening. In each one of these stages, different governments adapted electoral legislation to fit the prevailing political conditions. The first three stages corresponded to the regime's need to prolong and stabilize the ruling party's hegemony. The legislative reforms adopted during the fourth stage reflected the impossibility of prolonging the PRI's hegemony and, in the interest of avoiding political instability, the imperative of shifting to a more competitive terrain – albeit one in which the PRI fully expected to continue contesting and winning elections.

The Consolidation of Party Hegemony

Every political party entering public life faces the challenge of consolidating its own unity and cohesion. This task was especially complicated for Mexico's "official" party, which could have exercised a monopoly of political power (and sought to do so) but at the same time had to coexist with other legally registered parties. Because maintaining monopoly power requires rigid and vertical internal decision-making mechanisms, the party's hegemonic aspirations were incompatible with internal party democracy. Yet top-down decisions by the party elite had to be combined with an iron discipline among the rank and file, meaning that party members had to abide by decisions coming from the top even though their own particular interests suffered. There was always the risk, then, that dissatisfaction among the members and leaders who were not favored by the party's top-down procedures might lead them to secede from the party and join forces with opposition groups.

This option is not open to dissidents in a single-party system, but it is in a hegemonic-party system for the simple reason that the legal opposition is there as an alternative. Discipline in a single-party system is imposed by coercion (via, for example, Stalin's infamous purges or the German Nazi party's "night of the long knives"). However, in a hegemonic-party context coercion must be combined with mechanisms of dissuasion so that dissidents do not decide to switch parties (which, if it occurred in large numbers, might weaken the ruling party to the point that it could lose its hegemony).

In Mexico's hegemonic system, the only way to achieve this goal was to prevent (legally or illegally) the opposition from gaining any significant share of power. This meant that the only routes to political mobility were inside, not outside, the "official" party. When it became clear that outside of the "official" party there was nothing but political limbo, the party's members and mid-level leaders had no choice but to abide by the decisions of the party leadership. Nevertheless, it took some time to reconcile these antagonistic components of party life – top-down decisions by the party leadership and strong discipline among the rank and file (Meyer 1977).[4]

From 1924 to 1952, the process of presidential succession – in which the incumbent president chose his successor rather arbitrarily – caused dissension and breaks in discipline among those who felt they deserved the country's highest political office but had not been favored by the decision of the sitting president. In 1923, 1927, and 1929, these disagreements took the form of armed uprisings. As these were defeated, it gradually became clear to the postrevolutionary elite that resorting to arms was less and less effective as a means of political struggle (Medina Peña 1994). Thus, beginning in 1929 (the year the "official" party was founded), those not chosen by *dedazo* – the presidential index finger – opted to break with the party and challenge it at the ballot box. Although this latter strategy was less dangerous for the postrevolutionary regime, it still questioned the viability of "official" party hegemony.

If these dissidents had been able to make important gains, the incentive to continue along this path each time the ruling party selected its candidates would have produced a constant hemorrhaging of members, middle cadres, and top leaders. This would ultimately have made it impossible to maintain true "official" party hegemony. For this reason, when there were electoral divisions within the party in 1929, 1940, 1946, and 1952, governing elites responded by utilizing the heavy machinery of the state to squelch any possibility of success for those who challenged the regime. In each instance, the government harassed dissidents during the election campaign, practiced enough fraud to guarantee victory by the "official" candidate, and repressed post-election protests by backers of the opposition candidate (Reyna 1985).

It was, moreover, essential to prevent these internal divisions from giving rise to a permanent opposition party because any such alternative would have become a potential base for those who later on might also have decided to leave the party in disagreement with its decisions. This is why the Frente de Partidos Populares (Popular Parties Front), which had nominated Miguel Henríquez Guzmán for the presidency in 1952, was denied official party registration in 1954 (on the pretext of having organized an armed attack on a military barracks in northern Mexico, an

---

4 The "official" party's initial apex was its principal founder, former President Plutarco Elías Calles, the "maximum leader of the revolution." After 1936 it was the president, whoever the person occupying that post might be (Garrido 1986).

event that the government itself may have orchestrated so as to have grounds on which to deny *henriquistas* a party platform). In contrast, opposition that arose from outside the "official" party (the Mexican Communist Party [PCM] or the National Action Party, for example) did not pose such a threat. Nor did other parties that arose from splits within the "official" party but which consisted only of marginal groups (as was the case with the Popular Party [PP] in the late 1940s or the PARM in the early 1950s).

At the same time, the consolidation of presidentialist hegemony required that electoral processes be centralized by the federal government so that they could function as an instrument of control over state-level officials – including those who, even though they belonged to the "official" party, might challenge decisions emanating from the center. The federal government therefore enacted a new electoral law in 1946 with the double purpose of imposing strict discipline within party structures and tight control over state governments. Its main points were precisely to create disincentives for party leaders to organize factional movements and to centralize the organization of elections in the hands of the federal government (via the Ministry of the Interior) (Patiño Camarena 1994).

This initiative was successful over the longer term, and no split occurred within the PRI in association with the 1958 presidential succession. Disappointed contenders for the party's presidential nomination chose to abide by party discipline and remain within its ranks. Neither resort to arms nor an electoral challenge would have won them the power of the presidency, so it was preferable to remain within the party and receive lesser (but still lucrative) posts and opportunities. Similarly, state governors and local political bosses (*caciques*) were compelled to seek the president's approval and abide by his decisions in a disciplined way lest their power be sapped from the center through the federal government's control over electoral processes. By the late 1950s, then, both party hegemony and authoritarian presidentialism were consolidated, at least for the ensuing four decades.

The Controlled Opening

Two of Mexico's most progressive electoral reforms were enacted in 1964 and 1977. Both initiatives provided greater space for the opposition (especially in the federal Chamber of Deputies) by allocating to minority parties proportional representation seats based upon their overall electoral performance rather than votes obtained in relative-majority districts, which were won overwhelmingly by the PRI. In addition, the reform legislation relaxed the general requirements and conditions for opposition parties to maintain their legal registration, and it granted them some prerogatives to facilitate their survival and development (Paoli 1985).

Given the content of the reforms, it would even have been possible to think – as many national and foreign observers did at the time – that the governing elite had truly decided to democratize the political system. This was, of course, the manner in which the reform legislation was presented. But in reality, the reforms responded to growing signs that the political opposition might virtually (or actually) disappear from the electoral stage, leaving the PRI in a situation very much like that of a single party.

Indeed, the 1964 reform was largely a response to the fact that, six years earlier during the 1958 elections, the PAN had withdrawn its six federal deputies to protest what it considered to be an electoral fraud in that year's presidential election. When that occurred, the PRI was confronted with the prospect of being left as the only party with representation in Congress. It also perceived that the PAN might eventually withdraw altogether from the electoral field – a strategy that was in fact being seriously debated within the PAN (Castillo Peraza 1997). Thus the government decided to augment the incentives for the PAN to remain in the electoral arena, but at the same time to penalize the party for any subsequent attempt to withdraw its deputies as a gesture of political protest. Both points were codified in the 1964 electoral law.[5]

Something similar occurred before the 1977 electoral reform, which is widely recognized to have marked a significant (even if still limited) advance toward increased party competition. What motivated the government to accept this political opening was an internal crisis within the PAN that prevented it from nominating a candidate for the 1976 presidential race. Because the other two registered parties, the PPS and the PARM, had clearly fallen into the orbit of the PRI (systematically nominating the "official" party's candidate as their own), the PRI's candidate in effect ran against himself. This outcome evoked Soviet-style single-party elections. Thus the government once again recognized that it was time to open the electoral valve a little bit more by improving the conditions for party competition, as well as providing greater incentives for the political opposition in general.

Among other changes, the 1977 reform gave legal standing to several long-established leftist parties that had led a clandestine (or at least marginal) political existence (Semo 1997). Among the leftist parties newly incorporated into parliamentary life was the old Mexican Communist Party. Founded in 1919, it had sometimes collaborated with the "official" party until the latter broke with its "socialist" tendencies, after which there was a clear distancing between them (and the PCM became for a time a clandestine party). Other leftist parties, including those representing both Trotskyist and moderate socialist currents, were also incorporated into electoral politics under the terms of the new law. Along with the PCM, they thereafter began a slow but fruitful process of ideological and strategic moderation (for example, abandoning both the emblem of the hammer and sickle and the goal of carrying out a socialist revolution in Mexico). More important, they gradually fused, culminating in the creation of the Mexican Socialist Party (PMS) in 1985. On the right, a party with Christian origins, the Christian Democratic Party (PDC), likewise joined the parliamentary fray with legal standing.

5 See Lujambio and Marván Laborde 1997. Under the terms of the 1964 electoral legislation, elected deputies who declined to assume their position would have their political rights suspended for three years.

The 1977 reform was successful in one of its main objectives: revitalizing the party system. The system remained essentially hegemonic, but at least there was the guarantee that the PRI's presidential candidate would not run unopposed, as had occurred in 1976. In fact, in 1982 there were nine rival candidates for the presidency – even though the rules ensured that the PRI's nominee would still triumph.

The Regressive Reforms

The year 1982 marked the beginning of an extremely difficult period for the regime. The country fell into an economic crisis more severe than any it had experienced since the institutionalization of the 1910–1920 revolution. As a consequence, there was a real prospect that citizens would express their discontent at the ballot box by voting for opposition parties, old and new. Upon assuming the presidency, Miguel de la Madrid Hurtado (1982–1988) promised an "integral democracy" in which there would be a significant electoral opening. The government's expectation was that this political initiative would counterbalance the economic austerity program that it simultaneously adopted (De la Madrid 1984).

The De la Madrid administration did in fact relax political controls, and the opposition (especially the PAN) immediately began to win elections for various state- and municipal-level offices. The opposition's gains appeared particularly dramatic when compared to the nearly absolute electoral monopoly that the "official" party had long enjoyed. For this reason, the initial consequences of electoral opening created fear within the government, and halfway through his administration De la Madrid decided to backpedal on electoral matters. The regime then once again resorted to electoral fraud in its various forms.

The 1985 midterm federal elections and some state elections held during this period (in particular, those in Chihuahua and Durango in 1986) were marked by numerous, quite obvious instances of fraud committed to guarantee victory for the "official" party (Molinar Horcasitas 1987). The PAN was taking shape, albeit timidly, as a party that could challenge the PRI at the ballot box, at least at the regional level. Moreover, the economic development model adopted by the De la Madrid administration generated friction with the left-leaning, nationalist wing of the PRI itself. Some PRI members challenged the government from within, pushing for the party's internal democratization in order to open up the presidential nomination process. Later, when it became known that Carlos Salinas de Gortari (then the minister of budget and planning) would be the PRI's candidate, these dissident *priístas* exited the party and nominated their own candidate. Thus was launched the 1988 presidential candidacy of Cuauhtémoc Cárdenas, who also received the backing of a coalition of leftist parties. This kind of split within the PRI had not occurred since 1952 (Garrido 1993).

Faced by mounting challenges, first from the Right and then from the Left, the De la Madrid administration decided to revise federal electoral legislation. However, unlike the 1964 and 1977 reforms, this measure did not promote greater openness. On the contrary, it was a regressive reform whose main goal was to ensure the PRI's hegemony in what loomed as a tense, hotly contested presidential election in 1988. Whereas in 1964 the danger to be averted was that the PRI might end up virtually as a single party, in 1987 the risk was that the opposition's strength had increased to the point where it endangered the hegemony of the "official" party.

Of course, almost any legislation has to dressed up in progressive terms. Yet in the case of the 1987 electoral initiative, these aspects were purely cosmetic. In more substantive terms, the legislation significantly modified the composition of the federal Chamber of Deputies to ensure that the PRI would not lose its absolute majority there – which was an indispensable condition for preserving PRI hegemony and its control over the Congress (Castellanos 1996). Indeed, some of the modifications included in the 1987 law enabled the "official" party to hold on to an absolute majority that it otherwise probably would not have won at the polls (González Casanova 1990).

The key change concerned the number and distribution of proportional representation seats in the Chamber of Deputies. The number of proportional representation seats rose from 100 to 200 (compared to 300 relative-majority seats), and the majority party – which the PRI clearly remained – gained access to them for the first time. Moreover, under the so-called governability clause, the relative-majority party had the right to as many proportional representation seats as it needed to guarantee it an absolute majority (and political control) in the Chamber. This meant that, even if the PRI only obtained something like thirty percent of the total vote but remained the largest party, the final distribution of proportional representation positions would be made in such a manner that it would receive at least fifty percent plus one of the Chamber's seats. And in effect, in the 1988 congressional elections the PRI won only 239 relative-majority seats (47.8 percent of the total 500 seats in the lower chamber). It therefore received 12 proportional representation seats (thus giving it a majority of 251), and it also "bought" the support of several minority party deputies to give it an overall strength of 260 seats.

During the Salinas administration (1988–1994), the trauma of the 1988 elections convinced the governing elite that the opposition challenge would continue to grow unabated. Indeed, this is just what happened. The PAN and the center-left party founded by Cuauhtémoc Cárdenas in 1989 as a fusion of his 1988 electoral coalition and the PMS (the Party of the Democratic Revolution, PRD) together held an unprecedented 240 of the 500 seats in the 1988–1991 federal Chamber of Deputies (48.0 percent). This pushed the Salinas administration to implement a further regressive reform in 1990, which gave the PRI even greater guarantees that it would not lose its absolute majority in the Chamber of Deputies (Nuñez 1991).

The 1990 legislation included (in addition to the governability clause introduced in 1987) a "sliding scale" on which the largest party, in the event that it initially failed to win a full majority of seats, would receive two additional seats for each percentage point it obtained above 35 percent of the total vote. Under this new formula, the PRI would have obtained in 1988 – on the basis of the very same electoral performance – an additional 30 seats in the Chamber of Deputies because its 50.4 percent share of the vote was 15 percentage points above the level specified by law.

Those more progressive elements introduced in the 1990 electoral law – the creation of a Federal Electoral Institute (IFE) that was formally independent of the government, but which still remained under the control of the Ministry of the Interior and on which the PRI retained majority representation – again proved to be superficial and ineffective at moving the Mexican party system forward toward full competitiveness. The economic recovery that the Salinas administration was able to achieve during its first years in office also helped the PRI reestablish its electoral position, so that in the 1991 midterm federal elections the ruling party officially gained 13.6 percentage points more of the total valid vote than it had obtained in 1988 (64.0 percent versus 50.4 percent). Both the PAN and the PRD challenged the transparency and fairness of these elections. However, although there were citizen mobilizations against fraud in state elections in San Luis Potosí and Guanajuato, there was no post-election mobilization at the national level as there had been in 1988, mainly because the presidency was not in dispute.

In state elections during this period, the PAN won the first recognized opposition victory in a gubernatorial race in Baja California in 1989, thus ending sixty years of absolute PRI monopoly at this level. From then on, federal authorities also recognized other opposition wins in gubernatorial races (Guanajuato in 1991, Chihuahua in 1992). By the year 2000, the states of Aguascalientes, Baja California Sur, Jalisco, Nuevo León, Querétaro, and Zacatecas and the government of the Federal District were all in the hands of the opposition. In addition, opposition parties won municipal elections at an impressive pace. The PRI first lost a municipal election (to the PAN) in 1946, and it first lost a state capital in 1958. Yet by 1997, the PRI's share of the country's municipalities had fallen to 68.1 percent (1,365 out of a total of 2,003). The PAN and the PRD held 15.3 percent (306 municipalities) and 14.3 percent (286 municipalities), respectively, while smaller opposition parties together accounted for another 2.3 percent of these positions (BANAMEX 1998: 700).

Despite the PRI's strong electoral recovery in 1991, the Salinas government remained fearful of opposition advances at the state level. It therefore implemented a new electoral reform in 1993 that established better conditions for the PRI, ensuring that the "official" party would not lose its absolute majority in the federal Chamber of Deputies even by accident. The revised legislation again changed the formula for distributing the 200 proportional representation seats. Under its terms, these seats were allocated according to each party's share of the overall vote, regardless of the number of relative-majority seats each party had won. In 1988, the new formula would have provided the ruling party with 339 federal deputies (compared to the 251 it actually received), even before it acquired the backing of minority party deputies.

In making these changes, the Salinas administration exceeded the average of one important electoral reform in each six-year administration. But a third reform was still to come – one that was, however, neither planned nor sought by the governing elite. In this instance, an electoral reform was wrested from the government by the leftist opposition following the surprising public emergence of the Zapatista Army of National Liberation (EZLN) in Chiapas in 1994. The government was forced to make this concession because 1994 was also a year of presidential succession.

The regressive phase of Mexico's electoral evolution consisted of the 1987, 1990, and 1993 legislation. During this phase, in the face of opposition political forces that were still capable of being contained, the ruling elite imposed obstacles so that the opposition could not exceed certain limits. Furthermore, these initiatives preserved (even if artificially) regime control over two basic pillars of party hegemony: the PRI's absolute majority in the Chamber of Deputies, and ruling party control over electoral authorities (thus enabling the PRI to guarantee the election results that were necessary to fulfill the first objective).

The Forced Opening

The guerrilla conflict that erupted in Chiapas in January 1994 once again modified the correlation of forces among Mexico's parties. The broad social support won by the EZLN indirectly benefited the PRD, enabling it to demand that negotiations over electoral issues be reopened in order to guarantee conditions of greater fairness and impartiality in the 1994 presidential election. The PRD, which had rejected the Salinas administration's 1990 and 1993 reforms on the grounds that they were superficial and regressive, let it be known that it would not easily accept any verdict resulting from the August 1994 election unless there were significant amendments to federal electoral law. As a result, the Salinas administration adopted a third electoral reform. The legislation left intact the (pro-PRI) formula for determining the partisan composition of the Congress, but in exchange it granted election authorities somewhat greater autonomy. It thus became more difficult for the government to guarantee victory for the "official" party if the reported results did not faithfully reflect the popular will as expressed at the ballot box (Alcocer 1996).

The accelerated change in electoral legislation that occurred during the Salinas administration reflected what was at root a growing disequilibrium in the hegemonic-party system. This shift required hurried adjustments so as to prevent the system from "deteriorating" into one of its two possible alternatives, a genuinely competitive party system.[6] The strategy of not allowing the increasingly strong opposition to exceed limits that were safe for the PRI worked for a few more years. In the end, however, the government could not stop the opposition from finally gaining sufficient strength to demand conditions that would permit true electoral competitiveness, conditions under which the PRI's hegemony would no longer be sustainable. This opening was visible for the first time in the 1994 reform, and it

---

6 The other possible risk – that the PRI would become a de facto single party – had been left far behind, in 1982.

would henceforth be difficult for the government to hold back the advance of more equitable electoral legislation.

As noted above, the 1994 reform did not alter the formula for allocating proportional representation seats in the Congress, an arrangement that since 1987 had been increasingly favorable to the PRI. It did, however, substantially modify decision-making structures in the Federal Electoral Institute so that the PRI could no longer easily impose its will upon that body. The chairperson of the IFE's General Council remained the minister of the interior (as had been the case since 1946), but the Council's other members were now non-partisan citizen representatives (*consejeros ciudadanos*) nominated by the major political parties. Among the other measures adopted to make the electoral process more transparent, the reform legislation officially permitted international election observers – something that until then had been considered anathema by the Mexican government.

The period leading up to the August 1994 general elections was extraordinarily eventful. The EZLN's emergence dramatically modified the political scene, as did the fatal shooting of PRI presidential candidate Luis Donaldo Colosio in March – something that had not occurred since the assassination of president-elect Álvaro Obregón in 1928, the event that served as the catalyst for the formation of Mexico's first "official" party. There was, moreover, the serious prospect of major post-electoral conflict if the election results were not fundamentally credible. This risk was eventually avoided because there was a substantial difference between PRI candidate Ernesto Zedillo Ponce de León's final vote total and those of his principal adversaries.[7] But despite the PRI's comfortable victory, the government realized that the "official" party's hegemony could no longer be assured on the basis of cheating or regressive electoral legislation without endangering the country's political stability.

For these reasons, President Zedillo (1994–2000) argued that Mexico required a "definitive" electoral reform that fully established conditions for multiparty competition. Unlike those that preceded it, the Zedillo reform eliminated governmental control over the organization of elections and the tallying of their results. Henceforth even an outcome that was unfavorable to the PRI could not be overturned. More than anything else, it was this change that marked Mexico's entry into the sphere of genuine electoral competitiveness (Przeworski 1986).

The 1996 reform addressed two major points, both of which had in fact been subjects of debate since the 1987 regressive reform. First, it established a federal electoral authority that would no longer be subject to governmental control or influence by the ruling party. The IFE's chairperson, for example, was no longer the minister of the interior but rather an independent, non-partisan citizen. Second, it adopted a formula for constituting the federal Chamber of Deputies that

7 PRD candidate Cuauhtémoc Cárdenas, the rival most inclined to challenge the results, wound up in third place, with a vote total that was 33 percentage points lower than Zedillo's (Crespo 1995b).

significantly reduced the possibility that the PRI would be over-represented in that body. Henceforth the majority party's share of total Chamber seats could not exceed its share of the actual vote by more than 8 percentage points. The majority party could not, then, be assured that it would have an absolute majority in the Chamber of Deputies without having obtained an absolute majority of votes cast (Becerra, Salazar, and Woldenberg 1997).

These new rules meant that the PRI had to obtain, without resort to its old tricks and unfair advantages, more than 42 percent of the national vote in the 1997 congressional elections if it was to retain firm control over the federal Chamber of Deputies. However, even though the PRI used enormous amounts of public financing, and even though electoral observers reported that it still engaged in some illegal practices (in particular, illegally buying votes), it only won 39.1 percent of the total valid vote in these elections. This translated into a total of 239 seats (47.8 percent) in the 500-seat Chamber of Deputies. Thus for the first time the "official" party lost its absolute majority in the Chamber – and, with it, another pillar of party hegemony (Cansino 1998).[8]

From Hegemony to Simple Majority

In essence, the principal result of the 1996 reform was that the PRI was no longer a hegemonic party in the full sense of the word. After 1997, it came closer to fitting a dominant-majority model, but under much more competitive (though still somewhat unequal) conditions than had ever existed in Mexico.

The new distribution of power in the federal Chamber of Deputies was felt immediately. The PRI's four rivals at first formed a parliamentary "opposition bloc" through which they redistributed committee assignments and internal decision-making authority more fairly. The bloc did not survive because of differences on economic policy matters among the constituent parties, especially between the PAN and the PRD. Nevertheless, the PRI's primacy and its overwhelming capacity to impose its decisions (and, through it, those of the president) ceased to be the norm in Mexican legislative life. For example, the 1998 federal budget was for the first time the object of hard bargaining among parties represented in the Chamber of Deputies because it could no longer be automatically approved by the "official" majority, as had occurred for nearly seventy years. Some important presidential initiatives (including a bill addressing indigenous rights issues) were postponed because they, too, lacked automatic majority support. Things had clearly changed.

8 In the 1997 elections the PRD won 125 seats in the Chamber of Deputies, and the PAN won 121 seats. The remaining Chamber seats were distributed between two minor parties of more recent creation, 7 for the Labor Party (PT) and 8 for the Mexican Ecological Green Party (PVEM). The former organization had *salinista* origins (it had been supported by the president's older brother, Raúl), but it had a socialist orientation that made it ideologically more radical than the PRD. The latter party emulated European Green parties in programmatic terms, though in practice it was managed somewhat like a family business.

The fact that the PRI had lost its hegemony did not mean that it had lost power – much less that it no longer existed. But having emerged and ruled for seventy years as a hegemonic party, in the late 1990s the party set itself the task of continuing to win the presidency under newly competitive conditions. In doing so, the PRI had to take into account that over the years it had been discredited, in a manner not dissimilar to the Communist parties of Eastern Europe shortly before they were defeated.

Faced with these radically new circumstances, in late 1999 the PRI successfully carried out an internal primary to select its candidate for the 2000 presidential election. Because of the party's relative defeat in the 1997 federal legislative elections and the resulting discontent among *priístas*, voices arose within the party urgently calling for an internal reform that would permit rival groups and candidates to compete to become the PRI's nominees under fair conditions. At the local level, the PRI had suffered splits and defeats in Aguascalientes, Baja California Sur, Tlaxcala, and Zacatecas precisely because it rejected democratic candidate selection procedures. In contrast, in Chihuahua (where the PRI had lost the governorship to the PAN in 1992) an open primary election had proved so successful that the party was able to recover the governorship in 1998. Thus conditions favored a formally more open method for selecting the PRI's presidential candidate.

The winner of the primary held on November 7, 1999, was Francisco Labastida Ochoa. Labastida had served as both minister of agriculture and minister of the interior in Zedillo's cabinet, and he was widely understood to be Zedillo's favorite candidate. Because the president's favored candidate won, and because of some irregularities detected during the primary voting, the event's democratic credentials were strongly challenged from almost all sides. Nevertheless, the PRI avoided the main risk it had faced in the experiment – a major party schism. That itself placed the ruling party in a position from which it could once again aspire to win the presidential election, all the more so because the success of the internal primary produced new sources of support for the PRI and improved (even if only for a relatively brief period) its standing in public opinion polls.

For its part, the political opposition – which over the course of nearly four months in 1999 debated the possibility of nominating a common candidate as part of its efforts to defeat the PRI – wound up somewhat tarnished when it failed to present a united front for the 2000 elections. Moreover, in mid-1999 the opposition had failed to push through a new electoral reform that would have established controls on the amounts and sources of party campaign funds, tightened restrictions on the use of public funds for campaigns, curtailed such still-widespread illegal practices as the buying or coercing of votes, loosened the requirements for forming electoral coalitions, and established the conditions that would have fulfilled the 1996 constitutional mandate allowing Mexicans living abroad to vote in the 2000 elections. Although the opposition-controlled federal Chamber of Deputies had approved these measures, the PRI used its majority in the federal Senate to block their final approval.

The 2000 Elections and their Aftermath

To the surprise of nearly everyone (starting with *priístas*), PAN candidate Vicente Fox Quesada defeated PRI candidate Francisco Labastida by the substantial margin of 6.6 percentage points in the July 2000 presidential election.[9] The possibility that the PRI might well lose this crucial election had not been entirely dismissed beforehand. After all, with the exception of 1976 (when the PRI faced no registered opposition candidate), the historical trend was for the PRI's presidential candidate to win a share of the vote that was just slightly lower than what the party had received in the immediately preceding midterm congressional election, indicating that in 2000 Labastida might win something less than the 39.1 percent vote share that the PRI had received in the 1997 midterm elections. For the PRI to have won the election with only 35 to 37 percent of the valid vote, the opposition vote would have to have been divided almost equally between the two principal rival candidates. That outcome had seemed unlikely since 1998 because, whenever public opinion polls showed one opposition candidate gaining in strength, that candidate immediately began to draw away from his weaker rivals the support of voters who were more interested in the defeat of the PRI than the triumph of their own party or favorite candidate (Crespo 1998). This transferable vote became known as the "strategic vote" (*voto útil*), and it comprised the approximately 7 percent of the electorate that backed Fox but not the PAN.

However, the surprise in July 2000 lay not just in the fact, but also in the margin, of the opposition candidate's victory. This greatly facilitated both President Zedillo's and candidate Labastida's acceptance of the outcome. Although some public opinion surveys had forecast a result along these lines, many others had failed to do so – and some had been deliberately manipulated by the PRI and its media allies. These machinations confused both public opinion and the parties themselves, making it unclear who might win and by what margin.

On the whole, opinion polls projected that whoever won the election would do so by such a narrow margin that the second-place finisher would not readily accept the result. This scenario raised the distinct possibility of widespread public protests that might place in jeopardy the country's economic – and perhaps political – stability. In particular, a narrow victory by the PRI's candidate would have been suspect because there had been, in the weeks prior to the election, extensive denunciations of efforts by PRI operatives to buy or coerce votes in different parts of the country and among different sectors of the population. Thus if Labastida had won by a margin of three percentage points or less, opposition protests would almost inevitably have occurred.

9 Of the 36,778,272 votes validated by the Federal Electoral Institute, Fox won 43.5 percent (15,988,172 votes), Labastida received 36.9 percent (13,575,291 votes), PRD candidate Cuauhtémoc Cárdenas won 17.0 percent (6,257,353 votes), and 2.6 percent (957,456 votes) went to other candidates.

The margin of Fox's victory was important, then, because it permitted President Zedillo to recognize the outcome immediately, thus blocking any possibility of a PRI protest. At 11:15 p.m. on the night of the election, Zedillo appeared on national television to declare:

> Today we have been able to prove that ours is now a mature democracy, with solid and trustworthy institutions, and especially with a citizenry that manifests a great sense of civic consciousness and responsibility ... I have just telephoned Lic. Vicente Fox to express to him my sincere congratulations on his electoral triumph, and to assure him that the government I head is absolutely committed to collaborating with him between now and [his inauguration on] December 1 in all areas that may be important for the successful initiation of the next administration.[10]

The outcome on July 2 nevertheless surprised the PRI, which was not prepared for defeat. As the PRI and PRD had so much feared, voters split their ballots. This phenomenon had been quite unusual in Mexican elections and confirmed the plebiscitary character of the 2000 presidential election. Fox's candidacy drew approximately 1.5 million "strategic votes" (about 7 percent of the total) more than the congressional candidates sponsored by the "Alliance for Change," a coalition between the PAN and the PVEM. The result was a highly differentiated distribution of power, with the PAN winning 210 seats (42.0 percent of the total) in the federal Chamber of Deputies while the PRI won 211 seats (42.2 percent) and the PRD 53 seats (10.6 percent).[11]

The PRI's loss in the presidential race left the party without a mainsail, and in the immediate aftermath the party faced a high risk of schism. On the day after the election, PRI leader Dulce María Sauri tendered her resignation, but diverse elements within the party persuaded her to remain in her post until new national leadership elections – this time, without orienting instructions from a sitting president – could be held.

PRI unity hung by a thread. Several months of negotiations passed among key party figures, leaders of major affiliated organizations, PRI governors, and the Chamber of Deputies and Senate heads of the party's congressional delegation. The result was reformulated party statutes and more "horizontal" decision-making rules, changes necessitated by the fact that the vertical arrangements that had made internal party governance possible disappeared automatically when the PRI lost the presidency.

The new statutes, rules, and party principles were formally approved at the PRI's November 2001 national assembly. The assembly reaffirmed the party's traditional ideology of revolutionary nationalism and explicitly rejected the neo-liberal doctrines that the De la Madrid, Salinas, and Zedillo administrations had espoused. Although there were tensions and conflicts at the national assembly

---

10 *Reforma*, July 3, 2000.

11 The remaining seats were distributed among small parties. The 2000 election results were a particularly sharp reversal for the PRD, which had won 125 Chamber seats in 1997.

meeting, they did not produce an open split within the PRI. But the real test of fire lay ahead with the selection of new party leaders under more horizontal decision-making procedures – the first time since the party's founding that this process occurred without an incumbent president serving as "great elector" and "born leader."

Two rival groups contested the PRI's leadership. The first group was led by Roberto Madrazo, a former governor of Tabasco and an aspirant for the party's presidential nomination in 1999. Madrazo's key supporters included Elba Esther Gordillo, de facto leader of the powerful National Education Workers' Union (SNTE). The leader of the second group was Beatriz Paredes, a former governor of Tlaxcala who at the time led the PRI delegation in the federal Chamber of Deputies. The election (held in February 2002) was plagued by irregularities committed by both factions, but Madrazo's forces managed to prevail in the old arts of inventing votes, modifying ballots, and canceling opponents' votes that had long characterized the PRI regime. Party schism was closer than ever because, among other things, Madrazo won by the small margin of 1.6 percent of the ballots cast. His margin of victory came from his Tabasco stronghold (the state accounted for 4.2 percent of all votes), where he ostensibly beat Paredes by the improbable margin of 17 to 1.

Paredes and her supporters vigorously protested the fraud of which they had been victims, and the specter of schism floated in the air in the days following the election. But in the end Paredes calculated that her political future was more promising inside the PRI than outside it (a conclusion that Madrazo may not have reached, had he lost), and she observed party discipline. Thus the PRI passed its most difficult test after losing the presidency, giving it a stronger base for continuing as an opposition force and recovering its electoral strength (as the Communist party did in Russia in the 1990s). Nor can one discount the possibility of its eventual return to national power, as the PRI did in Chihuahua after losing control of the governorship in 1992.

Despite having survived the danger of schism, PRI leader Madrazo did not manage to gain control over all reins of party power. PRI governors operated quite independently, in line with their own interests. The same was true of PRI federal legislators, especially in the Senate (where the party held 60 of 128 seats, none of which would be up for election until 2006). The PRI's Senate delegation included some of its most experienced national leaders and was led by Manuel Bartlett, former minister of the interior during the Salinas administration and a former governor of Puebla. Bartlett continued to exercise strong influence over the traditional *priísta* elements who refused to collaborate with the "ultra-rightist" Fox administration,[12] and in coherent pursuit of this line, Bartlett consistently opposed

12 Shortly after President Fox was inaugurated in December 2000, Bartlett declared, "It can be good for Mexico if things go badly for Fox … We have to define clearly our profile as a popular party and struggle ceaselessly against the rightist Fox administration" (*Proceso*, November 12, 2000).

efforts by the new PRI leadership to find common ground with the Fox government and thereby advance major economic and political reform proposals. Moreover, Bartlett and like-minded elements within the PRI quite openly defied their party's leaders and accused them of betraying its most cherished principles.

For its part, the PRD – holding about a tenth of the seats in the Congress – also showed little inclination to cooperate with the Fox administration. Indeed, the party's radical wing attacked Amalia García's relatively moderate leadership for "collaborating" with the Fox government. In March 2002 García was replaced (in a disorganized election that was plagued with irregularities and severely questioned by *perredistas* themselves) by Rosario Robles, who succeeded Cuauhtémoc Cárdenas as governor of the Federal District in 1999 and represented the party's more radical wing. The PRD did not face the risk of division that confronted the PRI (the PRD has since its birth lived with internal splits and frictions among multiple groupings of party loyalists), and the Robles faction managed to unite the bulk of the party behind its opposition to collaboration with the Fox administration. Indeed, the party took the rather intransigent position that any reform measures enacted by the government should come from the PRD's own party platform.

In the year 2000, then, Mexico experienced the first peaceful alternation in national power in its entire history. Such changes had previously taken place via revolution, coup d'état, or civil war. Peaceful transition created a new opportunity to lay firm foundations for a democratic regime, though this will necessarily require significant changes in areas outside the party and electoral systems. However, the Fox administration faced a complicated panorama characterized by an extreme fragmentation of power – between the executive and legislative branches, between the lower and upper houses of Congress, and within the opposition parties that together held an absolute majority of seats in both the federal Chamber of Deputies and the Senate.

In effect, the challenge of governability in Mexico's incipient democracy lies first and foremost in the conduct of the main political actors. Many of the difficulties that the Fox administration initially encountered could be attributed to the president's own imperiousness, the lack of coordination within his administration, the PAN's difficulty in assuming its new role as governing party, and the obstructionist strategies adopted by powerful groups within the PRI and by the PRD's leadership. But above all, it proved difficult for Mexico's institutional framework to adapt to altered political conditions. The result was a badly divided government that, more than serving as a counterbalance to presidential power, constituted a brake on effective legislative and governmental action. In so doing, it represented a serious threat to the country's democratic governability.

References

Alcocer, Jorge. 1996. "Las recientes reformas electorales en México: perspectivas para una democracia." In *El desafío de la reforma institucional en México*, edited by Riordan Roett. Mexico City: Siglo Veintiuno.

BANAMEX (Banco Nacional de México). 1998. *México social, 1996–1998*. Mexico City: BANAMEX.

Becerra, Ricardo, Pablo Salazar, and José Woldenberg. 1997. *La reforma electoral de 1996*. Mexico City: Fondo de Cultura Económica.

Cansino, César, ed. 1998. *Después del PRI: las elecciones de 1997 y los escenarios de la transición en México*. Mexico City: Centro de Estudios de Política Comparada.

Castellanos, Eduardo. 1996. *Formas de gobierno y sistemas electorales en México, 1940–1994*. Mexico City: Centro de Investigación Científica Jorge L. Tamayo.

Castillo Peraza, Carlos. 1997. "De la fuerza a la maña: la lenta apertura del poder legislativo a la oposición entre los años 1943 y 1958," *Diálogo y Debate* (April-June): 29–40.

Crespo, José Antonio. 1994. "PRI: de la hegemonía revolucionaria a la dominación democrática," *Política y Gobierno* 1 (January-June): 47–77.

———. 1995a. "Hacia un nuevo modelo de dominación política: un enfoque comparativo entre México y Japón." Documento de Trabajo No. 27. Mexico City: Centro de Investigación y Docencia Económicas.

———. 1995b. *Urnas de Pandora: partidos políticos y elecciones durante el gobierno de Salinas*. Mexico City: Espasa-Calpe.

———. 1998. *¿Tiene futuro el PRI? Entre la supervivencia democrática y la desintegración total*. Mexico City: Grijalbo / Raya en el Agua.

Crespo, José Antonio, and Varun Sahni. 1998. "Del dominio al agotamiento: India y México," *Enfoque* 234 (July): 6–7.

De la Madrid, Miguel. 1984. *Las siete tesis rectoras*. Mexico City: Partido Revolucionario Institucional.

Duff, Ernst A., and John McCamant. 1976. *Violence and Repression in Latin America: A Quantitative and Historical Analysis*. New York: Free Press.

Duverger, Maurice. 1996 [1951]. *Los partidos políticos*. Mexico City: Fondo de Cultura Económica.

Garrido, Luis Javier. 1986. *El partido de la revolución institucionalizada: la formación de un nuevo Estado en México*. Mexico City: Siglo Veintiuno.

———. 1993. *La ruptura: la Corriente Democrática del PRI*. Mexico City: Grijalbo.

González Casanova, Pablo, ed. 1990. *Segundo informe sobre la democracia: México el 6 de julio de 1988*. Mexico City: Universidad Nacional Autónoma de México / Siglo Veintiuno.

Huntington, Samuel P. 1972. *El orden político en las sociedades en cambio*. Buenos Aires: Paidós.

Lujambio, Alonso, and Ignacio Marván Laborde. 1997. "La reforma de los 'diputados de partido,' 1962–1963," *Diálogo y Debate* (April-June): 41–75.

Medina Peña, Luis. 1994. *Hacia el nuevo Estado: México, 1920–1993*. Mexico City: Fondo de Cultura Económica.

Meyer, Lorenzo. 1977. "La etapa formativa del Estado mexicano contemporáneo (1928–1976)," *Foro Internacional* 17, 4 (April-June): 453–89.

Molinar Horcasitas, Juan. 1987. "Regreso a Chihuahua," *Nexos* 111 (March): 21–32.

———. 1991a. "La legitimidad perdida." *Nexos* 164 (August): 7–10.

———. 1991b. *El tiempo de la legitimidad: elecciones, autoritarismo y democracia en México*. Mexico City: Cal y Arena.

Nohlen, Dieter. 1995. *Sistemas electorales y partidos políticos*. Mexico City: Fondo de Cultura Económica.

Nuñez, Arturo. 1991. *El nuevo sistema electoral mexicano*. Mexico City: Fondo de Cultura Económica.

Paoli, Francisco. 1985. "Legislación electoral y proceso político, 1917–1982." In *Las elecciones en México: evolución y perspectivas*, edited by Pablo González Casanova. Mexico City: Siglo Veintiuno.

Patiño Camarena, Javier. 1994. *Derecho electoral mexicano*. Mexico City: Universidad Nacional Autónoma de México.

Pempel, T.J., ed. 1991. *Democracias diferentes: los regímenes con un partido dominante*. Mexico City: Fondo de Cultura Económica.

Przeworski, Adam. 1986. "Some Problems in the Study of Transitions to Democracy." In *Comparative Perspectives*. Pt. 3, *Transitions from Authoritarian Rule: Prospects for Democracy*, edited by Guillermo O'Donnell, Philippe C. Schmitter, and Laurence Whitehead. Baltimore, Md.: Johns Hopkins University Press.

Reyna, José Luis. 1985. "Las elecciones en el México institucionalizado, 1946–1976." In *Las elecciones en México: evolución y perspectivas*, edited by Pablo González Casanova. Mexico City: Siglo Veintiuno.

Sartori, Giovanni. 1980. *Partidos y sistemas de partidos*. Madrid: Alianza Universidad.

Semo, Enrique. 1997. "1977: la reforma política y la izquierda," *Diálogo y Debate* (April-June): 76–80.

3

Public Institutions and Electoral Transparency in Mexico

Silvia Gómez Tagle

Formally democratic political systems often do not meet the requirements of a true political democracy in which elections are the means by which citizens choose those who govern them. In Mexico from 1929 until 1977, a hegemonic-party system[1] prevailed in which, although there were several parties and elections were held regularly, only the Institutional Revolutionary Party (PRI) had a real chance to win. It was, in other words, an authoritarian system in which those who governed were not accountable to those who elected them. This system fostered corruption and impunity, and it placed the rule of law at risk.

Moving from an authoritarian hegemonic-party system to a functioning democracy requires three things: a transformation of the rules (electoral laws and institutions) in order to guarantee electoral transparency; the citizenry's confidence in elections as a means to achieve power; and the presence of competitive and autonomous political parties. The transformation of the Mexican party system and a shift toward democratization began in 1977, generating a dynamic of electoral reform that is still in play.

The three requirements for democratization (electoral reform, confidence in elections, and competitive parties) are in reality interdependent aspects of a single transition process. Because the central theme of this chapter is transparency in elections, questions concerning political parties and public opinion will be dealt with only in passing. Nevertheless, the discussion is not a restricted analysis of juridical norms; rather, it is an investigation into the relationship between these norms and political actors in a given historical context.

Any study of transparency in electoral processes implies analyzing the whole set of institutions that comprise the electoral system, as well as the more general question of what constitutes a transition to democracy. This latter topic is especially important in the Mexican case because, in the series of changes taking place between the mid-1970s and the late 1990s, there was no single moment that marked

---

Translated by Aníbal Yáñez-Chávez and Kevin J. Middlebrook.

1 For a definition of a hegemonic-party system , see Sartori 1994: 283. See also Huntington and Moore 1970 and Hemet, Rouquie, and Linz 1982.

the end of one political regime and the beginning of another.[2] Given the very gradual character of change, for many years it was even questionable whether one could speak of a political transition because the PRI and those in power were often able to bring the system back into equilibrium to compensate for any changes made in electoral rules and procedures.

Cotteret and Émeri define a functioning electoral system as "a set of procedures and juridical and material acts that lead to the designation of those who govern by those who are governed" (1973: 15), in which electoral law is understood as the result of a dynamic process of state-society interaction. "Electoral law simply registers the incessantly modified terms of these compromises" between political forces vying for power (1973: 3). From this perspective, transparency has as much to do with the electoral norms enshrined in law as with the functioning of institutions at a given historical moment. A determination of transparency is not limited to a single criterion. Rather, it must take into account the historical interaction of electoral rules and institutions, political parties, and public opinion.

If democracy presupposes a set of rules that organize competition for political power and offer the possibility of alternation in power through peaceful means, a key feature of a democratic system is that different groups may strive simultaneously for political power. The rules of the system safeguard the rights of minorities; they oblige those in power to submit to elections in which citizens can use peaceful means to change those who govern.

In authoritarian systems, in contrast, political control by a single group may be prolonged indefinitely even without popular support because the group can use its domination of the state apparatus to reproduce its power. Mexico provides a good example of how electoral laws and institutions can contribute to the stability of an authoritarian system at a time when there are no competing parties, and yet cause serious conflicts and a loss of legitimacy for the political system at a different moment in time.

If one accepts that there are no perfect democracies, then the question regarding the transition from an authoritarian regime to a democratic one becomes, "What are the degrees of imperfection that can be tolerated in a democratic regime before the institutional framework loses all meaning?" (Hermet, Rouquie, and Linz 1982). The meaning of democracy lies in establishing rules to channel the struggle for political power, demanding that those who govern are accountable to citizens and allow peaceful change of the political system. The institutions charged with organizing and certifying electoral results are the indispensable link between democratic rules and democracy in practice. The legitimacy of electoral processes depends largely upon whether these institutions are trustworthy.[3] Two fundamental

2 The term "political regime" is used here as defined by Levi (1995: 1362): a "set of institutions that regulate the struggle for power and the exercise of power, as well as the values that give life to those institutions."

3 If there is no means to force citizens and political parties to respect electoral rules, the entire process can fall apart because those who violate electoral law go unpunished.

issues are of importance here – electoral organization, and how the electoral process is evaluated (that is, how the actors or the outcomes are perceived).

Mexico: A Hegemonic-Party System

Democracy was not a core value for the political regime that emanated from the Mexican Revolution. Symbiotic ties between a powerful presidency and the ruling party allowed the sitting president to become the axis of national politics. Not only could he organize the various interest groups linked to his own party, but he could often control opposition social and political forces as well.

The absence of any autonomous centers of contending power – especially competing political parties – could be explained by the great hegemony of the PRI, the heir of the Mexican Revolution. This party's legitimacy stemmed originally from its connection to the broad social movement emanating from the 1910–1920 revolution. Because other political groups carried the stigma of being "counter-revolutionary," they found it extremely difficult to consolidate as autonomous centers of power. Indeed, it could be said that the PRI took advantage of the broad consensus it initially won from the Revolution and later established during the administration of President Lázaro Cárdenas (1934–1940) to impose an electoral system designed to prevent opposition parties from constituting a majority.

Mexico has held regular elections since the early 1930s. Yet until 1997 a single party controlled both the presidency and the Congress. Thus the PRI could pass legislation at will, and it frequently manipulated the electoral process. The president's control over core electoral issues allowed for elections that were free of conflicts that could jeopardize the PRI's hegemony. The difference in vote counts between the PRI and other parties was so great that charges that the electoral system lacked transparency were lost in the PRI majority.

From 1946 to 1976, four central aspects of electoral organization ensured the Mexican political system's stability in the electoral sphere: (1) the PRI maintained control over the legislative branch by holding a majority in Congress; (2) the requirement that political parties be registered in order to participate in elections allowed the president to control how many (and which) parties would compete electorally; (3) elections were organized and certified by institutions controlled by the president and the PRI; and (4) government funds were used to promote the ruling party.

Opposition parties were condemned to interminable defeats. Some – the Mexican Communist Party (PCM), the Popular Force Party (PFP),[4] and the Federation of Parties of the Mexican People (FPPM),[5] among others – were banned altogether.

---

4 The Popular Force Party was linked with *sinarquismo*, a movement of the extreme Right. It obtained its official registration in 1946 and competed in that year's presidential election, but it lost its registration in 1949 for committing illegal acts (profaning the monument to Benito Juárez in the Alameda park in downtown Mexico City). See Molinar Horcasitas 1991: 36.
5 The FPPM was organized in 1945 by a left-wing group of PRI dissidents. It was banned after the 1952 presidential election, in which its presidential candidate (General Miguel Henríquez

The only opposition party able to survive was the center-right National Action Party (PAN).

Over time, however, the PRI gradually lost the legitimacy it had inherited from the Revolution, and the electoral system it had designed to prevent the growth of other parties became a risk for the very stability of the political regime. Absent effective opposition parties, social discontent was often expressed outside of institutional channels, as occurred with the 1968 student movement, numerous dissident trade-union movements, and groups engaged in armed struggle against the established regime in the early 1970s.

In the 1976 general elections, the PRI was the only registered party to put forward a candidate for the presidency.[6] The PAN, hindered by internal divisions and its members' disgust with the lack of electoral transparency, chose not to field a presidential candidate. Other political forces, from both the Left and the Right, were blocked from competing in the contest because election authorities had not granted them official registration.[7]

The Stage of Political Pluralism

The most important political reform of this period took place in 1977. Jesús Reyes Heroles, then minister of the interior, proposed a series of changes in the party system and in electoral organization that were aimed at widening the possibilities for political representation. The goal was to "capture in the representative bodies the complicated national ideological mosaic of a majority current and of small currents which, while differing significantly from the majority, also make up part of the nation" (Reyes Heroles 1977: 9–16). The reforms and additions to 17 articles of the Mexican Constitution were published in the *Diario Oficial de la Federación* on December 6, 1977, and a new regulatory law was issued as well, the Federal Law on Political Organizations and Electoral Processes (LFOPPE).

This political reform also included complementary changes in other fundamental laws, including a constitutional amendment recognizing citizens' right to information[8] and an amnesty for political prisoners and fugitives. The latter action was an important incentive for many individuals involved in social struggles to join political parties and channel their activities through elections, rather than opting

---

Guzmán) made a very strong showing. See Martínez Assad 1982: 18.

6 As they customarily did, the Socialist Popular Party (PPS) and the Authentic Party of the Mexican Revolution (PARM) supported the PRI's candidate.

7 Party registration was granted by tshe Federal Electoral Commission (CFE), chaired by the minister of the interior. Moreover, the requirements to obtain registration were extremely difficult to meet.

8 The implementing legislation concerning citizens' right to information was not enacted until 2002. This law was in fact the most important legislative action taken to consolidate democracy in Mexico during the 2000–2003 period.

for direct action through peaceful means in social movements or through violent means in guerrilla groups.

Two fundamental features of the LFOPPE merit special note. First, the new law strengthened political pluralism by opening the possibility of registering new political parties. Second, it introduced the principle of proportional representation in the Chamber of Deputies, which allowed smaller parties to gain seats in Congress. After fifty years of defeats, the opposition enthusiastically seized this opportunity, and a number of new political parties were registered.[9]

The 1977 political reform defined political parties as "institutions in the public interest" and awarded them government subsidies to carry out their activities. Many survived thanks in large part to these subsidies, and their survival gave the regime an image of political pluralism.

Three new parties registered for the federal Chamber of Deputies elections in 1979: the Mexican Communist Party, the Socialist Workers' Party (PST), and the Mexican Democratic Party (PDM, the *sinarquista* heir to the PFP that had lost its official registration in 1949). They were joined in 1982 by the Revolutionary Workers' Party (PRT) and the Social Democratic Party (PSD). The PSD lost its conditional registration following the election because it failed to reach the 1.5 percent valid-vote threshold. The PARM also lost its registration for the same reason, but it won it back in 1985. In 1985 the Mexican Workers' Party (PMT) won registration as well. Thus the party system, which had essentially been closed from 1946 through 1976, gained vitality thanks to the participation of new organizations, even though some of them would not survive in the long run.

The makeup of the federal Chamber of Deputies changed as the number of single-member electoral districts (where the winner was chosen by a relative majority of the vote) rose from 196 to 300 and as 100 new deputies were elected according to a proportional representation formula (Patiño Camarena 1985: 222–27). The proportional representation seats were distributed by dividing the country into a minimum of three and a maximum of five party-list circumscriptions, and then allocating seats according to a party's proportional strength in each area. Only minority parties – defined in the LFOPPE as those that elected fewer than sixty deputies by a relative majority – had the right to the 100 proportional representation seats.

However, the new electoral legislation also sought to prevent minority parties from becoming majorities (Patiño Camarena 1985: 228). It specified that only fifty

---

9 To win "definitive registration," parties were required to demonstrate that they had a large membership distributed throughout the country. This was extremely difficult because it required organizing assemblies attended by hundreds of people who had to prove their identity before a notary public. In contrast, "conditional registration" allowed a political party to participate in elections, on the assumption that definitive registration would be granted after the elections on the basis of the votes received by the party in question. Any party not winning 1.5 percent of the valid votes cast in an election was to lose its registration (as occurred with the PARM in 1982), although the affected party could again request "conditional registration" in the following elections.

percent of the proportional representation seats would be distributed if two or more parties won ninety or more single-member districts, effectively limiting political pluralism. It also stipulated that any party winning sixty or more single-member districts would not receive any proportional representation seats. Furthermore, the federal Senate and state-level legislatures were not included in the reform.

The LFOPPE made no significant changes in the organization of elections. This responsibility continued to rest entirely with the Federal Electoral Commission (CFE), a body subordinate to the Ministry of the Interior (Secretaría de Gobernación) which, in turn, relied upon state governments to organize electoral processes. This institutional arrangement gave both the president and state governors the opportunity to manipulate electoral results. Certification of elections was in the hands of an electoral college in the Chamber of Deputies and another in the Senate. Both bodies were political in nature and clearly favored the majority party, the PRI.

During the early and mid-1980s, the center-right PAN offered the strongest challenge to the PRI and sparked the sharpest post-election disputes. Particularly bitter conflicts broke out over gubernatorial contests in Chihuahua and San Luis Potosí, as well as municipal elections in Culiacán, Sinaloa, and elsewhere. In contrast, although leftist parties multiplied in number, they did not become significant electoral competitors except in very limited areas such as the mountains of Guerrero and the Isthmus of Tehuantepec.

The tensions generated by conflicts between and among emerging parties, a citizenry in the process of organizing itself, and a politically controlled electoral system dominated by the federal executive led to pressures for additional reforms in 1986 and 1987. In particular, parties on both the left and the right demanded stronger guarantees for political minorities. The 1986 constitutional reform and the 1987 electoral law adopted some of the opposition's demands, including the creation of a special Tribunal for Electoral Disputes (Tribunal de lo Contencioso Electoral),[10] an increase from 100 to 200 in the number of proportional representation seats in the Chamber of Deputies, and the creation of the Federal District Representative Assembly – the first step toward restoring the political rights of residents in the nation's capital, whose government had been appointed by the federal executive since the mid-1920s.[11]

Yet in other important aspects, the 1986–1987 reforms represented a regression for democratization. First, the 1987 electoral law eliminated conditional registration for new parties, forcing any group that wished to form a party to fulfill the

10 However, the Tribunal only had administrative status. The final certification of elections remained in the hands of electoral colleges in the federal Chamber of Deputies (for deputies and the president) and Senate (for senators). See the reform to Article 74 of the Constitution.

11 Nevertheless, the heads of government (*jefe de gobierno*) in the Federal District (elected since 1997) and in its constituent administrative districts (*delegaciones*, elected since 2000), as well as the Federal District Legislative Assembly, have limited functions. Important reforms in the Federal District's governance are still pending.

stringent requirements of definitive registration before it could gain access to the electoral arena. Second, parties were represented in the Federal Electoral Commission in proportion to the votes they received in the previous election – a provision that allowed the PRI to hold an absolute majority of seats on the CFE.[12]

Mexico's party system could not be transformed overnight from a hegemonic system into a highly competitive plural system because there was never a "foundational pact" for altering the political regime. Instead, change took place gradually. From the mid-1980s onward the PAN slowly increased its electoral presence at the local, state, and national levels and expanded its support among business and middle sectors. The Left, by contrast, encountered numerous obstacles to its consolidation. It was splintered into multiple groups, and the PRI both usurped the language of the Left in its populist rhetoric and co-opted many leftist leaders and intellectuals. Problems of populism and political fragmentation plagued the National Democratic Front (FDN), formed around Cuauhtémoc Cárdenas's presidential candidacy in 1987–1988, and, later, the Party of the Democratic Revolution (PRD, formed in 1989). Although the FDN proved surprisingly effective at competing with the PRI among popular sectors in both rural and urban areas in the 1988 elections, it was comprised of highly disparate political organizations – the Mexican Unified Socialist Party (PSUM), the Party of the Cardenista Front for National Reconstruction (PFCRN), the PPS, the PARM, and diverse other social and political groups whose orientations ranged from the extreme left to the democratic center.

As a range of new political actors slowly emerged, Mexico's economic, intellectual, and political elites gradually disengaged from the PRI to form new autonomous power groups. The 1977 political reform marked the first step in the institutionalization of a more competitive struggle for power. Over time, Mexico moved from a phase in which votes literally did not count, to a stage in which votes were frequently miscounted because all of the electoral machinery was in the hands of the Ministry of the Interior and state governments dominated by the "official" party. The impact of increased political participation was thus constrained by the lack of electoral transparency.

The Struggle for Electoral Transparency

Because growing electoral competition was not accompanied by the institutional changes necessary to promote electoral transparency, post-electoral conflict became increasingly frequent at both the federal and state levels. The fact that electoral processes and the "winners" selected through them increasingly lacked legitimacy, combined with accumulated social discontent over Mexico's post-1982 economic crisis and growing resistance to authoritarianism, produced the 1987–1988 split in the ruling party that led to the formation of the FDN and extensive support for Cárdenas's presidential candidacy.

12 See Código Federal Electoral (1987), articles 162–65.

Cárdenas was never able to prove categorically that he won the 1988 presidential election, but the election's widespread irregularities have been well documented (Gómez Tagle 1994). Because certification of elections was through the electoral colleges in the federal Congress, the PRI traditionally had been able to impose its majority without difficulty. In 1988, however, this was not an option that could be legally justified because there was a chance that the legislature would come under opposition control. Election outcomes in 253 of Mexico's 300 relative-majority electoral districts were challenged through 523 legal briefs presented first to the Tribunal for Electoral Disputes and then to the electoral colleges (Tribunal de lo Contencioso Electoral 1988: 94–112). Opposition parties thus clearly signaled their refusal to accept the electoral outcome. Moreover, both the FDN and the PAN demanded that the packets containing marked ballots be opened in order to re-count the votes. The PRI refused, which cast even more suspicion upon the narrow presidential victory claimed by Carlos Salinas de Gortari.[13]

In light of the precariousness of his electoral triumph, President Salinas (1988–1994) pledged to carry out a major electoral reform. The most important feature of the 1989–1990 reforms was the creation of the Federal Electoral Institute (IFE). The IFE was to be an "autonomous," permanent body[14] with its own funding, a professional administrative staff, and a General Council chaired by the minister of the interior and comprised of "magistrate councilors" (*consejeros magistrados*), two congressional representatives, and one representative from each registered political party. The magistrate councilors were supposed to ensure the political independence of the IFE's decisions. In practice, however, they left the supervision of the electoral process to the body's president, and as a consequence the councilors never had much of an impact.[15]

The Salinas reforms left the overall size and composition of the federal Chamber of Deputies (300 relative-majority seats and 200 proportional representation seats) unchanged. However, the formula used to assign proportional representation seats was modified to favor the majority party. Under the terms of the legislation's so-called governability clause, the largest party in the Chamber of Deputies would hold seats disproportionate to its electoral strength up until it controlled sixty percent of the seats in the Chamber. This provision effectively nullified the democratizing impact of the 1986 constitutional reform that had increased the number of proportional representation seats to 200.

The 1989–1990 reforms also created a more powerful Federal Electoral Tribunal (TFE) to replace the electoral dispute tribunal that had been created in 1987.

---

13 Ballots from the 1988 elections were later burned, with the complicity of the PAN.

14 The IFE was in this regard different from the Federal Electoral Tribunal, which only formally convened during electoral periods.

15 See the reforms to Article 41 of the 1989 Constitution. For a study of the IFE's structure and functioning, see Gómez Tagle 1993.

Nevertheless, the TFE was still under the control of the executive branch,[16] and final word on electoral certifications remained in the hands of electoral colleges in the Chamber of Deputies and the Senate. The 1989 law also prohibited public officials from intervening in various ways in electoral processes,[17] but no one has ever been convicted of these "electoral crimes."

There were two important legal changes for parties in 1989 and 1990. First, common candidacies were eliminated, removing the option for multiple parties to support a single candidate without having formed a formal coalition. This measure specifically sought to preclude any recurrence of the threat that Cárdenas's jointly supported presidential candidacy had posed to the PRI in 1988. Second, conditional registration was reintroduced to permit new political parties to enter the electoral arena more easily. During the 1991 midterm elections, the Labor Party (PT, often identified at the time as pro-Salinas) and the Mexican Ecological Green Party (PVEM) registered with this status. Their presence further fragmented leftist support in the 1991 elections, thus compounding the Left's problems in the wake of the breakup of the 1987–1988 *cardenista* coalition.[18] In the 1991 congressional elections, PRI candidates won by a wide margin. Even though serious conflicts over the electoral process erupted in some parts of the country, the opposition's discontent with the results failed to win a wide hearing.[19] The PAN was generally satisfied because some local PAN successes during this period were recognized, including its victory in the gubernatorial race in Baja California (1989). The triumph of PAN gubernatorial candidate Vicente Fox Quesada in Guanajuato (1991) was not recognized, but the PRI ceded the post and permitted the appointment of an interim governor from the PAN. In contrast, the Party of the Democratic Revolution (PRD) – which still refused to recognize the legitimacy of the Salinas administration – was in no position to negotiate recognition of its local-level electoral victories. Although gubernatorial candidates like Fox in Guanajuato and Salvador Nava (who was supported by a coalition of several parties) in San Luis Potosí presented proof of electoral irregularities, the legal channels for challenging electoral outcomes proved ineffective.

Two other electoral reforms, implemented in 1993 and 1994, were enacted at a time when the PRI again held a majority in Congress. The opposition had since 1977 demanded some form of proportional representation in the federal Senate, and the 1993 legislation introduced the principle of minority representation in the

16 The method for electing TFE magistrates was similar to that for IFE councilors: the Chamber of Deputies elected them from a list proposed by the president. See Articles 41 and 60 of the federal Constitution and Federal Code of Electoral Institutions and Procedures (COFIPE), Book 6.

17 See Código Federal Electoral, article 341, and COFIPE, articles 338–344.

18 This problem was partially resolved when the Mexican Socialist Party (PMS), the successor to the PSUM, agreed to cede its registration so that Cárdenas could establish the Party of the Democratic Revolution (PRD).

19 For an assessment of the 1991 electoral process, see Gómez Tagle 1993.

upper chamber. It also increased the number of senators per state from three to four, with three being elected by majority vote and one assigned to the minority party garnering the second-most votes.[20]

Although the 1994 electoral reform did not affect the basic outlines of electoral organization, it nevertheless introduced important changes. For example, it replaced the IFE's magistrate councilors with six "citizen councilors" elected by a two-thirds vote (of those present) in the Chamber of Deputies from a list prepared by political parties.[21] The 1994 legislation resulted from growing pressures for political opening – especially the January 1994 armed rebellion led by the Zapatista Army of National Liberation (EZLN) – and the uncertainty produced by the assassination of PRI presidential candidate Luis Donaldo Colosio in March 1994. Nevertheless, civil society organizations and the political opposition were unable to win another important demand: removal of the minister of the interior from the IFE's General Council.

The new citizen councilors made their voices heard in the General Council, but they had little impact upon the conduct of the 1994 general elections because they had been appointed only three months beforehand. Moreover, the IFE's executive structure and its day-to-day activities remained under the control of the minister of the interior, who continued to serve as president of the IFE's General Council (Gómez Tagle 1997).

The 1994 reform eliminated electoral self-certification by assigning to the Federal Electoral Tribunal the final responsibility for certifying the election of federal deputies and senators. The IFE's General Council was given the power to certify the results of elections for proportional representation legislative seats, but the certification of presidential election results was still under the jurisdiction of the federal Chamber of Deputies. At the request of the IFE's General Council, the 1994 legislation also created a special prosecutor's office to investigate electoral crimes. However, this new office failed so abysmally in its duties that some civic organizations (including the Civic Alliance, AC) opted to abandon cases they had presented before it.[22]

The 1996 Electoral Reform

PRI candidate Ernesto Zedillo Ponce de León won the 1994 presidential election with 48.8 percent of the vote, slightly less than the official total reported for Salinas in 1988.[23] Yet Zedillo's victory was accepted by both the public and his principal adversaries, the PAN's Diego Fernández de Cevallos and the PRD's Cuauhtémoc Cárdenas. Two factors accounted for this acceptance. First, Fernández de Cevallos,

20 See Article 56 of the Constitution.
21 Prior to the 1994 reforms, the president presented the list of IFE candidates.
22 The failures of the special prosecutor's office were due largely to the inefficacy of established procedures and the fact that they placed a heavy probative burden upon grievants bringing cases before it. See Alianza Cívica 1994.
23 These percentages were calculated by the author from the total number of votes, including annulled ballots. See Gómez Tagle, ed. 1997: 42.

the strongest of the opposition candidates, recognized the outcome as legitimate, while third-place finisher Cárdenas had no strong basis on which to question the results. Second, the overall legitimacy of the election was strengthened by the reforms enacted earlier in 1994, including the appointment of citizen councilors at the IFE and the government's agreement for the first time to grant official status to Mexican and international election observers. The electoral process itself was, nonetheless, marred by numerous irregularities. Many of these problems were related to the opposition candidates' limited access to funding and the mass media, but others involved more flagrant legal violations such as vote-buying and coercion of voters (Alianza Cívica Observación 1994).[24] However, it proved impossible to "measure" precisely the impact of these irregularities upon the election results.

As in 1988, the PRI only won a simple majority of seats in the federal Chamber of Deputies in 1994. This meant that it was compelled to negotiate with other parties to achieve the two-thirds majority required to enact constitutional reforms. Yet various other factors also forced President Zedillo (1994–2000) to seek out the opposition's support. Foremost among these was the continuing political crisis provoked by the assassinations of Colosio and PRI party president José Ruiz Massieu (in, respectively, March and September 1994); the armed conflict in Chiapas; and post-electoral conflicts in Chiapas resulting from blatant irregularities in that state's gubernatorial election. To this was added the widespread citizen anger resulting from a sharp devaluation of the peso in December 1994 and the subsequent financial crisis.

It was in this context that the Zedillo administration undertook what it billed as a "definitive" electoral reform as part of a broader project of state reform.[25] The push for revised electoral legislation came largely from civil society organizations, as well as from opposition parties and members of the IFE's General Council (citizen councilors and party representatives), who called for a national forum to discuss political and electoral reforms. The proposals emanating from these meetings were sent to the Ministry of the Interior and the Congress (Minutes of the IFE General Council, April 7, 1995). What is most striking about them is that they reflected a consensus among the IFE councilors, the PAN, and the PRD.

The 1996 electoral reform was implemented in two stages. Consensus was reached on the necessary constitutional reforms in August. However, the electoral law itself (a revised version of the Federal Code of Electoral Institutions and Procedures, COFIPE) remained pending because of differences between the PAN and the PRD, on the one hand, and the PRI, on the other. In the end, the PRI majority in the Congress – facing the political deadline imposed by the approach of the July 1997 midterm elections – approved the revised electoral law without PAN or PRD support.

24 These violations included buying votes and voter identification cards (so they could be used by PRI loyalists), the use of public funds to influence or directly pressure voters to support PRI candidates by handing out packages of food and supplies, and making access to financial credits or social benefits contingent upon a vote for the PRI.

25 Zedillo's reform project also included other elements that in the long run would suffer a less fortunate fate, including a proposed constitutional reform on the rights of indigenous peoples.

The 1996 election law reforms did not modify the formal structure of the electoral institutions created during the Salinas administration. They were, nevertheless, of signal importance because they shifted the locus of power within the IFE and the TFE. This institutional transformation gave rise to a complicated process of role redefinition as the two main electoral institutions established their capabilities and areas of respective influence. But most important, it had a very important impact upon electoral transparency in Mexico – laying the basis for historic opposition party advances in the 1997 midterm elections (when the PRI lost its majority in the federal Chamber of Deputies) and the 2000 general elections (when the PRI lost control of the presidency) and essentially bringing post-election conflicts to an end.

The IFE's expanded autonomy was predicated upon a new relationship between the General Council and the legislative and executive branches of the federal government. This was achieved mainly through two actions: the minister of the interior no longer serves as *ex oficio* head of the IFE,[26] and political party representatives and congressional representatives (one federal deputy and one federal senator) are limited to a voice – but no vote – in IFE decisions. Under the terms of the 1996 law, only the nine councilors have both voice and vote in the General Council. The councilors, who serve nine-year terms, are elected in the Chamber of Deputies by a two-thirds vote of the members present.[27] The chair councilor (elected by members of the General Council) also acts as director of the IFE's entire executive apparatus.

The reformed IFE retains the main organizational features established 1991. Its administrative apparatus is organized into national secretariats (*vocalías*) and state- and electoral district-level delegations.[28] In principle, electoral councilors are not directly involved in managing the IFE's administrative operations. However, the councilors elected in 1996 reached a number of agreements that led them to become involved in the functioning of the entire institution through specialized commissions organized on various topics.

The 1996 constitutional reforms also created the Electoral Tribunal of the Federal Judicial Branch (TEPJF). The Electoral Tribunal, which replaced the TFE, became part of the federal judiciary (and thus independent of the federal executive), with faculties to resolve all electoral disputes at federal, state, and municipal levels. It is comprised of a High Court with seven magistrates and five regional courts with three magistrates each. Supreme Court justices choose (by a simple majority, in closed session) among three candidates for each magistrate seat and submit their recommendations to the Senate for final approval by a two-thirds vote of senators present. The changes embodied in the TEPJF had long been

26 The organization of elections had been under the control of the Ministry of the Interior since 1946.

27 See Article 41 of the Constitution, Section III, and COFIPE, Books 3 and 4. In 1996, the IFE councilors were selected through negotiations among the principal political parties.

28 Unlike members of the General Council, who are elected for fixed terms, state- and district-level councilors are appointed by the General Council for a particular electoral period.

advocated by opposition parties, and they significantly increased public confidence in the electoral process by ensuring that the certification of final results is the responsibility of a nonpartisan institution.

The Zedillo reforms also authorized the Supreme Court to intervene for the first time in court cases raising questions of constitutionality in electoral matters, whether they arise in federal cases or complaints involving state-level legislation.[29] Such cases can have a major impact upon state-level electoral legislation because state laws are often in conflict with principles that have been adopted over time at the federal level.[30] And for the first time, specific electoral appeals bodies and procedures were established as part of the constitutional system of checks and balances (De la Peza Cano 1999: 245).

The constitutional reforms adopted in 1996 also addressed a number of other important electoral issues. They granted Mexicans living abroad the right to vote; regulated public and private funding for political parties and set upper limits on election campaign spending; and established new oversight mechanisms for political party finances. However, when it came to the legal changes necessary to produce a new COFIPE, the PRI disavowed agreements reached during months of negotiations with opposition parties on constitutional reforms. Hence the electoral law that was finally approved in 1996 left many points pending (including the vote of Mexicans abroad and limits on campaign spending, which the PRI insisted upon raising).[31]

Finally, the 1996 constitutional reforms produced important changes in the representational formulas employed in both the federal Chamber of Deputies and the federal Senate. The Chamber of Deputies continues to have 300 deputies elected by a relative majority vote and 200 elected through a proportional representation formula. However, since 1996 the majority party is allowed only up to 8 percent overrepresentation, and an upper limit is set so that no party can have a qualified (two-thirds) majority in the Chamber. These provisions ensure that no party will be able to modify the Constitution on its own.

In the Senate, the model of representation based upon three senators from each state elected by majority vote and one selected from the best-performing minority party was modified in order to avoid the overrepresentation of a single party. Since 1996, the majority party holds two seats per state; the third seat goes to the minority

29 See Article 105 (section II.f) of the Constitution.

30 One important outcome in this regard was the reform of the Federal District's electoral law, through which inhabitants finally received the right to elect their government and the Federal District's representative assembly was granted expanded powers (becoming the Federal District Legislative Assembly). See Valdés 1998.

31 The total amount of campaign spending authorized by the PRI far exceeded what opposition parties considered prudent. However, new rules concerning the distribution of public funds for election campaigns meant that the PRI was no longer the only beneficiary of these higher limits. After 1996, resource allotments to political parties – both financing and media access – became somewhat more equitable. See COFIPE, Chapter 2.

party with the best electoral performance; and the fourth senator is selected via a proportional representation formula that takes into account different parties' share of the national vote. This scheme reduces majority party overrepresentation, but it also breaks with the ideal of equal representation for all thirty-one states and the Federal District.

The Performance of Electoral Institutions in 1997

When the nine IFE councilors[32] elected under the terms of the 1996 electoral law assumed office, the 1997 electoral process was already under way. They had, therefore, to accept many features of the electoral process as a *fait accompli*.[33] José Woldenberg assumed the position of chair councilor, and Felipe Solís Acero (the IFE's secretary of organization when it was created in 1991, and strongly identified with the PRI) became general secretary. Nearly all previous executive personnel remained in their posts, and only officials who had been the subject of serious complaints were removed.

Clara Jusidman, a member of the Civic Alliance and other citizens' organizations with equally high moral prestige among political parties, was appointed director of the Federal Voter Registry. The performance of this body had been criticized repeatedly during the Salinas administration because it was an instrument to manipulate voting lists. Jusidman's appointment thus further contributed to public confidence in the 1997 electoral process.

One of the IFE's most important responsibilities in 1997 was redistricting for the election of the 300 federal deputies chosen by majority vote. This was the first time that redistricting criteria were debated publicly, and all political parties participated in discussions of the various alternatives. Because this was a technical matter with broad implications for the legitimacy of the country's electoral institutions, parties had strong incentives to engage in this debate over Mexico's new electoral geography.

Among the most difficult negotiations were those concerning the IFE's budget and the amount of public funding that would go to political parties. The final budget allocated 2.46 billion pesos to cover the IFE's operating costs (including organization of the 1997 midterm elections) and 2.38 billion pesos for the parties, with the largest share going to the PRI.[34]

---

32 The councilors were José Barragán, Jesús Cantú, Jaime Cárdenas, Alonso Lujambio, Mauricio Merino, Juan Molinar Horcasitas, Jacqueline Peschard, José Woldenberg (chair), and Emilio Zebadúa. Barragán later resigned and was replaced by Enrique Ibarra.

33 See COFIPE, Transitory Article 11.

34 Different parties' shares of the budget were based upon the proportion of the total vote they had received in the 1994 general elections. Thus the PRI received 536 million pesos; the PAN, 336 million; and the PRD, 247 million. In the end, the vote of each registered citizen cost approximately 98 pesos in 1997 (Monge 1996: 35; Albarrán de Alba 1996: 31).

Despite the late date at which the new IFE leadership took responsibility for the electoral process, it performed exceedingly well during the July 1997 federal elections (Gómez Tagle 1998). The IFE's conduct won the approval of all political parties and the citizenry as well. Indesed, a post-election survey found that 70 percent of those interviewed believed the elections "very democratic, trustworthy, and legal" (Zebadúa 1997: 7). Even though the PRI disagreed with many decisions taken by the General Council, President Zedillo commended the IFE for the role it had played. The credibility of its actions was further supported by the principal electoral result: for the first time, the PRI failed to win a majority in the Chamber of Deputies, although it did maintain control of the Senate (Gómez Tagle 1998).

The Electoral Tribunal did not have any problems certifying the 1997 elections because there were relatively few challenges. A total of 204 complaints were filed with the TEPJF in the five regional courts, substantially fewer than in either 1991 or 1994 (Chávez 1997). The TEPJF's rulings were generally accepted because they did not appear to favor any one party.

Thus the juridical apparatus put in place by the 1996 reforms to oversee electoral conduct proved to be relatively effective. However, one problem persists: how to make (short) electoral periods compatible with slow juridical processes. Because of this mismatch in time frames, most attempts to challenge electoral authorities' decisions or political parties' actions through juridical channels have proved futile.[35] Even more worrisome is the fact that not all electoral misconduct is punished. For example, penalties are levied against officials who use public funds to benefit a candidate, but not against the candidate who benefits.

The Role of Electoral Institutions during the 1998–2000 Transition Period

Presidential elections in Mexico have always produced higher expectations and greater tensions than midterm congressional elections. Nevertheless, the 1997 elections gave President Zedillo an opportunity to assess the results of his strategy of establishing a "healthy distance" between the presidency and the PRI. What he discovered probably displeased him as much as it displeased the PRI because, in the month following the elections, the administration adopted a new posture. Indeed, Zedillo stopped talking about the virtues of a "healthy distance" between the presidency and the PRI and resumed a central role in his party's affairs, using the institution of the presidency to promote a larger PRI vote (Comisión Especial 2000).[36]

The IFE was inevitably affected by this shift in the political terrain. In fact, once the IFE severed its links with the federal executive, the PRI began to view it as an

---

35 See Articles 60 and 74 of the Constitution, and COFIPE, Book 7.

36 It is interesting to note in this regard that the Zedillo administration's Program for Education, Health, and Nutrition (PROGRESA), a very extensive targeted anti-poverty program, was established in August 1997.

institution that operated in opposition to the "official" party's interests. The PRI then adopted a stance of ongoing confrontation with the now-autonomous IFE (Aguirre 1999).

The following discussion examines the IFE's internal reorganization between 1998 and 2000, its role vis-à-vis political parties, and the performance of the Electoral Tribunal of the Federal Judicial Branch during this period.

Internal Reorganization of the IFE

Once the 1997 elections were over, the General Council proceeded to revise the executive structure that had been in place when the new IFE leadership assumed office in late 1996.[37] Solís Acero's appointment as general secretary and the fact that most senior executive personnel retained their positions after the 1996 reform represented efforts by the PRI to preserve its influence over the electoral process. For this reason, the electoral councilors decided to organize themselves in subject-specific commissions in order to oversee the performance of senior administrative personnel. The commissions focused upon funding for parties and political groups, parties' access to the mass media, the organization of electoral processes, the creation of a professional electoral service, electoral training and civic education, registration procedures for federal elections, and general administrative matters (Salcedo 1998: 19). The councilors' direct involvement in these areas of activity did, however, generate sharp conflicts. In particular, the PRI's representative before the General Council frequently criticized the electoral councilors' activism.

Frictions between the electoral councilors and the IFE's administrative staff finally exploded in a sharp conflict over the role played by Felipe Solís Acero, whom some councilors viewed as a defender of the Ministry of the Interior's and the PRI's interests. Solís Acero finally tendered his resignation in January 1998,[38] but there was no agreement within the IFE regarding who the replacement secretary general should be. This crisis lasted until April 1998, when, on a 7–2 vote, the General Council finally approved José Woldenberg's nomination of Fernando Zertuche Muñoz for the post (Roman 1998). What lay behind the delay was Zertuche's close identification with the PRI–led government over the course of a long career in public administration. The controversy over Solís and his replacement was a key moment in the IFE's institutional life, in which its independence was put firmly to the test.

The IFE and Political Parties

The 1996 electoral reform restricted new parties' participation in elections by (once again) eliminating conditional registration and increasing to 2.5 percent the minimum vote threshold for a party's continued electoral participation. However, the methods used by the IFE to determine whether parties meet other legal requirements

---

37 As part of the IFE's efforts to create a career electoral service, a total of 1,218 professional civil servants underwent a formal review before being granted tenure in their posts. See Gil Olmos 1998.

38 Gil Olmos 1997. Solís Acero was elected as a PRI federal deputy in the year 2000.

(primarily, that party members be spread throughout Mexico) became more transparent, and no serious complaints have been raised concerning them. In fact, between 1998 and 2000 two new parties were able to register, the Party of the Democratic Center (PCD, founded by Manuel Camacho Solís, a former member of the PRI, the former mayor of Mexico City during the Salinas administration, and a presidential aspirant in 1994 and 2000) and Social Democracy (DS, founded by Gilberto Rincón Gallardo, formerly of the PRD). Forty-one national political groupings (*agrupaciones políticas nacionales*) were also registered during this period, and the PARM (which had again lost is registration as a result of its poor showing in 1997) received a new registration. In addition, in advance of the 2000 elections, three small new parties allied themselves with the PRD: Democratic Convergence (CD), Party of the Nationalist Society (PSN), and Social Alliance Party (PAS) (IFE 2001).

One of the IFE's principal responsibilities is monitoring the use of public funds for political parties and their campaigns. It audited all parties after the 1997 elections and fined those that had not complied with legal requirements, including the PAN, PRI, and PT.[39] Of course, there is a wide gap between the amount of public funding allocated to parties and the upper limit on campaign spending, which means that the IFE has limited supervision over an important portion of party funding.[40]

In terms of the IFE's overall relationship with political parties, the most difficult challenge it faced during the 1998–2000 period involved its relations with the PRI. For example, the PRI appealed to the TEPJF in its successful effort to block a proposed rule change that would have directed state- and district-level IFE councils to conduct their activities through commissions, as the General Council had decided to do. The party also vigorously contested (though without success) the General Council's decision to create a special commission to investigate the use of government programs or public funds to benefit political parties in the 2000 general election.[41] In addition, the PRI objected to the actions of IFE councilors and decisions by the General Council concerning such matters as the right of Mexicans living abroad to vote, proposed rules for a professional electoral civil service, and the content of voter education programs.

However, the most significant of these conflicts arose from a complaint that PRD representatives presented to the General Council in November 1998 regarding the financing of the PRI's 1994 presidential campaign. The IFE councilors agreed

---

39 The PRI strongly objected to this sanction, going so far as to challenge the IFE's decision before the Electoral Tribunal of the Federal Judicial Branch (TEPJF). The challenge was denied.

40 In January 2000, prior to the general elections that July, the IFE awarded a total of 3.53 billion pesos (41.8 percent of its total budget of 8.45 billion pesos) to political parties. Thirty percent of these funds were distributed equally among all registered parties; the remainder was allocated in proportion to each party's share of the total vote in the 1997 elections.

to hear the case, even though it was not included on the regular agenda.[42] PRI leaders were furious that the Council had taken this position, and the exasperated PRI representative walked out of the General Council and did not return until March 1999 despite his legal obligation to attend (Schedler 1999). The internal confrontation ended only when the Council resolved that the PRD's complaint was "out of order and unfounded."[43]

The PRI also unleashed a media campaign to undermine the IFE's image, going so far as to promote impeachment proceedings (*juicio político*) to remove some electoral councilors. This complaint, in which the PRI was backed by the PT, targeted councilors Jesús Cantú, Jaime Cárdenas, Alonso Lujambio, and Emilio Zebadúa (Trejo Delarbre 1999). In August 1999, IFE comptroller Carlos Muñoz removed Cantú for "misuse of funds," officially reprimanded councilors Cárdenas and Zebadúa, and exonerated Lujambio.[44] Chairman Woldenberg, other councilors, and other political parties unanimously supported the accused and called for Muñoz's removal.

These internal tensions and repeated conflicts with the PRI damaged the IFE's public image. A March 1999 opinion poll on citizenship and institutions asked respondents the following question: "In general, how much confidence do you have in the following institutions, a lot or a little?" The Catholic Church scored highest (60 percent of those polled indicated they had a lot of confidence in it). The IFE scored a respectable 39 percent, but this rating was 9 percentage points lower than in January 1999, before its prolonged public fight with the PRI (*Este País* 1999).

Judicial Authorities and the Electoral Process

The IFE and judicial authorities (the Electoral Tribunal of the Federal Judicial Branch and the Supreme Court) have played fundamental, complementary roles in normalizing elections in Mexico. The IFE has had first responsibility for organizing all phases of the electoral process, from registering voters to auditing political parties on their campaign funds, use of public monies, and so forth. Both the TEPJF and the Supreme Court have served as guarantors of the correct interpretation of the law. The complementarity of their roles explains why the TEPJF has been able to amend IFE decisions on several occasions without provoking conflict between the two institutions.[45]

---

41 On these cases, see, respectively, Cossío Díaz and Franco G. S. 2000: 46 and IFE General Council resolution, December 17, 1999.

42 The case took on special importance because Andrés Manuel López Obrador, then president of the PRD, was in the audience.

43 IFE General Council minutes, May 25, 1999.

44 These councilors were charged with using official funds to purchase alcoholic beverages and for personal travel.

45 In general, the TEPJF's stance has been more cautious than the IFE's because the former has interpreted federal electoral law according to more conservative criteria.

These judicial institutions have had a great impact in local-level disputes, and in several instances opposition parties owed their success to the role played by them. For example, in February 1999 the Supreme Court intervened to reinstate an elected PAN municipal council in Valle de Bravo, State of México, that the state legislature had removed (Cossío Díaz and Franco G. S. 1999a: 51). Similarly, in state elections in Yucatán in 1998, the Electoral Tribunal intervened to award a proportional representation seat to the PRD that had been incorrectly assigned to the PRI (Cossío Díaz 1998). The TEPJF also resolved controversies over the re-election of municipal presidents in Chiapas and Coahuila, confirming that immediate reelection is not allowed to municipal council seats (Cossío Díaz and Franco G. S. 1999b). And in 1999 the PRD won the gubernatorial election in Tlaxcala because the TEPJF dismissed more than three hundred complaints filed by the PRI (Hernández Tamayo 1999).

The TEPJF has also demonstrated impartiality concerning different parties' participation in federal elections. A dispute over the use of symbols on electoral ballots became an important issue in the 2000 electoral process. The TEPJF prohibited the "Alliance for Change" from using a photograph of Vicente Fox Quesada on the ballot because it was not part of either the PAN's or the PVEM's formal party insignia.[46] On the other hand, the Electoral Tribunal ruled that the PRI could continue its long-established practice of using the colors of the Mexican flag (green, white, and red) in party symbols – while also establishing that any other party could use those colors as well (the PRD had been prohibited from doing so in 1989). Similarly, when the PRD filed a complaint concerning the PRI's campaign practices in 1994, the TEPJF finally determined that the complaint was without merit because the 1994 campaigns had "already been judged" (Méndez and Saldierna 1998). On the other hand, when Carlos Muñoz threatened to remove Jesús Cantú from the IFE, the Tribunal opted not to intervene in the dispute (*La Jornada*, August 15, 1999, p. 3).

Prelude to the 2000 Elections

When President Zedillo initially distanced the presidency from the PRI and from the electoral process, he enabled Mexico's electoral institutions to emerge from under the shadow of presidential power following the 1996 constitutional reforms and electoral law. However, when Zedillo experienced the PRI's setbacks in the 1997 midterm elections and realized there was a possibility of losing not just congressional seats and state governorships but the presidency as well, he began employing resources at the direct disposal of the president (such as funds for targeted programs to combat extreme poverty) in an organized, focused way to win support for the PRI. The PRI was, for example, able to win elections in all the municipalities in Nayarit and Michoacán where funds from the Program for Education,

---

46 The "Alliance for Change" was the coalition comprised of the PAN and the PVEM; its presidential candidate was Vicente Fox Quesada.

Health, and Nutrition (PROGRESA) had been widely distributed.[47] In 1998 the PRI also managed to win municipal races in many congressional districts in Michoacán where the PRD had won a majority in 1997 (Comisión Especial 2000).[48]

With political actors focused upon preparations for the 2000 general elections, negotiations began in mid-1998 for further electoral reforms. Driven by the PRD and the PAN, these drawn-out negotiations eventually produced agreements that were seconded by the PT and the PVEM in the Chamber of Deputies in March 1999. The proposed reforms redistributed government-provided access to electronic media, broadened the IFE's authority to monitor parties' campaign spending, and established spending limits for parties' primary elections. In addition, the sponsoring parties proposed rules that would have broadened citizen participation by enabling Mexicans living abroad to vote in Mexican embassies and consulates and by allowing Mexican citizens who lived abroad to make contributions to political parties.

To aid the development and strengthening of political parties, the proposed reforms also cleared the way for parties to form coalitions and field joint candidates in the 2000 elections. They gave coalitions a longer period in which to register (up to fifteen days before the deadline for candidate registration), and, in the case of coalition candidates, they provided that votes would accrue first to the sponsoring parties and then be combined to yield a total for the candidate. The proposal repealed the old requirement that members of social organizations had to be part of a political party in order to field candidates.

At first it appeared that the Ministry of the Interior was willing to discuss these election reform proposals. However, when it looked as though the opposition might field a coalition candidate in the 2000 presidential election,[49] the PRI decided to oppose further electoral reform. The 2000 elections therefore took place under the legal framework established in 1996.

What Is Missing for Mexican Democracy?

With the introduction of proportional representation in 1977 and the entry of several small, recently organized parties into the electoral arena, Mexico moved from a hegemonic-party system to one with a dominant party and several real opposition parties. The resulting dynamism in Mexico's electoral and party systems strengthened the country's institutional life, but it also generated new contradictions.

---

47 Even so, a PAN–PRD–PT coalition candidate won the governorship in Nayarit in July 1999.
48 In parallel with an IFE special commission established to investigate irregularities in the use of federal funds and bring cases before the Special Prosecutor for Electoral Crimes, opposition party members of the federal Chamber of Deputies established a special commission to prevent the abuse of federal funds in the 2000 elections. However, legal standards of proof made the task difficult.
49 Manuel Camacho Solís toured the country in an effort to promote this objective.

Opposition parties quickly came up against the limitations of a scheme designed to maintain PRI dominance. The system operated upon the basis of majority rule, as a democracy should. However, the other requirement that is fundamental in a democracy – respect for the rights of minorities – was not fulfilled. Citizens were not fully free to express their views, nor were there conditions in effect that would permit the minority to become a majority. In other words, there was not a "free confrontation between organized political groups that compete with each other to unite their demands and transform them into collective decisions" (Bobbio 1978: 33).

The process of constructing new political actors – through which economic and intellectual elites gradually detached themselves from the PRI to form autonomous power groups – was continually hindered by the lack of electoral transparency. This situation led to a social and political struggle for legal reforms that would establish more equitable rules for the electoral game.

The legitimacy crisis produced by extensive electoral fraud in 1988 forced Salinas de Gortari to carry out several electoral reforms. These initiatives sought to recover credibility by projecting an image of transparency in electoral institutions, with electoral organization changed at every level except the very top. When debate on Salinas's reforms began in 1990, some political parties, civil society leaders, and intellectuals welcomed the reforms as a step toward democracy. Others pointed out the reforms' serious limitations. In effect, the debate was over what degree of electoral transparency is needed in order for a democratic system to work.

The strengthening of civil society and political parties as real centers of auton-omous power finally forced the PRI, as well as the political groups that helped sustain it in power over the course of more than seven decades, to cede political space. From the late 1980s and through the year 2000, Mexico achieved alternation in power with the election of PAN and PRD governors in the states of Aguas-calientes, Baja California, Baja California Sur, Chiapas, Chihuahua, the Federal District, Guanajuato, Jalisco, Michoacán, Morelos, Nayarit, Nuevo León, Querétaro, Tlaxcala, Yucatán, and Zacatecas.[50] The process was furthered when the PRI won back the governorship in Chihuahua in 1998. Of course, the ultimate proof of the real possibility for party alternation in Mexico was the election of Vicente Fox Quesada, candidate of the opposition PAN–PVED "Alliance for Change" coali-tion, to the presidency in July 2000.

Under the 1996 round of electoral reforms, Mexican society won a strong presence in the political space represented by electoral institutions. Both the IFE and the TEPJF have played a major role in making votes count. The kinds of conflicts that have arisen among the IFE, political parties, and governmental insti-tutions indicate the range of interests that are affected by the IFE's actions (Baños Martínez 2000). Given the significant advances that have been made toward achieving a reasonable degree of transparency, it is extremely unlikely that a

---

50 In Chiapas and Nayarit, the gubernatorial elections were won by PAN–PRD coalitions that also included several smaller parties.

political party could win the presidency by fraudulent means, or hide a stolen election from the public. Autonomous electoral institutions have, then, become a key part of Mexico's new political geometry.

Nevertheless, many changes are required to consolidate democratic institutions in Mexico, and, despite partisan alternation in the presidency, electoral changes such as those proposed in 1999 remained pending well into the Fox administration. Part of the explanation was that Fox could not count on a majority in the Congress (or, at times, even the support of his own party's congressional delegation).[51] Other factors included opposition arising from forces closely identified with past PRI governments. The Congress made an important contribution to democratization processes in 2002 when it approved the Federal Law on Transparency and Access to Information (Ley Federal de Transparencia y Acceso a la Información), legislation that finally realized the rights formally guaranteed by constitutional reforms in 1977. However, the unfulfilled democracy agenda included such issues as the need to guarantee equity in terms of all parties' use of communications media and the economic resources (whether public or private) available to them.

The battle to democratize access to communications media has scarcely begun. In fact, the decree issued by President Fox on October 10, 2002, represented a step backwards. Not only was the decree issued without the agreement of the civil society organizations and political parties that had been working with the Ministry of the Interior since 2001 to develop new legislation regulating the mass media, but the measure also reduced from 12.5 percent to 1.25 percent the proportion of air time that electronic media are required to cede to the public "in lieu of tax payments." Moreover, whereas that time had previously been considered public-sector property and had been shared among public universities, state governments, the IFE, the National Human Rights Commission (CNDH), and other entities, it is now assigned exclusively to the Office of the Presidency. This change will substantially affect diverse political actors' access to electronic communications media, while significantly benefiting the president and the party that controls the federal executive (Salas 2002; Irízar 2002a).

Yet the developments since the July 2, 2000 elections that have most clearly underscored the serious deficiencies that still exist in Mexico's electoral system have involved the illegal use of money in election campaigns. Two prominent cases occupied both the IFE and the TEPJF during 2002 and 2003: legal violations involving the amount and foreign origin of funds that several individuals transferred to the "Friends of Fox" organization and, through it, to Fox's 1999–2000 presidential campaign, and the illegal diversion of funds from the Mexican Petroleum Workers' Union (STPRM) to PRI candidate Francisco Labastida's 1999–2000 presidential

51 Among the new political actors that appeared following the 2000 elections was the National Governors' Conference (CONAGO), formed in July 2002 by 17 PRI governors and 5 PRD governors. The CONAGO became a successful defender of federalism during the Fox administration by, among other things, forcing the federal government to increase the financial resources assigned to the states. See Guerrero 2002.

campaign. Both cases became known in 2001. However, it was not until nearly a year later that the IFE, because of its limited legal faculties to audit party resources and the consequent need to consult with the TEPJF, could begin formal investigations (Urrutia 2002: 3).

In the "Friends of Fox" case, the TEPFJ rejected arguments by the Ministry of Finance and Public Credit (SHCP) and the National Banking and Securities Commission (CNBV) that producing records concerning the organization's financial transfers would violate the legal right to privacy in banking transactions (Irízar 2002b). In May 2002 the TEPJF ordered the IFE to reopen its investigation into the matter, and the IFE's investigative commission sought to determine who had provided funding to the Fox campaign (Urrutia 2002). Among the individuals involved were Lino Korrodi Cruz (finance coordinator for the Fox campaign and a founder of "Friends of Fox"), Valeria Korrodi Ordaz, Carlota Robinson Kuachi, and Rito Padilla García (Guanajuato's secretary of government during Fox's term as governor and, after Fox became president, an advisor to the Ministry of the Interior).[52] Nevertheless, despite strenuous efforts by several of its electoral counselors, the IFE made very slow progress in its investigations. The Supreme Court had granted injunctions to the individuals under investigation, and the case placed Mexico's electoral and judicial institutions in direct confrontation with the presidency.

Nor was the IFE initially able to advance in its investigations into the PEMEX / STPRM case. The charge was that Rogelio Montemayor Seguy, former director of the state-owned Mexican Petroleum Company (PEMEX), and other senior PEMEX administrators had conspired with Carlos Romero Deschamps, Ricardo Aldana, and Jesús Olvera Méndez – all former union leaders and, during 2000–2003, members of Congress – to transfer some 640 million pesos from PEMEX, via the STPRM, to the Labastida campaign (Aranda 2002; Irízar 2002b). In early 2003 the Special Prosecutor for Electoral Crimes (FEPADE) took up the case and heard testimony from Labastida Ochoa himself, but the investigation still remained stalled because, as members of Congress, the three former union leaders enjoyed immunity from prosecution and there was not a majority in the Chamber of Deputies (the body responsible for judging such matters) willing to suspend it (Aranda 2002; Irízar 2002c, 2002d; Castillo García 2003). Nevertheless, in March 2003 the IFE concluded that the STPRM had transferred 500 million pesos to two civil associations linked to the Labastida campaign, and it fined the PRI one billion pesos (twice the amount of the illegal transfer, and the largest party fine in Mexican history) (Cuéllar and Urrutia 2003). The TEPJF confirmed this judgment in May 2003.

Both these cases thus revealed the risks that illicit campaign funding posed to legitimate democratic competition. They also underscored the limitations that still

---

52 There were also indications that some external funding for the Fox campaign had flowed through a Bancomer trust account managed by Carlos Rojas Magnon, a former senior official in the Office of the Presidency.

constrain those Mexican institutions responsible for monitoring election campaigns and investigating and punishing illegal acts.

Future electoral reforms in Mexico should address such issues as the allocation of government-provided access to electronic media, the IFE's authority to monitor parties' campaign spending, and the establishment of spending limits in parties' primary elections. Further action will also be necessary to implement the right to vote for Mexicans living abroad, expand the faculties of the Federal District's local governments and its legislative assembly, facilitate the formation of electoral coalitions and the fielding of joint candidates, and permit direct citizen participation through referendums.

In summary, political democracy has entered a consolidation phase in Mexico. There is a plural party system with three strong parties, and many obstacles have been overcome in the struggle to establish basic democratic rules. Mexico now faces new problems, not unlike those confronting other democracies around the world. One of the core challenges is how to prevent parties and elections from becoming mere competitive struggles among power elites. There is a serious risk that democracy will be perverted by the public relations strategies of mass communications media and the big money that can finance such campaigns.

The high rate of abstention in some local elections raises the possibility that Mexicans may have little interest in exercising the rights to electoral participation that took so long and such effort to win. This is one reason why the institutions responsible for organizing and judging elections continue to have a vital role to play. Their focus must remain upon guaranteeing equity and transparency. However, transparency on its own will not be sufficient to advance the democratic cause unless political parties motivate citizens to exercise their right to vote and prove capable of linking aspirations, needs, interests, and politics.

References

Aguirre, Alberto. 1999. "La reforma electoral de la oposición," *Masiosare* (supplement to *La Jornada*), April 18: 3–5.

Albarrán de Alba, Gerardo. 1996. "Las elecciones del 97 costarán casi 98 pesos por empadronado," *Proceso* no. 1047 (November): 31–32

Alianza Cívica. 1994. "Acuerdo del 28 de febrero de 1994 del Consejo General, por el cual sugiere a la Procuraduría General de la República concentrar las investigaciones relativas a los nuevo delitos electorales en una procuraduría especial." In *Informe de Alianza Cívica*, September. Mimeo.

Alianza Cívica Observación 1994. 1994. *Informe General.* August.

Aranda, Jesús. 2002. "Descarta la UEDO lavado y delincuencia en el Pemexgate," *La Jornada*, 17 May: 8.

Baños Martínez, Marco Antonio. 2000. "El IFE a nueve años," *Voz y Voto* 83 (January): 37–38.

Bobbio, Norberto. 1978. "¿Qué alternativas a la democracia representativa?" In *¿Hay una teoría marxista del Estado?*, edited by Norberto Bobbio et al. Puebla, Mexico: Universidad Autónoma de Puebla.

Castillo García, Gustavo.2003. "Labastida Ochoa compareció porque se le citó: Fromow," *La Jornada*, 11 January: 5.

Chávez, Víctor. 1997. "Caleficación del Tribunal Electoral." *El Financiero*, 18 July: 48.

Comisión Especial de la Cámara de Diputados. 2000. *Informe de la Comisión Especial de la Cámara de Diputados para la vigilancia del uso de recursos públicos federales con fines electorales.* June. Mimeo.

Cossío Díaz, José Ramón. 1998. "Yucatán: los dilemas de la justicia electoral," *Voz y Voto* 68 (October): 14–18.

Cossío Díaz, José Ramón, and Fernando Franco G. S.. 1999a. "La desaparición de los ayuntamientos," *Voz y Voto* 74 (April): 51–53.

———. 1999b. "Reelección a debate," *Voz y Voto* 80 (October): 47–48.

———. 2000. "Comisiones impugnadas," *Voz y Voto* 83 (January): 46–48.

Cotteret, Jean, and Claude Émeri. 1973. *Los sistemas electorales.* Barcelona: Oikus-Tau.

Cuéllar, Mireya, and Alonso Urrutia. 2003. "Con base en certezas razonables el IFE ratifica multa histórica al PRI," *La Jornada*, 15 March.

De la Peza Cano, José Luis. 1999. "Evolución de la justicia electoral en México." In *Derecho y legislación electoral*, edited by Gonzalo Moctezuma Barragán. Mexico City: Miguel Ángel Porrúa / Universidad Nacional Autónoma de México.

Este País. 1999. "Indicadores." *Este País* 101 (August): 27.

Gil Olmos, José. 1997. "Piden siete consejeros la remoción de Solís Acero, Secretario Ejecutivo del IFE," *La Jornada*, 8 October: 3.

———. 1998. "Evalúan a 56% de profesionales del IFE," *La Jornada*, 17 August: 7.

Gómez Tagle, Silvia. 1994. *De la alquimia al fraude en las elecciones mexicanas.* Mexico City: G y V Editores.

———. 1997. *La transición inconclusa: treinta años de elecciones en México.* Mexico City: El Colegio de México.

———. 1998. "Participación ciudadana y democracia posible," *Nueva Antropología* 54 (August): 9–29.

Gómez Tagle, Silvia, ed. 1993. *Las elecciones federales de 1991: la recuperación oficial.* Mexico City: La Jornada Ediciones.

———. 1997. *1994: elecciones en los estados.* Mexico City: La Jornada Ediciones / Centro de Investigaciones Interdisciplinarias en Ciencias y Humanidades, Universidad Nacional Autónoma de México.

Guerrero, Jesús. 2002. "Adjudican triunfo a la Conago por 40 mil millones a estados," *Reforma*, 16 December: 3A.

Hermet, Guy, Alain Rouquie, and Juan J. Linz. 1982. *¿Para qué sirven las elecciones?* Mexico City: Fondo de Cultura Económica.

Hernández Tamayo, Víctor. 1999. "Desecha el TRIFE todos los recursos de inconformidad que presenta el PRI," *La Jornada*, 12 January: 28.

Huntington, Samuel P., and Clement H. Moore. 1970. *Authoritarian Politics in Modern Society: The Dynamics of Established One-Party Systems.* New York: Basic Books.

IFE (Instituto Electoral Federal). 2001. *Memoria del proceso electoral federal.* Mexico City: IFE.

Irízar, Guadalupe. 2002a. "Afecta 12.5 a IFE y a partidos," *Reforma*, 19 October: 9.

———. 2002b. "Ratifica PRD denuncia por desvío en PEMEX," *Reforma*, 13 March: 13A.

———. 2002c. "Franquean a IFE en el caso PEMEX," *Reforma*, 22 March: 10A.

———. 2002d. "Investiga el IFE a 'Amigos de Fox'," *Reforma*, 16 May: 3A.

Levi, Lucio. 1995. "Régimen político." In *Diccionario de ciencia política*, by Norberto Bobbio et al.. Madrid: Siglo Veintiuno.

Martínez Assad, Carlos. 1982. *El henriquismo: una piedra en el camino.* Mexico City: Mastín Casillas Editores.

Méndez, Enrique, and Georgina Saldierna. 1998. "TRIFE: los gastos de campaña del PRI en 94 no son 'cosa juzgada'," *La Jornada*, December 23: 7.

Molinar Horcasitas, Juan. 1991. *El tiempo de la legitimidad*. Mexico City: Cal y Arena.

Monge, Raúl. 1996. "En el año electoral 1997, los partidos dispondrán de $1,380 millones; 42%, para el PRI," *Proceso* no. 1039 (September): 35–36.

Patiño Camarena, Javier. 1985. *Análisis de la reforma política*. Mexico City: Universidad Nacional Autónoma de México.

Reyes Heroles, Jesús. 1977. "Discurso de Chilpancingo," *Gaceta Informativa de la Reforma Electoral*, April–August. Mexico City: Comisión Federal Electoral.

Román, José Antonio. 1998. "Zertuche Muñoz nuevo secretario ejecutivo del IFE," *La Jornada*, April 8: 13.

Salas, Alejandro. 2002. "Señalan diputados a Fox que se caerá su decreto," *Reforma*, 12 October: 4A.

Salcedo, Edgar. 1998. "La duplicidad en el IFE," *Voz y Voto* 68 (October): 19–21.

Sartori, Giovanni. 1994. *Partidos y sistemas de partidos: marco para un análisis*. 2 vols. Madrid: Alianza.

Schedler, Andreas. 1999. "IFE: complicada imparcialidad," *Voz y Voto* 73 (March): 23–33.

Trejo Delarbe, Raúl. 1999. "El litigio en el IFE," *Nexos* 257 (May): 71–74.

Tribunal de lo Contencioso Electoral. 1988. *Elecciones 1988*. Mexico City: Tribunal de lo Contencioso Electoral.

Urrutia, Alonso. 2002. "Será reabierta la investigación sobre financiamiento de la campaña Foxista," *La Jornada*, 8 May: 3.

Valdés, María Eugenia. 1998. "Una nueva legitimidad en el Distrito Federal: las elecciones de 1997," *Nueva Antropología* 54 (August): 57–78.

Zebadúa, Emilio. 1997. "Fin del proceso," *La Jornada*, August 24: 7.

———. 1999. "La batalla por el IFE," *Reforma*, September 1: 2–3.

4

The Changing Mexican Voter,
1991–2000

Jorge Buendía

Mexico has experienced substantial political changes since the mid-1980s. As late as 1985, the Institutional Revolutionary Party (PRI) had never lost a governorship or a federal Senate seat, and it received 64.8 percent of the valid vote in that year's midterm elections. Twelve years later, the PRI received only 39.1 percent of the valid vote in the 1997 midterm elections, and it lost its absolute majority in the federal Chamber of Deputies. And in 2000, the PRI lost a presidential election for the first time since its founding in 1929. This was the culmination of a very slow process of political change.

Most of this political upheaval took place in the electoral arena. Understanding Mexico's political transition requires understanding its citizens' electoral calculus because voters have been the major agents of political change. The relevant question is: did voters themselves change, or were there changes in the exogenous factors that influence voting behavior? An important school of thought in political science argues, for example, that individual attitudes are fundamental in the creation and maintenance of democratic regimes.[1] If this is the case, the democratization of the Mexican polity must, at a minimum, be accompanied by changes in citizens' electoral calculus. More specifically, we should be able to document the emergence of new factors influencing individuals' vote choice and/or the relative decline of those elements that previously explained Mexicans' electoral behavior.

The purpose of this chapter is to assess the principal changes that Mexican voters underwent from 1991 through 2000. It first introduces some descriptive data concerning which social groups evidenced major changes in their level of support for Mexico's three major parties: the PRI, the center-right National Action Party (PAN), and the center-left Party of the Democratic Revolution (PRD). The essay then determines if electoral change at the aggregate level has been accompanied by

This chapter benefited from comments by Nancy Belden, María Amparo Casar, Federico Estévez, and Kevin J. Middlebrook. Rosario Aguilar provided invaluable research assistance. The author presented earlier versions of this work at the conference on "Dilemmas of Change in Mexican Politics," Center for U.S.–Mexican Studies, University of California, San Diego, October 8–9, 1999, and at the annual meeting of the American Association of Public Opinion Research, May 17–19, 2001, Montreal, Canada.

1 Almond and Verba 1963 is the seminal work in this regard.

important shifts at the individual level. In particular, the analysis focuses upon changes in the saliency of issues such as the state of the economy. Did the same factors shape Mexican voting behavior across different elections? If so, did their saliency (electoral impact) vary over time? Was the 2000 presidential election also a watershed in terms of the elements that determine Mexicans' voting behavior?

Before addressing these questions, it is important to caution that one must be careful when seeking to explain electoral change. If possible, hypotheses should be tested under the same conditions. That is, in order to demonstrate changes in issue saliency across elections, one must try to control for the maximum number of variables that can be considered alternative explanations. There is no such thing as a perfect research design, but a carefully constructed model can help evaluate the merits of alternative explanations.

Unfortunately, there is a lack of longitudinal survey data through which to observe changes and continuities in Mexican voting behavior. Thus this chapter examines only the four federal elections held in 1991, 1994, 1997, and 2000. Any observed change will probably have more possible explanations than there are cases to substantiate them. All explanations of change should, therefore, be considered tentative. The following analysis does, however, examine cross-sectionally the survey data for all four elections, and it compares the statistical results across these elections.

The Research Design

The research design employed in this analysis has four main features. First, all the survey data are drawn from national probability samples conducted in the aftermath of the 1991, 1994, 1997, and 2000 elections (see below). Second, the statistical model for each election includes the same variables, ensuring that any change identified in voter behavior will not be due to a different statistical specification. Changes in the statistical significance of the same variable from one election to another will indicate that the determinants of the vote are not the same across elections. Substantial shifts in the magnitude of a variable's coefficients (predicted probabilities) will indicate changes in issue saliency.

Third, some of the surveys used here are richer than others in terms of the available variables. However, adding additional variables would require a different statistical model for each election – which would, as explained above, limit the model's explanatory power across elections. Yet a drawback to this more rigorous approach is that the omission of relevant variables may mean a misspecified statistical model.

Finally, question-order effects cannot be ruled out as an alternative explanation of observed changes in voter behavior because the placement of the question concerning a voter's electoral choice (as well as some other questions) in the survey instrument varied across the four surveys. Nevertheless, with the minor caveats mentioned below, the wording of questions was practically identical from one survey to another.

The Data

As indicated above, this chapter draws upon four national probability samples conducted in the aftermath of the 1991 (N=5,000), 1994 (N=4,966), 1997 (N=2,033), and year 2000 (N=1,766) elections. All interviews were conducted face to face, using a box in which voters deposited a sheet marked with their electoral preference.

The two older surveys were sponsored by the Mexican government (Technical Advisory Unit, Office of the President) and are available at the survey data archive maintained by the Centro de Investigación y Docencia Económicas (CIDE) in México City. The 1997 and 2000 surveys are the Mexican version of the "Comparative Study of Electoral Systems" project. Consulta, S.A. de C.V., and Berumen and Associates were responsible for conducting the 1997 survey; Consulta, S.A. de C.V. had sole responsibility for the 2000 survey.

Trends in Partisan Support, 1991–2000

In the period from 1991 to 2000, the PRI lost ground in every federal election, while the PAN consistently advanced. The PRI's electoral support declined from 61.4 percent of the valid vote in 1991 (its best performance during this period) to 36.9 percent in the year 2000 (its worst showing) (see table 4.1). In contrast, the PAN's support increased from 17.7 percent of the valid vote in 1991 to 43.4 percent in 2000, the year in which it registered its best performance and won the presidency. The PRD's electoral support has been characterized by greater volatility. It won 25.7 percent of the valid vote in 1997 (its best showing over the 1991–2000 period), but its share slipped to 17.0 percent three years later.

Given the magnitude of the aggregate decline in the PRI's electoral support between 1991 and 2000, it is safe to assume that the party lost ground among all relevant social groups or categories. That was indeed the case. The PRI's share of the vote decreased among all age, gender, education, and income groups.

Table 4.1: **Results of Mexico's Federal Elections, 1991–2000, by Party** (percentage of valid vote)

Election Year	Type of Election	PAN	PRI	PRD	Other
1991	Midterm	17.7	61.4	8.3	12.6
1994	Presidential	26.7	50.1	17.1	6.1
1997	Midterm	26.6	39.1	25.7	8.6
2000	Presidential	43.4	36.9	17.0	2.7
Change, 1991–2000		25.7	−24.5	8.7	−9.9

Source: IFE 2000.
Note: In 1991, the "other parties" category included the PARM, PDM, PEM, PFCRN, PPS, PRT, and PT; in 1994, it included the PARM, PFCRN, PPS, PT, PVEM, and an alliance between the Opposition National Union (Unión Nacional Opositora) and the PDM; in 1997, it included the PC, PDM, PPS, PT, and PVEM; in 2000, it included DS, PCD, and PARM. See the List of Acronyms for individual party names.

Figure 4.1: **Educational Level and Electoral Support for Mexico's Institutional Revolutionary Party, 1991–2000** (percentage of survey responses)

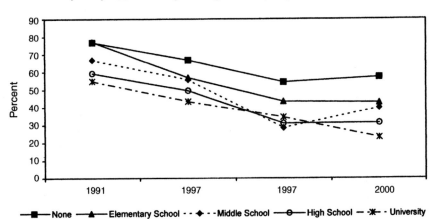

Source: Author's calculations based upon Presidencia de la República 1991 and 1994 national election surveys and Comparative Study of Electoral Systems, 1997 and 2000 Mexico Surveys.

Figure 4.1 tracks, for example, falling support for the PRI among all education categories. However, this decline was not uniform. Paradoxically, with the exception of the most educated voters, the declining trend was stopped or even reversed in the 2000 election.

This outcome can be easily explained by the fact that electoral backing for the PRI changed only slightly from 1997 to 2000 (falling from 39.1 to 36.9 percent). The most significant shift over this three-year period was the increase in support for the PAN and the loss of support for the PRD. In the 2000 election, the PRD paid the costs of being the incumbent party in Mexico City's government, the second most important political post in the country after the presidency.

Between 1991 and 2000, the PRI lost substantial support among the young and the very poor (the latter defined as families with an income of no more than one minimum wage). Its share of the vote declined by 34.8 and 32.2 percentage points, respectively, in these two populations. Given Mexico's sociodemographic profile, these were the groups whose backing the PRI could ill afford to lose.

The PRI fared better among groups whose electoral weight has been declining for many years: the illiterate and old people. Although these groups' support for the PRI remained substantial, the party also lost considerable ground among them (19.6 and 20.4 percentage points, respectively; see table 4.2).

The PRI's electoral decay was relatively similar among men and women and in urban and rural areas. Over the 1991–2000 period, the party lost 33.9 percentage points in urban areas and 35.8 percentage points in rural areas. Overall, then, the PRI's electoral base shrank substantially over the course of the 1990s, particularly after 1994. The decline occurred across all social groups, even among the PRI's traditional social bases.

Table 4.2: **Changes in Electoral Preferences in Mexico, by Party and Socio-demographic Category, 1991–2000** (percentage of survey responses)

Vote and Gender

Party	Female	Male
National Action Party (PAN)	23.7	26.5
Institutional Revolutionary Party (PRI)	−31.2	−31.5
Party of the Democratic Revolution (PRD)	10.1	9.4
Other parties	−2.7	−4.4

Vote and Income

Party	0–1 minimum wages	1–3 minimum wages	3–7 minimum wages	7 or more minimum wages
National Action Party	24.3	27.8	21.6	20.0
Institutional Revolutionary Party	−32.2	−32.0	−27.3	−32.1
Party of the Democratic Revolution	12.5	10.3	8.7	6.3
Other parties	4.6	6.1	2.9	−5.8

Vote in Urban and Rural Areas

Party	Urban	Rural
National Action Party	29.3	20.6
Institutional Revolutionary Party	−33.9	−35.8
Party of the Democratic Revolution	6.4	18.5
Other parties	−1.6	−3.1

Vote and Education

Party	None	Primary	Secondary	High School	University
National Action Party	7.4	25.9	28.1	23.5	22.8
Institutional Revolutionary Party	−19.6	−34.2	−27.0	−28.1	−31.8
Party of the Democratic Revolution	17.6	12.9	2.3	7.7	10.7
Other parties	−5.3	−4.6	−3.4	−3.0	−1.7

Vote by Age

Party	18–25 years	26–40 years	41–60 years	61 or more years
National Action Party	26.3	28.7	24.2	13.8
Institutional Revolutionary Party	−34.8	−33.4	−29.7	−20.4
Party of the Democratic Revolution	9.4	9.8	11.6	5.5
Other parties	−1.0	−5.0	−5.9	1.1

Source: Author's calculations based upon Presidencia de la República 1991 national election survey and Comparative Study of Electoral Systems, 2000 Mexico Survey.

Where Did PRI Voters Go?

The data for the 1991–2000 period indicate that the PAN benefited most from the PRI's decline. The PAN received 17.7 percent of the valid vote in the 1991 midterm federal elections, and it drew 43.4 percent of the vote in 2000.[2] The PRD's electoral strength grew by 8.7 percentage points between 1991 and 2000 (rising from 8.3 percent to 17.0 percent), but its gain was modest compared to PAN's.

With the exceptions of illiterate and rural voters, the PAN advanced at the PRI's expense in all categories. Rural voters also deserted the PRI, but they turned to the PAN and the PRD in equal proportions. In contrast, illiterate voters mainly shifted their support to the PRD. All other PRI deserters wound up in 2000 in the PAN's camp (although many of them had backed the PRD in 1997). What is really striking is that in 2000 the PAN performed particularly well among groups that traditionally ignored it. For instance, between 1991 and 2000 the PAN more than doubled its support among voters with a primary and secondary (middle-school) education and among rural voters (figure 4.2).

Figure 4.2: **Electoral Support for Mexico's National Action Party in Urban and Rural Areas, 1991 and 2000** (percentage of survey responses)

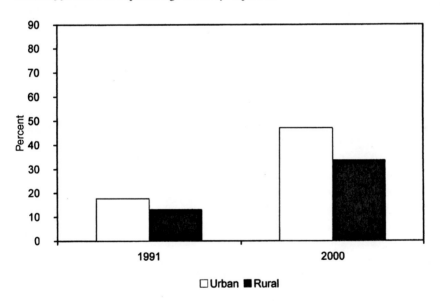

□ Urban ■ Rural

Source: Author's calculations based upon Presidencia de la República 1991 national election survey and Comparative Study of Electoral Systems, 2000 Mexico Survey.

2 The National Action Party (PAN) contested the 2000 elections in coalition with the Mexican Ecological Green Party (PVEM), the "Alliance for Change." The PRD also formed a coalition (the "Alliance for Mexico") for the 2000 elections; its partners were the Democratic Convergence (CD), Labor Party (PT), Party of the Nationalist Society (PSN), and Social Alliance Party (PAS).

The trends described up until this point show an acute deterioration of support for the PRI. However, it remains to be determined whether these changes at the aggregate level were accompanied by changes in the electoral calculus of individual voters. That is, does the Mexican voter now take into account considerations that he or she previously ignored? Or has the voter's electoral calculus remained stable despite changes at the aggregate level? The following section addresses these questions.

Determinants of Vote Choice, 1991–2000

Economic performance is probably one of the most powerful determinants of electoral choice in contemporary democracies. Countless studies have documented its impact upon voters' behavior. In this regard, Mexican citizens do not differ from voters elsewhere.

Cross-sectional studies of voting behavior in Mexico have found evidence of economic voting in the 1994 and 1997 elections (Poiré 1999; Magaloni 1999; Buendía 1995), and a longitudinal study by Brophy-Baermann (1994) found that poor economic performance has benefited the Left. A cursory review of electoral results and economic performance during the 1980s and 1990s certainly suggests the presence of economic voting. In 1982 the PRI obtained 69.3 percent of the vote, but in 1988 – after six years of economic crisis – its support shrank to 50.7 percent. In 1994 the PRI claimed 50.1 percent of the vote, but following the 1994–1995 economic crisis its share of the valid vote fell to 39.1 percent in 1997.

The data for the four elections analyzed here show that retrospective sociotropic voting was a strong determinant of the vote from 1991 to 1997, particularly in 1994 (see Appendix tables 4.6 through 4.9).[3] In 1994, the probability of supporting the PRI almost doubled (rising from 41.4 to 76.7 percent) if voters believed the national economy had improved over the previous year (table 4.7). The impact was not as large in 1991 and 1997; the probability of supporting the PRI rose by 20.8 and 15.5 percentage points, respectively, when the evaluation was positive (tables 4.6, 4.8). In 2000, however, the impact of national economic conditions was negligible. Indeed, positive evaluations of the national economy increased the probability of supporting the PRI by only 1.7 percentage points (table 4.9).

The reversal of the traditional pattern of economic voting in the 2000 election can be observed in figure 4.3. In all previous elections, positive perceptions of the

3 Question wording in the 1994, 1997, and 2000 surveys was very similar. In 1991, however, the three questions used had a more general meaning, referring to general conditions in the country rather than to economic conditions specifically. For instance, the retrospective sociotropic measure was: "In comparison to conditions in the country one year ago, how would you describe the country's current situation – better, the same, or worse?" ("Comparada con la situación que tenía el país hace un año, ¿cómo diría que es la situación actual del país?"). This question thus included an evaluation of economic conditions, but it was also measuring political and social conditions.

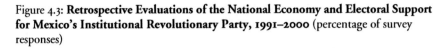

Figure 4.3: **Retrospective Evaluations of the National Economy and Electoral Support for Mexico's Institutional Revolutionary Party, 1991–2000** (percentage of survey responses)

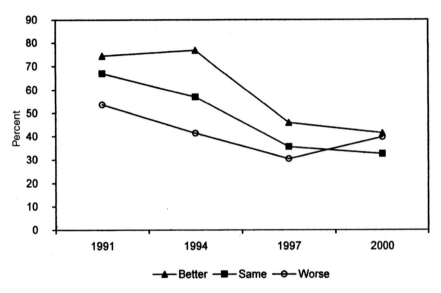

Source: Author's calculations based upon Presidencia de la República 1991 and 1994 national election surveys and Comparative Study of Electoral Systems, 1997 and 2000 Mexico Surveys.

national economy led people to support the PRI, while negative perceptions turned citizens against it. Notice that in 1991 and 1994 positive perceptions translated into a high level of support for the PRI (more than 70 percent), while in 1997 their impact was more limited. Yet in 2000 the electoral behavior of citizens with positive and negative assessments of the national economy did not differ at all. Considering that the Mexican economy grew at a high rate in 2000 (6.6 percent), this change in voting behavior is key to explaining the defeat of the ruling party.[4]

Two other items concerning economic voting are available in the four surveys analyzed here: retrospective and prospective "pocket-book" voting. Retrospective pocket-book voting was important in 1994 and to a lesser degree in 1991 and 2000. However, it did not affect electoral outcomes in 1997.

In the 2000 presidential election, voters' positive retrospective evaluations of their personal economic circumstances increased support for the incumbent PRI by 7.1 percentage points (from 33.9 to 41.0 percent; table 4.9). Yet this impact was quite low compared to what occurred in the previous presidential election in 1994. In that earlier year, retrospective pocket-book considerations made a difference of

---

4 The final section of this essay considers explanations for this watershed change in voting behavior.

Figure 4.4: **Prospective Evaluations of Personal Economic Circumstances and Electoral Support for Mexico's Institutional Revolutionary Party, 1991–2000** (percentage of survey responses)

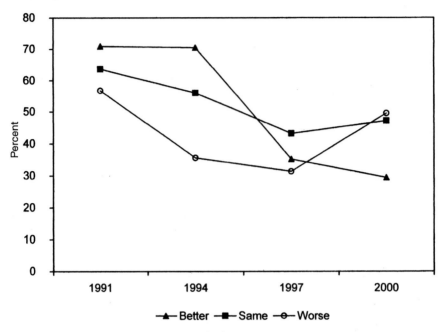

Source: Author's calculations based upon Presidencia de la República 1991 and 1994 national election surveys and Comparative Study of Electoral Systems, 1997 and 2000 Mexico Surveys.

29.1 percentage points (table 4.7). This measure, then, also shows the diminished influence of economic conditions on voting behavior in 2000.

In the period from 1991 to 1997, prospective pocket-book voting mattered the most in the 1994 presidential election (an increase of 34.9 percentage points for the PRI; table 4.7). In 1997, partisan preferences were scarcely influenced by judgments about the future state of voters' personal finances. In 2000, as in the previous presidential election, prospective pocket-book voting mattered (see tables 4.8 and 4.9 and figure 4.4).

However, unlike in previous elections, in 2000 it was the PAN and not the incumbent PRI that benefited from positive economic expectations (table 4.9). This was a significant break from previous Mexican voting patterns. As Magaloni and Poiré (2001: 27) have suggested, PAN nominee Vicente Fox Quesada was able to convince voters that he was the candidate who would demonstrate the greatest competence in managing the economy. Past memories of economic crises – especially the 1994–1995 financial crisis – were crucial to modifying citizens' electoral calculus. They no longer considered the PRI's presidential nominee to be the most competent candidate in economic matters.

The next section uses a statistical (multinomial logit) model to assess whether the relationships described thus far continue to hold after controlling for other variables.

Statistical Analysis of Voting Behavior

Models of voting behavior traditionally use as the dependent variable the different parties that comprise voters' choice set. Abstention is generally not included. Yet excluding abstention from the choice set can have important consequences for the analysis of voting behavior. Some theories (as well as common sense) dictate that abstention should be considered an integral part of the choice set.[5] For these reasons, the model used in this analysis includes abstention.[6] The dependent variable, then, has five possible outcomes: support for either (1) the incumbent party, the PRI; (2) the PAN; (3) the PRD; (4) a minor party ("Other parties"),[7] or (5) abstention.

The statistical model employed here is a multinomial logit model. The formula is:

$$\text{Prob}\ (Y = j) = \frac{e^{\beta j\, xi}}{1 + \sum\limits_{k=1}^{J} e^{\beta jxi}}$$

where j= 1,2,…, J.

$$\text{Prob}\ (Y = 0) = \frac{1}{1 + \sum\limits_{k=1}^{J} e^{\beta jxi}}$$

In this model, j_1=PAN, j_2=PRD, j_3=Abstention, and j_4=Other, while the PRI is the base category (Y=o).

The independent variables are: X_1=Retrospective evaluation of the national economy; X_2=Retrospective evaluation of the voter's personal economic circumstances; X_3=Prospective evaluation of the voter's personal economic circumstances; X_4=Political sophistication of the voter; X_5=Credibility of the electoral process;

5 See Burden and Lacy 1999; Aldrich 1993; and Buendía 2000 for a discussion of this issue.

6 A further benefit of adding abstention to a statistical model of voting behavior is that the number of cases available for analysis includes practically the entire sample. The only excluded cases are those survey respondents who did not answer the question concerning electoral preference.

7 Because of their small size, parties other than the PAN, PRD, and PRI were grouped in a single category. See the explanatory note in table 4.1 for the names of small parties competing in the elections analyzed here.

Table 4.3: **Determinants of Partisan Choice in Mexico, 1991–2000** (multinomial logit coefficients)

PRI versus PAN

Variable	1991		1994		1997		2000	
	Coeff.	T ratio	Coeff.	T ratio	Coeff.	T ratio	Coeff.	T ratio
Constant	-3.13	-11.29	-2.84	-10.90	-1.97	-4.36	-2.38	-3.95
Retrospective evaluation of the national economy	0.50	6.15	0.50	7.63	0.27	2.18	0.12	1.03
Retrospective evaluation of personal economic circumstances	-0.04	-0.46	0.30	4.41	0.12	1.07	0.26	2.41
Prospective evaluation of personal economic circumstances	0.02	0.12	0.57	4.87	-0.14	-0.45	-0.90	-6.90
Political sophistication	0.23	3.98	0.04	0.78	0.02	0.21	-0.18	-2.22
Lack of credibility in the electoral process	1.32	7.51	1.25	6.50	-0.06	-0.18	-0.79	-2.61
Female	-0.19	-1.88	-0.13	-1.47	-0.39	-2.32	-0.37	-2.40
South	0.35	2.07	-0.24	-1.64	-1.82	-6.99	0.19	0.99
Mexico City metropolitan area	-0.27	-1.53	-0.02	-0.17	-0.49	-2.01	-0.02	-0.10
Rural dweller	-0.41	-3.30	-0.22	-2.16	-0.24	-0.93	-0.29	-1.65
Age	-0.08	-1.43	-0.17	-3.37	0.13	1.41	-0.15	-1.63
Income	0.21	3.05	0.03	0.47	0.10	1.41	0.01	0.10
Education	0.13	4.41	0.14	5.70	0.16	3.53	0.18	2.27

PRI versus PRD

Variable	1991		1994		1997		2000	
	Coeff.	T ratio	Coeff.	T ratio	Coeff.	T ratio	Coeff.	T ratio
Constant	-4.12	-10.18	-4.23	-11.39	-1.04	-2.50	0.00	-0.01
Retrospective evaluation of the national economy	0.46	3.99	0.63	6.91	0.56	4.90	0.09	0.58
Retrospective evaluation of personal economic circumstances	0.37	2.94	0.37	3.92	-0.02	-0.21	0.43	3.11
Prospective evaluation of personal economic circumstances	0.30	1.40	0.86	6.01	0.09	0.35	-0.03	-0.23
Political sophistication	0.68	8.73	0.27	4.36	-0.02	-0.20	-0.17	-1.61
Lack of credibility in the electoral process	1.66	8.03	2.03	10.02	-0.39	-1.28	-0.44	-1.23
Female	-0.13	-0.93	-0.39	-3.32	-0.51	-3.23	-0.50	-2.52
South	0.31	1.20	0.98	6.57	0.05	0.25	0.05	0.21
Mexico City metropolitan area	0.62	3.20	0.65	3.84	1.67	8.18	0.38	1.73
Rural dweller	-0.68	-3.45	0.33	2.49	-0.19	-0.81	0.12	0.57
Age	-0.14	-1.70	-0.21	-2.94	-0.04	-0.44	-0.08	-0.68
Income	-0.05	-0.53	-0.18	-2.24	-0.05	-0.67	-0.12	-1.45
Education	0.01	0.34	0.09	2.85	-0.03	-0.77	0.22	2.07

Table 4.3, continued:

PRI versus Abstention

Variable	1991 Coeff.	1991 T ratio	1994 Coeff.	1994 T ratio	1997 Coeff.	1997 T ratio	2000 Coeff.	2000 T ratio
Constant	-0.90	-4.48	-1.01	-3.85	0.62	1.74	0.72	1.22
Retrospective evaluation of the national economy	0.32	5.44	0.21	3.15	0.40	4.07	-0.16	-1.21
Retrospective evaluation of personal economic circumstances	0.17	2.59	0.08	1.19	-0.10	-1.12	-0.22	-1.83
Prospective evaluation of personal economic circumstances	-0.17	-1.35	0.62	5.05	0.38	1.62	0.20	1.66
Political sophistication	-0.24	-5.01	-0.38	-7.55	-0.21	-3.02	-0.47	-4.98
Lack of credibility in the electoral process	1.84	13.21	2.03	11.48	0.37	1.52	0.07	0.27
Female	0.04	0.58	-0.15	-1.66	-0.43	-3.16	-0.40	-2.36
South	-0.23	-1.60	0.23	1.62	-0.37	-2.37	0.11	0.48
Mexico City metropolitan area	0.32	2.60	0.87	7.51	0.39	2.01	-0.04	-0.23
Rural dweller	-0.02	-0.24	-0.39	-3.50	0.15	0.81	-1.03	-4.97
Age	-0.19	-4.55	-0.25	-4.61	-0.19	-2.48	-0.56	-5.50
Income	-0.01	-0.19	-0.01	-0.19	0.06	1.10	0.08	1.26
Education	0.01	0.47	0.05	1.86	-0.04	-0.94	0.00	0.02

Summary Statistics for the Models

	1991	1994	1997	2000
N	4,442	4,177	1,660	1,312
Chi-squared	891.0	1,091.0	364.0	274.0
Likelihood ratio index	0.08	0.10	0.07	0.07
Percentage of correctly predicted cases	50.9	51.0	39.3	43.1
Null model	46.0	45.8	31.3	34.0

Table 4.4: **Determinants of Electoral Choice in Mexico, 1991–2000** (signs of logistic regression coefficients)

	PRI				PAN				PRD				Abstention			
	1991	1994	1997	2000	1991	1994	1997	2000	1991	1994	1997	2000	1991	1994	1997	2000
Retrospective evaluation of the national economy	–	–	–	NS	+	+	+	NS	+	+	+	NS	+	+	+	NS
Retrospective evaluation of personal economic circumstances	–	–	NS	–	NS	+	NS	+	+	+	NS	+	+	NS	NS	–*
Prospective evaluation of personal economic circumstance	NS	–	NS	NS	NS	+	NS	-	NS	+	NS	NS	NS	+	NS	NS

Notes: Economic evaluations are listed from best to worst. As evaluations of the state of the economy (in comparison to the previous year) become more negative, support for the PRI falls (represented by minus signs) and support for the PAN or PRD grows (represented by plus signs).

The PRI is the reference group. A variable is not statistically significant for the PRI if one or none of the reported comparisons is not significant.

Unless otherwise noted, all variables are statistically significant at a level of 0.05 or less.
* Significant at the 0.10 level
NS=Not significant

Source: Table 4.3.

Table 4.5: **Predicted Probabilities of Partisan Support in Mexico, 1991–2000: Economic Variables**

	PRI				PAN				PRD				Abstention			
	1991	1994	1997	2000	1991	1994	1997	2000	1991	1994	1997	2000	1991	1994	1997	2000
Retrospective evaluation of the national economy	-0.18	-0.20	-0.16	-0.06	0.08	0.12	-0.01	0.02	0.02	0.07	0.10	0.01	0.09	0.0	0.07	0.03
Retrospective evaluation of personal economic circumstances	-0.08	-0.12	0.02	-0.16	-0.03	0.08	0.04	0.04	0.03	0.04	0.0	0.10	0.06	-0.02	-0.05	0.02
Prospective evaluation of personal economic circumstances	0.01	-0.16	-0.05	0.16	0.0	0.05	-0.04	-0.19	0.01	0.05	-0.02	0.04	-0.05	0.05	0.07	-0.01

Source: Table 4.3.

X_6= Gender; X_7=South region[8]; X_8=Mexico City metropolitan area; X_9=Rural dweller (residence in localities with less than 2,500 inhabitants); X_{10}=Age; X_{11}=Income; X_{12}=Education.

Findings[9]

Statistical results from the analysis of each of the four surveys are shown in table 4.3; table 4.4 summarizes the results for the main variables for the four national elections held between 1991 and 2000. These results show that in all three of the elections held from 1991 to 1997, Mexicans behaved retrospectively in sociotropic terms. That is, as the state of the national economy declined, the probability of supporting the PRI also decreased. The negative electoral impact of bad economic conditions on the PRI vote was relatively consistent over the 1991–1997 period, ranging from 16 to 20 percentage points (see table 4.5).[10] However, this variable did not achieve statistical significance in the 2000 election. Given the high rate of economic growth that year, the defeat of the incumbent party was to a large extent due to its inability to make the state of the economy the most important electoral issue.

Egocentric retrospective evaluations did influence voters' choices in 1991, 1994 and 2000, but they did not do so in 1997. In the analyses of all four surveys, the statistical signs are in the expected direction: negative opinions diminished the likelihood of voting for the incumbent party. This variable had its strongest impact in 2000: the probability of supporting the PRI increased by 16 percentage points if people's personal finances were better off than they had been one year before (table 4.5). Both the PAN and the PRD benefited from deteriorating economic conditions, but it was the leftist PRD that profited most (a difference of 10 percentage points in 2000) from votes cast by citizens who perceived that their own economic circumstances had deteriorated. In the case of this variable, there was no observed break with past voting patterns.

Prospective evaluations mattered only in the 1994 and 2000 presidential elections. Prospective judgments do not seem to play a role in midterm elections, thus confirming the idea that these contests are essentially a plebiscite focused upon the economy and presidential performance (Magaloni 1999: 230).

Why do voters rely upon prospective judgments in presidential elections but not in midterm contests? There are two likely reasons. First, voters in midterm elections may believe that, because no new government will derive from the election, there is no reason to focus upon what policy changes the election will bring about. Moreover,

---

8 The South includes the states of Campeche, Chiapas, Guerrero, Oaxaca, Quintana Roo, Tabasco, Veracruz, and Yucatán.

9 The author used LIMDEP 7.0, version Nlogit 2.0, to perform the statistical analysis.

10 The statistical analyses were replicated with presidential approval included in the equation. As expected, the impact of economic conditions on the vote diminished. The only substantive change, however, was that retrospective evaluations of the national economy did not influence support for the PAN in 1997.

as a consequence of Mexico's highly presidential political system, they may believe that what Congress does makes little difference.

Second, this phenomenon may also result from the kind of electoral campaigns that political parties conduct. Although there are no systematic data to support this argument, it appears that Mexican political parties do not usually emphasize prospective issues in midterm elections. In 1997, for instance, opposition parties' television ads mainly focused upon the negative record of the incumbent PRI. Thus, because parties do not emphasize the potential policy changes that a new Congress might produce, it is harder for voters to take prospective issues into consideration.

In contrast, in presidential elections the candidates emphasize what their government will be like. Presidential campaigns usually represent an opportunity to break with the incumbent administration, while at the same time emphasizing the changes a new government will bring about. Similarly, parties' electoral campaigns seek to extrapolate the incumbent's current performance. If the record is positive, the incumbent party will project its past performance into the future; if it is negative, this is what the opposition parties will attempt to do.

Although the 2000 presidential election was similar to the 1994 election in the sense that prospective judgments mattered a great deal, the big change was in terms of who benefited from positive expectations. In 1994, positive expectations translated into increased support for the incumbent party (16 percentage points). In 2000, however, they translated overwhelmingly into support for Vicente Fox, the PAN candidate. Why?[11]

Conclusion

From 1991 to 1997, economic considerations clearly played an important role in electoral decision making in Mexico. Voters' behavior followed the rules of economic voting: if the economy improved, voters supported the incumbent, but if it did not, they turned against the party in power. In this process, Mexican voters gave most weight to retrospective sociotropic considerations.

Institutional factors (whether an election is a presidential or a midterm contest, for example) influence the salience of prospective economic considerations in the voting decision. In Mexico's 1991 and 1997 midterm elections, prospective economic judgments were absent from the electoral calculus. This was due in part to voters' belief that, at least in these years, the Congress could not alter the country's direction. But this phenomenon was also a consequence of electoral strategy because Mexican political parties tend not to emphasize prospective issues in midterm elections.

The historic 2000 presidential election represented both continuity and change in Mexicans' electoral behavior. First, pocket-book considerations did matter. As

---

11 This discussion does not examine the results for other variables included in the statistical model. For an analysis of the state of the economy and voter turnout in Mexico, see Buendía 2000.

expected, favorable personal economic circumstances translated into support for the incumbent PRI. Second, as in the 1994 election, prospective judgments influenced citizens' calculus. However, unlike what occurred in 1994, positive expectations benefited the leading opposition candidate, Vicente Fox, rather than the incumbent party's nominee. Third, unlike previous elections, in 2000 retrospective evaluations of the national economy did not influence electoral choice.

The changes in voters' electoral calculus appear large enough to account for the PRI's electoral defeat in 2000. The Mexican economy was growing strongly. While 55 percent of the electorate expected their personal well-being to improve over the course of the coming year, only 8 percent anticipated a deterioration in their personal economic circumstances.[12] Yet the ruling PRI could not connect its candidate with these perceptions and trends. Why was it unable to do so?

Three factors account for the findings reported above. They should be considered complementary rather than rival explanations.

First, the PRI's candidate, Francisco Labastida Ochoa, tried to dissociate his campaign from the incumbent administration of President Ernesto Zedillo Ponce de León (1994–2000). Hence, the strong economy did not become a campaign issue, and, more important, it was not linked to the PRI's candidate. PRI strategists identified the main issue of the campaign as "change," and they tried to appropriate this issue from Fox and other opposition candidates. Thus, instead of endorsing continuity (particularly a very strong economy), they literally ignored the government's achievements. The PRI apparently did not realize that the worst scenario for any long-time incumbent is a campaign centered upon the issue of change. This certainly helps to explain why the state of the national economy did not play a major role in the 2000 election.

Second, because of past experiences of economic crisis (especially the 1994–1995 crisis), voters "discounted" all the positive economic information they had at hand in 2000 (Magaloni and Poiré 2001). The 1994–1995 crisis was the most recent and painful evidence that the economy could be mismanaged by a PRI–led government. For this reason, positive economic indicators were not as credible as they had been before the 1994–1995 crisis. Hence they had a more limited impact upon vote choice in both 1997 and 2000.

Furthermore, Vicente Fox was able to persuade the electorate that he would be a more competent manager of the economy than the PRI's presidential candidate. He was able to do so in part because the 1994–1995 financial crisis made it almost impossible for the PRI to regain voters' confidence with respect to the economy. As Magaloni and Poiré argue (2001: 28), voters rewarded the PRI for good retrospective evaluations only "when they did not think a crisis was coming."

Third, the economy matters most to voters when times are bad. In good times, economic issues are not as salient. For example, when inflation is low, citizens do

---

12 These percentages are from a frequency table (created by the author) of prospective evaluations of personal economic circumstances in 2000.

not care about it; instead, they take low inflation for granted. Survey data show that voters are more likely to punish a government for bad economic conditions than to reward it for good economic performance (Buendía 2000). During the last years of the Zedillo administration (1997 and 2000 in particular), the Mexican economy registered its best performances of the decade. These circumstances help explain why economic voting mattered from 1991 to 1997 but not in 2000.

Mexico's 2000 election meant, then, both a rupture of the *ancien régime* and a break with previous voting patterns. Citizens' electoral calculus did change, and it facilitated partisan alternation in power. Moreover, it is likely that economic stagnation during 2001–2002 made voters more sensitive to economic issues in the 2003 midterm elections. Nevertheless, we still do not know whether the 2000 election was an exception in this regard or perhaps the beginning of a fundamental change in Mexicans' electoral behavior.

References

Aldrich, John H. 1993. "Rational Choice and Turnout," *American Journal of Political Science* 37, 1 (February): 246–78.

Almond, Gabriel A., and Sidney Verba. 1963. *The Civic Culture: Political Attitudes and Democracy in Five Nations.* Princeton, N.J.: Princeton University Press.

Brophy-Baermann, Michelle. 1994. "Economics and Elections: The Mexican Case," *Social Science Quarterly* 75, 1 (March): 125–35.

Buendía, Jorge. 1995. "Economics, Presidential Approval, and Party Choice in Mexico: The 1994 Elections." Mimeo. University of Chicago.

———. 2000. "El elector mexicano en los noventa: ¿un nuevo tipo de votante?" *Política y Gobierno* 7 (2): 317–52.

Burden, Barry C., and Dean Lacy. 1999. "The Vote-Stealing and Turnout Effects of Ross Perot in the 1992 U.S. Presidential Election," *American Journal of Political Science* 43, 1 (January): 233–55.

IFE (Instituto Federal Electoral). 2000. *Atlas electoral federal de México, 1991–2000.* Mexico City: IFE.

Magaloni, Beatriz. 1999. "Is the PRI Fading? Economic Performance, Electoral Accountability, and Voting Behavior in the 1994 and 1997 Elections." In *Toward Mexico's Democratization: Parties, Campaigns, Elections, and Public Opinion*, edited by Jorge I. Domínguez and Alejandro Poiré. New York: Routledge.

Magaloni, Beatriz, and Alejandro Poiré. 2001. "The Issues, The Vote, and the Mandate for Change." Paper presented at the international congress of the Latin American Studies Association, Washington, D.C., September.

Poiré, Alejandro. 1999. "Retrospective Voting, Partisanship, and Loyalty in Presidential Elections: 1994." In *Toward Mexico's Democratization: Parties, Campaigns, Elections, and Public Opinion*, edited by Jorge I. Domínguez and Alejandro Poiré. New York: Routledge.

Appendix

Table 4.6: **Economic Factors and Electoral Choice in Mexico, 1991** (percentage of survey responses)

Retrospective Evaluation of the National Economy

Party	Better	Same	Worse
Party of the Democratic Revolution (PRD)	5.2	7.8	14.6
Institutional Revolutionary Party (PRI)	74.4	67.0	53.6
National Action Party (PAN)	14.9	18.7	23.4
Other parties	5.5	6.5	8.4

Retrospective Evaluation of Personal Economic Circumstances

Party	Better	Same	Worse
Party of the Democratic Revolution	4.9	8.6	13.2
Institutional Revolutionary Party	72.5	67.3	57.2
National Action Party	17.3	17.9	18.2
Other parties	5.2	6.1	11.5

Prospective Evaluation of Personal Economic Circumstances

Party	Better	Same	Worse
Party of the Democratic Revolution	5.9	9.9	13.8
Institutional Revolutionary Party	70.9	63.7	56.8
National Action Party	17.5	19.7	18.6
Other parties	5.7	6.7	10.8

Source: Presidencia de la República 1991 national election survey.
Note: See the explanatory note in table 4.1 for those parties grouped in the "Other parties" category. Percentages in columns may not add to 100.0 because of rounding.

Table 4.7: **Economic Factors and Electoral Choice in Mexico, 1994** (percentage of survey responses)

Retrospective Evaluation of the National Economy

Party	Better	Same	Worse
Party of the Democratic Revolution (PRD)	4.6	11.4	18.4
Institutional Revolutionary Party (PRI)	76.7	56.9	41.4
National Action Party (PAN)	16.2	27.2	34.6
Other parties	2.4	4.5	5.8

Retrospective Evaluation of Personal Economic Circumstances

Party	Better	Same	Worse
Party of the Democratic Revolution	6.6	10.9	18.7
Institutional Revolutionary Party	72.3	56.6	43.2
National Action Party	18.5	27.8	32.5
Other parties	2.6	4.8	5.6

Prospective Evaluation of Personal Economic Circumstances

Party	Better	Same	Worse
Party of the Democratic Revolution	6.5	12.0	22.5
Institutional Revolutionary Party	70.5	56.0	35.6
National Action Party	20.3	27.1	35.3
Other parties	2.7	4.8	6.7

Source: Presidencia de la República 1994 national election survey.
Note: See the explanatory note in table 4.1 for those parties grouped in the "Other parties" category. Percentages in columns may not add to 100.0 because of rounding.

Table 4.8: **Economic Factors and Electoral Choice in Mexico, 1997** (percentage of survey responses)

Retrospective Evaluation of the National Economy

Party	Better	Same	Worse
Party of the Democratic Revolution (PRD)	21.7	35.0	36.5
Institutional Revolutionary Party (PRI)	45.9	35.5	30.4
National Action Party (PAN)	27.1	22.8	26.2
Other parties	5.2	6.7	7.0

Retrospective Evaluation of Personal Economic Circumstances

Party	Better	Same	Worse
Party of the Democratic Revolution	30.3	30.4	36.4
Institutional Revolutionary Party	38.3	38.8	33.1
National Action Party	25.2	22.9	25.3
Other parties	6.3	7.8	5.3

Prospective Evaluation of Personal Economic Circumstances

Party	Better	Same	Worse
Party of the Democratic Revolution	33.8	20.2	35.6
Institutional Revolutionary Party	35.2	43.2	31.3
National Action Party	25.5	24.8	22.2
Other parties	5.5	11.9	10.9

Source: Comparative Study of Electoral Systems, 1997 Mexico Survey.
Note: See the explanatory note in table 4.1 for those parties grouped in the "Other parties" category. Percentages in columns may not add to 100.0 because of rounding.

Table 4.9: **Economic Factors and Electoral Choice in Mexico, 2000**
(percentage of survey responses)

Retrospective Evaluation of the National Economy

Party	Better	Same	Worse
Party of the Democratic Revolution (PRD)	12.9	17.4	19.7
Institutional Revolutionary Party (PRI)	41.4	32.5	39.7
National Action Party (PAN)	44.1	45.8	39.4
Other parties	1.6	4.3	1.1

Retrospective Evaluation of Personal Economic Circumstances

Party	Better	Same	Worse
Party of the Democratic Revolution	12.5	18.1	22.7
Institutional Revolutionary Party	41.0	34.7	33.9
National Action Party	44.7	44.0	40.4
Other parties	1.9	3.2	3.1

Prospective Evaluation of Personal Economic Circumstances

Party	Better	Same	Worse
Party of the Democratic Revolution	15.1	17.8	33.0
Institutional Revolutionary Party	29.4	47.2	49.5
National Action Party	53.4	28.5	17.5
Other parties	2.1	6.5	0.0

Source: Comparative Study of Electoral Systems, 2000 Mexico Survey.
Note: See the explanatory note in table 4.1 for those parties grouped in the "Other parties" category.
Percentages in columns may not add to 100.0 because of rounding.

PART II
Parameters of a New Institutional Order

5

Changing Patterns of Executive-Legislative Relations in Mexico

Jeffrey A. Weldon

Over the course of the 1990s, Mexico moved gradually and imperfectly from a strongly presidentialist system, in which the chief executive exercised powers far beyond those defined by the 1917 Constitution, to one in which the president was generally restricted to his constitutional authority. President Ernesto Zedillo Ponce de León (1994–2000) often stated that he wished to be "merely" a republican president – not exercising metaconstitutional powers and intervening only minimally in the affairs of the ruling Institutional Revolutionary Party (PRI). By the end of his presidency, his wish had largely come true.

Yet the political institution that experienced the greatest change during the 1990s was not the Mexican presidency but the federal Chamber of Deputies, the lower house of Congress.[1] During the presidential administrations of Carlos Salinas de Gortari (1988–1994) and Zedillo, the Chamber of Deputies became more plural than ever before. Although the Chamber's practices and accomplishments did not differ materially from what had been observed over most of the preceding fifty years, a true revolution in parliamentary organization and procedures began to take shape during the 57th Legislature (1997–2000). Of course, the principal reason for this reorganization was that, for the first time in nearly seventy years, the ruling party did not have a majority. This outcome was due both to changing voter preferences and to important reforms that made the electoral system significantly more proportional.[2]

The author acknowledges research support from the Instituto Tecnológico Autónomo de México and the Instituto de Investigaciones Legislativas of the Cámara de Diputados. He is also grateful for excellent comments on an earlier version of this essay from Federico Estévez and Gabriel Aguilera, and for research assistance from Claudia Y. Carmona Monroy, Marco Antonio Fernández Martínez, María del Carmen Nava Polina, and Jorge Yáñez López.

1 Lujambio (1999) offers an excellent bibliography on recent research on the federal Chamber of Deputies.
2 Other studies of the 57th Legislature include analytic works by Rossell (2000) and Ugalde (2000) and a formal congressional report by Paoli Bolio (n.d.).

Presidencialismo

Although the branches of government are separated in Mexico, with independent electoral arrangements for selecting members of each body, Mexico can be characterized as a presidentialist system because the observed powers of the president go far beyond the authority that the Constitution grants to the executive branch. For many decades, the formal separation of powers did not mean much in practice because the president was able to dominate the other branches of government by metaconstitutional means – especially those that derived from the relationship between the president and the ruling party (Carpizo 1978: 190–99; Garrido 1989).

These metaconstitutional powers have historically depended upon three conditions beyond Mexico's constitutional architecture.[3] First, there must be unified government. If the opposition controls one or both chambers of Congress, then the president may not be able to win easy approval for his legislative proposals. Between 1917 and 1928, divided government was a frequent occurrence; at least, the party of the president did not always have a majority in the lower chamber of Congress. The Chamber of Deputies approved bills sponsored by the president at a rate typically below 50 percent. In contrast, as soon as a unified government solidified under the leadership of the Revolutionary National Party (PNR) in 1929, the approval rate of presidential bills increased significantly.

The second necessary condition for metaconstitutional presidential powers is that there must be strong discipline within the majority party. If the governing party has a low level of discipline, as has been common in the United States, the president will not be able to take full advantage of his legislative majorities.

In Mexico, this discipline was achieved historically via several complementary mechanisms. Among these, the prohibition on consecutive re-election of deputies (in force since 1933) inhibits legislators from representing their districts or states. Their constituents have no opportunity to reward or punish deputies or senators for their performance in Congress, so legislators look elsewhere for their cues. Early on, they decided that the best cue-givers were in the National Executive Committee (CEN) of the PNR and its successor parties (Weldon 1997a, 1997b). This is explained, in turn, by the second mechanism that centralizes control in the Chamber: nomination procedures in the postrevolutionary "official" party were generally very closed.[4] In its early years, the PNR had relatively open primaries (albeit often rigged

---

3 The author thanks Juan Molinar Horcasitas for this simple formula. Cosío Villegas (1973: 29) presents a cogent description of a similar formula. For details, see Weldon 1997a: 244–52.

Of course, the constitutional system must be presidential, with separate and independent powers for the executive. Mexico's 1917 Constitution created a presidency with much stronger powers than had existed under the 1857 Constitution (Carpizo 1978, 1988).

4 A party can select candidates according to one or more of several general methods. An open primary is an election open to any voter, regardless of party. A closed primary is an election in which only registered party members can vote. In closed conventions, an assembly of invited or elected delegates chooses the nominees, and participation is limited to only a few select militants.

in practice), but beginning in 1937 the party suppressed these procedures in favor of closed conventions (Goodspeed 1947: 295–96).[5] The Institutional Revolutionary Party, successor to the PNR, held closed primaries between 1946 and 1951, but the federal electoral law enacted in 1951 expressly prohibited parties from using primaries to select candidates (Medina 1978: 20–25).[6] Since then, the PRI has almost always selected its candidates through consensus among party leaders, with virtually no input from party militants. If this practice is replaced by more open procedures (federal electoral law once again permits primaries), then we should expect party discipline to decrease. Finally, a further factor that increases party discipline is the likelihood that loyalty will be rewarded. If the ruling party has a near monopoly upon elected and appointed positions in the federal and state governments, then legislators are more certain that the nominations the party offers to those who remain disciplined will eventually translate into electoral victories (Casar 1998; Nacif 1996). The "official" party won all governorships and Senate seats between 1929 and 1988 and lost very few congressional and state legislative districts or municipalities during the same period, so there was little doubt that party leaders could eventually deliver on their promises.

The third condition for metaconstitutional *presidencialismo* is that the president must also be the head of a centralized party. The discipline that the factors described above create must be channeled to the president, not just to the party leadership. The president must have the power to nominate all or most of his party's candidates – including, ideally, his successor (in a process known histori- cally in Mexico as the *dedazo*, referring to an incumbent's fingering his successor).

The Mexican president's capacity to name his successor – the ultimate in meta- constitutional powers – has always been considered a consequence of *presidencialismo* in Mexico. However, we should also consider what incentives existed for repre- sentatives elected to serve in the final three-year legislative term of a six-year presidential administration. In the first congressional term, party discipline was maintained, despite the fact that the Congress was inherited from the previous president,[7] because the deputies knew that the incumbent president could appoint them to bureaucratic posts or nominate them to another elective office. However, a president in the second half of his term could not credibly pledge to reward legislative loyalty because he would be out of office (in retirement or exile) just three months after the legislative term ended. The *dedazo* nevertheless allowed the president to impress upon his successor the commitments he himself made during his term. Given that the incoming president owed his office to the outgoing president, he could also be expected to protect some of the former president's

---

5 Garrido (1982: 220–21) states that in the new procedures, each of the party's constituent sectors would select its favored candidate and the CEN would choose among the pre- candidates, thus determining the balance among the sectors.

6 The term "closed primaries" was used by the PRI; see Medina 1978.

7 See González Casanova 1965 for a comparison of first and second congressional terms within the same six-year presidential term.

interests, including his promises to PRI legislators and other officeholders who followed the party line instead of their own better instincts. This tie between six-year presidential administrations was crucial for the maintenance of the system.[8] Therefore, the *dedazo* was not a consequence of *presidencialismo* but rather a necessary element in its preservation.

This was not the case between 1929 and about 1936, when former president Plutarco Elías Calles (1924–1928) dominated the official party (including federal deputies) as *jefe máximo* ("maximum chief"), while presidents for the most part were limited to their republican roles. The highly disciplined, term-limited deputies took their cues from the *jefe máximo,* not successive presidents.[9] However, by the end of the first half of his term, President Lázaro Cárdenas (1934–1940) had exiled Calles, united in himself the roles of chief executive and party chief, and begun to reorganize the party (Cornelius 1973; Weldon 1997b). Presidents who came to power after the *maximato* (the period of Calles's extraofficial political dominance) had significantly stronger influence over the Mexican Congress (Molinar Horcasitas and Weldon n.d.).

When all of these prerequisite conditions were fulfilled, the presidency had extensive metaconstitutional powers. As each one of the conditions was fulfilled in the 1920s and 1930s, presidential influence over legislation increased incrementally. Table 5.1 shows what action was taken in the Chamber of Deputies on presidential bills between 1917 and 1946 – before, during, and after the metaconstitutional conditions came into being. Just over one-third of the bills that President Venustiano Carranza (1917–1920) presented in the Chamber of Deputies were approved,[10] and less than 14 percent of the bills presented by President Adolfo de la Huerta (1920) were passed. The approval rate for President Álvaro Obregón (1920–1924) was below 38 percent. Calles was significantly more successful, at 70 percent, due in part to the organization of the lower chamber under Gonzalo N. Santos and the precursor of the PNR.[11]

---

8 Note that this commitment did not include policy questions; a new administration often changed economic policy dramatically. The commitments across administrations that needed to be respected were more personal and professional.

9 For analyses of the *maximato,* see Córdova 1995; Medín 1982; L. Meyer 1978; and L. Meyer, Segovia, and Lajous 1978.

10 On relations between Carranza and the Chamber of Deputies, see Marván Laborde 2002.

   Table 5.1 presents, by legislature, data on the approval of executive-sponsored bills. The data presented in the text refer to bills submitted by specific presidents. These numbers differ for two reasons. First, congressional and presidential terms overlap by three months. Second, some bills were approved well after they were first submitted, sometimes several years after the president who introduced them had left office.

11 The 1926–1928 alliance of revolutionary parties was unusually centralized and worked mostly to pass legislation that would pave the way for Obregón's subsequent administration (a transition that was foiled by the assassination of president-elect Obregón in 1928). See Santos 1984 and also J. Meyer 2002.

Table 5.1: **Action Taken on Executive-Sponsored Bills in Mexico's Chamber of Deputies, 1917–1946**

Legislature	Percent Approved	Percent Rejected	Percent Unresolved
27th (1917–1918)	37.6	2.4	60.0
28th (1918–1920)	33.3	1.4	65.3
29th (1920–1922)	17.7	1.3	81.0
30th (1922–1924)	45.7	3.1	51.2
31st (1924–1926)	50.6	5.2	44.2
32nd (1926–1928)	61.3	8.8	29.9
33rd (1928–1930)	81.1	2.5	16.4
34th (1930–1932)	70.8	6.5	22.6
35th (1932–1934)	82.3	10.1	7.6
36th (1934–1937)	95.0	1.6	3.5
37th (1937–1940)	96.8	0.8	2.4
38th (1940–1943)	97.4	0.4	2.2
39th (1943–1946)	97.0	2.4	0.6

Sources: Weldon 1997b: 22; 1997c: 129.
Note: The data refer to public bills, including constitutional reforms. They include bills introduced in the Chamber of Deputies by the executive branch, as well as those approved first by the Senate and subsequently considered in the lower chamber.

Presidential success in the legislature increased significantly after the PNR was formed in 1929. Over 83 percent of the bills presented by the presidents of the *maximato* (1928–1934) were approved, despite the fact that two of the requirements for metaconstitutional *presidencialismo* were not in effect during most of this period. There were many regional and local parties affiliated with the PNR, and loyalty to the CEN was not yet totally assured. However, these smaller parties were gradually dismantled after the "no re-election" clause was added to Article 59 of the Constitution during the presidency of General Abelardo Rodríguez (1932–1934). Even so, the third condition of metaconstitutional powers – the union of the presidency and the leadership of the party in the same person – was still far from satisfied. President Pascual Ortiz Rubio (1930–1932) had deep conflicts with Calles, and his legislative success rate was under 75 percent – significantly below that of Emilio Portes Gil's (1928–1930) 85+ percent rate and Abelardo Rodríguez's 90+ percent rate (Weldon 1997c: 123).

President Cárdenas had much better legislative success, due in part to the fact that he eventually also assumed the role of *jefe máximo*. Over 97 percent of his bills passed the lower chamber (Weldon 1997b: 20). Over the next two and a half decades, the executive's success rate in the Chamber of Deputies always exceeded 95 percent and sometimes reached 100 percent (Molinar Horcasitas and Weldon n.d.).

The approval rates for amendments to executive bills followed the same pattern as for bills sponsored by the president (Weldon 1997b; Molinar Horcasitas and

Weldon n.d.). Clearly, the model based upon the metaconstitutional conditions outlined above describes very well the growth of presidential power in Mexico. As these conditions have weakened over time, the model should also predict the decomposition of executive strength.

The first of the following sections describes how each of the conditions weakened during the 1990s, and the second delineates changes in the federal Chamber of Deputies' organization and rules. They are followed by presentation of evidence confirming that President Zedillo was, in fact, less successful than his predecessors in getting legislation through the lower chamber of Congress.

The End of Unified Government in the Chamber of Deputies

The electoral rules in force for the Chamber of Deputies during the 1979, 1982, and 1985 elections were strongly majoritarian. Three hundred of the Chamber's 400 seats were elected in single-member districts, and the 100 "proportional representation" seats were distributed in a somewhat inversely proportional manner that most benefited the smallest parties. These party-list seats were restricted to minority parties. The "official" Institutional Revolutionary Party won nearly all of the single-member districts,[12] and it always maintained at least two-thirds of the seats in the lower chamber – thereby guaranteeing that the Constitution could be modified without the consent of any of the opposition parties. The Senate was also elected by plurality during the whole 1979–1985 period, and the PRI never lost a Senate seat.

Although a new electoral law increased the number of party-list seats in the 1988 election to 200 and the total size of the Chamber of Deputies to 500 seats, the system was no less majoritarian. The rules stated that the party winning the most single-member districts would be guaranteed at least 251 seats in the Chamber, a bare majority. With a greater proportion of the vote, a party would receive its exact proportion of seats. This was the first of two "governability clauses," electoral rules developed to assure a majority to the winning party. This rule decreased the likelihood of divided government, thus enhancing the executive branch's power to govern. The system became strongly anti-proportional if the winning party captured less than half of the vote, but it was relatively proportional if the victorious party won between 50 and 70 percent of the vote. On the other hand, the remaining proportional representation seats were distributed in the same inversely proportional manner as before.[13]

Nevertheless, this electoral law was *too* proportional for the PRI. In the 1988 elections the ruling party garnered only 260 of the 500 seats in the federal Chamber of Deputies (Gómez Tagle 1997: 71), which meant unified government but not enough seats to guarantee party discipline. The blackmail potential of groups

---

12 On average, the PRI lost fewer than six single-member districts per election; author's calculations based upon data presented in Gómez Tagle 1997: 70–71.

13 For details on the disproportionality of the system, see Molinar Horcasitas and Weldon 1990: 240–42. On the motives behind this reform, see Molinar Horcasitas and Weldon 2001.

within the PRI increased as the party's majority in the Chamber decreased. The solution was to create a "moving escalator:" the party with the most single-member districts and at least 35 percent of the vote would be guaranteed 251 seats, and for every percentage point above 35 percent (up to 60 percent), it would get an additional two seats. Beyond that point, it would receive its proportional share up to 70 percent. Opposition parties continued to receive seats by the somewhat inversely proportional method previously in effect. If the party with the most single-member districts did not win at least 35 percent of the valid vote, then each party would get a total number of seats proportional to its vote.

After one test of the new formula – in the 1991 federal legislative election, when the PRI won 320 seats (Gómez Tagle 1997: 72) – the opposition parties deemed the governability clause too favorable to the PRI. In September 1993, this electoral formula was replaced by a system without a majority-assuring mechanism. Proportional representation seats would be distributed in a parallel manner to the single-member districts, proportional to the total valid vote. The maximum number of seats that any party could win was 315 (63 percent of the Chamber), and no party could win more than 300 seats unless it won at least 60 percent of the vote. Thus the PRI limited its ability to reform the Constitution – an action that requires a two-thirds vote in each chamber – without the consent of at least one major opposition party. Moreover, for the first time the larger opposition parties were awarded proportionally more seats than the smallest parties. It was still very likely that the majority party would be strongly overrepresented (usually by 10 to 15 percentage points), but the 300–seat limit was an important concession. In fact, in the 1994 general elections, the PRI (with just over 50 percent of the vote) ended up winning 300 seats.

This parallel system was modified for the 1997 elections so that no party could ever secure more than 300 seats in the Chamber of Deputies and no party could be overrepresented by more than 8 percentage points. This meant that the winning party had to garner at least 42.2 percent of the vote in order to win a majority of the seats.[14] In close races, this party also had to capture a sufficient number of single-member districts to achieve a majority. Thus if no party won at least 42.2 percent of the effective vote[15] or if the distance between first and second place was sufficiently small, no party would hold a majority in the Chamber of Deputies.

In the 1997 midterm elections, the PRI received 39.1 percent of the valid vote and 40.0 percent of the effective vote. This translated into only 239 seats in the federal Chamber of Deputies, 12 short of a majority. For the first time in nearly seven decades, the "official" party had failed to win a majority in the lower chamber. Table 5.2

14 This was because (.422 + .08) x 500 = 251. If a party reached this minimum threshold, it would also have to win at least 167 of the 300 single-member districts to obtain a majority: (.422 x 200) + 167 = 251.

15 The effective vote is the total vote of all parties that reach the 2 percent minimum threshold. A party's share of the effective vote is usually a point or two higher than its share of the national vote, depending upon how many votes went to parties that failed to reach the threshold.

Table 5.2: **Results of Mexico's 1997 Elections and Seats in the Chamber of Deputies**

Party	Percent of Valid Vote	Percent of Effective Vote	Single-member Districts	Party-list Seats	Total 1997 election	Total 30 April 2000
PRI	39.1	40.0	165	74	239	245
PAN	26.6	27.2	64	57	121	117
PRD	25.7	26.3	70	55	125	116
PVEM	3.8	3.9	0	8	8	5
PT	2.6	2.6	1	6	7	12
PC	1.1	—	—	—	—	—
PDM	0.7	—	—	—	—	—
PPS	0.3	—	—	—	—	—
Independents	—	—	—	—	—	5
Total	99.9	100.0	300	200	500	500

Sources: IFE n.d.; Lujambio 2000; Chamber of Deputies at www.cddhcu.gob.mx.
Note: See the List of Acronyms for individual party names.

reports the distribution of the party vote and Chamber seats. A number of deputies changed parties or became independents, so the last column in table 5.2 shows the number of deputies in each parliamentary group as of September 30, 1999.

On the basis of their performance in the 1997 elections, the National Action Party (PAN) and Party of the Democratic Revolution (PRD) together just missed achieving majority status in the Chamber of Deputies. The PRI could not form a majority with just one of the small parties, significantly reducing the blackmail power of the Labor Party (PT) and the Mexican Ecological Green Party (PVEM). Possible minimum winning (majority) coalitions at the beginning of the 57th Legislature were the following: PRI–PRD, PRI–PAN, PRI–PVEM–PT, PRD–PAN–PVEM, and PRD–PAN–PT.

Organization of the Chamber of Deputies, 57th Legislature

At the time of its adoption in 1979, the Congressional Organic Law (Ley Orgánica del Congreso General de los Estados Unidos Mexicanos) did not contemplate the possibility of non-majoritarian internal government.[16] Until the August 1999 reforms to this law, the governing body of both the lower and upper legislative chambers was the High Commission (Gran Comisión), which could only be formed if a party had an absolute majority in the chamber in question.[17] The High Commission's members could only come from the majority party, a situation that was no longer acceptable in the new pluralism of the 1990s.

16 *Diario Oficial de la Federación* (hereinafter *Diario Oficial*), May 25, 1979.
17 This was assumed under the federal electoral laws in effect between 1979 and 1985 and guaranteed under the 1988–1991 laws.

A new coordinating body – the Commission on Agenda Control and Political Concertation (CRICP) – was created informally in the Chamber of Deputies (but not in the Senate) in 1991; it was formalized by a reform to the Organic Law in 1994.[18] The CRICP assumed responsibility for nominating members to committees, along with most administrative tasks, while the High Commission became little more than the caucus of the majority party. CRICP participants included the coordinator of each party with representation in the Chamber, plus other members to be named by the High Commission – thus guaranteeing that the majority party would also hold a majority in the CRICP. This still worked well for the 56th Legislature (1994–1997), in which the PRI had 300 members and controlled both the High Commission and the CRICP.

After the 1997 elections, however, no party had an absolute majority in the Chamber of Deputies, so it was impossible to form the High Commission. This meant that no one could name the extra members to the CRICP. The new governing body would have one member from each party, as per the terms of the Congressional Organic Law, but any three members would constitute a majority. Thus the PRD (or PAN) in combination with the PVEM and the PT would have a majority on the CRICP even though they together controlled no more than 28 percent of the combined seats in the Chamber. In response to this novel situation, the parties' leaders came up with a sensible solution. By parliamentary agreement, the new CRICP would comprise only the five leaders of the parliamentary groups, but each committee member's vote would be weighted according to the number of deputies that his or her party had at the beginning of the term. Therefore, the coalitions within the CRICP would mirror those that were possible on the floor of the Chamber.

After a great deal of debate, a defeat on the floor of the Chamber, more debate and compromises, and alterations made by the Senate, the Congressional Organic Law was modified significantly during the summer of 1999.[19] This was one of the greatest accomplishments of the 57th Legislature – a nearly complete reorganization of the lower chamber that will permit more efficient and equitable internal government.

First, the reforms lengthened the term of the Chamber's Executive Committee (Mesa Directiva) from one month to one year, making this body much more professional. The new legislation also reduced the committee's size to seven members: the president (hereafter, "speaker"), three vice presidents, and three secretaries (all deputies), all of whom are elected by a two-thirds majority vote. Given that no party can control more than 60 percent of the Chamber's seats, the plurality within the lower chamber will at least be partially reflected in the Executive Committee.

Second, the CRICP was replaced by the Political Coordination Board (Junta de Coordinación Política), which is comprised of the coordinators of the parties with representation in the Chamber. Its members still have weighted votes depending upon the size of the party caucus, but since 1999 the weights have been adjusted to

18 *Diario Oficial,* July 20, 1994.
19 Ley Orgánica del Congreso General de los Estados Unidos Mexicanos, *Diario Oficial,* September 3, 1999.

reflect defections from or additions to a party over the course of the legislative term. The Political Coordination Board has functions similar to those of the CRICP: it nominates members to committees, proposes the budget, and presents resolutions to the Executive Committee and the Chamber membership.

Third, the 1999 reforms created the Conference for Steering and Scheduling Legislation (Conferencia para la Dirección y Programación de los Trabajos Legislativos). It is comprised of the members of the Political Coordination Board (the party leaders), with the speaker serving as chair. Decisions are taken either by consensus or by weighted vote. The speaker votes only to break a tie. The Conference establishes the general legislative program, the legislative calendar, special rules for debate and amendment, and the daily program. It also has the power to pressure committees to bring their legislation to the floor of the Chamber in a timely manner.[20]

Fourth, the 1999 reform legislation also established a new administrative director of the Chamber of Deputies, the secretary general. The person who holds this position is not a deputy. He or she is nominated by the Conference and elected by a two-thirds majority vote of the full Chamber. After several votes, the Chamber of Deputies finally elected J. Fernando Franco González Salas, former president of the Federal Electoral Tribunal (TFE), as the first secretary general.[21]

Similar reforms were enacted in the Senate, where the High Commission was also eliminated.

The Committee System of the 57th Legislature

Legislative committees in 1997 were less successful than the CRICP had been in reflecting possible floor coalitions in the Chamber of Deputies. Because the PRI had in the past often been highly overrepresented in committees (Lujambio 1995: 190–97; Martínez Gallardo 1998), the opposition parties wanted to guarantee a division that was as proportional as possible. After much negotiation, the CRICP finally named the committees, but it failed to reproduce exactly the relative weight of each party in the Chamber – a failure that would cause problems later on.

The membership target for each committee was 30 deputies. In the 57th Legislature, the PRI usually had 14 members on each committee, the PRD and PAN had 7 each, and the PVEM and PT had 1 each. Each committee chair had a double vote in the event of a tie.[22] This meant that the PRI, if it happened to control the chair, could control a committee with the support of one small party. The PRI was not

---

20 Some of the bills introduced during the 58th Legislature (2000–2003) considered the Conference redundant and sought to eliminate it, reassigning its duties to either the Political Coordination Board or the Executive Committee.

21 There was general dissatisfaction with the office of the secretary general during the 58th Legislature, and a number of bills proposed splitting it into an administrative secretary and a parliamentary secretary, the latter of which would be responsible for following the progress of bills through committee to the Chamber floor and for coordinating the Chamber's research operations.

overrepresented per se; in fact, it was underrepresented by about one percentage point. It was, rather, the small parties that were overrepresented (with about double the level of representation they merited), but the PVEM and PT clearly required minimum representation on each committee. An arrangement under which the PRI was purposely underrepresented at 13 members, with the other parties' representation unchanged, would have yielded a total committee membership of 29, thus re-creating all possible floor majorities in the committees. In this scenario, the PRI could only have achieved a majority with one large opposition party or with both small parties, and it would have taken three opposition parties acting together to form a majority (Weldon 1998).

The distribution of committee seats among parties was the origin of many intractable problems in the 57th Congress. Several important measures that had majority support on the floor of the Chamber of Deputies were killed in committee. One example involved the proceedings against Governors Roberto Madrazo of Tabasco and Víctor Cervera Pacheco of Yucatán, on which the Mexican Ecological Green Party joined the PRI in opposing their impeachment on charges of electoral fraud and corruption (and, in the latter case, for having served as governor beyond the constitutionally limited six-year term). The committee report (*dictamen*) required a joint vote of the interior and justice committees, on each of which the PRI and PVEM together had 15 of the 30 members. The preliminary vote in each committee (meeting jointly) was tied. The rules allow a second vote so that committee chairs can break a tie, but the chair of the interior committee was a PAN member and the chair of the justice committee was from the PRI. Thus the tie could not be broken, and the impeachment proceedings did not emerge from committee – despite majority support for such action on the floor of the Chamber of Deputies.[23]

The 1999 reforms to the Congressional Organic Law reduced the number of committees from 42 regular committees (and many more special committees) to 27 regular committees. The new legislation stipulated that there should be no more than thirty deputies on each committee, and that no deputy can belong to more than two committees. Committees are now formally authorized to establish subcommittees, and the Political Coordination Board must formally consider the committees' proportionality so as to guarantee that each party has its fair share of these positions. However, many committees had very little legislative work during the 57th Legislature, and several had no bills at all on their docket (Weldon and Yáñez López 1999).

Legislative Procedure in the Chamber of Deputies, 57th Legislature

Every three years, the federal Chamber of Deputies is completely renewed with freshman legislators. In the past, executive branch officials and the Chamber's permanent

---

22 Chairpersons were also distributed proportionally among the parties.

23 The impeachment proceedings would have been dropped in the PRI–controlled Senate, but the Chamber of Deputies was denied the possibility of making a political statement.

staff guided (or misguided) these newcomers so that they could produce legislation in a timely manner. However, these "coaches" were less influential in the politically plural 57th Legislature, and a number of initial mistakes in the legislative process gave some credence to PRI assertions that opposition parties were not ready to govern.

One early fumble involved the rejection of the 1998 omnibus tax modification package (Miscelánea Fiscal), which is voted upon every year with the federal budget. It reached the floor of the Chamber on December 4, 1997, after having been reported out of the finance committee with unanimous support. Members of both the PAN and the PRD had heard rumors that the other party intended to abstain, so each party planned to abstain – assuming that the PRI's affirmative votes alone would ensure approval of the bill. Later, however, the PAN and PRD deputies independently changed their positions. Each group decided to vote against the bill, believing that the other opposition party would abstain and that the PRI's votes, combined with the other party's abstentions, would still suffice to pass the legislation. Eventually the PAN and PRD learned of each other's planned stratagem, and a rebellion (directed particularly against the PAN leadership) broke out on the floor of the Chamber during the vote. The tax bill was finally rejected when 240 deputies voted in favor and 243 opposed it (with 4 abstentions), despite the legislation's unanimous support before it reached the floor.[24]

Voting down the tax bill was problematic enough, but Speaker Pro-tem Pablo Gómez (a PRD deputy) made matters worse by declaring that the legislation was dead. The proper procedure would have been to hold a vote in which members were asked either to send the bill back to committee or to kill it, but no such vote was held. Article 72 of the Mexican Constitution states that a bill that is rejected on the floor of the Congress cannot be reintroduced until the following legislative session (which was scheduled to begin on March 15, 1998), a situation that would have left the government to function without the proposed tax adjustments. The deputies wisely decided to ignore the constitutional norm, and on December 11, 1997, members of the PRI, PAN, PRD, and PT introduced a new omnibus tax package. It was approved on the floor of the Chamber the following day by a vote of 450 in favor and 5 against, with 5 abstentions.

A similar case in April 1999 ended inconclusively. A proposed constitutional reform that would have given members of the Supreme Court the power to introduce legislation did not receive the necessary two-thirds majority (the vote was 234 in favor and 209 against).[25] The Chamber's speaker tried to send the bill back to committee without a vote, but after arguments with other members of the Executive Committee, he claimed the bill had been rejected. The subsequent status of this important piece of legislation was never clarified.

24 Rarely are there such perfect examples of a prisoner's dilemma.
25 This initiative would have permitted the Supreme Court to introduce bills affecting the judicial branch. Proponents believed that Supreme Court justices would introduce better legislation because of their expertise and experience, while opponents claimed that the justices would not be able to rule neutrally on the constitutionality of their own legislation.

In the 1998 spring legislative session, the PAN once again tried to introduce legislation prohibiting any party from using Mexico's national colors in its party emblems (as the PRI does). However, because PRI opposition to past PAN bills on this subject had frozen them in committee, PAN deputies sought to achieve their purpose by employing a parliamentary device called an *excitativa* (something akin to a discharge petition in the U.S. House of Representatives, but without binding provisions) rather than introducing a new bill. Prior to the 1999 reforms to the Congressional Organic Law, committees were (unreasonably) expected to issue reports within five days. If a committee held a bill for a longer period, a member might ask the speaker to send an excitativa to the committee to report out the bill. PAN deputies recalled that years earlier their party had submitted a bill in the Chamber of Deputies barring any party from using the combination of red, green, and white in its symbols, and they requested an excitativa to bring the bill to the floor of the Chamber for reconsideration.

There were, however, two problems with this strategy. First, an excitativa only *suggests* to a committee that it should report out the bill in question. If the committee fails to act, the speaker can only propose to the full Chamber that the bill be reassigned to another committee.[26] Thus an excitativa is in no way equivalent to presenting legislation or forcing a report on a bill. Second, the PRI discovered that it had indeed reported out the bill in question – with a negative recommendation – earlier in the decade, meaning that the excitativa was not even in order. This situation created considerable embarrassment for the PAN, whose only remaining option was to present a new bill. On April 30, 1998, on a vote of 244 to 224, the Chamber of Deputies approved the PAN's new bill and sent it to the Senate – where it became one of several pieces of opposition legislation rejected by that body's PRI majority.[27]

Reforms in the Legislative Process

Reforms that were approved in November 1997 restricted the rights of federal deputies to amend legislation on the floor of the Chamber. Because the regular procedures for amending bills on the floor are arcane and contradictory, floor

26 This rule was modified by parliamentary practice during the 58th Legislature. When the second excitativa is issued, the speaker assigns a date by which the bill should be reported. If the committee has not reported out the bill by that date, a third excitativa could result in the bill being reassigned to another committee. Some bills proposed that such legislative initiatives be brought directly to the floor for a vote without a committee report, but the Executive Committee (wisely) ignored the excitativas on these same bills.

27 The other pieces of opposition legislation rejected by the Senate included a bill reducing the value-added tax (December 1997) and an electoral reform (Summer 1999).

The Senate amended several bills and returned them to the Chamber of Deputies, including the Cinematography Law (Senate amendments removed some of the more radically protectionist provisions) and legislation lowering of the minimum age for deputies and senators (the Senate decreased the age for senators but rejected lowering the age for deputies to 18).

amendments have never been particularly common. Now, however, they are nearly impossible (Weldon 1998). According to the revised rules:

> No proposal modifying any article or group of articles can be put to debate, but a deputy can present a modification as part of his argument against a bill. If an article or group of articles submitted for detailed discussion is rejected by the Chamber, that part of the report is sent back to the committee for a new elaboration, taking into account the debate, and the committee report will be presented to the Chamber at a later date.[28]

During the intervening period, the remainder of the bill is suspended. It cannot be sent to the Senate or to the president until the committee reports on the questioned articles, perhaps including the amendments. Nothing in the rules forces the committee to accept the amendments in its report, making this a completely closed rule. Since the reforms, the number of bills amended on the floor has not been reduced to zero, but there were floor amendments on only three occasions between January 1998 and April 2000.

The new rules sought to control congressional committees by requiring that all committee reports be published forty-eight hours prior to debate on a bill unless the CRICP (now the Conference for Steering and Scheduling Legislation) grants an exception.[29] Moreover, minority reports that dissent from majority committee reports can only be considered if they are published at least forty-eight hours before the day that the report is discussed and voted upon.[30] This raises the possibility that the Conference might allow a bill to come to the floor of the Chamber within the forty-eight-hour limit but not permit any related minority reports.

The 1998, 1999, and 2000 Budgets: Climbing the Learning Curve

The Chamber of Deputies alone approves appropriations items in the federal budget, so during the 57th Legislature the PRI–controlled Senate could not veto its actions. This situation made budget politics a good test of the metaconstitutional conditions outlined earlier in this chapter. The Constitution and the budget laws permit deputies to modify the budget as they see fit, and the president apparently does not have the power to veto their actions.[31] Therefore, if *presidencialismo* was

---

28 Article 19, "Acuerdo parlamentario relativo a las sesiones, integración del orden del día, los debates y las votaciones en la Cámara de Diputados," *Diario Oficial,* November 11, 1997.

29 Articles 12 and 13, "Acuerdo parlamentario," *Diario Oficial,* November 11, 1997.

30 Article 17, "Acuerdo parlamentario," *Diario Oficial,* November 11, 1997. If there are several minority reports, they are considered in order of the sponsoring parties' parliamentary strength.

31 The uncertainty results from the fact that only one chamber approves the budget, and the veto is constitutionally authorized as a clause in Article 72 that describes legislative procedures for bills approved by *both* chambers. Constitutional scholars are almost unanimous in claiming that the president lacks a veto over the budget (Burgoa 1994: 692; Carpizo 1978: 86–87; Tena Ramírez 1985: 263–67). In practice, however, presidents frequently vetoed appropriations during the 1920s and 1930s, and at the time the Chamber of Deputies did not complain that the vetoes were unconstitutional. In fact, the Chamber occasionally overturned a veto – without, of course, the intervention of the Senate. See Weldon 2002b.

indeed weakened during the 1990s, during the 57th Legislature the Chamber should have modified the budget more often and more extensively than in the past (Weldon 2002b).

The evidence seems to support this hypothesis. The three budgets that the Chamber of Deputies approved in the 57th Legislature (for fiscal years 1998, 1999, and 2000) were heavily modified in committee. However, during the first two years of this legislature, no amendment was offered unilaterally, by the Chamber alone. The deputies were reluctant to modify the budget without the approval of the Ministry of Finance and Public Credit (SHCP).

When considering the 1998 budget, federal deputies challenged both the government's spending and taxation proposals. On the spending side, they increased revenue sharing with the states,[32] and on the revenue side the political opposition reduced the value-added tax (*impuesto al valor agregado*, IVA) from 15 to 12 percent. Because tax bills also come before the Senate, PRI members of the upper chamber were able to veto the cut in the IVA. Using the fiasco over the omnibus tax package to discredit the opposition, the PRI successfully deflected public opinion away from its veto of the tax cut and toward the opposition's supposed incompetence. Opposition deputies may have made a tactical error in separating the IVA from the rest of the omnibus tax package and approving the two bills separately. By dividing them, they allowed the PRI to defeat the IVA reduction in the Senate without having to reject the entire tax bill (and appear somewhat irresponsible as a result). Nevertheless, PAN deputies succeeded in raising the tax on beer and alcohol (revenues that they had planned to use to pay for the cuts in the IVA), thereby canceling out any potential gains from a lower IVA. All relevant parts of the budget were approved before the December 15, 1997 recess.

The opposition was more successful in the budget game during fiscal year 1999. The Zedillo administration had included in its budget bill a tax increase on telephones, which the PAN strongly opposed. This time, the opposition held its ground, taking the budget negotiations into overtime. In special session (December 15–31, 1998), the opposition – particularly the PAN – insisted upon excluding the telephone tax, holding out to the very last day. The administration ultimately capitulated. On the spending side, there were generalized reductions in expenditures, including especially deep cuts for the Federal Electoral Institute (IFE).[33]

---

32 In Puebla, however, Governor Manuel Bartlett found a way to read the law that was contrary to the PAN's expectations. The PRI governor assigned resources from federal revenue sharing to municipalities inversely to population size. Because opposition-controlled municipalities are among the largest in the state, the increased expenditures went primarily to towns where the PRI enjoyed the strongest partisan support.

33 The advantage the opposition expected to derive from cutting the IFE's budget was difficult to divine. One reason might have been revenge for sanctions the IFE had levied against opposition parties for irregularities in their financial reports. However, reducing its budget made it more difficult for the IFE to monitor and ensure clean elections – something that was clearly in the interest of opposition parties.

The budget process for fiscal year 2000 handed both victories and defeats to the opposition coalition. The PAN and PRD found enough common ground to propose significant unilateral amendments to President Zedillo's bill – increasing revenue-sharing payments to the states, setting a higher debt limit for the Federal District, and raising social expenditures for certain groups. A portion of the needed funds were to come from resources that would otherwise have gone to the federal government bureaucracy, and another portion from reduced spending on the post-1995 bank bailout.[34] The PRI, in contrast, wanted to maintain the bank bailout appropriations at the levels requested by the Ministry of Finance and Public Credit. The budget committee for fiscal year 2000 included 14 members from the PRI, 7 each from the PAN and the PRD, 1 from the PT, and Marcelo Ebrard, an independent originally assigned to the committee by the PVEM. The PAN, PRD, and Ebrard supported the opposition amendments, while the PRI had the PT's support for a version of the bill closer to what the SHCP had proposed.[35] The result was a 15–15 tie vote in committee, which prevented the bill from being reported out of committee before the end of the Chamber's regular session on December 15, 1999.[36]

These budget negotiations had broader implications as well. The PT had earlier entered into a formal alliance with the PRD and three other small parties for the 2000 elections, and the PVEM had allied with the PAN. Therefore, the alignment of the PT and the PVEM with the PRI on the budget issue questioned the stability of the opposition electoral blocs.

Because the budget bill was not passed during the regular congressional term, a special session of Congress was convened. The small parties, following the lines of the alliances established for the 2000 elections, cooperated with the PAN and the PRD to report out the appropriations bill on December 21. For its part, the PRI opted to introduce a minority report. What followed were some of the closest votes in the Chamber's history. The committee report was defeated on the floor by a vote of 246 in favor and 248 against, with 2 abstentions. This outcome allowed the PRI's minority report to come to debate and a vote. The first vote on the PRI version ended in a tie, with 246 votes both for and against it. There is no tie-breaking procedure on the floor of the Chamber of Deputies (the bill is not defeated, nor does anyone hold a tie-breaking vote); instead, the vote is held again. On the second vote, the PRI's minority report was defeated by one vote, 247 in favor and 248 against.

34 The Bank Savings Protection Fund (FOBAPROA) was a program established in 1990 to accept loan portfolio transfers from Mexico's commercial banks in exchange for higher levels of bank capitalization. Under the terms of the bank rescue plan initiated in 1995, troubled banks transferred loan portfolios to FOBAPROA and received promissory notes in exchange. The Bank Savings Protection Institute (IPAB), which inherited FOBAPROA's liabilities, was charged with establishing a new system for protecting bank deposits by the year 2005.

35 The PVEM tried to remove Ebrard from his committee seat so that his replacement would support the PRI's version of the bill, but the PAN and PRD quashed this attempt on the floor of the Chamber.

36 The revenue portions of the budget had been approved with little controversy and on time.

The special session ended on December 21, 1999, and a second special session was convened for the following week. This time, the budget committee reported out a compromise bill – signed by all parties, including the PRI – that contained many of the opposition's amendments. The Conference proposed a special rule to debate and vote on the bill. This procedure, although common in the U.S. House of Representatives, is highly unusual in Mexico's Chamber of Deputies. The measure ruled out points of order against the timing of the bill so that it could be presented without the requisite publication in the *Gaceta Parlamentaria*. It also allowed amendments without committee approval, which is normally required. Moreover, the special rule permitted the consideration of four amendments (technically, minority reports) regardless of whether the committee report itself was approved, even though the Chamber's by-laws permit the debate of minority reports only after the committee bill (or sections of it) has been defeated on the floor. This was a creative way of ending stalemates in committee.

The special rule was passed on the floor, and the committee report was approved by a vote of 465 to 8, with 10 abstentions. The PRD minority report, which would have completely eliminated funds for the bank bailout, was defeated by a vote of 140 in favor and 243 against, with 106 abstentions (mostly PAN members). The PAN amendment, which would have forced the administrators of the bailout funds to publish the names of the beneficiaries, failed by a vote of 245 in favor and 246 against. The first PRI amendment, which increased the amount of funding for the bank bailout, was approved, 246 to 245. During the vote, the speaker of the Chamber of Deputies, Francisco Paoli Bolio of the PAN, walked out and did not cast a vote on this question.[37] The PRI then attempted to restore social spending to something closer to what the Ministry of Finance and Public Credit had originally requested. In a series of nine votes, the Chamber of Deputies approved the committee version of the subsections of the article in question by a margin of between two and four votes, thus maintaining the spending levels desired by the opposition. The second PRI amendment, which would have shifted money among social spending categories, was defeated by a vote of 245 to 248.

Although the two opposition amendments went down to defeat and one PRI

---

37 The PAN had expected Paoli Bolio to vote with the rest of the party, which would have created a tie. Afterwards, some PAN members – including the party's candidate for the presidency – wondered aloud if his absence had not been induced. Paoli Bolio first refused to answer and then said that it was a decision of conscience. In January 2000 he was called on the carpet by the party's National Executive Committee, and he reportedly resigned from the party – but not the Chamber of Deputies speakership – in protest. In February, Paoli Bolio announced that he would henceforth abstain in all votes, following the model of the British speakership.

Political scientists who study legislatures usually assume that the speaker is approximately the median voter of the assembly. This is a convenient stylized fact that is useful for formal models. In this case, we know for certain that Paoli Bolio was exactly the median voter, at least on the IPAB question.

amendment passed, on the whole the political opposition gained in this budgetary approval process because the committee bill reflected the bulk of what the opposition parties most wanted.

For its part, at some point between December 21 and December 28, 1999, the PRI decided that instead of trying to ally with one or two small parties in order to pass its version of the budget bill, it would win over deputies one by one. It did in fact convince enough deputies to vote with the PRI or to absent themselves from the Chamber that it was able to prevail (by one vote) on the two key amendments. After this experience, the PRI began to lobby deputies outright to switch parties. By April 2000, the PRI ranks had swelled to 245 members due to defections from the PAN and especially the PRD.

There were also lessons learned from the 57th Legislature's budgetary experiences. The deputies recognized that the floor-amendment procedures were awkward and confusing, and so the rules were formalized and streamlined in practice for the 58th Legislature (2000–2003).[38] Floor amendments are now explicitly permitted, but only after the committee report has been approved in general. Moreover, committees can no longer veto floor amendments to their bills.

Conditions for Metaconstitutional Presidentialism in the 57th Legislature

The 57th Legislature offered a perfect testing ground for determining whether the conditions that created *presidencialismo* in the 1920s and 1930s were responsible for a breakdown in presidential influence during the Zedillo administration. Obviously, the first necessary condition – unified government – no longer held, given that the PRI lost its majority in 1997.

The second condition – strong party discipline – largely remained in force. The candidate selection process remained centralized for the 1997 elections, though it opened up somewhat for the year 2000 elections.[39] There were, however, fewer seats available to distribute to disciplined PRI members. By September 1999, opposition governors controlled the states of Aguascalientes, Baja California, Baja California Sur, Guanajuato, Jalisco, Nayarit, Nuevo León, Querétaro, Tlaxcala, and Zacatecas; the PRD controlled the Federal District; and the PRI fell short of a majority in a number of state legislatures. Therefore, although the discipline observed in the Chamber of Deputies remained high, it likely was very strained.

---

38 However, the rules of Congress were not amended, nor did the 58th Legislature witness any proposals to alter legislative procedures in any of the several bills that amended the rules.
     See Heller and Weldon 2001 for a discussion of the rules and their consequences from a social-choice perspective.

39 The PRI later announced that it would hold either open or closed primaries to select congressional candidates for the 2003 midterm election, a development that should eventually decrease party discipline.

Prior to 1998, it was impossible to develop party cohesion scores for the Chamber of Deputies because roll-calls were not made public. Since October 1998, roll-call votes have been recorded electronically, and some of the votes are published online in the *Gaceta Parlamentaria* (at www.gaceta.cddhcu.gob.mx).

For the purposes of this analysis, party cohesion was measured as the largest percentage of party members voting in the same way – for, against, or abstaining. Cohesion scores in the U.S. Congress usually are a function of a dichotomous decision (for or against).[40] However, in the Mexican Chamber of Deputies, abstentions are significant. They averaged 3.2 percent of all votes in the period studied (totaling 129 votes on one occasion), and so these cohesion scores should be trichotomous. An abstention is a relatively easy way to dissent from a party position, but it remains a dissenting vote. Sometimes abstentions are the highest vote count in a party; thus in these cases cohesion would be based on the percentage of abstentions. The cohesion score, therefore, is the maximum share of votes within a party, divided by the total number of party members who voted.[41] Cohesion scores can range from 0.333 to 1. In the former case, a party would be evenly divided among members in favor, against, and abstaining; in the latter, all members would have voted in the same direction.[42]

Between October 6, 1998, and April 30, 2000, the PRI's discipline was exceptionally high – reaching 99.6 percent for all votes (see table 5.3). The party's cohesion was slightly lower (99.1 percent) on private bills.[43] PRI cohesion remained very high when the party voted against either the PRD or the PAN.[44]

---

40 The most common measure of intraparty cohesion is the Rice (1928) index: $|(\%_{YES} - \%_{NO})|$. The score runs from 0 (half voting each way) to 1 (all voting together). This score is not useful when the vote is commonly trichotomous.

41 Members not voting are not included in these calculations. Often an absence is just an absence, although sometimes (as in the Paoli Bolio case) nonattendance may be strategic. Distinguishing among such cases is, however, nearly impossible.

42 Often, a single member of the PVEM voted on a roll-call. A cohesion index cannot be computed when the denominator is zero, and it is trivial when only one member votes. In these cases, therefore, PVEM scores were not included in the analysis.

43 These are authorizations for individuals to accept medals from foreign countries or to work for foreign governments, usually in consulates or embassies.

44 Brady, Cooper, and Hurley (1979) suggest a "party vote" variable, in which at least 50 percent of one party votes against 50 percent of the other in a two-party system. This measure is less satisfactory in a system in which there are five parties and three voting options. For this reason, this study specifies cohesion scores when all parties voted together or a major or minor party voted against the other major parties.

Cox and McCubbins (1993) propose a party leadership vote, which measures cohesion when the leader and whip of each party vote together against the leader and whip of the other party. This cohesion score also works best in a two-party system. Further complicating matters, in Mexico's Chamber of Deputies the leadership (coordinators and vice-coordinators) of each of the three main parties numbers at least half a dozen individuals, and they are liable to change during the course of a legislature.

Table 5.3: **Party Cohesion in Mexico's Chamber of Deputies, October 1998–April 2000**
(percentages)

Type of Vote	Party				
	PRI	PAN	PRD	PT	PVEM
All votes	99.6	93.5	92.5	93.6	98.1
	(1.0, 296)	(11.2, 296)	(12.8, 296)	(13.3, 276)	(7.2, 243)
Public bills	99.7	93.9	93.8	93.0	98.9
	(1.1, 258)	(11.1, 258)	(11.6, 258)	(13.9, 238)	(5.5, 205)
Private bills	99.1	90.8	83.8	97.6	92.7
	(0.8, 38)	(11.6, 38)	(16.6, 38)	(8.3, 38)	(12.5, 34)
Party votes	99.6	92.2	92.8	88.9	97.5
	(1.3, 159)	(12.6, 159)	(13.9, 159)	(16.4, 140)	(8.0, 118)
Major party votes	99.6	92.0	93.5	89.0	97.3
	(1.3, 152)	(12.8, 152)	(13.4, 152)	(16.4, 136)	(8.2, 112)

Source: Data for "all votes," "party votes," and "major party votes" are from Weldon 2002a. All calculations are by the author.

Note: Public bills include procedural votes in the Chamber of Deputies. "Party votes" means that a plurality of at least one party voted in a different sense than the other parties. "Major party votes" means that one of the three largest parties (PRI, PAN, PRD) dissented from the other two.

In the body of the table, standard deviations and the number of votes are reported in parentheses.

See the List of Acronyms for individual party names.

Cohesion within the PAN measured 93.5 percent for all votes during the October 1998-April 2000 period. As in the case of the PRI, cohesion among PAN deputies was higher for public bills (93.9 percent) than for private bills (90.8 percent). However, unlike the PRI, cohesion among PAN deputies declined on votes where one of the three major parties dissented (92.0 percent). This was because PAN backbenchers frequently voted against their leadership and with the PRD when the rest of the party voted with the PRI, as they did on the many bank bailout votes or on sure-to-fail amendments (Heller and Weldon 2001).

PRD cohesion was the lowest of all the parties represented in the 57th Legislature, averaging 92.5 percent for all votes during the period studied. Much of the difference was due, however, to much lower party cohesion on private bills (83.8 percent), on which PRD deputies frequently voted against or abstained. Sometimes they voted against foreign decorations for members of the cabinet, but on occasion they voted against granting permission for Mexican citizens to work in foreign embassies. Private bills are cheap protest votes, and the symbolic targets were likely not the individuals mentioned in the bills but rather the Ministry of the Interior (Secretaría de Gobernación), which prepares the documentation. Cohesion among PRD deputies was higher on public bills (93.8 percent), and it was also higher (and higher than cohesion among PAN deputies) on bills on which one major party dissented (93.5 percent). It is possible that the PRD promoted certain amendments even though the party knew they would be defeated, a tactic that rallied PRD deputies but split PAN deputies (Heller and Weldon 2001).

Cohesion scores for the PVEM were lower than those for the PRI but higher than those for the PAN and PRD. Their levels were surprisingly high given that it was a new party with a relatively underdefined ideology beyond environmentalism. The PT also had high discipline in the 1998–1999 period. These were, moreover, parties that switched easily between supporting the PRI on one vote and the opposition on the next. However, the PT's discipline decreased in the 57th Legislature's last year. The party served as a way station for dissident deputies who left the PRD or the PAN and became independents, then joined the PT, and sometimes finally wound up in the PRI. As a consequence, during the period studied the PT had the lowest cohesion score (0.89) of any of the five parties on major party votes.

We should expect party discipline to remain strong in the near future in part because Mexico's "no re-election" restrictions still apply. Political parties continue to debate the merits of reversing these restrictions and reintroducing the possibility of re-election. However, such reforms always appear to be just around the corner. Almost everyone now favors them, but only the PAN has made the re-election issue a high priority.

The third condition for metaconstitutional powers is that the president must be head of the party. For a variety of reasons,[45] President Zedillo insisted that he wanted to be a republican president, and he rejected the privileges that Mexican presidents have always held in internal party politics (though there is little doubt that Zedillo installed allies in the party leadership). Zedillo figuratively cut off his finger – and, in so doing, ended the tradition of the *dedazo* – when he promised not to intervene in the year 2000 presidential succession. In November 1999, the PRI organized a national open primary to choose its candidate for the presidency, Francisco Labastida Ochoa. Although Zedillo denied that he had a favorite among the five primary candidates, there was little doubt that he preferred Labastida, who had served as Zedillo's minister of the interior until the spring of 1999. There was, then, no full-fledged dedazo – though perhaps the stump of Zedillo's figuratively amputated finger pointed toward Labastida, at least in the minds of primary voters.

Nevertheless, Zedillo did not interfere much in local political campaigns. During the course of his administration very few gubernatorial candidates were considered to be presidential selections, and most gubernatorial candidates now compete in relatively open party primaries.[46] Of course, given the election of PAN candidate Vicente Fox Quesada to the presidency in July 2000, one should anticipate a weakening of presidential influence on the federal Chamber of Deputies.

45 These considerations related in part to the way in which Zedillo ended up as an accidental presidential candidate in 1994, following the assassination of PRI presidential candidate Luis Donaldo Colosio.

46 Some of these governors, such as Patricio Martínez in Chihuahua, were "undisciplined" to the extent that they challenged the Ministry of the Interior even more than PAN governors had done.

Thus for the 57th Legislature, the first condition for metaconstitutional presidential powers was negated. The second was questioned, not through institutional reforms such as permitting re-election but through the weakening of the third condition.

Evidence of Presidencialismo in the 57th Legislature

This subsection examines the Mexican Congress's legislative output during the Salinas and Zedillo administrations. It demonstrates that legislative production is very different when the metaconstitutional conditions are relaxed. Overall, deputies have become more active in proposing and approving their own legislation, and executive dominance of the legislative process has declined. The data for this analysis were gleaned from the *Diario de los Debates*.[47]

The 57th Legislature (1997–2000) was the first in seventy years in which no party held an absolute majority. In these circumstances, the PAN was the median voter in the Chamber of Deputies;[48] in the 133 votes between October 6, 1998, and April 30, 1999, in which the yeas prevailed, the PAN voted with the winning coalition in all but three instances (Lujambio 2000: 12–13).[49] Over the October 1998–April 1999 period there were seven instances in which the PRI voted against and lost to an opposition coalition. Out of the 297 votes between October 1998 and April 2000, the PRI was in the prevailing coalition 264 times and the PAN was on 260 occasions.

As has been common since 1988, the PRD was the party most frequently on the losing side in legislative voting. Of a total of 297 votes, the PRD was in the winning coalition only 189 times. On 84 votes, it was defeated by a coalition that included at least the PRI and the PAN. These latter two parties voted together on more than three out of every four roll-calls. On 12 votes, the PRI and PRD voted together in a winning coalition against the PAN, but in each of these votes, either the PVEM or the PT joined the PRD. It never voted with the PRI alone.

47 These data were collected by María del Carmen Nava Polina and Jorge Yáñez López under the author's supervision, with funding from the Instituto Tecnológico Autónomo de México and the Instituto de Investigaciones Legislativas of the Cámara de Diputados. Unlike summaries of bills published periodically by the Chamber of Deputies, these data take into account intergenerational effects (the many bills that are introduced in one legislature and resolved in a future legislature). This data base also disaggregates committee reports into their component bills more effectively than the summaries provided by the Chamber of Deputies or by the PAN (witness the confusion over the *excitativa* that was ruled out of order). Many of the data for the 1988–1997 period were originally presented in Nava Polina, Weldon, and Yáñez López 2000; the numbers are slightly adjusted here to make them comparable to data for the 1997–2000 period, which are based upon the author's analysis of Cámara de Diputados records.

48 Spatial analysis (Weldon 2002a) of roll-call votes in the 57th Legislature has confirmed that the left-right alignment of the parties was PRD, PT, PVEM, PAN, and PRI. Note that the PRI was to the *right* of the PAN, and that the median deputy in the Chamber was from the PAN. The method used in this analysis was W-NOMINATE (Poole and Rosenthal 1997).

49 Lujambio (2000) excludes losing propositions from his analysis.

On five votes, the PRI prevailed in an affirmative vote alone, with all the other parties voting against. On ten votes, the PRI prevailed in a negative vote when the other parties voted in favor. (Two of these required simple majorities, and the other eight votes required two-thirds majorities, which the PRI could easily defeat.) On seven additional votes, the PRI prevailed with the support of either the PT or the PVEM. However, on only one vote did the PRI win with the support of both these small parties. In all of the other cases of votes in which a majority was required, the PRI prevailed with less than a minimum winning coalition because of higher participation rates among PRI deputies (Weldon 2002a).

The degree to which President Zedillo shied away from sending bills to the politically divided Chamber of Deputies is noteworthy. During the 57th Legislature, only 69 of his bills arrived at the Chamber of Deputies (including bills that the executive had originally sent to the Senate and which then went to the Chamber for review after passage by the upper chamber). Overall, the executive branch was responsible for less than 10 percent of all legislation that reached the Chamber of Deputies, a much smaller proportion than in the previous three legislative sessions. In comparison, Salinas was responsible for 42.3 percent of the bills presented in the second half of his administration (1991–1994). Indeed, Zedillo himself submitted 34.2 percent of all legislation considered in the Chamber of Deputies during the first half of his term, when the PRI had a comfortable 60-percent majority (see table 5.4).

Of the 69 executive-sponsored bills presented to the Chamber during the 1997–2000 period, 14 were required legislation that the executive submits each November (the budget, the revenue law, the omnibus tax bill, the fiscal coordination law, and related bills).[50] Another 14 bills requested congressional authorization for the president to leave the country, and all of them originated in the Senate – presumably because they dealt with foreign relations, the prerogative of the upper chamber. (A further 19 legislative proposals also originated in the Senate.) All initiatives regarding the Ministry of Finance and Public Credit must originate in the Chamber of Deputies, and 18 bills fell into this category (in addition to budget bills).[51] However, only 4 substantive executive bills, unrelated to the SHCP, began their trajectory in the lower chamber: amendments to the industrial property law, amendments to the administrative procedures law, a pharmaceutical-chemical control law, and a firearms bill.[52]

There were 23 substantive bills that Zedillo could have sent to either chamber on his own authority. He chose to send 19 (82.6 percent) of them to the Senate, where he apparently felt that his legislation would be better attended. Zedillo may have

50 One additional bill, which created the Superior Auditing Authority (Órgano Superior de Fiscalización), was originally introduced in the 56th Legislature but considered and finally approved in the 57th.
51 These bills also include some tax and banking legislation, as well as legislation regulating commemorative coins.
52 The industrial property and pharmaceutical-chemical control laws were approved unanimously.

Table 5.4: **Sponsors of Public Bills in Mexico's Chamber of Deputies, 1988–2000**

Legislature	Executive	Percent	Deputies	Percent	Legislatures	Percent	Senate	Percent	Total
				Sponsor					
54th (1988–91)	72	22.7	244	78.0	0	0.0	1	0.3	317
55th (1991–94)	135	42.3	178	55.8	3	0.9	3	0.9	319
56th (1994–97)	91	34.2	164	61.7	11	4.1	0	0.0	266
57th (1997–2000)	69	9.8	566	80.3	32	4.5	38[a]	5.4	705
Total	367	22.9	1,152	71.7	46	2.9	42	2.6	1,607

Sources: For 1988–1997, Nava Polina, Weldon, and Yáñez López 2000; for 1997-2000, author's analysis of Cámara de Diputados data.

[a] This category includes 7 revenue bills presented by senators in the Chamber of Deputies as the chamber of origin.

preferred this route because, on controversial bills with the potential to divide the PRI, intra-party differences could be patched over while the bill lingered in committee. He therefore faced fewer political risks in the Senate than in an open vote in the Chamber of Deputies. The bill to privatize electrical power generation, which was sent to the Senate, may have been an example in this regard.[53]

For their part, members of the Chamber of Deputies presented a record number of bills during the 57th Legislature – a total of 566. This was substantially more than twice the volume of any of the preceding three legislatures, and it was near three and a half times the number of bills initiated by deputies during the 56th Legislature. Indeed, this proportion of member-initiated legislation (80.3 percent) was even higher than that achieved by the 54th Legislature (1988–1991), when the PRI held only 52 percent of the seats in the Chamber of Deputies.

It is interesting to note that state legislatures were very active in the 57th Legislature, presenting a total of 32 bills.[54] Not surprisingly, opposition-controlled states (including the Federal District) accounted for 20 of these initiatives. The state of Nuevo León introduced 8 bills; the Federal District Representative Assembly submitted 5; and Baja California introduced 6.

The PAN and the PRD each presented more than one-fifth of the public bills considered in the 57th Legislature. Each party's total (156 initiatives) was roughly twice the number of bills that the PRI introduced (79) (see table 5.5). The PRI appeared reluctant to introduce legislation at the beginning of the session; indeed,

53 It was somewhat ironic, therefore, that it was the PRI contingent on the Senate's energy committee that squelched Zedillo's energy bill during the 58th Legislature.

54 Article 71 of the Mexican Constitution grants authority to introduce bills to the president, deputies, senators, and state legislatures. In the last case, bills requesting federal action are first introduced in a state assembly according to the requirements established by the respective state constitution (typically, governors, state-assembly deputies, municipalities, and private citizens have the right to introduce such bills). If the initiative is approved, it is forwarded to the Congress and introduced as a regular bill.

Table 5.5: **Deputy-Sponsored Public Bills in Mexico's Chamber of Deputies, by Party, 1988–2000**

Party	54th (1988–91)	Per-cent	55th (1991–94)	Per-cent	56th (1994–97)	Per-cent	57th (1997–2000)	Per-cent	Total
					Legislature				
PAN	102	32.2	39	12.2	75	28.2	156	22.1	372
PARM	41	12.9	11	3.4	—	—	—	—	52
PFCRN	7	2.2	7	2.2	—	—	—	—	14
PPS	22	6.9	13	4.1	—	—	—	—	35
PRD	23	7.3	43	13.5	41	15.4	156	22.1	263
PRI	19	6.0	29	9.1	11	4.1	79	11.2	138
PT	—	—	—	—	1	0.4	25	3.5	26
PVEM	—	—	—	—	—	—	43	6.1	43
Independents	1	0.3	3	0.9	13	4.9	9	1.3	26
Coalition with PRI	14	4.4	21	6.6	6	2.2	43	6.1	76
Opposition coalition	5	1.6	1	0.3	3	1.1	19	2.7	34
Committee	9	2.8	11	3.4	14	5.3	31	4.4	65

Sources: For 1988–1997, Nava Polina, Weldon, and Yáñez López 2000; for 1997–2000, author's analysis of Cámara de Diputados data.

Note: The percentages are based upon the total number of bills considered in the Chamber of Deputies. They do not, therefore, add up to 100.0.

The PT had no representatives in the 54th and 55th legislatures. The PVEM had no representatives in the 54th, 55th, and 56th legislatures. The PARM, PFCRN, and PPS were not represented in the 56th and 57th legislatures.

See the List of Acronyms for individual party names.

PRI deputies presented only 11 bills in the first year of the session. However, taking up the slack left by the executive branch, they presented 68 bills during the second year. The PVEM and PT introduced 43 and 25 bills, respectively – far above their relative weight in the Congress.

Sponsoring bills is relatively easy. What is more indicative of success is the proportion of legislation introduced by various political actors that is ultimately approved. Table 5.6 demonstrates that Zedillo was much less successful than his predecessors in this regard. Between 1988 and 1997, the executive branch on average introduced 66.2 percent of all of the legislation that the Congress eventually approved. During the 57th Legislature, however, this proportion fell to 29.3 percent. In contrast, federal deputies accounted for 56.3 percent of all approved bills. The last time the deputies had been responsible for a majority of legislation approved in the Chamber of Deputies was in the 31st Legislature (1924–1926), before the foundation of the PNR (Weldon 1997b: 125). Between 1928 and 1997, the president had always sponsored at least 60 percent of the bills passed by the Chamber, and during the 1950s this proportion approached 100 percent.

Table 5.6: **Sponsors of Approved Bills in Mexico's Chamber of Deputies, 1988–2000**

Legislature	Executive	Percent	Deputies	Percent	Legislatures	Percent	Senate	Percent	Total
				Sponsor					
54th (1988–91)	71	59.0	38	34.5	0	0.0	1	0.9	110
55th (1991–94)	133	62.1	77	36.0	1	0.5	3	1.4	214
56th (1994–97)	90	75.0	29	24.2	1	0.8	0	0.0	120
57th (1997–2000)	63	29.3	121	56.3	6	2.8	25[a]	11.6	215
Total	357	54.2	265	40.2	8	1.2	29	4.4	659

Sources: For 1988–1997, Nava Polina, Weldon, and Yáñez López 2000; for 1997-2000, author's analysis of Cámara de Diputados data.
[a] This category includes one revenue bill presented by a senator in the Chamber of Deputies as the chamber of origin.

The bills that the executive branch sent to the Chamber of Deputies met with extraordinary success during the 57th Legislature, and Zedillo's legislative record actually improved over time as his administration learned that sending fewer bills increased the rate of approval. Nevertheless, approval ratios were below historical averages. Between 1988 and 1997, the lower chamber approved 98.7 percent of all executive bills (see table 5.7), clear evidence of metaconstitutional presidentialism. The approval rate dropped to 91.3 percent in the 57th Legislature, and for the first time in many years, two presidential bills were rejected – the omnibus tax reform (which was defeated by "accident") and the original bill concerning the Bank Savings Protection Fund (FOBAPROA). Part of Zedillo's bank bailout proposal received a negative report in committee, and it was replaced with a version of the bill that the PAN had introduced. On December 12, 1998, the Chamber accepted the report (thus rejecting the executive's bill) by a vote of 325 in favor and 159 against.[55]

The Chamber of Deputies was less generous with bills that the deputies themselves presented. Only 20.8 percent of the bills introduced by deputies were approved in the 57th Legislature. This was better than the 54th and 56th Legislatures, when the approval rate for deputies' bills was under 17 percent (see table 5.8). However, it was much lower than the approval rate achieved during the 55th Legislature, when 38.5 percent of deputies' proposals were approved. Nevertheless, the success of deputies in the 57th Legislature should not be measured simply by percentages, where the high denominator (583)[56] lowers the percentage rate. Instead, it is remarkable that the Chamber approved 121 deputy-sponsored bills during this period. The previous best performance in recent decades in this category was by the 55th Legislature (1991–1994), with 77 bills in three years – less than two-thirds the number produced by the politically plural 57th Legislature.

Table 5.9 compares the approval rates of bills submitted by federal deputies

55 Seven PRI deputies voted with the opposition on this bill.
56 This total includes 17 bills that had been introduced in earlier legislatures.

Table 5.7: **Action Taken on Executive-Sponsored Public Bills in Mexico's Chamber of Deputies, 1988–2000**

Legislature	Approved	Percent	Rejected	Percent	Unresolved	Percent	Total
			Action Taken				
54th (1988–91)	71	98.6	0	0.0	1	1.4	72
55th (1991–94)	133	98.5	0	0.0	2	1.5	135
56th (1994–97)	90	98.9	0	0.0	1	1.1	91
57th (1997–2000)	63	91.3	2	2.9	4	5.8	69[a]
Total	357	97.3	2	0.5	8	2.2	367

Sources: For 1988–1997, Nava Polina, Weldon, and Yáñez López 2000; for 1997-2000, author's analysis of Cámara de Diputados data.
[a] One bill was withdrawn and is not, therefore, included in the total.

Table 5.8: **Action Taken on Deputy-Sponsored Public Bills in Mexico's Chamber of Deputies, 1988–2000**

Legislature	Approved	Percent	Rejected	Percent	Unresolved	Percent	Total
			Action Taken				
54th (1988–91)	38	15.6	27	11.1	179	73.4	244
55th (1991–94)	77	38.5	13	6.5	110	55.0	200
56th (1994–97)	29	16.2	22	12.3	128	71.5	179
57th (1997–2000	121	20.8	29	5.0	433	74.3	583
Total	265	22.0	91	7.5	850	70.5	1,206

Source: For 1988–1997, Nava Polina, Weldon, and Yáñez López 2000; for 1997-2000, author's analysis of Cámara de Diputados data.

according to the deputies' party affiliation. In the last three legislatures in which the PRI held a majority of Chamber seats, 42.1 percent, 58.1 percent, and 25.0 percent, respectively, of PRI bills were approved. This proportion fell to 22.6 percent (a total of 19 bills) in the 57th Legislature, although this approval rate was still above the rates achieved by the PAN and the PRD (18.6 percent and 13.8 percent, respectively).

The PRD approval rates for the 1988–2000 period ran somewhat contrary to conventional wisdom. As one would have expected, no PRD bills were approved during the first half of the Salinas administration (table 5.9), a period during which the government retaliated against the PRD for the strong challenge it had posed in the 1988 presidential race. However, it is difficult to explain how one-fifth of the PRD's bills (9 of 45) were approved in the second half of Salinas's presidency (1991–1994) because it seems unlikely that bias against the party would have dissipated so quickly. Among the bills sponsored by the PRD and approved by the Chamber were constitutional modifications affecting church-state relations, educational

Table 5.9: **Action Taken on Deputy-Sponsored Bills in Mexico's Chamber of Deputies, by Party, 1988–2000** (percentages)

	Action Taken											
	Approved				Rejected				Unresolved			
Party	54th	55th	56th	57th	54th	55th	56th	57th	54th	55th	56th	57th
		Legislature				Legislature				Legislature		
PAN	7.8	28.6	8.6	18.6	9.8	6.1	11.1	8.1	82.4	65.3	80.2	73.3
PARM	9.8	33.3	—	—	2.4	8.3	—	—	87.8	58.3	—	—
PFCRN	14.3	14.3	—	—	28.6	0.0	—	—	57.1	85.7	—	—
PPS	0.0	29.4	—	—	18.2	29.4	—	—	81.8	41.2	—	—
PRD	0.0	20.0	6.8	13.8	39.1	8.9	9.1	8.1	60.9	71.1	84.1	73.3
PRI	42.1	58.1	25.0	22.6	0.0	0.0	16.7	8.3	57.9	41.9	58.3	69.0
PT	—	—	0.0	28.0	—	—	0.0	16.0	—	—	100.0	56.0
PVEM	—	—	—	14.0	—	—	—	9.3	—	—	—	76.7
Independents	100.0	0.0	30.8	22.2	0.0	0.0	15.4	22.2	0.0	100.0	53.8	55.6
Coalition with PRI	35.7	63.6	66.7	34.9	0.0	0.0	0.0	2.3	64.3	36.4	33.3	62.8
Opposition coalition	40.0	0.0	0.0	34.6	0.0	0.0	0.0	7.7	60.0	100.0	100.0	57.7
Other parties	—	100.0	0.0	—	—	0.0	100.0	—	—	0.0	0.0	—
Committee	100.0	90.9	57.1	34.4	0.0	0.0	0.0	0.0	0.0	9.1	42.9	65.6

Source: For 1988–1997, Nava Polina, Weldon, and Yáñez López 2000; for 1997–2000, author's analysis of Cámara de Diputados data.

Note: The "other parties" category includes bills that were reported in later legislatures, after the party in question was no longer represented in the Chamber of Deputies. Included here are, for example, one bill each sponsored by the PST and the PSUM in the 55th Legislature, and a total of five bills sponsored by the PARM, PPS, and PST in the 56th Legislature.

The PT had no representatives in the 54th and 55th legislatures. The PVEM had no representatives in the 54th, 55th, and 56th legislatures. The PARM, PFCRN, and PPS were not represented in the 56th and 57th legislatures.

See the List of Acronyms for individual party names.

reforms, part of the September 1993 electoral reform, legislation requiring that 30 percent of all candidate slots be filled by women (though this bill was subsequently modified by the Senate), and reforms to the consumer protection law. The supposed early flirtation between the PRD and the Zedillo administration only registered as a 6.8 percent approval rate for PRD bills during the 1994–1997 period. However, as one would have expected, the approval rate of PRD–sponsored initiatives increased to 13.8 percent (22 bills) after the PRI lost majority control in the Chamber of Deputies.

During the 57th Legislature, the Chamber approved 18.6 percent of the PAN's total initiatives (table 5.9). In absolute terms, however, the PAN was responsible for more legislation approved (30 bills) than any other party.

In percentage terms, the PT was the most successful party in the 57th Legislature (table 5.9). Seven of its 25 bills (28.0 percent) were approved. The PT (which began

Table 5.10: **Amendments to Executive-Sponsored Bills Approved by Mexico's Chamber of Deputies, 1988–2000**

Legislature	Type of Amendment						
	Committee	Percent	*Floor*	Percent	*None*	Percent	Total Approved
54th (1988–91)	40	56.3	5	7.0	31	43.7	71
55th (1991–94)	64	48.1	53	39.4	59	44.4	133
56th (1994–97)	46	51.1	11	12.2	44	48.9	90
57th (1997–2000)	25	39.7	5	7.9	37	58.7	63
Total	175	49.0	74	20.7	171	47.9	357

Source: For 1988–1997, Nava Polina, Weldon, and Yáñez López 2000; for 1997–2000, author's analysis of Cámara de Diputados data.
Note: The percentages do not sum to 100.0 percent because some bills were amended both in committee and on the floor of the Chamber.

the legislative session with 7 deputies and grew to as high as 13 thanks to defections from other parties) represented no more than 2.6 percent of all legislators, but it was responsible for 3.3 percent of approved bills.

Nearly 10 percent of all bills presented in the 57th Legislature were introduced jointly by two or more parties. Sometimes all five parties and independent deputies cosponsored legislation. Not surprisingly, a relatively high percentage of bills that were jointly sponsored and whose sponsors included the PRI were approved (34.9 percent). However, a nearly identical 34.6 percent of the bills presented by opposition coalitions (a total of nine bills) were also approved, indicating that a broad-spectrum opposition alliance is not totally unworkable in the Mexican Congress and that a limited common legislative program might be feasible.

One of the more telling statistics from the years when *presidencialismo* was taking shape concerned the proportion of executive bills amended in the Chamber of Deputies. As presidents became more powerful in the 1920s and 1930s, the proportion of their bills that was amended during the legislative process declined dramatically. Even during the period from the 54th through the 56th Legislatures (1988–1994), an average of 45.6 percent of the executive's bills were not amended either in committee or on the floor of the Chamber (table 5.10). The proportion of unamended executive-sponsored bills increased to 58.7 percent in the 57th Legislature, but much of the difference can be explained by changes in legislative rules. In the 55th Legislature (1991–1994), 39.4 percent of all presidential bills were amended on the floor of the Chamber. During the 57th Legislature, however, floor amendments were virtually prohibited (or only allowed when the Conference permitted them). As a result, only four executive bills were amended on the floor during the 57th Legislature. The proportion of executive bills amended in committees also declined, but to a lesser degree.[57]

57 One of the two executive bills defeated on the floor of the Chamber of Deputies (the 1998 omnibus tax package) had been amended in committee.

Table 5.11: **Sponsors of Constitutional Reforms in Mexico, 1988–2000**

	Sponsor				
Legislature	*Executive*	Percent	*Deputies*	Percent	Total
54th (1988–1991)	2	2.2	90	97.8	92
55th (1991–1994)	6	10.5	50	87.7	57
56th (1994–1997)	6	23.1	45	86.5	52
57th (1997–2000)	2	1.2	148	87.6	169
Total	16	1.6	333	90.0	370

Source: For 1988–1997, Nava Polina, Weldon, and Yáñez López 2000; for 1997-2000, author's analysis of Cámara de Diputados data.
Note: The total includes other sponsors of constitutional reforms, including the federal Senate and state legislatures.

It is worth noting that many of the executive bills that were approved without modification during the 57th Legislature (including the 14 travel authorizations) were not susceptible to amendment.[58] Moreover, the deputies appeared reluctant to modify some of the more technical economic bills, such as changes in tax formulas. However, most major executive-sponsored bills were amended in committee.[59]

One surprising finding in this analysis is that during the 1988–2000 period Mexico's president was directly responsible for only 1.6 percent of the constitutional reforms introduced in the Chamber of Deputies. Between 1988 and 2000, 370 constitutional amendment initiatives were submitted to the lower chamber (table 5.11). Of these, the deputies themselves introduced 333; only 16 were submitted by the executive branch, and the remaining 20 were sponsored by senators or state legislatures.[60] Even during the Salinas administration, when it is generally thought that the president was the source of the many constitutional reforms, the great majority of these bills originated, at least formally, in the Chamber of Deputies. This pattern continued in the 57th Legislature, when the executive branch sponsored only 2 of the 169 constitutional reforms considered in the lower chamber. Because constitutional amendments require a two-thirds majority in both the lower and

58 Nonetheless, the Chamber of Deputies did in fact amend the first travel request that Zedillo submitted, temporarily deleting some destinations from his itinerary.

59 In comparison, during the 56th Legislature (1991–1994), 64 percent of the bills introduced by deputies were approved without amendment. In the first two years of the 57th Legislature, 66 percent of these bills were amended in committee, 17 percent were amended on the floor of the Chamber, and only 34 percent went unchanged. See Nava Polina, Weldon, and Yáñez López 2000.

60 Several bills were introduced jointly by deputies, senators, and the executive. Many constitutional scholars consider these initiatives (classified here as deputy-sponsored legislation) to have been illegally processed because the congressional rules appear to specify that bills can only be introduced in a chamber by its own members. This rule was unabashedly violated in the 58th Legislature, when senators introduced several dozen revenue bills in the lower chamber.

upper chambers, these reforms are often negotiated among the parties before they are introduced in Congress. Perhaps the parties that are expected to support constitutional amendments sign on from the beginning, thus inhibiting the president from presenting the reform.

Conclusion

Executive-legislative relations in Mexican have undergone substantial change since the mid-1990s. Divided government after 1997 did not bring about a total breakdown in *presidencialismo*, but the old practices of executive domination over the Congress diminished significantly. Most of the president's bills were still approved in the Chamber of Deputies during the 1997–2000 period, but the executive's rate of success was far lower than the historical average.

In the shift in executive-legislative relations that followed the 1997 elections, what explained the relative strength of the executive even as metaconstitutional conditions weakened? Was the president still successful because of these metaconstitutional powers, or did something else better explain the phenomenon? The first condition for metaconstitutional presidentialism was, of course, negated by divided government. Throughout the 1990s, party discipline seemed unreasonably high not only for the PRI but also for all other political parties, at least in comparison with parties in other North American and Latin American countries.[61] Indeed, levels of party cohesion in Mexico during these years more closely resembled European parliamentary systems (Bowler, Farrell, and Katz 1999). As for the unity of president and party leader, President Zedillo certainly tried to avoid using the metaconstitutional powers that other presidents of Mexico enjoyed. Therefore, the third condition for metaconstitutional presidentialism was at least somewhat weakened.

The most dramatic consequence of divided government for executive-legislative relations was that the president sent less legislation to the hostile Chamber of Deputies. He instead delegated bills to PRI deputies or, more likely, sent bills to the more politically congenial Senate – which contributed indirectly to Zedillo's high level of legislative success. If a president sends only routine finance bills and the budget package to the Chamber of Deputies, it is very likely that nearly all of his legislation will get through Congress. In marked contrast, major initiatives such as the post-1995 bank bailout, the creation of a new comptroller's office, and several judicial reform proposals met strong opposition in the lower chamber. These bills would have died had deputies not made meaningful amendments to the original bills.

Legislative procedures also inhibited congressional independence during the 1997–2000 period. It was always procedurally difficult to amend bills on the floor

---

61 Although it is relatively easy to explain the PRI's extraordinary party discipline, it is harder to do so for the other parties. The PAN may have had high discipline because of its relative homogeneity and more closed nominating procedures, but the splits within the PAN during the 57th Legislature were the most dramatic of any party (in a qualitative, not quantitative, sense).

of Mexico's Chamber of Deputies, and reforms adopted in 1997 made it even harder to do so. Amendments are easily made in committee, but the "original sin" of the 57th Legislature was the malapportionment of committee seats. It was not easy for opposition deputies to report out controversial bills when the PRI was united in opposition, and when the opposition did succeed in getting its bills reported out of committee, rookie errors on the floor sometimes torpedoed their efforts. Of course, even when opposition deputies managed to win approval for their legislative initiatives on the floor of the Chamber, the PRI-controlled Senate vetoed the bills.

The 57th Legislature was exuberant in its introduction of new legislation. Mexico had never seen as active a Chamber of Deputies. Ironically, this actually made the Chamber appear inefficient. Deputies significantly increased the numerator (bills approved), but they so flooded the denominator (bills introduced) that the approval rate was low and gave the impression that little was being accomplished. Moreover, by dealing with so many of their own bills, the deputies neglected their responsibilities regarding many of the executive's initiatives. Of course, this is how it should be in a republican system.

A new phase in executive-legislative relations opened with the PRI's historic defeat in the July 2000 presidential election, and the even more plural 58th Legislature marked a (temporary?) end to metaconstitutional *presidencialismo* in Mexico. President Vicente Fox Quesada's (2000–2006) National Action Party held under 42 percent of the seats in the Chamber of Deputies during the 2000–2003 period. Despite its loss of the presidency, the PRI usually had one or two more deputies than the PAN in its Chamber ranks, and its numerical advantage was even greater in the Senate.

Party discipline remained high during the 58th Legislature, with the PAN showing the highest levels of cohesion (above 97 percent as of December 2002) among the three main parties represented in the Chamber. Without the benefit of a *priísta* president to maintain discipline, the cohesion of the highly fractious PRI declined to approximately 95 percent. The PRD's cohesion matched that of the PRI during most of the 58th Legislature. Therefore, the second condition for metaconstitutional presidentialism continued to hold – though the PRI's and PAN's roles were reversed.

The third condition was also highly questioned. Certainly neither Fox nor the *panistas* considered the president to be the PAN's *jefe máximo*, and party discipline was coordinated through the party's national executive committee rather than the Ministry of the Interior or the president's office. Press reports often exaggerated, however, the real ideological and programmatic differences that existed between President Fox and the PAN's congressional delegations. In practice, most PAN deputies and senators supported the president, and Fox himself (if not his entire cabinet) was reliably *panista*.

Therefore, the first and third conditions for metaconstitutional *presidencialismo* were severely weakened after 2000, with quite remarkable consequences. Through December 2002, the success rate for executive-sponsored bills submitted to the

Chamber of Deputies fell to under 86 percent,[62] and less than one-quarter of all legislation approved by the lower chamber was sponsored by the executive branch. Indeed, nearly every single bill from the executive that could be amended was modified either in committee or on the floor in either the Chamber of Deputies or the Senate.[63] For their part, deputies were more active than ever, introducing 986 bills in the first 28 months of the 58th Legislature. About one-fifth of the bills introduced by the PAN and the PRD were approved, while approximately 15 percent of the PRI's bills were passed.

The great test for *presidencialismo* in Mexico lies with future election results. If the president's party does not have a majority in the Chamber of Deputies, then the pattern established between 1997 and 2003 will continue (not all of the executive's bills will be approved, most will be substantially modified, and deputies will pass much of their own legislation). However, if the president's party wins a majority of seats in the lower chamber, then a future president might have the legislative success of Salinas or of Zedillo between 1994 and 1997. Or has the principle of separation of powers taken hold so firmly in Mexico that even a Chamber of Deputies in which the president's party holds a majority will not automatically approve everything that the executive sends its way?

References

Bowler, Shaun, David M. Farrell, and Richard S. Katz. 1999. *Party Discipline and Parliamentary Government.* Columbus: Ohio State University Press.

Brady, David, Joseph Cooper, and Patricia A. Hurley. 1979. "The Decline of Party in the U.S. House of Representatives, 1887–1968," *Legislative Studies Quarterly* 4 (3): 381–408.

Burgoa, Ignacio. 1994. *Derecho constitucional mexicano.* 9th ed. Mexico City: Porrúa.

Cámara de Diputados. 1997–2000. *Diario de los Debates de la H. Cámara de Diputados, LVII Legislatura.* Mexico City: Cámara de Diputados.

Carpizo, Jorge. 1978. *El presidencialismo mexicano.* Mexico City: Siglo Veintiuno.

Carpizo, Jorge, ed. 1988. *El sistema presidencial mexicano (algunas reflexiones).* Mexico City: Instituto de Investigaciones Legislativas, Universidad Nacional Autónoma de México.

Casar, María Amparo. 1998. "Executive-Legislative Relations: The Case of Mexico." Working Paper #84. Mexico City: División de Estudios Políticos, Centro de Investigación y Docencia Económicas.

Córdova, Arnaldo. 1995. *La Revolución en crisis: la aventura del maximato.* Mexico City: Cal y Arena.

Cornelius, Wayne A. 1973. "Nation Building, Participation, and Distribution: The Politics of Social Reform under Cárdenas." In *Crisis, Choice, and Change: Historical Studies in Political Development,* edited by Gabriel A. Almond, Scott C. Flanagan, and Robert J. Mundt. Boston: Little, Brown.

---

62 Although certainly low by historical standards, this rate was perhaps not so bad given the PAN's minority status in the Chamber.

63 This statement does not refer to travel authorizations. However, in April 2002 opposition parties in the Senate rejected the president's request to travel to Canada and the United States – the first time that this had occurred in either chamber.

Cosío Villegas, Daniel. 1973. *El sistema político mexicano.* Mexico City: Joaquín Ortiz.

Cox, Gary W., and Mathew D. McCubbins. 1993. *Legislative Leviathan: Party Government in the House.* Berkeley: University of California Press.

Garrido, Luis Javier. 1982. *El partido de la revolución institucionalizada: la formación del nuevo estado en México (1928–1945).* Mexico City: Siglo Veintiuno.

———. 1989. "The Crisis of Presidencialismo." In *Mexico's Alternative Political Futures,* edited by Wayne A. Cornelius, Judith Gentleman, and Peter H. Smith. La Jolla: Center for U.S.–Mexican Studies, University of California, San Diego.

Gómez Tagle, Silvia. 1997. *La transición inconclusa: treinta años de elecciones en México.* Mexico City: El Colegio de México.

González Casanova, Pablo. 1965. *La democracia en México.* Mexico City: Era.

Goodspeed, Stephen Spencer. 1947. "The Role of the Chief Executive in Mexico: Politics, Powers, and Administration." Ph.D. diss., University of California.

Heller, William B., and Jeffrey A. Weldon. 2001. "Legislative Rules and Voting Stability in the Mexican Chamber of Deputies." Paper presented at the annual meeting of the Midwest Political Science Association, Chicago, April.

IFE (Instituto Federal Electoral). n.d. *Estadísticas de las elecciones federales de 1997.* Diskettes. Mexico City: IFE.

Lujambio, Alonso. 1995. *Federalismo y Congreso en el cambio político de México.* Mexico City: Universidad Nacional Autónoma de México.

———. 1999. "Entre el pasado y el futuro: la ciencia política y el Poder Legislativo en México." In *La ciencia política en México,* edited by Mauricio Merino. Mexico City: Consejo Nacional para la Cultura y las Artes / Fondo de Cultura Económica.

———. 2000. "Adiós a la excepcionalidad: régimen presidencial y gobierno dividido en México," *Este País* 107 (February): 2–16.

Martínez Gallardo, Cecilia. 1998. "Las legislaturas pequeñas: la evolución del sistema de comisiones en la Cámara de Diputados de México, 1824–2000." *Licenciatura* thesis, Instituto Tecnológico Autónomo de México.

Marván Laborde, Ignacio. 2002. "Ejecutivo fuerte y división de poderes: el primer ensayo de esa utopía de la Revolución Mexicana." In *Gobernar sin mayoría: México 1867–1997,* edited by María Amparo Casar and Ignacio Marván Laborde. Mexico City: Taurus / Centro de Investigación y Docencia Económicas.

Medín, Tzvi. 1982. *El minimato presidencial: historia política del maximato.* Mexico City: Era.

Medina, Luis. 1978. *Evolución electoral en el México contemporáneo.* Mexico City: Comisión Federal Electoral.

Meyer, Jean. 2002. "La diarquía (1924–1928)." In *Gobernar sin mayoría: México 1867–1997,* edited by María Amparo Casar and Ignacio Marván Laborde. Mexico City: Taurus / Centro de Investigación y Docencia Económicas.

Meyer, Lorenzo. 1978. *El conflicto social y los gobiernos del maximato.* Vol. 13 of *Historia de la Revolución Mexicana.* Mexico City: El Colegio de México.

Meyer, Lorenzo, Rafael Segovia, and Alejandra Lajous. 1978. *Los inicios de la institucionalización: la política del maximato.* Vol. 12 of *Historia de la Revolución Mexicana.* Mexico City: El Colegio de México.

Molinar Horcasitas, Juan, and Jeffrey A. Weldon. 1990. "Elecciones de 1988 en México: crisis del autoritarismo." *Revista Mexicana de Sociología* 52 (4): 229–62.

———. 2001. "Reforming Electoral Systems in Mexico." In *Mixed-Member Electoral Systems: The Best of Both Worlds?,* edited by Matthew Soberg Shugart and Martin P. Wattenberg. New York: Oxford University Press.

———. n.d. *Procedimientos legislativos de la Cámara de Diputados, 1917–1964.* Series I, vol. 1, book

2 of *Enciclopedia parlamentaria de México.* Mexico City: Instituto de Investigaciones Legislativas, Cámara de Diputados. Forthcoming.

Nacif, Benito. 1996. "Political Careers, Political Ambitions, and Career Goals." Working Paper #51. Mexico City: División de Estudios Políticos, Centro de Investigación y Docencia Económicas.

Nava Polina, María del Carmen, Jeffrey A. Weldon, and Jorge Yáñez López. 2000. "Cambio político, presidencialismo y producción legislativa en la Cámara de Diputados." In *La Cámara de Diputados en México,* edited by Germán Pérez Fernández del Castillo. Mexico City: Cámara de Diputados / Facultad Latinoamericana de Ciencias Sociales–México. Forthcoming.

Paoli Bolio, Francisco José, ed. n.d. *La Cámara de Diputados en la LVII Legislatura.* Mexico City: Cámara de Diputados.

Poole, Keith T., and Howard Rosenthal. 1997. *Congress: A Political-Economic History of Roll Call Voting.* New York: Oxford University Press.

Rice, Stuart A. 1928. *Quantitative Methods in Politics.* New York: Alfred A. Knopf.

Rossel, Mauricio. 2000. *Congreso y gobernabilidad en México.* Mexico City: Cámara de Diputados / Porrúa.

Santos, Gonzalo N. 1984. *Memorias.* Mexico City: Grijalbo.

Tena Ramírez, Felipe. 1985. *Derecho constitucional mexicano.* 21st ed. Mexico City: Porrúa.

Ugalde, Luis Carlos. 2000. *The Mexican Congress: Old Player, New Power.* Washington, D.C.: Center for Strategic and International Studies.

Weldon, Jeffrey A. 1997a. "The Political Sources of *Presidencialismo* in Mexico." In *Presidentialism and Democracy in Latin America,* edited by Scott Mainwaring and Matthew Soberg Shugart. Cambridge: Cambridge University Press.

———. 1997b. "El crecimiento de los poderes metaconstitucionales de Cárdenas y Ávila Camacho: su desempeño legislativo, 1934–1946," *Diálogo y Debate* 1 (1): 11–28.

———. 1997c. "El presidente como legislador, 1917–1934." In *El Poder Legislativo en las décadas revolucionarias, 1908–1934,* edited by Pablo Atilio Piccato Rodríguez. Series I, vol. 1, book 3 of *Enciclopedia parlamentaria de México.* Mexico City: Instituto de Investigaciones Legislativas, Cámara de Diputados.

———. 1998. "Committee Power in the Mexican Chamber of Deputies." Paper presented at the international congress of the Latin American Studies Association, Chicago, September.

———. 2002a. "Factores institucionales y políticos de la disciplina partidaria en la Cámara de Diputados en México, 1998–2002." Paper presented at the Latin American Congress of Political Science, Salamanca, Spain, July.

———. 2002b. "The Legal and Partisan Framework of the Legislative Delegation of the Budget in Mexico." In *Legislative Politics in Latin America,* edited by Scott Morgenstern and Benito Nacif. Cambridge: Cambridge University Press.

Weldon, Jeffrey A., and Jorge Yáñez López. 1999. "Avanzan comisiones; se acentúa inigualdad," *Reforma* (Mexico City), June 17.

6

Democratization, Judicial and Law Enforcement Institutions, and the Rule of Law in Mexico

Beatriz Magaloni and Guillermo Zepeda

Important institutional innovations in the judicial sphere accompanied Mexico's process of democratization. In particular, a constitutional reform in 1994 established a more independent and powerful Supreme Court that can effectively exercise a veto in the legislative process (through its power of judicial review) and arbitrate conflicts among different branches and levels of government. The reform reduced the number of justices from twenty-five to eleven and replaced the system of lifetime appointments with fifteen-year terms. The president nominates justices, but they must be approved by a two-thirds vote of the federal Senate.[1] Thus, so long as the president's party lacks a two-thirds majority in the Senate, this new institutional arrangement limits presidential influence upon the composition of the federal judiciary.

The 1994 constitutional reform also introduced two major changes in judicial procedure. Through so-called constitutional actions, the Supreme Court now has the authority to interpret the constitutionality of laws. Constitutional actions can be promoted by 33 percent of the members of the federal Chamber of Deputies or Senate against a federal law or an international treaty; by 33 percent of the members of a state legislature against a state law; by the federal attorney general (Procurador General) against a federal or state law or an international treaty; or by the leadership of any political party officially registered before the Federal Electoral

The authors wish to thank the Tinker Foundation for financial support for this project and researchers at the Centro de Investigación para el Desarrollo, A.C. (CIDAC) for their comments and suggestions.

1 The 1994 constitutional reform also established a controversial Judicial Board (Consejo de la Judicatura) with responsibility for administering the federal judiciary and, in particular, selecting judges and overseeing judicial promotions. Prior to 1994, the Supreme Court was nominally in charge of promotions, but because the president had a strong, unilateral influence over the Court's composition, the executive was also able to shape indirectly promotions within the federal judicial branch (Magaloni 2003).

The new Judicial Board is comprised of seven members. Four are nominated by the federal judiciary (the president of the Supreme Court also serves as president of the Board), two by the Senate, and one by the president. After some initial difficulties, the Supreme Court decided to acquire jurisdiction over the Board's decisions.

Institute against a federal electoral law.[2] The Supreme Court's decisions have general effects beyond the individual case under consideration (that is, they are immediately binding in legal terms) only when eight justices vote in favor of a ruling and when the decision involves questions of constitutional interpretation.

Second, so-called constitutional controversies permit the Supreme Court to adjudicate conflicts among different branches or levels of government with respect to the constitutionality of their acts. Thus, the Court now has the authority to resolve conflicts between the executive and the legislative branches; between the federal government and one or more states; and between governors and municipal governments. Most of the constitutional controversies presented before the Court thus far have involved disputes between municipal authorities and governors of different partisan affiliations. The Court is, then, emerging as a key arbiter in the practice of Mexican federalism.[3]

In light of a long tradition of judicial subservience in Mexico dating to the turn of the twentieth century, the establishment of a Supreme Court that serves as a true constitutional tribunal and arbiter of federalism certainly constitutes an important change.[4] Yet as significant as the 1994 constitutional reform was, it has thus far had limited consequences for citizens' everyday lives. Indeed, with only a few exceptions, since the mid-1990s the Court has mainly ruled upon issues that are far removed from the concerns of the ordinary citizenry. For example, the overwhelming majority of the constitutional actions decided by the Court thus far have dealt with constitutional interpretations of electoral laws, a highly salient topic for political parties but not necessarily for ordinary citizens.

More generally, it is important to note that, under the terms of the 1994 constitutional reform, individual citizens have only limited direct access to the Supreme Court. They cannot initiate constitutional actions, although citizen-promoted cases can still reach the Court because it retains the right of *certiorari* (the right to reexamine cases first considered in lower-level federal courts). This is one reason why it will be some time before the effects of these Supreme Court and procedural reforms recast the criteria of judicial interpretation employed by lower-level courts. A stronger and more independent Supreme Court certainly moves the Mexican judiciary in the right direction, but a fundamental transformation of prevailing practices in the federal judiciary and a significant reform of state-level judiciaries (where most civil and criminal cases are heard) and law enforcement institutions

2 Local political parties can also promote an action of unconstitutionality against state-level electoral laws.

Judicial review of electoral laws was not originally part of the 1994 constitutional reform. This provision was added in 1996.

3 The Supreme Court is also responsible for ruling on conflicting interpretative criteria established by the federal courts of appeal (*tribunales colegiados*).

4 For an analysis of the Supreme Court reform and its significance for the system of checks and balances and federalism in Mexico, see Magaloni and Sánchez 2001 and Magaloni 2003.

(public prosecutors, agents responsible for investigating crime, and the police) are still pending.

Indeed, the most pressing public demand regarding the Mexican legal system involves rising public insecurity and state authorities' failure to investigate, prosecute, and punish crime effectively. As in other Latin American countries, democratization in Mexico was accompanied by a weakening of the state as an enforcer of contracts and rights and by a consequent increase in public insecurity.

In order to assess the state's performance in an area of vital concern to Mexican citizens, this chapter explores the relationship between democratization, crime, and the rule of law during the late 1990s. In the analysis that follows, we seek answers to two key questions. First, was the wave of crime and violence that Mexico experienced during the 1990s the product of democratization? Some observers have argued that the increased incidence of crime resulted from the dismantling of authoritarian rule and the loosening of societal controls. An adequate assessment of this issue can only come from systematic cross-sectional analysis, and so we examine democratization and crime in a broadly comparative context. We demonstrate through econometric analysis that what drove higher crime rates in emerging democracies such as Mexico was not political change per se, but rather two other processes associated with it – poor economic performance and growing income disparities.

Second, to what extent was the higher incidence of crime in Mexico during the 1990s the result of failures by judicial and law enforcement institutions? In order to address this question, we investigate the geography of crime across different Mexican states and, again through econometric analysis, test the extent to which different aspects of institutional capacity, political change (partisan alternation in power), and socioeconomic indicators drive crime rates. We show that poor performance by state-level judicial and law enforcement institutions was in fact a significant factor in rising public insecurity during the late 1990s, and we argue that fundamental reforms in this area should hold a high place on the public policy agenda facing Mexico's new democracy.

Our empirical analysis focuses upon the performance of law enforcement institutions at the state level rather than at the federal level. We take this approach because, in Mexico's federal system, states are responsible for prosecuting and punishing the overwhelming majority of crimes. Federalism, however, poses a major challenge in this area because policies to combat crime cannot be designed and implemented from the top downward. Rather, successful action in this area requires a coordinated effort among the states.

Democratization, Economic Crisis, and Crime in Latin America

Not only does Latin America have the highest rates of homicide in the world, but, together with sub-Saharan Africa, the region experienced the greatest increase in criminal behavior during the 1990s. Measured in terms of the rate of intentional

Table 6.1: **Homicide Rates in Selected Latin American Countries, 1970s/1980s and 1980s/ 1990s** (homicides per 100,000 inhabitants)

Country	Late 1970s/Early 1980s	Late 1980s/Early 1990s
Colombia	20.5	89.5
Brazil	11.5	19.7
Mexico	18.2	19.0
Venezuela	11.7	15.2
Trinidad and Tobago	2.1	12.6
Peru	2.4	11.5
Panama	2.1	10.9
Ecuador	6.4	10.3
United States	10.7	10.1
Argentina	3.9	4.8
Costa Rica	5.7	4.1
Uruguay	2.6	4.4
Paraguay	5.1	4.0
Chile	2.6	3.0

Sources: Ayres 1998 and Zepeda 2001 (for Mexico in 1997).

homicide, Colombia, El Salvador, Brazil, and Mexico ranked as the four most dangerous places to live in the region (Fajnzylber, Lederman, and Loayza 1998; Ayres 1998).

Table 6.1 displays data concerning the frequency of homicide per 100,000 inhabitants in selected Western Hemisphere countries in the late 1970s/early 1980s and in the late 1980s/early 1990s. Except for Costa Rica, Paraguay, and the United States, this form of violent crime increased throughout the region. The rate of increase was particularly dramatic in Colombia, Peru, Panama, and Brazil. In Mexico, the murder rate did not grow significantly over this period, but (as indicated below) the incidence of robbery did. The reasons for this widespread explosion in violent crime are not altogether well understood.

Since the early 1980s, Latin America has undergone two fundamental transformations. First, in the years after 1982, there was a sharp economic decline followed by structural adjustment and market-oriented reforms. These processes increased income inequality in the region (IADB 1999). Second, most Latin American countries also experienced transitions from authoritarian rule to more democratic forms of governance – even though in some counties (Peru and Venezuela, for example) there was a reversion toward authoritarianism. The near-simultaneity of these changes has led some observers to conclude that democracy *causes* an increase in public insecurity. In contrast, we argue that it was the correlation between democratization, on the one hand, and economic collapse and rising income disparities, on the other, that produced the empirical association between democratic political change and the increase in violent crime.

Table 6.2: **Determinants of the Rate of Intentional Homicide in Fifty-Two Countries**

	Model 1		Model 2	
Independent Variable	Coefficient	Standard Error	Coefficient	Standard Error
Constant	.18***	.07	−.02	.09
Income (per capita GDP)	−.02**	.01	−.01	.01
Democracy	.05**	.02	.01	.02
Democracy x Democracy	−.004*	.002	−.001	.001
Inequality			.02***	.003
Average rate of growth (1990–1997)			−.01***	.003
	N=46		N=42	
	Adjusted R²=.18		Adjusted R²=.77	

Sources: Burnham and Burnham 1997; Heston, Summers, and Aten 2002; POLITY98 data base.
Note: See the accompanying text for the countries included in this analysis.
*   Significant at the .10 confidence level
**   Significant at the .05 confidence level
*** Significant at the .01 confidence level

To determine whether crime was a response to the dismantling of authoritarianism and democratization, or a result of economic collapse and rising income disparities, we performed regression (ordinary least squares) analyses on a data set compiled by the United Nations on crime rates in fifty-two countries.[5] The measure of crime was the average number of intentional homicides per 100,000 inhabitants between 1995 and 1997, as reported in the sixth United Nations World Crime Survey. The explanatory variables employed in this analysis were the level of democracy (as measured in the POLITY 98 data base),[6] income inequality (defined as the ratio of the income of the richest twenty percent of the population to the income of the poorest twenty percent), average rates of growth in gross domestic product (GDP) during the 1990s, and GDP per capita.[7] Our hypothesis is that if an empirical relationship exists between the level of democracy and the rate of violent

5 Unfortunately, Chile is the only Latin American country included in the United Nations data base on comparative crime rates. The other countries are: Albania, Armenia, Australia, Azerbaijan, Bahamas, Belarus, Belgium, Bulgaria, China, Croatia, Cyprus, Czech Republic, Denmark, Estonia, Fiji, Finland, Germany, Greece, Hong Kong, Hungary, India, Ireland, Israel, Jordan, Kuwait, Kyrgyzstan, Latvia, Lesotho, Lithuania, Malaysia, Moldova, Norway, Poland, Portugal, Republic of Korea, Romania, Russian Federation, Singapore, Slovakia, Slovenia, South Africa, Spain, Sri Lanka, Sweden, Switzerland, Thailand, Turkey, Uganda, Ukraine, United Kingdom, and Zimbabwe.

6 The POLITY Project is a widely used source of cross-national, longitudinal data on the authority characteristics of political systems, including different regimes' place on an authoritarianism-democracy continuum. For overviews of the project, see Gurr 1974 and Gleditsch and Ward 1997.

7 The economic data are drawn from Heston, Summers, and Aten 2002.

crime, it is because of an intervening structural variable that reflects the socio-economic characteristics of some democratizing countries. In other words, we believe that the observed association between democracy and violent crime is spurious.

The results of this analysis are reported in table 6.2. In the first model, we explored the impact of income (per capita GDP) and democracy on homicide rates without controlling for the rate of economic growth and the level of income inequality. In the analysis, the democracy variable was squared in order to test the hypothesis that the relationship between the level of democracy and the rate of violent crime takes the form of an inverted U (that is, higher crime rates should be observed at middle levels of democracy or in democratizing countries). The signs of the democracy and the democracy-squared variables should, therefore, be positive and negative, respectively.

The results indicate that there is indeed a correlation between democratization and the incidence of violent crime, and that the effect of democracy is curvilinear. There was less crime in authoritarian countries (those with low values on the democracy index) and in democratic nations (those with higher values) during the 1990s. Medium levels of democracy, such as those found in newly democratizing countries, were associated with more crime.

Table 6.2 also reports the results of a second regression analysis, in which we controlled for the socioeconomic variables mentioned above. In this analysis, the effect of democracy on crime disappeared. From these results we conclude that what appears to produce higher crime rates in newly established democracies is not political change per se, but rather the socioeconomic conditions associated with it. In particular, most of these so-called Third Wave democracies came about as a result of economic collapse (Haggard and Kaufman 1995; Geddes 1999).[8] Consequently, economic conditions have a highly significant effect upon the incidence of violent crime; indeed, the less a country grew during the 1990s, the higher its crime rate. Income inequality also had the predicted effect; greater inequality was associated with more crime.

These are only tentative findings because our analysis was limited to a subset of countries for which comparable crime rate data were available.[9] Yet the evidence indicates that part of the dilemma in building the rule of law in democratizing countries stems from the structural context (namely, poor economic performance and increased income disparities) in which democratization has taken place.

Nevertheless, as we seek to demonstrate in this chapter for the Mexican case, rising crime rates are also the product of state failure. Many judicial and law enforcement institutions – including courts, prosecutors' offices, and the police – are incapable of detecting and punishing crime. In fact, in some instances these

---

8 Samuel P. Huntington (1991) argued that a "third wave" of democratization began in 1974.

9 In future work, we plan to increase the number of countries included in the regression and perform an analysis of differences (namely, what factors cause an increase in crime rates rather than the absolute incidence of crime).

institutions operate as authoritarian enclaves because, accustomed to enforcing laws in authoritarian settings, they cannot meet their obligations under more open political conditions. They either violate individual rights when enforcing the law, or they allow crimes to go unpunished.

The Criminal Justice System in Mexico

In Mexico, local judiciaries, local prosecutors' offices, and the police are responsible for detecting, prosecuting, and punishing most crimes. Yet the performance of judicial and law enforcement institutions at the state level varies widely. In some states, the judiciary is extremely subservient to politicians, and in de facto terms there is no separation of powers. Local public prosecutors control significant decisions in the most important criminal trials, and they exercise strong influence over judicial promotions. In other states, the judiciary is more independent, but it is poorly financed and understaffed. In only a very few states (Aguascalientes, for example) is there a well-functioning judiciary.[10]

The federal judiciary also plays an important role in criminal trials because it has jurisdiction over federal crimes (those associated with drug-trafficking, for instance). In addition, through its review of requests for injunctions (*amparo* proceedings), the federal courts of appeal (*tribunales colegiados*) review the decisions of state-level superior courts (*tribunales superiores de justicia*). This means that, as a practical matter, many criminal cases wind up being examined by the federal judiciary.

Furthermore, federal courts of appeal and the federal district courts are responsible – again, through amparo proceedings – for judging the legality and constitutionality of laws and other governmental actions that directly affect individual rights. Federal courts have interpreted their tremendously important roles in a very narrow way, generally limiting themselves to enforcing the principle of legality rather than interpreting laws, lower courts' decisions, or governmental actions in light of the Constitution. In other words, the federal judiciary has conceived of itself merely as an agent of the politicians who enact laws. Indeed, even in cases in which federal courts do question the constitutionality of laws, amparo decisions concerning a law's constitutionality do not have general effects. Rather, the decision is binding only in the specific case before the court, and it does not establish a judicial precedent for future cases.[11]

One might anticipate that the federal courts' heretofore limited influence will eventually grow because of the important process of judicial reform initiated in Mexico in the mid-1990s. A Supreme Court that more actively exercises its role in constitutional interpretation should have a significant demonstration effect in this regard, and the influence that partisan political actors formerly exercised over judicial nominations and promotions will decline. Yet the prevailing criteria for

---

10 A systematic assessment of the state-level judicial system is beyond the scope of this chapter.
11 This is the so-called Otero clause (*cláusula* Otero) in Mexican law.

judicial interpretation are still extremely formalistic. For example, federal courts dismiss most amparo suits on the basis of highly formalistic arguments (Rubio, Magaloni, and Jaime 1994), which partly explains why most complaints of human rights violations filed against prosecutors' offices and the police are heard by human rights commissions rather than the federal judiciary.

It is important to reemphasize, however, that local public prosecutors and the police play the most important part in criminal cases because the law grants them tremendous discretion both in the period before a trial takes place and during the trial itself.

The public prosecutor's office (*ministerio público*, MP) is responsible for investigating and prosecuting crimes. Governors appoint prosecutors, who then freely appoint and remove MP agents. These agents serve various functions in Mexico's criminal justice system. First of all, they are in charge of investigating a crime when one is reported. The MP has a monopoly over investigative and prosecutorial actions, meaning that if for some reason it refuses to investigate a crime, the victim has virtually no legal recourse because no other authority can compel the MP to initiate an investigation. Federal courts can now review the MP's formal decision not to prosecute.[12] However, they lack jurisdiction over the broader investigative and prosecutorial process, which in practice means that if the MP simply decides to file away a crime report (which, as we will see below, constitutes its most frequent course of action), the victim is left without any legal options.

Prosecutors' enormous legal discretion promotes arbitrariness. Indeed, failures by the MP to investigate and prosecute crimes constituted the most common form of human rights violation in Mexico in the late 1990s. In 1998, for example, the National Human Rights Commission (CNDH) received approximately 50,000 complaints of human rights abuses. Two-thirds of these complaints were related to the operation of the criminal justice system, and nearly fifty percent of the recommendations issued by the CNDH were directed against prosecutors' offices (Zepeda 2001).

Once MP agents identify a suspect and decide to prosecute, judicial authorities must issue an arrest warrant in order to bring him or her before a court of law. If the police arrested the accused in the act of committing a crime, they must bring the suspect before a judge within forty-eight hours. The judge then decides whether there are sufficient grounds to try the suspect on the basis of the evidence presented by the prosecutor (*averiguación previa*). Within a seventy-two-hour period, the judge must issue an order remanding the accused to trial (*auto de formal prisión*). Unless the suspect has been released on bail, the trial takes place while the accused is in jail.

12 In 1995 President Ernesto Zedillo Ponce de León (1994–2000) introduced a reform that permitted citizens to seek a court injunction against the MP's decision not to prosecute (*ejercer la acción penal*). However, it is still too soon to judge the effectiveness of this measure. Part of the problem lies in the fact that the Zedillo reform granted very limited jurisdiction to the judiciary in such matters.

Agents of the MP are also responsible for representing the victim(s) during a trial. Victims of crime cannot appoint their own attorneys to defend their interests, nor do they have any formal rights during these proceedings. Therefore, if the MP does a poor job in handling the case, or if it decides to desist in the prosecution, those most directly affected have no legal option.

This does not mean that trial proceedings are biased against victims. In fact, nine out of ten suspects brought to trial are convicted (Zepeda 2001). The extremely high levels of impunity found in Mexico are the result not of a lenient judiciary, but rather the product of failures on the part of law enforcement institutions. The root problem is that only about 3 percent of criminal suspects ever end up before a court of law.

High conviction rates by the judiciary are not that uncommon in other countries. What is striking about judicial proceedings in Mexico is that criminal cases are largely decided upon the basis of what transpires before the trial takes place, during the investigative and prosecutorial phases. The small proportion of suspects brought before a court of law are those who the police caught in the actual act of committing a crime (*en flagrante delicto*) or who were unable to bribe authorities in prosecutors' offices to secure their release.

Public defenders assigned to the courts legally represent the overwhelming majority of suspects brought to trial. This means that, as a practical matter, most defendants are unable to offer testimonial or forensic evidence beyond that which MP agents gather during their investigation and present at the outset of the trial. As a consequence, judges issue their rulings based largely upon the prosecutor's claims. The MP thus plays the central role in the criminal justice system – as investigator, prosecutor, and a key actor in trial proceedings.

In the sections below, we develop and apply a methodology for assessing the performance of these judicial and law enforcement institutions.

Crime and Judicial Performance in Mexico During the 1990s

The Geography of Crime

During the 1990s, crime and violence moved to the forefront of both public and policy makers' attention. In the quarterly surveys conducted since March 1998 by *Reforma* newspaper, some 60 percent of respondents have consistently identified crime, violence, and public insecurity as the main challenges facing Mexico City. Indeed, between 65 and 80 percent of respondents have regularly indicated that they were afraid to ride public buses, take taxis, walk the streets, go to the bank, or use automatic bank teller machines. Moreover, most citizens believe that crime and insecurity are partly the product of police corruption and the inefficiency of those public institutions responsible for prosecuting and punishing criminals.[13]

---

13 In the same *Reforma* surveys, close to 60 percent of respondents have stated that they believe that police forces are corrupt, and 30 percent have expressed the view that the "overwhelming majority of policemen are committing the crimes."

Figure 6.1: **Crimes Reported to State-Level Public Prosecutors' Offices in Mexico, 1991–2000**

Source: Zepeda 2001, with data from the Instituto Nacional de Estadística, Geografía e Informática (INEGI).

Although President Ernesto Zedillo Ponce de León (1994–2000) proposed a series of policy initiatives to combat crime, none of them was notably effective. His "National Program for Public Safety, 1995–2000" allocated emergency funding to state governments that had to be devoted entirely to public safety programs,[14] and it sought to create better instruments for screening, monitoring, and sanctioning police corruption and the so-called infiltration of criminals into the police. In addition, Zedillo reformed important aspects of Mexico's criminal justice system, increased legal sanctions, and involved the army directly in the fight against crime. Even so, crime rates were barely affected.

Figure 6.1 reports the trend in crimes reported to state-level public prosecutors' offices between 1991 and 2000. There was a 90-percent increase in reported crime rates over this period, with a sharp jump after the 1994–1995 financial crisis and a monotonically rising trend until 1997. Crime rates did not continue rising after 1997, but neither was the trend reversed. The Mexican case thus corroborates what Fajnzylber, Lederman, and Loayza (1998: 26) found in their large cross-national study of crime in Latin America and the Caribbean: after an initial shock, an increase in crime is felt for a long period, suggesting that countries can be engulfed in crime waves that are hard to turn around.

Although crime is a national problem in Mexico, some states and cities are particularly affected by it. For example, robbery rates are high in big cities, while homicide is a severe problem in poor areas. In order to delineate more clearly the

14 After 1999, these funds became a permanent transfer from the federal government to states.

geography of crime in Mexico, table 6.3 presents several different measures of the phenomenon. The average number of crimes per 100,000 inhabitants reported to local prosecutors' offices between 1996 and 2000 (column 2) provides a sense of the longer-term trend with regard to public insecurity in the states. Table 6.3 further reports the number of robberies, homicides, and total crimes per 100,000 inhabitants over the 1996–2000 period.

The states with the highest incidence of robbery are Baja California, the Federal District (Mexico City), Baja California Sur, Quintana Roo, and Chihuahua. Note, however, that these states are not those where murder is most prevalent. Murder is an acute problem in the poorer states of Guerrero, Chiapas, Oaxaca, the State of México, and Michoacán. Many of these killings are assassinations carried out in the context of political conflicts between peasants and landlords, powerful local political bosses, and their paramilitary organizations. The incidence of robbery is highly correlated (0.80) with the total number of crimes reported, but murder is a crime of a different nature. It does not correlate closely with other crimes.

Table 6.3 also reports the estimated frequency of unreported crime (the so-called black number, or *cifra negra*) for each state, data that were drawn from the first victims survey conducted by the Citizens' Institute on Insecurity (Instituto Ciudadano Sobre Inseguridad, A.C.). On average, 61 percent of all crimes in Mexico remain unreported, which means that statistics on reported crime vastly underestimate the actual level of public insecurity.

State-level estimates of unreported crime are useful for comparing the propensity in different areas to report crimes. The inhabitants of the Federal District head the list; they fail to report 76 percent of the crimes that actually occur. The State of México (73 percent), Guerrero (72 percent), and Morelos (72 percent) follow. In marked contrast, the inhabitants of Baja California Sur show the highest propensity to report crimes; only some 43 percent of crimes in the state go unreported.

What factors account for differences in the propensity to report crimes? At a cross-national level, there is a high correlation between citizens' perceptions of the effectiveness of law enforcement institutions and their tendency to report crimes (Kangaspunta, Joutsen, and Ollus 1998). In a national victims survey conducted in Mexico in 2001, the principal reasons given for not reporting a crime were: "a waste of time," 47 percent; "the tardiness of procedures before the Ministerio Público," 11 percent; and "fear," 9 percent (Zinser 2001).[15] Thus, state-level differences in unreported crime partly reflect citizens' distrust of law enforcement institutions.

Unreported crime data for 2001 were employed to estimate an average total crime rate for each of Mexico's 31 states and the Federal District (table 6.3, column 6). The index of the incidence of crime reported in table 6.3 (column 7) is the average of

---

15 In the United States, the main reason for not reporting crime is that the object was recovered or the criminal did not succeed. Only 2.8 percent of victims fail to report a crime because they believe the police are not effective, and only 1.2 percent fail to do so because of fear. See the U.S. Department of Justice's 1999 victims survey at www.ojp.usdoj.gov/bjs/pub/pdf/ cvus99.pdf.

Table 6.3: **The Geography of Crime in Mexico, 1996–2000** (crimes per 100,000 inhabitants)

State	Total Reported Crimes	Robberies	Murders	Unreported Crimes[a]	Estimated Total[b]	Crime Index[c]	Crime Group Number[d]
Guerrero	1,002.8	322.2	45.1	72	2,578.7	64.9	4
Distrito Federal	2,694.0	1,684.8	10.3	76	8,531.0	61.4	4
Morelos	2,015.9	693.5	19.7	72	5,183.7	52.2	4
State of México	1,515.3	612.2	25.5	73	4,097.0	52.1	4
Oaxaca	1,216.7	256.8	28.8	64	2,163.0	44.4	4
Chiapas	893.4	204.5	32.5	61	1,397.4	44.0	4
Tabasco	2,534.1	644.2	12.7	65	4,706.1	41.6	4
Chihuahua	2,408.8	958.4	17.9	60	3,613.2	40.9	4
Colima	2,070.3	579.4	20.3	54	2,430.4	36.6	3
Quintana Roo	2,446.3	1,042.3	11.0	63	4,165.3	36.6	3
Michoacán	868.8	288.9	24.3	55	1,061.9	33.1	3
Yucatán	3,028.7	716.3	1.5	63	5,157.0	31.9	3
Tamaulipas	1,557.2	614.2	15.7	61	2,435.6	31.6	3
Baja California	4,671.6	1,945.4	18.5	50	4,671.6	31.5	3
San Luis Potosí	1,679.8	384.5	10.6	64	2,986.4	29.2	3
Campeche	1,520.6	398.0	9.6	69	3,384.6	28.3	3
Sinaloa	728.0	403.2	18.0	63	1,239.6	27.2	2
Puebla	1,049.8	358.4	14.3	64	1,866.4	26.8	2
Sonora	1,656.0	560.2	14.8	45	1,354.9	24.2	2
Nayarit	916.9	321.1	11.7	67	1,861.5	23.8	2
Durango	1,395.2	418.3	8.6	62	2,276.5	22.8	2
Jalisco	1,434.0	626.2	10.6	55	1,752.6	22.0	2
Nuevo León	1,660.1	515.2	4.5	63	2,826.7	21.5	2
Baja California Sur	3,177.0	1,351.7	8.4	43	2,396.7	21.4	2
Veracruz	900.8	239.4	10.8	63	1,533.8	21.0	1
Tlaxcala	814.1	217.1	13.4	56	1,036.2	20.8	1
Coahuila	1,056.5	410.0	7.2	62	1,723.8	18.1	1
Querétaro	1,543.9	552.0	5.0	58	2,132.0	18.0	1
Guanajuato	1,091.2	344.6	6.5	58	1,506.9	16.0	1
Aguascalientes	1,283.8	444.7	3.7	56	1,634.0	13.7	1
Hidalgo	854.4	230.7	5.7	54	1,003.0	12.1	1
Zacatecas	925.4	275.9	5.1	52	1,002.5	11.5	1

Source: Authors' calculations based upon data from the Centro de Investigación para el Desarrollo, A.C. (CIDAC) and the Instituto Nacional de Estadística, Geografía e Informática (INEGI).
Notes: States are listed in rank order based upon the incidence of crime index (data column 6).
[a] Data concerning unreported crimes are from the national victims survey conducted by the Instituto Ciudadano de Estudios sobre la Inseguridad Pública.
[b] Total crimes are estimated by factoring in estimates of unreported crimes.
[c] The index of the incidence of crime is an average of total estimated crimes plus murder. Each of these values is standardized to a base of 100. Thus, the average counts murder and total crimes equally.
[d] Groups are constructed on the basis of the crime index. Group 4 includes the eight states for which the index is highest; Group 3 includes the next eight highest-ranking states; and so on.

two measures: the estimated total number of crimes per 100,000 inhabitants,[16] and the incidence of murder per 100,000 inhabitants.[17] The index of the incidence of crime thus weights murder equally in order to reflect the relative importance of this form of violent crime. Each of these variables is standardized to a base of 100.

By this index, Guerrero, the Federal District, Morelos, the State of México, Oaxaca, Chiapas, Tabasco, and Chihuahua were the eight states where public insecurity was most acute in the late 1990s. However, these states stood out for somewhat different reasons: Guerrero, Oaxaca, and Chiapas were notable for their murder rate; crimes against property dominated in the Federal District; and Morelos, the State of México, Tabasco, and Chihuahua had above-average measures of *both* robbery and murder. Because we have standardized the variables, the index values can also be employed to compare states. Thus, public insecurity in Chihuahua (with an index value of 40.9) was twice as great as in Tlaxcala (with an index value of 20.8).

Finally, the last column in table 6.3 classifies states into one of four categories, based upon the index described above. The eight states (listed above) in Group 4 were those with the highest incidence of crime in the late 1990s. States in Group 3 also had an incidence of crime above the national mean,[18] while the incidence of crime in those states in Group 2 was below the national average.[19] The states in Group 1 had the lowest levels of public insecurity.[20]

The Performance of State-level Law Enforcement Institutions

How have different Mexican states responded to rising crime rates? Do states devote enough resources to combating crime, and how efficiently do they employ them? What are the chances that a reported crime will be investigated, or that the individual(s) who commit it will be apprehended, prosecuted, and convicted? In order to address these questions, we have constructed a database (based upon information from the National Institute for Statistics, Geography, and Informatics, INEGI) that permits us to judge the effectiveness of state-level criminal justice systems and thereby evaluate the institutional performance of different states' responses to crime.

The first variable we consider in this analysis involves the state-level resources available to investigate and prosecute crime. Our index of resources (table 6.4, column 2) encompasses the total number of *ministerio público* agents per 100,000

16 We exclude murder from the estimated total number of crimes.
17 We do not employ the incidence of robbery (which constitutes about 40 percent of all crime) in the index because it is already encompassed in the measure of total crime.
18 Listed in descending rank order, the other states in Group 3 were Colima, Quintana Roo, Michoacán, Yucatán, Tamaulipas, Baja California, and Campeche.
19 The states in this group were Sinaloa, Puebla, Sonora, Nayarit, Durango, Jalisco, Nuevo León, and Baja California Sur.
20 This group included Veracruz, Tlaxcala, Coahuila, Querétaro, Guanajuato, Aguascalientes, Hidalgo, and Zacatecas.

Table 6.4: **The Performance of Mexican Law Enforcement Institutions, 1996–2000**

State	Index of Resources	Investigative Efficiency	Percent of Arrest Warrants Enforced	Weighted Conviction Rate	Performance Index	Performance Group Number
Baja California Sur	89.6	47.5	16.3	18.0	78.9	4
Coahuila	69.6	46.9	16.1	18.0	72.9	4
Nayarit	73.0	7.5	21.0	26.1	70.7	4
Colima	45.3	29.8	23.5	19.3	68.2	4
Veracruz	57.2	36.7	20.8	15.0	67.4	4
Guanajuato	59.8	40.9	21.1	12.1	67.3	4
Sonora	54.5	33.4	21.0	16.5	66.8	4
Aguascalientes	56.7	32.4	18.5	15.6	63.6	4
Puebla	51.8	61.5	14.6	8.4	63.1	3
Durango	64.3	43.6	12.7	13.4	62.0	3
Querétaro	51.4	26.9	20.6	15.3	61.8	3
Campeche	66.2	37.5	12.3	14.6	60.8	3
Tabasco	51.5	39.4	11.3	18.7	60.3	3
Chihuahua	60.0	35.6	12.3	16.1	59.7	3
Michoacán	63.7	19.4	15.9	17.9	59.7	3
Zacatecas	67.2	24.7	14.2	16.3	59.6	3
Jalisco	58.5	53.8	14.0	6.5	59.3	2
Nuevo León	27.9	37.5	20.4	13.3	57.5	2
Hidalgo	53.2	38.7	16.5	9.3	57.0	2
Sinaloa	61.1	21.8	14.8	15.9	56.9	2
San Luis Potosí	64.5	16.2	13.4	14.6	52.9	2
Morelos	65.9	31.3	13.7	7.4	52.7	2
Distrito Federal	44.9	33.1	9.3	16.1	51.3	2
Tamaulipas	59.1	25.9	8.6	15.3	50.8	2
Quintana Roo	63.4	42.1	9.0	6.0	50.1	1
Baja California	33.8	22.9	15.3	15.4	49.7	1
State of México	20.7	41.7	18.3	4.6	46.6	1
Tlaxcala	53.2	49.4	2.8	8.6	46.2	1
Chiapas	66.0	12.0	11.3	9.9	44.8	1
Guerrero	70.8	21.2	7.3	5.8	41.7	1
Oaxaca	67.9	15.4	4.2	9.7	39.0	1
Yucatán	15.1	19.1	8.8	17.6	38.2	1

Source: Instituto Nacional de Estadística, Geografía e Informática (INEGI).
Note: States are listed in rank order based upon the performance index (data column 5).

inhabitants in a state, the total number of employees in prosecutors' offices per 100,000 inhabitants, and the average number of crimes reported in each state per MP agent. We constructed the index by standardizing each these three measures to a base of 100 and then averaging the three values.

States vary widely in their resource capacity to combat crime. Consider, for example, the number of crimes reported per individual MP agent. On average, between 1996 and 2000 each agent was responsible for investigating 425 reported crimes a year, a heavy case load that helps explain why many state authorities have a limited capacity to respond to victims' demands. Indeed, the resource shortage in some states is alarming. In Yucatán over the 1996–2000 period, each MP agent averaged 1,800 cases per year.

Our second measure of judicial performance seeks to capture the efficiency of criminal investigations. Here we start by noting that the effectiveness of the criminal justice system does not depend upon bringing every case to trial; there are, in fact, other ways of successfully concluding a criminal investigation (*averiguación previa*). Figure 6.2 shows all the possible paths that an investigation can follow within the agencies of the MP. Effective investigations are (1) cases in which the MP determines that there is a crime to prosecute, identifies and formally detains a suspect (3.3 percent of all investigations), or arrests a suspect and brings him or her before a court of law (3.1 percent of all investigations);[21] or (2) cases in which state-level authorities determine that they have no jurisdiction in the matter (for example, because the crime is defined as a federal offense) (4.3 percent of all investigations), or which are closed ("permanently filed") for reasons other than "prescription" (failure of the investigation) (8.6 percent of all investigations). The cases that are permanently filed for "other reasons" (for example, the MP determines that there is no crime to prosecute, the suspect dies, or the victim forgives the crime, in those instances in which the law permits him or her to do so) constitute 7.8 percent of all investigations. The overall efficiency of state-level criminal investigations is the sum of the values for each of these paths. In the year 2000, for example, local prosecutors' offices had an overall investigative efficiency of 18.5 percent.

The other paths delineated in figure 6.2 mark ineffective investigations. Of the 2,353,186 crimes reported to local prosecutors' offices in 2000, 43.2 percent remained "pending investigation" – that is, there was no further processing of the case after the initial presentation of a crime report. Another 24.9 percent of all cases were "provisionally filed" until more evidence was acquired, but in practice most of these cases were never reconsidered. Finally, in 4.8 percent of the cases prosecutors failed to bring the accused into court even after investigators established that a crime had occurred and identified a suspect. Overall, in the year 2000 state-level public prosecutors failed to conduct effective investigations into 81.5 percent of reported crimes (the sum of the cases that were pending investigation, provisionally

---

21 A suspect can be arrested without being formally detained.

Figure 6.2: **Crimes Under Investigation at the State Level in Mexico, 2000** (percentages)

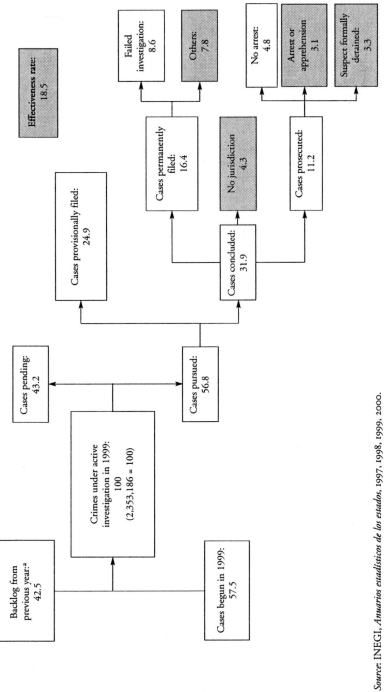

Source: INEGI, *Anuarios estadísticos de los estados*, 1997, 1998, 1999, 2000.
[a] This category only includes the backlog from 1998.

filed, prescribed, or in which the MP failed to bring a suspect, once identified, before a court of law).

Why does the MP so frequently fail to conduct effective investigations? It is, of course, difficult to provide a precise answer to this question, but we can posit a series of hypotheses. First, some of the reported crimes that the MP does not investigate may involve minor offenses that authorities simply choose to ignore in order to concentrate their attention and resources on more important matters. We note, however, that there were serious offenses among the reported crimes not investigated by the MP. Nor is a lack of resources with which to conduct investigations necessarily the problem. In fact, there is a modest negative pair-wise correlation (−.11) between the index of resources and the measure of investigative effectiveness in table 6.4.

Yet a third possibility is that local prosecutors' offices do not employ their available resources effectively. Agents of the MP may not be well-qualified professionally; they may ignore modern investigative methods, or they may not know how to employ forensic laboratories or other resources in support of their investigations. Finally, corruption may be part of the problem. Given their monopoly over investigation and prosecution, prosecutors' offices and MP agents possess impressive legal discretion, which they can employ selectively and arbitrarily. Whether a reported crime is investigated may thus depend upon such criteria as whether a bribe was paid, or whether the victim or the suspect had special political influence.

Following the approach depicted in figure 6.2, we calculated the effectiveness of each state's criminal investigations for the period between 1996 and 2000 (table 6.4, column 3). The worst performing state was Nayarit, where only 7.5 percent of reported crimes were investigated effectively. Chiapas (12.0 percent), Oaxaca (15.4 percent), San Luis Potosí (16.2 percent), and Yucatán (19.1 percent) followed. The best performers were Puebla (61.5 percent) and Jalisco (53.8 percent).

The third variable we employ is the proportion of arrest warrants that are effectively enforced. When a court issues an arrest warrant, it means that both MP authorities and the court have determined that there is a crime to prosecute and a suspect has been identified. The issuance of a legal warrant allows the police to arrest a suspect and bring him or her before a court of law and thereby initiate a criminal trial. However, on average over the 1996–2000 period, the police only enforced 14.4 percent of the arrest warrants issued at the state level. Failure to enforce a warrant might mean that the suspect had disappeared, or that the police might have purposely chosen not to enforce it because they had been bribed or because the suspect enjoyed political influence.

Table 6.4 reports (column 4) the percentage of arrest warrants that the police enforced in each state between 1996 and 2000. Tlaxcala performed worst in this area, with only 2.8 percent of its warrants enforced, but the proportion was only slightly higher in Guerrero (7.3 percent) and the Federal District (9.3 percent). In contrast, the police in Colima (23.5 percent), Guanajuato (21.1 percent), Sonora

(21.0 percent), Veracruz (20.8 percent), Querétaro (20.6 percent), and Nuevo León (20.4 percent) were much more effective in this regard.

Fourth, we consider the conviction rate (the percentage of crimes reported that ended with a conviction) achieved in different states over the 1996–2000 period. For a conviction to occur, a crime report must follow a long and cumbersome path: the investigation must be effective (that is, the suspect must be identified, arrested, and brought before a court of law), and, after hearing evidence at trial, the judge must convict the criminal. As we have noted, most reported crimes go unpunished because the MP fails to investigate the matter, or because the police fail to enforce an arrest warrant in the case.

Because murder is a particularly serious crime, we posit that a measure of conviction rates should weight this crime more heavily for the simple reason that failing to investigate, prosecute, and convict a murderer is a much more serious lapse by state authorities than not convicting someone for car theft. Moreover, most murders are reported, and when a corpse is found, an investigation must necessarily begin.

Between 1996 and 2000, an average of 18 percent of all murder investigations in Mexico ended with a conviction. There was, however, substantial variation among states in the murder conviction rate. In the State of México, murder suspects were convicted in only 6 of every 100 cases. Chiapas and Guerrero, two of the states with the highest incidence of murder, also had extremely low conviction rates (7.2 and 8.1 percent, respectively). The highest average conviction rates in murder cases during the 1996–2000 period were in Tabasco (31.1 percent), Nayarit (29.5 percent), Baja California Sur (29.3 percent), Yucatán (28.8 percent), and Coahuila (27.2 percent).

We derived a weighted conviction rate by calculating separate rates for murder and for other crimes, and then averaging the two. Column 5 in table 6.4 reports the average (weighted) conviction rate for each state for the 1996–2000 period.

We are now in a position to calculate a summary performance index for state-level judicial and law enforcement institutions. Each of the variables discussed above and reported in table 6.4 was standardized to a base of 100; the overall index value (column 6) is the average of the four variables weighted equally. On the basis of the resulting index scores, Mexico's 31 states and the Federal District are grouped from best (4) to worst (1) in terms of institutional performance. Baja California Sur was the best-performing state; its judicial and law enforcement institutions were twice as effective as those of most of the states in the worst-performing group (Durango, Yucatán, Oaxaca, Chiapas, the Federal District, Guerrero, Tlaxcala, and the State of México).

It is worth noting that during the 1996–2000 period poorer states exhibited some of the worst performance in terms of the efficiency of their judicial and law enforcement institutions. This is not to say that inadequate institutional performance in this area can be attributed solely to poverty. After all, the Federal District is among Mexico's wealthiest localities, but it registered below-average institutional performance. The same was true in the case of Baja California. These examples strongly suggest that factors other than poverty also influence the performance of judicial and law enforcement institutions, a topic that ranks high on the agenda for future research in this area.

The Magnitude of the Challenge Posed by Crime and Public Insecurity

What is the magnitude of the challenge that states face in combating crime and public insecurity? States with more crime naturally face bigger challenges. But depending upon the efficacy of their judicial and law enforcement institutions, some are better equipped than others to address the problem.

To estimate the magnitude of the challenge posed by crime and public insecurity, we can compare our index of the overall incidence of crime and our institutional performance index. A measure of magnitude can be derived by dividing a state's group number on the institutional performance index by its group number on the incidence of crime index. For example, Aguascalientes is in the top group (4) in terms of its institutional performance, indicating the good overall effectiveness of its judicial and law enforcement institutions. This state also falls into the group with the lowest incidence of crime (1). Therefore, its ratio of performance to crime is 4, from which we conclude that Aguascalientes ranks among the states that are best equipped to combat crime and public insecurity. A ratio of 3 means that a state's institutions are still able to meet the challenge, but that they must increase their efforts if they are to dissuade criminal behavior in the future. A ratio of 2 means that the state can barely meet the challenge posed by crime and public insecurity, while a ratio smaller than 1 means that crime exceeds the state's capacity to combat it.

Table 6.5 presents the ratio of institutional performance to the incidence of crime in different states. States are ordered from the best-equipped to the least-equipped in terms of their capacity to combat crime and public insecurity. By this measure, only Aguascalientes, Coahuila, Guanajuato, and Veracruz had a well-developed capacity in this area during the 1996–2000 period. Querétaro and Zacatecas were also capable of meeting the challenge, but they faced the need to increase their efforts to dissuade criminals. For the remainder of Mexico's states (particularly those falling below the line represented by Colima in table 6.5), the challenge appears to be enormous. The Federal District, for example, fell into the lowest group (4) in terms of the incidence of crime, yet its judicial and law enforcement institutions registered a below-average performance (group 2). Chiapas, Guerrero, the State of México, and Oaxaca faced the greatest challenges: their crime rates were among the highest during the 1996–2000 period, and their judicial and law enforcement institutions were among the worst performers.

Table 6.5: **The Magnitude of Mexico's Challenge in Combating Crime**

State	Performance Group (A)	Crime Group (B)	Ratio A:B
Aguascalientes	4	1	4.0
Coahuila	4	1	4.0
Guanajuato	4	1	4.0
Veracruz	4	1	4.0
Querétaro	3	1	3.0
Zacatecas	3	1	3.0
Baja California Sur	4	2	2.0
Hidalgo	2	1	2.0
Nayarit	4	2	2.0
Sonora	4	2	2.0
Durango	3	2	1.5
Puebla	3	2	1.5
Colima	4	3	1.3
Campeche	3	3	1.0
Jalisco	2	2	1.0
Michoacán	3	3	1.0
Nuevo León	2	2	1.0
Sinaloa	2	2	1.0
Tlaxcala	1	1	1.0
Chihuahua	3	4	0.8
Tabasco	3	4	0.8
San Luis Potosí	2	3	0.7
Tamaulipas	2	3	0.7
Distrito Federal	2	4	0.5
Morelos	2	4	0.5
Baja California	1	3	0.3
Quintana Roo	1	3	0.3
Yucatán	1	3	0.3
Chiapas	1	4	0.3
Guerrero	1	4	0.3
State of México	1	4	0.3
Oaxaca	1	4	0.3

Sources: Tables 6.3, 6.4.

Do Institutions Matter?

One key question is whether the performance of judicial and law enforcement institutions shapes criminal behavior. Ever since the publication of Gary S. Becker's seminal article on this subject (1968), the economics profession has emphasized incentives in the analysis of the determinants of criminal behavior. According to Becker, "some individuals become criminals because of the financial and other rewards from crime compared to legal work, taking account of the likelihood of apprehension and conviction, and the severity of punishment" (p. 390). If crime rates can be shown to respond to rewards and punishments embedded in a state's institutional setting and the pattern of law enforcement, local authorities can more effectively be held accountable for the problem. Moreover, to the extent that criminal behavior responds to incentives of this kind, informed policy initiatives should be better able to reduce the incidence of crime. If, on the hand, crime rates depend principally upon deeply rooted socioeconomic phenomena such as income inequality, poverty, or social anomie, policy makers will be able to do less in the medium term to combat crime.

In assessing this issue in the Mexican context, we conducted an econometric analysis employing three dependent variables: the index of the overall incidence of crime, the average homicide rate, and the average robbery rate between 1996 and 2000.[22] The independent variables were the institutional performance measures discussed above, as well as several socioeconomic and political variables.

The measures of institutional performance included our summary index for the 1996–2000 period. However, we also disaggregated the index into its component parts in order to assess their individual impact upon the dependent variables. Thus, we included the index of resources, the measure of investigative efficiency, the percentage of arrest warrants executed by police, and the weighted conviction rate. Each institutional measure was an average for the 1996–2000 period.[23] We anticipated that each of these variables would have a negative effect upon the dependent variable, meaning that more resources, greater investigative efficiency by MP agents, a larger percentage of arrest warrants served, and a higher conviction rate should be associated with less crime.

The socioeconomic controls included a state's average per capita growth rate during the 1996–2000 period. This period witnessed a serious economic crisis in 1994–1995 followed by a fast aggregate economic recovery – albeit one that was not uniformly distributed across different Mexican states. Consistent with the cross-sectional regression results presented earlier in this essay, we expected to find higher crime rates in states that experienced a sharper economic collapse and a more mediocre recovery after the 1994–1995 financial crisis.

We employed a variety of indicators to measure poverty: the percentage of a state's population that cannot read and write, GDP per capita in 2000, and the marginality index compiled by the National Population Council (CONAPO). This last measure was derived from a factor analysis of a series of municipal-level socioeconomic indicators (the extent of illiteracy, the percentage of the population earning less than two minimum wages, and the percentage of households without

22 We performed a series of regression analyses, some with the average figures reported in the text and others with yearly data, using pooled time-series analysis with fixed and random effects. Here we report the results of the simpler regression with average figures, although these findings were mostly confirmed by the pooled time-series analyses.

23 In the pooled time-series regression analyses, we employed yearly figures for each of these measures.

such basic services as piped water, electricity, and access to sewerage).[24] We expected to observe a higher incidence of murder in poorer states and more robbery in richer states.

Our analysis also considered the possible impact of urbanization, which is defined as the percentage of a state's population living in localities with more than 15,000 inhabitants. We expected a positive effect upon the incidence of crime and robbery, and a negative effect upon the frequency of murder.

As a political variable, we employed the average number of years over the 1996–2000 period that a party other than the ruling Institutional Revolutionary Party (PRI) governed a state. Consistent with the cross-sectional evidence presented in table 6.2, we did not expect democratization (measured as rule by an opposition party) to produce an increase in crime rates.

The results of our analysis are reported in table 6.6. We found strong evidence that the quality of judicial and law enforcement institutions does matter. The first model of the incidence of total crime indicates that a state's overall crime rate during the period from 1996 to 2000 was significantly shaped by its institutional performance: better institutional performance reduced crime (producing a negative coefficient for the institutional-performance variable).[25] We also found strong evidence that economic performance significantly influenced crime rates. The coefficient for the growth-rate variable is negative and highly significant, meaning that there was more crime in those states experiencing a worse economic performance during the 1996–2000 period. In addition, the results indicated that both the level of urbanization and the extent of poverty (as measured by the rate of illiteracy) were associated with more crime.

However, there was no evidence that partisan alternation in power increased the incidence of crime. On the contrary, there appeared to be less crime in states where the opposition governed for a longer period between 1996 and 2000 (the opposition-government variable has a negative coefficient, almost reaching statistical significance with a T-value of 1.61).

These variables together explained 57.0 percent of the variance among states in the overall incidence of crime during the 1996–2000 period. We thus conclude, in line with our initial expectations, that crime is produced jointly by poverty, poor economic performance, and the failure of judicial and law enforcement institutions. Our statistical analysis found no evidence that democratization creates more crime.

The second and third statistical models employed average murder rates and average robbery rates, respectively, as the dependent variables. These models also

---

24 Because these variables are highly correlated, table 6.6 only reports results with regard to illiteracy. The text discusses results for the other two variables.

   We also tested whether the proportion of young male adults (ages 18 to 25) in a state's total population affected crime rates, but this variable did not have a statistically significant effect.

25 This variable was robust to any specification.

Table 6.6: **The Effects of Institutional Performance on Crime Rates in Mexico, 1996–2000**

Independent Variable	Model 1: Incidence of Crime	Model 2: Murder	Model 3: Robbery
Institutional performance index	−0.67***	(0.18)	
− Index of resources		0.08 (0.13)	−0.30 (5.46)
− Investigative efficiency		−0.19 (0.39)	−22.19** (10.74)
− Arrest warrents enforced		−0.22*** (0.08)	7.81 (14.42)
− Weighted conviction rate[a]		−0.47* (0.26)	−2.52 (7.11)
Average per capita growth rate	−341.35** (144.39)	−76.09 (103.3)	414.58 (5,164.43)
Illiteracy	1.06** (0.51)	0.90** (0.42)	−8.96 (15.19)
Urban population	53.19*** (16.37)	22.04* (11.32)	1,314.41** (541.34)
Opposition government	−7.76 (4.82)		
Constant	42.38** (18.78)	17.34 (11.43)	209.42 (850.91)
	N = 32	N = 32	N = 32
	$F_{(5, 26)} = 6.00$	$F_{(7, 24)} = 3.39$	$F_{(7, 24)} = 3.15$
	Prob > F = 0.0008	Prob > F = 0.007	Prob > F = 0.016
	R^2 = 0.57	R^2 = 0.53	R^2 = 0.50
	Root MSE = 9.85	Root MSE = 7.30	Root MSE = 332.16

Note: This table displays the results of regression analyses with heterosedastic consistent errors (standard errors in parentheses).
  * Significant at the .10 confidence level
 ** Significant at the .05 confidence level
*** Significant at the .01 confidence level
[a] In the case of murders, the analysis employed the average conviction rate for murder.

disaggregated the institutional performance index into its component elements in order to assess which aspects of judicial and law enforcement institutions have the most important effect upon crime.

In the second model, two of the institutional variables had negative coefficients and were statistically significant, indicating that higher conviction rates and more consistent enforcement of arrest warrants reduced a state's murder rate. However, our measures of a state's available resources and investigative effectiveness did not have a statistically significant impact upon murder rates. We thus conclude that murder was more prevalent where killers were able to escape arrest (either because the police failed to capture them, or because suspects were able to buy off the police) and where the criminal justice system failed to convict them. As expected, poverty was associated with higher murder rates, but contrary to our initial expectations, we also found more murders in more urbanized states.

In the third statistical model, the variable representing investigative effectiveness had a significant effect upon robbery, meaning that the MP can deter thieves by carrying out more effective investigations. However, the other institutional variables had no such impact. Finally, we found that average robbery rates were higher during the 1996–2000 period in more urbanized states, and that the level of illiteracy had no statistically significant effect upon the incidence of robbery. Note, though, that the coefficient for the illiteracy variable has the opposite sign in the second and third models. When GDP per capita was employed as a measure of poverty, the variable's coefficient was positive and statistically significant, meaning that there was more robbery in richer states. We can thus conclude that murder and robbery rates were both more prevalent in urban areas over the 1996–2000 period, yet poorer states showed higher murder rates while richer states experienced higher robbery rates.

We also added to the analysis variables for the sanctions that states impose upon those committing serious crimes. One sanctions variable represented the average length (in years) of the prison terms imposed for intentional homicide, while the other sanctions variable represented the length (in months) of jail sentences given for robbery. However, neither of these variables yielded statistically significant results, and therefore we do not report results for the regressions that included these variables. Thus, it appears that state judicial authorities are not able to deter criminals simply by increasing the severity of punishment. Rather, as our statistical models demonstrate, what they need to do to deter crime is to improve substantially the institutional performance of their law enforcement operations: carry out more effective investigations, apprehend more criminals, and convict them more often.

What is the relative impact of socioeconomic and institutional variables upon crime rates? To what extent can states deter crime by improving their institutional performance? In order to address these questions, we simulated the results of our first statistical model for the institutional performance index, urbanization, poverty, and economic growth rates. Figure 6.3 presents these simulations based upon the institutional performance index and three levels of urbanization: "predominantly rural," "semi-urban," and "predominantly urban."[26] The remaining explanatory variables were held to their mean values.

26 A predominantly rural state is defined as a state with a level of urbanization one standard deviation below the mean urbanization level; a semi-urban state is one with an average level of urbanization; an urban state is defined as a state with a level of urbanization one standard deviation above the mean.

Figure 6.3: **The Simulated Effect of Institutional Performance on the Incidence of Crime in Mexico, by Level of Urbanization, 1996–2000**

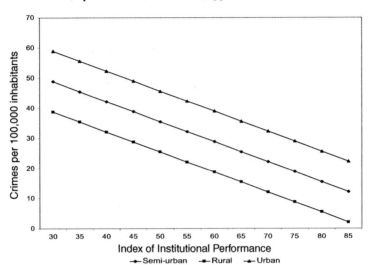

This exercise demonstrates that the performance of judicial and law enforcement institutions has a powerful effect upon the incidence of crime. For the 1996–2000 period, a ten-point increase in the institutional performance index (one standard deviation) led to a reduction of 6.6 crimes per 100,000 inhabitants. This means that if the worst-performing states (Yucatán, Oaxaca, and Guerrero) increased their institutional performance to the level of the best-performing ones, they could reduce their crime rates by 63.2 percent.[27] Urbanization had equally notable effects. A predominantly urban state had 20.2 more crimes per 100,000 inhabitants than a predominantly rural one, and 10.1 more crimes than a semi-urban state.

Figure 6.4 simulates our model with regard to the impact of growth rates and poverty upon the incidence of crime between 1996 and 2000. The simulation shows that economic performance also had a very significant effect in this regard. Indeed, an increase of one standard deviation in the indicator for average growth rates (equivalent to a one-percentage-point increase in the average per capita growth rate, from 5 percent to 6 percent a year) produced a reduction of 3.4 crimes per 100,000 inhabitants. This means that, ceteris paribus, if Oaxaca (with one of the worst average growth records during the 1996–2000 period) had experienced the growth record of Querétaro (the best performing state, with an average per capita growth rate of 7 percent over the period in question), its incidence of crime

27 The simulated reduction of crime rates was derived by calculating the expected crime rate in a semi-urban state with a performance index of 40, and comparing it with a semi-urban state with a performance index of 80. The incidence of crime dropped from 42.2 to 15.5 per 100,000 inhabitants.

Figure 6.4: **The Simulated Effect of Economic Growth and Poverty on the Incidence of Crime in Mexico, 1996–2000**

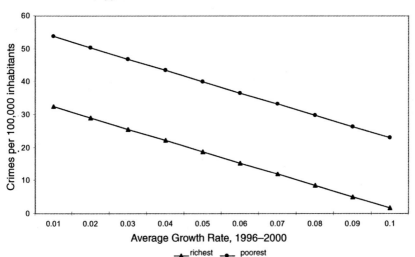

would have been 43.3 percent lower.[28] Crime is, then, extremely sensitive to economic performance.

Poverty also had a powerful effect upon the incidence of crime. Ceteris paribus, states with the largest number of poor inhabitants (as measured by the rate of illiteracy) – including Chiapas, Oaxaca, and Guerrero – had 21.3 more crimes per 100,000 inhabitants than the richest states. We emphasize, however, that after disaggregating our index of the overall incidence of crime, poverty showed mixed effects – increasing murder rates, but reducing robbery rates.

Conclusion

In the course of this chapter we have argued that important institutional changes pertaining to the federal judiciary accompanied the process of democratization in Mexico. The most significant development was the establishment in 1995 of a more independent and powerful Supreme Court that can veto legislation through its power of judicial review, resolve disputes among different branches of government, and serve as an arbiter of federalism. Yet the reform of state-level judiciaries and law enforcement institutions (prosecutors' offices, MP agents, and the police) is still pending. As we have shown, these institutions are not yet capable of meeting their

28 This percentage was derived by comparing the expected crime rate in an average-wealth state with an economic growth rate of 1 percent (39.4 crimes per 100,000 inhabitants) with the expected rate of an average-wealth state with a growth rate of 6 percent (22.2 crimes per 100,000 inhabitants).

core responsibility of protecting citizens against crime, despite the fact that Mexicans consider this matter to be one of the most important problems facing the country.

The explosion of crime is not unique to Mexico; since the 1980s, crime rates have increased dramatically in almost all Latin American countries. Our cross-sectional analysis demonstrated that crime rates have been higher in democratizing countries than in either authoritarian regimes or established democracies. Yet it appears that the sharp rise in crime rates cannot be attributed to political change per se; rather, this phenomenon appears to be the result of the socioeconomic conditions in which democratization occurred. Indeed, as in other "Third Wave" democratization processes, political change in Mexico was accompanied by profound economic difficulties and greater income disparities – conditions that led to an increase in crime. In fact, our cross-sectional econometric analysis found that the less a country grew during the 1990s and the greater its income disparities, the higher its crime rate *regardless* of its level of democracy.

However, these findings do not mean that crime is solely the product of under-lying socioeconomic conditions. Our in-depth empirical investigation of crime rates in Mexico between 1996 and 2000 indicates that the explosion in crime had two main causes: economic recession, and the failure of judicial and law enforce-ment institutions.

These institutions are often extremely corrupt. Not only do they allow crime to go unpunished because of their incompetence, but in some instances they have actually been "captured" by criminals. The victims of crime have no legal recourse when public prosecutors refuse to investigate a crime and bring charges against a suspect because prosecutors hold a monopoly over such actions. In the absence of legal rights for victims of crime and effective checks on prosecutors' offices, some state-level law enforcement institutions operate as de facto authoritarian enclaves. Indeed, the overwhelming majority of the complaints filed before the National Human Rights Commission are related to the criminal justice system.

Our analysis has shown that crime rates respond strongly to policy-sensitive variables – that is, the pattern of law enforcement within a state. We developed a new methodology for assessing the performance of law enforcement institutions, focusing upon four factors: the resources that states devote to combating and investigating crime; the investigative effectiveness of public prosecutors' offices; whether the police effectively enforce arrest warrants; and the conviction rates achieved by law enforcement institutions and local judiciaries in their efforts to punish criminals.

Policy makers confronting a high incidence of crime possess a menu of "carrot and stick" policies that, if well designed and effectively implemented, will actually deter crime. For example, we found that simply increasing the severity of punish-ment is not an effective deterrent. Rather, there must be a dramatic increase in the effectiveness of law enforcement so that criminals are deterred by the higher probability of being detected, apprehended, and convicted. In the case of robbery, increasing investigative effectiveness matters most; in the case of murder, the key factors are the capacity of police forces to enforce arrest warrants and the probability of conviction.

These institutional explanatory variables have a robust effect upon the incidence of crime even after controlling for socioeconomic factors. Hence, even though crime is caused by some elements over which state-level politicians may not have much control (at least in the short term), our analysis indicates that crime rates in Mexico are extremely sensitive to variations in the character of local judicial and law enforcement institutions. This conclusion represents our more positive finding. The bad news is that the level of these state-level institutions' overall effectiveness is appallingly low. Thus, establishing the conditions necessary to reduce substantially existing problems of crime and public insecurity will not be easy.

Mexico's federal institutions imply that it is not possible to implement a nation-wide policy of crime prevention. State-level institutions – especially public prosecutors' offices and local judiciaries – are the main players in this area. The federal government can coordinate states' crime prevention efforts by, for example, creating better information systems on criminal organizations that operate across state boundaries and by allocating to the states more federal funds to combat crime. The allocation of these funds should take into account both prevailing crime rates *and* state-level efforts to combat crime, so that funding decisions reward those states that make more effective efforts to reduce crime.

Future prospects for combating violent crime in Mexico will depend heavily upon the state-level incidence of crime and prevailing patterns of law enforcement. Based upon the information in table 6.3, we can identify three different scenarios. The most optimistic scenario centers on those states with a low incidence of crime (groups 1 and 2) and efficient patterns of law enforcement (groups 3 and 4): Aguascalientes, Coahuila, Guanajuato, Veracruz, Querétaro, Zacatecas, Baja California Sur, Nayarit, Sonora, Durango, and Puebla. We believe that these states will be able to deter criminal behavior effectively because, on the one hand, they possess quite efficient law enforcement institutions and, on the other hand, criminal activity is not that prevalent.

The pessimistic scenario centers on states with a high incidence of crime (groups 3 and 4) and poor performance by law enforcement institutions (groups 1 and 2). These states may confront serious problems with crime over an extended period. Even better economic conditions may not reverse trends in the incidence of crime because poor law enforcement creates strong incentives for criminal behavior to perpetuate itself. Although improved economic conditions would certainly be helpful in this regard, it will require a tremendous effort on the part of law enforcement institutions to prevent crime from perpetuating itself in these states.

Oaxaca, Chiapas, the State of México, and Guerrero confront the greatest challenges because they have both the highest incidence of crime (group 4) and the worst institutional performance (group 1). Yucatán, Quintana Roo, and Baja California follow; their incidence of crime is slightly lower (group 3), but they are among the states with the worst institutional performance (group 1). The Federal District and Morelos also face a pessimistic scenario because they are among the states with the highest incidence of crime (group 4) and the second-worst institutional performance (group 2). Similarly, Tamaulipas and San Luis Potosí have a high incidence of crime (group 3) and a quite deficient performance by law enforcement institutions (group 2).

Yet a third scenario falls between these optimistic and pessimistic extremes. Whether this third group of states remains engulfed by violent crime (as in the pessimistic scenario) or effectively reduces crime rates (the optimistic scenario) will depend upon such factors as economic performance and state-level efforts to combat criminal behavior. Some states – Colima, Campeche, Michoacán, Chihuahua, and Tabasco – possess quite efficient law enforcement institutions (groups 4 and 3) but still face a high incidence of crime (groups 4 and 3). The future for them is slightly more optimistic because, although they confront very high crime rates, their prevailing pattern of law enforcement is such that they might be able to deter criminals effectively, particularly if economic conditions improve significantly. Jalisco, Nuevo León, and Sinaloa face moderate crime rates (group 2), yet their law enforcement performance is quite deficient (group 2). Thus, these states will need to improve markedly their law enforcement efforts if they want to prevent an explosion of criminal behavior. Finally, although Tlaxcala and Hidalgo have low crime rates, their law enforcement performance is dismal. Because their law enforcement institutions are incapable of deterring violent crime, they are vulnerable to a higher incidence of crime in the future.

Further democratization at the state level will, we believe, increase incentives for local politicians to attempt to confront more effectively the challenges they face in combating crime. As we have shown, partisan alternation in power at the local level is not responsible for an increase in crime rates. The correlation between the incidence of crime and opposition government between 1996 and 2000 was in fact negative. The states governed by opposition parties during this period actually had lower crime rates, in part because the opposition managed to win power in richer and faster-growing states. However, beyond the partisan identity of local governments, intensified political competition will allow voters to hold local politicians accountable for their performance in office, one aspect of which will be how well they confront the problem of violent crime. Whether Mexican voters actually hold local politicians accountable on the crime issue, and the extent to which elections generate the correct political incentives to improve the performance of law enforcement institutions, are questions that constitute an agenda for future research.

References

Ayres, Robert L. 1998. *Crime and Violence as Development Issues in Latin America and the Caribbean.* Washington, D.C.: World Bank.

Becker, Gary S. 1968. "Crime and Punishment: An Economic Approach," *Journal of Political Economy* 76 (3): 169–217.

Burnham, R.W., and Helen Burnham. 1997. *United Nations World Surveys on Crime Trends and Criminal Justice Systems, 1970–1994: Restructured Five-Wave Data.* Washington, D.C.: National Institute of Justice, U.S. Department of Justice.

Fajnzylber, Pablo, Daniel Lederman, and Norman Loayza. 1998. *Determinants of Crime Rates in Latin America and the Caribbean: An Empirical* Assessment. Washington, D.C.: World Bank.

Geddes, Barbara. 1999. "Authoritarian Breakdown: An Empirical Test of a Game Theoretic Argument." Paper presented at the annual meeting of the American Political Science Association, Atlanta, September.

Gleditsch, Kristian S., and Michael D. Ward. 1997. "Double Take: A Re-examination of Democracy and Autocracy in Modern Politics," *Journal of Conflict Resolution* 41 (June): 361–82.

Gurr, Ted Robert. 1974. "Persistence and Change in Political Systems, 1800–1971," *American Political Science Review* 74 (December): 1482–1504.

Haggard, Stephan, and Robert R. Kaufman. 1995. *The Political Economy of Democratic Transitions.* Princeton, N.J.: Princeton University Press.

Heston, Alan, Robert Summers, and Bettina Aten. 2002. *Penn World Tables Version 6.1.* Philadelphia: Center for International Comparisons, University of Pennsylvania. October.

Huntington, Samuel P. 1991. *The Third Wave: Democratization in the Late Twentieth Century.* Norman: University of Oklahoma Press.

IADB (Inter-American Development Bank). 1999. *Facing Up to Inequality in Latin America.* Washington, D.C.: IADB and Johns Hopkins University Press.

Kangaspunta, Kristina, Matti Joutsen, and Natalia Ollus, eds. 1998. *Crime and Criminal Justice in Europe and North America, 1990–1994.* Helsinki: European Institute for Crime Prevention and Control.

Magaloni, Beatriz. 2003. "Authoritarianism, Democracy, and the Supreme Court: Horizontal Accountability and the Rule of Law in Mexico." In *Horizontal Accountability in Latin America,* edited by Scott Mainwaring and Christopher Wellna. Oxford: Oxford University Press.

Magaloni, Beatriz, and Arianna Sánchez. 2001. "Empowering Courts as Constitutional Veto Players: Presidential Delegation and the Supreme Court in Mexico." Paper presented at the annual meeting of the American Political Science Association, San Francisco, September.

Remmer, Karen L. 1991. "The Political Impact of Economic Crisis in Latin America in the 1980s," *American Political Science Review* 85 (3): 777–800.

Rubio, Luis, Beatriz Magaloni, and Edna Jaime. 1994. *A la puerta de la ley: el estado de derecho en México.* Mexico City: Cal y Arena.

Zepeda, Guillermo. 2001. "La procuración de justicia." Ph.D. diss. Facultad de Derecho, Universidad Nacional Autónoma de México.

Zinser, Adolfo. 2001. "La cifra negra," *Reforma* (Mexico City), 29 June.

7

Decentralization, Democratization, and Federalism in Mexico

Alberto Díaz-Cayeros

For many years, Mexican federalism was dismissed as false or insignificant (Riker 1964). The degree of political centralization was enormous, and the regime's democratic credentials were highly suspect. These features were regarded as reasons enough to believe that the formal institutional arrangement of the territory was unimportant. Thus, with the exceptions of Robert E. Scott's (1959) fine study of Mexican politics and Merilee S. Grindle's (1977) analysis of agricultural policy, little scholarly research addressed the role of federalism. In fact, most of a half-century's research on Mexico suggested that all politics was national.

Political scientists were among the principal perpetrators of the centralist myth. Historians, in contrast, have long highlighted the importance of federal arrangements in the nineteenth century and at the beginning of the twentieth century (Benson 1954; Carmagnani 1993, 1994; Hernández Chávez 1996). Recent work by Jeffrey W. Rubin (1997) has also called considerable attention to the mismatch between what careful studies of regional political processes were suggesting about the importance of federalism and local politics, and the centralist conventional wisdom of how the Mexican political system worked. The dual trends since the 1980s toward decentralization and democratization should dispel any doubt as to whether Mexico is a federal country.[1]

The renewal of federalism has in fact become one of the most important issues of political debate in contemporary Mexico. As in other Latin American countries, political change has been the central force leading to decentralization and height-

The author thanks the Centro de Investigación para el Desarrollo, A.C. (CIDAC) for providing a conducive environment in which to carry out research on federalism in Mexico, and especially colleagues at CIDAC for contributing greatly to his thinking on the topic. The database employed in this chapter was developed at CIDAC; Jacqueline Martínez Uriarte painstakingly collected the electoral data used here. Diego Szteinhendler provided able research assistance. The author also acknowledges insightful comments from Beatriz Magaloni, Jorge I. Domínguez, and Kevin J. Middlebrook on previous versions of this chapter. Of course, all mistakes and interpretations remain his sole responsibility.

1 The peculiar characteristics of Mexico's federal arrangement, especially its high degree of centralization in fiscal authority and the long dominance of one political party at all levels of government, do deserve further comment (see below).

ened demands to make federalist arrangements work better (see Haggard 1999; Rojas 1999; and Willis, Garman, and Haggard 1999). The greater political pluralism that now characterizes Mexico, coupled with the demise of the dominant-party system, has led to a vindication of the periphery vis-à-vis the center. However, the periphery in Mexico is very diverse, as reflected in the political, social, and economic features of each state. Indeed, one of Mexico's greatest development challenges is the coexistence of extreme poverty in some regions with the economic dynamism of richer areas. The pressing political challenge is to identify a federal arrangement that can hold together such dissimilar realities.

It is in the "provinces" (the term often used to describe everything that is not Mexico City) where one observes the most responsive and accountable representative governments, and where elections came to be accepted as the only legitimate way to win and hold power even before electoral democratization occurred at the national level. In many states and municipalities, citizens have been accustomed both to divided government (Lujambio 2001) and to partisan alternation in office (Díaz-Cayeros and Martínez Uriarte 1997) since the early 1990s. Of course, it is also in the "provinces" that some of the most authoritarian traits of Mexico's post-revolutionary political regime have been preserved (Snyder 1999), and local[2] bosses or *caciques* still control important sources of patronage. Yet such clientelistic exchanges are constrained by the availability of discretional funds from the federal government, and they are increasingly circumscribed to such specific regions as the states of the Yucatán Peninsula and the Gulf of Mexico coast.

Within this context, democratization has been associated with decentralization and federalism. Although the trends toward greater democratization and decentralization are likely to continue, this chapter argues that the future of federalism in Mexico is uncertain. Processes of political change at the local level have taken on a dynamic of their own, independent of national trends. With the defeat of the formerly hegemonic Institutional Revolutionary Party (PRI) in the 2000 presidential election, political authority has become fragmented. State and municipal officials' demands for the devolution of power and resources are for the most part the consequence of their greater accountability to voters, although entrenched local bosses are as interested in such matters as the most progressive, democratic elements. Yet at the federal level, Mexico still retains fiscal and political institutions designed for a centralized dominant-party system.

As state and municipal governments go about satisfying citizens' demands, they need not be concerned about the sources of funds or the taxes levied to generate their financial resources. Much has been said regarding local governments' dependence upon federal revenue transfers. The other side of the coin, however, is that local governments are not accountable for the way in which taxes are levied in Mexico. Changing this misalignment in the institutional design of fiscal federalism will not be easy because powerful political actors do not have incentives to co-operate in

2 In this chapter, the term "local" refers to either state or municipal levels of government, or both.

order to redesign existing arrangements. Governors and municipal presidents only seek to redress old grievances against the political center and concentrate their efforts on obtaining more fiscal resources and improved conditions for their localities.

However, if federalism is merely a fight over scarce federal resources, its future is rather bleak. In order to establish a "new" federalism, in which states and the federal government work together to enhance local autonomy and accountability while the federal government preserves a compensatory role for disadvantaged regions, political actors will need to overcome obstacles generated (paradoxically) by the very success of democratization and decentralization. Governors and municipal presidents will need to risk losing popularity by increasing local taxation, and the federal government must devolve the authority to levy taxes even at the cost of less efficient tax collection.

This chapter is organized as follows. The first section examines regional inequality in Mexico from a comparative perspective, highlighting the point that this will be one of the main challenges in the political economy of Mexican development in future years. The second and third sections analyze the processes of decentraliza-tion and democratization unfolding in Mexico, stressing the prevailing configuration of fiscal authority and financial transfer systems and the ascending role of governors and other local political actors. The fourth part discusses the tensions between decentralization and democratization, viewed through the lens of tax collection efforts by local governments.

The chapter ends by considering the shortcomings of Mexican political institu-tions as arenas for redefining the federal pact and setting an an agenda for debate about the future of federalism in Mexico. The extent to which such an agenda can be advanced depends upon politicians' capacity to turn existing institutions into effective instruments of choice, co-operation, and consensus building – rather than into arenas in which conflicts are perceived as zero-sum and the political game becomes impossible to play. That is the principal challenge facing Mexican federal-ism in the years to come.

Regional Inequality, Poverty, and Redistribution

The starting point for understanding federalism in Mexico is to note the high degree of regional inequality prevailing in the country (Díaz-Cayeros 1995). Excluding petroleum-producing states, the difference between the richest area (the Federal District) and the poorest one (Chiapas), as measured by state gross domestic product (GDP) per capita, was on the order of 6 to 1 in 1999. That is, Mexico City (the Federal District) had a per capita GDP of about US$10,000, which was approximately six times greater than that of Chiapas (US$1,700).[3] Inequalities of

3 The 1999 ratio was very similar to that which obtained in 1993. With the onset of the 1994–1995 peso devaluation and financial crisis, state GDP levels collapsed in U.S. dollar terms. However, once economic recovery began, these levels (and inequality ratios) returned to the earlier pattern.

this magnitude persist even when GDP data are adjusted for variations in purchasing power parity among different regions.[4]

Perhaps one might think that Mexico's regional disparities are not large when compared, for example, with those in Indonesia, where the difference in per capita GDP between East Kalimantan and East Nusa Tenggara is on the order of 19 to 1. However, as reported in table 7.1, when differences between regional price levels in Indonesia are adjusted for purchasing price parity (and oil production is excluded from the calculations), the ratio between per capita GDP in the richest area (Jakarta) and in the poorest one (East Nusa Tenggara) is 6.5 to 1, a pattern quite similar to Mexico's.[5]

Other countries with a federal system and a level of development comparable to Mexico's also have a 6 to 1 ratio between the richest and poorest regions, as is the case in Brazil and Russia. It may be, however, that long-established democracies are more likely to reduce regional differences. In India, a much poorer federal country but one with a longer record of democratic politics, the difference in GDP per capita between Delhi and Bihar is on the order of 4 to 1, closer to the regional disparities observed in developed nations. In post-unification Germany, for example, the difference between the richest and the poorest Land is 3.5 to 1, and when the eastern Länder are excluded from the calculation, the gap is only 2 to 1. That difference is similar to what is found in other advanced industrial democracies, including Canada (2.5 to 1), Spain (2.2 to 1), and the United States (2.2 to 1) (see table 7.1).

Is regional inequality a characteristic of underdevelopment? Figure 7.1 displays information concerning regional disparities and economic development levels for all the largest countries of the world, including both federal and centralized systems and both democracies and authoritarian regimes.[6] It shows that regional disparity (measured through the coefficient of variation, which is the standard deviation divided by the mean) is in fact correlated with the level of development, as measured by national GDP per capita.

Figure 7.1 identifies in boldface type the political systems that are organized as federations. Almost all the world's large countries, regardless of the nature of their political regime or their degree of regional disparity, are formally organized as federations.[7]

4 The author calculated Mexican states' GDP per capita at purchasing power parity for 1989, based upon data from Zepeda Miramontes 1992. However, as noted above, per capita GDP levels and states' rank ordering in 1999 were not very different from those at the end of the 1980s, except for the oil-boom effects still observed in Campeche and Tabasco in the late 1980s.

5 Even if mining activity (primarily petroleum production) is excluded from the Mexican calculations, the difference between the Federal District and Oaxaca is still on the order of 6 to 1.

6 The one large country omitted is Pakistan, for which regional GDP data were not available.

7 If China, Italy, and Spain are also considered to be quasi-federal systems, only Asian cases contradict the contention that all large countries are federations. Indonesia is moving toward something more similar to federalism, so Japan is in fact the only country depicted in the graph that is likely to retain a highly centralized political arrangement.

Table 7.1: **Regional Inequality in Selected Countries, 1980s–1990s**

Country	Maximum per capita income	Minimum per capita income	Maximum/ minimum ratio	Coefficient of ratio variation	Typical log deviation
Germany (1995)	Hamburg (DM 78,861)	Mecklenburg (DM 22,463)	3.51	0.38	0.17
Without Eastern Länder	NA	Rheinland (DM 38,665)	2.04	0.25	0.10
Brazil (1985)	Federal District (Cr 0.1651)	Piauí (Cr 0.0233)	7.09	0.4873	0.22
Without Federal District	Sao Paulo (Cr 0.1372)	Piauí (Cr 0.0233)	5.89	NA	NA
India (1991)	Delhi (Rps 10,177)	Bihar (Rps 2,655)	3.83	0.38	0.15
Italy (1989)	Lombardia (LIT 26,858,969)	Calabria (LIT 11,285,278)	2.38	0.26	0.12
United States (1990)	Connecticut (US$17,600)	Mississippi (US$7,860)	2.25	0.19	0.08
Russia (1992)	Yakutia Sakha (Rbl 116,845)	Kabar-Balk (Rbl 19,943)	5.86	0.41	NA
Spain (1987–1989)	Baleares (Index=109.2)	Extremadura (Index=49.0)	2.23	0.20	0.09
Canada (1990)	Northwest Terr. (CD $37,900)	Newfoundland (CD $15,200)	2.49	0.30	0.13
Indonesia (1984)	East Kalimantan (Rps 3,869,000)	East Tenggara (Rps 198,200)	19.52	1.27	0.33
Without mining and PPP-adjusted	Jakarta (Rps 1,191,900)	East Nusa Tenggara (Rps 184,400)	6.46	0.56	0.19
Japan (1990)	Tokyo (Y 4,238,000)	Okinawa (Y 1,880,000)	2.25	0.16	0.06
China	Shanghai (US$1,527)	Guizhou (US$164)	9.31	0.81	0.22
Without Beijing and Shanghai	Guandong (US$519)	Guizhou (US$164)	3.16	NA	NA
Mexico (1999)	Distrito Federal (35,500 pesos)	Chiapas (6,000 pesos)	5.86	0.48	0.19
PPP-adjusted (1989)	Distrito Federal (US$15,141)	Oaxaca (US$2,299)	6.59	NA	NA

Sources: Author's calculations based upon the following: for Brazil, *Anuario Estadístico Brasileño, 1991* (data at constant 1970 prices); for Canada, Watts 1999 (data in Canadian dollars); for China, Ohmae 1995; for Germany, *Der Spiegel* 18/1996; for India, Cashin and Sahay 1996 (data in 1990 current rupees); for Italy, PDS n.d.; for Indonesia, Hill 1992; for Japan, Barro and Sala-i-Martin 1995 (data in constant 1985 yen); for Mexico, INEGI (for 1999) and Zepeda Miramontes 1992; for Russia, Neuber 1994; for Spain, EUROSTAT (index calculated with the 1986-1988 mean, EUR12=100); for the United States, Barro and Sala-i-Martin 1995. NA= Not available   PPP=Purchasing power parity

Figure 7.1: **The Relationship between Regional Disparities and the Level of Economic Development in Selected Countries, 1980s–1990s**

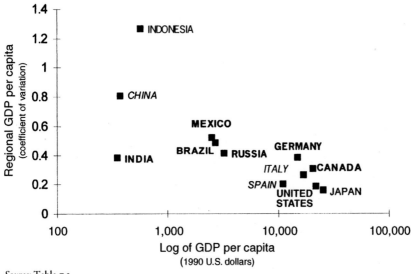

Source: Table 7.1.

Except for China, Indonesia, and Pakistan, in the year 2003 all the large countries in the world were also democracies – although it should be noted that the links between size, federalism, and democracy are not well understood.[8] This pattern suggests that, regardless of the level of economic development, federalism is the most common institutional arrangement for large countries.[9]

The high correlation between regional inequality and underdevelopment suggests that as countries become richer, they might also become less regionally unequal.[10] The basic pattern undermines Simon Kuznets's (1963) hypothesis suggesting that regional inequality takes the shape of an inverted U, reaching the highest levels at intermediate levels of development.[11] Hence an argument suggesting that large countries at intermediate levels of development (such as Brazil or Mexico) should tolerate a large degree of regional inequality *because* they are at intermediate levels

8 For a seminal analysis of the relationship between size and democracy, see Dahl and Tufte 1973; for a specific focus on federalism, see the insightful comments in Riker's classic study (1964).

9 The degree of centralization within federal systems varies greatly. The basic point to be stressed is that federalism is a mode of power allocation that seems to be necessary whenever the population and territory of a country are large. The converse, however, is not true; some countries with small populations and territories have federal systems.

10 India is the anomaly in this regard.

11 The Kuznets hypothesis is often discussed in terms of household inequality, but the mechanics of the argument rely upon regional distributions of income. Of course, it is possible that the hypothesis could hold for a larger sample of countries.

of development does not seem to be supported by the evidence.

Why are richer countries regionally more equal? This could be the consequence of "natural" economic processes (as neoclassical economic growth theory suggests), or it could be attributable to specific forms of governmental intervention. Although it is difficult to measure the relative weight of each of these factors, there is no doubt that developed countries have put into place policies aimed at reducing regional inequalities and increasing national integration, including federal grants to less developed regions and equalization transfer programs. In developed countries, public debate about regional development has produced political arrangements that make financial transfers among regions possible. Federalism (or quasi-federal arrangements, as in Italy and Spain) has been a basic institutional framework necessary to achieve this.

Discussions about such issues in Mexico reflect the perceived need to generate a system of transfers and federal grants to compensate poor regions, notwithstanding the political difficulties involved in convincing rich regions to pay for such compensation. Yet the debate is not unique to Mexico. In Brazil and Russia, for instance, discussions about federalism arouse tensions because rich regions perceive that, given the level of development in the country as a whole, they can ill afford to send resources to poor regions, thereby perhaps undermining their own prospects for growth and development. From this perspective, redistribution must wait for rich regions to pull the country to a higher level of development. Poor regions, however, tend to have disproportionate power in the political arena (formally through malapportionment, as in the case of the Brazilian Northeast, or informally through blackmailing the federal government with threats of secession, as in Russia). The question of how to strike a balance between these opposed views of public policy on regional inequality is likely to become the most important tension in Mexican federalism in future years.

The cogency of these issues reflects the fact that the character of different Mexican regions' insertion into global trade, finance, and technology networks has produced differential regional growth based upon the market access and competitive advantages available to each state, city, or region. In the period between 1960 and 1988, one could speak of a long-term regional convergence process, in which the richest states tended to grow less rapidly than poorer ones so that an eventual catch-up was possible. However, since 1988 the empirical evidence of convergence is inconclusive (Díaz-Cayeros 1995; Arroyo 1999; Navarrete 1995; Alzati 1998).

Poor states experienced dynamic growth in some earlier periods, but during the 1990s regional differences in economic development appear to have increased. In figure 7.2, the vertical axis depicts average per capita GDP growth rates in Mexican states between 1993 and 2000, while the horizontal axis shows the per capita GDP of each state in 1993 U.S. dollars. If regional convergence were occurring, one should observe a downward sloping trend in which poorer states grew faster than richer ones. Yet figure 7.2 shows no such trend. If anything, during the 1993–2000 period there appeared to be a tendency for richer states to register higher rates of GDP growth per capita.

Figure 7.2: **Divergence in Economic Performance in Mexico's States, 1990s**

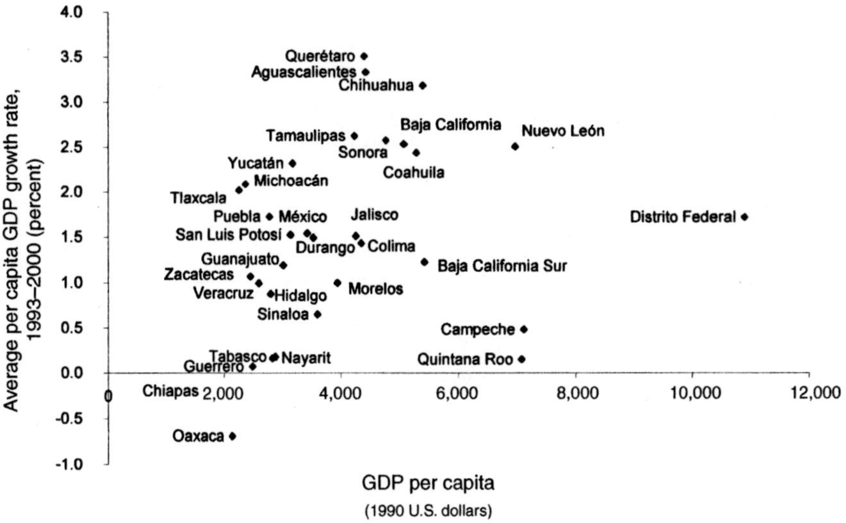

Source: Author's calculations based upon data from the Instituto Nacional de Estadística, Geografía y Informática (www.inegi.gob.mx)

The outlier to the right of figure 7.2 is the Federal District. If we were also to exclude from the analysis Campeche and Quintana Roo – whose comparatively high per capita GDP reflects their internationally oriented economies based upon, respectively, petroleum and tourism (Cancún) – one could even argue that there was some divergence in economic performance during the 1990s, with most data points aligning along an upward-sloping diagonal. But considering the full sample, the fact is that the data points (Mexican states) are scattered all over, which yields a statistically insignificant relationship between initial (1993) gross domestic product per capita and economic growth over the 1993–2000 period.

Depending upon the way that regional gross domestic product is measured, the available data suggest that regional inequality in Mexico increased during the 1990s. In fact, regional inequality at the turn of the twenty-first century was about 10 to 20 percent greater than in the 1960s and 1970s (Courchene, Díaz-Cayeros, and Webb 2000). This shift was probably an unintended consequence of the change in the model of development. During the period of import-substitution industrialization, economic activity was concentrated in a few cities, but income levels were not so different across regions because the economy was closed and flows of financial resources and migrants somewhat equalized regional differences. Although there is debate as to whether trade liberalization has had a discernible effect upon regional development in Mexico (Garza 2003; Tamayo-Flores 2001; Hiskey 2001), the transformation of regional economies due to the investment flows generated by the North American Free Trade Agreement (NAFTA) is quite noticeable in cities in the North and Center regions of the country.

During the 1970s there was considerable concern in Mexico about the degree of regional inequality that economic development was generating. Public policies that were designed to create regional poles of development or provide financial compensation to poor regions largely failed (Palacios 1989). In fact, federal public investment was not concentrated in poor regions, but instead tended to reinforce the growth of wealthier areas. Nevertheless, improvements in education and in the provision of such public goods as health care and infrastructure greatly improved conditions in poorer states, allowing for the economic convergence that was observed during those years.

Yet trade liberalization and the shift to a market-led model of economic development have changed conditions radically. Regions with poor infrastructure, deficient human capital, and local governments incapable of providing public goods are not able to take advantage of new economic opportunities; instead, they face greater challenges from increased global competition than before. At the same time, fiscal and macroeconomic imperatives have prevented the federal government from boosting growth in poor regions through increased federal expenditures. In contrast, regions that are better endowed with human capital and physical infrastructure are taking advantage of the NAFTA and the associated flows of trade, finance, and technology, and they are growing like never before.

In fact, two factors appear to explain the speed with which different Mexican states were able to recover after the December 1994 peso crisis: the degree to which a state's economy is internationalized (measured as the proportion of state GDP comprised by exports and imports; Díaz-Cayeros n.d.), and a state's human capital endowment. Those states with the best economic performance after the crisis were concentrated in the North. The top performers (Aguascalientes, Baja California, Coahuila, and Querétaro) have been particularly successful at attracting foreign investment in the manufacturing sector. The worst performers clustered in the Center and West regions and included the Mexico City area and agricultural states like Morelos, Nayarit, San Luis Potosí, and Sinaloa. In overall terms, then, different regions' competitive advantages are clearly connected to how much a region can profit from global markets, which in turn depends greatly upon the level of education of its people.

This pattern of differential growth and regional inequality has momentous political implications. Rich states will press the federal government to allow them to keep the financial resources that will permit them to continue in the virtuous cycle of growth / increased public provision of trade infrastructure and human capital / growth. Poor states, on the other hand, will press for federal programs that compensate them for their initial disadvantages, as well as additional resources to redress the new problems generated by economic globalization. Although the country as a whole benefits from free trade and open international markets, in poorer regions international competition poses challenges that – unless addressed by appropriate public policies – could well result in further impoverishment.

Governors in poor regions will have to convince the federal government that it is in the benefit of the country as a whole for them to receive financial compensation. But how successful they are in voicing and obtaining their demands will depend upon their potential for disruption, the degree of representation they hold within the larger political system, and the willingness of rich states to preserve the federal pact. It is the political process that will determine whether federal public policies will be designed in such a way that resources generated in wealthier regions will remain there, in order to promote further economic growth, or whether they will be redirected toward poorer regions, even if this does not maximize the national potential for growth. The issue goes beyond the philosophical question of what type of federalism Mexicans want, although this is obviously a central dimension in the discussion. Rather, it involves rethinking the institutional design of federalism and the system of federal financial transfers in such a way that, while promoting the growth of richer regions, these arrangements will produce policies that also translate into greater welfare for poorer states.

Waiting for market forces to mitigate "naturally" uneven growth and poverty is not a viable option. To be sure, migration to wealthier areas and the resulting increased flow of financial resources to poorer ones may well occur. But migration can become a politically contentious issue, and financial flows are not likely to be directed toward poor states – at least in the short or even medium run. Some form of federal public action is, therefore, essential. Yet how to design public policies in such a way that the poor are not left behind and the rich are willing to pay for compensatory programs is still an open question, to which we turn next.

Decentralization and Mexico's Complex System of Financial Transfers

Decentralization is one of the most important political processes that has accompanied democratization in Mexico. Democratization has been expressed primarily in the electoral arena, through increased guarantees for free and fair elections and, most important, partisan alternation in power in local and federal offices. Over the course of the 1990s, in vast areas of the country the long-dominant PRI abided by the will of the electorate and ceded power when it lost elections. At the same time, opposition parties gained access to office or accepted PRI victories, no longer crying fraud whenever they were defeated. Decentralization, in turn, has occurred in multiple issue-areas and policy arenas, from education, to health care, to the construction of physical infrastructure.

Decentralization finds its clearest expression in the way in which the system of financial transfers from the federal government to states and municipalities was reformed during the 1990s. The share of total tax revenue going to states and municipalities steadily increased during the decade.[12] In 1998 the federal government established a special budgetary item, the so-called budget item 33 contributions

12 For a discussion of the revenue-sharing system, see Arellano Cadena 1996.

(*ramo* 33 *aportaciones*), in order to streamline and make more transparent the allocation and distribution of federal conditional and unconditional transfers to local governments.[13] Efforts have also been made to improve the mechanisms for managing state and municipal debt (Hernández Trillo, Gamboa, and Díaz-Cayeros 2002).

Notwithstanding these important changes, federal-local relations in Mexico are still characterized by an enormous centralization of tax authority in the hands of the federal government. This situation, in turn, translates into state and municipal governments' extreme financial dependence upon federal transfers. Such extreme centralization is the consequence of a longer-term process that this author has analyzed elsewhere (Díaz-Cayeros 1997). However, the turning point came in the mid-twentieth century when the federal government began to claim exclusive authority over some forms of revenue.

During the second half of the twentieth century, the federal government consolidated the process of fiscal centralization by declaring itself the only level of government permitted to levy taxes on foreign trade, natural resources (including all petroleum and mining concessions), banks, and insurance institutions, as well as excise taxes on electricity, tobacco, natural gas, matches, distilled alcohol, forestry products, and beer.[14] States theoretically retained the capacity to levy an income tax, payroll taxes, sales taxes, and other taxes not explicitly listed in Article 73 of the Constitution. However, apart from payroll taxes, no state actually exercises this authority (although states did levy sales taxes until 1979). Over time, therefore, the federal government came to monopolize almost all sources of revenue. In exchange for states' refraining from using fully their own tax authority, the federal treasury transferred shares of tax revenue (*participaciones*) to the states, and these transfers increasingly came to constitute the most important source of local government finance.

The shift to fiscal centralization was not, though, simply a product of constitutional changes. Instead, it required a federal-local compromise. More specifically, the system of tax coordination characterizing the contemporary Mexican federation was the product of a deal struck between federal authorities and state governments in 1947 (Díaz-Cayeros 1997). Under the terms of this compromise, local politicians delegated financial power to the president, in exchange for access to patronage channeled through federal bureaucracies and attractive careers in the federal legislature and bureaucracies.[15] Institutional rules such as no immediate re-election

13 Analyses of these transfers are found in Guerrero et al. 1998; Courchene and Díaz-Cayeros 2000; and Levy 1998.

14 See Article 73, section 29, of the Constitution.

15 Robert E. Scott characterized the centralization of Mexican politics after the mid-twentieth century in the following terms: "[The weakening of the local machines] was coupled with the ever-increasing financial dependence of the formal state governments upon the central authorities, because just as the growing complexities of social and economic life called for greater expenditures by governmental agencies, the national government was busily preempting most of the major sources of tax revenue for itself. This forced the local officers to go to Mexico City, hat in hand, seeking grants from the national government to satisfy the demands of their constituents" (1959: 135).

for members of Congress (which ensured that offices were always available to be filled by local politicians) and the ruling PRI's effective control of the electoral process facilitated the implementation of this compromise. The compensation for the loss of local financial independence and fiscal initiative came from electoral success: during the heyday of PRI hegemony, local politicians securing a nomination from the party were certain of attaining office because they had the full support of the national party. At its origin, local and national politicians were both better off with this arrangement, and they were therefore willing to abide by it. However, the losers were democratic politics and federalism.

The tradeoff for local politicians between electoral success and financial dependence reflected the overwhelming power of the federal government, but local-level elites willingly accepted this arrangement. Pablo González Casanova (1965), writing about Mexican politics in the early 1960s, described the resulting situation in the following terms:

> The states' dependence upon the central government is a political, military, and financial fact. From the application of the Constitution to remove governors from office, to the political functions of military zone chiefs, to the activities of interior ministry agents, to the deputies and senators who make a political career in the capital city, to states' scarce financial resources and their extreme financial dependence upon the federal budget, to the possibility of a one-hundred-percent variation in the amount of federal aid to a state, indeed all the way to a political calendar that gradually accentuates the power of the president over the course of his presidential term – all these facts imply that the political instruments crafted to achieve a system of "checks and balances," like the one Madison proposed, do not function in the contemporary Mexican reality (p.41).

As the next section will show, political conditions in Mexico have changed rapidly since the early 1990s, but the system of revenue sharing and federal financial transfers has not. The specific system of revenue sharing now in place emerged in 1980 with the introduction of the value-added tax, while the existing arrangements for federal financial transfers are the result of the gradual transformation of ad hoc grants to local governments into comprehensive federal budgetary items. These transfers were initially for regional development (budget item 26, which was created in the 1980s and became the most important source of funds for the National Solidarity Program, PRONASOL), but in 1998 the transfers to local governments for education, health care, and social infrastructure were consolidated into budget item 33. Explaining the evolution of each of these funds far exceeds the scope of this chapter. However, it should be sufficient to note that the system that has emerged is characterized by two features: a large degree of decentralization in spending (more than half of national expenditures are now carried out by subnational governments, even if this spending is nominally part of the federal budget), coupled with an even higher degree of centralization in taxation (municipal and state governments together only collect around five percent of national revenue).

Table 7.2: **Mexican States' Financial Dependence Upon the Federal Government, 1999** (pesos per capita and percentages)

State	State's self-generated revenue	Car property taxes (all shared)	Revenue sharing (net of municipal shares)	Education transfers	Health care transfers	Public safety transfers	Other transfers	Federal public investment	Total resources	State's self-generated revenue as percentage of tax revenue	State's self-generated revenue as percentage of total resources
Aguascalientes	105.4	126.9	1,123.1	1,209.8	230.7	70.4	129.7	343.4	3,339.4	17.1	7.0
Baja California	358.0	100.3	1,166.1	1,079.7	142.2	88.9	59.5	311.3	3,306.0	28.2	13.9
Baja California Sur	91.1	87.0	1,588.9	1,963.2	417.3	256.6	178.4	167.1	4,749.6	10.1	3.7
Campeche	504.6	74.3	1,743.8	1,611.4	321.5	130.6	188.2	397.8	4,972.2	24.9	11.6
Coahuila	273.1	161.1	1,107.4	1,118.8	127.7	60.2	72.3	511.0	3,431.6	28.2	12.7
Colima	126.7	119.2	1,426.0	1,433.2	330.0	105.4	154.9	190.3	3,885.7	14.7	6.3
Chiapas	261.5	36.3	1,031.2	1,203.7	178.7	51.7	138.5	1,395.0	4,296.6	22.4	6.9
Chihuahua	362.2	74.8	998.6	907.7	131.0	51.9	68.6	586.4	3,181.2	30.4	13.7
Distrito Federal	2,075.5	375.5	1,392.7	1,261.0	98.5	38.1	131.3	4,131.8	9,504.4	63.8	25.8
Durango	141.5	73.6	965.7	1,363.9	210.3	84.2	157.3	348.7	3,345.2	18.2	6.4
Guanajuato	199.5	100.2	805.9	740.9	115.3	37.6	60.3	446.0	2,505.7	27.1	12.0
Guerrero	143.7	46.0	758.0	1,385.3	243.0	45.3	167.0	1,107.9	3,896.2	20.0	4.9
Hidalgo	111.9	61.2	808.8	1,267.8	180.4	55.1	145.1	541.6	3,171.9	17.6	5.5
Jalisco	225.8	154.8	933.0	707.6	142.0	31.5	68.6	379.8	2,643.1	29.0	14.4
State of México	135.8	57.0	917.6	648.8	145.8	28.8	48.3	639.5	2,621.6	17.4	7.4
Michoacán	112.0	74.4	736.5	1,070.1	133.8	42.8	91.4	850.2	3,111.2	20.2	6.0
Morelos	267.9	78.4	925.5	1,042.3	174.6	57.9	98.4	238.6	2,883.6	27.2	12.0
Nayarit	181.9	64.0	1,120.1	1,470.3	230.3	67.9	149.8	268.9	3,553.2	18.0	6.9

State	State's self-generated revenue	Car property taxes (all shared)	Revenue sharing (net of municipal shares)	Education transfers	Health care transfers	Public safety transfers	Other transfers	Federal public investment	Total resources	State's self-generated revenue as percentage of tax revenue	State's self-generated revenue as percentage of total resources
Nuevo León	426.6	276.5	1,127.3	795.1	121.5	51.2	66.7	334.8	3,199.7	38.4	22.0
Oaxaca	55.2	23.9	692.9	1,247.0	159.5	43.3	164.6	1,119.5	3,505.9	10.2	2.3
Puebla	123.3	82.8	772.0	761.3	99.9	35.7	99.5	552.9	2,527.4	21.1	8.2
Querétaro	144.3	117.8	1,153.4	1,035.9	188.5	63.4	132.8	248.9	3,085.0	18.5	8.5
Quintana Roo	306.7	162.5	1,166.7	1,341.5	287.9	80.6	136.7	207.7	3,690.3	28.7	12.7
San Luis Potosí	96.4	95.2	817.5	1,199.5	128.6	57.0	89.5	793.1	3,276.8	19.0	5.8
Sinaloa	211.4	87.4	1,052.0	957.4	140.3	54.9	90.7	346.7	2,940.8	22.1	10.2
Sonora	339.8	119.1	1,222.9	1,042.2	201.0	95.1	92.4	516.4	3,628.9	27.3	12.6
Tabasco	221.9	81.1	2,835.8	1,098.4	200.9	67.9	155.5	247.8	4,909.3	9.7	6.2
Tamaulipas	258.8	146.1	1,035.0	1,172.9	196.5	72.4	86.0	494.4	3,462.1	28.1	11.7
Tlaxcala	120.6	50.4	1,047.1	1,236.6	201.7	69.4	182.6	251.9	3,160.3	14.0	5.4
Veracruz	86.2	59.5	902.0	979.6	100.4	31.5	99.5	815.0	3,073.7	13.9	4.7
Yucatán	184.7	112.3	899.8	999.0	188.6	55.2	147.7	368.2	2,955.5	24.8	10.0
Zacatecas	101.5	43.4	933.8	1,329.5	149.5	49.1	139.9	335.9	3,082.6	13.4	4.7
Coefficient of variation	1.31	0.66	0.36	0.24	0.39	0.61	0.34	1.14	0.34		

Source: Courchene and Díaz-Cayeros 2000.

Note: The calculation of each state's self-generated revenue as a percentage of its total resources (column 12) includes car property taxes (a federal tax that is fully shared with states) with other forms of self-generated revenue.

Table 7.3: **Mexican Municipalities' Financial Dependence Upon State and Federal Governments, 1999** (pesos per capita and percentages)

State	Municipalities' self-generated revenue	State revenue sharing	Federal revenue sharing	Municipal Social Infrastructure Fund	Municipal Strengthening Fund	Total resources	Municipalities' self-generated revenue as percentage of tax revenue	Municipalities' self-generated revenue as percentage of total resources
Aguascalientes	148.0	270.1	171.7	111.5	148.0	849.3	25.1	17.4
Baja California	228.5	262.0	21.3	50.4	143.3	705.5	44.6	32.4
Baja California Sur	376.2	374.7	70.9	181.9	145.3	1,149.0	45.8	32.7
Campeche	79.3	420.0	83.6	255.7	147.7	986.3	13.6	8.0
Coahuila	119.3	250.7	26.5	71.5	152.6	620.6	30.1	19.2
Colima	95.3	337.7	149.5	165.0	150.9	898.4	16.4	10.6
Chiapas	18.5	254.3	13.1	263.7	144.7	694.3	6.5	2.7
Chihuahua	196.1	234.6	32.5	80.8	150.0	694.0	42.3	28.3
Distrito Federal	—	—	149.5	—	—	149.5	—	—
Durango	74.3	232.5	79.0	157.1	155.0	697.9	19.3	10.6
Guanajuato	94.8	194.4	27.9	131.3	150.1	598.5	29.9	15.8
Guerrero	69.2	180.6	101.8	304.6	149.4	805.6	19.7	8.6
Hidalgo	67.5	195.8	118.7	191.0	151.1	724.1	17.7	9.3
Jalisco	175.7	222.7	19.5	74.3	149.6	641.8	42.1	27.4
State of México	140.6	221.7	11.2	71.1	148.4	593.0	37.6	23.7
Michoacán	61.0	176.3	55.4	161.1	151.8	605.6	20.8	10.1
Morelos	37.3	223.9	119.3	102.0	147.2	629.7	9.8	5.9
Nayarit	55.6	269.2	132.8	156.8	153.4	767.8	12.1	7.2

State	Municipalities' self-generated revenue	State revenue sharing	Federal revenue sharing	Municipal Social Infrastructure Fund	Municipal Strengthening Fund	Total resources	Municipalities' self-generated revenue as percentage of tax revenue	Municipalities' self-generated revenue as percentage of total resources
Nuevo León	212.8	267.4	24.3	59.6	149.6	713.7	42.2	29.8
Oaxaca	30.2	169.5	128.1	257.9	147.9	733.6	9.2	4.1
Puebla	0.4	183.5	48.2	179.0	147.8	558.9	0.2	0.1
Querétaro	151.2	276.7	75.4	160.0	147.8	811.1	30.0	18.6
Quintana Roo	301.4	260.5	100.1	165.6	138.1	965.7	45.5	31.2
San Luis Potosí	51.2	197.7	76.6	181.3	151.3	658.1	15.7	7.8
Sinaloa	141.1	248.7	20.8	82.0	153.1	645.7	34.4	21.9
Sonora	163.0	288.3	21.2	73.1	150.1	695.7	34.5	23.4
Tabasco	38.3	703.0	53.9	167.1	148.7	1,111.0	4.8	3.4
Tamaulipas	87.7	246.4	30.3	95.5	151.2	611.1	24.1	14.4
Tlaxcala	28.0	259.9	154.7	162.0	149.5	754.1	6.3	3.7
Veracruz	48.6	220.9	19.4	177.7	148.7	615.3	16.8	7.9
Yucatán	45.2	215.0	127.6	209.0	150.5	747.3	11.6	6.0
Zacatecas	65.4	221.3	130.7	190.5	153.6	761.5	15.7	8.6
Coefficient of variation	1.41	0.63	0.99	0.82	0.32	0.89		

Source: Courchene and Díaz-Cayeros 2000.

Tables 7.2 and 7.3 summarize the most important financial resources available to, respectively, state and municipal governments. (To enhance comparability, all the data are provided in per capita terms.) The second column in each table lists the resources that each level of government collects using its own fiscal authority. These funds constitute a state's or a municipality's "own revenue" in the sense that their collection and administration, as well as the legislation determining the base, rates, and conditions for the payment of these taxes, are local. Local governments also obtain substantial resources from fees and user charges, which, although they are not taxes in a strict sense, are included in the "own revenue" columns in tables 7.2 and 7.3. The last two columns in each table provide measures of local governments' financial autonomy: the proportion that a local government's own revenue comprises of all its tax revenues (an amount that includes transfers agreed upon through the federal/local revenue-sharing system), and the proportion that its own revenue comprises of its total financial resources. The intermediate columns in tables 7.2 and 7.3 list all the different transfers from higher-tier governments (the federal government in the case of states, and federal and state governments in the case of municipalities) received by subnational governments.

Financial transfers to state governments first include car property taxes, consisting of the federal tax levied on new cars (*impuesto sobre automóviles nuevos*) and *tenencia*, a property tax on both new and used cars (see table 7.2). Although these are federal taxes, under existing revenue-sharing arrangements they are transferred in full to the states according to what is called a "derivation principle," whereby richer states receive more revenue because they have a larger tax base (that is, more cars).[16]

The fourth column in table 7.2 reports fiscal transfers to states via the federal revenue-sharing system, payments which are comprised mainly of general tax revenues (*fondo general de participaciones*, FGP) and some shared excise taxes. States keep 80 percent of FGP monies; they must transfer at least 20 percent to municipalities. The formulas for transfers from this fund have increasingly incorporated population as a major determinant in allocating monies, which explains the relatively equal distribution of these resources in per capita terms. However, it is important to highlight the extremely disproportionate allocation that goes to Tabasco, an outcome which is explained by inertia in the revenue-sharing formulas – originally defined at a time when that oil-producing state enjoyed great bargaining power.

The next four columns in table 7.2 concern the education, health care, public safety, and other transfers within federal budget item 33. Education comprises the most important component of these transfers. The primary concern where these funds are concerned is that the formulas for their allocation give great weight to

16 Taxing automobiles became a controversial issue in Mexico when in 2001 the PRI governor of Chihuahua, Patricio Martínez (1998–2004), attempted to tax cars smuggled into his border state, thereby making them quasi-legal. The federal government adamantly opposed his initiative and threatened to withhold transfers via the revenue-sharing system if the state went ahead with its proposed tax.

covering the payroll of what were, prior to the decentralization of basic education, federal schools and teachers. States differed greatly in the proportion of their schools that were either state- or federally supported. Hence, a state like Nuevo León (where only half of the schools were federally supported) receives far fewer resources in this category than does the Federal District (where all basic education was federal).[17]

Of the four funds reported in this section of table 7.2, public safety monies are the most unequally distributed. They exhibit a measure of dispersion (the co-efficient of variation) as large as that for car property taxes. It is hardly surprising that the measure of dispersion for car property taxes is similar to that for regional GDP; after all, car ownership is highly correlated with the level of economic development. But it is unclear why public safety funds should also display such dispersion, unless criminality is also distributed across the country in line with the degree of development.[18]

Column 9 reports federal public investment funds directed to states. These are federal development projects such as roads, ports, and water infrastructure. Other than a state's own revenue (regarding which there is a very high degree of dispersion among states), this is the most unequally distributed resource among all the funds reported in table 7.2. The Federal District received a very disproportionate share of these funds in 1999, although given the nature of this transfer, there is no way to know whether this will continue to be the case in the future.[19] The main point to be made concerning these resources, however, is that they constitute substantial amounts that can produce great imbalances among states – and they are primarily devoted to communications and transportation infrastructure, precisely those purposes that might be most important for regional development in an era of economic globalization.

In the case of municipal governments, table 7.3 reports data on four kinds of financial transfers. First, the amounts shown in column 3 are FGP funds initially transferred from the federal government to the states, which in turn must transfer them to municipalities. States could in theory transfer even more funds to their municipalities, but in practice the overwhelming majority of them distribute only what is required by federal law (that is, 20 percent of FGP monies). The second transfer (column 4) consists of monies from the Municipal Development Fund (FFM) that the federal government directly provides to municipalities. Because the formula employed in allocating these resources rewards local property tax and water-usage fees collection, the distribution of these funds closely parallels states' general level of economic development. In contrast, the third transfer – the Muni-

---

17 For discussions of the "federalization" of education, see Merino 1998 and Latapí and Ulloa 2000.

18 See the chapter by Beatriz Magaloni and Guillermo Zepeda in this volume.

19 There are very large differences between the amount of federal public investment funds authorized and those actually spent, and regional patterns in the distribution of these funds often change dramatically from year to year (see Díaz-Cayeros 1997). The figures reported in table 7.2 are calculations based upon actual expenditures in 1996.

cipal Social Infrastructure Fund (FISM) – is allocated by precisely the opposite criterion. The resources in this fund are the heirs of the National Solidarity Program (a strategy for poverty alleviation adopted during the administration of President Carlos Salinas de Gortari [1988–1994]),[20] and they are distributed according to a complex poverty formula.[21] Finally, there is a fourth fund within budget item 33, the Municipal Strengthening Fund (FORTAMUN), which is allocated to municipalities according to their population, almost on an equal per capita basis.[22]

Several of these funds are conditioned in different ways, in the sense that there are restrictions upon their use by the recipient level of government. In general, revenue-sharing funds carry no conditions. Similarly, FORTAMUN funds come with only quite general suggestions concerning their preferred use. In contrast, public safety funds must be used in conjunction with federal programs; education and health care funds are clearly earmarked to pay the salaries of teachers, doctors, and nurses; and infrastructure funds (FISM monies, plus a small state social infrastructure fund) are highly conditioned and come with very clear spending guidelines and monitoring procedures. Federal investment funds are really controlled by the federal bureaucracy, although to the extent that state governments contribute their own resources, they might have some voice in the implementation of federal programs.

The two summary issues to highlight in tables 7.2 and 7.3 appear in the last two columns and in the final row: subnational governments' low degree of financial autonomy, and the large variation in the size of financial transfers across states. Taking as the relevant measure each state's own revenue as a percentage of its total resources in 1999 (table 7.2, column 12), state financial autonomy ranged from a low 2.3 percent in Oaxaca to a high 25.8 percent in the Federal District. Nuevo León, the industrial powerhouse of the North, approximated the Federal District at 22.0 percent, but it was still highly dependent upon federal revenue transfers.

There was somewhat greater financial autonomy at the municipal level (table 7.3, column 9), with several states in the 30-percent range. Those states are either comparatively developed ones in the North and West (Nuevo León, Chihuahua, Baja California, and Jalisco) or small states with an important tourist destination that produces substantial property tax (*predial*) revenue (for example, Loreto in Baja California Sur and Cancún in Quintana Roo).

However, subnational governments' overall dependence upon federal government transfers is the highest observed among members of the Organisation for Economic Co-operation and Development (OECD), including both centralized and federal regimes. It is, moreover, quite high by international standards (see World Bank 2000, table A1).

20 For analyses of the National Solidarity Program (PRONASOL), see Dresser 1991, Bailey 1994, and Molinar Horcasitas and Weldon 1994.
21 For analyses of these funds, see Mogollón 2002 and Levy 1998.
22 The minor differences in the amounts shown in table 7.3, column 5, reflect alternate population totals.

The coefficient of variation summarizes differences in the distribution of financial transfers across states. This indicator has a value of 0.52 for the distribution of per capita GDP. Thus, any value greater than that in the last row of either table 7.2 or 7.3 means that the distribution of resources from a given fund is more unequal than the regional distribution of national wealth. The discussion in the previous section suggested that state GDP dispersion in Mexico is high by international standards. Except for education, health care, state revenue-sharing, and FORTAMUN funds, in 1999 federal transfers were distributed more unequally than state GDP.

This pattern, however, is not necessarily either good or bad. There would, for example, be strong reasons for poverty alleviation funds to be distributed unequally, so that poorer regions receive more resources than richer ones. At the same time, the best economic incentives are those provided to subnational governments in revenue-sharing funds such as those from the Municipal Development Fund, which allocates resources according to local tax collection efforts rather than in equal per capita terms. Under both criteria – the extent of poverty or the vigor of local tax collection efforts – the distribution of funds would be highly unequal. Hence, evaluating variations in financial transfers across states depends fundamentally upon understanding what each of those funds seeks to accomplish. Yet the existence of multiple federal transfer funds in Mexico is the product of incremental change, not part of an overarching design that links together federal, state, and municipal governments. A considered assessment of the purpose of Mexico's revenue transfer system is, therefore, one of the main pending issues on the federalism agenda (Courchene and Díaz-Cayeros 2000).

In and of itself, incrementalism in public policy is nothing to complain about. Gradual change ensures that major mistakes can be avoided, although it may also entrench vested interests and permit bureaucracies to "capture" specific programs or projects. However, the problem with incrementalism in this instance is that changes in the system of federal grants and transfers to subnational governments have not kept pace with the momentous shifts in the political system. The mismatch between the arrangement of Mexican fiscal federalism, and the expanded role for governors and local politicians that has accompanied democratization, has produced increasing demands for change that have thus far been accommodated only by further incremental changes (mostly related to increasing the percentages that states and municipalities can expect from federal transfers). Yet this situation is creating perverse incentives for local government tax collection and furthering subnational units' dependence upon the federal government (Díaz-Cayeros 1997). Because the federal revenue collection system concentrates resources, personnel, and the most important taxes, states and municipalities have little, if any, taxation authority – even though fiscal authority is perhaps the most essential prerequisite for effective political authority.

There are differences in the extent to which states and municipalities use the limited fiscal authority they still retain, but this variance is highly correlated with

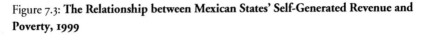

Figure 7.3: **The Relationship between Mexican States' Self-Generated Revenue and Poverty, 1999**

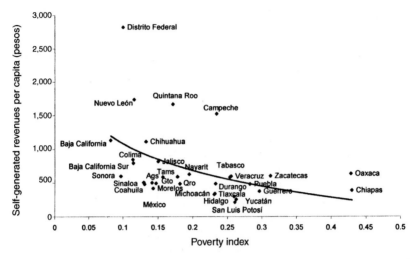

Source: Table 7.1 and author"s calculations of the Foster-Greer-Thorbecke (FGT) poverty index based upon 1990 census data from the Instituto Nacional de Estadística, Geografía e Informática (www.inegi.gob.mx). See the accompanying text for the parameters of the poverty index.

the level of economic development. Figure 7.3 depicts the strong inverse correlation existing between the sum of self-generated revenue from both state and municipal governments (as reported in tables 7.2 and 7.3) and the extent of poverty (measured by the Foster-Greer-Thorbecke [FGT] poverty index).[23] This relationship brings us back to the concern articulated earlier in this chapter: left on their own, the capacity of states (and municipalities) to command resources will depend upon their level of development. As a consequence, unless federal transfers are assigned to them, those areas most in need of improved human capital and infrastructure will have fewer resources to devote to them.

If the division between wealthier states with taxation capacity and poorer ones without it were consistently mobilized into political differences (with, for example, one party winning in rich states and another one in poor states), serious conflicts might arise. The next section describes the impact of democratization on local politics in Mexico, and the following one analyzes the mismatch generated by decentralization and democratization – and the degree to which we can anticipate a mobilization of regional differences within the Mexican party system.

23 The FGT index is a general measure of poverty, which in its simplest form is a head-count ratio of the proportion of households below a stipulated poverty line. In figure 7.3, the author calculated the poverty index from 1990 census data (see www.inegi.gob.mx), with a poverty line of less than 2 minimum wages and with a parameter $\alpha=2$ (which gives greater weight in the index to the poorest among the poor). For a general discussion of the FGT index in the Mexican context, see Mogollón 2002.

Democratization and the Politics of Governors

Mexico has experienced a gradual but continuous process of democratization, which is evident in the evolution of presidential and federal legislative election results. Although most observers have concentrated their attention at the federal level, there is increasing awareness that an explosive process of democratization has also occurred at state and municipal levels. Figure 7.4 shows the evolution of support for the PRI and the competitiveness of federal elections between 1979 and 1997. The bars (based on the right-hand axis) depict the gradual decline in PRI support, which was only interrupted by two events: the surprising performance of Cuauhtémoc Cárdenas in the 1988 presidential election,[24] and the equally surprising recovery of the PRI in 1991, which was mostly due to the popularity at the time of President Carlos Salinas.

The lines in the graph (based on the left-hand axis) show the evolution in the degree of competitiveness in Mexico's 300 single-member congressional districts, as measured by the Laakso-Taagepera effective number of parties.[25] Considering that a competitive district is one in which at least 1.7 effective parties are present, one can see that in 1979 only half of the districts had anything resembling real partisan competition. In a dominant-party setting, as Juan Molinar (1991) has argued, this might actually be an overestimation because in many of those districts a fragmented yet minuscule opposition had no chance whatsoever of defeating the PRI – although the number of parties was high precisely because of this fragmentation. The crucial issue, however, is the overall trend. By 1994 the PRI faced some degree of electoral threat in all 300 single-member districts.

Figure 7.4 also shows the evolution of two additional thresholds of electoral competitiveness – with more than 2.35 effective parties, and with more than 3.0 effective parties. At these thresholds, the PRI's decline was less continuous. In part this was because the 1988 election results were characterized by a surge in the fragmented vote for parties supporting the Cárdenas candidacy within the National Democratic Front (FDN), which fielded separate candidates in the congressional elections. However, even at these multiparty thresholds, the trend was for the PRI to face stiffer challenges. In fact, in the 1997 midterm elections, PRI candidates came in third (in seven congressional districts) for the first time.

This is a generally well-known story. Somewhat less well known is the process of democratization at the local level (Rodríguez and Ward 1995; Ward and Rodríguez 1999). By 1999, ten states and the Federal District were governed by a party other than the PRI. During the period between 1989 and 1997, seven states became

24 Cárdenas's supporters claimed that he actually won the election. Although the truth of the matter is difficult to ascertain, there is no doubt that the results were rigged to increase the votes claimed by the PRI's candidate, Carlos Salinas de Gortari.

25 The effective number of parties is the inverse of the sum of the squared vote shares of each party competing in an election. Hence, it is the inverse of the Herfindahl-Hirschman measure of fragmentation.

Figure 7.4: **The Changing Competitiveness of Mexican Federal Elections, 1979–1997**

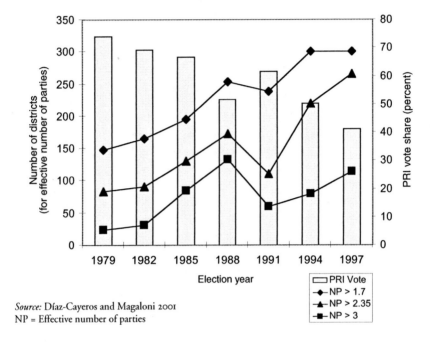

Source: Díaz-Cayeros and Magaloni 2001
NP = Effective number of parties

accustomed to the dynamic of divided government (Lujambio 2001), a condition that has become increasingly common. At the municipal level, more than half of Mexico's state capital cities have experienced partisan alternation in office. Moreover, by 1997 the combined population under the jurisdiction of National Action Party (PAN) and Party of the Democratic Revolution (PRD) local authorities almost equaled that under PRI government, and by mid-1999 the PAN and the PRD had governed municipalities in every state. The number of municipalities governed by parties other than the PRI still represents a modest proportion of Mexico's more than 2,400 local jurisdictions, but the PRI is strongest in small rural municipalities while the PAN and PRD are much stronger in urban zones. And even in rural districts, the PRI now faces increasing challenges, particularly from the PRD.

A particularly striking feature of the local dynamics of PRI support is that, although in the past local elections tended to follow federal trends, during the 1990s a clear differentiation between federal and local elections emerged. In most states, the support that the PRI receives in local elections is greater than its federal support. Perhaps the most striking manifestation of this process is the way in which governors are quickly becoming the axes of state politics and key players in national coalition building. Governors were the principal political players in the 1930s, before the consolidation of a hegemonic-party system, and they made a comeback in the 1990s.

Table 7.4: **Results of Gubernatorial Elections in Mexico, 1993–1999** (percentage of valid votes)

State	Year	PRI	PAN	PRD	Number of Parties	Coalition	Winner	Previous winner
Coahuila	1993	65.5	27.0	0.0	2.0		PRI	PRI
Chiapas	1994	50.4	9.2	34.9	2.6		PRI	PRI
Morelos	1994	75.8	7.9	0.0	1.6		PRI	PRI
Tabasco	1994	57.5	2.6	38.7	2.1		PRI	PRI
Baja California	1995	42.3	50.9	3.3	2.3		PAN	PAN
Guanajuato	1995	32.9	58.1	7.0	2.2		PAN	PAN
Jalisco	1995	36.6	51.9	3.9	2.4		PAN	PRI
Yucatán	1995	48.7	44.4	3.0	2.3		PRI	PRI
Michoacán	1995	38.9	25.5	32.4	3.1		PRI	PRI
Campeche	1997	48.0	3.1	41.2	2.5		PRI	PRI
Colima	1997	42.6	38.2	16.3	2.8		PRI	PRI
Distrito Federal	1997	25.6	15.6	48.1	3.1		PRD	PRI
Nuevo León	1997	41.9	48.5	3.2	2.4	PRD+PVEM	PAN	PRI
Querétaro	1997	39.5	45.4	7.4	2.7		PAN	PRI
San Luis Potosí	1997	49.5	41.4	9.1	2.4		PRI	PRI
Sonora	1997	41.8	31.6	23.5	3.0		PRI	PRI
Chihuahua	1998	50.3	42.2	5.5	2.3	PT+CDP	PRI	PAN
Zacatecas	1998	39.8	13.5	46.7	2.5		PRD	PRI
Durango	1998	39.9	30.3	8.4	3.3		PRI	PRI
Veracruz	1998	49.0	27.2	17.9	2.9		PRI	PRI
Aguascalientes	1998	38.0	53.1	6.9	2.3		PAN	PRI
Oaxaca	1998	48.9	10.2	37.6	2.6		PRI	PRI
Tamaulipas	1998	54.9	26.6	16.1	2.5		PRI	PRI
Puebla	1998	55.5	29.7	11.2	2.4		PRI	PRI
Sinaloa	1998	47.5	32.7	18.1	2.7		PRI	PRI
Tlaxcala	1998	44.3	8.6	34.0	2.4	PRD+PT +PVEM	Coalition	PRI
Baja California Sur	1999	37.4	6.3	55.9	2.2	PRD+PT	Coalition	PRI
Hidalgo	1999	53.5	32.1	14.4	2.4		PRI	PRI
Quintana Roo	1999	44.4	17.4	36.1	2.8		PRI	PRI
Guerrero	1999	49.8	1.7	47.7	2.1	PRI+PRS and PRD+PT+PRT	PRI	PRI
Nayarit	1999	44.8	52.9	0.0	2.1	PAN+ PRD+PT	Coalition	PRI
State of México	1999	42.5	35.5	22.0	2.8	PAN+PVEM and PRD+PT	PRI	PRI

Source: Diaz-Cayeros and Magaloni 2001

Note: See the List of Acronyms for individual party names.

Figure 7.5: **Electoral Competitiveness and Support for the Institutional Revolutionary Party in Mexico's 2000 Federal Elections**

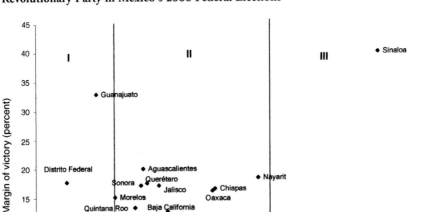

Source: Author's calculations based upon data from the Instituto Federal Electoral (www.ife.org.mx).

Before 1993, the PRI had lost only three gubernatorial elections. However, as table 7.4 shows, over the 1993–1999 period (a time span during which all gubernatorial posts were renewed), the PRI lost the governorship in eleven states. Even in those states in which the PRI was able to win, the threat of an opposition victory was real. Indeed, during this period the PRI was able to win more than fifty percent of the gubernatorial vote in only four states: Chihuahua, Hidalgo, Puebla, and Tamaulipas.

The "number of parties" column in table 7.4 reveals that gubernatorial elections during the 1993–1999 period were characterized by either two- or three-party (candidate) races. The number of effective parties was calculated taking into account the possibility for electoral coalitions; where a coalition competed, the coalition was counted as a single party. Although it was not true that the PRI lost wherever opposition parties were able to forge a coalition, there was evidence of a trend for the opposition to win in states where two-party races emerged. The PRI clearly benefited from the fragmentation of the opposition; indeed, most of the races it won between 1993 and 1999 were in multicandidate settings. Nevertheless, overwhelming PRI victories in gubernatorial elections had clearly become a thing of the past.

Figure 7.5, which depicts the relationship between margin of victory and PRI support in the year 2000 federal elections, further illustrates the erosion of the

PRI's electoral dominance. The horizontal axis shows PRI support in the state; the vertical axis marks the margin of victory or loss for the PRI. Except for Sinaloa, the home state of PRI presidential candidate Francisco Labastida Ochoa, there was no state in which the PRI received more than 50 percent of the valid vote (as shown by the empty area labeled III).

The other quadrants in figure 7.5 divide the space into high-competition (a margin of victory of less than 10 percent) and low-competition (a margin of victory of more than 10 percent) areas, according to PRI electoral strength. Most PRI–controlled states fall into the area labeled IV, in which there was no overwhelming margin of victory. The region denoted II mostly comprises states with PAN victories in two-party (candidate) races. Quadrant I includes Guanajuato (an outlier, reflecting the home-state effect for PAN presidential candidate Vicente Fox Quesada) and the Federal District (in which three-party competition is fierce), where the PRI placed third.

These patterns of electoral competition have momentous implications for the behavior of governors. No matter which party they belong to, state executives in Mexico (rightfully) feel that they won their post in highly competitive contests based upon their own merits, not those of their party or the federal government. In particular, PRI governors do not think that the president was responsible for their electoral success.

These views reflect a profound change in political expectations. Presidential power was long the cornerstone of the Mexican political system. Presidents wielded great authority through the metaconstitutional powers of *presidencialismo* (Weldon 1997) in a hegemonic- or dominant-party system. Besides appointing his own cabinet, a Mexican president could control PRI nominations for all important federal elective posts, as well as governorships and sometimes even municipal presidencies. Through the federal administrative bureaucracy, the president could decide what projects were undertaken in each state, in line with national priorities. Moreover, he could also discipline rebellious or incompetent governors through the "dissolution of powers" provision in the Constitution, or simply by forcing them to resign. Neither chamber of the Congress played a role in checking presidential power, and the Supreme Court issued few (if any) judicial interpretations that constrained the executive branch. In such circumstances, governors behaved more like appointed federal bureaucrats than elected officials.

But this situation is now a thing of the past. The new players in the Mexican political system are the governors. For example, for several decades the candidates for the PRI's presidential nomination always emerged from among the members of the appointed federal cabinet, but in the year 2000 election all major contenders for the presidency were, or had recently been, governors. At the time of the primary organized to choose the PRI's nominee, Manuel Bartlett and Roberto Madrazo were governors of, respectively, Puebla and Tabasco, while Francisco Labastida Ochoa had been governor of Sinaloa before joining President Ernesto Zedillo Ponce de León's (1994–2000) cabinet. Among the opposition candidates, the PAN's

Vicente Fox had served as governor of Guanajuato, and the PRD's Cuauhtémoc Cárdenas had governed the Federal District (and, before that, his home state of Michoacán).

The erosion of presidential power also has important implications for legislators' behavior. Federal deputies and senators have regained some of the prominence they lost in the 1930s. Although ambitious politicians may still find congressional office of limited attraction because of the "no re-election" rule, budget battles and enacting legislation have become major political events in which deputies and senators are key actors. Deputies and senators are, moreover, increasingly likely to form coalitions with the governor of their home state because they realize that subnational political careers are not only feasible but highly rewarded. As a consequence, federal deputies have become more parochial in their demands.

Party discipline in the Congress is still strong, but peripheralizing forces are felt whenever a major piece of legislation is debated. Nowhere is this more evident than in budget discussions, which have become inextricably linked to the federal revenue transfer system. As the next section shows, there is an institutional mismatch in the evolution of decentralization and democratization in Mexico because, although pressures are mounting to redesign the federal pact, political configurations are not conducive to reaching agreements in this area. Moreover, there is no forum in which the new, democratically elected players can convene and effectively make choices to carry out the changes they might all agree are necessary.

Local Revenue Collection and the Federal Arrangement

The process of constructing a complex system of fiscal federalism in Mexico was long and convoluted. Although most observers think that current arrangements evolved rationally over time, the system's development was in fact a highly contingent process strongly shaped by the peculiarities of Mexican political development – namely, the character of the hegemonic- or dominant-party system. As noted above, the centralization of revenue collection and subnational governments' heavy dependence upon federal transfers were the consequence of local actors' willingness to abdicate their taxation authority in exchange for political rewards.[27] The system of revenue sharing was constructed from the local level upward as federal revenue transfers gradually substituted for taxes raised by state and municipal governments. In contrast, the trend since the 1980s in favor of decentralization through a very rapid divestment of federal government spending responsibilities has been more of a top-down phenomenon. Both processes have generated a very strong mismatch between the established system of intergovernmental transfers and the evolution of political forces in states and municipalities.

As processes of democratization and decentralization advance, federal deputies

---

26 Local actors' financial dependence has actually been exacerbated by their capacity to press the federal government successfully for ever larger flows of resources.

and senators increasingly seek to cultivate local sources of political support, rather than simply trying to please the president or national political elites. Deputies in particular have an incentive to expand the flow of federal resources to their districts in order to lay the bases for their possible future political advancement to senatorial or gubernatorial posts. To the extent to which their expenditures are decentralized to states and municipalities and the Congress exercises more stringent oversight over their activities, federal bureaucracies are also becoming less powerful. In short, politics in Mexico is becoming local.

Moreover, conflicts between state governors and the federal government are increasingly common. On several occasions since the early 1990s, PAN governors in the comparatively wealthy states of Baja California and Nuevo León have threatened to abandon the federal system of revenue sharing because they believe that the formulas employed in calculating transfers do not treat their states fairly. Ernesto Ruffo, whose election in Baja California in 1989 was the first PAN gubernatorial victory to be recognized by national authorities, claimed that the federal government withheld funds from his state.[28] Similarly, in 2001 the PRI governor of Chihuahua, Patricio Martínez, attempted to levy taxes on cars illegally smuggled into his state, notwithstanding the fact that both taxes on new cars and the prosecution of smuggling are strictly areas of federal jurisdiction.

Bitter conflicts have also occurred within states over the system of federal revenue transfers and the formulas determining their allocation. Perhaps the most famous instance involved Manuel Bartlett, then the PRI governor of Puebla, and the PAN municipal government in the state's capital city. In 1998 they clashed sharply over the formulas used by the state to distribute federal funds to municipalities. Governor Bartlett had issued a law concerning the allocation of state transfers to municipalities that was highly redistributive, thereby ensuring that poorer municipalities would receive far more resources than wealthier cities. Those poorer municipalities happened to be governed predominantly by the PRI, while the richer cities were ruled by the PAN (Mogollón and Díaz-Cayeros n.d.).

The question that emerges from these examples is whether Mexico's prevailing institutional arrangements can accommodate these emerging centripetal forces, while at the same time protecting a federal sphere for effective collective choices. Since 1997 the federal Chamber of Deputies has successfully passed budget and income bills without a clear majority from a single party. However, political fights over these issues have become increasingly bitter, and party leaders' efforts to maintain control over their delegations have at times failed. The most important debates have occurred within the Chamber precisely because it has exclusive authority over the federal budget.

---

27 It was ironic that, following the PAN's presidential victory in the year 2000, PRI and PRD governors claimed that the federal government unfairly withheld resources from their states – just as Ruffo had done a decade earlier. See "Fustiga CONAGO ante Congreso Plan de Fox," *Reforma*, November 11, 2002.

Nevertheless, the strongest future tensions are likely to arise between and among states. The gap between those states exhibiting better economic performance (given the more beneficial character of their insertion into world markets and their more favorable human capital endowments) and stagnant regions with reduced prospects for economic development may be widening – and politicians might take advantage of this. The risk is that political mobilization of the rift between richer and poorer states could result in an utter lack of agreement about the current system of revenue sharing and an unwillingness to devise a new one. Given that states control so few sources of taxation, their efforts would be devoted not to taxing and spending according to citizen demands (supposedly one of the virtues of federal arrangements) but rather to obtaining as many resources as possible from the national government in what would quickly become a zero-sum game.

However, the residual taxation authority that states and municipalities retain provides a guide to the prospects for breaking such a zero-sum interaction. If participating in a federal arrangement simply becomes a fight over a pie of fixed size, richer states will see no particular advantage to joining in. But if states can tax and thereby increase the amount of resources available to them, the relationship becomes a cooperative bargaining game rather than a zero-sum one. In a bargaining situation, players can decide to cooperate (thereby achieving a superior outcome for everyone) or they can fall into disagreement (an outcome in which each player goes his or her own way). The reason bargaining might break down – thus making everyone worse off – is that players might not be able to agree about how to distribute the gains resulting from working together in a federation.

Hence, we can think of debates over revenue sharing and transfer formulas as disagreements over how to allocate the benefits of federation. The incentives to belong to a federation depend upon both the distribution being offered to each state and the state's opportunity costs (as reflected in the disagreement outcome). Revenue collection by subnational governments provides a good estimation of how that disagreement outcome is configured, and an analysis of revenue collection and local capacity to tax reveals that the rift between richer and poorer states – the former wanting to break from the federal pact, and the latter seeking to preserve a highly redistributive system – is likely to widen in the future.

What determines why some states and municipalities collect more revenue from their own tax sources than others? In essence, the answer is overwhelmingly economic in nature: the more economically developed a state or municipality is, the more it is able to collect fiscal resources for its future development. This, however, is not the full story. Estimates of the variance in revenue collection across Mexican states reveal that important political considerations lie beneath the obvious economic correlates – political dimensions that might become mobilized and make compromises over federalism very hard to reach.

Table 7.5 presents the results of an analysis of variance in total subnational tax collection per capita in Mexico in 1999. The table includes estimates for both overall subnational revenue and its components (states' and municipalities' own revenue,

Table 7.5: **Determinants of Mexican States' and Municipalities' Self-Generated Revenue Collection**

Dependent Variable / Independent Variables	Total Local Self-Generated Revenue	States' Self-Generated Revenue	Municipalities' Self-Generated Revenue
Constant	−1.32	−0.42	−3.10
	(1.56)	(2.75)	(2.70)
GDP per capita (log)	1.17	1.50	1.14
	(0.18) ***	(0.34) ***	(0.39) ***
GDP growth,	−13.54	−18.69	−9.82
1996–1999	(3.04) ***	(6.11) ***	(6.89)
Revenue sharing	−0.18	−0.78	0.17
per capita (log)	(0.24)	(0.31) **	(0.41)
PRI electoral	−0.10	0.84	−3.52
support, 1997	(1.07)	(1.82)	(1.36) ***
Opposition governor	0.26	0.36	0.19
	(0.11) **	(0.21) *	(0.17)
R^2	0.72	0.51	0.62
F	20.94	4.93	8.50

Sources: Data concerning gross domestic product (GDP) per capita and the average annual rate of GDP growth between 1996 and 1999 are from the Instituto Nacional de Estadística, Geografía e Informática (www.inegi.gob.mx). Electoral results for 1997 are from the Instituto Federal Electoral (www.ife.org.mx). Information concerning opposition governors is from table 7.3.

Note: T-statistics in parentheses. These are heteroskedastic consistent standard errors corrected by White method.
*** Significant at the .01 level
** Significant at the .05 level
* Significant at the .10 level

obtained from tables 7.2 and 7.3 and measured in logarithms). The independent variables employed in this analysis are both economic and political in nature.

The first two economic variables are controls that take into consideration a state's income level and its growth performance: logarithms of per capita GDP and the average annual rate of GDP growth between 1996 and 1999.[28] Because both revenue collection and per capita GDP are measured in logarithms, the coefficient of this latter variable indicates the income elasticity of revenue sharing. One would expect per capita GDP to have a strong, positive effect upon subnational governments' capacity to generate their own revenue, while the rate of economic growth

28 Unreported estimates were also made using the Foster-Greer-Thorbecke poverty index. However, given the very high correlation between that index and per capita GDP, only one of the development-level variables could be included because of problems of multicollinearity. Because gross domestic product has a very straightforward quantitative interpretation, it is preferable to a poverty index as a control for the effect of the level of economic development on taxation.

should have a marginally positive effect. In addition, the revenue sharing variable (also measured as a logarithm, based upon tables 7.2 and 7.3) controls for the disincentive effects that the current revenue-sharing system might have on subnational units' generation of their own revenue. That is, when the level of economic development is held constant, one would anticipate that states receiving larger amounts of revenue-sharing funds would make less active efforts to collect their own taxes for the simple reason that they are not compelled to exert fiscal effort.

The two political variables tested are electoral support for the PRI in the 1997 midterm federal elections and the presence of an opposition governor (from either the PAN or the PRD) in a given state. With regard to the first of these variables, one would expect PRI strength to have a negative effect upon subnational governments' revenue collection because the places where the erstwhile dominant party was strongest in the late 1990s were characterized by highly clientelistic sociopolitical relations, so that privileged groups and individuals were often exempted from paying local taxes. Such tax exemptions were not part of a formal process; rather, they represented compliance failures that were encouraged and protected by local governmental authorities. And with regard to the second political variable, PAN and PRD governors had an imperative to reduce their dependence upon transfers from a PRI-led federal government. They should, therefore, have been more willing to incur the costs involved in strengthening tax collection efforts, eliminating privileges, and otherwise broadening the tax base in order to secure more financial resources. This dummy variable should, then, be positively associated with larger local tax revenues.

The findings reported in table 7.5 show that, except for the economic growth variable, all the expectations are fulfilled and all the coefficients are statistically significant. Growth had a negative effect upon variance in subnational units' revenue collection, suggesting that the taxes levied at the state and municipal levels in the late 1990s were not dynamic (that is, they were not very responsive to variations in the rate of economic activity). This is probably good news for local governments because it means that they are less vulnerable to downturns in the economic cycle than is the federal government, whose revenue collection is particularly linked to the international price of petroleum and general economic activity (via value-added and income taxes).

Distinguishing between state and municipal revenue collection efforts reveals that the effects of economic activity were strong for state governments' finances but less so for municipal governments' revenue situation (table 7.5, columns 3 and 4). This could be explained by the fact that municipal revenue comes mostly from property taxes, which are unlikely to be strongly affected by changes in economic activity (or, at least, affected more slowly). This view is further reinforced by the value of the coefficient for elasticity of GDP, which is larger than 1. An elasticity greater than 1.0 means that the response of tax collection to economic activity (GDP per capita) is more than proportional. Thus, the government of a richer state can be expected to collect, at the margin, tax revenues 1.5 times the difference in per

Figure 7.6: **The Simulated Effect of Support for Mexico's Institutional Revolutionary Party on Municipal Revenue Collection**

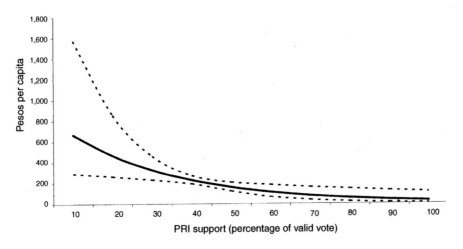

Source: Coefficients reported in Table 7.5, using CLARIFY software.

capita GDP between it and a poorer state. Note, however, that this effect stems from the level of economic activity rather than from the rate of economic growth, and that it is not very strong (although still elastic) in the case of municipal finances.

The impact of the political variables was very different in the cases of municipal and state government revenue collection. Electoral support for the PRI did have a negative effect upon municipal revenue, but the presence of an opposition party governor only had a positive impact upon state government revenue collection. This finding suggests that municipal-level PRI politicians were more likely to grant tax privileges to their bases of political support, while opposition governors were hard pressed to meet citizens' spending demands and therefore sought additional resources with which to do so. In overall terms, the dominant dynamic in sub-national revenue systems in the late 1990s appeared to be that opposition governments sought to reform tax collection, and that they were willing to assume the political costs of increasing taxes and eliminating privileges. There may have been greater leeway to make such changes at the state level than at the municipal level.

In order to gain greater insight into the effect that PRI electoral support had upon municipal revenue collection in the late 1990s, figure 7.6 simulates what level of tax collection our model predicts at different levels of PRI support. The analysis employs CLARIFY statistical software (Tomz, Wittenberg, and King 2001), which provides estimates of both the predicted effects of the independent variables and the range of uncertainty in the predictions.

Like the coefficient in table 7.5, figure 7.6 shows that greater PRI electoral support was associated with less municipal tax collection.[29] Indeed, it suggests that in localities where the PRI received 70 percent or more of the vote, municipal governments collected virtually no revenue. Because the analysis controls for the level of economic development, this outcome is a function of party hegemony rather than the result of the correlation between poverty level and PRI support.

The most interesting patterns are in the intermediate ranges, where one clearly sees the powerful effect of electoral competition upon revenue collection. In localities in which the PRI's support fell from 50 to 40 percent, revenue collection increased by more than 100 pesos per capita.[30] In an environment in which the majority of Mexican municipalities collected less than 100 pesos of revenue per person, this was a very powerful effect.

Further research would be necessary to ascertain whether this relationship holds in an analysis based upon information for a number of years. Nevertheless, the important finding here is that the fiscal performance of Mexico's subnational governments during the late 1990s was highly partisan: opposition party politicians had incentives to improve local tax collection, while PRI politicians were inclined to depend upon federal handouts. If this finding is coupled with the observation that opposition governments were more prevalent in wealthier, more urban states and municipalities, a troubling prospect emerges.

PRI politicians may prefer a system of financial transfers that basically sends resources to poorer regions, while PAN and PRD politicians would prefer more state and municipal autonomy. If the existing system of fiscal federalism in Mexico does not provide a forum where the states can resolve their differences, the gap in political practices between richer and poorer states may widen. National politics may increasingly reflect the divide between those states where poverty and stagnation are prevalent and those areas where more rapid growth and more favorable insertion into international markets result in improved welfare for their inhabitants. Whether the country can withstand such divisions is an open question.

Conclusion

This chapter has analyzed Mexican federalism in the context of processes of democratization and decentralization. The discussion opens up a very clear agenda for debate over the future of federalism. How can one design a federal system so as to mitigate the disequilibria generated by uneven regional growth? What are the limits of redistribution in federal transfers, both through revenue sharing and via other social policy funds? How does one structure funds so that they do not

---

29 The dotted lines in figure 7.6 delineate 95 percent-confidence-level bands, which measure the range of error in these point predictions.

30 At levels of PRI electoral support lower than 40 percent, the spread between the confidence-level bands is so wide that one cannot really determine what occurred with municipal revenue collection when PRI strength decreased even further.

increase subnational units' dependence upon the federal government? Which taxes should most appropriately remain under federal control, and which ones should be devolved to which level of subnational government? What should the Senate's role be in the federal system, particularly with regard to the federal budget? In which arenas or decision-making institutions can governors and their finance ministers voice their demands and propose new revenue-sharing arrangements? The answers to these questions will determine whether Mexico's federal pact for the twenty-first century can be redesigned without provoking the intense political conflicts that produced so much chaos and instability in the nineteenth century.

References

Alzati, Fausto. 1998. "The Political Economy of Growth in Mexico." Ph.D. diss., Harvard University.

Arellano Cadena, Rogelio, ed. 1996. *México, hacia un nuevo federalismo fiscal.* Mexico City: Fondo de Cultura Económica / Gobierno del Estado de Puebla.

Arroyo, Francisco. 1999. "Panorama regional de México, 1980–1996: dinámica del producto interno bruto en las entidades federativas." Unpublished manuscript.

Bailey, John. 1994. "Centralism and Political Change in Mexico: The Case of National Solidarity." In *Transforming State-Society Relations in Mexico: The National Solidarity Strategy,* edited by Wayne A. Cornelius, Ann L. Craig, and Jonathan Fox. La Jolla: Center for U.S.–Mexican Studies, University of California, San Diego.

Barro, Robert, and Xavier Sala-i-Martin. 1995. *Economic Growth.* New York: McGraw-Hill.

Benson, Nettie Lee. 1954. *La diputación provincial y el federalismo mexicano.* Mexico City: El Colegio de México.

Carmagnani, Marcello. 1994. *Estado y mercado: la economía pública del liberalismo mexicano, 1850–1911.* Mexico City: Fondo de Cultura Económica.

Carmagnani, Marcello, ed. 1993. *Federalismos latinoamericanos: México, Brasil, Argentina.* Mexico City: El Colegio de México.

Cashin, Paul, and Ratna Sahay. 1996. "Internal Migration, Center-State Grants, and Economic Growth in the States of India." *IMF Staff Papers,* 43 (1): 123–71.

Courchene, Thomas, and Alberto Díaz-Cayeros. 2000. "Transfers and the Nature of the Mexican Federation." In *Achievements and Challenges of Fiscal Decentralization: Lessons from Mexico,* edited by Marcelo M. Giugale and Steven B. Webb. Washington, D.C.: World Bank.

Courchene, Thomas, Alberto Díaz-Cayeros, and Steve Webb. 2000. "Historical Forces: Geographical and Political." In *Achievements and Challenges of Fiscal Decentralization: Lessons from Mexico,* edited by Marcelo M. Giugale and Steven B. Webb. Washington, D.C.: World Bank.

Dahl, Robert A., and Edward R. Tufte. 1973. *Size and Democracy.* Stanford, Calif.: Stanford University Press.

Díaz-Cayeros, Alberto. 1995. *Desarrollo económico e inequidad regional: hacia un nuevo pacto federal en México.* Mexico City: Centro de Investigación para el Desarrollo, A.C. / Miguel Ángel Porrúa / Fundación Naumann.

——. 1997. "Political Responses to Regional Inequality: Taxation and Distribution in Mexico." Ph.D. diss., Duke University.

——. n.d. "Notas sobre crecimiento y distribución regional del ingreso." Centro de Investigación para el Desarrollo, A.C., Mexico City. Unpublished manuscript.

Díaz-Cayeros, Alberto, and Beatriz Magaloni. 2001. "Party Dominance and the Logic of Electoral Design in the Mexican Transition to Democracy," *Journal of Theoretical Politics* 13 (3): 271–93.

Díaz-Cayeros, Alberto, and Jacqueline Martínez Uriarte. 1997. "Towards a Model of Budgetary Allocation and Revenue-sharing in Mexico's Local Governments." Paper presented at the international congress of the Latin American Studies Association, Guadalajara, Mexico.

Dresser, Denise. 1991. *Neopopulist Solutions to Neoliberal Problems: Mexico's National Solidarity Program.* Current Issues Brief no. 4. La Jolla: Center for U.S.–Mexican Studies, University of California, San Diego.

Garza, Gustavo. 2003. "The Dialectics of Urban and Regional Disparities in Mexico." In *Confronting Development: Assessing Mexico's Economic and Social Policy Challenges,* edited by Kevin J. Middlebrook and Eduardo Zepeda. Palo Alto and La Jolla: Stanford University Press and Center for U.S.–Mexican Studies, University of California, San Diego.

González Casanova, Pablo. 1965. *La democracia en México.* Mexico City: Era.

Guerrero, Juan Pablo, et. al. 1998. "La descentralización de los fondos de aportaciones federales (ramo 33): análisis preliminar de sus efectos y riesgos." Centro de Investigación y Docencia Económicas, Mexico City.

Grindle, Merilee S. 1977. *Bureaucrats, Politicians, and Peasants in Mexico: A Case Study in Public Policy.* Berkeley: University of California Press.

Haggard, Stephan. 1999. "The Politics of Decentralization in Latin America." In *Decentralization and Accountability of the Public Sector in Latin America,* edited by Javed Burki, Guillermo Perry et al. Proceedings of the annual World Bank Conference on Development in Latin America. Washington, D.C.: World Bank.

Hernández Chávez, Alicia, ed. 1996. *¿Hacia un nuevo federalismo?* Mexico City: Fondo de Cultura Económica.

Hernández Trillo, Fausto, Rafael Gamboa, and Alberto Díaz-Cayeros. 2002. "Determinants and Consequences of Bailing Out States in Mexico," *Eastern Economic Journal* 28 (3): 365–80.

Hill, Hal. 1992. "Regional Development in a Boom and Bust Petroleum Economy: Indonesia since 1970," *Economic Development and Cultural Change* 40 (2): 351–79.

Hiskey, Jonathan T. 2001. "The Political Economics of Crisis-Based Development in Mexico." Paper presented at the annual meeting of the American Political Science Association, San Francisco.

Kuznets, Simon. 1963. "Quantitative Aspects of the Economic Growth of Nations: Distribution of Income by Size," *Economic Development and Cultural Change* 11 (2, part II): 1–80.

Latapí, Pablo, and Manuel Ulloa. 2000. *El financiamiento de la educación básica en el marco del federalismo.* Mexico City: Fondo de Cultura Económica.

Levy, Santiago. 1998. "Análisis metodológico de la distribución de los recursos en el ramo 33." In *Instrumentos de distribución de los recursos del ramo 33.* Mexico City: Comisión de Desarrollo Social, Cámara de Diputados.

Lujambio, Alonso. 2001. "Democratization through Federalism? The National Action Party Strategy, 1939–2000." In *Party Politics and the Struggle for Democracy in Mexico: National and State-Level Analyses of the Partido Acción Nacional,* edited by Kevin J. Middlebrook. La Jolla: Center for U.S.–Mexican Studies, University of California, San Diego.

Merino, Gustavo. 1998. "Las transferencias federales para la educación en México: una evaluación de sus criterios de equidad y eficiencia," *Gestión y Política Pública* 7 (2): 355–99.

Mogollón, Olivia. 2002. "De la discreción a las fórmulas: mecanismos de distribución de recursos decentralizados para alivio a la pobreza." Master's thesis, Instituto Tecnológico Autónomo de México.

Mogollón, Olivia, and Alberto Díaz-Cayeros. n.d. "Federalismo fiscal, pobreza y sesgo partidista:

los recursos financieros de los municipios en Puebla." Centro de Investigación para el Desarrollo, A.C. Unpublished manuscript.

Molinar, Juan. 1991. "Counting the Number of Parties: An Alternative Index," *American Political Science Review* 85 (4): 1383–91.

Molinar Horcasitas, Juan, and Jeffrey A. Weldon. 1994. "Electoral Determinants and Consequences of National Solidarity." In *Transforming State-Society Relations in Mexico: The National Solidarity Strategy*, edited by Wayne A. Cornelius, Ann L. Craig, and Jonathan Fox. La Jolla: Center for U.S.–Mexican Studies, University of California, San Diego.

Navarrete, Juan. 1995. "Convergencia: un estudio para los estados de la República Mexicana." Documentos de Trabajo del CIDE, no. 42. Mexico City: División de Economía, Centro de Investigación y Docencia Económicas.

Neuber, Alexander. 1994. "Fiscal Federalism or Fiscal Separatism? A Second Look at the Russian Federation in 1992–93." European Bank for Reconstruction and Development. Typescript.

Ohmae, Kenichi. 1995. *The End of the Nation State: The Rise of Regional Economics*. New York: The Free Press.

Palacios, Juan José. 1989. *La política regional en México, 1970–1982*. Guadalajara, Mexico: Universidad de Guadalajara.

PDS (Partito Democrático della Siniestra), n.d. "Un modello regionale di ispirazione federalista." N.p.

Riker, William H. 1964. *Federalism: Origin, Operation, Significance*. Boston: Little, Brown.

Rodríguez, Victoria E., and Peter M. Ward, eds. 1995. *Opposition Government in Mexico*. Albuquerque: University of New Mexico Press.

Rojas, Fernando. 1999. "The Political Context of Decentralization in Latin America." In *Decentralization and Accountability of the Public Sector in Latin America*, edited by Javed Burki, Guillermo Perry et al. Proceedings of the annual World Bank Conference on Development in Latin America and the Caribbean. Washington, D.C.: World Bank.

Rubin, Jeffrey W. 1997. *Decentering the Regime: Ethnicity, Radicalism, and Democracy in Juchitán, Mexico*. Durham, N.C.: Duke University Press

Scott, Robert E. 1959. *Mexican Government in Transition*. Urbana: University of Illinois Press.

Snyder, Richard. 1999. "After the State Withdraws: Neoliberalism and Subnational Authoritarian Regimes in Mexico." In *Subnational Politics and Democratization in Mexico*, edited by Wayne A. Cornelius, Todd A. Eisenstadt, and Jane Hindley. La Jolla: Center for U.S.–Mexican Studies, University of California, San Diego.

Tamayo-Flores, Rafael. 2001. "Mexico in the Context of the North American Integration: Major Regional Trends and Performance of Backward Regions," *Journal of Latin American Studies* 33 (2): 377–407.

Tomz, Michael, Jason Wittenberg, and Gary King. 2001. *CLARIFY: Software for Presenting and Interpreting Statistical Results* (Version 2.0). Cambridge, Mass.: Harvard University (www.gking.harvard.edu).

Ward, Peter M., and Victoria E. Rodríguez. 1999. *New Federalism and State Government in Mexico: Bringing the States Back In*. Austin: Lyndon B. Johnson School of Public Affairs, University of Texas-Austin.

Watts, Ronald L. 1999. *Comparing Federal Systems*. 2nd ed. Kingston, Ontario: McGill-Queen's University Press.

Weldon, Jeffrey A. 1997. "The Political Sources of *Presidencialismo* in Mexico." In *Presidentialism and Democracy in Latin America*, edited by Scott Mainwaring and Matthew Soberg Shugart. Cambridge: Cambridge University Press.

Willis, Eliza, Christopher da C.B. Garman, and Stephan Haggard. 1999. "The Politics of Decentralization in Latin America," *Latin American Research Review* 34 (1): 7–56.

World Bank. 2000. *Entering the Twenty-first Century*. World Development Report 1999/2000. Oxford: Oxford University Press.

Zepeda Miramontes, Eduardo.1992. "Perspectivas regionales del desarrollo humano en México: 1990." Documentos de Trabajo Fundación Friedrich Ebert, no. 41. Mexico City: Friedrich Ebert Stiftung.

PART III
Key Political Actors:
Pillars of the Old Regime –
Foundations of the New?

8

A New Scenario for Mexican Trade Unions: Changes in the Structure of Political and Economic Opportunities

Graciela Bensusán

The purpose of this chapter is to examine the ways in which changes in Mexico's political and economic environment since the 1980s have affected Mexican trade unionism – its organizational forms, its power resources and capabilities, and its strategies. Although the dominant form of trade unionism in Mexico during the second half of the twentieth century was state-corporatist, it is important to distinguish here between this more traditional type and the "new trade unionism," whose declared aim is to supercede the subordinated style of action that characterized the former.

This distinction is necessary because one of the assumptions that informs this analysis is that neoliberal policies[1] and the transformation of Mexico's post-revolutionary political regime have had differing impacts depending mainly upon such factors as the degree of labor union autonomy vis-à-vis the government and employers, the characteristics of union leaderships (for example, their different sources of legitimacy), and the extent of internal union democracy. All of these elements translate into a greater availability of resources, strategies, and innovative capacities to meet the challenges posed by a new economic and political context.

Another assumption underlying this discussion is that Mexico's new external market-oriented development model, and the policies that preceded or accom-panied its implementation, have increased the power of capital to impose con-

The author thanks Kevin Middlebrook for his pertinent comments and suggestions with regard to this chapter, as well as Landy Sánchez and Soledad Aragón for their support in preparing it. Much of the information and the approach utilized in this essay are from the trinational research project "Trade Union Strategies in the Face of Neoliberal Restructuring," which the author directed between 1996 and 1998 with financial support from the National Council of Science and Technology (CONACYT) and the Programa Interinstitucional de Estudios de la Región de América del Norte, administered by El Colegio de México.

Translated by Aníbal Yáñez-Chávez and Kevin J. Middlebrook.

1 Neoliberal policies are defined here as those that are guided by the conviction that: "a) market deregulation is generally the best way to increase the efficiency of resource allocation; b) increased efficiency is the best way to promote overall economic growth; c) maximizing growth (as opposed to satisfying basic needs for all, or reducing poverty, or reducing inequality) should be the main goal of economic policy;" Robinson 1998:2.

ditions upon governments interested in attracting or retaining private-sector investments. This shift has mainly resulted in a decline in labor unions' economic power to achieve gains for their members. Nevertheless, this tendency manifests itself in distinct ways and gives rise to different types of responses, depending upon the specific characteristics of unions and the sectors in which they operate. Those unions that continued to pursue conservative tactics not only failed to recover their earlier strength, but they also failed totally to represent their members' interests. In some cases, however, conditions permitted unions to recover some of their leverage through non-traditional means (including greater involvement in production issues, resort to real worker mobilizations, and rank-and-file-backed confrontations with employers). Thus one of the main hypotheses developed here is that, although some of the old sources of labor power (such as the historic alliance with postrevolutionary governments) ceased to be of much use under Mexico's new circumstances, other sources of leverage that previously held no significance (such as international alliances with foreign trade unions and with nongovernmental organizations [NGOs], or labor union connections with networks of intellectuals and research centers) became indispensable to meet the challenge of capital's growing power.

This chapter employs the concept of the structure of political and economic opportunities to analyze the conditions surrounding Mexican trade unionism in an overall context of neoliberal restructuring. The concept is drawn from studies of social movements and refers to the "external factors that may influence the rise or decline of political opportunities for a given movement to operate, considering a given level of resources of power" (McAdam 1982: 85, cited by Robinson 1998: 20). It generally highlights the opportunities that labor unions have to attain their objectives through different political and institutional arrangements (Robinson 1998: 10). However, the concept is expanded here to include the economic realm because, as Robinson notes, unions are formed and act in both political and economic spaces. Thus the discussion also addresses the opportunities that unions have to defend workers' interests through collective bargaining and contact with firms. Yet it should be noted that the boundaries between political and economic opportunities are sometimes difficult to draw, and on occasion the two are blurred and mutually reinforcing (although it is still useful to make the distinction precisely to show this interaction).

There are numerous elements shaping the structure of political and economic opportunities in which labor unions function. They include: (1) shifts in the power of the state and of business; (2) institutional changes, ranging from new trading arrangements such as the North American Free Trade Agreement (NAFTA) to the exclusionary impact of new workplace institutions; and (3) economic factors such as long-term structural tendencies or external financial shocks (Robinson 1998). Because of limitations of space, this chapter will not describe these changes in detail in the Mexican context.[2] Insofar as possible, however, it will evaluate the impact of these different elements upon Mexican trade unionism.

---

2 See Bensusán 1998 for a more detailed discussion of these transformations in the Mexican labor context.

Following and expanding upon McAdam (1996), this analysis examines the structure of political opportunities in terms of: (1) the political system's degree of openness, understood as the opportunities that are available for trade union organizations to exercise influence in the political sphere (through political parties, the legislative and executive branches of government, and so forth); (2) the character of political alliances among elites and the opportunities they permit labor organizations to support or change governmental policies; (3) the political influence of other actors, including NGOs and labor unions in other countries; (4) the limits to the state's capacity for repression; and, finally, (5) the space available for labor issues on the national political agenda.

The Nature of Mexican Trade Unions

The organized labor movement that took shape in Mexico during the early twentieth century was of the "state corporatist" type (as defined by Schmitter [1992]), in the sense that it was closely linked to the birth of the postrevolutionary political system and its subsequent operation in the context of import-substitution industrialization. One of its most characteristic features – its obligatory nature – was the legacy of practices followed by the Mexican Regional Labor Confederation (CROM) when it controlled a part of the state apparatus during the presidency of Álvaro Obregón (1924–1928). The CROM's privileged political position enabled it to create various institutional mechanisms to help broaden its membership, confront the power of employers, and defeat its adversaries in the labor movement. These practices – in such matters as union registration, collective bargaining, the operation of so-called exclusion clauses (which de facto created a closed or union shop), and strikes – gave labor organizations important coercive powers in exchange for strong government control over labor affairs. They were widely criticized by dissident labor elements outside the CROM – and, indeed, by the CROM itself when it was no longer in government. Nevertheless, they became institutionalized in 1931 with the adoption of Mexico's first federal labor law, and they were legitimated through the advances that unions won because of their political connections (Bensusán 1992).

The symbiotic relationship between the markedly statist character of Mexico's labor legislation and an authoritarian, corporatist political system gave rise to a system of interest intermediation with monopolistic features. Its vertical and centralized structure took shape more upon the basis of governmental convenience than upon the needs for representation. In this arrangement, internal democracy ran counter to labor unions' function of enforcing discipline with regard to government policies, and it led to a primary preference for institutional (judicial and political) sources of labor power – to the detriment of other power resources, including mobilization, solidarity and coordination among worker organizations (which in Mexico was confused with vertical control), or a strong identification between the leadership and the rank and file (which was replaced by discursive appeals to the ideology of the Mexican Revolution).[3]

Many of these features proved to be serious limitations when the traditional trade union movement was forced to confront the challenges posed by neoliberal economic restructuring, preventing organized labor from exercising any real counterweight to government policies. This leads us to hypothesize that the relatively greater negative impact of neoliberal restructuring upon the interests of wage earners in Mexico (compared to its impact in countries such as the United States and Canada)[4] was due more to the subordinate nature of Mexican unions and the constraints under which they operate (mainly having to do with unions' inability to oppose government policies or to innovate in marshalling power resources and designing strategies adapted to new circumstances) than to the characteristics of neoliberal economic restructuring itself.[5]

In its historical origins, the Confederation of Mexican Workers (CTM) – the Mexican labor confederation that still groups the largest number of unionized workers – was the product of intense mobilizations and the convergence of diverse political currents. However, to the extent that during the second half of the twentieth century the Mexican regime consolidated its authoritarian and corporatist features, the CTM became a pillar of control over wage earners and in defense of the system. Although it is true that the CTM always aspired to organizing and representing all salaried workers, and that it became the dominant force in the labor movement (which translated into, for example, control over most of the labor representatives elected to tripartite conciliation and arbitration boards and the National Minimum Wage Commission, CNSM), this inclusive organization grew ever closer to the model of "business unionism" prevalent in the United States. It did so because of its lack of internal democracy, its acceptance of the established economic model, and the importance that it gave to institutional mechanisms in its efforts to extend its influence and prevail over its trade union adversaries.

It is, however, important to highlight the elements that make Mexican trade unionism distinctive. The most significant contrasts are with the voluntary character of trade unionism in established democracies and the different relationship that unions in these countries have with the state.[6] Because of the existence of

---

3 On the characteristics of the relationship between unions and the state, see Bizberg 1990 and Middlebrook 1995.

4 Bensusán and Robinson (1998) compare the impact of neoliberal policies in Canada, Mexico, and the United States.

5 In short, it is a question of considering to what extent actors are able to counteract the restrictions imposed upon them by an adverse economic situation.

6 In Mexico, so-called entrance and separation exclusion clauses do not permit workers to decide whether or not they join an organization, or when and how they leave it. Instead of strengthening unions' bargaining power against employers, these clauses became an instrument of political control and reduced union leaders' incentives to gain the active support of rank-and-file workers or develop innovative strategies for more effective representation. Given that union formation and the creation of unionized workplace majorities have been

exclusion clauses in collective contracts, a union's right to demand the signing of a contract even if it has merely two workers signed up as members (although, once a strike takes place, it may have to prove that it has the backing of the majority of employees in a given workplace), a legal prohibition against an employer replacing striking workers, and striking workers' right to receive back wages (generally an amount equal to half the pay due them for the days lost to the strike, except in the case of solidarity strikes – which are permitted in Mexico), Mexican unions have had considerably more institutional means at their disposal to increase their membership and threaten their adversaries than do unions in other countries. Nevertheless, the obverse side of this situation has been strong governmental control over organizational and bargaining processes, so that the mechanisms that should strengthen unions in their confrontation with capital become in practice instruments used to discipline workers.

As a result of these different factors, that part of the Mexican labor movement that was allied with the government (with which it maintained substantial political exchanges as a fundamental strategy) grew over time without much grassroots effort. In contrast, unions that did not form part of the "official" labor movement – those that were truly independent of government and employers – found it virtually impossible to gain a presence within major firms, especially those located in strategically important sectors. Thus state-owned enterprises and major private firms in the most dynamic economic activities (the automobile manufacturing industry, for example) enjoyed special protection against organizing efforts by unions linked to the Authentic Labor Front (FAT) and other such groups.[7]

In comparative perspective, then, the obstacles that truly independent Mexican unions faced in their organizing efforts were never much different in practice than those faced by workers in other countries with regimes that are openly unfavorable to collective action. Beginning with "red" trade unionism in the 1920s and continuing through the labor insurgency of the 1970s, the struggles by some workers in the early 1990s to shake off CTM control, and the attempts by the FAT to gain a foothold in the *maquiladora* (in-bond processing) industry, there is in Mexico a long history of defeats for independent unions at the hands of "official," government-allied unionism, the state, and employers.[8] Yet what might have been seen as weak-

---

(with few exceptions) the result of deals "from above" that are not always linked to workers' desire to organize, it is understandable why workers' interests have often been set aside – and the interests of the trade union bureaucracy given precedence – in difficult circumstances such as the economic crises of the 1980s and mid-1990s. This situation would not have been possible to sustain had there been a tradition of democratic trade unionism, with a leadership that had to be accountable to those it represented.

7 On the links between the Mexican state and trade unions over the course of import-substitution industrialization, see Aziz 1989, Bizberg 1990, and Middlebrook 1995.

8 This history brings to mind the difficulties that U.S. unions face as they seek to overcome all kinds of company maneuvers designed to defeat union certification campaigns. In this regard, the study by the North American Commission for Labor Cooperation (CCL 1997) of U.S.

nesses of independent labor organizations during the heyday of state-corporatist trade unionism – their lack of state support and their tendency to be closely aligned with various social movements and nongovernmental organizations – could become strengths in Mexico's new context of economic restructuring and political opening. Whether this proves to be the case depends, of course, upon the extent to which these potential resources are used to design innovative labor strategies and put them into practice.

It is useful, therefore, to establish criteria that will allow us to locate Mexican trade unions according to their principal characteristics and the strategies that they adopt in the face of political and economic change.

A Typology of Labor Organizations

Labor organizations in contemporary Mexico may be grouped according to the following characteristics: (1) the main source of their economic and political resources (whether from the state or society); (2) their relationship with the state (autonomy or subordination) and their stance with regard to neoliberal economic policies (whether they support or challenge them); (3) their relationship with employers (cooperation, subordination, or confrontation); (4) their degree of internal democracy and the incentives (positive or negative) that exist for labor leaders to seek rank-and-file support in order to achieve an organization's principal objectives.

Following these criteria, Mexico's various trade unions can be grouped into one of three types:[9]

- *State-corporatist*: Labor organizations of this type are characterized by their dependence upon the state to obtain political and material resources. Thus the institutional mechanisms that guarantee an organization control over its members (exclusion clauses), its participation in government posts (including representation on tripartite bodies), and its political representation (a presence in national and state-level legislatures, municipal presidencies, governorships, and other elected positions) comprise its main power resources. Given the authoritarian characteristics of Mexico's postrevolutionary political regime, the government's interest in preventing trade unions (especially major confederations and federations and the nationally-organized industrial unions) from exercising coercive

---

employers' use of the threat of plant closings to prevent unionization suggests that the right to organize is not fully guaranteed in either Mexico or the United States, although the shortcomings arise from markedly different legal orders in the two countries. For further discussion, see Bensusán 1999.

9 This discussion will refer principally to the Confederation of Mexican Workers (CTM), the Mexican Telephone Workers' Union (STRM), and the Authentic Labor Front (FAT). These three organizations exemplify well the organizational characteristics, weaknesses and strengths, and economic and political strategies typical of, respectively, state-corporatist, social, and "movement" unionism.

power to threaten the accumulation process led to these labor organizations'
subordination to the government and, as a consequence, their near-permanent
support for the economic policies that it implemented. State-corporatist unions
also traditionally maintained an implicit and increasing relationship of subordination to employers, accepting their demands on matters of productivity,
workforce flexibility, and so forth.

State-corporatist unions are, moreover, typically characterized by a lack of
internal democracy, by the presence of strongly centralized organizational
structures, and by the fact that their leaders' relationship with the rank and file is
based upon top-down control over members in local units that are atomized and
have scant power. Large national confederations such as the CTM, the CROM,
and the Revolutionary Confederation of Workers and Peasants (CROC), as
well as federations representing public sector employees and the most important
national industrial unions – including the Mexican Mining and Metalworkers'
Union (SNTMMSRM), the Mexican Petroleum Workers' Union (STPRM),
and the General Union of Mexican Electrical Workers (SUTERM) – all con-
form to this type of trade unionism.

State-corporatist trade unionism historically sought to preserve its space in
the state apparatus and in political spheres in exchange for backing government
policies. Both at the macroeconomic level (through their participation in various
economic stabilization pacts) and in collective bargaining at the company level,
labor organizations of this type have sought above all to preserve their position
as the main interlocutor with private enterprise and the government, ceding
ground on such matters as wage and benefit levels and the quality of jobs in
expectation of an uncertain recuperation at some unknown future time.

• *Social Trade Unionism*: Unions of this type derive their resources from both the
state (making use of available institutional advantages) and other sources –
whether from their own rank and file, from ties with other trade union and
political actors, or from their ability to bargain with employers. Many of the
organizations in this category previously belonged to the ranks of state-
corporatist trade unionism. However, beginning in the mid-1980s they began to
take their distance from the "official" labor movement – so much so that, by the
1990s, they constituted a separate category of trade unionism. Although unions
of this type have not openly broken with the state, they have diversified their
power resources and thereby significantly increased their autonomy vis-à-vis the
state, their ability to criticize the neoliberal economic model, and their capacity
to form external alliances.

Labor organizations of this type have also strengthened their capacity to
bargain with employers. Indeed, many of the incentives for their members come
from the advantages they have secured via their union contracts in such areas as
wages, fringe benefits, training programs, agreed-upon flexibility, and so forth.
These unions are characterized by average levels of internal democracy. They
typically have democratically elected leaders, although the national leadership

often has a strong presence in union organizational structures and exercises relatively centralized decision-making authority (a legacy of their state-corporatist past). It should be noted, however, that some social trade unions are seeking higher levels of internal democracy. Examples of this trajectory can be found in the Mexican Telephone Workers' Union (STRM), the Mexican Electricians' Union (SME), and, more generally, the members of the Federation of Unions of Goods and Services Enterprises (FESEBES) and the National Union of Workers (UNT).

- *"Movement" Trade Unionism*: Labor organizations of this kind are distinguished by their insistent challenges to the neoliberal economic project and, at times, by their open confrontations with the state. A similar attitude has also character- ized their relations with employers; they generally adopt quite rigid positions in their efforts to defend the rights they have already won. These labor groups systematically use mobilizations, strikes, or work stoppages as means of pressur- ing both the state and private employers. Moreover, "movement" trade unionism adopted a combative position in struggles for both collective bargaining rights and union democratization and independence during the 1970s.

    "Movement" trade unionism relies fundamentally upon the support of its members and its relations with other social movements (the urban popular movement, the women's movement, and so forth) to obtain material and political resources. Its organizational structures give a greater weight to membership meetings and collegiate bodies, and these organizations often have recourse to methods of direct democracy such as referenda, plebiscites, and so forth.

    Organizations that can be grouped in this category include those once belonging to the May 1 Inter-Union Coordinating Network (CIPM),[10] incipient labor movements in the service sector, unions of university employees (such as the Independent Union of Metropolitan Autonomous University Workers, SITUAM), and dissident elements within the National Education Workers' Union (SNTE), SUTERM, and STPRM. This type of trade union- ism is broadly inclined to link up with social movements, while at the same time maintaining radical and ideologically sectarian political positions (Sánchez 1998).[11]

    Even though in its origins the FAT had a number of "movement" union characteristics, over the course of the 1990s it evolved more toward social trade unionism. One consequence was that the FAT's single most important member union, the Union of Metal, Steel, and Iron Industry Workers (STIMAHCS),

---

10 The CIPM included industrial workers through territorial forms of association, as well as through production, distribution, and consumption cooperatives (Román and Velasco 1998). The organization practically ceased functioning after late 1998.

11 It should be noted in this context that "movement" unions have often held positions similar to those of the Zapatista Army of National Liberation (EZLN). Indeed, the CIPM's declaration of principles proclaims that one of its goals is to "translate the Zapatista demands to the urban field" (Román and Velasco 1998).

Table 8.1: **A Typology of Mexican Labor Organizations**

Type of Labor Organization	Main Source of Economic and Political Resources	Relationship with the State	Relationship with Employers	Degree of Internal Democracy
State Corporatist	State	Subordination and support	Cooperation / complicity	Low (predominance of negative incentives)
Social	Societal / state	Autonomy and conditional support	Cooperation	Medium (combination of negative and positive incentives)
Movement	Societal	Autonomy and critical positions	Resistance and conditional cooperation	High (predominance of positive incentives)

Sources: Robinson 1998, Bensusán 1998.

became part of the National Union of Workers in 1997 – without abandoning its movement positions or its hopes of building an alternative development model. In fact, the UNT's broad agenda clearly indicates an inclination toward a similar goal. The fact that the UNT adopted positions in favor of transforming public policy explains in part the CIPM's failure, because this latter organization was forced to share more critical spaces within the labor movement with more powerful organizations such as the STRM.

The Impact of Neoliberal Restructuring upon the Structure of Economic and Political Opportunities for Labor

The Structure of Economic Opportunities

Stabilization and Adjustment in the 1980s

The adoption of neoliberal policies in Mexico in the 1980s sharply altered the structure of economic opportunities under which trade unions operated. The informal sector grew rapidly, inflation-adjusted wages stagnated or declined, many social benefits were cut back, and employment fell in the most heavily unionized sectors. There were no palliatives forthcoming from state and municipal governments, not even when parties in opposition to the long-ruling Institutional Revolutionary Party (PRI) were victorious at the polls. At the same time that opportunities for exchanges with the federal government diminished, state-corporatist unions found it impossible to make up for these losses by increasing their economic power through direct negotiations within firms or through expanded participation in vital discussions concerning productivity and workforce training. To the contrary, the capacity of foreign investors to impose their conditions upon Mexico increased significantly with global and regional economic integration,

Table 8.2: **The Structure of Economic Opportunities for Mexican Trade Unionism, 1972–2002**

	1972–1982	1983–1988	1989–1994	1995–1999	2000–2002
Monetary policy	2	−1	0	−1	−1
Commerial policy	2	1	0	0	0
Fiscal policy	2	−1	−1	−1	−1
Social policy	2	−2	−1	−2	−1
Labor legislation	2	−2[a]	−2[a]	−2[a]	−1
Employers' positions vis-à-vis					
unions	1	−1	−1	−1	−2

Coding Scheme: -2 = Very unfavorable; -1 = Somewhat unfavorable; 0 = Neutral; 1 = Somewhat favorable; 2 = Very favorable

Note: These scores refer principally to state-corporatist unions and to workers located in key sectors of the independent labor movement.

[a] These values correspond to advantages that workers obtained based upon labor legislation. If one were to take into account the advantages obtained by labor leaders, the sign of the values would change because of the institutional advantages that union leaders derive from federal labor law.

The author gratefully acknowledges the assistance of Dr. Alicia Puyana in the elaboration of this table.

which is why proposals to address the country's problems were unilateral and why workers' interests were left defenseless.

The difficult period that began with the 1982 external debt crisis meant not only a change in national economic policy, but more profoundly a transformation of the country's model of development. The import-substitution industrialization (ISI) model had made it possible for the Mexican economy to expand at an average real rate of 7.2 percent per year during the first half of the 1970s. The model was based upon the expansion of internal demand; the protection of domestic industry via tariffs, subsidies, credits, and so forth; an expansionary monetary policy; and increasing public spending (Lustig 1994). During the ISI period, trade unions – especially those in strategic sectors dominated by state-owned enterprises – occupied a key position in the political arena and enjoyed optimal conditions to win rising real wages without having to mobilize.

However, even though problems with the ISI model had been evident since the early 1970s, corrective measures were postponed because of the petroleum-led economic boom that occurred during the second half of that decade. A not very prudent fiscal policy (based almost exclusively upon income from oil exports) and a disequilibrium in the trade balance combined with high international interest rates, worsening terms of trade, and an interruption in the in-flow of foreign capital to produce the acute economic crisis of 1982 (Heredia 1997).

Table 8.2 illustrates schematically how the structure of economic opportunities changed for Mexican trade unionism during the 1980s. The situation was highly favorable for labor organizations between 1972 and 1982 because monetary and fiscal policies permitted the growth of real wages in the private sector and, especially, in state-owned firms (De la Garza and Herrera 1992). In the trade arena, protection of domestic industry provided a certain leeway for collective bargaining at the firm level, while the government made substantial investments in health care, education, and subsidies for transportation and food that improved the living standards of urban workers and indirectly supplemented their incomes (Friedman, Lustig, and Legovini 1995). Furthermore, labor legislation permitted the expansion of the unionized work force and provided legal instruments for the consolidation of "official" labor organizations, simultaneously blocking openings for independent trade unionism. It was precisely the combination of these legal mechanisms and government policy that contained employers' hostility toward "official" unions.

However, over the next two decades the adoption (in successive stages) of a new development model and adjustment measures aimed at correcting recurrent economic crises and counteracting the effects of the post-2001 U.S. recession completely modified the economic scene, radically reducing the margin for exchanges between the state and organized labor. The years between 1983 and 1988 were particularly difficult and stood in sharp contrast with the earlier situation. During this period the government deployed the "Immediate Program for Economic Reordering" (PIRE) in an attempt to lower aggregate demand. Its main components were a reduction of the public deficit (achieved by cuts in government spending) and the devaluation of the peso (Heredia 1997). The sharp fiscal adjustment resulted in reduced public social spending, a contraction in wages for public employees (directly affecting the most important segment of the labor movement), and tax increases (reducing the margin that employers had in their bargaining with unions) (Lustig 1994). At the same time, the devaluation of the peso caused a decline in real incomes and an increase in the price of most goods (many of which were produced with imported inputs), thus further reducing workers' purchasing power (Friedman, Lustig, and Legovini 1995).

Beginning with the PIRE and in subsequent economic programs as well, holding down wages became a fundamental variable in government efforts to reduce inflation. For example, during the 1983–1998 period real wages (both official minimum wages and contract-determined wages) fell by between 7.7 and 10.5 percent annually, depending upon the category.[12] Employment grew by 0.4 percent per year during this same period, a rate that was insufficient to keep pace with the growth of the economically active population (Friedman, Lustig, and Legovini 1995: 336).

Mexico's accession to the General Agreement on Tariffs and Trade (GATT) in 1986 accelerated the process of trade liberalization and steadily diminished the importance of the domestic market. As a result, competitive economic pressures intensified and the mobility of capital increased. After the debt crisis and the nationalization of privately owned banks in 1982, the Mexican government's

---

12 In marked contrast, the real value of the legal minimum wage had grown by 113.6 percent between 1960 and 1979 (Bensusán 1998, table 8, and Lustig 1994).

priority was to recover its credibility with international financial institutions, foreign investors, and the national private sector. These concerns were further accentuated by the 1987 crisis.[13] As a consequence, the meaning of the government's "populist" alliance with unions was completely transformed, becoming an instrument of survival for labor leaders and a means of disciplining workers. Labor policy was placed in the service of employers, who had within their reach the instruments necessary to limit the power of trade unions and to begin to make collective bargaining agreements more flexible (De la Garza 1993).

Economic Restructuring in the 1990s

Between 1989 and 1994 the Mexican economy experienced a certain recovery. There was a modest resumption of growth (gross domestic product [GDP] grew by 3.4 percent per year in real terms) and inflation declined (Hernández Laos 1999). Policy makers controlled inflation through a combination of stabilization policies and structural change. Stabilization policies were implemented through a series of economic pacts among government, organized labor, and the private sector that featured stringent efforts to eliminate budget deficits and monetary policy based upon a flexible (although controlled) exchange rate moving within a specified range. Structural change meant increased trade liberalization (whose adverse effects on domestic industry were partly offset by an increase in foreign investment in other sectors, including the maquiladora industry), deregulation of prices for many goods and services, and the privatization of public enterprises (Hernández Laos 1999).

These changes led to a modest recovery of manufacturing wages between 1990 and 1993.[14] However, privatizations and increased foreign competition also meant major restrictions upon collective bargaining. Trade liberalization compelled manufacturing firms to implement significant changes in the production process, which in turn led to important modifications in collective contracts as companies sought increased flexibility in the organization of production. Most Mexican trade unions were unprepared to confront these transformations (De la Garza 1993).

Another sign of the weakening influence of trade unions during this period was the virtual elimination of wage differences between unionized and non-unionized workers. The former were some 40 percent higher than the latter in 1982, but this gap

13 The most obvious expression of the 1987 crisis was the sharp decline in the Mexican stock market in October. The crisis was accompanied by high inflation rates, leading to a 42 percent devaluation of the peso vis-à-vis the U.S. dollar, cutbacks in public spending, and a drop in real wages. There was a wave of popular protests, and labor groups opposed to government policies emerged (including such organizations as the Frente Intersectorial en Defensa del Empleo [Intersectoral Front in Defense of Employment]). For its part, the Labor Congress (CT), the umbrella organization grouping the "official" organized labor movement, called for a general strike that was never carried out (although the SME and the STRM did strike). See Bolívar 1990: 49–50, and Trejo Delarbre 1992: 283–86.

14 For details, see the data compiled by the National Institute of Statistics, Geography, and Informatics (INEGI) [www.inegi.gob.mx].

fell to about 10 percent in 1989 and only 3 percent in 1992. Similarly, significant differences between the wages of workers producing tradable versus non-tradable goods were eliminated, while other variables – gender, level of education, geographic location, or whether or not workers were employed in the maquiladora sector – began to exert greater influence upon wage trends (OCDE 1997: 98 and 78n).

It should be noted that there was a substantial increase in public social spending during this period. Indeed, programmable social spending rose from 5.7 percent of GDP in 1988 to 9.1 percent in 1994.[15] However, many of these funds were allotted through the National Solidarity Program (PRONASOL), so that general subsidies for basic consumption were replaced by programs oriented toward the urban population in extreme poverty. As a result, there was little direct income benefit for members of trade unions, and outcomes such as this affected the bases for consensus within state-corporatist unions. Table 8.2 indicates how government social policy during this period was unfavorable for trade unions.

In late 1994, as a consequence of an overvalued exchange rate, a large deficit in the balance of trade, and a series of destabilizing political events (the Chiapas rebellion and the assassination of high-level political figures, including Luis Donaldo Colosio, the PRI's designated presidential candidate), the peso experienced a sharp devaluation and the Mexican economy once again fell into crisis. In the years that followed, workers felt the negative effects of both economic instability and structural changes, not only as a result of the policies implemented by the administration of President Ernesto Zedillo Ponce de León (1994–2000) but also because of the cumulative effects of the earlier changes. Especially between 1995 and 1997, labor unions faced a restrictive monetary policy and stringent government efforts to control wage increases, a major fiscal adjustment that produced significant cuts in social spending, and accelerating trade liberalization (see table 8.2).

The level of unemployment in Mexico had remained low since the 1980s because most firms adjusted to changed economic circumstances by compressing wages rather than by dismissing employees (Hernández Laos 1999: 146), but it rose significantly during the 1994–1995 economic crisis. Moreover, the new jobs that were created were often of poor quality, as evidenced by the increasing number of workers without fringe benefits or social security coverage and the growing proportion of non-wage work in the economically active population, which reached more than 50 percent (OCDE 1997: 95–102; OCDE 1999: 81, table 4).[16] These factors, as well as the historical alliance with the PRI regime that nullified the "official" labor movement's opportunities to oppose government economic policy and present alternatives, led unions to accept wage losses in exchange for maintaining jobs.

15 See Poder Ejecutivo Federal 1994.
16 Although the Organisation for Economic Co-operation and Development (OECD) estimates that the informal sector made up between 20 and 44 percent of non-agricultural employment in Mexico during the mid-1990s, the International Labour Office (ILO) calculates that this sector constituted about 57 percent of the non-agricultural work force at the time (OCDE 1999: 81).

During the 1980s period of economic stabilization and adjustment, limiting wage increases was an important instrument in the government's efforts to control inflation. However, following trade liberalization and the surge of foreign investments that preceded the approval of the NAFTA, the government also sought to keep wages low in order to consolidate one of Mexico's principal comparative advantages vis-à-vis its new trading partners. As a consequence, inflation-adjusted wages remained low, ending the 1990s below the level they had reached at the beginning of the decade – a further indication of unions' notable loss of economic power.

The available data paint a truly depressing picture. Official minimum wages lost 74.6 percent of their purchasing power between 1982 and 2001 (Juárez Sánchez 2002: 35). The greatest decline during the 1990s occurred in the context of the 1994–1995 financial crisis, with minimum wages rising 17.6 percent in 1995 while the annual rate of inflation was 52 percent.[17] A similar pattern held in contract-based wage increases in federal-jurisdiction economic activities, suggesting that most unions were incapable of enforcing a more balanced allocation of the costs of the economic crisis. Thus in 1995 the average increase in contract-based wages was only 12.3 percent, almost forty percentage points below the rate of inflation. Even after economic recovery began in 1997, average contract-based wages in federal-jurisdiction activities barely equaled the rate of inflation (STPS 2001: 15). For the 1982–2000 period as a whole, the inflation-adjusted value of salaries paid by the Mexican Social Security Institute fell by 48.8 percent, while average contract-based wages declined by 59.3 percent. Average real wages in the manufacturing sector fell by 38.4 percent, compared to a decline of 21.1 percent in the maquiladora industry (Juárez Suárez 2000: 35).

The asymmetries in labor costs between Mexico and its North American economic partners were accentuated by successive peso devaluations and wage caps that were calculated to keep wage increases below the rate inflation – even after labor productivity in Mexico began to rise. Whereas in 1980 Mexico's hourly labor costs in the manufacturing sector were equivalent to 23 percent of U.S. labor costs, in 1997 they had fallen to about 10 percent of the U.S. level. Even though the differences between Mexico and the United States in average economic productivity are still very large, the even greater degree of wage disparity (in the late 1990s average Mexican wages in manufacturing were about one-eighth those in the United States) produces a labor yield in Mexico that is practically twice the size of that in Canada and the United States. That is, while in Canada and the United States the value added per unit of wages paid was equal to 1 in the late 1990s, in Mexico the same measure was somewhat greater than 2 (Hernández Laos 1997: 88). Moreover, beginning in 1994 Mexico's increases in labor productivity in the manufacturing industry (albeit starting at a lower level) were greater than those in the United States (Poder Ejecutivo Federal 1998: 61).

---

17 In the year 2000 the rate of increase in the minimum wage (10 percent) finally exceeded the inflation rate (9 percent).

One important consequence of economic restructuring during the 1990s was the loss of jobs in sectors with high union density (see below). These economic activities had been dominated by the powerful national industrial unions that comprised the core of state-corporatist trade unionism. Even though some unions gained through their expansion into sectors with previously low unionization rates, these large national industrial unions did not recover from this structural economic transformation. At the same time, workers in these industries lost a significant part of their contract benefits and purchasing power.

Corporatist arrangements themselves played a fundamental role in the implementation of these adjustment policies and structural changes. They did so primarily by ensuring that these transformations occurred without serious distributive conflicts, either over wages at the macroeconomic level or in firm-level collective bargaining. Employers realized that "official" trade unions would not be an obstacle to their efforts to modernize production, and for this reason they were able to innovate in the use of technologies and in forms of work organization while at the same time cutting labor costs.

Although the established institutional rules remained in place, the private sector preferred dialogue with "official" labor organizations (whether real or simulated, through the expansion of so-called protection contracts that conceal employers' complete control in the workplace) to opening up individual relations with workers, particularly in economic activities with a strong trade union tradition. This was, for example, the case in the automobile manufacturing industry, where employers and the government helped the CTM regain the political control it had lost in the 1970s by expanding into the new assembly plants established in north-central and northern Mexico (Bensusán and Bayón 1998).

In some sectors and regions, employers maintained low rates of unionization (and sometimes avoided unionization completely) through political deals that, in exchange, offered "official" labor organizations the opportunity to expand in the service sector or among non-wage workers. This development marked the beginning in Mexico of anti-union trends paralleling those in the United States. Examples of this phenomenon in states governed by the center-right National Action Party (PAN) included the electronics maquiladoras in Guadalajara, Jalisco, and the manufacturing industry in Chihuahua.[18] At the same time, employers opposed even more actively the entry of independent union organizations like the FAT into the maquiladora industry concentrated along the Mexico–U.S. border. In doing so, they raised the costs of independent unionization for workers. In the

18 One example of no unionization and extreme labor flexibility in the Guadalajara electronics industry is IBM, where a subcontracting agency provides production personnel and is in charge of manufacturing operations (Partida 1999: 253). There are other industrial zones in Jalisco (El Salto, for example) where there is an important concentration of foreign-owned, high-productivity electronics firms and where what predominates is pro-business and "letterhead" unionism, characterized by low levels of workplace conflict and union subordination to employer policies. See De la O 1999: 204–18.

Honeywell, General Electric, and Han Young cases, firings or plant closings ended workers' efforts to free themselves from CTM control.[19]

From the outset of the economic restructuring process, Mexican labor legislation (which did not undergo any significant modification whatsoever) protected the interests of capital by guaranteeing its strategy of competing through low wages and high productivity. Indeed, as numerous studies have shown, employers encountered no major institutional obstacles to their efforts to increase productivity and competitiveness.[20] Thus labor legislation proved useless to protect workers' rights, but it kept the corporatist shackles intact and gave the government the means to repress expressions of non-conformism. All of this increased the power of capital and weakened trade unions' bargaining ability.

The discretionary character of legal protection based upon governmental influence over tripartite conciliation and arbitration boards (*juntas de conciliación y arbitraje*),[21] government control of wages, and the absence of a system of representation providing wage earners with real autonomy, were all factors preventing the emergence of a counterweight capable of achieving a more balanced distribution of the costs resulting from neoliberal economic policies. These same policies might have had a less adverse impact upon wage earners if state intervention in the market had been less extensive, or if there were an effective rule of law in Mexico. These considerations highlight the interaction of economic and political opportunity structures and the way in which they have jointly determined the possibilities for trade union action.

The Structure of Political Opportunities

Political Opening and Limitations on Presidentialism

The greater openness of the Mexican political system after 1988 produced two changes that radically modified the political role of unions, whether as vehicles for mobilizing electoral support for the PRI or as barriers to ideological or political currents offering alternatives to the ideology and politics of the Mexican Revolution.

19 The impact of the post-2001 U.S. recession on the maquiladora industry, where significant numbers of jobs were lost as exports to the U.S. market contracted, also increased the difficulties that the UNT experienced in establishing a presence in the industry. Just in the period from December 2000 to December 2001, official data showed a decline of 226,454 jobs in the maquiladora sector (Bossio Rotondo 2002: 26).

20 Exchange-rate policy was much more important in this regard. See Hernández Laos 1997.

In their efforts to take advantage of their increasing leverage vis-à-vis the government and unions and prepare for a democratic regime change that might weaken existing political controls and the repressive capacity of the state, employers aspired to low-profile labor legislation with limited individual and collective rights. The idea was to operate without unions as an instrument for the conduct of labor relations, stripping them of their coactive power and thereby clearing the way for direct employer relations with workers. From 1989 onward, proposals for labor legislation reform emanating from the business sector had this goal, which represented a potential threat for state-corporatist unions highly dependent upon institutional resources.

21 On the functioning of conciliation and arbitration boards in union registration cases, see Middlebrook and Quintero 1998.

First, the increasing transparency and fairness of the electoral process and the expanding political presence of opposition parties (especially the PAN and center-left Party of the Democratic Revolution, PRD) transformed the party system and placed new competitive demands upon candidates of the "official" PRI. This occurred just at the time that unfavorable results of neoliberal economic policies eroded the support that the labor leadership – and, more generally, the authoritarian and corporatist character of the regime as a whole – had among rank-and-file workers.

The PRI's changing electoral circumstances during these years clearly reflected the consequences of having abandoned its commitments to popular sectors and the scant achievements (when not crashing failures, as in 1994–1995) of the country's new economic model. Although the PRI obtained 68.4 percent of the total valid vote in the 1982 presidential election, its share of the vote fell to 50.4 percent in 1994 and to 36.1 percent in the year 2000, when the opposition "Alliance for Change" (with Vicente Fox Quesada as its presidential candidate) won the election with 43.5 percent of the vote. In the federal Chamber of Deputies, the PRI obtained 74.1 percent of the seats in 1982, while that percentage fell to 47.8 percent in 1997 (depriving it of a majority in the Chamber) and to 36.8 percent in 2000 (before recovering somewhat to 44.8 percent in 2003). For their part, both the PAN and the PRD, while experiencing some electoral ups and downs, generally improved their positions. In sum, in 1988 the PRI lost the qualified majority in the Chamber of Deputies that had permitted it to enact constitutional reforms without the support of other parties; in 1997 it lost the simple majority in the Chamber required to approve or modify regular legislation (a departure that implied a substantial shift in the balance of political power); and in the year 2000 it lost the presidency (Becerra, Salazar, and Woldenberg 2000: 474; Aguayo Quezada 2000).

Up until 1988 the PRI had exercised absolute dominance over Mexico's thirty-one state governments and the Federal District. Yet a decade later, opposition parties controlled the governorship in nine states (the PAN in six, the PRD in three). Among the PRI's losses were two border states (Baja California and Chihuahua, the latter of which was recovered by the PRI in 1998) and the economically and politically vital Federal District (governed since 1997 by the PRD) (Pacheco 1999a, 1999b).

It is worth underscoring that opposition party victories at the local (state) level did not necessarily translate into more favorable conditions for workers. Some opposition administrations continued to uphold the status quo in their labor policies. Moreover, such fundamental issues as the minimum wage are decided at the federal level. During the 1990s, PAN administrations generally respected the hegemonic position of the CTM,[22] and they were careful about taking decisions

---

22 In Chihuahua during the *panista* administration of Governor Francisco Barrio (1992–1998), the CTM played a leading role by participating in negotiations for an agreement (titled "State Coordination for Labor Improvement") to modernize labor relations in the state. However, these negotiations ended without any conclusive results. In essence, the agreement transferred to the local level the concerns put forward in the May 1992 "National Agreement to Raise Productivity." See Bensusán and Reygadas 2000; on the Barrio administration in general, see Aziz 1994.

Table 8.3: **Labor Representation in Mexico's Chamber of Deputies, 1979–2003**

Year	1979	1982	1985	1988	2000	2003
Total Institutional Revolutionary Party (PRI) deputies	296	299	289	261	211	222
Labor deputies	93	99	96	59	19	19
Labor deputies as proportion of PRI deputies (percent)	31.4	33.1	33.2	22.6	9.0	8.6
Union affiliation of labor deputies						
CTM	45	50	51	NA	11	9
SNTE[a]	12	15	14	NA	4	NA
CROC	11	12	11	NA	1	2
FSTSE[a]	9	6	7	NA	1	3
SNTMMSRM	4	5	6	NA	NA	1
CROM	2	3	3	NA	2	1
STFRM	2	1	1	NA	0	1
SNTSS[a]	2	2	2	NA	0	1
CGT	1	1	0	NA	0	NA
COR	1	1	NA	NA	NA	NA
FENASIB[a]	0	1	1	NA	0	NA
Others	3	1	NA	NA	NA	1

Sources: Author's calculations based upon data in Reyes de Campillo 1996: 164, and, for 2000 and 2003, the Institutional Revolutionary Party's (PRI) parliamentary group in the Chamber of Deputies.

Notes: Unions affiliated with the PRI's so-called popular sector are denoted with [a]. Deputies from these organizations are included among the total labor deputies listed in the second line of the table. See the List of Acronyms for individual union names.

NA = Not available

(such as providing openings for trade unions opposed to the CTM) that might discourage investment in the maquiladora sector. In the Federal District during the late 1990s, the PRD administration did not produce any major changes in relations with trade unions, such as increasing transparency regarding collective bargaining agreements so as to make "protection contracts" impossible or improving the political opportunities for independent trade unionism.

Nor have these opposition parties become allies of the "new trade unionism." The FAT and some other organizations within this current have affinities with the PRD that have led them to put forward congressional candidates on the PRD's party-list nomination slates. However, the poor list ranking assigned to those candidacies in 1994 and 1997 apparently reflected the PRD's scant interest in having legislators from the independent trade union milieu. Even so, in the wake of

Vicente Fox's historic defeat of the PRI in the 2000 presidential election, there were some expectations that both the "new trade unionism" and opposition parties might gradually find ways to strengthen their alliances (even if only at certain conjunctures) around such key issues as the reform of federal labor legislation, the rejection of further privatizations of state-owned firms, or wage policy (which is still in the hands of the federal executive because of its control over the National Minimum Wage Commission).

Table 8.3 demonstrates the scope of the labor movement's political decline during the 1990s, as measured by the number of seats that union leaders held in the federal Chamber of Deputies. The total dropped from 59 seats in 1988 to just 19 in 2000, when the PRI suffered its greatest electoral defeat. Although the PRI recovered some ground in the 2003 midterm elections, the number of labor deputies remained constant at 19. This pattern reflected the declining importance of this particular power resource for state-corporatist unions as a consequence of Mexico's greater electoral competitiveness and political pluralism.

A second decisive aspect of political change in Mexico during the 1990s was the declining politico-administrative power of the presidency as a consequence of neoliberal economic restructuring (particularly the privatization of the most important state-owned enterprises), the electoral growth of the opposition, and internal and external pressures for democratization of the regime. These processes reduced the executive's capacity to grant favors to allied union leaders and fulfill the terms of the old postrevolutionary social pact with labor. Similarly, the loss of the PRI's majority in the federal Chamber of Deputies in 1997 increased the odds that presidential initiatives might be defeated in the Congress, especially as opposition parties for the first time took on a key role in defining economic policy.

The Repressive Capacities of the State

From 1982 until the early 1990s, the repressive policies that the Ministry of Labor and Social Welfare (STPS) pursued in support of employers and government-allied union leaders largely explained why independent workers' struggles were so unsuccessful. Of course, there were times when state repression was also used against traditional labor leaders. The most conspicuous instance of this involved Joaquín ("La Quina") Hernández Galicia, the powerful leader of the Mexican Petroleum Workers' Union. Hernández Galicia was arrested in January 1989 for alleged violations of firearms laws, although the underlying reasons were his opposition to the partial privatization of Petróleos Mexicanos (PEMEX, the state-owned oil company) and his decision to permit union members to vote freely in the 1988 presidential election, which resulted in the victory of opposition candidate Cuauhtémoc Cárdenas in the oil workers' districts.[23] Another prominent case was that of Agapito González Cavazos, the leader of CTM–organized workers in the

---

23 Hernández Galicia was sentenced to eleven years in prison. After years of legal appeals and political lobbying, he was finally released in December 1997 (*La Jornada*, December 17, 1997).

maquiladora industry in Matamoros, Tamaulipas. In February 1992, while in the midst of contract negotiations with maquiladora owners' associations, the federal government arrested him on charges of tax evasion, with the clear intent of curbing his combative leadership style.[24]

The signing of the NAFTA, the 1994–1995 economic crisis, and the gradual advance of democracy all reduced the margin for presidential discretion in using repressive means to resolve labor conflicts. These changes accounted in part for an apparently neutral presidential stance toward such developments as the appearance of the "Union Movement and the Nation" Forum (Foro El Sindicalismo ante la Nación), the CIPM (now disbanded), and the UNT.[25] However, the institutional resources inherited from Mexico's authoritarian regime are still deployed against labor protest movements, even though they are sometimes of doubtful constitutionality. In 1998, for example, the receivership provision (*requisa*) in federal labor law was used to nullify a strike by Aeroméxico flight attendants.

Nevertheless, it is certainly the case that the opportunities for independent labor mobilization without the risk of overt repression are greater now than they have been in several decades. The factors contributing to this situation include the weakening of presidentialism, the limited options facing traditional union leaders, greater political pluralism, and generalized popular discontent with government economic policies. More open political conditions have undermined the strength of the CTM and other PRI–affiliated labor organizations, which no longer have easy recourse to repression or co-optation to maintain their control over the rank and file. Having supported government economic policies that were detrimental to workers' interests and lost their traditional role in the distribution of social welfare benefits, old-style corporatist organizations have sacrificed what remained of their credibility.

At the same time, dissident labor forces have used timely alliances with opposition political parties, social movements, and international trade union allies to increase their influence over public opinion and government policies. These shifts have strengthened the position of alternative labor groups promoting greater autonomy vis-à-vis the state, increased political pluralism within labor organiza-

24 González Cavazos, who in the early 1980s helped local maquiladora workers win a 40-hour work week with 56 hours' pay, was freed after paying a fine. Even though the government sought to sideline him by establishing a rival CTM union in the area, by 1993 González Cavazos was again involved in contract negotiations. This time, however, he showed a greater willingness to cooperate with employers. See Carrillo and Kopinak 1999: 117, 124–25.

25 With the death of long-time CTM leader Fidel Velázquez in June 1997 and the PRI's electoral defeats in July 1997, there was a new opportunity for the realignment of forces within the labor movement. In the CTM, the succession followed the course outlined in the confederation's statutes and the candidacy of Leonardo Rodríguez Alcaine was accepted without public objections. However, the situation was different within the CT. There were important defections from this umbrella organization, including the National Union of Social Security Workers (SNTSS), the STRM, and other members of the FESEBES in August 1997 (*La Jornada*, June 22, 1997, p. 14; *La Jornada*, August 28, 1997, p. 41).

tions, closer union involvement in production decisions within the firm, and a critique of neoliberal economic policies. The UNT and the National Assembly of Workers (ANT) have, for example, sought to exploit these conditions to pressure for modifications in Mexico's market-oriented development model, and their protests have encountered considerable public support.[26]

The Space for the Labor Agenda

The post-1997 composition of the Congress has provided a space favorable for questioning neoliberal economic policies. At the same time, for the first time since at least the 1920s, the conditions are present to prevent a top-down institutional-ization of labor-state-capital relations. In fact, political opening has produced an opportunity to advance debate on the institutional arrangements that are needed to replace the postrevolutionary labor relations order (which was at once protectionist of workers' social interests and authoritarian and corporatist in political content), end government intervention in workplace organization, and provide unions with opportunities to represent their members' interests.

In the late 1990s both the center-right PAN and the center-left PRD offered proposals for institutional reform aimed at democratizing labor relations. Their legislative initiatives would make it possible to transform the nature of union organizations and significantly improve opportunities for independent trade unionism, eliminating the existing corporatist shackles and widening the space for dialogue over such issues as productivity and training. However, because of the mistrust that prevails on the political scene and in the trade union milieu, these proposals were rejected not only by "official" labor organizations (in all likelihood, the main losers in a democratizing reform of state-labor relations) but also by some adherents of the "new trade unionism." These latter groups feared that, over the course of the legislative reform process, anti-union pressures from employers and the international financial institutions would prove stronger than the influence exerted by labor reformists and their political allies over the character of the new labor order (Bensusán 2000, 2001a). These considerations temporarily removed labor issues from mainstream political debates and precluded discussions of crucial issues such as the quality of the jobs generated by Mexico's success in exporting manufactured goods, the continued stagnation of real wages, and the need to extend social benefits and legal protections to the large informal sector.

The political alternation that occurred in the presidency in December 2000 generated widespread expectations that it might be possible to adopt a major reform of federal labor law. There were, in fact, several steps in that direction, including the installation of the STPS–convened "Roundtable on Labor Updating

26 For example, as part of the protest movement that the UNT organized against President Zedillo's budget proposals for 1999, the STRM temporarily shut down facilities (though it did not suspend telephone service) belonging to the Mexican Telephone Company (Teléfonos de México, TELMEX). Interviews conducted at the time with TELMEX customers indicated considerable support for the UNT's broader agenda. See *Reforma*, December 5, 1998, p. 4).

and Modernization" ("Mesa para la Actualización y Modernización Laboral") in mid-2001. Nonetheless, the space available for the agenda advanced by the "new trade unionism" proved very limited. The more conservative positions held by the CT and by the business sector tended to dominate these discussions (Bensusán 2001b).

New Allies: NGOs and Labor Unions in Other Countries

Finally, among the elements shaping labor's new political environment are the increased presence of nongovernmental organizations (the Mexican Action Network Against Free Trade [RMALC], for example) and external support from unions in Canada and the United States aimed at broadening cooperation and designing common strategies to confront the growing power of transnational firms. In the latter case, the election of John Sweeney as president of the American Federation of Labor–Congress of Industrial Organizations (AFL–CIO) brought about an important change in that organization's policies, including increased emphasis upon expanding relations with the Mexican labor movement. Sweeney's trip to Mexico City in January 1998 to inaugurate the American Center for International Trade Union Solidarity (Centro Americano para la Solidaridad Sindical Internacional) was the first such visit by an AFL–CIO president in some seventy years. Although Sweeney's agenda included meetings with the CTM leadership, the CTM no longer monopolized ties with the AFL–CIO, as had traditionally been the case. On this occasion, AFL–CIO officials also met with UNT representatives, with whom they discussed the possibility of more effective use of the grievance procedures created under the NAFTA's so-called labor side agreement, a topic that the CTM was never interested in.

In September 1999, the AFL–CIO signed separate cooperation agreements with the CTM, the UNT, the Metropolitan Autonomous University (UAM), and the National Autonomous University of Mexico (UNAM). These regular exchanges – including trade union leaders, labor attorneys, and university researchers from both Mexico and the United States – gave rise to joint publications, a systematic sharing of information concerning the maquiladora industry, and mutual support for trade unions denouncing violations of Canadian, Mexican, and U.S. labor laws. These activities also provided proof of the advantages of trade union cooperation in the context of regional economic interdependence.[27]

The presence of labor organizations from other countries has been utilized most effectively by independent unions seeking to distance themselves from traditional corporatism and refound their domestic and external alliances. These groups have

27 The topics examined at a meeting held between the AFL–CIO and the UNT in Washington, D.C. in April 1999 indicate the scope of the agenda for cooperation between the two organizations. They included the NAFTA and the North American Agreement on Labor Cooperation, the unionization of migratory workers, sectoral alliances, and the training of organizers and researchers. The author thanks the American Center for International Trade Union Solidarity, Mexico City, for this information.

Table 8.4: The Structure of Political Opportunities for Mexican Trade Unionism, 1972-2000

	1972–1982		1983–1987		1988–1996		1997		2000	
	Tradi-tional unionism	Inde-pendent unionism	Tradi-tional unionism	Inde-pendent unionism	Tradi-tional unionism	Inde-pendent unionism	Tradi-tional unionism	Inde-pendent unionism	Tradi-tional unionism	Inde-pendent unionism
Character of the Political System (open vs. closed)	2	-2	2	-2	2	-2	-2	1	-1	1
Unity or Division within the Ruling Party (PRI)	2	-2	2	-2	-1	1	-2	1	-2	2
Availability of allies in the government	2	-1	1	-2	1	-1	1	0	1	0
Availability of allies allies outside the government										
– Opposition parties, nongovernmental organizations, and social movements	-1	1	-1	1	-2	2	-2	2	-2	2
– Employers	1	-2	-1	-2	1	-2	1	-2	1	-2
Repressive capacity of the state	2	-2	2	-2	-1	-2	-1	-1	2	2
Political agenda	2	-1	-2	-2	-2	-1	-2	1	-2	2

Coding Scheme: -2 = Very unfavorable; -1 = Somewhat unfavorable; 0 = Neutral; 1 = Somewhat favorable; 2 = Very favorable

Note: During the 1988–1996 period the closed character of the political system still favored traditional unionism because of its alliance with the government and its representation in Congress (where the PRI held a majority), but the traditional labor movement did not take advantage of this situation to improve the chances for its legislative initiatives.

used such ties to undercut state-corporatist unions' established position as exclusive representatives of workers' interests.[28] More generally, the greater presence of external actors and the existence of NAFTA–based mechanisms to oversee the protection of workers' rights have contributed significantly to increased transparency in the labor relations sphere. The most frequent vices and transgressions (so-called protection contracts that legally enshrine employers' unrestricted control over workplace relations, limitations on the organization of independent trade unions, the absence of fair rules to resolve inter-union disputes, and so forth) have been publicized, thereby putting an end to the isolation that characterized the old corporatist system and creating new constraints on its expansion. Table 8.4 summarizes these major tendencies in the evolution of political opportunities for both traditional and independent trade unionism.

In overall terms, then, the legacies of Mexico's protectionist and statist import-substitution development model and its authoritarian and corporatist political system meant that the adoption of neoliberal economic policies after the mid-1980s both weakened the established labor movement and produced a profound crisis of representation for wage earners. The dramatic drop in real wage levels (to their lowest levels since the mid-1960s) and the elimination any wage premium for unionized workers clearly indicated that there were no effective counterweights to the power of capital. The government was able to place the costs of economic adjustment squarely onto the backs of workers, establishing a model of integration into the world economy that is based upon low labor costs and rising productivity.

The problem for the Mexican labor movement, therefore, is not limited to altering union strategies so that workers can extract greater advantages from the new economic and political context. Neoliberal economic restructuring has led virtually everywhere to the erosion of old resources of union power, but the impact of these policies has been deeper in Mexico. An adequate response to them requires a change in both the political regime and in the nature of trade unionism, leaving state corporatism and coercion behind in order to move toward a configuration more in tune with democracy. Whatever kind of trade unionism prevails in the future (whether of a more narrow, "bread and butter" type, or one linked to social movements, with a broader agenda), these arrangements – approximating plural-ism or social corporatism – would be based upon voluntary union membership, union autonomy from employers and the state, and internal union democracy.

However, one must recognize that the profound changes produced by two decades of neoliberal economic transformation and gradual democratization also present certain limitations. First, economic statism (exercised in favor of the banks and other private-sector interests close to governing circles) and labor legislation that is authoritarian (even if formally protectionist and pro-union) in character have not disappeared. These arrangements no longer seek to protect the weakest sectors, such as workers and the owners of small and midsize businesses. Rather,

28 The RMALC's role during the NAFTA negotiations is a preeminent example.

they ensure Mexico's international comparative advantages and the interests of investors by maintaining low wages and docile unions. For these reasons, established corporatist controls remain useful and (at least until the PRI lost control of the federal executive in 2000) maintaining the historic alliance between the state-corporatist union leadership and the government was still worthwhile – even if the margins for presidential maneuver were much narrower and workers were excluded from the benefits.

Second, insofar as democracy in Mexico is still fragile and the traditions of independent social organization (whether involving unions or social movements) are incipient, the prevailing political elements are not auspicious for a broader transformation of the labor movement. The balance of factors is still weighted against a trade unionism that would place more trust in its own resources (closer ties to the rank and file, or new alliances with social movements) and in favor of one that relies predominantly upon institutional sources of power, including provisions in labor law, exclusion clauses in contracts, and the support of the state. This situation reflects more than the fact that potential allies among social movements sometimes tend to border dangerously on illegality, or the old disagreements between state-corporatist and independent unions. The bias against change also results from the unfavorable economic context and the fact that state-corporatist unions have become badly discredited because of their clear inability to achieve wage gains, which makes these traditional organizations even more fearful of the consequences of losing their coercive powers.

The Impact upon Union Strategies

The CTM and the "Official" Labor Movement

The CTM, the organization that groups the majority of unionized workers in Mexico, exemplifies traditional behavior in the union sphere. During the 1980s and 1990s it was primarily devoted to preserving its space in the state apparatus and on the political scene, in exchange for its willingness to accede to neoliberal economic policies (which the CTM accepted as inevitable) and their negative impact upon the membership it represented. At the macroeconomic level through a series of national economic pacts,[29] as well as at the microeconomic level in the collective bargaining agreements it negotiated with employers, the CTM was intent upon preserving its position as the privileged interlocutor with capital and the government. To do so, it was willing to make major concessions in terms of wage and

29 In December 1987 the CTM joined the government and representatives of the private sector in signing an Economic Solidarity Pact (PSE) designed to control inflation and restore macroeconomic stability. This agreement, under various names, was renewed continuously through 1996. Among other provisions, the pacts controlled increases in the prices of both public and private goods and established wage caps calculated according to the anticipated rate of inflation (which invariably turned out to be lower than the actual rate of inflation). For details, see Bensusán 1992, 1998, and Zapata 1995.

fringe benefit levels and the quality of jobs. The CTM leadership argued that this strategy would save jobs and increase Mexico's economic competitiveness, which would eventually produce renewed economic growth and an improvement in working conditions.

Labor members of the PRI's congressional delegation supported nearly the entire range of neoliberal reforms enacted during the late 1980s and early 1990s, including those that entailed constitutional or legal changes in the rural property regime and those that permitted the privatization of state-owned firms and broadened opportunities for foreign investment. Their main objections to the neoliberal agenda focused upon reforms to the national social security system, although after some minor modifications they approved these changes as well.[30] Only in the case of federal labor legislation did CTM opposition remain firm. Indeed, even though international organizations backed neoliberal reformers in advocating the deregulation of labor markets (OCDE 1997), the CTM leadership systematically rejected – openly in the case of Fidel Velázquez, and via behind-the-scenes maneuvering in the case of Leonardo Rodríguez Alcaine – changes that threatened its corporatist privileges or reduced its role in the flexibilization of labor norms. More than real veto power, however, the CTM's success in this struggle may have been due primarily to the fact that its interests coincided with those of the government in not wanting to alter the legal instruments permitting control over labor conflicts.

Something similar occurred with the CTM's position regarding the NAFTA. It accepted the NAFTA negotiations and gave unconditional backing to President Carlos Salinas de Gortari's (1988–1994) decision to pursue the agreement. The CTM limited itself to insisting that the worker rights provisions included as a "side agreement" (the product of lobbying by NAFTA opponents in the United States and Canada) not touch directly the issue of freedom of association or endanger the membership monopolies its affiliates held based upon domestic labor legislation. Here again, the CTM's demand coincided with the Mexican government's interest

---

30 In 1992 the administration of President Carlos Salinas de Gortari (1988–1994) established the Retirement Savings System (SAR). After negotiating some changes to the original proposal, but without winning full participation in the new system's administrative bodies, the CTM supported the initiative. For an analysis of the CTM's initial demands and the results it finally obtained, see Bertranou 1995: 12–17.

In December 1995 the Mexican Congress adopted (on the basis of the PRI's legislative majority, without the endorsement of opposition parties) a revised social security law establishing new rules for pensions, effective from July 1997. The legislation replaced the "pay-as-you-go" system administered by the Mexican Social Security Institute (IMSS) with an individually capitalized social security system operated by Retirement Fund Administrators (AFOREs), which are supervised by the National Commission on Retirement Savings (CONSAR). The 1995 reform also separated health and social services from the retirement pensions system. On the reform and its implications, see Murillo 1999: 65. For critical opinions regarding the reform (including initial CTM and CT opposition to the privatization of social security), see Mussot 1996.

in maintaining low wages and docile trade unions as a basis of comparative economic advantage, which in good measure explained the CTM's success in bargaining on this point.[31]

Although the CTM's conservative short-term economic strategy did not differ substantially from the policies adopted by unions confronting the challenge of economic restructuring in other countries, it must be noted that the CTM did not adopt any long-term strategy aimed at renewing its power resources, despite the erosion of old methods of exerting national political pressure and the loss of state support in the CTM's confrontations with capital. The change in the CTM's leadership after the death of Fidel Velázquez in June 1997 brought neither a renewal in strategy nor an open debate concerning the viability of the course the confederation had followed over the previous fifteen years. On the contrary, the CTM's new leadership (headed by SUTERM union boss Leonardo Rodríguez Alcaine) gradually lost its prominent role even within the Labor Congress (CT) itself, where other voices strove to prevent the total collapse of that structure by radicalizing their discourse concerning the negative impact of government economic policies on workers.[32]

In terms of unionization initiatives, the CTM continued to trust in the top-down arrangements that had in the past allowed it to consolidate its presence. In key export activities and other sectors with low levels of unionization (services, for example), the CTM coerced employers into allowing it to unionize work sites and gain control of collective contracts, in exchange for its guarantee of labor discipline. A similar strategy also allowed the CTM to protect unionized jobs in economic activities that experienced radical restructuring (textiles, for example). This approach permitted the CTM to conserve its position in many sectors, recuperate lost terrain in others (in automobile manufacturing, for example, where independent unions had gained a significant presence during the labor insurgency of the 1970s), or even expand the rate of unionization in the manufacturing industry as a whole.

The CTM's unionization strategy did not, however, take into account the possibility that old-style practices might be exhausted in the near future, or the fact that exclusion clauses have become a very questionable practice in the context of advancing political democracy. The confederation also faced growing difficulties in the form of pressures from U.S. employers seeking to avoid union representation altogether (successfully, in case of many maquiladora plants and in the electronics industry) and the state's reduced capacity to repress rank-and-file discontent or to sustain traditional union leaders against internal challenges. In addition, the PAN and PRD proposals for labor law reform place in doubt the future of exclusion clauses, and they seek greater transparency and less arbitrary handling of workers'

---

31 On Mexican and U.S. unions' positions regarding the NAFTA, see Bensusán 1994 and Ruíz 1997.

32 In its efforts to maintain its hegemony within the Labor Congress, the CTM sought systematically to weaken viable alternatives to state-corporatist unionism. Its disputes with the FESEBES and the STRM ended in these organizations leaving the CT.

organizational efforts by ending government control over the registry of unions and their leaderships.

The CTM has, moreover, made no systematic effort to increase the active commitment of its affiliated members by strengthening its representational structures at the workplace level. To the contrary, when challenged by internal dissidents, the confederation often responded with repression. The PRI–led government invariably supported this policy, above all in export sectors such as automobile manufacturing and maquiladora production. However, the slow advance of democratization – especially greater public resistance to the official use of violence following the revolt by the Zapatista Army of National Liberation (EZLN) in Chiapas in 1994 – made such actions increasingly problematic.

The CTM's unwillingness (or incapacity) to mobilize in defense of workers' interests and the dependent nature of its bargaining relationship with employers and the government doomed its strategy to failure. The CTM leadership maintained its control over the trade union apparatus, but the agreements the confederation reached with the government were not translated into significant gains for its members. For example, in 1992 the CTM and the government signed a "National Agreement for the Promotion of Productivity and Quality" that linked wage increases to improved productivity at the firm level. However, employers found it easy to push aside the demands of a negotiating counterpart that was subordinated to the state and incapable of posing a real threat to business interests. Without government support or a serious mobilizational capacity, the CTM found it very difficult to extract concessions from employers facing increased competition and pressures to cut labor costs.

Similarly at the macroeconomic level, the limited negotiating capacity of subordinated actors like the CTM and other "official" unions in the CT contributed to a highly unequal distribution of the costs and benefits of economic restructuring and, over time, eroded the legitimacy of tripartite pacts. For this reason, agreements on such matters as the principles for a "new labor culture" did not constitute a real counterweight to the interests of capital and the state. In this regard, the Mexican experience differed substantially from that of labor organizations in other countries (automobile workers' unions in Brazil, for example) where authentic workers' representatives with a defined strategy and real mobilizational capacity were able to soften the impact of neoliberal restructuring (Bensusán and Bayón 1998).

Finally, it is worth noting that the CTM's economic strategy during the late 1980s and the 1990s was based largely upon the modernizing idiom of the government and employers. The confederation did not set its own objectives around which it could seek the support of the rank and file and of the broader public affected by neoliberal policies. On the contrary, the CTM supported the government's strategy of isolating those groups like the RMALC and the PRD that articulated views critical of the economic adjustment process, trade liberalization, and the NAFTA. Even after the turn to neoliberalism, the CTM insisted upon defending at all costs its alliance with the government and the PRI, arguing that the new policies were "inevitable" and promising that renewed economic growth would bring improved conditions for workers. This approach distanced the rank and file even more from the CTM's top leadership because fifteen years of retreats and sacrifices did not lead to anything other than successive economic crises and feeble recoveries.

In terms of its political strategy, the CTM maintained its corporatist affiliation with the PRI during the 1980s and 1990s even after the governments that took office under the party's name adopted policies that gravely affected the interests of CTM members. The confederation became an unconditional supporter of the old regime, betting on the PRI's keeping and rebuilding power (where it had been lost) while at the same time resisting efforts to end the tradition of group-based party affiliation. Having identified the main opposition political parties (the PAN and the PRD) as possible threats to maintaining its corporatist privileges, the CTM's whole political strategy was aimed at smearing them and depicting them as enemies of workers' interests. Similarly, rather than raising pressures to change Mexico's new economic model, the CTM spoke out against social movements like the EZLN that adopted extreme positions against neoliberalism, taking advantage of the EZLN's emergence to remind the government of the important role that the traditional labor movement had to play in controlling labor discontent.

During the 1990s the CTM's reduced but still significant presence in Congress and in local governments continued to be a source of material resources. Nevertheless, at the same time that its ties to the federal executive were affected by the president's reduced room for maneuver in a context of neoliberal reform and expanding democratization, the CTM's legislative seats proved less and less useful to its affiliates because they were obtained through an implicit bargain in which the confederation agreed not oppose neoliberal policies or defend proposals by opposition parties that favored the interests of workers. This was one more example of the way in which the CTM's future was seriously compromised by its conservative responses to the new conditions created by economic and political change.

The "New Trade Unionism"

Those labor groups opposed to the de facto monopoly that the CTM and other government-allied organizations have held over Mexican unions have always faced significant obstacles. However, when neoliberal economic policies were adopted with the main features of political authoritarianism still intact, legal and political conditions became even more adverse for any organization seeking to represent workers while maintaining independence from government.

It is remarkable that the FAT has survived over a period of some forty years without government support and in the face of strong employer resistance to accepting it as an interlocutor. It has been able to do so because of its ability to mobilize alternative resources – especially ties with labor organizations in other countries and ties to Mexican social movements – and its capacity to adapt to changing conditions. Similarly, unions like the SME and the STRM (following the election of a new leadership in 1976) were able to maintain a greater degree of autonomy within the umbrella-like CT because of their members' higher educational level and their leaders' ability to maneuver successfully in an authoritarian environment without losing rank-and-file support. As a result, they had a solid basis for becoming interlocutors with employers and even (during the Salinas administration) the federal executive.

Political liberalization and the state's declining capacity for repression opened additional opportunities for a "new trade unionism" based upon a critique of traditional corporatism and the search for alternative power resources. Yet this option still remains a minority within the Mexican labor movement, and it faces many obstacles and uncertainties. In the year 2000 the National Union of Workers, the organization founded in 1997 as an alternative to traditional trade unionism, had a membership of about 326,000 workers in federal-jurisdiction economic activities.[33] Its affiliates included unions in both the service sector (unions representing universities, the Mexican Social Security Institute, and telephone, aviation, and transportation workers, among others) and the industrial sector (unions representing workers in the automobile and metalworking industries, among others), organizations that confronted very different issues and faced quite distinct bargaining conditions in terms of employers' power. Similarly, there were important divergences of perspective among UNT members concerning the economic and political strategies to be followed, depending upon different unions' origins and inclinations. The STRM, for example, had a greater affinity for social trade unionism, while the FAT was closer to movement trade unionism. For these reasons, the following discussion identifies only some of the (still evolving) strategies pursued by the organizations comprising the UNT.

A Successful Bargaining Experience at the Local Level
One of the cases that contrasts most sharply with the CTM's failure to build a coalition of interests with capital in order to achieve mutual benefits (even in sectors it dominates, such as automobile manufacturing) is the success achieved by the Mexican Telephone Workers' Union through the negotiating strategy it adopted when confronting the privatization and restructuring of TELMEX. Indeed, the STRM is the most-cited exception in discussions of the unilateral methods that were generally employed in the restructuring of production at state-owned and

---

33 These data are from the Ministry of Labor and Social Welfare's National Associational Registry (Registro Nacional de Asociaciones), 2000.

The Mexican Constitution (Article 123, clause 31) distinguishes between local- and federal-jurisdiction economic activities. Although the federal labor code applies to both categories, its application in the former case is the responsibility of state governments. Federal-jurisdiction activities (including the petroleum and petrochemical, mining, railroad, electrical power generation, steel and metalworking, automobile, textile, sugar, and banking industries) are distinguished by their strategic importance and/or the especially large number of workers employed in them.

private firms in Mexico during the late 1980s and the 1990s. By renouncing its previous statist positions and accepting greater functional flexibility in the organization of work, the STRM achieved a real voice in processes of change that could have gravely affected the jobs and working conditions of its members. The transformation process was not yet complete at the end of the 1990s, and its final outcome depends upon a number of factors (including the type of labor relations established in firms that emerge to compete with TELMEX).[34] Nonetheless, the STRM's experience clearly demonstrates that internal democracy and rank-and-file participation make it difficult to postpone indefinitely a consideration of workers' interests and require union leaders to design courses of action aimed at strengthening the union's negotiating power.[35]

The STRM's position toward the NAFTA and the opening of the telecommunications industry in Mexico similarly reflected a coalition of interests with TELMEX. The union backed the company's demands for a transitional period before telecommunications deregulation that would permit it to increase productivity and better face challenges from competitors. Later, the STRM sketched out a long-term project for the telecommunications sector in which TELMEX would continue to play a central role in Mexico's development. Parallel to this, it stepped up its criticisms of neoliberal economic policies, the absence of redistributive measures, and indiscriminate deregulation, warning that under existing conditions increased competitive pressures would end up damaging the interests of TELMEX workers by causing a generalized drop in the telecommunications sector's labor costs.

However, as one can deduce from this list of criticisms, the STRM's relative success in mediating the industrial restructuring process remains subject to threat. Even more to the point, its experience does not constitute a viable model for other UNT affiliates with fewer organizational resources and significantly less market-based bargaining leverage, such as university employees or workers in the small and midsized automobile parts or garment manufacturing firms that constitute the bulk of the FAT's membership.

Although its activities are less well known and of more modest scope than the successes achieved by the STRM, the FAT also played a central role in various

---

34 The STRM agreed to make the collective bargaining agreement with TELMEX more flexible, committed itself to increasing the company's productivity, participated in the formation of focus groups, and supported a strong worker training program. It did so in exchange for company commitments to protect workers' jobs, prevent abuses of labor flexibility (the union has a voice when tasks are redesigned or workers are reassigned), ensure safe and healthy working conditions, and maintain – and, in some skill categories, improve – workers' incomes, especially by awarding productivity bonuses. In contrast, workers in some of the firms that compete with TELMEX in long-distance service are organized by "letterhead" unions, have collective bargaining agreements that include only what it required by law, and face high job insecurity. See Sánchez 1998.

35 Sánchez 1998 analyzes the STRM's power resources and capabilities and the strategies it adopted in the face of industrial restructuring.

initiatives in which unions won a real voice in company affairs and gained tangible benefits for their members. The FAT has placed a priority on bilaterally negotiated forms of workplace flexibility that do not endanger jobs and that contribute to increased productivity. The case of Sealed Power, an automobile parts company, offers a key example of this strategy at the micro level. The STIMAHCS, after encountering years of strong employer resistance, finally displaced a CTM-affili-ated union and won control of the Sealed Power collective bargaining agreement in the late 1970s.[36] The company, which produces parts for Ford Motor Company and must therefore maintain high levels of quality, came to recognize the benefits of cooperation for both management and labor. Indeed, insofar as the FAT-affiliated STIMAHCS demands quality treatment of workers and therefore enjoys their real backing, the company has concluded that its long-term industrial relations situa-tion is even more favorable than with the CTM because the STIMAHCS can deliver on the commitments it makes in dealing with new production challenges.[37]

The Long-term Strategy of Independent Unions

In the short term, the STRM and the FAT have managed to negotiate innovative arrangements without selling out their members' interests. Over the longer term, both organizations aspire to expanding their power resources and moving toward a new model of trade unionism. Within the UNT, however, it is not yet clear whether this model (based upon workers' voluntary union membership and a broad alliance with social movements struggling for an alternative model of development) will be widely accepted, or whether what will prevail is a more syndicalist and politically conservative vision of labor action. This uncertainty is registered in experiences as different as the UNT's presence (even while holding opposing positions) side by side with traditional unions in negotiations with the administration of President Vicente Fox (2000–2006) over reform of the federal labor law, and its mobilization of workers against the government's orthodox economic policies.[38]

Nevertheless, positions within the UNT have increasingly converged upon the need to create institutional conditions that will eliminate the inherited vices of authoritarian corporatism and reestablish collective bargaining as an authentic bilateral space for determining workplace conditions. This, in turn, presupposes intro-ducing substantial changes in labor legislation, which is why the UNT publicly

---

36 Author's interview with Benedicto Martínez, secretary general of the STIMAHCS, Mexico City. Martínez recognized the importance of worker participation in the company's quality control programs. At Sealed Power, union delegates have a strong presence on the factory floor, where they are actively involved in dealing with workers' needs.

For a discussion of the FAT's other experiences in the metalworking industry, see Peón 1990 and Hathaway 1997: 26.

37 Author's 1995 interview with a Sealed Power production manager, reported in Bensusán, García, and Von Bülow 1996.

38 Many of the UNT's affiliated organizations supported the SME's opposition to the privati-zation of the electrical power industry. See La Jornada, September 28, 2002.

presented in mid-2002 its own proposal for labor law reform. The proposal's most important provisions aimed at eliminating the possibility of governmental control over organizing and bargaining processes, cleaning up the process of collective contracting, democratizing unions' internal governance, and guaranteeing an independent system of labor justice (UNT 2002). Taking this initiative led the UNT to seek out new political allies (especially within the PRD, but also including federal deputies and senators from other parties' parliamentary groups) in order to promote its proposal and simultaneously block the adoption of a more limited labor law reform – one that might leave in place the possibility of controls on union action – negotiated among employer representatives, the government, and the CT in the "Roundtable on Labor Updating and Modernization" that the minister of labor and social welfare convened in June 2001.[39]

Gaining Political Power Through Transnational Action

The new opportunities created by Canadian and U.S. trade unions' interest in what happens on the Mexican labor scene have been most effectively exploited by independent labor organizations. Traditional Mexican unions tended to believe that this interest merely reflected Canadian and U.S. unions' protectionist concerns about job flight to Mexico. However, the FAT in particular adopted a different strategy toward the NAFTA than the CTM or even the STRM, seizing the opening created by the NAFTA debate to expand considerably its political role. An organization with a membership of no more than ten thousand workers in small and midsized firms, the FAT became the pillar of the RMALC, which led the struggle in Mexico against the NAFTA and successfully forged alliances with NAFTA opponents in Canada and the United States. Together they demanded the adoption of special provisions to safeguard the interests of workers and protect the environment.

Since the implementation of the NAFTA, the FAT has worked through the RMALC network and its international alliances to promote international efforts to embed minimum labor standards in trade and investment agreements. Its international activities have increased its organizational capacity and political leverage (though not its membership size) beyond its direct capacity for social representation, which has in turn given it a stronger voice in international forums. At the same time, the FAT's alliance with the United Electrical, Radio, and Machine Workers of America (UE) in the United States has provided it a greater presence in maquiladora firms. It has devoted part of its resources to cadre formation, joint actions with U.S. organizations along the Mexico–U.S. border, and protests of labor rights violations filed with the national administrative offices created by the NAFTA–based North American Agreement on Labor Cooperation.[40]

---

39 On the PRD's proposal for labor law reform and its points of convergence with the UNT's proposal, see Escobar Toledo 2002: 7–8.

40 As part of its efforts to improve union organizing conditions, the UNT has also used alliances constructed during the NAFTA negotiations to present jointly with U.S. labor organizations

The Organizational and Mobilizational Bases of Independent Unionism

Although the international dimension is of growing relevance to Mexican labor organizations, both the FAT and the STRM have also taken care to build support among their rank and files. This approach may come especially naturally to the FAT as an opposition organization that not only never received government subsidies, but was also forcibly excluded from organizing in key industries such as automobile manufacturing and maquiladora plants. This background explains why the FAT is more willing than any other Mexican labor organization to do without exclusion clauses as an institutional resource for expanding or maintaining its membership.[41]

The STRM historically enjoyed significant institutional advantages (both exclusion clauses in its work contract and the monopoly character of TELMEX) in its efforts to assure a strong membership base, but more recently it has struggled to maintain them. Deregulation in the telecommunications industry has brought the union face to face with two types of problems: how to prevent new telecommunications companies from signing "protection contracts" that give them competitive advantages in terms of labor costs and working conditions, and how to defend unionized jobs within TELMEX at a time when the company threatens to expand subcontracting arrangements if the union does not meet its demands for reductions in labor costs. The STRM has, therefore, sought to use external alliances as part of its effort to win support from workers in the new telecommunications companies, and it is devoting more attention to preparing the cadres who are directly involved in organizational activities – tasks that were perceived to be of marginal importance during earlier periods when unionizing telecommunications workers was a sure thing.

During the late 1990s the FAT and the STRM also sought to build their organizational and mobilizational capacities in other ways. For example, along with other independent groups, they occupied the political space abandoned by "official" trade unions when the latter ceased participating in open-air May Day demonstrations. At the same time, the FAT and the STRM joined efforts – first in the "Union Movement and the Nation" Forum, and later within the UNT – in order to increase the economic and political power resources at their disposal.

The UNT, created when the organizations that made up the FESEBES (except the SME) seceded from the Labor Congress in October 1997, represented the most important break within the "official" labor movement in several decades. This self-styled alternative to state-corporatist unions has adopted many of the FAT's critical positions toward government economic policies, and it has built upon the STRM's negotiating experiences on productivity issues and the mobilizations in defense of social security led by the National Union of Social Security Workers (SNTSS).

(via the national administrative offices established under the terms of the North American Agreement on Labor Cooperation) denunciations of so-called protection contracts that favor employers and impede unionization. See Bensusán 2002.

41 This is still an isolated position within the UNT.

Yet the UNT's longer-term strategy for confronting Mexico's altered economic and political landscape is still not well defined. Although it promotes rank-and-file mobilizations in support of its positions and has radicalized its critique of the neoliberal economic model and government policies (approximating in this regard the line maintained by the FAT), it also sits alongside traditional unions in negotiations with employers on issues of importance to its members, including reform of federal labor legislation. The UNT has thus occupied a position somewhere between social and movement trade unionism. This ambivalence has reflected a difficult coexistence within the organization between more conservative elements that fear abandoning traditional corporatist alliances in order to take better advantage of the opportunities opened up by growing political pluralism, and groups that are clearly convinced that they cannot negotiate with old-style union leaders without endangering their own credibility as a political alternative.

The UNT's expansion came at the expense of the CT and the May 1 Inter-Union Coordinating Committee, which had formed in 1995. As an organization closely associated with movement trade unionism, the CIPM's most important reference point was the EZLN and other peasant and urban-popular movements. The FAT maintained its support for the grouping for some time, but the CIPM was weakened when leading independent labor organizations (particularly unions of university employees) formed the UNT. Rather than join the UNT itself, the CIPM opted to foster insurgencies within state-corporatist unions in an effort to democratize (and avoid further atomization of) the labor movement. Its preference for mobilizational strategies and its rejection of negotiations with employers made it the most radical alternative in the Mexican labor agreement. However, dwindling support forced its dissolution in 1999.

In addition to participating in the UNT, the STRM and FAT have also pursued other alliances and mobilizational strategies. For example, in response to the lingering effects of Mexico's devastating 1994–1995 economic crisis, the STRM radicalized its discourse and openly questioned the PRI's lack of commitment to the interests of the country's majorities. It also pushed for the formation of the Workers' Social Movement (MST), a political grouping that obtained official status in 1999 with the goal of negotiating with political parties to defend workers' demands. For its part, the FAT has participated actively in the organization of citizen polls (*consultas a la ciudadanía*) on such topics as economic policy and freedom of association.

The Power Resources and Capabilities of Mexican Unions

Traditional Trade Unionism

The old-line labor movement has concentrated its main efforts upon guaranteeing that the corporatist rules of the game continue to exclude independent labor organizations from key economic sectors. This explains why the CTM and its allies have resolutely defended the established legal order, even though it has long ceased to be of much use in protecting workers' interests because the functioning of the institutions that it regulates depends upon the government's policy stance.

The economic and political power of Mexican unions has long rested upon exclusion clauses and the legal requirement that all employers sign a collective bargaining agreement when an officially registered union so demands. These mechanisms made "official" trade unions the main instrument through which employers worked to flexibilize legal and contractual arrangements that might obstruct their competitive strategies and, above all, their efforts to prevent an autonomous trade unionism from becoming a real force. More generally, after the defeat in the late 1940s of labor organizations opposed to Fidel Velázquez and the labor movement's subordination to government, the CTM stopped using mobilizational strategies and basically relied upon state support to expand its presence and become employers' favored labor counterpart.

The CTM has concentrated more recent organizational efforts on such non-wage workers as street vendors, taxi drivers, and transport employees in an effort to extend its influence and win new members in the rapidly expanding informal sector. Given that the enterprises in which they are employed are often of questionable legality, these workers are susceptible to political manipulation. For this reason, higher unionization rates in some sectors cannot be interpreted as evidence of a real increase in labor strength.

The Evolution of Unionization Rates

Because of structural factors such as those outlined above, because the widespread presence of exclusion clauses in collective contracts makes union membership a de facto condition of employment rather than a voluntary commitment to a truly representative organization, and because state-corporatist unions' organizational successes are often the product of government support, the rate of unionization in Mexico cannot be taken as a reliable indicator of unions' economic and political power or a measure of their capacity (or willingness) to mobilize against public policies they oppose. Nevertheless, the evolution of unionization rates in federal-jurisdiction economic activities and in the manufacturing industry highlight both important sectoral trends and shifts in the balance of influence between CT affiliates and independent union organizations.

In 1978 unionized workers made up 16.2 percent of the employed population (Zazueta and De la Peña 1984). This proportion declined over the following two decades, so that by 1997 unionized workers represented only 12.9 percent of the employed population (Aguilar 2001). With regard to the population that could potentially be unionized (non-agricultural employees and workers 14 years of age and older), the unionization rate was 27.9 percent in 1978 (Zazueta and De la Peña 1984) and 16.3 percent in 1997 (Aguilar 2001).[42]

---

42 The population that could potentially be unionized in 1997 was calculated by subtracting the number of agricultural workers from the total employed population. See Aguilar 2001.

Given the absence of official data on unionization levels, these calculations could have been affected by uncertainties concerning the size of the unionized labor force in local-jurisdiction economic activities. Apart from this difficulty, however, two factors might account for the evident decline in unionization rates since the late 1970s: transformations in the labor market caused by increasing numbers of informal-sector workers and salaried workers hired under subcontracting arrangements (conditions that make unionization much more difficult), and the growing inefficacy of traditional means of union expansion (involuntary affiliation via exclusion clauses, collective bargaining agreements negotiated by labor leaders and employers without rank-and-file participation, and so forth) in a context in which many foreign investors prefer to avoid unionization altogether.

Similarly, an analysis of the economically active population that really can be unionized (workers with full-time jobs) shows that in 1978 the national rate of unionization was as high as 50 percent. Unionization rates reached 80 percent in economic activities in which only those who were ineligible to join blue-collar unions (management personnel) were excluded from these organizations (Zazueta and De la Peña 1984). By 1997, the unionization rate calculated in this matter had fallen to 40.9 percent (Aguilar 2001).[43] In this instance, the expansion of subcontracting arrangements and growing employer resistance to unionization appear to be the main factors behind the decline in unionization rates.

In contrast, a comparison of the data prepared by Zazueta and De la Peña in 1978 with those published by the North American Commission for Labor Cooperation (CCL 1997) shows a significant growth in the rate of unionization in federal-jurisdiction economic activities, from 34.2 percent in 1978 to 51.4 percent in 1994 for all the industrial branches under federal jurisdiction. It is possible that some part of this increase resulted from underreporting in 1978,[44] because activities such as automobile manufacturing had been placed under federal jurisdiction only a few years before (in 1975). However, if these data are accurate, they would indicate that "official" unions actually expanded their relative influence during a critical stage in the evolution of these important economic industries (see table 8.5).

A slightly different picture emerges if we compare the previous data with those obtained in January 2000 from the STPS's National Associational Registry and other sources of information on the employed workforce. These data indicate a unionization rate of 46.8 percent of privately owned activities under federal labor jurisdiction – that is, 4.6 percentage points below the rate reported by the North American Commission for Labor Cooperation for 1994.

---

43 For 1997, the population that could readily be unionized was calculated upon the basis of the number of workers receiving social security benefits from either the IMSS or the Social Security Institute for State Workers (ISSSTE). See Aguilar 2001.

44 On the basis of data from the STPS's National Associational Registry, Zazueta and De la Peña (1984: 392) reported that unionized workers under federal jurisdiction (those covered by Title "A" of the federal labor code) numbered 1,061,263 in 1978.

Table 8.5: Unionization Rates in Mexican Private-Sector Industries under Federal Labor Jurisdiction, 1978–1999

Industrial Activity	1978			1994			1999		
	Workers	Union members	Unionization rate	Workers	Union members	Unionization rate	Workers	Union members	Unionization rate
Total	1,922,460	657,212	34.2	2,557,122	1,314,431	51.4	2,259,394	1,057,042	46.8[a]
Textiles	250,833	104,727	41.8	97,337	80,536	82.7	80,863	56,333	69.7
Electrical power generation	157,653	82,647	52.4	87,473	77,503	88.6	155,396	76,826	49.4
Cinematographic industry	18,283	2,702	14.8	26,513	18,124	68.4	-	12,923	-[b]
Rubber	20,706	9,021	43.6	46,232	9,121	19.7	22,988	8,169	35.5
Sugar	50,947	40,330	79.2	184,863	63,631	34.4	26,906	43,653	-[c]
Mining and metalworking	393,374	192,185	48.9	178,141	60,306	33.9	260,135	97,499	37.5
Petroleum and natural gas	146,681	63,766	43.5	94,462	81,648	86.4	78,504	46,074	58.7
Cement and limestone	16,561	4,357	26.3	32,898	11,069	33.6	46,172	8,829	19.1
Automobile	110,846	11,443	10.3	139,772	59,178	42.3	165,787	49,527	29.9
Chemicals	151,191	15,233	10.1	123,068	27,339	22.2	217,149	45,592	21.0
Cellulose and paper	44,325	7,594	17.1	47,635	20,066	42.1	47,615	15,958	33.5
Vegetable oils	12,203	5,642	46.2	16,400	8,529	52.0	10,583	829	7.8
Food products	291,959	16,607	5.7	210,316	61,439	29.2	208,303	87,005	41.8
Bottling	87,528	13,458	15.4	152,275	81,197	53.3	110,551	59,296	53.6
Railroads	103,047	81,626	79.2	95,706	36,432	38.1	23,376	132,557	-[c]
Wood and wood products	31,070	3,646	11.7	30,765	7,037	22.9	26,892	4,708	17.5
Glass	26,688	893	3.3	19,072	12,901	67.6	27,656	10,231	37.0
Tobacco	8,565	1,335	15.6	6,095	3,667	60.2	6,594	3,188	48.3

Industrial Activity	1978			1994			1999		
	Workers	Union members	Unionization rate	Workers	Union members	Unionization rate	Workers	Union members	Unionization rate
Banks and credit unions				259,164	95,163	36.7	159,805	56,382	35.3
Other federal-jurisdiction activities[d]				709,035	499,545	70.5	694,206	430,596	62.0
Unspecified activities			—	—	—	—	—	11,266	—[b]

Sources: Except as noted below, the data for 1978 are from Zazueta and De la Peña 1984; for 1994, CCL 1997; and for 1999, author's calculations based upon Instituto Nacional de Estadística, Geografía e Informática (INEGI, at www.inegi.gob.mx), "Encuesta industrial mensual" (December 1999), and Registro Nacional de Asociaciones (data effective January 31, 2000). Data for the mining and metalworking and for the petroleum and natural gas industries are from INEGI, Censo económico 1999 (preliminary data). Data for "other federal-jurisdiction activities" in 1994 and 1999 were compiled by the author from the following sources: for the Mexican Social Security Institute (IMSS), IMSS web page (December 1999); for telecommunications, Presidencia de la República, Quinto informe de gobierno (1999); for federal automobile transportation and maritime transportation, INEGI, XII censo de transportes y comunicaciones, 1994 (data for December 1993); for aviation, Dirección General de Aeronáutica Civil (December 1999); for the Universidad Nacional Autónoma de México (UNAM), UNAM web page (December 1999); for NOTIMEX, Sindicato de Trabajadores de NOTIMEX (Departamento de Personal, February 2000); for the Colegio de Bachilleres, Sindicato Nacional de Trabajadores del Colegio de Bachilleres (Departamento de Personal, December 1999).

Notes:
[a] The overall unionization rate in 1999 only refers to industrial activities for which data on both total employed personnel and unionized workers were available.
[b] Unionization rates were not calculated for the cinematographic and "not specified" categories in 1999 because data on total employed personnel were not available.
[c] Unionization rates were not calculated for the sugar and railroad industries in 1999 because the number of affiliates that unions claimed was greater than the reported number of workers employed.
[d] This category includes the Mexican Social Security Institute (IMSS), telecommunications, federal transportation activities (automobile, maritime, and air transportation, the National Autonomous University of Mexico (UNAM), NOTIMEX (the government news agency), the Colegio de Bachilleres, and construction. Activities that could also be registered as local-jurisdiction industries were excluded from this category.

In more disaggregated terms, between 1978 and 1994 unionization rose in 14 of the 18 branches of federal-jurisdiction industry for which information is available. This translated into an overall increase in the rate of unionization in industry. By 1999, however, the unionization rate had fallen in 12 of those branches and risen in only four of them.[45] There was also a decline in the percentage of unionized establishments between 1992 and 1995 (from 50.2 percent to 42.2 percent) that was greater than the drop in industrial employment. Indeed, while employment fell by only 4 percentage points, the rate of unionization fell by 8 points.[46]

Other indicators of the impact of neoliberal policies on unionization during the 1990s confirm a loss of membership in the large national-industrial unions (those unions that organize workers across state lines in the same economic activity) that historically comprised the heart of the Mexican labor movement. These organizations were strongly affected by industrial restructuring and plant closures. Indeed, whereas industrial and national-industrial unions represented 36 percent of all unionized workers in 1978, they accounted for only 27 percent of the unionized workforce in 1999.[47] At the same time, there was an increase in the number of unionized workers in other sectors, including public services and some branches of the manufacturing industry (rubber, mining and metallurgy, food products, and bottling).[48]

More generally, the Labor Congress's overall importance in the labor movement declined significantly between the late 1970s and the late 1990s. Whereas in 1978 the CT had 4.5 affiliates for every member of an independent union employed in federal-jurisdiction economic activities (Zazueta and De la Peña 1984), by the year 2000 this ratio had fallen to 1.8:1.[49] A total of 326,873 of the 488,581 (66.9 percent)

---

45 Between 1978 and 1994 the rate of unionization fell in the textile, electrical power generation, petroleum and petrochemical, movie, cement, automobile manufacturing, chemical, paper and cellulose, food products, bottling, wood products, glass, and tobacco industries. By 1999, the rate had risen again in the rubber, mining and metallurgy, food products, and bottling industries. Data for 1978 are from Zazueta and De la Peña 1984; for 1994, from CCL 1997; for 1999, from the STPS's National Associational Registry [www.stps.gob.mx], January 2000.

Although the information in table 8.5 concerning rates of unionization in different federal-jurisdiction industries in 1994 and 1999 comes from the same source (the STPS's National Associational Registry), the variations observed in these two years could in some instances be due to problems of data collection – and not just to real declines in the level of unionization resulting from job losses produced by the 1994–1995 economic crisis or changes in the labor movement's organizational capacity.

46 Author's calculations based upon data in INEGI 1993a, 1993b, 1995.

47 Data for 1978 are from Zazueta and De la Peña 1984; data for 1999 are the author's calculations based upon information from the National Associational Registry [www.stps.gob.mx], January 2000.

48 Author's calculations based upon data from the STPS's National Associational Registry [www.stps.gob.mx], January 2000.

49 Author's calculations based upon data from the STPS's National Associational Registry [www.stps.gob.mx], January 2000.

unionized workers who were not affiliated with the CT belonged to the UNT. However, some 70 percent of the UNT's total membership belonged to a single organization, the National Union of Social Security Workers.[50] Nevertheless, the UNT had become the second most important union organization in Mexico, still smaller than the CTM but larger than traditional confederations such as the CROC and the CROM.

As for the distribution of the unionized workforce by individual labor organization, the available information does not indicate any major changes as a result of either Mexico's new economic policies or shifts in state-labor relations. Between 1993 and 1995, the CT's three largest organizations – the CTM, CROC, and CROM – experienced an absolute decline in their memberships, but they increased their relative share of the unionized workforce in the manufacturing industry (by six percentage points in the case of the CTM, and by half a percentage point each in the cases of the CROC and CROM). With some differences between them, the CTM and the CROM both increased their shares of the unionized labor force in the chemical, paper, machine and metalworking, and other manufacturing industries, while they lost ground in the non-metallic minerals and basic metals industries. It was precisely in the latter two industries that the CROC's membership increased as a proportion of the unionized workforce.

Organizational Structure and Discursive Orientation
Throughout the 1980s and 1990s the CTM preserved its vertical organizational structure (featuring powerful leadership bodies and weak membership units) and the undemocratic practices that made possible top-down control over decision making. As a consequence, the confederation's established leadership was able to suppress internal dissidence and block leadership challenges at minimal cost. Indeed, the relatively orderly succession following the death of Fidel Velázquez indicated that internal controls and discipline continued to function quite efficiently, even though some internal divisions did show in heated disputes between Secretary General Rodríguez Alcaine and some members of the CTM's national executive committee over economic interests in the auto-transport sector.[51]

Whatever the CTM's capacity for mobilization at the end of the 1990s, its strategies had been badly discredited in the eyes of rank-and-file members after more than fifteen years of near-continuous defeats. It had been unwavering in its

---

50 Author's calculations based upon data from the STPS's National Associational Registry [www.stps.gob.mx], January 2000.

51 A series of struggles took place among national executive committee members in July 1999. One dispute pitted José Ramírez Gamero, leader of the Auto-transport Industry Union, against Armando Neyra, the CTM's secretary of finances. Gamero accused the executive committee of using his union as its "economic booty," specifically charging that Neyra had fostered internal splits within it. For his part, Rodríguez Alcaine backed the creation of a new auto-transport workers' union in an attempt to undercut Ramírez Gamero (*La Jornada*, July 26, 1999, p. 44).

commitment to renouncing confrontation in exchange for the government's support for maintaining its coercive unionization capacity and control over its affiliates. The CTM also renounced using the coordinating capacity it derived from its hegemony within the Labor Congress and in key economic activities (automobile manufacturing, for example). What was especially striking was the lack of a CTM strategy that might permit it to recover from its economic losses given the significant increases in productivity that had occurred over the course of the 1990s (Hernández Laos 1997).

Even at the level of ideological discourse, the CTM's position was badly eroded during the 1980s and 1990s. The government began to abandon its commitment to revolutionary ideology as early as 1982. For example, during his presidential campaign and the early part of his administration, President Miguel de la Madrid (1982–1988) radically altered his discourse by giving greater priority to the need for economic austerity than for social justice. This shift was, of course, accentuated during Carlos Salinas de Gortari's presidential term (1988–1994). The CTM lost credibility in this context by adopting the government's modernizing discourse at a time when government policies demanded continuous sacrifices from workers.[52]

In overall terms, the CTM's position was weakened by dual processes of economic and political opening. During the 1990s, the labor candidates sponsored by the PRI found it more and more difficult to prevail in transparent and truly competitive elections (see table 8.3). Over time, democratic advances also made it more difficult for the CTM leadership to employ repression against the rank-and-file opposition that predictably arose to its conservative strategy. The emergence and growing strength of the UNT were one consequence of the CTM's failure to respond more assertively to altered economic and political conditions.

The New Trade Unionism

Beginning in the 1990s, Mexico's most important independent labor organizations redoubled their efforts to increase their analytic, organizational, and strategic capacities, especially their ability to assess political and economic conditions and devise appropriate responses. They increased their interactions with universities and professional associations, seeking out specialists to advise them in areas such as labor law. External alliances also proved to be an important means of expanding their organizational strengths. These shifts are summarized in table 8.6.

The FAT and the STRM are representative of what has been achieved by independent labor groups. The FAT, for example, established an outstanding international presence through the RMALC and its publication, the magazine *Alternativa*. In fact, it became an important source of information on Mexican labor and social problems linked to trade liberalization and globalization, with a certain credibility in public opinion circles. Similarly, the STRM established alliances with Canadian and U.S. unions in the telecommunications sector, and it has participated actively

---

52 On the shift in government discourse and the labor policies associated with it, see Bensusán 1987.

Table 8.6: **The Power Resources and Capacity of Mexico's New Trade Unionism**

Power Resources	Uses of Power Resources	Increased Capacity
Material resources	Number and quality of staff	Strategic and discursive
Selective incentives	Communication channels	
Members' identification with, and commitment to, the union and its objectives	Willingness to participate in activities supporting the union	Mobilization
Inter- and intra-union solidarity	Scope and scale of potential collective actions	Mobilization and coordination
Union institutions that reinforce class identity and common class interests	Tendency to perceive common interests and negotiate divergent claims	Coordination
National and international activists and political linkages with other progressive social movements and with intellectuals	Quantity and quality of information Volume of creative ideas Credibility that union demands represent a public interest	Discursive and strategic
Influence with, and links to, political parties	Union capacity to influence the political and legislative agendas and outcomes in these areas Union tendency to perceive and situate its program in the broadest class or national agenda	Strategic, discursive, and legislative

Source: Robinson 1998.

in the Postal, Telegraph, and Telephone International. Both the FAT and the STRM have taken advantage of such alliances to file complaints about labor rights violations in Mexico and the United States before the national administrative offices created by the North American Agreement on Labor Cooperation. These grievance processes, which require close cooperation among unions in the NAFTA countries, may not have greatly modified the conditions under which organizing efforts take place, but they have certainly focused public attention upon existing obstacles to exercising the right of association. Over the longer term, such public awareness will benefit the organizing efforts undertaken by independent unions.

The creation of the UNT formed part of independent labor organizations' efforts to improve their coordination capacity and mobilize the additional material resources required to carry out a complex strategy to promote economic and political change. The UNT's main goal has been to democratize the labor movement and the political regime as prerequisites for altering Mexico's neoliberal economic policies.[53] However, the UNT's problems have been greater than its achievements. With the exception of the STRM and the SNTSS (which together have move than 265,000 members), the federation's affiliates have very limited resources. This harsh economic reality has greatly constrained what the UNT has been able to accomplish. Among other things, it has limited the group's ability to expand its own membership and create the research and analytic capacities that would increase its strategic capabilities.

One must therefore conclude that, although some factors favor a renewal of the power resources at the disposal of the "new trade unionism," the prospects for the consolidation of this tendency are still unclear. Among other reasons, it is not yet certain whether available resources and capabilities will really be translated into achievements that permit organized labor to regain sufficient economic and political power to constitute a real counterweight to capital, or to win adoption of public policies that will again be oriented toward socioeconomic redistribution.

Future Perspectives on Mexican Unions' Economic and Political Power

The overlapping processes of political and economic opening that Mexico experienced from the mid-1980s through the 1990s established new conditions for organized labor. A significant electoral reform in 1996, the PRI's loss of its majority in the federal Chamber of Deputies in 1997 and its defeat in elections to choose a governor for the Federal District that same year, and its historic loss of the presidency in the year 2000 elections were all landmarks on the road to electoral transparency and greater political openness. Similarly, the signing of free-trade agreements with Canada and the United States and later with the European Union made economic liberalization largely irreversible, regardless of which party prevails in a particular election.

In this context, the margins for political exchanges like those that historically characterized relations between the PRI and "official" unions will continue to narrow. Labor organizations such as the CTM that continue seeking privileged unionization and contract-negotiation arrangements that do not confront business interests and lack real rank-and-file support will be hard-pressed to obtain any positive results in an economic and political environment that is increasingly hostile to these

53 The UNT's main programmatic positions were presented in its proposal for a "Reform of the State, of Society, and Production" ("Reforma del Estado, Social y Productiva"). The document proposed a leading role for unions in the formulation of public policies at the national, sectoral, regional, and local levels. Yet within the UNT there is considerable diversity of opinion about how to respond to different opportunities and constraints, as well as about how to use alternative sources of power to move beyond the strictures of state-corporatist labor relations (UNT 2000).

outmoded approaches. The future prospects for a trade unionism that is not based upon the authentic representation of workers' immediate interests is likely to be bleak.

One key factor shaping the future balance of forces between state-corporatist and independent unions will be the outcome of efforts to reform federal labor legislation. Even though traditional controls on workers have weakened, legal arrangements that preserve membership monopolies and permit state intervention to inhibit or repress labor conflicts mean that, under the status quo, workers pay high costs if they challenge entrenched labor leaders or seek to secede from established organizations. However, both the PAN and PRD have proposed labor code reforms that would democratize labor relations and guarantee freedom of association. Under an institutional framework that eliminates governmental control over union organizing and union demands, establishes an independent system of labor justice, and creates space for bilateral worker-employer agreements on productivity and distributional issues at the national, regional, and sectoral levels, union leaderships with credibility among their rank and file and the willingness to mobilize in support of their demands and attract new social and political allies will have much greater opportunities to win economic and political power.

This is the reason why, in the wake of political alternation in the presidency in 2000, the old-style labor movement focused its strategy on defending the institutional status quo and demonstrating that it remained a key factor in maintaining labor governability. The CT thus agreed to participate in controlled negotiations to reform federal labor legislation. This process was coordinated by Minister of Labor and Social Welfare Carlos Abascal, a former president of the Mexican Employers' Confederation (COPARMEX) who had promoted a dialogue between that organization and legendary labor leader Fidel Velázquez concerning a "new labor culture." These roundtable discussions were not destined to produce any profound change in established institutional arrangements. Indeed, on the presumption that existing political conditions would not permit congressional approval of constitutional amendments (which would be necessary to eliminate, for example, the conciliation and arbitration board system controlled by the federal executive), the principal negotiating parties essentially limited themselves to discussing restricted changes that would leave unaltered union leaders' established prerogatives and rules that permit officially recognized unions to maintain artificial representational monopolies against workers' will and at the expense of internal union democracy. Although the UNT participated in this negotiating effort and submitted proposals that would have ended the corporatist labor relations regime, its protests were systematically rejected in favor of more conservative positions advanced by representatives of the CT and major employer organizations (particularly the COPARMEX and the Private Sector Coordinating Council, CCE).[54] In the end, the UNT withdrew from the negotiations

54 For this reason, it was important that the UNT elaborated its own full-blown proposal for reform of the constitutional and legal order governing labor relations. By doing so, it consolidated a position favoring institutional reform within the "new trade unionism."

As this experience clearly indicated, the advance of electoral democracy will not automatically bring about the changes necessary to promote a regime of voluntary trade unionism, under which an organization's resources and capabilities are fully under union control and based upon real representation. So long as the government seeks to contain redistributive pressures following a wage loss such as that experienced by Mexican workers since 1982, and so long as the government fundamentally maintains the economic policies implemented thereafter, the old-style labor movement will have an opportunity to preserve – if not its historical political alliance – a relatively privileged relationship with the federal government, even under PAN control.

Nevertheless, there is no doubt that old-style unionism will continue to lose influence in an increasingly competitive (and more transparent) political environment, and that this transition will over time favor a new form of unionism capable of responding more effectively to evolving challenges in the world of work. Under these new conditions, increasing importance will accrue to the strategies, power resources, and capabilities that the "new unionism" deploys to alter old labor institutions and orient itself toward organizational forms that are more appropriate to the defense of rank-and-file interests in Mexico's new structure of political and economic opportunities.

References

Aguayo Quezada, Sergio. 2000. *El almanaque mexicano.* Mexico City: Grijalvo.

Aguilar, Javier. 2001. *La población trabajadora y sindicalizada en México en el periodo de la globalización.* Mexico City: Fondo de Cultura Económica.

Aziz Nassif, Alberto. 1989. *El estado mexicano y la CTM.* Mexico City: Centro de Investigaciones y Estudios Superiores en Antropología Social.

———. 1994. *Chihuahua: historia de una alternativa.* Mexico City: La Jornada / Centro de Investigaciones y Estudios Superiores en Antropología Social.

Becerra, Ricardo, Pedro Salazar, and José Woldenberg. 2000. *La mecánica del cambio político en México.* Mexico City: Cal y Arena.

Bensusán, Graciela. 1987. "Una década de política laboral en México: salarios y empleo, 1977–1986." In *Políticas públicas en América Latina,* edited by Rogelio Hernández and Gonzalo Varela. Mexico City: Facultad Latinoamericana de Ciencias Sociales.

———. 1992. "La institucionalización laboral en México: los años de la definición jurídica, 1917–1931." Ph.D. diss., Facultad de Ciencias Políticas y Sociales, Universidad Nacional Autónoma de México.

———. 1994. "Entre candados y dientes: la agenda laboral del Tratado de Libre Comercio," *Perfiles Latinoamericanos* 4 (January-June): 109–41.

———. 1998. "El sindicalismo mexicano: análisis a nivel nacional." Final report for the project on "Estrategias sindicales frente a la reestructuración neoliberal y el Tratado de Libre Comercio de América del Norte." Consejo Nacional de Ciencia y Tecnología / Programa Interinstitucional de Estudios de la Región de América del Norte. Mimeo.

———. 1999. *Estándares laborales después del Tratado de Libre Comercio de América del Norte.* Mexico City: Facultad Latinoamericana de Ciencias Sociales–México / Friedrich Ebert Stiftung / Plaza y Valdés.

————. 2000. *El modelo mexicano de regulación laboral.* Mexico City: Plaza y Valdés.

————. 2001a. "La reforma de la legislación laboral." Paper prepared for the Red de Investigadores y Sindicalistas de Estudios Laborales. Mimeo.

————. 2001b. "La agenda y la política laboral en transición," *Veredas* (Universidad Autónoma Metropolitana-Xochimilco) 2: 77–89.

————. 2002. "Los sindicatos y la gobernanza global." In *Gobernanza global en América Latina*, edited by Claudio Maggi. Caracas, Venezuela: Nueva Sociedad.

Bensusán, Graciela, and Cristina Bayón. 1998. "El sindicalismo del sector automotriz mexicano." Mimeo.

Bensusán, Graciela, Carlos García, and Marisa Von Bülow. 1996. *Relaciones laborales en las pequeñas y medianas empresas de México.* Mexico City: Fundación Friedrich Ebert / Juan Pablos Editor.

Bensusán, Graciela, and Luis Reygadas. 2000. "Relaciones laborales en Chihuahua: un caso de abatimiento artificial de los salarios," *Revista Mexicana de Sociología* 62, 2 (April-June): 29–57.

Bensusán, Graciela, and Ian Robinson. 1998. "Comparative Chapter: National-Level Analysis." Final report for the project on "Estrategias sindicales frente a la reestructuración neoliberal y el Tratado de Libre Comercio de América del Norte." Consejo Nacional de Ciencia y Tecnología / Programa Interinstitucional de Estudios de la Región de América del Norte. Mimeo.

Bertranou, Julián. 1995. "La política de la reforma a la seguridad social en México: análisis de la formulación del Sistema de Ahorro para el Retiro," *Estudios Sociológicos* 37 (January-April): 3–23.

Bizberg, Ilán. 1990. *Estado y sindicalismo en México.* Mexico City: El Colegio de México.

Bolívar, Augusto. 1990. "El período de la transición a la modernidad." In *México en la década de los ochenta: la modernización en cifras*, edited by Rosa Albina Garavito and Augusto Bolívar. Mexico City: Universidad Autónoma Metropolitana–Azcapotzalco / El Cotidiano.

Bossio Rotondo, Juan Carlos. 2002. "Crisis y reestructuración de la maquila de exportación," *Trabajadores* 31 (July-August): 23–30.

Carrillo, Jorge, and Kathryn Kopinak. 1999. "Condiciones de trabajo y relaciones laborales en la maquila." In *Cambios en las relaciones laborales*, edited by Enrique de la Garza and Alfonso Bouzas. Mexico City: American Federation of Labor–Congress of Industrial Organizations / Frente Auténtico del Trabajo / Universidad Autónoma Metropolitana / Universidad Nacional Autónoma de México.

CCL (Comisión para la Cooperación Laboral). 1997. *Cierre de empresas y derechos laborales.* Dallas, Tex.: North American Commission for Labor Cooperation.

De la Garza, Enrique. 1993. *Reestructuración productiva y respuesta sindical en México.* Mexico City: Universidad Nacional Autónoma de México / Universidad Autónoma Metropolitana–Iztapalapa.

De la Garza, Enrique, and Francisco Herrera. 1992. "Las transformaciones del sindicalismo en México," *Cuadernos de Trabajadores* (Centro Nacional de Promoción Social) 6 (October): 11–16.

De la O, María Eugenia. 1999. "La transformación de las relaciones laborales y la contratación colectiva en Jalisco." In *Cambios en las relaciones laborales*, edited by Enrique de la Garza and Alfonso Bouzas. Mexico City: American Federation of Labor–Congress of Industrial Organizations / Frente Auténtico del Trabajo / Universidad Autónoma Metropolitana / Universidad Nacional Autónoma de México.

Escobar Toledo, Raúl. 2002. "Las reformas a la legislación laboral: la propuesta del PRD," *Trabajadores* 31 (July-August): 7–11.

Friedman, Santiago, Nora Lustig, and Adriana Legovini. 1995. "Mexico: Social Spending and Food Subsidies during Adjustment in the 1980s." In *Coping with Austerity: Poverty and Inequality in Latin America*. Washington, D.C.: Brookings Institution.

Hathaway, Dale. 1997. "Mexico's Frente Auténtico del Trabajo: Organizing Beyond the PRI and Across Borders." Paper presented at the international congress of the Latin American Studies Association, Guadalajara, Mexico.

Heredia, Blanca. 1997. "La transición al mercado en México: desempeño económico e instituciones políticas." In *México en el desfiladero: los años de Salinas*, edited by Marcelo Cavarozzi. Mexico City: Facultad Latinoamericana de Ciencias Sociales / Juan Pablos Editor.

Hernández Laos, Enrique. 1997. "México: costo laboral y competitividad manufacturera." In *Costos laborales y competitividad industrial en América Latina*, edited by Edward Amadeo, José Márcio Camargo, Gustvao Gonzaga, Enrique Hernández Laos, Daniel Martínez, Álvaro Reyes, Héctor Szretter, and Víctor E. Tokman. Geneva: International Labour Office.

——. 1999. "Apertura comercial, productividad, empleo y contratos de trabajo en México." In *Productividad y empleo en la apertura económica*, edited by Víctor E. Tokman and Daniel Martínez. Lima, Peru: International Labour Office.

INEGI (Instituto Nacional de Estadística, Geografía e Informática). 1993a. *Encuesta Nacional a Trabajadores Manufactureros*. Mexico City: INEGI.

——. 1993b. *Encuesta Nacional de Empleo, Salarios, Tecnología y Capacitación en el Sector Manufacturero*. Mexico City: INEGI.

——. 1995. *Encuesta Nacional de Empleo, Salarios, Tecnología y Capacitación en el Sector Manufacturero*. Mexico City: INEGI.

Juárez Sánchez, Laura. 2002. "Los trabajadores de México a dos décadas de neoliberalismo económico," *Revista Trabajadores* (Universidad Obrera de México) 29: 7–12.

Lustig, Nora. 1994. *México: hacia la reconstrucción de una economía*. Mexico City: Fondo de Cultura Económica.

McAdam, Doug. 1982. *Political Process and the Development of Black Insurgency, 1930–1970*. Chicago, Ill.: University of Chicago Press.

——. 1996. "Political Opportunities: Conceptual Origins, Current Problems, Future Directions." In *Comparative Perspectives on Social Movements: Political Opportunities, Mobilizing Structures, and Cultural Framings*, edited by Doug McAdam, John D. McCarthy, and Mayer N. Zald. Cambridge: Cambridge University Press.

Middlebrook, Kevin J. 1995. *The Paradox of Revolution: Labor, the State, and Authoritarianism in Mexico*. Baltimore, Md.: Johns Hopkins University Press.

Middlebrook, Kevin J., and Cirila Quintero. 1998. "Las juntas locales de conciliación y arbitraje en México: registro sindical y solución de conflictos en los noventa," *Estudios Sociológicos* 47 (May-August): 283–316.

Murillo, Sandra. 1999. "¿Quiénes podrán acceder a una pensión de retiro? La reforma del IMSS y las tendencias recientes del trabajo en México." Master's thesis. Facultad Latinoamericana de Ciencias Sociales–México.

Mussot, María Luisa. 1996. *Alternativas de reforma de la seguridad social*. Mexico City: Friedrich Ebert Stiftung / Universidad Autónoma Metropolitana–Xochimilco.

OCDE (Organización para la Cooperación y el Desarrollo Económicos). 1997. *Estudios económicos de la OCDE*. Mexico City: OCDE.

——. 1999. *Estudios económicos de la OCDE*. Mexico City: OCDE.

Pacheco, Guadalupe. 1999a. "Caleidoscopio electoral: elecciones en México." Mimeo.

——. 1999b. "El péndulo regional," *Voz y Voto* 80: 36–41.

Partida, Raquel. 1999. "Nuevas condiciones de trabajo en la industria electrónica de Guadalajara: el caso de IBM y Solectron." In *Cambios en las relaciones laborales*, edited by Enrique de la

Garza and Alfonso Bouzas. Mexico City: American Federation of Labor–Congress of Industrial Organizations / Frente Auténtico del Trabajo / Universidad Autónoma Metropolitana / Universidad Nacional Autónoma de México.

Peón, Joaquín. 1990. "Sealed Power Mexicana (SPM), planta Naucalpan, Edo. de México," *Revista Calidad Total* (Fundación Mexicana para la Calidad Total), 3.

Poder Ejecutivo Federal. 1994. *Sexto informe de gobierno*. Mexico City: Presidencia de la República.

——. 1998. *Cuarto informe de gobierno*. Mexico City: Presidencia de la República.

Reyes del Campillo, Juan. 1996. *Modernización política en México: elecciones, partidos y representación, 1982–1994*. Mexico City: Universidad Autónoma Metropolitana–Xochimilco.

Robinson, Ian. 1998. "Introduction." Final report for the project on "Estrategias sindicales frente a la reestructuración neoliberal y el Tratado de Libre Comercio de América del Norte." Consejo Nacional de Ciencia y Tecnología / Fideicomiso para Estudios de América del Norte / Programa Interinstitucional de Estudios de la Región de América del Norte. Mimeo.

Román, Richard, and Edur Velasco. 1998. "The Restructuring of Labor Control in Mexico." Paper presented at the international congress of the Latin American Studies Association, Chicago, Illinois, September.

Ruiz, Martha. 1997. "El sindicalismo en México ante el Tratado de Libre Comercio de América del Norte." *Licenciatura* thesis. Universidad Nacional Autónoma de México.

Sánchez, Landy. 1998. "Entre la apertura comercial y la transición política: la estrategia del STRM." Master's thesis. Facultad Latinoamericana de Ciencias Sociales–México.

Sánchez, Sergio. 1998. "La Coordinadora Inter-sindical 1 de mayo." Mimeo.

Schmitter, Philippe C. 1992. "¿Continúa el siglo del corporativismo?" In Philippe C. Schmitter and Gerhard Lembruch, *Neocorporativismo: más allá del estado y el mercado*. Mexico City: Alianza Editorial.

STPS (Secretaría del Trabajo y Previsión Social). 2001 "Programa Nacional de Política Laboral, 2001–2006," *Diario Oficial de la Federación*, December 17.

——. 2002. "Base de datos del Registro Nacional de Asociaciones" [www.stps.gob.mx].

Trejo Delarbre, Raúl. 1992. "Sexenio de cambios aplazados: política laboral y sindicalismo, 1982–1988." In *México: auge, crisis y ajuste*, edited by Carlos Bazdresch, Nisso Bucay, Soledad Loaeza, and Nora Lustig. Mexico City: Fondo de Cultura Económica.

UNT (Unión Nacional de Trabajadores). 2000. "Propuesta de la Unión Nacional de Trabajadores para el nuevo gobierno." Mimeo.

——. 2002. "Anteproyecto de reforma al artículo 123 constitucional y a la Ley Federal del Trabajo" [www.unt.org.mx/1ft/reformas.htm].

Zapata, Francisco. 1995. *El sindicalismo mexicano frente a la reestructuración*. Mexico City: El Colegio de México / Instituto de Investigaciones de las Naciones Unidas para el Desarrollo Social.

Zazueta, César, and Ricardo de la Peña. 1984. *La estructura del Congreso del Trabajo: Estado, trabajo y capital en México*. Mexico City: Fondo de Cultura Económica.

9

Rural Producers' Organizations and the State in Mexico: The Political Consequences of Economic Restructuring

Horacio Mackinlay

S tudies of corporatism in Mexico have generally focused upon the three sectors – peasant, worker, and "popular" – that have traditionally comprised the Institutional Revolutionary Party (PRI), the party that emerged from the Mexican Revolution and held national power (under different names) between 1929 and the year 2000. The PRI's structure was supposedly designed to give priority representation to the least fortunate groups in Mexican society, the so-called social sector. Midsize and large business interests were not formally included in order to symbolize the party's autonomy vis-à-vis capitalist classes. This does not mean that business groups were excluded from the corporatist framework; rather, their relationship with the state differed from that of the social sector. Because of this difference, no existing study provides an integrated vision of rural producers' organizations (both peasant organizations and businesses) and their changing relations with the state.

This chapter examines producers' organizations and their place in Mexico's traditional rural corporatist system. In particular, it analyzes changes in this system following the implementation of neoliberal economic reforms in the late 1980s and in the 1990s, focusing mainly upon developments through the end of the last PRI administration in December 2000 but also making some observations about events occurring early in the administration of President Vicente Fox Quesada (2000–2006). There have been profound changes in the scale and form of state intervention, in the organization of production in the context of global economic integration, and in the legal framework governing agricultural, livestock, and forestry activities. As a consequence, the conditions facing social actors in rural Mexico have also been transformed.

Large corporations operating in domestic and foreign markets are playing a central role in the transformation of rural Mexico. Peasants devastated by neoliberal economic policies are also experiencing a process of land disentailment. The resulting crisis is affecting important groups of midsize and even large-scale family farmers who in the past enjoyed the protection of trade barriers and state intervention in the countryside, and in the process it is altering relations between rural producers' organizations and the state.

Translated by Aníbal Yáñez-Chávez and Kevin J. Middlebrook.

To comprehend fully the changes that have occurred in this relationship, it is helpful to examine the origins of relations between rural producers' organizations and the Mexican state. The following section overviews key developments between 1929 (when the postrevolutionary governing party was founded) and 1988 (when the process of neoliberal economic reform accelerated and the rural corporatist system fell into crisis). The discussion focuses, in turn, upon the peasant (or social) sector and the rural business (or private) sector.

Mexico's Corporatist System, 1929–1988

The Social Sector

The social sector in rural Mexico was principally defined in terms of land tenure. The social-property regime included *ejidos* and agrarian communities, whose lands could not be seized, transferred, sold, or reassigned. The *ejido*, a collective form of land ownership that was the principal vehicle for the distribution of land during Mexico's postrevolutionary agrarian reform, was constituted from latifundia or private properties that exceeded the size limits established by agrarian law.[1] Agrarian communities were the product of the restitution or confirmation of indigenous communities' rights to lands they had held since time immemorial.[2]

This property regime was designed to prevent peasants who had benefited from the agrarian reform from losing their lands in commercial transactions, as well as to prevent these lands from again becoming private property. *Ejidatarios* and *comuneros* had exclusive use of parceled croplands within these properties,[3] and they made decisions about the use of common areas and resources – water, pastures, forests, financial credit, and various forms of government support – in general assemblies (Pérez Castañeda 2002). According to both agrarian law and official government discourse, individuals in the social sector were supposed to be the main beneficiaries of the government's economic development and social welfare initiatives.

---

1 Since 1940, the upper limits to private ownership have been 100 hectares of irrigated land, 200 hectares of rain-fed land, 400 hectares of good pasture land, 800 hectares of mountainous land or pasture land in arid zones, and between 150 and 300 hectares of land devoted to such specific crops as cotton, bananas, sugarcane, and coffee. See Ley Federal de Reforma Agraria (1985), articles 249–50.

2 In fact, most so-called agrarian communities were formed by people who were not indigenous but who occupied the lands in question, while many authentically indigenous communities received *ejido* lands due to the fact that they could not prove that their lands had been taken from them illegally.

    According to government statistics, Mexico's agrarian reform created 29,162 ejidos and restored land to 2,366 communities. This involved approximately 103 million of the 197 million hectares in Mexico. More than 3.5 million peasants in the social sector benefited from the reform (SRA 1998: 313).

3 In so-called collective ejidos and certain indigenous communities, land was worked collectively and not parceled to individuals. However, there were comparatively few such cases.

The National Peasants' Confederation

The preeminent rural organization in postrevolutionary Mexico was the National Peasants' Confederation (CNC), the central pillar of the rural corporatist system. Formed in 1938 and promoted "from above," the CNC was, during its early years, practically the only social organization with a presence in the countryside. In most states, it was the main route for gaining access to land. The CNC's territorial structure began at the level of the ejido's leadership bodies (*comisariado ejidal*) and continued upward through the regional (municipal peasant committees), state (agrarian community leagues), and national (the national executive committee) levels. CNC members generally held their affiliation as part of a collective organization (ejidos, agrarian communities, groups of land petitioners, producer cooperatives), although the CNC also allowed for individual affiliation, as in the case of small property owners (Mackinlay 1996: 172). In fact, the CNC automatically viewed all ejidatario and comunero beneficiaries of Mexico's agrarian reform as members of both the CNC and the PRI. It was a "massive, collective, and often involuntary incorporation into the party in power" (Paré 1985: 89).

Ejidos enjoyed a special position in state development projects only during the presidency of Lázaro Cárdenas (1934–1940). With the end of his administration, during the "agrarian counterreform" period between 1940 and 1958, the ejido's privileged place was taken over by family farmers. Because ejidatarios would continue (despite increasing difficulties) to produce corn and other staple crops with little or no outside assistance, the government began to see them not as an agent whose development should be fostered, but rather as a political and electoral instrument of the "official" party. This process went hand in hand with the unleashing of PRI–connected local bosses, who often took control of ejido leadership bodies and developed an illegal land market for their own benefit while they simultaneously appropriated scarce development resources (Gordillo 1988a: 151–53). In this context, the CNC's role in the political system – besides serving as a link between peasants and government agencies – shifted to party work.[4] This involved coordinating demonstrations of support for the ruling party (carting people to political rallies) and mobilizing rural voters in favor of PRI candidates.

Although there was eventually a "correction" in the government's anti-ejido policies, the general orientation of economic policy toward the countryside did not change during the period of "stabilizing development" (1958–1970). The government created certain compensatory mechanisms to support the ejido sector, and it resumed land distribution (maintaining the tendency to allocate marginal lands to peasants for strictly political reasons). Monies from the World Bank and the Inter-American Development Bank were also used to create investment funds providing

---

4 In certain regions, the peasant-state relationship was established directly with government agencies rather than through the CNC. This was, for example, the case in regions where land distribution antedated the formation of the CNC. See Baitenmann 1997 on the case of central Veracruz.

credit to small producers. In addition, the federal government established or revamped several state-run companies and public development agencies, including the National Basic Foods Company (CONASUPO), in order to increase its role in regulating the market for basic goods.

Yet contrary to their stated purposes, these supports mainly benefited midsize and large-scale family farmers – that is, market-oriented producers pursuing a capitalist rationality based upon wage labor and the search for profits. The government's rural programs contributed much less to the peasant economy that relied upon family labor and production partly for a family's own consumption, thus pursuing a rationality focused less upon profit-making than reproducing the domestic economic unit.[5] As a consequence, the peasant population began to falter in the role it had been assigned – namely, to supply low-cost food and raw materials to Mexico's secondary and tertiary sectors.

Beginning in the mid-1960s, prices for basic goods – especially corn and beans – dropped so low that a permanent crisis took root among peasant producers of basic grains. They were unable to shift to other crops because they lacked access to sufficient credit and technology. In contrast, family farmers not only received most government production supports, but they were also much more successful in shifting their focus to more commercially viable crops.

The agricultural crisis coincided with a severe political crisis. Opposition to the CNC had first appeared in the late 1940s when the General Union of Mexican Workers and Peasants (UGOCM) was organized in northern Mexico as part of Vicente Lombardo Toledano's Popular Party (CEHAM 1989). Then, in the early 1960s, some rank-and-file members in northern Mexico split from the CNC to form the Independent Peasant Confederation (CCI), a development that caused alarm in high political circles (Bartra 1985: 79–93). In the early 1970s, a new split in the CNC gave rise to the Mexican Agrarian Confederation (CAM). However, these organizations were finally co-opted by the regime and became affiliated with the PRI as part of the party's peasant sector. Indeed, although the UGOCM, CCI, and CAM all challenged the CNC for power and political clientele, they eventually became "official" organizations with subordinate positions in the rural corporatist system.[6]

---

5 For a definition of the Mexican peasantry and its relationship with family farmers, see CEPAL 1982. This discussion does not mention agribusiness corporations or stockholding commercial associations because, during the period in question, these enterprises were not engaged in primary agricultural or livestock production. Because of the legal restrictions imposed by the 1917 Constitution, only individuals could own or rent land under the private-property land tenure regime. Agribusinesses and other commercial associations were thus restricted to the processing and commercialization of food products.

6 In the 1980s and 1990s other groups also affiliated with the PRI and became part of its peasant sector. These included the Northwestern Peasant Alliance (ALCANO), Peasant Torch (Antorcha Campesina), and the National Coordinating Network of Societies and Unions of Peasants and Settlers (CONSUCC).

In the 1970s, however, peasants began to mobilize outside of "official" bodies and to form independent organizations whose agenda went beyond the struggle for land to include demands for fair crop prices, bank credit, infrastructure projects, wage increases, and improved working conditions for agricultural workers. Toward the end of the decade, peasant movements – especially those focused upon the struggle for land – clustered together in the "Plan de Ayala" National Coordinating Network (CNPA), a vast network of organizations that provided mutual support and mobilized to promote their demands (Bartra 1985: 94–154).

Given the statist orientation of the administrations of Presidents Luis Echeverría (1970–1976) and José López Portillo (1976–1982), the economic and political crises of the 1970s prompted increased state intervention in rural affairs. There was a proliferation of investment funds, credit institutions, and state-run firms to regulate the market for basic goods, provide low-cost inputs, and participate directly in the production of primary products for agribusiness. In this context, the CNC focused its strategy upon rural economic organization. Over the course of the 1970s, it formed producers' unions, ejido unions, credit unions, unions of cooperatives, mutual insurance associations, rural production societies, and collectiveinterest rural associations (ARICs) (Rello 1990). Even though increased public investment cushioned the impacts of the crisis and provided temporary relief from the effects of declining production, such measures could not resuscitate production over the long term. Agricultural production levels again plummeted when government financial support for agriculture was cut back after the onset of Mexico's debt crisis in 1982.

The powerful CNC–linked economic organizations created in the 1970s initially clashed with the agrarian sector's traditional land distribution structure as the leaders of these economic units gained the upper hand in the Confederation's national leadership. Political alliances, networks, and loyalties shifted as a result. At the same time, new strongmen often established monopolies in these economic organizations, and corruption and political clientelism flourished thanks to the expanded flow of state resources (Mackinlay 1991).

These developments were accompanied by efforts to reinforce strong legal and political controls over ejidos exercised through their own internal structure and authorities. State intervention in ejidos extended to such issues as production, financing, and marketing decisions. Thus a complex corporatist system took shape, headed by the federal government and resting to a greater or lesser extent upon the CNC, which de facto became part of the federal public administration. Such was the degree of symbiosis that many peasants made no distinction between the CNC and the government.

However, just as the CNC could not block the CNPA's mobilizations during the 1970s, in the 1980s it could not contain new groups that mobilized in search of autonomy. These groups, which joined together in the National Union of Autonomous Regional Peasant Organizations (UNORCA), sought better economic conditions for their members.[7] In doing so, they lodged harsh criticisms against state interventionism and paternalism.

The onset of trade liberalization, galloping inflation, and generally deteriorating economic conditions in the second half of the 1980s sparked rural mobilizations that once again escaped the CNC's control. These actions were led by the UNORCA, the organization that by the end of the decade was at the vanguard of peasant struggles (Fox and Gordillo 1991).

The UNORCA and Other Independent and Autonomous Organizations

In the UNORCA's view, state intervention inhibited the economic, organizational, and political initiative of producers in Mexico's social sector. The ejido could be productive and generate wealth for its members, but it was prevented from doing so by excessive – and poorly conceived – governmental intervention and the involvement of private intermediaries who skimmed off the producers' surplus. According to Gustavo Gordillo, one of the UNORCA's leaders, the organization's main position was that rural communities needed to take control of their economic and social life in order to generate self-managed processes autonomous from the government bureaucracy. By so doing, peasant communities could make optimum use of state resources and redefine relations with the market to their benefit (Gordillo 1988a, 1988b).

Organizations within the UNORCA network built an authentic social movement that catalyzed important struggles and mobilizations (De la Fuente and Mackinlay 1994). They had the support of intellectuals and militants from the leftist movement of the 1970s (including Hugo Andrés Araujo, Gustavo Gordillo, and Adolfo Orive), as well as from leaders who had built their careers in government programs established between 1970 and 1982 to foster development in the social sector.

In contrast to the CNPA, whose radical stance brought it into direct confrontation with the state and led to its decline in the mid-1980s, the UNORCA network sought dialogue with the government and the negotiated resolution of its demands. Its political orientation, combined with the links that its leaders had with certain groups within the federal bureaucracy, encouraged the Ministry of Programming and Budget (SPP) to begin testing a system of "social concertation" (*concertación social*) with UNORCA. This system, introduced as part of a national planning law enacted by the administration of President Miguel de la Madrid (1982–1988), sought to coordinate with these rural interlocutors the design and implementation of development programs.[8]

In contrast to the CNC, whose members were automatically considered part of the PRI, the UNORCA's affiliates were able to follow their own inclinations in the partisan political arena. Several important CNC economic organizations developed

---

7 The UNORCA adopted the CNPA's organizational model and established a network of organizations rather than a centralized body.

8 Bartra et al. 1991; Moguel, Botey, and Hernández Navarro 1992.

close ties with the UNORCA and participated in its mobilizations. Yet even though UNORCA developed an autonomous ideology and pursued independent political actions, its most important leaders had close ties to Carlos Salinas de Gortari, his brother Raúl, and other high-level public officials.[9]

That the UNORCA was at the vanguard of peasant struggles in the late 1980s did not mean that the CNC was on the verge of extinction. The CNC was in fact many times larger – in terms of both individual members and the number of organizations under its control – than the UNORCA, and the CNC's privileged position vis-à-vis the state still made it attractive for rural organizations to affiliate with it or remain under its umbrella. Yet the UNORCA was unique – and uniquely important – in terms of the influence of its programmatic positions (particularly regarding the reorganization of ejidos and peasant enterprises within a framework of self-management) and its demand that state intervention in rural affairs be transformed so as truly to benefit the social sector (see UNORCA 1989). Many CNC organizations identified with these positions, and rank-and-file CNC members frequently participated in UNORCA mobilizations. Other independent organizations also adopted the UNORCA's positions regarding the "struggle for autonomy" and "control of the surplus."[10]

The Private Sector

Private landowners are often thought of as family farmers and counterpoised to "peasant" ejidatarios. This dichotomy is incorrect, however. Many ejidatarios are commercially oriented, and many private landowners adhere to the typical peasant logic of production as reproduction of the household and family labor. Indeed, most private landowners in Mexico are small peasant producers.[11]

In official agrarian ideology, "smallholders" (*pequeños propietarios*) are holders of land under the private-property legal framework, regardless of the size of their plots. Because Mexico's agrarian reform law prohibited latifundia, by definition large landowners could not exist. Thus in order to distinguish among landowners by property size, it was customary to differentiate between "authentic small-holders" (peasant holders of small plots) and simply "small landowners" (owners of midsize and large rural holdings). The latter category ranged from medium-scale family farmers to family-run enterprises engaged in large-scale production for the domestic and international markets.

9 One should remember that Mexico's omnipresent postrevolutionary state prevented most social organizations from developing with genuine autonomy.

10 These organizations included the Coalition of Urban, Peasant, and Popular Democratic Organizations (CODUC), the Cardenista Peasant Union (CCC), the Independent Confederation of Agricultural Workers and Peasants (CIOAC), the General Worker-Peasant-Popular Union (UGOCP), the National Farm Workers' Union (UNTA), and some remaining fractions of the now-divided CNPA.

11 For statistical data on this point, based upon information from the 1970 agricultural census, see CEPAL 1982: 114, 123.

Contrary to common belief, Mexico's postrevolutionary agrarian reform did not just distribute land under the social property statute. It also created a significant amount of private property through the adjudication of national lands and the formation of agricultural colonies. Many such colonies and even fairly large private properties were created in the irrigation districts opened up in northern Mexico during the "agrarian counterreform" period.[12]

The ejidatarios who belonged to the social sector and peasant smallholders were kept separate in political and party terms. As noted above, the former were included in the PRI's peasant sector, while the latter were incorporated into its popular sector through the National Confederation of Smallholders (CNPP). However, this distinction (designed to separate peasants artificially, based upon land tenure criteria), while important in terms of political action, was less clear-cut in the case of government development programs, which sometimes included peasant smallholders in the social sector. Government agencies often recognized (correctly) that the two groups shared common social conditions, and that authentic smallholders therefore also deserved special treatment – though not as preferential as that granted to ejidatarios and comuneros.

The following sections present a brief overview of the main private-sector organizations active during the 1929–1988 period, focusing primarily upon their origins, relations with the state, and organizational and political trajectories.

The National Confederation of Smallholders

The National Confederation of Smallholders was created in 1946 to represent and defend the interests of private landowners engaged in agricultural, cattle-raising, and forestry activities. Formed at the government's initiative, the CNPP was integrated into the PRI's popular sector via the National Confederation of Popular Organizations (CNOP).[13] Given the peasant condition of most rural smallholders, it would have been more logical to place the CNPP in the party's peasant sector. However, the deliberate goal was to separate the CNPP from the CNC in matters of party and legislative action (Hardy 1984).

The CNPP was most active in the agrarian sphere, providing legal defense for landowners threatened by land distribution and advising them about how to

12 As part of an overall reordering of land tenure, the agrarian reform shaped social property endowments through collective land distributions and private property arrangements through individual allocations (Pérez Castañeda 2002).

    There are no data available on private land distributions because these were registered in the Public Property Registry (Registro Público de la Propiedad), which made no distinctions concerning the origin of rural private properties – many of which antedated the agrarian reform era.

13 In contrast to the PRI's more homogeneous worker and peasant sectors, the very heterogeneous popular sector includes segments of the population that are neither workers nor peasants, ranging from owners of small businesses and merchants, to public employees and middle-class professionals, to such grassroots urban elements as newspaper vendors, shoeshine boys, and lottery ticket vendors.

obtain from agrarian reform authorities the "certificates of non-affectability" that hindered land distribution procedures.[14] In the productive sphere, the CNPP registered ten national producers' unions, though most of them existed only on paper.[15] Although in principle the CNPP was comprised of an army of small land-owners, in fact it was controlled by owners of midsize and large private properties. As the political arm of private agricultural landowners affiliated with the PRI, the CNPP had some importance until the mid-1970s,[16] after which it declined in significance.

The CNPP's fall from influence occurred during the Echeverría administration, when it backed the president in a clash with the business sector over land distributions in the fertile agricultural valleys of Sinaloa and Sonora. The CNPP supported the Ocampo Pact (a leadership organization that included the social sector's CNC, CCI, CAM, and UGOCM) and endorsed the government's agrarian policy despite its impact upon many private landowners (C. de Grammont 1988: 398). The CNPP's close ties to government policies then became its weakness: family farmers realized that they were better off distancing themselves from the state, precisely in order to have greater bargaining power. This led some of them either to affiliate with opposition parties (especially the National Action Party, PAN) and or to restrict their participation to nonpartisan organizations focused solely upon economic and agricultural issues.

Unlike the social-sector rural organizations, which had the means to force their members to participate politically, the CNPP had few ways to force its rank and file to mobilize around it. Because it could not rival its social-sector counterparts in electoral and political mobilization and could not represent the interests of large-scale family farmers, the CNPP was never able to generate much of a presence within the PRI. For this reason, the number of popularly elected positions assigned to it was never very high.[17]

14 These certificates were developed during the Cárdenas administration to pacify private landowners who were unhappy with the government's land reform policy. They proliferated after 1940 to counteract ejido-oriented legislation (Escárcega and Caraveo 1989).

15 Although other producers' unions had a certain importance for a time, the most important CNPP unions in the late 1990s were the National Sugarcane Union (Unión Nacional Cañera) and the National Coffee Producers' Union (Unión Nacional de Productores de Café). The former mainly comprised small-scale private peasant producers and some ejidatarios; the latter represented large-scale coffee growers. However, these unions operated relatively autonomously from the national confederation.

16 Like the CNC, which has traditionally claimed to include among its members all peasants in the social sector who benefited from land distribution, the CNPP claims to represent 2.5 million rural landowners, the same number of Mexicans who have "rural landowner" legal status. See CNPR 1996.

17 The relative importance of different PRI–affiliated organizations could be measured in terms of the number of candidacies they controlled for seats in federal and state legislatures and other elected posts, including municipal presidencies and governorships.

The National Cattlemen's Confederation

In 1936, Mexico's leading ranching associations formed the National Cattlemen's Confederation (CNG). This occurred after negotiations in which the government granted cattlemen a series of privileges (including twenty-five-year "cattle-raising concessions" that allowed cattlemen to accumulate enormous tracts of pasture lands) in exchange for the cattlemen's support for the economic and social reforms undertaken by President Cárdenas (Escárcega 1990: 203–9). The CNG also won the monopoly right, through obligatory membership, to represent all livestock producers, including all beef and milk producers, hog farmers, poultry raisers, beekeepers, and other livestock producers.

Because of the proliferation of livestock subsectors after the 1960s, by 1975 the CNG included 1,427 local livestock associations grouped into 44 regional unions, 121 local hog farmers' associations organized in 5 regional unions, 120 local beekeeper associations joined into 2 national unions, and 15 national registry associations (CNG 1993: 15). The organization also fulfilled some administrative functions. For example, the Ministry of Agriculture empowered it to issue export permits, as well as sanitary guidelines for transporting cattle from one part of Mexico to another.

The growth of the cattle industry was based predominantly upon an extensive production model rather than an intensive-entrepreneurial one.[18] As Michelle Chauvet has argued, cattlemen's economic power was based upon "the ownership of large areas rather than the result of being an efficient sector that promoted change and modernization" (1999: 14). Hence, as in the case of the CNPP, one of the CNG's main functions was legal in nature: to defend cattlemen in agrarian litigation and to support them by issuing certificates of non-affectability that hindered the land distribution process.[19]

The CNG is not in principle a political organization, nor is it formally affiliated with any political party. However, it historically has been conspicuously close to the PRI. For example, the CNG traditionally received a quota of positions in the PRI's representative bodies even though it was not formally linked to the party. CNG members, who formally entered the PRI through the popular sector's CNPP, usually held the chairmanship of the federal Chamber of Deputies' Livestock Commission. At the regional level, some cattlemen allied with PRI power groups were known to form private armies to repress peasant movements, as occurred in Chiapas, Guerrero, the Huasteca region (a mountainous area at the juncture of the states of San Luis Potosí and Veracruz), and southern Veracruz.

18 Cattle were primarily fed on natural pastures, with deleterious impacts upon vast areas of forest and jungle.

19 The limits to small property in the livestock sector are not calculated upon the basis of a fixed land area, but rather upon the area required to raise up to 500 head of cattle (or the equivalent, for other types of livestock); Ley Federal de Reforma Agraria (1985), article 249. This area was calculated in terms of region-specific "pasture coefficients" established by the Ministry of Agriculture. It is an extremely high territorial limit given Mexico's sociodemographic characteristics.

The CNG enjoyed relative autonomy vis-à-vis the state apparatus by virtue of not formally being a part of the PRI. However, because it wielded great influence as a representative of cattlemen landowners, for years it was able to maintain a privileged position (and had few political confrontations) with state and federal governments.

The CAADES and the CNPH

Organizations of private agricultural landowners in Mexico took shape under guidelines established by the 1932 agricultural associations law. This legislation abolished the late nineteenth-century chambers of agriculture that had grouped by individual state all large landholders and hacienda owners. In an effort to divide agricultural producers and involve them in the postrevolutionary state's modernizing projects, the 1932 law instead licensed organizations by type of activity. One important characteristic of these associations was that they often became auxiliaries of state and federal governments in planning and implementing agricultural policy.

The earliest such associations were formed in Sinaloa and Sonora. In Sinaloa, a state-level agricultural associations law enacted in 1932 brought horticultural producers together in a single state-wide organization, the Confederation of Agricultural Associations of Sinaloa (CAADES). CAADES, which was empowered to collect state taxes on agricultural activities, became a powerful instrument for the coordination and organization of business (González 1994:107). In contrast, the organization of Sonora's agricultural producers was not the result of a law obliging producers to join together; instead, it arose from an initiative by two key regional associations (in Hermosillo and Ciudad Obregón) that regrouped in 1963 to form the Confederation of Agricultural Producers of Sonora (COAES) (C. de Grammont 1988: 396). The CAADES, meanwhile, expanded its activities beyond Sinaloa and, during the 1950s and 1960s, backed the establishment of three prominent national producers' unions in the cotton, chickpea, and horticulture industries. Thus producers from the two states with the highest degree of agricultural development were the vanguard in efforts to organize agricultural business interests.

The National Union of Horticultural Producers (UNPH) was established in 1961 with the backing of CAADES. One year later, the UNPH obtained the concession to grant official certificates of origin and establish shipping guidelines, which enabled it to regulate the supply and foreign trade of fruits and vegetables. This forced producers throughout Mexico to form state-level associations in order to participate in setting crop-planting and export quotas. Around 1990, the UNPH (by then known as the National Confederation of Horticultural Producers, CNPH) claimed to have 22,000 members grouped into 245 local associations in 24 states (CNPH 1991: 31). Although private landowners predominated, the CNPH also included ejidatarios.

Over the course of thirty years, the CNPH became an efficient organization offering its affiliates a number of services. It created a space in which producers from different regions could discuss common problems, and membership dues allowed the CNPH to hire national and international consultants to carry out technical and market research. Even more important, however, was the CNPH's promotion and defense of Mexican exporters' interests abroad and its lobbying of U.S. congressmen and government officials. With eight operational offices, eight regional offices, and thirteen representatives in U.S.–Mexico border cities, seaports, and airports, the CNPH had a considerable infrastructure. Despite complaints about the CNPH's favoritism toward long-standing members (which had a basis in the organization's statutes), this organizational infrastructure made the CNPH an important promoter of fruit and vegetable growers – indeed, probably a more efficient one than the Ministry of Agriculture would have been (González 1994: 105–20).

The National Agricultural and Livestock Council

The relationship between agricultural producers and the Mexican state began to disintegrate when growers came face to face with a new round of agrarian reform. The crisis of peasant agriculture that began in the mid-1960s, combined with the end of the Bracero Program (the contract-labor program, in effect between 1942 and 1964, under which Mexican farm workers were sent to work temporarily in the United States), increased land distribution pressures upon the irrigated lands of northwestern Mexico. Many of these lands exceeded the upper limits that agrarian law established on individual property size.[20] A series of administrative decisions granting lands to peasant groups in Sinaloa and Sonora in the mid-1970s provoked strong protests from growers led by the CAADES and COAES and backed by large national business organizations, including the Mexican Employers' Confederation (COPARMEX) and the Private Sector Coordinating Council (CCE).

During the tensest months of the conflict between the agrarian bourgeoisie and the federal government (June to September 1976), the COPARMEX, the CCE, the National Confederation of Chambers of Industry (CONCAMIN), the Confederation of National Chambers of Commerce (CONCANACO), the National Chamber of Manufacturers (CANACINTRA), and the Mexican Bankers' Association (ABM) all supported the CAADES-led protest. However, because of the gravity of the political crisis and the imminent end of the Echeverría administration, the business sector eventually toned down its opposition. The conflict ended with the government-authorized distribution of enormous expanses of land (organized as collective ejidos) in the Yaqui and Mayo valleys to peasants who had been agricultural workers on these properties (Gordillo 1988b: 102; Rello 1987).

The nationalization of Mexico's banking industry in 1982 widened the gap between business interests and the state. Agricultural producers opted for a closer relationship with national business interests in the urban-industrial sector, which had already begun a process of autonomous organization. In 1984, the CCE created

---

20 So-called hidden latifundia were often legally registered under other individuals' (generally family members) names.

the National Agricultural and Livestock Council (CNA), which was open to all producers regardless of whether they formed part of the social or the private sector. The CNA began with 17 member organizations and 27 associate organizations, the former consisting of growers' associations and the latter consisting of agroindustrial and financial groups that control the agricultural and food production chain. By 1992, CNA membership had grown to 34 organizations (including 26 powerful producers' associations from regions with high agricultural potential) and 59 associate organizations (C. de Grammont 1995a: 81–82).

Neither the CNG nor the CNPH joined the CNA, but many of their members (including CAADES) did become affiliates. Over time, the CNA became the principal representative of the bulk of Mexico's growers and a significant number of ranchers. It included small, midsize, and large-scale family farmers who formed part of member organizations, as well as large agroindustrial corporations that formed part of associated organizations. Family farmers were mainly responsible for primary production, while agroindustrial conglomerates (barred from owning or renting land) focused upon the processing and commercialization of food products.[21]

Once the agricultural and agrarian policy context became more favorable for the private sector during the De la Madrid administration, the relationship between business and government improved markedly. As a consequence, the CNA enjoyed government favor as state elites sought links with what they viewed as modern, dynamic business representatives. Indeed, after the mid-1980s the CNA became the main organization representing the agricultural business sector vis-à-vis the Mexican government.

It is worth emphasizing that the CNA was formed at the initiative of business interests themselves. It was not the product of legislation, nor does it fulfill any administrative functions at the behest of the government, as was the case with previous producers' associations. In this regard, the formation of the CNA marked an important change in agricultural and livestock business interests' traditionally subordinate relationship vis-à-vis the state. During the late 1980s the CNA's key demands included a reduction in the state's role in economic production in order to allow market forces to prevail; legal protection for private land ownership (although the CNA accepted the coexistence of the private and social sectors); the transfer of many state functions to agricultural producers, including the administration of irrigation districts; and a reduction in government subsidies to agriculture and livestock raising, subject to the removal of controls on consumer prices.

The CNA's position regarding Mexico's accession to the General Agreement on Tariffs and Trade (GATT) in 1986 was ambiguous. On the one hand, many CNA

---

21 Transnational corporations such as Anderson Clayton, Ralston Purina, International Multifoods, Nestlé, Carnation, Campbell's, Kellogg's, General Foods, McCormick, and Kraft have long had operations in Mexico, but barriers to land ownership limited their activities. See Arroyo, Rama, and Rello 1985; Morett Sánchez 1987.

affiliates (especially family farmers) remained closely linked to the domestic market because their growth had been dependent upon protectionist barriers. On the other hand, large agroindustrial conglomerates and family farmers capable of competing in both domestic and foreign markets were interested in market opening. Because of the CNA's free-market ideology, it could not oppose trade liberalization. However, in order to lower production costs and make Mexican products more competitive in export markets, the CNA pushed for tariff reductions on agricultural inputs – goods that often competed with items produced by state-run companies. In cases in which these imports might compete with CNA members' products, the organization emphasized the need for variable tariffs that were adjusted seasonally, thereby minimizing harm to national producers. It also demanded that protective tariffs be lifted very gradually (C. de Grammont 1988: 401–6).

Traditional Corporatism in Rural Mexico

Until the end of the De la Madrid administration, corporatism in rural Mexico was linked to a virtual one-party system in which the PRI's and the state's spheres of action blended together. Although the De la Madrid administration took important steps to open the economy and cut public expenditures, the fundamental features of the old interventionist, protectionist, populist state persisted. Trade liberalization was still at an early stage, having affected only limited numbers of rural producers.

Within the social sector, the corporatist system had both territorial and functional bases. Where land distribution and the handling of agrarian demands were concerned, ejidos and agrarian communities were closely tied to the Ministry of Agrarian Reform (SRA). On economic issues, they were linked to the Ministry of Agriculture and Water Resources (SARH) and other public agencies established to promote agricultural and livestock development.

Within the private sector, the corporatist system was based primarily upon promoting the interests of ranchers and family farmers within a closed, state-centered economy.[22] The government channeled a whole range of subsidies to producers in order to compensate for agricultural products' low prices. In the case of fruit, vegetable, and livestock production, organizations like the CNG, CAADES, and CNPH carried out administrative functions delegated to them by state and federal government bureaucracies.

Beginning in the mid-1980s, the rise of the CNA somewhat altered corporatist arrangements affecting private agricultural producers. Although this independent organization did not directly fulfill a public function, it did represent agricultural business interests before the state. Something similar occurred in the social sector

---

22 However, the interests of small peasant landowners (particularly those affiliated with the CNPP) were scarcely taken into account. Although they represented the vast majority of private landowners and were sometimes considered part of the social sector, they benefited less from state intervention than did ejidatarios.

with the rise of the UNORCA, whose member organizations declared themselves independent of the state. Although their organizational efforts were not entirely autonomous, they did have a greater degree of autonomy than other social sector organizations.

Two points are especially relevant here. First, in the private sector, PRI–affiliated organizations such as the CNPP were subordinated to the state to a much greater degree than were unaffiliated producers' groups. When unaligned business organizations' interests differed from those of the government, they were sometimes capable of presenting strong opposition to government policies. This was especially the case with the CAADES and the COAES, though less so with the CNG.

Second, the nature of private-sector rural business organizations' subordination to the state differed markedly from that of peasant organizations in the social sector. The difference lay in the fact that business organizations were the main beneficiaries of the government's economic policies. In contrast, peasant (social-sector) organizations were in an inferior position economically and politically despite the fact that they could reap some partial benefit from public policies.

These differences can be explained in terms of class. Prosperous farmers were part of the economically dominant classes, and their relations with – and access to – representatives of the state were on a more or less equal basis.[23] Poor peasants were economically subordinated to the system, and thus in political terms they were more subordinated than prosperous farmers.

The Historical Significance of Mexico's Agrarian Reform, 1917–1992

The 1988 elections, in which the PRI barely managed to hold on to the presidency, marked a turning point in the evolution of Mexico's postrevolutionary authoritarian regime. Up until that time, political power in rural areas had for decades been exercised in an antidemocratic, largely unchecked manner; after these elections, key features of the system began to change as the regime's legitimacy declined.

Mexico's postrevolutionary agrarian reform restructured the overall system of rural property relations. By giving many country people access to land in the form of social and private property, it significantly redistributed the nation's wealth and created opportunities for social mobility for considerable segments of the population – although it failed in its objectives of generating sustained development and eliminating poverty and intolerable social inequities. Even though the government's policies especially benefited commercially oriented family farmers, they also helped poor peasants – albeit inefficiently, clientelistically, and with political and electoral objectives.

One traditional explanation for the difficulties that rural producers encountered is that the price system established for agricultural products in the early 1940s subsidized urban-industrial development at the expense of rural producers' capacity

23 For a theoretical discussion on the class aspects of corporatism, see, for example, Panitch 1992.

for accumulation (Shwedel 1992).[24] More recently, some analysts have also emphasized a complex set of factors that slowed productivity growth and hindered the development of a culture promoting productivity. These elements included the inefficiency and authoritarianism of state agencies, the political orientation of much state intervention, and the generalized corruption that accompanied public funding in both the social and private sectors.

Despite these negative aspects, the agrarian reform was crucially important for Mexico's political stability and the PRI's hold on power. It made an enduring contribution to the postrevolutionary pacification of the countryside and, later, to the peasantry's subordination to the established regime and the PRI's electoral machine. For decades the PRI could depend upon the "green vote." It could do so not only because extensive state economic intervention produced a real majority preference for the "official" party in the countryside, but also because electoral irregularities were easier to perpetrate in rural areas, where opposition parties had greater difficulty monitoring the vote.

In 1988, many rural polling places still reported between 90 and 100 percent of their votes for the PRI, even though in nearby *monitored* polling locations the PRI's share of the vote was much lower. Given Carlos Salinas de Gortari's very narrow margin of victory over leftist opposition candidate Cuauhtémoc Cárdenas in the 1988 presidential race, one can assert with confidence that the rural vote – legally and illegally obtained – tipped the scale in favor of the PRI's candidate (López 1988).

The Corporatist System and the Salinas Reforms, 1989–1994

President Carlos Salinas de Gortari (1988–1994) implemented a series of radical reforms that ended the long era of government economic intervention and social welfare statism that Cárdenas had initiated in the 1930s. These measures opened a new period in which the market became the primary regulator of economic activity, thus establishing economic and commercial rules of the game that were unknown to rural producers. The principal features of the reforms implemented during the first three years of the Salinas administration were the dismantling or privatization of the state-owned enterprises that supported agricultural production; unilateral commercial opening for many products imported from the United States and Canada, even before the negotiation of a free-trade agreement with those countries; the reorganization of financial, credit, and insurance systems; the elimination of guaranteed prices for most basic crops (except corn and beans); and the deregulation of agricultural, livestock, and forestry activities (Encinas et al. 1995).

---

24 This unfavorable situation especially affected the peasant economy. Family farmers' better access to government production supports and subsidies allowed them to compensate for low prices.

The Social Sector

In the course of his presidential campaign, Salinas proposed renewing the alliance between peasants and the state. The PRI's electoral platform adopted demands from autonomous peasant organizations regarding such matters as the proposal to transfer some government functions to producers. Once in office, Salinas appointed Gustavo Gordillo undersecretary for policy and social consensus in the Ministry of Agriculture and Water Resources. At the same time, the autonomous organizations agreed to join the Permanent Agrarian Congress (CAP), a leadership body that involved Mexico's twelve leading "official" and autonomous organizations[25] in establishing a new dialogue between the organized peasant movement and the state.

Although some leaders of autonomous organizations appreciated the points of convergence between their demands and the PRI's platform, others feared the Salinas administration's "attempts at co-optation and neocorporatism ... in the name of consensus and modernization in the countryside" (quoted in Hernández Navarro 1992: 238). Nevertheless, they decided to participate in government initiatives so as not to be excluded from policy decisions concerning the divestment of state-owned enterprises or the distribution of promised resources for rural development. For the first time, social-sector organizations not aligned with the PRI were recognized interlocutors with government, and it was in this context that the CNC called for the formation of a broad "new peasant movement."

During this period the CNC underwent a major revamping to turn it into the image and likeness of the UNORCA. Hugo Andrés Araujo, a former UNORCA leader, was appointed CNC organizational secretary in 1989 and then general secretary in 1992. Along with some statutory changes to democratize the CNC and combat internal fiefdoms and strongmen, the CNC's economic organizations were placed front and center. The CNC, together with the CAP, began to work closely with the SARH's Undersecretariat for Policy and Social Consensus to establish production agreements for rural organizations and to dismantle state-owned rural enterprises.

Thus resources began to flow toward rural producers' organizations through "concertation agreements," and the assets of many state-owned firms were transferred to producers' groups. The CNC was the main beneficiary of these transfers to the social sector, confirming that the autonomous peasant movement had been drawn into a political dynamic that depended upon the state much more than before. The UNORCA, whose leaders were now on the side of government, was relegated to the background. The CNC displaced it as the principal coordinator of the network of rural producers' organizations, leaving the UNORCA to represent its own affiliates (Mackinlay 1996: 207ff.).[26]

25 The seven autonomous organizations included the ALCANO, CCC, CIOAC, CODUC, UGOCP, UNTA, and UNORCA; the five "official" organizations included the CAM, CCI, CNC, National Movement of the Four Hundred Peoples (MNCP), and UGOCM.

26 Although the CNPP did not form part of the CAP, it received the same treatment in the concertation process as did other organizations.

However, even though CAP affiliates received a goodly share of the assets trans-ferred by the state, the proportion was smaller than expected. Once the divestment and privatization process was set in motion, private capital captured the most profitable state-owned enterprises, while the social sector took control of the least productive ones and those with poor prospects.[27] Furthermore, in early 1990 Carlos Hank González (a traditional PRI politician linked to the business sector) was appointed head of the SARH and Luis Téllez (a main architect of the 1992 reforms to Mexico's agrarian legislation) was appointed undersecretary of planning. These appointments marked the beginning of the end of Gustavo Gordillo's influence; in 1992 he left his post at SARH for a less important position in the Ministry of Agrarian Reform.

The National Solidarity Program and Neocorporatist Experiences

Another key Salinas initiative was the National Solidarity Program (PRONASOL). At first this anti-poverty program concentrated mainly upon urban popular groups and, in the countryside, indigenous groups. However, after the decay of the concertation process, it was expanded to cover a large portion of Mexico's rural population. PRONASOL undertook multiple actions in increasingly wide spheres of activity as the Salinas administration progressed. These included social assistance programs (daycare centers, corn mills, cultural activities, public health services, school scholarships); infrastructure projects (repair of irrigation works; construc-tion of dams, levees, and canals; electrification of water wells; drainage and road projects in rural villages); support of productive activities (promotion of handi-crafts, small-scale credit for corn and bean cultivation, financing of peasant enter-prises in the social sector); programs for agricultural day-laborers; and programs to raise rural employment levels (Mackinlay and De la Fuente 1994).

Although some PRONASOL monies were derived from the sale of state-owned enterprises, most of its funds were resources earmarked for regional development that had previously been disbursed through various public agencies and state governments but which were now centralized in a single program controlled directly from the president's office. A particular feature of PRONASOL was that it depended upon the activities of small committees ("solidarity committees," each

27 Among the most important assets that were sold to the private sector were the following: the large supermarkets, food products manufacturing companies, storage facilities, and ware-houses that had formed part of the CONASUPO complex; Mexican Balanced Foodstuffs (ALBAMEX), a state-owned producer of livestock feed; 58 of the 62 government-owned sugar mills; tobacco processing plants; agrochemical companies producing fertilizers; and, in the coffee sector, the distribution company, the most important industrial plant, and the Café Mexicano trademark. The social sector received some CONASUPO warehouses, storage facilities, and rural stores; the administrative offices, warehouses, transportation equipment, and other assets of TABAMEX (Tabacos Mexicanos); palm and wax (*candelilla*) investment funds; sawmills and assorted equipment for forestry activities; coffee-processing plants belonging to the Mexican Coffee Institute (INMECAFE); and four sugar mills (De la Fuente and Mackinlay 1994: 121–38).

specializing in one area of action) and individual and/or group participation. There was an attempt to make the committees responsible for PRONASOL–funded projects, and renewed support was conditional upon their meeting set goals (SEDESOL 1993).

In the countryside, solidarity committees displaced the regional and national peasant organizations (both "official" and autonomous) through which some of these resources had previously been distributed. The idea was to create new institutions of political representation for rural dwellers, different from the previous ones both in their structure and in terms of political practices and relationships. Leading members of the Salinas administration apparently believed that an alternative territorial structure built around the 5,000-plus Solidarity committees could displace existing corporatist organizations and form the basis for a "Solidarity Party" that could substitute for the PRI.[28] The solidarity committees did not survive beyond the Salinas administration (and could, therefore, be called a failed neocorporatist experiment), but PRONASOL did have the effect of disarticulating traditional peasant organizations.

Although PRONASOL had little involvement in the dismantling of state-owned enterprises, it did intervene in the strategically important coffee sector on the grounds that there were large numbers of indigenous producers. The dismantling of the Mexican Coffee Institute (INMECAFE) in 1990 was unlike most other such operations carried out by the Salinas administration because it escaped the government's rigid political control. An independent organization that had emerged from the autonomous movement of the 1980s, the National Coordinating Network of Coffee Producers' Organizations (CNOC), was able to break the CNC's organizational monopoly and create a situation of political and organizational diversity. A whole range of organizations – especially the Statewide Coordinating Network of Coffee Producers of Oaxaca (CEPCO) and the CIOAC, but also the Coalition of Urban, Peasant, and Popular Democratic Organizations (CODUC), the General Worker-Peasant-Popular Union (UGOCP), and the National Farm Workers' Union (UNTA) – participated alongside the CNOC and the CNC (Ejea and Hernández Navarro 1991). The fact that these independent organizations were able to consolidate their position demonstrated the failure of neocorporatist attempts to replace the old national corporatist organizations with new subnational "official" institutions in coffee-producing states (Snyder 1999: 298–99).

State Reform during the Salinas Administration

"State reform" during the Salinas administration left autonomous peasant organizations in disarray. Their development strategy was based upon making government actions more efficient, not sudden deregulation and liberalization of the economy and state agencies' withdrawal from the production process. Lacking adequate

---

28 This neocorporatist initiative was set aside in late 1991 so as not to alienate the PRI's old guard. See the essays in Cornelius, Craig, and Fox 1994.

administrative and technical training and special programs to ease the transition, the recipients of most parastatal holdings were unable to reap full benefit from the transfers. As a consequence, the results anticipated from the transfers did not materialize. This negative situation was exacerbated by an overall deterioration of the agricultural sector's economic condition, which was partly due to the drastic economic measures that had been undertaken.

The social-sector organizations also ran up against local and regional interest groups (backed by CNC strongmen) that boycotted the autonomous organizations' self-management efforts. Except for a handful of cases (one of which was the coffee sector), then, there were very few organizational initiatives of this kind that enjoyed any measure of success in the first half of the Salinas administration.[29]

The Reform of Article 27

The radical economic measures that Salinas implemented during the first half of his administration were followed, in the second half, by the most thoroughgoing constitutional and legislative reforms in Mexico since the adoption of the 1917 Constitution. These reforms brought an end to land distribution and transformed the entire system of land ownership – privatizing social property (both individual and communal plots), significantly broadening the prerogatives of private landowners by legalizing "hidden latifundia," and permitting for the first time the establishment of rural commercial associations with stockholders in the area of primary agricultural production. Prior to the Salinas reforms, such associations could not be directly engaged in agricultural production; instead, they were required either to purchase needed agricultural and livestock products or to enter into partnerships with farmers or ranchers to obtain them. However, under the new regulations, these associations can control up to 2,500 hectares of irrigated land and 5,000 hectares of rain-fed land (that is, 25 times the size limit for individual small property). The new legislation also modified regulations on forestry and water resources, mining, fisheries, and so on, making the rules for the purchase, use, and exploitation of natural resources more flexible.[30]

When in late 1991 President Salinas sent to Congress his proposal to reform Article 27 of the Mexican Constitution, peasant organizations were taken by surprise. Except for the CNC, which supported the reforms unconditionally, organizations in the CAP expressed strong reservations about privatizing ejido lands. They initially supported only the formation of agrarian tribunals, bodies responsible for the adjudication of land disputes that were to be autonomous from the executive

---

29 For more details on the policy of social concertation and the dismantling of state-owned enterprises in the rural economy, see De la Fuente and Mackinlay 1994. On the privatization process in general, see Concheiro and Tarrío 1998.

30 For a comparison of the legal framework that existed during the agrarian reform era (1917–1992) and the new one created as a result of the Salinas reforms, see Pérez Castañeda 2002. For an overall analysis of the whole range of legislative reforms on rural issues, including those dealing with other natural resources, see Mackinlay and De la Fuente 1996.

branch. Over time, divergent positions emerged among peasant organizations over whether to support the reforms, reject them, or remain neutral. Sometimes different leaders of the same organizations took contradictory stances on the issue.

In the February 1992 parliamentary debate over implementing legislation for the Article 27 reforms, the CAP adopted a constructively critical position. However, when the government did not take into account any of its proposals, its distance from the Salinas administration deepened. Thus in August 1992 in Hermosillo, Sonora – during the last of three CNC–sponsored meetings of peasant organizations convened to discuss the package of government financial supports being offered in connection with the reforms – an UNORCA leader denounced the new agrarian legislation, the state's economic withdrawal from the countryside, and free trade.

This speech aborted the CNC's attempt to establish its hegemony over the construction of a "new peasant movement." Although none of the autonomous organizations seceded from the CAP, many preferred to maintain some independence vis-à-vis the government rather than becoming mere appendages of the CNC (Hernández Navarro 1994: 127). Nevertheless, the government co-opted some of their leaders, which contributed to the discrediting of the CAP. The revolt by the Zapatista Army of National Liberation (EZLN) in Chiapas in January 1994 intensified divisions and regroupings within both "official" and autonomous agrarian organizations.

These developments affected at least indirectly two of the Salinas administration's other rural initiatives, the Program for the Certification of Ejidal Rights and the Titling of Urban Plots (PROCEDE) and the Direct-Support Program for the Farm Sector (PROCAMPO). PROCEDE was designed to regularize ejido property and strengthen juridical security in tenure arrangements. However, even though the government vigorously promoted PROCEDE, this voluntary program encountered substantial distrust among ejidatarios. This reaction, combined with technical and legal difficulties, prevented the program from attaining its objective of regularizing land tenure under the social-property regime during Salinas's term in office.

PROCAMPO, announced in 1993, was a program designed to mitigate the impact of the government's withdrawal of guaranteed-price subsidies as part of its accession to the North American Free Trade Agreement (NAFTA). As first established, PROCAMPO provided a direct cash subsidy on a per-hectare basis to producers of nine basic crops (corn, beans, wheat, sorghum, soybeans, barley, rice, cotton, and safflowers).[31] Several months later the government also established a program of direct supports for coffee producers. In doing so, it responded partly to the CNOC's political and organizational skills. However, the principal consideration – especially in the aftermath of the Zapatista rebellion – was that a substantial proportion of the coffee sector's indigenous farmers are concentrated in Chiapas and Oaxaca.

---

31 Direct cash subsidies are permitted under international trade rules on the grounds that they supposedly do not distort prices in the way that universal subsidies do.

The Private Sector

Shortly after assuming the presidency, Salinas unilaterally opened Mexico's borders to many agricultural imports. This action demonstrated his interest in signing a free-trade agreement with Canada and the United States. Internally, Salinas justified this decision on the basis that it gave Mexicans access to cheap food imports as a way of fighting inflation, and it forced Mexican producers to increase their yields or run the risk of succumbing to foreign competition.[32]

In a similar vein, in June 1990 the government deregulated the fruit and vegetable sector, eliminating quotas and export-permit requirements. Deprived of its authority to regulate the production and export of fruits and vegetables, the CNPH disintegrated; a majority of state-level CNPH delegates decided in a national assembly that their participation was pointless, and they opted to withdraw (González 1994). As a consequence, the CNPH's informational, promotional, and advisory work, as well as its defense of producers' interests abroad and its maintenance of open communications among fruit and vegetable producers throughout Mexico, are no longer taking place (González 1994: 112). However, it is important to underscore that it was the producers themselves who decided the fate of the confederation. Even if it lost the administrative functions it once had, the CNPH could have been preserved in order to carry out some of its important tasks in a new economic context.

The CAADES offers an interesting contrasting example in this regard. It also lost its administrative faculties and was obliged to alter its modus operandi as a consequence of market deregulation. Nevertheless, this organization remains one of the strongest producers' associations in Mexico. Its members produce more than sixty percent of the country's exported fruits and vegetables (C. de Grammont 1995a: 83).

The reforms to Mexico's agrarian law found universal support in the private sector. This did not mean that all private producers had been viscerally opposed to the agrarian reform; in fact, many private landowners (often products of the agrarian reform themselves) were respectful of the two forms of land tenure – social and private – enshrined in the Constitution. In economic terms, these individuals (typically owners of small and midsize farms producing for the domestic market) favored a system based upon family property that was regulated, subsidized, and protected by tariffs. They became alarmed when the Salinas administration began implementing its neoliberal economic policy measures so decisively.

However, others in the private sector saw Mexico's agrarian reform as the root of all evil in the countryside. They especially viewed the policy of land distribution as an obstacle to capital investment. Those holding these views tended to be owners

---

32 Already in 1988, the De la Madrid administration had – in accordance with GATT requirements – eliminated the quota system and regional restrictions affecting cattle exports to the United States. It similarly eliminated permit requirements and tariffs on most livestock products. See Pérez Espejo 1997: 54–60.

of family-operated companies that were on the verge of surpassing the legal limits on property size and representatives of agroindustrial groups and large domestic and transnational firms. In general, export-oriented producers and those with the potential to compete in an open economy agreed with Salinas's free-trade and other neoliberal policies (C. de Grammont 1995a: 86–88).

Despite their differences regarding agrarian reform and macroeconomic policy, both camps agreed upon the need to stop land distribution, liberalize the ejido land market, and end state tutelage of the social sector. Only a few months earlier, the CNA, together with other leading Mexican business organizations, had made a series of similar, though less radical, proposals. They included calls to legalize the rental of ejidal lands and permit commercial associations between investors and ejidatarios. However, these proposals stopped short of totally transforming the rural social-property regime (CNA et al. 1990).

Prior to the Article 27 reforms, family farmers had an important influence over the CNA's policies. This body favored a gradual transition to a more open market economy and a more tenuous trade opening, and some of its most prominent members even protested against what they perceived to be excessive trade liberalization at the beginning of the Salinas administration (C. de Grammont 1996: 44). By the time of the reforms, however, there had been a change in the CNA leadership consonant with the shifts in government policy. With the election in 1992 of Eduardo Bours of the Bachoco Group (a preeminent poultry consortium) to the CNA presidency, the current representing large corporations – many of which were created as a result of the privatization of state-owned rural enterprises – became predominant.

Once the Salinas administration had won passage of the constitutional reforms affecting land and natural resources, rural producers' organizations turned their full attention to the NAFTA negotiations. The CNC, CNA, CNG, and the National Confederation of Rural Property Owners (CNPR)[33] participated in the government's advisory council on the agricultural and livestock sector. However, the main voice on the government's negotiating team was the Foreign Trade Business Organizations' Coordinating Network (COECE), which grouped representatives of 180 production branches and which only the CNA joined. The hegemony that the CNA achieved as representative for the private agricultural sector allowed it practically to replace the CNG as speaker for the livestock industry in these negotiations. Many of the CNG's affiliates expressed their viewpoint in the COECE through the CNA (Pérez Espejo 1997: 23).

As for the CAP, once the rural reforms were completed, it belatedly joined the government's trade advisory council. It was, however, unable to modify the NAFTA's agricultural section, which proved to be extremely disadvantageous for the Mexican countryside. Moreover, in the final phase of the NAFTA negotiations,

33 The CNPP became the National Confederation of Rural Smallholders (CNPR) after the Article 27 reforms.

the Mexican government made new concessions in the few areas (sugar, citrus, and vegetables) where the negotiations had favored Mexico (Encinas et al. 1995: 55).[34]

The agrarian reforms and economic liberalization also had important repercussions among private-sector organizations. The most striking case involved key groups of poultry farmers, dairymen, feedlot owners, and hog farmers who – discouraged by the CNG's general ineffectiveness and its passivity regarding the NAFTA – chose to present their interests through the CNA. In fact, many of them left the CNG despite the legal requirement that they be represented by that organization (Pérez Espejo 1997: 23).

The livestock sector's situation further illustrates the realignments that took place between business interests and the state during the NAFTA negotiations. Although Mexico's negotiators did protect the position of cattlemen within Mexico's national territory, they could not defend their priorities in the foreign trade arena. Major groups that previously had been protected from foreign competition were left out in the cold.

Indeed, ranchers benefited from the new agrarian law, which allows producers to shift land from livestock raising to forestry without having to abide by the limits governing the size of private property in the forestry sector. Moreover, a portion of land devoted to livestock raising can be shifted to agricultural use as long as the overall limits on agricultural holdings are respected.[35] Thus land-extensive ranching, although problematic in environmental and social justice terms, remains protected.

In contrast, the livestock sector did not benefit from the overall direction of Mexico's new economic policy. Along with producers in other activities, it had to face both domestic market deregulation and increased foreign competition. A few groups – northern Mexico's exporters of cattle on the hoof, owners of strictly feedlot-fed cattle, and some transnational consortiums able to diversify production on both sides of the border to meet the needs of Mexican and U.S. markets – benefited under the NAFTA. Nevertheless, the NAFTA hurt most producers – cattlemen in the tropics, dairymen, hog farmers, and everyone producing for the domestic market. The livestock sector as a whole has lost ground under the NAFTA because it lacks export potential and because the domestic market is now open to imports from the north.[36]

---

34 Following William Clinton's victory in the 1992 U.S. presidential election, the Mexican government had to accept changes in the preliminary version the NAFTA that it had negotiated with the administration of President George Bush (1988–1992).

35 The only new category of individual small property created by the 1992 reforms was in the forestry sector. Previously nonexistent, private property holdings in forestry were limited to 800 hectares. The other individual limits were left as before, with the exception that commercial associations can multiply them by a factor of twenty-five. See Ley Agraria (1992), articles 119, 123.

36 See Pérez Espejo 1997 for a discussion of the NAFTA's impact upon the Mexican livestock sector.

The crisis in agricultural production worsened suddenly in 1993, shortly after the end of the legislative reform process. In mid-1993, owners of small and midsize agricultural and livestock properties who were hard-hit by free trade, skyrocketing interest rates, and an acute profitability crisis mobilized against the government's macroeconomic policies and particularly against the banking system, which was beginning to foreclose on delinquent loans. This debtors' movement, known as "El Barzón" (named for the yoke ring to which an ox-drawn plow is attached), began in the state of Jalisco, spread rapidly to states in northern Mexico, and then took on a national character. Sparked by private producers who were threatened with losing their collateral, the movement grew to include producers from the social sector (C. de Grammont 1995b, Rodríguez and Torres 1996, Mestries 1997). Many indebted farmers from the CNA, CNPR, and CNG gravitated toward El Barzón, which would become a major player among rural organizations during the administration of President Ernesto Zedillo (1994–2000).

Changes in the Corporatist System under Salinas

Although the central elements of political authoritarianism were preserved, the Salinas administration did much to dismantle Mexico's welfare state and limit the postrevolutionary tradition of state interventionism. As a result, the country entered fully into a new, neoliberal epoch. Where the corporatist system's evolution in the countryside was concerned, the Salinas administration was a period of transition. There was a break in the economic and property relations that lay at the center of corporatist ties, but the government did not surrender the reins of political control. Indeed, it attempted to devise alternative, neocorporatist mechanisms of control in several instances. Although most of these experiments failed or did not outlive the Salinas administration, social-sector organizations were weakened as a result of the way in which the government implemented its economic and social assistance programs.

In its early years, the Salinas administration had manipulated the autonomous organizations in the CAP with promises of projects and resources. When the time came for reforms to Article 27, most of the organizations distanced themselves from the government (though without abandoning the CAP). Nevertheless, the fact that some of these groups' leaders were co-opted led to their fragmentation or loss of support among the rank and file. Very few autonomous organizations retained any degree of initiative.

Private-sector organizations established during the era of state interventionism, such as the CNPH, were swept away by the Salinas administration's neoliberal policies. The remainder, such as CAADES, had to adjust their strategies to the country's new free-market orientation. The CNA, whose leadership shifted to the business faction most closely identified with neoliberal policies, became the real interlocutor with government. This organization rivaled and partially displaced the CNG in the livestock sector. Other partisan agrarian-oriented organizations, such as the CNPR, gradually lost even more influence.

Overall, the reforms to Mexico's agrarian legislation lowered the traditional barriers that had separated the social sector and the private sector. As a consequence, indebted producers came together in El Barzón regardless of their land tenure regime.

Consolidation of Structural Changes, Democratic Transition, and Abandonment of the Countryside during the Zedillo Administration

Deepening Neoliberalism and Mexico's Growing Agricultural Crisis

The sharp devaluation of the peso in December 1994, at the very outset of President Ernesto Zedillo's term in office, imposed the need for even more austere handling of public funds than had prevailed under Salinas. Federal funds for the agricultural, livestock, and forestry sectors declined in relative terms year by year, and the government continued to dismantle important state agencies still active in the countryside. The National Basic Foods Company (CONASUPO), the once gigantic conglomerate whose most important enterprises had already been privatized in the two preceding administrations, continued to shed its functions. In late 1998, when CONASUPO's role was restricted to a limited regulation of the corn and beans markets, the government decreed that the agency would be gone within a year, along with the government subsidy for tortillas.

At the same time, the pace of trade opening continued to quicken. Beginning in 1995, the government, probably under pressure from large domestic and transnational agribusiness corporations,[37] began duty-free importation of "sensitive" products (corn, beans, barley, powdered milk, and potatoes) at levels above the quotas stipulated in the NAFTA (De Ita 1999). The government justified raising import levels on the grounds that they helped meet consumer demand and also exerted downward pressure on the prices of basic consumption goods – even though imports at these levels harmed domestic producers by forcing them to sell their products at depressed prices or, when they could find no buyers, to warehouse their crops. By late 1999, nearly 230,000 tons of beans – mostly from the states of Chihuahua, Durango, Nayarit, Sinaloa, and Zacatecas – had accumulated in storehouses because producers had been unable to sell them in the domestic market.

After CONASUPO's disappearance, producers of corn and other basic grains had to establish a direct relationship with the market. No longer able to rely upon government credit, subsidized guaranteed prices, and other supports, these growers were forced to seek alternative financing and marketing channels. The transition from the previous era of strong state intervention in grain markets was very difficult. It was marked by improvisation, disorganization, monopolistic practices,

---

37 These included Arancia, Archer Daniels Midland, Cargill, Continental, Dreyfus, Maseca, and Minsa, which together controlled a large share of the basic grains market. These corporations have access to U.S. government-subsidized export financing, which gives them liquidity and lowers their costs.

and contraband – all of which hindered the development of new marketing systems and efficient, competitive market institutions.

In the absence of sufficient credit from development institutions and private banks, producers turned to moneylenders or attempted to finance production themselves by selling their labor. New forms of agricultural subcontracting began to emerge in commercial agriculture, whereby large corn-milling companies like Minsa and Maseca advanced farmers cash or in-kind payments for their crops in order to guarantee their access to raw materials. And given that the Article 27 reforms had lifted restrictions on stockholding commercial associations, large corporations reappeared as a social actor in rural Mexico and began to fill their new role under the neoliberal economic model, establishing contracts with farmers in which property titles served as collateral.

The impact of neoliberal policies has been overwhelming. Rural Mexico's economic and social situation has deteriorated alarmingly. Average annual growth rates in the agricultural and livestock sector have been very low or even negative. Production costs have escalated because of accumulated inflation. Credit has shrunk drastically, and food and agricultural imports have risen in both volume and value. Except for 1995 and 1999, Mexico recorded a trade deficit throughout the 1990s (Fritscher 1999). The rural population in poverty has swelled.[38] Deforestation, erosion, forest fires, floods, landslides, and the loss of biodiversity have created an environmental disaster (AMUCSS et al. 1998).

New Forms of State Intervention: Toward the Dissolution of Traditional Corporatist Networks?

Although the state's presence in rural Mexico is greatly reduced in comparison to the 1970s and 1980s, in some areas government economic intervention is more direct than in the past. This is because generalized production subsidies have given way to targeted subsidies like PROCAMPO that provide per-hectare payments to growers.[39] This Salinas-era initiative was initially designed to support producers of basic crops during the NAFTA–mandated fifteen-year phase out of import barriers. However, given the depth of Mexico's agricultural crisis and Mexican producers' generalized dissatisfaction with the high level of subsidies that U.S. and Canadian farmers receive, it is likely that the program will remain in place.

38 Assessments of the incidence of poverty differ considerably because there is no consensus about measurement criteria. According to a World Bank study published in 2002, some 73 percent of the approximately 25 million rural dwellers (a quarter of Mexico's total population) were poor, and half of these (36.5 percent of the total rural population) lived in extreme poverty. See *La Jornada*, June 2, 2002.

39 In the late 1990s PROCAMPO benefited some 3 million agricultural producers in an area of nearly 14 million hectares. Sixty-three percent of its beneficiaries had landholdings that averaged no more than 2 hectares, and approximately 85 percent belonged to the social sector. Set initially at US$100 per hectare, this support had lost nearly 30 percent of its inflation-adjusted value by the end of the 1990s.

The other principal programs to support Mexican agricultural producers – all of which provide direct cash payments or in-kind subsidies and were carried over from the Zedillo administration by the government of President Vicente Fox – are the Alliance for the Countryside and Supports and Services for Agricultural and Livestock Marketing (ASERCA), both of which focus upon farmers with middle and high production potential. In addition, there are initiatives under the Ministry of Agriculture, Livestock, and Rural Development (SAGAR)[40] that target specific branches of agricultural production and a temporary employment program.[41] However, the overall budget to support rural producers is very small compared to what was available in the period before neoliberal economic reform began – and especially in comparison with the subsidies and supports available to U.S. and Canadian producers.

Perhaps the Zedillo administration's most important innovation in its assignment of resources to the rural sector (also retained by the Fox administration) was its decision to implement a decentralization policy that transferred government resources and functions to individual states. This was a laudatory goal, but peasant organizations claimed that decentralization strengthened state governors' discretionary powers and excluded producers' social and economic organizations. The outcome was "the strengthening of local bosses, inefficiency, and the exclusion of most peasants and rural producers from planning, decision making, implementation, and assessment with regard to federal resources for agricultural, livestock, and forestry development" (AMUCSS et al. 1998: 3). This deliberate policy of excluding social-sector organizations from their traditional role was based upon the assumption that they are corrupt and inefficient.

One area in which the state has been in clear retreat – and which will have a significant impact upon political relations in the Mexican countryside – is in its control over ejidos and agrarian communities. The Article 27 reforms reduced the state's influence by introducing a new property regime and limiting its legal attributes in the handling of agrarian demands. Post-1992 agrarian legislation retains the categories of ejido and agrarian community, but neither has much to do with the earlier idea of social property. These forms of land tenure now approximate private property. Individual parcels are still subject to certain limitations on their transfer or use as collateral, but these restrictions do not prevent them from being sold or made subject to other commercial practices. What continues to distinguish them is that ejidos and agrarian communities generally retain common areas (pastures, forests, water resources, mines, and so forth) whose fate must be decided in general assemblies of all co-owners (see Pérez Castañeda 2002).

---

40 SAGAR replaced the SARH at the beginning of the Zedillo administration.

41 Most of the agronomy departments and research programs at both public and private universities are not well linked to rural production activities.

Although it is not absolutely necessary to regularize land tenure in order to implement the new rules established by the 1992 agrarian law, the trend toward privatization was reinforced by PROCEDE. This program, which was introduced at the end of the Salinas administration, grants separate titles both for common areas and for parcels and urban house plots. By late 2002, it had reached approximately 75 percent of all ejidos and agrarian communities. The remainder comprises agrarian units that either did not accept the program (it is voluntary) or that have legal problems (mostly derived from the inefficiency and corruption of the old agrarian reform administrative apparatus) that must be aired in the agrarian tribunals.

Few people would question the need for significant reform of Mexico's system of rural social property, especially considering the vast illegal market that previously existed for ejido land and which has now been legalized and made subject to a uniform set of rules throughout the country. One might, however, object to specific features of the new statutes for land ownership (both private and social) and of the program for regularizing land tenure, PROCEDE. Although this chapter cannot deal with these issues in depth, some points merit mention.

Ejido assemblies have more authority than before in the land title regularization process, and they still decide the use and allocation of such common property as forests, pastures, and mineral resources within ejido boundaries. This can be a very delicate matter during the titling process. There have been situations in which common areas have been converted to individual parcels without duly weighing the impact upon the ecosystem. Absent the requirement to carry out environmental impact studies, ejido assemblies have sometimes exercised their rights over common areas "in a visceral and thoughtless, not to say irresponsible, manner" (Pérez Castañeda 1998: 65).

These circumstances have produced two seemingly contradictory phenomena: at the same time that parceled and jointly held properties are becoming increasingly fragmented, control over parceled ejido properties is becoming concentrated in the hands of fewer stakeholders – although this does not necessarily lead to the joining of contiguous parcels. PROCEDE's shortcomings have contributed to a process of disentailment that is disorderly and destructive of natural resources, and there is no guarantee that ejido lands will not revert to irregular tenure patterns once the PROCEDE process is completed.

As a result, particularly after PROCEDE has completed land titling, the state will intervene in agrarian units' internal affairs much less than it did in the past. The individualization of property ownership and land tenure greatly undermines corporatist relations based upon the control of local bosses. Ejido *comisarios*, the presidents of the ejido executive bodies who were formerly charged with electoral mobilization and political control on behalf of the PRI, have seen their influence wane. Not only have their land tenure responsibilities been reduced, but they no longer handle financial credits, development funds, or other forms of governmental support. This means that the clientelist and corporatist practices once carried out through ejido commissariats will dissipate.[42]

A further example of less extensive but more direct state intervention can be found in programs designed to fight rural poverty, particularly the Zedillo administration's Program for Education, Health, and Nutrition (PROGRESA).[43] The budget cuts that occurred between 1994 and the year 2000 reduced anti-poverty expenditures significantly; the lowest point was 1999, when overall anti-poverty spending fell to 0.96 percent of gross domestic product. Following its "new federalism" strategy, the Zedillo administration decentralized many of PROGRESA's constituent programs and continued the policy of excluding local, regional, and national peasant organizations from the distributional arena (Pineda 2002).

Unlike PRONASOL, whose budget went mainly to various social assistance programs and public works projects in urban areas, PROGRESA targeted rural groups and restricted its support to education, food, and healthcare.[44] In its zeal to make social spending more efficient, PROGRESA emphasized individual relationships with target populations via localized and selective programs. Thus, whereas PRONASOL's rural programs financed small-scale production projects and provided credit, PROGRESA totally ignored agricultural production and distributed its supports on an entirely individual basis. One consequence was that it divided rural communities between families that were its beneficiaries and those that were not.

Because PROGRESA effectively suspended work with collectively organized groups, it was impossible for government officials to build a neocorporatist political operation around it. Nevertheless, this did not mean that PROGRESA beneficiaries were not pressured to vote for the PRI. During the Zedillo administration it was not unusual for PROGRESA benefits to be given out at public events, or for these events to coincide with election day. At other times, individuals linked to the PRI threatened people by telling them that they would lose their PROCAMPO checks or not obtain land titles through PROCEDE if they failed to vote for the "official" party. Such stratagems (noted by opposition parties and

---

42 These practices may disappear at an uneven pace throughout the country because custom awards the commissariats different degrees of power in different places (author's interview with Héctor Robles Berlanga, director of research and publications for the Procuraduría Agraria, Mexico City, August 1999).

43 This program replaced PRONASOL in 1997.

44 During the Zedillo administration, the federal government ended anti-poverty programs in urban areas. The only subsidies that remained for the urban poor were for the consumption of milk and tortillas. These basic-product subsidies were also maintained for the rural population via the 23,000 outlets that CONASUPO Distributors (DICONSA), managed by the Ministry of Social Development (SEDESOL), operated in economically marginal areas. However, these subsidies were reduced by some 75 percent over the course of the Zedillo administration, on the basis of the argument that such subsidies should be restricted to the most marginal rural and urban areas. See *Masiosare* (supplement to *La Jornada*), October 13, 2002.

independent electoral observers alike) remained all too common, however vigorously the Zedillo government argued that such traditions had been superseded.

Although Vicente Fox and the "Alliance for Change" (the electoral coalition between the National Action Party, PAN, and the Mexican Ecological Green Party, PVEM) won the year 2000 election in urban areas, the PRI continued to receive a relatively high proportion of the vote in rural communities. However, more than the result of coercion or imposition, this outcome should be seen as the product of the political culture that prevailed in impoverished rural areas during the PRI's long national reign. It was a long-established custom to exchange votes for particular social and economic benefits – an attitude that had a certain logic when elections were generally uncontested and no party other than the PRI could possibly win.[45] Moreover, one must recognize that the PRI enjoyed real popularity in many regions, where it was responsible for obtaining the few benefits that the rural population had received.

The initial indications were that the Fox administration's anti-poverty programs would not be used in a clientelistic manner,[46] although in PRI–controlled states old political practices persisted. The poorest groups of the population will remain vulnerable to political manipulation, but the Federal Electoral Tribunal (IFE) and the Electoral Tribunal of the Federal Judicial Branch (TEPJF) and their state-level counterparts make it more and more difficult to exercise traditional forms of authoritarian political control.

The following section analyzes rural producers' primary expression of opposition to government policy during the Zedillo administration: the struggle to restructure overdue bank loans.

Mobilizations over Delinquent Loans and Import Policy

Despite a series of restructuring plans that development banks and private financial institutions put forward during the Zedillo administration, Mexico's post–1995 economic crisis prevented many farmers from repaying their debts. At the same time, both public and private financial institutions severely restricted the flow of credit to the agricultural and livestock sector. In this context, El Barzón led extensive mobilizations to draw domestic and international attention to the loan crisis. Although rural in its origins, the movement soon extended to urban areas as it drew in bankrupt owners of small businesses and middle-class consumers threatened with the loss of their investments or loan collateral.

A few months prior to the December 1994 peso devaluation, El Barzón split into two factions. One was El Barzón-Unión, which sought to ally with the Party of the Democratic Revolution (PRD) and pressure the government from the opposition.

---

45 The difficulty was that this attitude proved hard to change when the PRI lost its monopoly of power. See Fox 1996: 252–53, based upon observations in Bonfil 1990.

46 The Fox administration continued PROGRESA as the Opportunities Program (Programa Oportunidades), with no major changes in its philosophy or forms of operation.

The other was El Barzón-Confederación, which declared itself independent of all political parties but had ties to the PRI. In the end, the alliance with the PRD strengthened El Barzón-Unión, making it the main debtors' organization in Mexico and politicizing its demands. From its initial struggle in defense of family patrimony, it went on to denounce neoliberalism and to champion a less exclusionary economic model. In contrast, El Barzón-Confederación practically disappeared.

Traditional producers' associations (including the CNC, CNPR, CNA, CNG, and CAP) and business organizations were unwilling to engage in a battle to restructure overdue loan portfolios. Indeed, the CAP barred El Barzón's agrarian faction (AgroBarzón) from becoming one of its members. Similarly, Mexico's large business organizations (the CONCAMIN, COPARMEX, CONCANACO, CANACINTRA, and the CNA) were reluctant to defend individuals indebted to the banks. The stance taken by these organizations sparked breakaways among their rank and file, who then appealed to AgroBarzón for legal advice and representation.

Many indebted ejidatarios, especially those with good land and an entrepreneurial bent, also joined AgroBarzón. This organization – the first agrarian movement to include both private property owners and ejidatarios – started to blur the differences that once separated the social and private sectors. In the context of Mexico's 1994–1995 economic crisis, common interests united farmers without regard to old divisions.

El Barzón sought to use mass mobilizations to open channels of negotiation with governmental authorities, but these channels never fully materialized. Mexican family farmers producing primarily for the domestic market – once the main beneficiaries of public policy in agriculture – had little place in government development schemes during the 1990s, and they were certainly not a priority in the neoliberal economic model. During the Zedillo administration, the Ministry of Finance and Public Credit (SHCP) prevailed over the SAGAR in shaping government policy toward the agricultural and livestock sector. As a result, the government neither strongly pressured commercial banks to make concessions to debtors nor made any significant concessions itself. Contrary to its past practice of trying to co-opt social movements, this time the government (guided by SHCP authorities) opted for minimal negotiation with El Barzón. The government's failure to address the *barzonistas'* demands pushed them into an increasingly oppositional stance.[47]

In October 1999, El Barzón mobilized 200 members in a "Caravan for the Dignity of the Mexican Countryside" that coincided with debates on the year 2000 budget. Departing from Ciudad Juárez, Chihuahua on the Mexico–U.S. border, the protesters finally reached the Federal District in December, where they organized sit-ins, demonstrated in front of SHCP offices, and burst into the federal Congress building on horseback. These mobilizations and spectacular actions

47 This discussion of El Barzón draws upon C. de Grammont 2001.

finally forced governmental authorities to meet with the *barzonistas*, although no major agreements were reached.

The El Barzón protests paralleled positions taken by a network of organizations comprised of the Mexican Association of Social-Sector Credit Unions (AMUCSS), the National Association of Trading Companies for Rural Producers (ANECPC), the Mexican Network of Peasant Organizations in Forestry (Red MOCAF), the CNOC, and the UNORCA.[48] These organizations began to work together during the Zedillo administration, forming an informal coalition that was active in criticizing government economic policies and offering alternative proposals. However, with the exception of the UNORCA and the CNOC, none of these groups had the capacity to mobilize large peasant contingents. Instead, they carried out their campaigns in the mass media.[49]

Among the initiatives that this coalition undertook was the formulation of alternative budgets for the agricultural, livestock, and forestry sectors in 1997, 1998, and 1999 (AMUCSS et al. 1998, 1999). Because of these organizations' lobbying during the 2000 federal government budget negotiations and the pressure exerted by El Barzón's street mobilizations, in December 1999 the Senate approved legislation requiring the executive branch to charge duties of 30 percent on agricultural imports that exceeded NAFTA quotas. Moreover, after long negotiations, opposition party and PRI deputies in the federal Chamber of Deputies finally agreed to increase social spending, despite President Zedillo's position on this matter.

This was a significant victory, but it did not mark the end of protests by rural producers. In early 2000, bean producers from throughout Mexico denounced "the excessive imports authorized by the Ministry of Commerce and Industrial Development (SECOFI), over and above the quotas agreed in the NAFTA, the contraband that goes unpunished ... and the inefficiency and greed of private marketing and distribution systems."[50] In February 2000, El Barzón protesters occupied the international bridge connecting Ciudad Juárez with El Paso, Texas, and in mid-March it joined with the Democratic Peasant Union (UCD)[51] in a new wave of mobilizations. Protesters again used horses to block access to public buildings, peddled beans on the streets of Mexico City, and demanded measures that

---

48 When the UNORCA distanced itself from the government following the Salinas reforms, this once predominantly pro-PRI organization diversified its political alliances. Some of its leaders (acting as individuals) allied with the PRD, while others remained in the PRI. In 2000, the UNORCA's leader argued that this shift had not affected the organization's autonomy or divided it internally because greater partisan independence allows the organization to win new political spaces; see *Masiosare* (supplement to *La Jornada*), March 5, 2000. Altogether they occupied three federal congressional seats, four local congressional seats, and five municipal presidencies, most of them won during the 1997 federal and local elections.

49 The CAP also issued media statements criticizing Mexico's import policies.

50 See the paid advertisement in *La Jornada*, January 28, 2000, p. 12.

51 The UCD, with close ties to the PRD, is comprised mainly of migrant workers who brought vehicles from the United States into Mexico illegally. Their core demand was that these vehicles (numbering about 2 million) be legalized.

would allow the sale of more than 200,000 tons of beans held in storage warehouses. These demonstrations coincided with coffee growers' mobilizations led by the CNOC, which for the first time employed street mobilizations by staging marches in twelve different states.

What had appeared in December to be a significant victory proved not to be one in practice because the Zedillo administration refused to implement the measures enacted by the Chamber of Deputies. In particular, it failed to implement duties on imports that exceeded NAFTA quotas, and in March 2000 it reduced the federal budget once again. The SAGAR's budget was cut by 230 million pesos (US$24 million), 200 million of which had been assigned to the Alliance for the Countryside.

Soon thereafter, El Barzón organized a day of protest in eight states to demand that "End Point," a government program for restructuring overdue loans, be extended. *Barzonistas* blockaded 26 bank branches and the headquarters of the Mexican Bankers' Association in Mexico City. On April 10 (the anniversary of Emiliano Zapata's assassination), hundreds of livestock producers from the National Dairymen's Association (Asociación Nacional de Ganaderos de Leche), UCD members, and other groups blockaded the entrance to SECOFI headquarters for hours. The farmers demanded an end to imports of milk products and milk substitutes, while UCD members demanded legal registry for their vehicles. The PRD's demand that the government renegotiate the agricultural chapter of the NAFTA began to resonate among rural producers.

Once again, the response to these various mobilizations was heartening. SAGAR authorities conceded that, during the first four months of 2000, they would schedule imports within NAFTA quotas so as not to harm domestic producers, and they further agreed to allow the sale of stored domestic production. Additionally, they invited producers' organizations to participate in supervising custom-houses in order to halt contraband. Governmental authorities also reached agreement with 80 regional producers' organizations to form an Interstate Bean Council (Consejo Interestatal de Frijol) to plan activities in that branch of agriculture. Furthermore, milk producers obtained a commitment that SAGAR would review sections of the tariff code dealing with milk products, and coffee producers received a significant increase in funding for the Coffee Support Program (Programa de Apoyo al Café).[52] Nevertheless, the *barzonistas* did not win an extension of debt payment schedules, nor was there much immediate progress in resolving the problem of illegally imported vehicles.

In sum, in the months prior to the July 2000 general elections, protests organized independently by El Barzón, the CNOC, cattle ranchers, bean farmers,

---

52 However, coffee producers did not win any concessions to their demand that the government halt cheap coffee imports used in the manufacture of instant coffee (which, because they do not come from Canada or the United States, do not fall under the NAFTA's free-trade provisions).

and the UCD took place at the same time and in the same streets. These were among the very first mobilizations launched by farmers affected by the government's neoliberal policies, but they lacked tactical or political coordination. In part for this reason, farmers and indebted producers only won modest concessions, many of which were never honored by the government. And, of course, they did not even minimally alter the overall direction of economic policy.

The rural producers' mobilizations that began in late 1999 and continued through mid-2000 obviously also had objectives related to the July 2, 2000, presidential election. These ranged from winning immediate policy concessions, to supporting (even if in a disguised manner) their partisan political preferences, to demonstrating their future negotiating leverage. They certainly succeeded in revealing the substantial differences in perspective and political divisions that existed among the organizations participating in these protests. Yet they also showed that mass mobilizations could exert significant pressure upon local and federal governmental authorities by disrupting road traffic and provoking urban chaos. However, this experience further demonstrated that one consequence of the decade's neoliberal reforms was that governmental authorities have reduced faculties to address the problems highlighted by protestors.

Rural Producers' Organizations at Century's End

The Social Sector and the Crisis of the Old Corporatist System

When on January 1, 1994, the Zapatista Army of National Liberation initiated an indigenous uprising in Chiapas, Mexico's peasant organizations joined the ensuing debate. They demanded a series of changes in both the government's and society's overall treatment of indigenous peoples and in specific policies affecting the countryside. However, as the government intensified its neoliberal policies during the remainder of the 1990s, the CAP's financial dependence upon the government and its generally moderate stance prevented it from capitalizing upon the political impact of the *zapatista* rebellion and winning major policy concessions.[53] As a result, its profile on the national political stage diminished sharply. Only the UNORCA played a more dynamic opposition role, though even it limited its protests to media declarations rather than mobilizing rank-and-file members in street protests.

What analysts such as the CAP's general coordinator did succeed in doing was calling attention to the fact that the Article 27 reforms had "weakened the social and organizational fabric of ejidos and agrarian communities," so much so that if the trend continues, the ejido – the essence of Mexico's postrevolutionary rural

53 The CAP led none of the street demonstrations staged by rural producers' organizations in 1999–2000. The fact that it limited its protests to occasional declarations concerning its disagreement with government policies reflected not only its dependence upon government financial support (rather than members' contributions), but also the fact that its policy positions had to be coordinated with all of its members, many of which were "official" organizations.

history – "could disappear altogether" (*La Jornada*, May 25, 1999). Indeed, by the end of the Zedillo administration, an alarming number of ejidos either had been abandoned or were renting their property because their members lacked the financial wherewithal to work the land themselves. Farming activities now provide a decreasing share of rural families' subsistence, particularly among small producers who are forced to rent their land and seek work as agricultural day-laborers, join the ranks of the urban under-employed, or migrate to the United States to find employment.[54]

This structural change may have profound implications. As long as the peasantry itself is in transition, it will be difficult for social-sector peasant organizations (originally configured mainly to promote agricultural production) to prosper. This situation is expressed in practical terms by the fact that, with the passage of time, they have less and less to do. These organizations lost their agrarian role when the Salinas administration closed the door on further land distribution (except, perhaps, in Chiapas). With the dismantling of the welfare-providing, intervention-ist state, they lost their political role as interlocutors in the design of public policies and frequent intermediaries in the distribution of public funds. What meager development funds that are available from the government are now distributed to individuals or small groups of producers. In short, the neoliberal reforms of the late 1980s and the 1990s transformed the economic and political landscape so radically that traditional peasant organizations were left without a viable project.

With the gradual weakening of the PRI's overall political position during the 1990s, the corporatist system of representation declined in significance in the Mexican countryside. The three sectors that comprised the PRI still had an electoral reason to exist, but the ruling party's capacity to reward the allied leaders of social organizations with elective offices or other public posts was in sharp decline even before it lost the presidency in the year 2000. During the Salinas and Zedillo administrations, increasing numbers of big business representatives were designated as PRI candidates for elected office via the heterogeneous CNOP, pushing aside candidates from the peasant and workers' sectors.[55]

The CNC, whose reform-minded leadership was closely identified with President Salinas, resumed its old ways at the beginning of the Zedillo administration when

---

54 According to a typology of ejido producers developed by the SARH and the Economic Commission for Latin America and the Caribbean (ECLAC), most ejidatarios with plots of 2 to 10 hectares in size earn between 18 and 40 percent of their total income from agricultural and livestock activities. The remainder of their income derives from wage work, micro-enterprise activities, and remittances from the United States (De Janvry, Gordillo, and Sadoulet 1997: 175).

55 For instance, during the year 2000 electoral campaign, the CNC complained bitterly that only 6 of the PRI's 34 gubernatorial candidates, and only 14 of the party's 367 candidates for the federal Chamber of Deputies, were from the peasant sector. Similarly, the Confederation of Mexican Workers (CTM) lamented that only 15 of the 90 candidates it had proposed were included on PRI slates for congressional seats.

Beatriz Paredes became its leader in August 1995. Again dominated by the power brokers who for decades controlled the PRI regime's official policies in the countryside, the organization still has an undeniable strength in many regions. Nevertheless, the PRI's defeat in the year 2000 presidential election produced new difficulties for the CNC, and its future is indissolubly linked to the now highly factionalized former ruling party. Heladio Ramírez, the former governor of Oaxaca who had succeeded Paredes in 1998, took advantage of the power vacuum within the PRI that resulted from the absence of presidential arbitration of internal disputes and, for the first time in CNC history, engineered his re-election as the organization's secretary general in August 2001. But now without state support, the CNC has had to learn to function as an opposition force, taking positions that are strongly critical of government policies. However, like the majority of organizations that comprise the CAP, the CNC is on the whole discredited, weakened, and divided by the continuing divisions provoked by Ramírez's reelection.

Despite this situation, legislators identified with the peasant social sector from the PRI, the PT (Labor Party), and the PRD (some of whom had participated in autonomous movements during the 1980s) elaborated a proposed Law of Rural Development (Ley de Desarrollo Rural). This initiative obliged the government to promote planning where agricultural and livestock activities were concerned, provide training for rural producers, establish financing and marketing mechanisms that would break with neoliberal orthodoxy, and undertake other actions that implied much greater public spending than the government had considered. When it was first drafted during the Zedillo administration, the bill was the object of disdain by the neoliberal faction that dominated the PRI. Nevertheless, a PRD–PAN legislative coalition in the federal Chamber of Deputies approved the measure (against PRI opposition) in April 2000. It had remained blocked in the Senate until December 2000, when a PRD–PRI coalition approved the measure (now against the opposition of the governing PAN).

The legislation elicited President Fox's first use of his veto power. However, it also forced the Fox administration to negotiate in December 2001 an alternative Law of Sustainable Rural Development (Ley de Desarrollo Rural Sustentable) that was more acceptable to the government. More generally, within the context of PRI and PAN governments' sustained assault on the peasant social sector, this experience also recognized the surprising policy space that had been won by a coalition of federal legislators from diverse parties committed to winning better treatment for peasants and the owners of small and midsize family farms.

In overall terms, the fact that social-sector corporatist organizations are in crisis in terms of their original function of representing the peasantry's interests does not mean that they have no utility for the government as mechanisms of political control.[56] The stances taken by organizations affiliated with the CAP (especially those that have been identified with struggles for autonomy and independence,

---

56 See Schmitter 1974 for a discussion of the different functions of corporatist organizations.

from which one might have expected a more combative attitude) amply demonstrate this point. Especially notable were their decision not to cooperate with El Barzón and their moderate stance during the rural producers' mobilizations that took place in the first half of 2000.

Although there is no conclusive evidence that the Zedillo administration brought direct pressures to bear upon CAP affiliates not linked to the PRI, it is hardly unusual for the Mexican state to offer financial support to particular groups – without necessarily openly co-opting them – in order to secure a less hostile attitude on their part. Without explicitly forbidding "controlled" organizations to play a somewhat oppositional role (especially when their failing to do so would have cost them all grassroots support) in such matters as massive street demonstrations and the creation of dangerous alliances with groups such as El Barzón, the government might have insinuated that there would be reprisals in terms of its financial support for these organizations. Alternatively, their leaders may have acted cautiously because they anticipated such a turn of events.

The fact that this kind of political understanding (more explicit for some organizations than others) prevailed became evident when the government attempted to change the rules of the game. In August 2001 the CAP organized a series of street mobilizations to protest the agricultural policies of the recently inaugurated Fox administration. Although the mobilized contingents came not just from CAP members but also from unaffiliated organizations, the government sought to end blockades of roads and streets by negotiating with the CAP over the partial restoration of its budget for productive projects – but without making any concessions to the CAP's more substantial demands for sharply modified agricultural policies and the renegotiation of the NAFTA's chapter on agriculture and livestock.[57]

---

57 See Hernández Navarro 2001. According to this source, the Fox administration restored over half of the budget for productive projects that had been established in 2000, when the PRI still controlled the presidency. If the value of these projects was in fact the approximately US$10 million reported by Hernández Navarro (19), the government incurred quite modest costs in maintaining the CAP's corporatist apparatus.

Paradoxically, El Barzón was conspicuously absent from the August 2001 demonstrations. Indeed, during the first two years of the Fox administration it did not demonstrate a force comparable to what it displayed at the end of the Zedillo administration. This may be due to the fact that many of its members had renegotiated their overdue loans, or because generally lower bank interest rates somewhat eased their difficulties. Nevertheless, another financial crisis or a shift in political conditions (such as the wave of producers' mobilizations that occurred in late 2002 and early 2003) might well produce a resurgence of the movement.

The year 2003 marked the tenth year of the NAFTA transition period, when tariff restrictions were removed on all agricultural and livestock products except corn, beans, and powdered milk (the only products with fifteen-year transition periods). The prospect of intensified competition from Canada and the United States elicited strong reactions from rural producers in Mexico in late 2002 and early 2003.

In these negotiations, unsuccessful efforts by Minister of Agriculture Javier Usabiaga to end official financing for the archaic corporatist system concluded with the government's strange recognition of the CAP as "the sole interlocutor for peasants' demands."[58] In taking this approach, Usabiaga was following the example of Minister of Labor and Social Welfare Carlos Abascal, who sought to maintain good relations with the PRI-identified Labor Congress (CT). By doing so, however, he breathed artificial life into the rural corporatist system. These developments demonstrated that the corporatist system, although retaining only a very diminished capacity for political control (and certainly nothing comparable to its central role in regime legitimation and peasant control during the PRI era), can still exert pressure upon the government bordering on blackmail.

The Private Sector and the New Corporatist Relationships
In the business sector, during the 1990s the CNA consolidated its position as the most important interlocutor with government regarding public policies affecting the agricultural and livestock sector. This organization fully accepts the new market and commercial rules that have been instituted, and since the end of the Salinas administration it has come to represent predominantly the interests of large domestic and foreign corporations that are either oriented toward foreign markets or that operate simultaneously in Mexico's domestic market and abroad.

This does not mean, however, that the CNA has totally abandoned family farmers tied to the domestic market or the interests of members who have been adversely affected by trade liberalization. As any organization would do, the CNA continually demands greater government support for rural producers, improvements in how institutions work, and so forth.[59] Nevertheless, considering that there are heterogeneous interests within the organization and that the interests that dominate are those of the large agroindustrial groups noted above, it is possible that members who are less well represented may eventually withdraw from the organization – if they manage to survive in the marketplace at all. If they do retain their membership, it will presumably be to reap the small advantages to be derived from affiliation with one of the few rural producers' organizations that has some influence on the government.

Although some of its individual members may have participated in the protests and mobilizations that occurred in 2000, the CNA seeks to maintain a dialogue with the government that permits it to keep its members' political behavior within acceptable limits. In other words, the CNA fulfills the core functions that corporatist theory assigns to this type of body: defending and representing the

58 Hernández Navarro 2001: 19. As Hernández Navarro notes, not even the PRI had gone this far in characterizing the CAP's role.

59 Although the CNA cannot lodge complaints leading to investigations of unfair trade practices (this must be done by the producers' organizations that are most directly affected by such practices), hog farmers and other groups affiliated with the CNA presented such complaints during the Zedillo administration.

interests of its affiliates vis-à-vis the state, and exercising a measure of political control over those members.[60]

Second in overall political importance in the private sector is the CNG, which lost ground to the CNA when large numbers of poultry farmers, dairy farmers, cattle ranchers, and hog farmers left its fold during the Salinas years. However, the crisis in livestock production pushed the CNG to take a more combative stance against free trade and neoliberal economic policies during the Zedillo administration. It retook the initiative by backing anti-dumping complaints against imports of beef and pork products from the United States and the European Union. Nevertheless, its position is still far weaker than it was prior to the NAFTA negotiations (Pérez Espejo 1997: 38–41).

For its part, the CNPR remains marginalized in national politics. Its very limited presence mainly reflects the fact that the Article 27 reforms ended its chief functions, which consisted of defending its members against agrarian reform. Moreover, its essence was as a party organization, which no longer has a place among the business-organization models that now predominate in Mexico's agricultural and livestock sector.

In general terms, the business sector certainly has greater opportunities (particularly through the CNA) to promote its members' interests than does the social-peasant sector. Nonetheless, it also faces some limitations resulting from the dismantling of the interventionist state and the deregulation of economic activities. In essence, state actions are now limited to the provision of direct subsidies, which, although clearly insufficient, are all that the country's straightened financial circumstances permit. In domestic controversies, the state can at best play the role of conciliator – and, more often than not in such matters, it is only an observer with little possibility of acting effectively, even when different groups accustomed to a formerly powerful state role insist upon addressing their concerns to it. And in the matter of international disputes, the government is only a channel through which producer organizations can reach the dispute panels established by the NAFTA. It can do little to defend them internationally, and it is necessarily bound by the decisions of such bodies.[61]

---

60 In contrast, the CAP (the CNA's equivalent in the social-peasant sector) has lost the first function, retaining only the second.

In general, the universe of members represented by business organizations has declined dramatically.

61 It is difficult and costly to prove that the rules prohibiting "dumping" and other unfair trade practices have been violated. Only the most powerful producers' organizations can take on such cases. As a practical matter, then, social-sector organizations and many business groups are unable to defend themselves against such practices when they occur.

Conclusion: Rural Corporatism in the Twenty-First Century

Mexico's neoliberal transformation destroyed most of the economic, political, and social conditions that had sustained traditional corporatist relations in the countryside. Old political structures are being dissolved not so much because of the rise of democratic practices and a strong civil society, but because of the state's withdrawal from the multiple spheres in which it once intervened. In turn, rapid changes in rural society have shaped a new corporatist structure in which the main actors vis-à-vis the state are large Mexican and transnational agribusiness corporations. This shift was visible even within the PRI's traditional system of interest representation; whereas big business interests were once expressly excluded from the party, they became more directly represented during the 1990s. However, following the PRI's defeat in the year 2000 presidential election, these interests occupied an even more central place in the Fox administration.

Regional and national peasant organizations dating from the agrarian reform era, as well as family farmers' organizations established during the period of protectionism and state intervention, have lost many of their traditional functions. The fact that these groups have been pushed aside is partly the consequence of neoliberal reform. However, these organizations also became marginalized because they lacked sufficient clout to win their demands. Their failure in this regard reflected in part the absence of a tradition of independent, autonomous societal organization in Mexico.

Important strata of the Mexican peasantry and family farmers are being forced out of agriculture. In those sectors where peasants and the owners of small and midsize family farms are still holding on fundamentally as agricultural producers (and not just part-time and subsistence farmers), and in the few (mainly export-oriented) agricultural activities that are expanding, new relationships are taking shape between producers and the market economy that involve novel forms of association and, frequently, different political practices.

For example, in tobacco (Mackinlay 1999a, 1999b) and sugar cane production (Singelmann 2003), producers' organizations are playing more expansive roles as they negotiate with large domestic and transnational firms over prices for their products, contracting conditions, employees' benefits, and so on. New forms of association between small farmers and large firms have also emerged (generally without the state's presence) in basic grains and in fruit and vegetable production. Similarly, novel linkages are emerging between peasant firms and export markets. Although still few in number, there are documented success stories involving fruit- and vegetable-producing ejido cooperatives (Runsten 2000), ejido associations of tobacco producers (Léonard and Mackinlay 2000), and some peasant groups exporting organic coffee, despite the depression in world market prices for this crop.[62]

---

62 There is a large bibliography on coffee producers. See, for example, the references in Ejea and Hernández Navarro 1991 and Snyder 1999.

Expanding vegetable and fruit production in northwestern Mexico has also brought significant changes to agricultural day-laborers. Many of these workers are indigenous persons, women, and children (Lara 1998). Although they are difficult to organize because of their temporary-worker and part-time peasant status, day-laborers are beginning to evidence new forms of political expression.

These varied examples illustrate the fact that Mexico's peasants and small farmers are striving to stay alive in the marketplace. They are developing survival strategies and, in some cases, incipient processes of capital accumulation. However, these processes do not as yet involve large layers of the rural population, nor do they significantly affect the well-being of those who are involved in them. To the contrary, the new contracts and working conditions are generally disadvantageous to agricultural workers and small farmers.

The enormous changes occurring in rural Mexico are still at such an early stage in their evolution that it is impossible to predict their outcome. Further studies of the countryside will undoubtedly reveal more about the "new rurality" that is taking shape. However, unless new institutional arrangements develop to benefit agricultural workers and farmers, or unless something occurs to undermine the disproportionate advantages that large domestic and transnational agribusiness corporations enjoy in the market, the overwhelming majority of Mexican farmers face a situation of deteriorating production and social decomposition. The specific consequences of this trend are still unknown, but they will be monumental in scale.

References

AMUCSS (Asociación Mexicana de Uniones de Crédito del Sector Social), ANECPC (Asociación Nacional de Empresas Comercializadoras de Productores del Campo), CNOC (Coordinación Nacional de Organizaciones Cafetaleras), Red MOCAF (Red Mexicana de Organizaciones Campesinas Forestales), and UNORCA (Unión Nacional de Organizaciones Regionales Campesinas Autónomas). 1998. "Por un presupuesto que valore justa e integralmente al campo: priorizar soberanía alimentaria y desarrollo de la agricultura campesina sustentable." Mimeo.

AMUCSS (Asociación Mexicana de Uniones de Crédito del Sector Social), ANECPC (Asociación Nacional de Empresas Comercializadoras de Productores del Campo), CNOC (Coordinación Nacional de Organizaciones Cafetaleras), Red MOCAF (Red Mexicana de Organizaciones Campesinas Forestales). 1999. *20 demandas para un presupuesto 2000*. Mexico City: AMUCSS, ANECPC, CNOC, Red MOCAF.

Arroyo, Gonzalo, Ruth Rama, and Fernando Rello. 1985. *Agricultura y alimentos en América Latina: el poder de las transnacionales*. Mexico City: Universidad Nacional Autónoma de México / Instituto de Cooperación Iberoamericana.

Baitenmann, Helga. 1997. "Rural Agency and State Formation in Postrevolutionary Mexico: The Agrarian Reform in Central Veracruz, 1915–1992." Ph.D. diss., New School for Social Research.

Bartra, Armando. 1985. *Los herederos de Zapata*. Mexico City: Era.

Bartra, Armando, et al. 1991. *Los nuevos sujetos del desarrollo rural*. Cuadernos de Desarrollo de Base, no. 2. Mexico City: ADN Editores.

Bonfil, Guillermo. 1990. *México profundo: una civilización negada*. Mexico City: Consejo Nacional para la Cultura y las Artes / Grijalbo.

C. de Grammont, Hubert. 1988. "Los empresarios agrícolas, un grupo en consolidación." In *Las sociedades rurales hoy*, edited by Jorge Zepeda Patterson. Zamora, Mexico: El Colegio de Michoacán.

———. 1995a. "Neocorporativismo o descorporativización, dilema del Consejo Nacional Agropecuario." In *Globalización, deterioro ambiental y reorganización social en el campo*, edited by Hubert C. de Grammont. Mexico City: Juan Pablos Editor.

———. 1995b. "Nuevos actores y formas de representación social en el campo." In *El impacto social de las políticas de ajuste en el campo mexicano*, edited by Jean-Francois Prud'homme. Mexico City: Instituto Latinoamericano de Estudios Transnacionales / Plaza y Valdés.

———. 1996. "La organización gremial de los agricultores frente a los procesos de globalización de la agricultura." In *Neoliberalismo y organización social en el campo mexicano*, edited by Hubert C. de Grammont. Mexico City: Universidad Nacional Autónoma de México / Plaza y Valdés.

———. 2001. *El Barzón: clase media, ciudadanía y democracia*. Mexico City: Plaza y Valdés / Instituto de Investigaciones Sociales, Universidad Nacional Autónoma de México.

CEHAM (Centro de Estudios Históricos sobre el Agrarismo en México). 1989. *Historia de la cuestión agraria mexicana*, vol. 8. Mexico City: CEHAM / Siglo Veintiuno.

CEPAL (Comisión Económica para América Latina y el Caribe). 1982. *Economía campesina y agricultura empresarial*. Mexico City: Siglo Veintiuno.

Chauvet, Michelle. 1999. *La ganadería bovina de carne en México: del auge a la crisis*. Mexico City: Universidad Autónoma Metropolitana–Azcapotzalco.

CNA (Consejo Nacional Agropecuario), COPARMEX (Confederación Patronal de la República Mexicana), CONCANACO (Confederación de Cámaras Nacionales de Comercio), Asociación Mexicana de Casas de Bolsa. 1990. *Propuestas del sector agropecuario para la reactivación productiva del campo*. Mexico City: Instituto de Proposiciones Estratégicas.

CNG (Confederación Nacional Ganadera). 1993. *Informe de Labores*. Mexico City: CNG.

CNPH (Confederación Nacional de Productores de Hortalizas). 1991. "La exportación de hortalizas mexicanas frente al Tratado de Libre Comercio con Norteamérica." Culiacán, Sinaloa. Mimeo.

CNPR (Confederación Nacional de Propietarios Rurales). 1996. *CNPR: documento básico*. Mexico City: Secretaría de Organización, CNPR.

Concheiro, Luciano, and María Tarrío, eds. 1998. *Privatización en el mundo rural*. Mexico City: Departamento de Producción Económica, Universidad Autónoma Metropolitana–Xochimilco.

Cornelius, Wayne A., Ann L. Craig, and Jonathan Fox, eds. 1994. *Transforming State-Society Relations in Mexico: The National Solidarity Strategy*. La Jolla: Center for U.S.–Mexican Studies, University of California, San Diego.

De Ita, Ana. 1999. "Libre mercado de granos: propiedad privada," *La Jornada*, April 13.

De Janvry, Alain, Gustavo Gordillo, and Elisabeth Sadoulet. 1997. *Mexico's Second Agrarian Reform*. La Jolla: Center for U.S.–Mexican Studies, University of California, San Diego.

De la Fuente, Juan, and Horacio Mackinlay. 1994. "El movimiento campesino y las políticas de concertación y desincorporación de las empresas paraestatales, 1989–1994." In *Campo y ciudad en una era de transición*, edited by Mario Bassols. Mexico City: Departamento de Sociología, Universidad Autónoma Metropolitana–Iztapalapa.

Ejea, Gabriela, and Luis Hernández Navarro, eds. 1991. *Cafetaleros: la construcción de la autonomía*. Cuadernos de Desarrollo de Base, no. 3. Mexico City: Coordinadora Nacional de Organizaciones Cafetaleras.

Encinas, Alejandro, Juan de la Fuente, Horacio Mackinlay, and Gonzalo Chapela. 1995. "Movimiento campesino y reforma neoliberal." In *El campo mexicano en el umbral del siglo XXI*, edited by Alejandro Encinas. Mexico City: Espasa Calpe.

Escárcega, Everardo. 1990. "El principio de la reforma agraria." In *Historia de la cuestión agraria mexicana*, vol. 5. Mexico City: Centro de Estudios Históricos del Agrarismo en México / Siglo Veintiuno.

Escárcega, Everardo, and Efrén Caraveo. 1989. *Inafectabilidad agraria y pequeña propiedad*. Mexico City: Centro de Estudios Históricos del Agrarismo en México.

Fox, Jonathan. 1996. "National Electoral Choices in Rural Mexico." In *Reforming Mexico's Agrarian Reform*, edited by Laura Randall. New York: M. E. Sharpe.

Fox, Jonathan, and Gustavo Gordillo. 1991. "Entre el Estado y el mercado: perspectivas para un desarrollo autónomo en el campo mexicano." In *Los nuevos sujetos del desarrollo rural*, edited by Armando Bartra et al. Mexico City: ADN Editores.

Fritscher, Magda. 1999. "El maíz en México: auge y crisis en los noventa," *Cuadernos Agrarios* 17–18: 142–63.

González, Humberto. 1994. "Política liberal y corporativismo: las asociaciones de empresarios agrícolas." In *Estado y agricultura en México: antecedentes e implicaciones de las reformas salinistas*, edited by Enrique Ochoa and David E. Lorey. Mexico City: Universidad Autónoma Metropolitana–Azcapotzalco.

Gordillo, Gustavo. 1988a. *Estado, mercados y movimiento campesino*. Zacatecas, Mexico: Universidad Autónoma de Zacatecas / Plaza y Valdés.

———. 1988b. *Campesinos al asalto del cielo: de la expropriación estatal a la apropiación campesina*. Mexico City: Siglo Veintiuno.

Hardy, Clarisa. 1984. *El Estado y los campesinos: la CNC*. Mexico City: Centro de Estudios Económicos y Sociales del Tercer Mundo / Nueva Imagen.

Hernández Navarro, Luis. 1992. "Las convulsiones rurales." In *Autonomía y nuevos sujetos sociales en el desarrollo rural*, edited by Julio Moguel, Carlota Botey, and Luis Hernández Navarro. Mexico City: Siglo Veintiuno.

———. 1994. "De Zapata a Zapata: un sexenio de reformas estatales en el agro," *Cuadernos Agrarios* (nueva época) 8–9: 122–40.

———. 2001. "Usabiaga se baja del ring." *La Jornada*, August 21.

Lara, Sara. 1998. *Nuevas experiencias productivas y nuevas formas de organización flexible del trabajo en la agricultura mexicana*. Mexico City: Procuraduría Agraria / Juan Pablos Editor.

Léonard, Eric, and Horacio Mackinlay. 2000. "¿Apropiación privada o colectiva? Viscisitudes y expresiones locales de la desincorporación del monopolio estatal Tabacos Mexicanos, S.A. de C.V.," *Alteridades* (Universidad Autónoma Metropolitana–Iztapalapa) 19: 123–41.

Ley Agraria. 1992. Mexico City: Secretaría de Agricultura y Recursos Hidráulicos.

Ley Federal de Reforma Agraria. 1985. Mexico City: Secretaría de la Reforma Agraria.

López, Arturo, ed. 1988. *Geografía de las elecciones presidenciales de México*. Mexico City: Fundación Arturo Rosenblueth.

Mackinlay, Horacio. 1991. "La política de reparto agrario en México, 1917–1990." In *Procesos rurales y urbanos en el México actual*, by Alejandra Massolo et al. Mexico City: Universidad Autónoma Metropolitana–Iztapalapa.

———. 1996. "La CNC y el 'nuevo movimiento campesino,' 1989–1994." In *Neoliberalismo y organización social en el campo mexicano*, edited by Hubert C. de Grammont. Mexico City: Universidad Nacional Autónoma de México / Plaza y Valdés.

———. 1999a. "Institutional Transformation in the Tobacco Sector: Collective or Individualized Bargaining?" In *Institutional Adaptation and Transformation in Rural Mexico*, edited by Richard Snyder. La Jolla: Center for U.S.–Mexican Studies, University of California, San Diego.

———. 1999b. "Nuevas tendencias de la agricultura de contrato: los productores de tabaco en Nayarit después de la privatización de Tabamex." In *Empresas, reestructuración productiva y empleo en la agricultura mexicana,* edited by Hubert C. de Grammont. Mexico City: Instituto de Investigaciones Sociales, Universidad Nacional Autónoma de México / Plaza y Valdés.

Mackinlay, Horacio, and Juan de la Fuente. 1994. "PRONASOL y el campo: ¿un viraje motivado por los sucesos de Chiapas?" In *ChiaPaz y la transición democrática: libertad, justicia, democracia,* edited by Grupo Parlamentario del Partido de la Revolución Democrática. Mexico City: Cámara de Diputados.

———. 1996. "Las reformas a la legislación y a la política crediticia relativas al medio rural." In *La sociedad rural mexicana frente al nuevo milenio,* edited by Hubert C. de Grammont and Héctor Tejera, vol. 3. Mexico City: Instituto Nacional de Antropología e Historia / Universidad Nacional Autónoma de México / Plaza y Valdés.

Mestries, Francis. 1997. "La crisis financiera rural y el Agrobarzón," *Cuadernos Agrarios* 15 (January–June): 72–93.

Moguel, Julio, Carlota Botey, and Luis Hernández Navarro, eds. 1992. *Autonomía y nuevos sujetos sociales en el desarrollo rural.* Mexico City: Siglo Veintiuno.

Morett Sánchez, Jesús Carlos. 1987. *Agroindustria y agricultura de contrato en México.* Chapingo, Mexico: Pueblo Nuevo / Universidad Autónoma Chapingo.

Panitch, Leo. 1992. "El desarrollo del corporativismo en las democracias liberales." In *Neocorporativismo: más allá del estado y el mercado,* edited by Philippe C. Schmitter and Gerhard Lehmbruch. Mexico City: Alianza Editorial.

Paré, Luisa. 1985. "Movimiento campesino y política agraria en México, 1976–1982," *Revista Mexicana de Sociología* 47 (4): 85–111.

Pérez Castañeda, Juan Carlos. 1998. "La regulación y la desamortización de la propiedad (comentarios al Procede)." In *Propiedad y organización rural en el México moderno,* edited by Julio Moguel. Mexico City: Universidad Nacional Autónoma de México / Consejo Nacional de Ciencia y Tecnología / Juan Pablos Editor.

———. 2002. *El sistema de propiedad agraria en México.* Mexico City: Editorial Palabra en Vuelo.

Pérez Espejo, Rosario. 1997. *El Tratado de Libre Comercio de América del Norte y la ganadería mexicana.* Mexico City: Instituto de Investigaciones Económicas and Facultad de Medicina Veterinaria y Zootécnia, Universidad Nacional Autónoma de México.

Pineda, Fernando. 2002. "Las políticas sociales de combate a la pobreza en México: el caso del Programa de Educación, Salud y Alimentación (Progresa), 1997–2002." Master's thesis, Facultad de Ciencias Políticas y Sociales, Universidad Nacional Autónoma de México.

Rello, Fernando. 1987. *Burguesía, campesinos y Estado en México: el conflicto agrario de 1976.* Geneva: United Nations Research Institute for Social Development.

Rello, Fernando, ed. 1990. *Las organizaciones de productores rurales en México.* Mexico City: Facultad de Economía, Universidad Nacional Autónoma de México.

Rodríguez, Guadalupe, and Gabriel Torres. 1996. "El Barzón y Comagro: dos estrategias frente a la modernización neoliberal del campo," *Cuadernos Agrarios* 10 (July–December): 70–94.

Runsten, David. 2000. "Mexican Ejidal Agriculture and the World Market: Advantages and Disadvantages of a Cooperative." Paper presented at the international congress of the Latin American Studies Association, Miami, Fla., March.

Schmitter, Philippe C. 1974. "Still the Century of Corporatism?" *Review of Politics* 38 (January): 85–131.

SEDESOL (Secretaría de Desarrollo Social). 1993. *La solidaridad en el desarrollo social: la nueva relación entre sociedad y gobierno.* Mexico City: Coordinación de Comunicación del Programa de Solidaridad, SEDESOL.

Shwedel, Kenneth. 1992. "El TLC y el cambio estructural en el campo." In *La disputa por los mercados: TLC y sector agropecuario*, edited by Alejandro Encinas, Juan de la Fuente, and Horacio Mackinlay. Mexico City: Cámara de Diputados / Diana.

Singelmann, Peter. 2003. "La transformación política de México y los gremios cañeros del PRI," *Revista Mexicana de Sociología* 65(1): 117–52.

Snyder, Richard. 1999. "After the State Withdraws: Neoliberalism and Subnational Authoritarian Regimes in Mexico." In *Subnational Politics and Democratization in Mexico*, edited by Wayne A. Cornelius, Todd Eisenstadt, and Jane Hindley. La Jolla: Center for U.S.–Mexican Studies, University of California, San Diego.

SRA (Secretaría de la Reforma Agraria). 1998. *La transformación agraria: origen, evolución, retos y testimonios*. Mexico City: SRA.

UNORCA (Unión Nacional de Organizaciones Regionales Campesinas Autónomas). 1989. *UNORCA: documentos para la historia*. Mexico City: Costa Amic.

10

Business and Politics in Mexico

Matilde Luna

Mexico's changing economic and political environment during the 1990s opened new avenues of political action to the business sector. The country's market-oriented policies and increased integration into the world economy, the 1994–1995 financial crisis, and the demonstrated international competitiveness of some Mexican firms all had important impacts upon the economic and political differentiation of Mexican business, its leadership, and the structures through which its interests are represented.

In the political arena, the shift toward increasingly meaningful party politics diversified the constellation of political actors and the range of strategies available to the private sector. Regime liberalization also modified the main institutional context for business political action. In 1996, for example, reforms to the Law on Chambers of Industry and of Commerce removed the requirement that all businesses belong to such associations. The original law, enacted in 1936, was one of the pillars of the country's system of interest representation. It had underpinned multiple agreements among government, labor, and business, and, more recently, the economic pacts that served as the basis for liberalizing the Mexican economy after the mid-1980s.

Entrepreneurs and their associations played an important role in promoting these developments. They espoused market-oriented policies, politics based upon parties, and greater social participation.[1] In particular, their proposals sought to counteract the enormous weight of the executive branch in policy making. The business sector challenged presidentialism throughout the 1980s and 1990s, demanding a democratic political system and becoming increasingly active in party politics. The archetypal case was business leader Manuel J. Clouthier, presidential candidate of the National Action Party (PAN) in 1988.

This chapter examines the changes that have occurred in the Mexican business sector's political involvement, in its position within the political system, and in its

Translated by Aníbal Yáñez-Chávez and Kevin J. Middlebrook.

The author is grateful to Kevin Middlebrook for his comments on an earlier version of this chapter.

1 See, for example, Luna 1992 on the business sector's political participation from 1970 to 1987 and the institutional impact of these changes.

forms of organization. It also explores the dilemmas that business faces in the transformed context of an internationalized economy, democratization, and intense competition among political parties. Business associations – the private sector's foremost institutional political representatives – are the main focus of discussion. Their role is examined in two spheres of public space, politics and policy making.

The principal lines of analysis involve identifying changes in economic governance and in the private sector's political action strategies. Of particular interest is the emergence of forms of business organization alternative to the corporatist traditions that formerly characterized the postrevolutionary regime, as well as the appearance of new forms of bargaining and distinctive political agreements. The multiple changes associated with Mexico's more complex and competitive economic and political environment are challenging the traditional forms of social order consolidated through corporatist and clientelist social coordination mechanisms, in which there was little difference between politics and policy.[2] In order to evaluate these changing tendencies, this chapter assesses various forms of economic governance – corporatism, associations, networks, and, to a lesser degree, community – as well as different types of private-sector collective action strategies.[3]

Corporatism is based upon hierarchical structures and obligatory membership in bureaucratic and asymmetrical organizations. These social organizations, which are strongly dependent upon the government, are national in scope and hold a monopoly over representation. Such characteristics make these organizations an appropriate participant in agreements dealing with aspects of macroeconomic policy. Tripartite agreements – in which the principal actors are the government, business associations, and top-down, centralized labor confederations – are a natural extension of corporatism and a preferred way of formulating national policies. They are based upon formally equal representation of the participating social actors, which generally act at a distance from their affiliates.

Association governance is based upon private organizations in which membership is voluntary. However, even though members choose to join them, affiliation with these organizations is still somewhat obligatory in the sense that they have (or seek) government recognition. Associations function in a more competitive or pluralistic institutional context and usually (unlike corporatist groupings) offer incentives to attract their members.

---

2 This conceptualization is based upon Offe 1975. Offe proposes a set of decision-making models, each with its own possibilities and limitations. Non-distinction between politics and policies corresponds to the consensus model, which tends toward a perverse politicization of the policy sphere. Offe distinguishes this model from such others as the legal-rational model and the directed-rationality model.

3 This definition of different forms of governance is based upon Hollingsworth and Boyer 1997, Schmitter 1992, and Luna 1997. Luna 1997 proposes an analytic model to study changes in strategies for formulating science and technology policies, distinguishing among strategies based upon organizational and normative principles: the state, the market, the community, and networks.

Networks are built upon informal, voluntary relationships of multilateral exchange. Personal relationships, trust, cooperation, and flexible structures feature in these forms of governance. Because of their flexibility, networks are appropriate in complex economic and social environments, although (unlike corporatist organizations) they tend to generate uncertainty over the rules and outcomes of interaction.

Community, in turn, is found in circumscribed or closed social spaces. It is based upon an informal membership that evolves slowly over time. Exchange is based upon trust and social solidarity, and compliance stems from moral and social norms.

There are several major collective action strategies available to the business sector: action aimed at the public policy sphere, particularly economic policy; partisan action involving a close relationship between business associations and political parties; and normative action aimed at modifying the organizational principles and values that govern social and political life.[4]

Organizations' institutional dynamism depends upon three main types of factors: external elements, internal factors, and those related to the institutional traditions that constrain and give meaning to the implementation of different practices. External factors include, for example, market pressures to achieve greater competitiveness and changes in the institutional context, which in the case of the Mexican business sector also involve a more competitive political environment. Among the most important internal elements are changes in the balance of forces among different political factions, in forms of leadership, and in modalities of action.

In order to analyze these different issues, the remainder of the chapter is divided into five main sections. The first provides background, reviewing the business sector's traditional position within the Mexican political system and describing business's main representational structures. The second part considers the paramount political tensions of the late 1980s and early 1990s. The third section assesses business's political conduct over the course of the 1990s in terms of its various collective action strategies, the rearticulation of political currents, and the content of public debates. The fourth part discusses a series of phenomena during the 1990s related to the private sector's organization and reorganization on the basis of different models of economic governance. The fifth and concluding section explores the role of business in Mexico's transformed economic and political order.

---

4 This analytic proposal is based upon Luna and Tirado 1992, which presents a conceptual framework to examine business organizations' structure and actions, and Tirado and Luna 1995, which analyzes the Private Sector Coordinating Council (CCE) through the early 1990s on the basis of this and other distinctions.

The Institutional Context: The Non-Distinction between Politics and Policies

This opening section outlines some features of the relationship between business and politics in Mexico that can be considered traditional. By doing so, it establishes a baseline from which to evaluate the direction and significance of changes in the business sector's political conduct during the 1980s and 1990s.

Business and the Political Regime

The relationship between business and politics in Mexico traditionally conformed to a corporatist model that defined the mechanisms for representation and inter-mediation of private-sector interests as well as those for cooperation and political control. Within this corporatist framework, business and labor associations played important political roles.

Under the 1936 Law on Chambers of Industry and of Commerce, different confederations or chambers held a monopoly upon representation in their respective sectors, and businesses were required to be members of the confederation or chamber in their area. Despite these associations' enormous heterogeneity and the fact that the law did not cover all organizations (making some affiliations voluntary), the most important organizations conformed to the corporatist pattern.

The government generally negotiated separately with labor and business representatives, but what prevailed on the ground was a broad, informal social pact. The government acted as arbiter based upon both the political power it derived from Mexico's strongly presidentialist system and the economic influence it gained through extensive state intervention in the economy. The formal balance of power in pacts between business and labor rested upon workers' incorporation into the "official" Institutional Revolutionary Party (PRI) and the formal exclusion of entrepreneurs from political party life, a situation that persisted until the early 1980s. It was at that point that businessmen – particularly business associations – became actively involved in party politics.

The System of Interest Representation

There is a very great variety of business associations in Mexico, some organized by economic sector and others by region. The most important groupings are linked together in hierarchical national umbrella organizations, most of which operate with a strong degree of centralized control. These associations developed in a non-competitive institutional context and, therefore, had a weak relationship with their members. Their function has been more one of formal representation than the active intermediation of members' interests.

The big national sectoral organizations are grouped in the Private Sector Coordinating Council (CCE). Figure 10.1 depicts the CCE's composition during the mid-1990s. Of special note in figure 10.1 are the multiplicity of associations in the financial sector – the Mexican Bankers' Association (ABM); the Mexican

Figure 10.1: **Membership in Mexico's Private Sector Coordinating Council**

	Private Sector Coordinating Council (CCE)							
Principal constituent organizations	ABM	CMHN	AMIB	AMIS	CONCAMIN	CNA	CONCANACO	COPARMEX
Organizational base					75 chambers 42 associations	27 organizations	261 chambers	57 centers
Approximate number of affiliates	30	37	25	59	125,000	250,000	500,000	30,000
Percentage of CCE affiliates[a]	0.003	0.004	0.003	0.006	13.8	27.6	55.2	3.3
Sectors represented	Finance	(Mixed)	Finance	Insurance	Industry	Agriculture	Commerce	(Mixed)

Source: Luna and Tirado 1992.
Note: See the List of acronyms for the names of individual organizations.
[a] Percentage of the CCE's 905,151 indirect offiliates in mid-1990s.

Association of Stock Investment Firms (AMIB); and the Mexican Association of Insurance Firms (AMIS) – and the inclusion of two multisectoral organizations, the Mexican Employers' Confederation (COPARMEX) and the Mexican Council of Businessmen (CMHN, which includes a number of large Mexican economic consortiums).

The CCE's asymmetrical structure – based upon "one association, one vote" decision making – led to overrepresentation of the CMHN's large economic groups and underrepresentation of small and midsize businesses, which lacked a representational space proportional to their numbers. In fact, although large corporations represented only 0.01 percent of the CCE's indirect membership, they controlled 50 percent of the votes (Luna and Tirado 1992).

There are several private-sector associations that fall outside of the CCE's system of representation. The most important ones are the organizations linked to foreign trade, which have developed in a more pluralistic institutional context. Some of them are affiliated to international bodies, such as the American Chamber of Commerce–Mexico and the Mexican Chapter of the International Chamber of Commerce. Other national associations related to international trade are the Mexican Business Council for International Affairs (CEMAI), which is a CCE member without voting rights; the National Council on Foreign Trade (CONACEX); and the National Association of Mexican Importers and Exporters (ANIERM).

The Political Environment in the 1980s and 1990s

The 1980s were characterized by significant political activism on the part of Mexican business (Tirado and Luna 1995). This activism was one consequence of the 1982 bank nationalization, which shattered the established nexus for economic policy development (especially the link between private companies and government agencies in the financial sector) and demonstrated the executive branch's potential to act unilaterally. In the lengthy confrontation that ensued between the state and the national private sector, the traditionally radical business current – led by the COPARMEX, but including the Confederation of National Chambers of Commerce (CONCANACO) and the National Agricultural and Livestock Council (CNA) – dominated public debate.

The private sector's political activism during the 1980s was inspired both by economic and political liberalism and by social-Christian doctrines. It was directed at promoting a new economic, political, and social model that would assign a leading role to business and protect the private sector against further unilateral decision making by the government. Business leaders from the liberal-conservative current (including the COPARMEX, CONCANACO, and CNA) advocated a "social market economy," a democratic political system that fostered party politics (in practice, a PRI–National Action Party system), and social participation through "subsidiary associations."[5] Based upon the COPARMEX's ideological affinity with the center-right PAN, the current's leaders supported political participation by business in this party.

In the late 1980s, several events changed the shape of state-private sector conflict in important ways. Among them were the opening of the Mexican economy, especially Mexico's adhesion to the General Agreement on Tariffs and Trade (GATT) in 1986; the signing of economic pacts among government, labor, and business to control inflation and accelerate economic liberalization (in particular, the privatization of the commercial banking sector), beginning in late 1987; and the political advance of the center-left National Democratic Front (FDN), which mobilized unexpectedly strong opposition to the PRI in the 1988 presidential election.

One key development during this period was the weakening of the liberal-conservative business current in public perceptions and the strengthening of "elitist" organizations, known as such for their members' economic weight. The CMHN, ABM, AMIB, and AMIS constituted the axis of a liberal-pragmatic current within the private sector. This change in the balance of private sector forces became apparent when the central focus of private-sector activism shifted from partisan political action to more routine economic and administrative policy-making activities designed to consolidate new economic policy guidelines concerning

5 This current is termed "liberal conservative" because of the content of its political messages. For an extensive characterization of political currents in the business sector during the 1980s, see Luna 1992.

liberalization, a downsizing of the federal government's regulatory functions, and, above all, privatization. It was also visible in the increasingly strong ties between the government and those business organizations comprising the liberal-pragmatic current.

One major consequence of the elitist or pragmatic-liberal current's growing influence was leadership change in the CCE during the late 1980s and early 1990s, actions orchestrated by prominent CMHN members Claudio X. González, Agustín Legorreta, and Rolando Vega. It was during these years that the CCE became the chief signatory to the controversial 1987 Economic Solidarity Pact and a champion of trade liberalization, privatization, and foreign investment (Luna and Tirado 1993). Together with the government, the CCE implemented novel mechanisms for tripartite collaboration among business, government, and labor, along with not-so-novel mechanisms of top-down control over its members. In doing so, it relied upon the broad membership base of the National Confederation of Chambers of Industry (CONCAMIN), CONCANACO, and CNA, organizations that stipulated affiliation for all businesses in their respective sectors.

Within Mexico's new policy framework of privatized state firms and policies designed to encourage international competitiveness, big economic groups began to emerge and consolidate their position.[6] They included both traditional economic groups and business consortiums that developed during the economic reform period (especially nontraditional exporting firms that established strategic alliances with foreign capital, many of which became midsize multinational firms). Studies of the changing structure of the private sector between 1987 and 1992 have found that Mexican private businesses significantly increased their importance as a proportion of all large businesses operating in the country and in terms of their contribution to total economic activity (Garrido 1998, 1999).[7] A considerable number of these large industrial conglomerates dominated their respective sectors, and several of these clusters were closely associated with financial institutions.

There was, however, growing uneasiness within the private sector about the concentration of decision-making power in the CCE and the close identification of the pragmatic-liberal and liberal-conservative currents with, respectively, the PRI and the PAN. The pragmatic-liberal current (encompassing particularly the CMHN, ABM, and AMIB) had directly benefited from the privatization of state-owned companies, export promotion policies, and the government's protection of the financial sector in the negotiations over the North American Free Trade Agreement (NAFTA). Particularly noteworthy was the unprecedented participation of CMHN members Claudio X. González and Gilberto Borja in, respectively, the administrations of Presidents Carlos Salinas de Gortari (1988–1994) and Ernesto Zedillo

6 Between 1991 and 1994, the number of "billionaire" Mexican businessmen rose from two to twenty-four (although this number was subsequently reduced as a consequence of the 1994–1995 economic crisis). For a critical assessment of these large industrial firms' contributions to the private sector and the Mexican economy as a whole, see Garrido 1998: 399.

7 Firm size was defined by total sales as a percentage of gross domestic product.

(1994–2000). Moreover, in 1993 CMHN members and other financial-sector leaders made large contributions to Zedillo's presidential campaign in response to a request from Salinas and the president of the PRI (*Proceso*, March 8, 1993, p. 6).

Entrepreneurs' political involvement with the PAN was even more notable. During the 1980s and 1990s a group of prominent *panistas* arose from the private sector. Most were owners of small and midsize businesses, and some were former local COPARMEX and CONCANACO leaders. These businessmen competed for elected offices, winning gubernatorial races in Guanajuato, Jalisco, and several northern Mexican states.

Business associations' demands for democratization slackened somewhat when the FDN emerged and ran Cuauhtémoc Cárdenas as its presidential candidate in 1988, mainly because many elements in the private sector viewed Cárdenas as a threat. Nevertheless, business leaders continued to run as the candidates of various parties, changing the traditional rules of the political system but without clearly establishing new norms of political behavior for entrepreneurs as citizens, as a sector, or as politicians.

Business's Political Conduct in the 1990s

The private sector's political activities during the 1990s were marked by internal conflicts, despite a brief period of unity during the NAFTA negotiations. These conflicts arose because of the realignment of political currents within the private sector and the predominance of business associations in the policy sphere.

Internal Conflicts

Toward the end of the 1980s, the overall unity that had characterized the private sector during the corporatist era began to weaken. Moreover, by the early 1990s conflicts no longer centered upon business relations with government; instead, confrontations were increasingly among entrepreneurs (Luna and Tirado 1993). For instance, following the signing of the Pact for Stability, Competitiveness, and Employment (PECE) in October 1992, some business associations challenged their representatives' authority to negotiate an agreement of this nature on behalf of the private sector. Some entrepreneurs also objected to specific items contained in the PECE, such as price controls. The dissident associations branded CCE leaders as "pro-government" and demanded that the Council function simply to coordinate its member organizations and not try to speak for the entire business sector. Similar tensions surfaced in rivalries over the CCE presidency, over the extent of the Council's overall authority and responsibilities, and over the appropriateness of obligatory membership in industrial and business chambers and confederations.

The main contenders in the conflict over the CCE presidency for the 1989–1990 period were, on one side, the liberal-conservative current led by the COPARMEX and the CONCANACO and backed by the CNA and, on the other side, the big economic groups represented by the CMHN and financial-sector associations.

Because none of the Council presidency candidates reached the vote threshold prescribed in the by-laws, an interim president was elected (from the CMHN) for a six-month period and later confirmed for an additional year. At the same time, the relevant by-laws were reformed so that in future elections each organization, in order of seniority, would present a slate of candidates. This reform gave the CONCANACO (created in 1917 and hence the oldest organization in the CCE) the opportunity to present the first slate, which produced the CCE president for the 1991–1992 period. This development eased the marginalization of small and midsize industrial and commercial firms and those outside the Mexico City metropolitan area, which were organized in associations like the CONCANACO, the COPARMEX, the CONCAMIN, and the National Chamber of Manufacturers (CANACINTRA).

As noted above, disputes surrounding the CCE presidency exposed disagreements within the business community over the Council's level of authority, the policies it advocated, and the degree to which it was representative of the sector as a whole. There was an especially vigorous debate over obligatory membership in business chambers. The merchants grouped in the CONCANACO defended mandatory membership, arguing that their organization was a legitimate representative and that the elimination of this membership requirement would atomize merchant' interests. However, the greatest controversy surrounded the relative importance of macroeconomic and microeconomic priorities in Mexico's development strategy, particularly the role that the government should play.

The Public Debate

Mexico entered the 1990s with an open economy and relative macroeconomic stability. However, industrialization had stagnated, and some business groups began looking to microeconomic reform to help firms achieve real competitiveness in the framework of a more open economy (Luna 1995). Government and business agreed in general that microeconomic reform was a priority if the country was to advance to a new stage of development, but there were profound differences over who should promote the reforms and how. Public officials and some business groups (including the Mexican Bankers' Association and the CMHN) declared that microeconomic reform was mainly the responsibility of private firms. In contrast, organizations such as the COPARMEX, the CONCANACO, and the CANACINTRA warned that microeconomic efficiency depended not only upon each firm's internal organization, but also upon a competitive and efficient economic environment and an effective and well-articulated industrial policy.

The main targets of criticism were Mexico's recently privatized commercial banks and the Ministry of Finance and Public Credit (SHCP), which were said to be responsible for the constant shortage of capital and the absence of fiscal incentives to expand production. The Ministry of Commerce and Industrial Development (SECOFI) also received criticism for not developing an industrial modernization plan.

This debate, precipitated by the 1994 presidential election and fanned by the effects of the post-1994 banking crisis, transferred the CCE's peculiar internal asymmetry into the political arena and produced a realignment of political currents within the private sector. These currents now became differentiated based upon the following dichotomies: producers versus financiers, large versus small firms, and location in the Mexico City metropolitan area versus other regions of the country. The new divisions replaced ideological and political affinities between business associations and political parties as the main axes of political differentiation within the private sector.

It was upon this basis that discussions emerged over the role that government, business associations, and the private sector as a whole should play in economic development, and that policy proposals were developed regarding how to create the requisite conditions for improving firms' economic performance.

The Realignment of Political Currents

Two major political currents dominated the CCE during the 1990s: (1) the pragmatic-liberal current comprised of financial groups and large exporting firms, represented especially by the CMHN, the ABM, the AMIB, and (2) a critical-liberal current composed of business organizations with a broad base among small firms (the AMIS, CANACINTRA, CONCANACO, COPARMEX, and CNA).[8] Their differences arose over the relative downgrading of the domestic market's importance under Mexico's new economic strategy and firms' differential capacity to adapt to trade opening and the government's deregulation processes. More specifically, the factors leading to the emergence of the critical-liberal current included the plight of small firms and industries focused on the domestic market and different business groups' discontent over the centralism characteristic of the main national business organizations.

The critical-liberal current was distinctive for both its composition and its proposals. It united organizations with historically different political positions, ranging from the COPARMEX (with its radical anti-government positions and ties to the Roman Catholic Church) to the CANACINTRA (with its traditionally strong ties to government). The new current also embraced organizations that had previously not participated in public debate, including the Mexican Association of Insurance Institutions, which had formerly been aligned with the financial sector.

Under COPARMEX leadership and with input from the CANACINTRA, the critical-liberal current capitalized on many businesses' unhappiness with Mexico's economic policy orientation and with large economic groups' control of CCE leadership. As a group, the current's members supported a series of private-sector proposals for the 1994–2000 presidential period that featured demands for a new industrial policy.

8 The new critical-liberal current was very much in evidence during the 1994 presidential succession (Luna and Tirado 1999a).

The pragmatic-liberal current (the CMHN, ABM, and AMIB) was, however, much better established because of its longer history and its members' economic importance. The current's position was strengthened during the NAFTA negotiations by the creation of the Foreign Trade Business Organizations' Coordinating Network (COECE). The COECE, which assumed national political importance during the early 1990s, bolstered the pragmatic-liberal current's position by combining the basic CCE structure with a set of organizations oriented toward foreign trade, a group that formerly had been outside the CCE's system of representation but that became strategically important under trade opening.

The CONCAMIN maintained a position midway between these two currents. Although its decisions often tipped the balance in favor of the pragmatic-liberal current (as was the case, for example, with the CCE succession in 1990), its positions remained closer to those of the critical-liberal current, as will be seen below.

Both currents continued to recognize the value of competition as a fundamental element of economic dynamics. However, they differed regarding the government's economic role and the best means to achieve competitiveness in world markets. The pragmatic-liberal current emphasized macroeconomic conditions and the international market, while the critical-liberal tendency placed greater attention upon microeconomic policies and the domestic market. The former assumed a causal relationship between trade liberalization and increasing firm competitiveness driven by market pressures; the latter argued that government should play an important role in leveling the playing field and thereby creating expanded opportunities for business competition.

In particular, the critical-liberal current highlighted the lack of sufficient financial resources and fiscal stimuli for production, thus placing the traditional opposition between financial capital and industrial capital on the public agenda. In addition, it emphatically demanded a national industrial policy that would take into account not only the specific conditions of different industrial branches, but also the situation of production units in terms of size, technological capability, and regional disequilibria.

Along these lines, the critical-liberal current called for solid government financial support for an industrial policy, along with infrastructure modernization, deregulation at the state and municipal levels, promotion of business partnerships, and, especially, appropriate enforcement of legislation regarding economic competition and a broadening of collaborative arrangements between government and business associations so as to involve all businesses in policy design (Luna 1995). The CONCAMIN seconded these proposals, noting that a new national industrial policy should eliminate distortions carried over from Mexico's protectionist period, reduce the concentration of production and eliminate oligopolistic interests, address small and midsize firms' organizational lags, and halt "excessive" regulation of economic activity.

For most of the 1990s, the CCE leadership was controlled by heads of associations affiliated with or sympathetic to the critical-liberal current. Mainly as a result of the changes made to the CCE's electoral procedures in the early 1990s – but also reflecting the breadth of support organized around the critical-liberal perspective – the CCE presidency was held successively by the leaders of the CONCANACO (Nicolás Madhauar), the CONCAMIN (Germán Cárcova), the COPARMEX (Héctor Larios), and the CNA (Eduardo Bours). As a consequence, the discourse of the critical-liberal current and that of the CCE remained relatively in tune with one another. The CCE, however, often emphasized the conjunctural character of a new industrial policy and the need to support firms relatively less able to compete in a radically altered economic context.

Unstable Unity

The NAFTA negotiations in the early 1990s provided an ephemeral but significant moment of unity among business interests and between business and government. This unity was largely attributable to the nature of the negotiations themselves, which pushed business groups to cooperate in order to seek advantages for the private sector as a whole. However, unity was also encouraged through new mechanisms of communication and collaboration and by certain political conditions. The most important political conditions were:

- The desire to achieve common objectives, including stable access to external markets, a just balance in dispute resolution arrangements, complementarity of the Mexican economy with its trading partners, and the exclusion of petroleum from the negotiations;
- Validation of COECE member organizations' independent positions through a confidentiality agreement that granted the COECE the exclusive right to announce to the public the advances made in the negotiations with Canada and the United States;
- Changes in the CCE's by-laws that encouraged the Council, when faced with the urgency of presenting a united business front, to promote a relative opening in its affairs that better accommodated the interests of small businesses;
- The prospect that business interests not taken specifically into account in the NAFTA negotiations would be protected via such governmental initiatives as programs to modernize midsize, small, and "micro" firms;
- The representational situation of small firms, whose heterogeneity and organizational instability and the strong individualism of their owners (Puga 1994) posed obstacles to the creation of a small-business organization capable of functioning as a counterweight to "elitist" organizations and large economic groups.

One element that undermined private-sector unity in the 1990s was government protection of the financial sector. Despite demands by Mexico's industrialists that the government open the financial sector to foreign competition, the purchasers of recently privatized banks repeatedly maintained that the financial system should be phased into the NAFTA framework gradually. This disagreement within the private sector had its parallel within the government, with the SECOFI endorsing a faster opening while the SHCP and banking officials remained much more conservative with regard to how fast and how much to liberalize the financial sector. The COECE's president strongly criticized the commercial banks for failing to provide sufficient support for Mexico's productive apparatus and for lagging in terms of the extent and speed of their liberalization.

Business and Party Politics

The various business currents' affinities with different political parties, which had been so clear in 1988, became blurred over the course of the 1990s. In a context of greater political competition, business organizations' political preferences and align-ments became more diversified.[9] Organizations with significant financial resources expanded and professionalized their relationship with parties. For example, the CCE created a liaison commission in order to influence the debates and decisions of the federal Congress. Some business leaders even switched their partisan allegiance, regardless of the ideological affinities between their associations and particular political parties.[10]

The most politically active entrepreneurs during the 1990s were those affiliated with the PAN, which captured a number of governorships over the course of the decade.[11] Entrepreneurs also achieved a greater presence in the federal Congress, running as candidates for the PAN, PRD, and PRI. In 1999, thirty PAN business-men, five from the PRD, and one from the PRI were members of the federal Chamber of Deputies (Ortiz 2000). In addition, two members of the exclusive CMHN (Miguel Alemán and Alberto Santos de Hoyos, both of the PRI) became federal senators, representing the states of Veracruz and Nuevo León, respectively.

One notable aspect of these processes has been the PRD's efforts to attract entrepreneurs and business organizations. Toward this end, in 1998 the PRD created an undersecretariat for business affairs within its National Executive Committee. It also established a set of state-level organizations called "Business Roundtables," through which business organizations that are independent of national business chambers have joined the PRD.[12] In 1999, the PRD had business roundtables in

9 The COPARMEX's decision to more or less distance itself from the National Action Party (PAN) allowed an economically and politically heterogeneous group of businessmen and business organizations to converge around a common economic program. This development, in turn, enabled the critical-liberal current to ascend to the leadership of the CCE.

10 One example of this phenomenon was textile producer Ricardo Villa Escalera, the PAN's candidate for governor of the state of Puebla who in 1999 became a member of the PRD's National Business Coordinating Network.

11 Entrepreneurs who won gubernatorial races as PAN candidates included Ernesto Ruffo Appel in Baja California, Vicente Fox Quesada in Guanajuato, Alberto Cárdenas in Jalisco, and Fernando Canales Clariond in Nuevo León.

12 Groups that have affiliated with the PRD through these roundtables include the National Association of Industrial Manufacturers (Asociación Nacional de Industriales de la Trans-

the Federal District and in the states of Chiapas, México, Morelos, Puebla, and Sinaloa.

The Rise of New Organizational Forms

When considering business and politics in Mexico in the broad sense, the 1990s were clearly a period of considerable dynamism in the forms of business organization. The altered economic and political environment increasingly revealed the limitations of corporatist arrangements as tensions among business interests mounted, fracturing the unity of the business class that typically characterizes corporatist regimes. In contrast to the relative stasis of the past, competition became a central value in Mexico's new economic paradigm. Because of intensifying market pressures, firms were challenged to identify innovative ways of interacting with government agencies, social actors, and other companies in order to obtain the information, financial, and even knowledge resources necessary to expand their competitive capacities. The internationalization of the economy, for its part, substituted supranational spaces for the national negotiating spaces that were the arena of corporatist agreements and large hierarchical organizations. At the same time, economic globalization underscored the importance of local forms of economic governance, insofar as they can help firms confront the drastic changes arising from a more internationalized market (Hirst and Thompson 1996).

Transformations in institutional context also diversified the range of political actors that are relevant to Mexican business and produced a more competitive environment. One such change was the elimination in 1996 of obligatory membership in business associations. This reform challenged business associations' capacity to survive by forcing them to adopt incentives to prevent members from deserting them and to expand their financial resources. Paradoxically, the 1996 revised chambers law itself established one important membership incentive. Although the law states that membership in business and industrial chambers is voluntary, it authorizes chambers to register firms in SECOFI's Mexican Business Information System (Sistema de Información Empresarial Mexicano) and to charge fees for registering and updating information (*Diario Oficial de la Federación*, January 2, 1997).[13]

International Networks

As national-level pacts declined as a mechanism for collaboration between government and business (their role practically ended after the 1994–1995 crisis), new forms of multilateral cooperation emerged that were similar to those put in

---

formación), which arose from a split within the CANACINTRA in the 1980s; the business section of the El Barzón debtors' organization; the Tlalnepantla Industrialists' Association; and several of the "business cells" originally created by the PRI.

13 The incentives that associations themselves have created are discussed below.

place under the COECE for the NAFTA negotiations. Independent of its specific results, the COECE – a joint creation of the private sector and government – was widely recognized as a successful experiment in collaboration among entrepreneurs and between business and government.[14]

The starting point for the COECE was the CCE's institutional structure, which was broadened with the addition of business associations linked to foreign trade and modified to ensure input from the bottom up. One important impetus for creating a coordination and communication system for business was the need for a grand alliance that could mitigate Mexico's negotiating disadvantages vis-à-vis its NAFTA neighbors to the north. However, it was also important to retain the CCE's sectoral and regional structure, which was essential for generating information on each industrial sector and branch, organizing cooperation among businesses in different branches on the basis of commodity chains, and involving a broad number of Mexican entrepreneurs in the consultation process.

The interactions with the U.S. and Canadian governments and U.S. and Canadian businesses combined negotiations by sector and negotiations by topic. They addressed such issues as unfair competition, intellectual property rights, and rules of origin. According to several participants in the NAFTA process, personal networks were the key to effective communication, with COECE members acting as consultants to Mexican government agencies, representatives of the national business community, and liaison with their U.S. and Canadian counterparts. Such complex communications and the coordination of both internal and external strategies would have been impossible in the CCE's highly hierarchical institutional system.

Corporatist Retreats, or Mere Coordination of Interests?

In the late 1990s, two new organizations arose in Mexico's strategically important financial and export sectors with the objective of uniting existing associations in these areas and promoting their activities in the international market. These bodies were the Financial Coordinating Council (CCF, established in 1998) and the Mexican Foreign Trade Council (COMCE, created in 1999). Both are empowered to represent the general interests of their respective sectors before governmental authorities and private organizations and to be the "official" spokespersons for their members.

The CCF, under the leadership of the Mexican Bankers' Association, originally linked together ten associations of financial institutions. These included the Mexican Association of Stock Investment Firms and the Association of International Financial Intermediaries, which represents over one hundred institutions.

The COMCE emerged less obtrusively under the leadership of the Mexican Business Council for International Affairs (CEMAI), a nonvoting member of the CCE. Unlike the CCF, which simply links existing organizations, the COMCE

---

14 Studies of the COECE include Alba 1997, Puga 1994, and Luna and Puga 1998.

requires that its member associations cease to exist as separate bodies. Its affiliates include the National Council on Foreign Trade and the COECE. However, one important association, the National Association of Mexican Importers and Exporters (ANIERM), decided not to participate (*El Financiero*, April 15, 1999). ANIERM's refusal to join apparently reflected the fact that the COMCE only represents the interests of exporters, while ANIERM's membership includes importing businesses as well.

Association Governance

Some business groups with a national presence in the industrial sector have approximated the goal of association governance by creating semi-private bodies offering services to companies. One example is the Foundation for Innovation and Technology Transfer for Small and Midsize Firms (FUNTEC), created by the CONCAMIN in 1994. Another is the Technology Transfer Unit (Unidad de Transferencia de Tecnología) created by the CANACINTRA in 1993, which offers technological, commercial, and financial services to members. FUNTEC in particular has assumed representative functions before joint public-private bodies that spur technological modernization, helping them promote coordinated activities among large firms, business associations, and research centers (De Gortari and Luna 1997, Casalet 2000).

Regional Cooperation

Regional programs operated by national business associations have had relatively little impact in Mexico. Nevertheless, in both industry and in the agricultural and livestock sector, local-level specialized chambers and associations have begun to establish multilateral relationships between their members and state universities and research institutions, as well as with governmental agencies. These networks have appeared more or less spontaneously. They are generally oriented toward gaining access to information and knowledge resources for the benefit of their members, adapting technologies, or standardizing products and processes.

One study of these networks found that specialized associations at the municipal and state levels are the actors most frequently involved in establishing links among academic institutions, local governments, and small firms in traditional industries (Luna and Tirado 1999b). Based upon an analysis of network dynamics, Luna and Tirado determined that these specialized associations may be able to establish cooperative relationships with other actors and fulfill an important monitoring function to ensure that their objectives are fulfilled. Along with their geographical proximity to members, one of the main incentives for collaboration that municipal- and state-level associations can provide is their capacity to share members' specialized knowledge about their production processes and general business needs.

These network relationships generally have been based upon learning through interaction, and participants' specific capabilities usually matter less than their capacity for cooperation. Most such networks are local. However, some have had sufficient financial, organizational, informational, and knowledge resources to develop into international networks. In effect, their dynamism has brought them into the global environment.

Although credit unions have little chance to follow such an internationalizing trajectory, they nevertheless demonstrate the crucial role of cooperation in the market era. Between 1989 and 1998, the number of credit unions in Mexico rose from 142 to 383 (Luna and Puga 1998). Because they are based upon social solidarity and voluntary exchange, these institutions approximate forms of community governance. They are able to provide businesses with financial resources, technical assistance, bulk purchases, and other commercial services through the mutual support of their members – generally small agricultural and industrial producers or merchants.

In summary, one useful way to portray the trends that prevailed among Mexico's corporatist business organizations in the 1990s is to place these organizations along an axis that runs between two extremes of economic governance. At one pole lies the state, which is connected to national space; at the other pole is the market, which is shaped by international forces. Although shifts during the decade in forms of business governance and in the character of business associations' relations with the state and the market were neither uniform nor unilinear, they did highlight the fact that there are diverse forms of economic governance, each with its own logic, and that these relationships are still in flux.

Conclusion: The Private Sector's Dilemmas in a New Era

National businesses face a key challenge within Mexico's increasingly complex economic and political environment – the need to differentiate their strategies for collective action. In order to meet this challenge, they must first recognize the distinction between politics and policies. If the Mexican private sector fails to make this distinction, the result could be the politicization of the policy sphere. This is precisely what happened between 1976 and 1982, when conflicts between government and business created a governability crisis and threatened the stability of both the economy and the political system (Luna 1992). At that time, the problem of representation inherent in corporatism's top-down controls was temporarily resolved through the creation of the CCE and the largely unregulated entry of entrepreneurs into partisan politics.

There are two reasons why the reappearance of politicization in early twenty-first-century Mexico would likely have much more profound effects than in the 1976–1982 period. First, an internationalized environment makes the Mexican economy much more vulnerable to shocks. Second, the fact that Mexico has not yet completely consolidated a democratic regime based upon multiparty political competition and the rule of law makes its political system very fragile.

In general terms, long-established corporatist arrangements in the private sector face three interrelated challenges: internationalization, which has reduced the relative importance of national bodies in the design of public policies; political democratization, which has undermined the control mechanisms that necessarily form part of a corporatist regime; and increased competition among political parties, which has decentralized the relationship between business and government.

In the field of public policy, some Mexican business organizations have shown an ability to evolve. Although their transformation is still incomplete, they demonstrate that it is possible to draw upon an institutional capital whose dynamism goes beyond mere organizational survival. Such dynamism requires the development of cooperation mechanisms and incentive systems to resolve the dilemma between competition and cooperation. It also requires raising the quality of representation and articulating political fields on different geographic scales. In other words, the future viability of corporatist-type organizations depends upon their capacity to create associations that are more administratively and territorially decentralized, less isolated from their social bases, and more flexible in their structure.

In countries such as Italy and Germany, the resurgence of functional collaboration agreements has been possible because of the presence of decentralized decision-making structures and social organizations' capacity to capitalize on the opportunities that their particular resources presented. This type of economic governance has succeeded in counteracting networks' perverse effects, including uncertainty about the rules for (and results of) cooperation (Regini 1998).

Such outcomes do not imply the disappearance of large national organizations, but they do require capacity building in business associations to the point that they can coordinate multiple interests and manage conflicts that appear in the process of developing and implementing policies. Indeed, these associations will only be able to prosper in the future if they mobilize their political resources to coordinate diverse interests. This was the basis upon which the critical-liberal current built its grand alliance in the 1990s, enabling it to establish control over the CCE. However, it is also likely that the pronounced centralization of national business organizations, as well as the dearth of information and lack of deliberation that prevail within many business associations, contributed to this alliance's limited impact upon the main lines of national economic policy.

The relationship between business and politics in a more narrow sense has been a leading topic of debate among entrepreneurs ever since the creation of the CCE, an organization that some business leaders considered turning into a political party. The issue gained special saliency in the 1980s when these debates hinged upon whether entrepreneurs should participate in political parties as individuals or as a sector.

This question retained its relevance in the context of greater political competition during the 1990s. One case is particularly noteworthy because of the individual's connection with the CCE, the elite of Mexican business associations. Eduardo Bours was president of the CCE in 1999 when he urged the private sector to give its financial support to Francisco Labastida's primary campaign to win the

PRI's presidential nomination. Bours later became Labastida's campaign finance director, a development that sparked spirited exchanges among members of the CMHN and a protest by Juan Sánchez Navarro, a leading private-sector ideologue and promoter of private-sector associations. A similar case involved Silvestre Fernández Barajas, a former president of the CONCAMIN, former PRI federal deputy, and candidate in the PRI's gubernatorial primary in the Federal District in 1999.

Given the traditionally hierarchical structure of interest representation in Mexico, partisan political identification by business associations provokes conflict both among the top organizations and between these national groups and locally based associations whose members' political preferences are increasingly diverse. One should recall in this regard that the PRI's first gubernatorial defeats were at the hands of entrepreneurs running as PAN candidates.

However, because of the rising influence of Mexico's legislative branch and the country's experiences with political alternation in power at the state and federal levels, new representational mechanisms and political practices have emerged to redefine the business-politics relationship. Entrepreneurs increasingly participate in politics as individuals, holding elected office under various political party banners. The CCE has created a liaison commission that aims to influence congressional debates, and the CCE and similar bodies now hold dialogues with candidates from various parties to discuss economic policy proposals.

In sum, distinguishing between economic and political interests within business organizations has meant recreating these organizations' relationship with the political sphere. The result has been that political parties and other social organizations now have a greater influence on the design and direction of public policies in Mexico.

The presidential victory of PAN candidate Vicente Fox Quesada in July 2000 synthesized the new relationship between business and politics that had been fostered during the 1980s and 1990s. Among other things, the first years of the Fox administration made evident the danger of politicization of the policy sphere. Despite Fox's initial statement that his administration "was one of businessmen and for businessmen," relations among the federal executive, the Congress, and business associations such as the CMHN and the CCE (whose president for 2000–2002 was Claudio X. González, a former president of the CMHN, CCE president during 1985–1987, and a close advisor to the Salinas administration) proved difficult. The CCE refused to sign the "national political accord" proposed by President Fox, and there were multiple political conflicts over proposed reforms to fiscal and tax policy, federal labor law, educational policy, and the terms under which foreign investors could participate in the electrical power sector. Moreover, investigations into the financing that entrepreneurs had provided for Fox's presidential campaign made evident the urgent need to distinguish between politics and policies and to regulate the new relationship between entrepreneurs and partisan politics.

References

Alba, Carlos. 1997. "La COECE: un caso de cooperación entre los sectores público y privado en México," *Comercio Exterior* 4 (2): 149–58.

Casalet, Mónica. 2000. "The Institutional Matrix." In *Developing Innovation Systems: Mexico in a Global Context*, edited by Mario Cimoli. London: Pinter.

De Gortari, Rebeca, and Matilde Luna. 1997. "Las asociaciones empresariales ante la tecnología," *El Cotidiano* (Universidad Autónoma Metropolitana–Azcapotzalco) 13 (81): 22–29.

Garrido, Celso. 1998. "El liderazgo de las grandes empresas mexicanas." In *Grandes empresas y grupos latinoamericanos*, edited by Wilson Peres. Mexico City: Siglo Veintiuno / Comisión Económica para América Latina y el Caribe.

——. 1999. "El caso mexicano." In *Las multinacionales latinoamericanas: sus estrategias en un mundo globalizado*, edited by Daniel Chudnovsky, Bernardo Kosacoff, and Andrés López. Mexico City: Fondo de Cultura Económica.

Hirst, Paul, and Grahame Thompson. 1996. *Globalization in Question: The International Economy and the Possibilities of Governance*. Cambridge: Polity Press / Cambridge University Press.

Hollingsworth, J. Rogers, and Robert Boyer. 1997. "Coordination of Economic Actors and Social Systems of Production." In *Contemporary Capitalism: The Embeddedness of Institutions*, edited by J. Rogers Hollingsworth and Robert Boyer. Cambridge: Cambridge University Press.

Luna, Matilde. 1992. *Los empresarios y el cambio político: México 1970–1987*. Mexico City: Instituto de Investigaciones Sociales, Universidad Nacional Autónoma de México / Era.

——. 1995. "Entrepreneurial Interests and Political Action in Mexico: Facing the Demands of Economic Modernization." In *The Challenge of Institutional Reform in Mexico*, edited by Riordan Roett. Boulder, Colo.: Lynne Rienner.

——. 1997. "Modelos de colaboración entre el sector privado, el gobierno y los académicos." In *Gobierno, academia y empresas en México: hacia una nueva configuración de relaciones*, edited by Rosalba Casas and Matilde Luna. Mexico City: Instituto de Investigaciones Sociales, Universidad Nacional Autónoma de México / Plaza y Valdés.

Luna, Matilde, and Cristina Puga. 1998. "Institutional Dynamism in Traditionally Corporatist Settings." Paper presented at the World Congress of Sociology, International Sociological Association, Montreal, Canada, July–August.

Luna, Matilde, and Ricardo Tirado. 1992. *El Consejo Coordinador Empresarial: una radiografía*. Mexico City: Instituto de Investigaciones Sociales, Universidad Nacional Autónoma de México.

——. 1993. "Los empresarios en el escenario del cambio: trayectoria y tendencias de sus estrategias de acción colectiva," *Revista Mexicana de Sociología* 55 (2): 243–71.

——. 1999a. "Las organizaciones empresariales." Working paper. Mexico City: Instituto de Investigaciones Sociales, Universidad Nacional Autónoma de México.

——. 1999b. "The Contribution of Business Associations to the Configuration of Knowledge Networks in Mexico." Paper presented at "Triple Helix in Latin America," Rio de Janeiro, June.

Offe, Claus. 1975. "The Theory of the Capitalist State and the Problem of Public Policy Formation." In *Stress and Contradiction in Modern Capitalism: Public Policy and the Theory of the State*, edited by Leon N. Lindberg et al. Lexington, Mass.: Lexington Books.

Ortiz, Alicia. 2000. "Empresarios y democracia." Working paper. Facultad de Ciencias Políticas y Sociales, Universidad Nacional Autónoma de México.

Puga, Cristina. 1994. "Las organizaciones empresariales en las negociaciones del TLC." In *Los empresarios ante la globalización*, edited by Ricardo Tirado. Mexico City: Instituto de Investigaciones Legislativas, Universidad Nacional Autónoma de México.

Regini, Marini. 1998. "Still Engaging in Corporatism? Recent Italian Experience in Comparative Perspective." Paper presented at the World Congress of Sociology, International Sociological Association, Montreal, Canada, July–August.

Schmitter, Philippe C. 1992. "Comunidad, mercado, estado ¿y las asociaciones? La contribución esperada del gobierno de intereses al orden social." In *Teorías del neocorporativismo: ensayos de Philippe Schmitter*, edited by Rigoberto Ocampo. Mexico City: Universidad Iberoamericana / Universidad de Guadalajara.

Tirado, Ricardo, and Matilde Luna. 1995. "El Consejo Coordinador Empresarial: de la unidad frente al 'reformismo' a la unidad para el TLC (1975–1993)," *Revista Mexicana de Sociología* 57 (4): 27–60.

Mexico's Armed Forces:
Marching to a Democratic Tune?

Roderic Ai Camp

M exico's pattern of civil-military relations is unique among Latin American countries, constituting a significant case study in the withdrawal of the armed forces from direct political intervention. As a consequence of the Mexican Revolution of 1910–1920, the Mexican military became the first in the region to emerge from the remnants of popular or guerrilla forces that had destroyed the established armed forces. The only other Latin American countries where this has happened are Cuba after 1959 and Nicaragua after 1979. These popular origins have flavored how the officer corps views itself and, to some degree, how the average citizen views the military.

As a result of the military's gradual withdrawal from direct participation in political affairs over the course of the 1920s and 1930s, along with the inauguration in 1946 of the first elected civilian president since 1913, Mexico achieved an enviable reputation as the Latin American country with the longest record of military subordination to civil rule. Nevertheless, questions remain about the stability of this relationship and about what conditions might spur Mexico's armed forces to a more active political role.

The three conditions most likely to alter the well-established pattern of military subordination to civil rule are the spread of societal violence, represented by guerrilla groups; increased militarization of various sectors in response to rising levels of criminal activity, including urban crime and drug trafficking; and the creation of partisan civilian alliances with factions in the armed forces as part of the natural pattern of political pluralization. The fact that there have been significant changes in all three of these areas since the mid-1990s alters to some degree the dynamic that has characterized civil-military relations in Mexico in recent decades.

When President Ernesto Zedillo (1994–2000) took office in December 1994, the Mexican military remained steadfast in its support of constitutional government. The armed forces did so despite the fact that they faced an eleven-month-old rebel movement in Chiapas; had provided inadequate security to the governing party's initial presidential candidate, Luis Donaldo Colosio, who was assassinated in March 1994; had witnessed increased drug trafficking and drug-related violence, including corruption of the armed forces at the highest levels; and had experienced one of the worst economic crises in Mexican history. Moreover, the military shared an unpleasant history with the incoming president who, as the former secretary of education, had allowed public school textbooks to lay blame upon the military for its role in the 1968 massacre of student demonstrators in Mexico City.

The last half of the 1990s presented many new challenges to the armed forces and saw the development of patterns within the military that differed from those existing prior to 1994. These included shifting attitudes within the officer corps that have implications for the military as an institution and for its relations with civilian governmental leadership.

Changes in the Armed Forces since 1994

Structural Reorganization

One of the most significant changes – specifically involving the army, by far the most influential service among the Mexican armed forces[1] – is the desire among a new generation of officers to reform many aspects of military professionalization and organization. The desire for reforms, which was expressed in an internal army document in June 1995 – just eighteen months after the public appearance of the Zapatista Army of National Liberation (EZLN) in January 1994 – makes clear the level of dissatisfaction with the army's technical training, abilities, hierarchy, promotion system, and strategy. The authors of this document were responding to the Zapatista movement, to the army's expanded mission in drug eradication, and to its increased role in internal police tasks. The document details a number of weaknesses, several of which hold broad implications both for the armed forces as an institution and for civil-military relations.[2]

A key organizational reform advocated in the document is an increased emphasis upon regional commanders, decentralizing control away from the minister of defense and placing greater reliance upon the decision-making authority of zone commanders.[3] It is difficult to measure the extent to which decentralization of decision making has taken place since 1995, but one recognizable organizational change is the rapid growth in the number of military zones, which as of 2003 numbered forty-four.[4] The location of the newly created zones is also noteworthy, reflecting the armed forces leadership's security concerns regarding drug trafficking and guerrilla activity on the part of both the EZLN and the Popular Revolutionary Army (ERP), which appeared in the summer of 1996. The new zones include the 37th – State of México (central Mexico), the 38th – Chiapas (southern Mexico), the

---

1 Seventy-seven percent of the armed forces are army/air force troops under the command of the Ministry of Defense, compared to only 23 percent under the Department of the Navy.

2 For a more detailed treatment of the weaknesses identified in the internal document, see Camp 1999.

3 These two- and three-star generals are Mexico's highest-ranking active duty officers.

4 The navy is divided into six naval regions and twenty-two zones, and the air force is separated into three regions comprising a total of eighteen air bases.

39th – Tabasco (Gulf coast), the 40th – Baja California Sur (northwestern Mexico), the 41st – Jalisco (western Mexico), the 42nd – Chihuahua (northern Mexico), the 43rd – Michoacán (west central Mexico), and the 44th – Oaxaca (southern Mexico).

Giving regional commanders more authority has produced two visible, seemingly contradictory, results. The rationale behind this change was that former zone and regional commanders had been overly dependent upon the minister of defense. The remedy was to replicate the U.S. army's practice of assigning greater authority to the on-scene commander. Division General Miguel Ángel Godínez Bravo, commander of the forces arrayed against the EZLN, illustrated this increased autonomy when he announced military policy in the region and apprised the domestic and international press of his views.[5] The contradictory result appears in the career of Division General Jesús Gutiérrez Rebollo, who for nearly five years (contrary to established army policy) was allowed to command the 15th zone in Jalisco as well as the 12th regional command of the multiple-state area. During his tenure, Gutiérrez Rebollo used both commands to promote his own drug trafficking-related activities.[6]

The second major organizational reform advocated in the internal army report was better cooperation between the air force and the army to create Airborne Special Forces units, small mobile forces of approximately 100 soldiers that can be activated against both drug dealers and guerrillas.[7] In 1995 the Ministry of Defense set up a combined Army and Air Force Study Center in Mexico City that included four separate schools – intelligence, human resources, administration, and logistics. There is no published evidence that inter-service rivalries exist in Mexico. However, graduates of the Advanced War College (ESG), the army's second-tier military academy, have little respect for their naval peers.[8]

The third organizational change is increased contact with civilian professionals, especially government officials, as well as an expanded corps of civilian employees within the armed forces. The Mexican military is the most insular of all armed forces in Latin America. It has little contact with civilians, and civilians have limited contact with the officer corps. As part of its new emphasis upon internal security issues and higher-caliber education, in 1981 the Ministry of Defense established a third-tier academy – the National Defense College (CDN) – for

---

5 Author's communication with a *New York Times* correspondent who attended a private press conference held by Godínez Bravo.

6 See the documents provided by the government when General Gutiérrez Rebollo was appointed Zedillo's drug czar in March 1997.

7 Sixty-four of these units existed in the late 1990s, but only one (assigned to Mexico City) was fully trained and staffed (Grayson 1999: 30).

8 The elite graduates of the Advanced War College have traditionally received staff and command diplomas, which are almost essential to reaching two-star rank. These diplomas have proved to be a source of conflict, as will be seen below.

This discussion is based upon the author's interviews with recent graduates of the War College; this pattern is the same one that the author discovered in 1990.

officers from all three services.[9] Recent generations of students taking the CDN's year-long course of study have included an expanded number of civilians, along with Mexican colonels and generals and other officers of equal rank. The CDN plans to increase the number of civilian participants to six, a sizable group given that CDN classes average in the twenties.[10] Additional contact with civilians occurs through study in civilian institutions. In 1980, only eighteen officers were enrolled in master's or doctoral programs in civilian institutions. The number increased to 40 in 1985, 68 in 1995, and 142 in 1998. These officers were enrolled at the National Autonomous University of Mexico (UNAM), the National Polytechnic Institute (IPN), the Universidad Iberoamericana, and Universidad Anáhuac, all located in Mexico City (see www.sedena.gob.mx).

Institutional Growth

The second major change in the Mexican armed forces since the mid-1990s is their rapid expansion. When Carlos Salinas de Gortari became president in December 1988, the armed forces totaled 179,305 personnel. When Ernesto Zedillo succeeded Salinas in 1994, the armed forces totaled 218,000 active duty officers and soldiers. By July 1997, their numbers had risen to 236,575. In just the first thirty months of his presidency, then, Zedillo added 22,000 personnel, and by 1998 the armed forces had grown to 238,000.[11]

Even more extraordinary than the overall growth of military personnel in Mexico's army, air force, and navy has been the dramatic expansion in the number of officer candidates enrolled in military academies and officers graduating from the respective services' war colleges. During the six years of the Salinas administration (1988–1994), all army and air force academies combined averaged 1,246 graduates yearly, similar to levels during the preceding administration of Miguel de la Madrid (1982–1988). Yet in 1995 – just months after Zedillo took office and a year

9 The Ministry of Defense also streamlined educational administration in 1996 by placing the Army/Air Force University under the jurisdiction of the General Directorate of Military Education, one of the traditional departments within the Ministry of Defense. In the late 1990s, the former director of the National Defense College, General Gerardo Vega García, held this post. One indication of the significance of the military education system for military careers is that Vega García went on to become minister of national defense.

10 The navy and air force have always maintained close contact with civilians through their military educational programs. Three-quarters of the instructors at the Heroic Naval College (Colegio Heróico Naval) in the port of Veracruz and the Air College (Colegio Áereo) in Jalisco are civilian. In contrast, the entry-level academy for the army, the Heroic Military College (Colegio Heróico Militar) in Mexico City, employs military personnel almost exclusively. Because no detailed histories of the founding and evolution of these academies exist, it is difficult to explain why they differ in this regard. It may be that the naval and air force academies' more recent origins and their heavier reliance upon technology from abroad (which increased their contacts with U.S. programs) explain their openness to both foreign and civilian expertise.

11 The number has probably grown slightly. The budget that the Ministry of Defense submitted in May 1999 indicated that the army and air force alone then totaled 183,296 soldiers.

after the Zapatista uprising – the army and air force enrolled 1,659 officer candidates and officers in their academies. By 1996 these academies had 5,300 men and women in their classrooms, a fourfold increase in two years. The growth pattern continued unabated into 1997, with 7,981 enrolled (Poder Ejecutivo Federal 1997: 5; 1998: 5).[12]

The unprecedented expansion of the officer corps – and, to a lesser extent, troop strength more generally – resulted from a confluence of national security concerns. The primary causes of greater staffing needs were the stalemated Zapatista rebellion in Chiapas, the spread of small but aggressive ERP guerrilla attacks in numerous Mexican states, the expanded drug-interdiction mission of all military services, and the extraordinary growth in criminal activity, all of which placed heavy demands upon the armed forces and stretched their logistical abilities.

The most immediate consequence of this rapid force expansion has been the military's increased visibility. The growth in the officer corps itself suggests two potential outcomes. First, it may be more difficult to maintain the controls over officer training and socialization that have typified the Mexican armed forces. Second, analysts have always argued that the military's small size has imposed a structural limitation upon its direct involvement in the political sphere. With growth of the armed forces, this limitation could weaken or even disappear.

The Mexican armed forces typically do not make their troop assignments known in any detail, either to the general public or to the federal Congress. However, since 1990 the president has reported the armed forces' combined surveillance activities on land, sea, and in the air. The expansion of the physical area under active patrol corresponds closely to changing personnel patterns. In 1990, the armed forces reported a total surveillance area of 1.4 million kilometers. By 1991 surveillance tasks had nearly doubled to cover 2.4 million kilometers. Throughout 1993, just before the outbreak of armed rebellion in Chiapas, the armed forces were covering 4.2 million kilometers.[13] Twelve months later, that figure had more than tripled to 14.2 million kilometers, and it remained at that level during the initial years of the Zedillo administration (Poder Ejecutivo Federal 1997: 5). In 1997, surveillance rose to 22.9 million kilometers, and for the first six months of 1998, the military had already covered 14.5 million kilometers (Poder Ejecutivo Federal 1998: 5). Since 1995, the Ministry of Defense has spent nearly a quarter (24.6 percent) of its budget on fighting drug traffickers, and by December 1996, 1,493 troops were

12 An interesting paradox is that the minister of defense has not mandated a change in class size at either the Advanced War College or the National Defense College (author's interview with a member of the 1997 class at the Advanced War College and the author's personal observations while lecturing before the 1998–1999 National Defense College class). Although class sizes at the two institutions increased somewhat in the 1990s, both remain quite small. As a consequence, officers who are not staff and command graduates are performing tasks traditionally reserved for elite army or air force officers.

13 The figures are reported at the beginning of the following year. The rebellion broke out on January 1, 1994, eleven months before Salinas left office.

trained to work with Mexico's attorney general. In 1999, the Ministry of Defense reported that 36,341 soldiers and officers were assigned to drug-related missions. All of these figures suggest a dramatic increase in the armed forces' responsibility in performing anti-drug trafficking missions, alone or with civilian agencies.

New Professionalism?

The third major change in the early years of the Zedillo administration, discussed in considerable detail in the 1995 internal army report, was the army officer corps' dissatisfaction with the caliber of training in their academies. The quality of this training has direct technical, psychological, and social implications for the armed forces.

The technical side of this issue is most easily addressed. Graduates of the Heroic Naval College (Colegio Heróico Naval) in the port of Veracruz or its counterpart in Mazatlán had been receiving the equivalent of a college degree, while graduates of the army's Heroic Military College (Colegio Heróico Militar) were given only a preparatory certificate. Moreover, the army required only a secondary, not a preparatory, education of students wishing to enroll at its academy. This requirement has since been changed. All entering cadets must have prior preparatory training, and graduates of the Heroic Military College now leave with a *licenciatura*, the equivalent of a college degree.[14]

For decades, the psychological implication of a weak professional program made many officers feel intellectually inferior to their civilian counterparts. Given the academic caliber of their classes, especially after civilian government officials began attending private universities and graduate schools, their attitudes had a basis in fact.[15] Furthermore, the Ministry of Defense, cognizant of the fast-changing pace of warfare as illustrated by the 1991 Gulf War and the war in Bosnia, recognized the need to increase the military's electronic capabilities.[16] Their experiences with the Zapatistas, who used the Internet to battle the military on the field of public opinion, made a deep impression on the high command. In 1997 the military educational system began offering a new computer engineering degree (Poder Ejecutivo Federal 1997: 14), and computer capabilities at the National Defense College were brought up to the level of their civilian government counterparts.

The second consequence of the military's increased emphasis upon educational quality is its potential for altering the officer corps' social attitudes. Requiring

14 For a detailed analysis of changes in the educational curriculum and their consequences, see Camp 1998.

15 This was not true of naval officers, who graduated with a well-respected engineering degree and college equivalency. Military Medical Corps officers graduate from the Military Medical School, one of the foremost institutions in Mexico. The high quality of military medical training was illustrated in dramatic fashion when President Zedillo ordered the Central Military Hospital to admit the late Nobel Prize-winning author Octavio Paz, believing that civilian treatment of his cancer was not adequate.

16 See Camp 1999: 4.

officer cadets to have a preparatory education before entering the Heroic Military College modifies somewhat the social origins of potential officers. Mexicans who complete preparatory school (the equivalent of a pre-college academic track) come from families with higher socioeconomic backgrounds. Unlike government and intellectual leaders, the Mexican military is drawn overwhelmingly from working-class and lower-middle-class backgrounds. In addition, the desire to increase the proportion of civilian lecturers and instructors raises the potential for expanding and legitimizing diverse points of view among officers. This is illustrated by the fact that the Advanced War College, which in the past drew its lecturers almost exclusively from among career officers, is now emulating the National Defense College by bringing in prominent Mexicans, including leading opposition figures, to address advanced classes. Students report that in the late 1990s several military instructors openly encouraged students in the classroom to support the National Action Party (PAN), a partisan posture completely unthinkable several years ago.[17] Although this remains an exceptional experience, it illustrates initial cracks in what has long been an unpoliticized milieu.

Americanization Influences

Not only have Mexico's armed forces upgraded their internal educational caliber, but they have also sought to improve their professional training through military assistance programs in the United States. At some time in their career, most senior officers take short, specialized courses related to their military occupational specialty. According to figures from the U.S. International Military Education and Training (IMET) program, Mexico received more assistance than any other Latin American country in 1996 and 1997, and during those years it sent the largest number of students to the School of the Americas' staff and command course at Ft. Benning, Georgia, and to the Inter-American Air Force Academy (Latin American Working Group 1998: 189).[18] Mexican soldiers also received training in two special areas – riverine operations (to prepare them for intercept patrols to stop drug trans-shipments) and military public relations (to improve their image with the public and in the Mexican media).

Educational statistics for Mexico's leadership demonstrate that members of the officer corps have studied in the United States more frequently than any other group. From 1978 to 1998, Mexico's armed forces sent 4,173 people to study in the United States; 2,675 (64.1 percent) were trained during the Zedillo administration. These figures contrast markedly with the tenor of the overall relationship between the Mexican and U.S. militaries,[19] in which the Mexican military is so suspicious of contacts between U.S. military personnel and its own officers that it requires prior

---

17 Author's communication from a recent U.S. guest officer in the third-year class.

18 In 1997, 305 soldiers attended courses at Ft. Benning, and 260 enrolled in courses at the Inter-American Air Force Academy at Lackland Air Force Base in Texas. See Meisler 1998: A4, and the Latin American Working Group's web site at www.ciponline.org/facts.

formal authorization for social contacts with U.S. officers (or, for that matter, civilian foreigners). The Mexican government has expelled U.S. military attachés for gathering "information too aggressively and has imposed early retirement on senior officers who had become too friendly with the U.S. mission" (Cope 1996: 191).

Among Mexican officers at the rank of general, 41 percent are known to have trained abroad, and all but a handful received their education in the United States. Top military officers acquire even more extensive foreign training than the average general officer; 80 percent have studied abroad, and 73 percent did so in the United States. Despite the well-documented tensions between U.S. and Mexican military personnel over the years, Mexico has accepted monies from the International Military Education and Training program. The Mexican navy has had an officer in every U.S. Navy Command College class since 1960; moreover, "the high quality of these naval officers can be seen in the fact that thirty-three graduates have risen to flag rank, and six have gone on to lead the navy." Most important of all, Mexican officers have both studied and taught at the U.S. Army School of the Americas and attended all senior service war colleges (Cope 1996: 193).

There is no question that the United States has become the major influence in terms of Mexican military doctrine (Williams 1984: 196). More important, the United States acquired this influence in two ways – through the curricular materials used in Mexican military academies and by administrative design. When Mexican specialty arms programs were modernized in the late 1960s and early 1970s, the process was surely influenced by the fact that Mexican officers who had studied in the United States between 1964 and 1968 had received training in how to establish military schools. The pattern was repeated from 1971 to 1976 (Piñyero 1989: 116).

Mexican officers have trained at dozens of U.S. military schools and bases since World War II, but the most influential schools have been each service's war college: the Army School of the Americas at Ft. Benning, Georgia; the Inter-American Air Force Academy at Lackland Air Force Base, Texas; and the Naval Small Craft Instruction and Technical Training School at Rodman Naval Base, Panama. "These three institutions all present, in Spanish, professional courses that use U.S. curriculum models filtered through the platform delivery of a sophisticated inter-American faculty. Since the early 1960s the Inter-American Defense Board has operated the Inter-American Defense College (IADC), based at Ft. McNair, in Washington, D.C." (Ramsey 1994: 74–75).

19 A U.S. member of the Inter-American Defense Board in the 1990s described meetings of the Joint Mexico–U.S. Defense Commission as follows: "[It] was a bilateral forum which accomplished little in the eyes of the U.S. delegates. We held meetings every three months and exchanged briefings on topics of each delegation's choosing. So while we used these meetings as a vehicle to promote a better understanding of U.S. interests and programs in Latin America or on doctrinal issues, such as training, the Mexicans tended to brief us on topics such as their role in 'civil defense' of Mexico City during intense pollution, i.e., support to civilian authorities. They never briefed us on topics such as operations in Chiapas, for example" (letter to the author, March 25, 1997).

Ten percent of Mexican officers who have studied in the United States completed the U.S. Army Staff and Command School course at Ft. Leavenworth, Kansas.[20] However, the U.S. course most frequently completed by influential Mexican officers is the staff and command course offered by the Inter-American Defense College in Washington, D.C. Sixteen navy and army officers completed this course between 1952 and 1975. Since 1975 the course has enrolled at least one Mexican officer each year. Two graduates – Admirals Miguel A. Gómez Ortega and Luis C. Ruano Angulo – became secretaries of the navy. Five naval officers graduated from the U.S. Naval War College in Newport, Rhode Island, and three of them became navy secretaries.

The Inter-American Defense College, located on the same military post as the U.S. National Defense University (formerly the Army National War College), is fundamentally an inter-American institution offering a war college diploma. Its faculty are employed by the Inter-American Defense Board, not by the U.S. Department of Defense (Ramsey 1993: 39). The course consists of a nine-month curriculum (similar in scope to that of the National War College) that covers political, social, economic, and military theory. A major curricular theme is the internal threat created by poverty, disease, and social and economic injustice. Speakers from U.S. colleges and the U.S. government address the students, who include officers at the rank of lieutenant colonel and colonel, as well as some civilians. Small groups of students study topics such as labor organizations, labor and social security, human communications, education, religion, housing, and health and nutrition. They also write short research theses ("Inter-American Defense College" 1970: 21–23).

The School of the Americas has generated controversy for decades because some of its Latin American graduates later participated in notorious human rights abuses, leading critics to assert that U.S. training was responsible for these abuses.[21] Mexican graduates of the School of the Americas and its predecessor in the Panama Canal Zone have taken courses in a variety of specialties, including infantry and

---

20 These data are drawn from information on Mexican officers of general rank compiled as part of the author's Mexican Political Biographies Project.

21 There is little evidence to support a connection between the school's training and the actions of its graduates. As Cope (1995: 22) notes, 59,000 students have graduated from the school since its inception, less than 0.5 percent were guilty of misconduct, and most of these attended one- to two-week technical courses, allowing for little instructor influence. Nevertheless, in response to these accusations, the U.S. Congress trimmed the school's budget, eliminating its recruitment funds in July 1999.

In recent years, critics of the School of the Americas have argued that graduation from the program conveys prestige and power on the officers when they return to their home institutions. The present author has made this same point about the careers of Mexican officers. Yet a high-ranking Mexican officer stated that the view that training from, or holding a post in, the United States is beneficial to an officer's career was incorrect. Instead, he argued, top staff viewed these assignments as rewards for individual officers, not as credentials enhancing their upward mobility elsewhere in the armed forces.

airborne tactics, naval intelligence, and counter-insurgency. The 40–week command and general staff course is patterned on its sister course at Ft. Leavenworth, but it is taught in Spanish and classes are attended jointly by Latin American and U.S. officers ("U.S. Army School of the Americas" 1970: 89). The course does indeed have a specific political bias as part of its mission, which is to promote democratic values and, since 1990, respect for human rights (Fishel and Fishel 1997: 4).[22]

Mexican officers have shared extensive experiences in the United States. Whether those experiences have exerted a cohesive, visible influence upon Mexican military policy or civil-military relations is not clear (Fitch 1979: 361). In fact, three elements may reduce the impact of these shared experiences. First, most of the courses that Mexican officers take are of short duration (one to two weeks) and technical in nature, which allows for little interaction with U.S. instructors. Second, officers who graduated from courses taught in the Panama Canal Zone (the case until 1984) received their instruction in Spanish and in a Latin American setting, two factors that undercut the impact of new ideas presented from a different cultural and professional perspective (Cope 1995: 23). Third, brief periods of training – especially in the case of adults – are generally not sufficient to displace existing beliefs about the military's role in society or its relationship to the civilian population, beliefs that are different in the United States and Mexico (Fitch 1993: 22). A RAND Corporation evaluation of the effectiveness of international military training in the United States concluded that such training has "almost no influence over ... civil-military relations" and exerts only marginal influence, positive or negative, on the development of the officer's nation.[23]

Despite the factors that may mediate against foreign training's socializing impact, careful analysts of these training programs suggest several possible influences that may well have significant professional and political consequences. Because they are not direct, they are easily overlooked. First and foremost, the learning strategies employed in U.S. military academies are new to Mexican officers. The greatest impact of U.S. training upon these officers may well be showing them the legitimacy of exploring alternative ways to solve operational and strategic problems. Until 1995, apparently, no such approach was used at Mexican military academies below the level of the National Defense College, whose own approach may well be the product of officer experiences in the United States. General Félix Galván López, who as defense minister created this school, had previously served as assistant military attaché in Washington, D.C. and lectured frequently at the Inter-American Defense College, with which Mexico's National Defense College shares many similarities.

22 In fact, the School of the Americas is the only U.S. army academic institution where human rights instruction is incorporated into every course. For a detailed discussion of the content of the human rights program, see Ramsey 1994: 78 and 1995.

23 This is the most comprehensive evaluation of the actual socializing consequences of such training. See Taw 1993: 7, 15. A much earlier study by Lefever (1976: 90) found little evidence that U.S. training had influenced the political role of the armed forces.

Because the CDN produces the "cream of the crop" among officers reaching the rank of general, it legitimizes methodological approaches and curricular orientations previously ignored in Mexican military academies. There is strong evidence that the Advanced War College made significant changes in its programs following the publication, in the summer of 1995, of an internal national defense document that criticized severe failures in domestic military education and called for increased training in the United States (Camp 1999). Furthermore, recent directors at the Advanced War College have begun to emulate the National Defense College approach, bringing in distinguished civilian lecturers, including nationally prominent politicians. Their presentations produce a favorable environment for student officers to analyze civil-military relations.

A second potential way that U.S. training programs influence Mexican participants is through personal contacts with U.S. military personnel, both students and instructors. Fitch suggested that these contacts provide "myriad opportunities for the U.S. to communicate its policy preferences and its view of local politics" (1993: 16). In the 1950s and 1960s, the dominant message that the U.S. military attempted to convey was opposition to local and global communism, consistent with the Mexican military's perception of communism as anti-national, anti-Catholic, anti-Western, and anti-military. In the 1980s and 1990s, the United States concentrated on a strategy of low-intensity conflicts, which focuses upon domestic threats to national security (drug trafficking, terrorism, and guerrillas) and upon the need to win the "hearts and minds" of the non-combatant population, providing a new and important argument for promoting democracy and respect for human rights (Fitch 1993: 24–26).

Third, the need to communicate in English is an indirect means through which Mexican officers participating in U.S. programs expose themselves to external intellectual influences well beyond those related to military topics. Learning English as a second language opens the door to other types of literature not available in Spanish (Amos et al. 1979: 2).[24]

There is little question that Mexican officers are affected by their training in the United States. It is evident that they have passed on some intellectual influences and that these have filtered down through the armed forces. The influences emerge most strongly in domestic educational programs, primarily at the National Defense College. As the political environment in Mexico has become increasingly open, these perspectives have reinforced the methodological shift favoring pluralism, paralleling the trend in the body politic.[25] Nevertheless, attitudes toward mission and civil-military relations remain largely determined by professional training at home.

---

24 The author's book on the Mexican military, which remains unpublished in Mexico, offers a revealing example. The minister of defense obtained a manuscript copy, which circulated widely throughout the officer corps (author's interview with a member of the presidential staff, Mexico City, July 1992). The author also received, mysteriously, a 20–page, single-spaced commentary with suggestions and criticisms from an unidentified high-ranking officer.

Dissension in the Ranks

The development within the armed forces that has received most attention in Mexico and abroad involves the increasing number of military officers breaking ranks and airing their grievances in the mass media and in the political arena. The underlying thread that ties these incidents together is the state of civil-military relations. For example, in December 1994 José Francisco Gallardo, a young, brash, fast-track brigadier general, wrote an article recommending the establishment of a military ombudsman, the implication being that disputes within the armed forces were being ignored or suppressed by senior commanders. To punish Gallardo for raising this issue in the civilian arena, the armed forces arrested him on unrelated charges involving misuse of military funds. Gallardo was court-martialed and imprisoned for several years.[26]

The second case (which received substantial attention in the U.S. media) was that of Division General Jesús Gutiérrez Rebollo, reputedly one of the Mexican army's most successful commanders in the drug war. Based upon this reputation, in 1997 the minister of defense recommended Gutiérrez Rebollo to become President Zedillo's first drug czar, a recommendation passed on to General Barry MacCaffray, director general of the U.S. Drug Enforcement Agency between 1996 and 2000. Less than three weeks after assuming his post, Gutiérrez Rebollo was arrested on charges of drug-related corruption – to the embarrassment of the Ministry of Defense, the president of Mexico, and General MacCaffray. Gutiérrez Rebollo responded by alleging that his arrest was intended to shift attention away from the defense minister, who, purportedly, operated his own drug ring.[27]

In December 1998, Lt. Col. Hildegardo Bacilio Gómez, a member of the army medical corps, led a peaceful march of some fifty soldiers, along with two senators from the Party of the Democratic Revolution (PRD), down Mexico City's main thoroughfare. If one ignores Bacilio Gómez's broader political statements and his accusations of government corruption, the central issue for the marchers – all of whom had legal problems in the military – was the arbitrariness of military justice, the absence of the same constitutional protections enjoyed by civilians, and the

---

25 For example, the high command has insisted upon learning U.S. techniques from its public affairs officers so that it can present its own story to the Mexican public and enhance its image in the mass media.

26 In response to repeated demands by such groups as the Inter-American Organization of Human Rights, President Vicente Fox Quesada (2000–2006) released – but did not pardon – Gallardo.

27 Based upon a thorough interrogation of all junior officers and noncommissioned officers in Gutiérrez Rebollo's command, there is no question that he was deeply involved with known traffickers. These ties were established over several years. The real question is why Mexican military intelligence and the U.S. Drug Enforcement Agency were unaware of these blatant associations. See Dillon 1998.

inability of military personnel to appeal their cases to the high command.[28] Some high-ranking officers privately supported the marchers' complaints, as did the more astute observers in the Mexican media. Even more notable, the chief administrative officer at the Ministry of Defense went so far as to state in a press conference that some of the complaints were credible.

One of the most recent incidents to expose the armed forces to public criticism concerns the role of the army troops who comprise the president's military staff. In Mexico, the army provides logistical support and security for the president. These troops, headed by an influential chief of military staff, are a brigade composed of five battalions (three infantry, one special forces, and one artillery). The existence of an army brigade that takes its orders directly from the president has created tensions within – and, more recently, outside – the military. Within the military, there is a perception that officers who serve on the presidential staff are "politicized" and that their careers benefit from their close contact with the president and his cabinet. An analysis of promotion records substantiates this perception; these officers typically reach general rank more quickly, and all recent chiefs of military staff have become division generals, Mexico's highest active-duty rank.[29]

Because of their political duties, presidential staff officers envision themselves as an elite unit within the military, and some fellow officers view them as operating outside of conventional army units. Most presidential staff officers hold the same junior position as a regular army officer, but the presidential chief of staff typically spends many years in this unit and in presidential guard battalions.[30] Retired Division General Álvaro Vallarta Cecenã explored this issue in July 1999 and claimed that there are no differences between officers and soldiers in regular units and those in the presidential guard. He asserts that both are subject to the Code of Military Justice and that the minister of defense is ultimately responsible for the conduct of both groups. In short, Vallarta Cecenã argues that this is a non-issue;

---

28 These allegations corresponded generally to those voiced by General Gallardo during the administration of Carlos Salinas de Gortari (1988–1994) and by General Gutiérrez Rebollo and his family.

    Another case arose when the military arrested Colonel Pablo Castellanos García in March 1997 for passing confidential military information to the media. He was tried and convicted by a military court and sentenced to five and a half years in prison. His civilian lawyer stated repeatedly that he was not allowed to present any argument in his client's defense, once again raising questions concerning how the armed forces treats the legal rights of its own personnel. See *Proceso*, May 30, 1999 [www.proceso.com.mx]. See also the May 24, 1999, column by Miguel Ángel Granados Chapa in *El Diario de Yucatán* [www.sureste.com], in which he linked his case to those of Gallardo and Bacilio.

29 These include Generals Arturo Cardona Marino, Carlos Bermúdez Dávila, and Miguel Ángel Godínez Bravo.

30 Miguel Ángel Granados Chapa, author of the newspaper column "Plaza Pública," has examined the careers of chiefs of staff extending back to the time of President Miguel Alemán (1946–1952). For more details, see Camp 1995.

critics who portray tensions between the two groups, he adds, are misleading the public (*Reforma* 1999).[31]

Information on the presidential military staff's role in the 1968 massacre of student protestors in Tlatelolco Plaza in Mexico City glaringly contradicts General Vallarta Ceceña's assertion that the minister of defense has some control over troops who report directly to the president.[32] The recently published papers of then secretary of defense General Marcelino García Barragán report that President Gustavo Díaz Ordaz's (1964–1970) chief of staff, General Luis Gutiérrez Oropeza, secretly positioned ten military sharpshooters, dressed in civilian clothing, in apartment buildings surrounding the plaza. These officers were responsible for instigating the bloody confrontation between regular army troops and students (Scherer García and Monsiváis 1999).[33] The defense minister had no prior knowledge of these men or their assignment;[34] they reported directly to General Gutiérrez Oropeza, and the general reported directly to the president.[35]

31 Article 15 of the Organic Law of the Mexican Army and Air Force outlines the presidential staff and its missions.

32 General Luis Garfías Magaña, former head of the congressional national defense committee, also contradicts Vallarta Ceceña's interpretation, suggesting that the presidential military staff, through abuses, has created favorites in the military, demoralized members of the regular armed forces, and reduced the army's prestige. As Sergio Aguayo Quezada, an expert on Mexican national security and one of the few careful students of this subject, recently remarked, the presidential military staff and guards are operationally controlled by the presidency, but they are administratively responsible to the Ministry of Defense. The results "are permanent tensions between the presidential military staff and the Ministry of Defense." Although it is unlikely that an incident like the Tlatelolco massacre could be repeated, the lines of command technically make such a scenario possible. See Aguayo Quezada's discussion in *El Diario de Yucatán*, July 1, 1999 [www.sureste.com].

33 For a synopsis in English, see Dillon 1999.

34 The policy implications for the Mexican military's command hierarchy are even more significant when one considers that Gutiérrez Oropeza, a lowly brigadier general at the time, was operating autonomously from the minister of defense. The image of the regular military suffered tremendously as a result of the student massacre, and there were numerous consequences for the armed forces as an institution.

35 For a succinct summary of the details, see Beltrán del Río 1999. Gutiérrez Oropeza began his presidential staff career as an aide to President Adolfo Ruiz Cortines in May 1958, acted as chief of aides to Gustavo Díaz Ordaz when he served as minister of the interior (1958–1964), and then became Díaz Ordaz's chief of staff as a brigadier general in 1964. Díaz Ordaz placed a great deal of trust in him after he protected the president from normal school students in Chihuahua during the 1964 presidential campaign. According to *Excélsior*, Gutiérrez Oropeza was briefly relieved of his command for "misinterpreting orders" in 1968, but he served out the presidential term as chief of staff. He then became director of military industry from 1970 to 1973, a departmental-level post in the Ministry of Defense. According to Division General Luis Garfías Magaña, his classmate at the Advanced War College, Gutiérrez Oropeza was the only officer who did not reach three-star (division general) rank (*Excélsior*, September 28, 1997).

The other major source of dissension arose within the army, not between the army and other services or special civilian-oriented units. The 1995 internal army report called for revisions in the general promotion process, although it did not specify what steps should be taken. Nevertheless, it is clear that the demand for a more objective procedure came in response to inequities in the promotion process at the higher ranks. The widespread perception that the process is seriously flawed and that favoritism abounds provokes deep divisions within the military leadership, weakens its institutional cohesiveness, and creates frictions that could potentially be manipulated by civilian interests (Camp 1999: 12). One source of these perceptions is that ministers of national defense have tended to favor different military occupational specialties – such as the infantry, artillery, and cavalry (armored) – depending upon their own specialty.

Consequences for Civil-Military Relations

Naturally, the key question for most observers regards the consequences of these changing patterns for civil-military relations. The single most important characteristic of this relationship to keep in mind is that the broad outlines of civil-military interactions are determined by the larger societal setting. That setting affects institutional patterns as well as the collective attitudes of the officer corps.

The contextual variable that most distinguishes Mexico from the rest of Latin America is that the nature of its political regime led to an atypical linkage between the country's political parties and the armed forces. Given the monopoly of a one-party system, the Mexican military's only ally was the Mexican state or the Institutional Revolutionary Party (PRI) that had dominated the state since 1929. The military was never drawn into political conflicts with other parties, for either personal or ideological reasons,[36] nor did it become involved in the intense partisan encounters that characterized most of the region in the 1970s and 1980s.

However, the political landscape began to shift rapidly after 1989, and this change became significant for civil-military relations when opposition parties gained control of the federal Chamber of Deputies in 1997. The executive branch

---

36 The last serious military contender for the presidency was General Miguel Henríquez Guzmán, who ran as an opposition party candidate in 1952. A significant group of officers opposed President Miguel Alemán's (1946–1952) choice of Adolfo Ruiz Cortines as his successor, and they campaigned openly for General Henríquez Guzmán. Alemán punished these officers by granting them permanent leaves, essentially quashing their active-duty careers. (The most notable figure in this movement in terms of his later political career was Marcelino García Barragán, minister of defense during the 1968 student movement. García Barragán was forced out of the army from 1950 to 1958.) An important contemporary political thread to General Henríquez Guzmán is Cuauhtémoc Cárdenas, who campaigned for him as a student in 1951. Cárdenas is the son of General Lázaro Cárdenas (president of Mexico from 1934 to 1940) and godson of General Francisco Múgica, hence well connected to many Mexican officers.

continued to dominate the legislative agenda through the 1990s, but the potential existed – for the first time since the 1930s – for the military to seek out allies among the leadership of political parties other than the PRI. Although this did not occur formally, retired officers from all branches of the armed forces joined the Party of the Democratic Revolution and the National Action Party, and other officers signed on as party advisers. These included Division General Luis Garfías Magaña, who from 1994 to 1997 chaired the Chamber of Deputies' national defense committee as a member of the PRI and then joined the PRD in August 1997.[37]

The incident involving Lt. Colonel Bacilio Gómez, referred to earlier, illustrates the potential consequences of partisan political involvement in military affairs. The fact that two PRD senators joined Bacilio Gómez in his march down the Paseo de la Reforma contributed significantly to the demonstration's political clout and to the media attention it attracted. Along these same lines, the fact that officers and instructors at the Advanced War College have openly expressed sentiments in favor of the PAN suggests a gradual breakdown of the officer corps' nonpolitical posture.

Nevertheless, despite the fact that Vicente Fox Quesada's populism attracted many officers to the PAN, there was no evidence in the late 1990s of widespread associations, either direct or indirect, between the officer corps and opposition party leaders. In other words, opposition parties were as yet unwilling or unable to make political allies of members of the armed forces. Perhaps even more important, even after opposition parties gained control in the federal Chamber of Deputies, they were unable to force the defense minister to testify regarding specific policy questions. Instead, General Enrique Cervantes Aguirre met with legislators on his own turf at the Ministry of Defense, in effect allowing the military to shield the exchange from public scrutiny. All political parties were represented at the first of these meetings. In May 1999 armed forces commanders met with the Senate's national defense committee, again at the Ministry of Defense. Only one opposition party member attended.[38] The secretary of the Senate committee complained that "the Ministry of Defense maintains complete silence, and the defense committee is headed by a general who is more interested in helping his institution [than in helping Congress]" (Aguayo Quezada 1999).

Federal legislators made it clear to the media that they remained uninformed, as had their PRI predecessors, regarding military activities and budget matters. The *panista* secretary of the federal Chamber of Deputies' national defense committee complained in late 1998 that the proposed 1999 budget was "too general on military expenditures" and that Congress needed more information in order to evaluate the

37 Garfías Magaña has distinguished roots in the military, as well as antecedents that would reinforce a tendency to support plural politics. His father, General Luis Garfías Espinosa de los Monteros, was interim chief of staff to President Francisco I. Madero (1911–1913).

38 The others were PRI senators – Pedro León, Laura Pavón, Dionicio Pérez Jácome, General Marco Antonio Valdivia, and General Álvaro Vallarta Ceceña, head of the Senate national defense committee. Adolfo Aguilar Zinser, an independent, was the one non-PRI member.

armed forces' functions (Martínez McNaught 1998). The legislators also revealed that they had received no data from the navy or the army on the costs of combating drug traffickers, even though they had specifically requested this information. In fact, the budget made no mention of monies allocated for the armed forces' primary missions: the rebellion in Chiapas, drug interdiction, disaster relief, reforestation, and social projects (Barajas 1999). Both the PAN and the PRD tried to augment their information about the military by hiring technical advisers, a first in Mexico.[39]

The social setting's second major impact upon civil-military relations and civilian images of the military stems from an extraordinary increase in criminal activity, some of it drug related and the rest associated with a major economic downturn that reached crisis levels just as Zedillo took office. This situation led to the most controversial issue in civil-military relations in the late 1990s – the militarization of society.

The military's involvement in civil police matters had already risen significantly during the administrations of Miguel de la Madrid and Carlos Salinas de Gortari, largely because of an expanding mission in drug interdiction and eradication. Pressured by the United States, Mexico's civilian leadership (especially under Salinas) increased the role of the military because this institution was viewed as relatively uncorrupted when compared with the civilian police.

Retired officers and officers on leave have long served in state-level judicial police units and as police chiefs in various Mexican cities. Their first wholesale use came in the Zedillo administration, when hundreds of officers and troops were assigned to specific Mexico City neighborhoods in order to reduce the high crime rate, a rapidly rising priority among urban Mexicans. That effort, begun in 1994, did not yield much in the way of positive results. Nevertheless, in July 1999 the minister of defense decided to transfer 4,899 soldiers to the government's fledgling Federal Preventative Police, an agency created in January 1999 to combat organized crime across state boundaries.[40] In its 1999 report to Congress, the Ministry of Defense noted that a total of 47,411 soldiers were dedicated to combating drugs and protecting strategic installations.[41]

The most important effect of the troop transfer was to increase, very visibly, public discussion about what the armed forces' missions should be and the degree to which they should involve tasks traditionally performed by civilians. Representatives of the PRD, for example, argued that public security is not a military mission. Of course, the military has in fact performed public security tasks for decades.[42] What has changed is the extent of their involvement in performing such

39 For example, retired Colonel Miguel Ángel Rosas Paradavell was an adviser to the PRD congressional delegation in 1998–1999.

40 *El Financiero* (International Edition), July 12, 1999. The transfer also included 352 Humvee vehicles and 1,862 nine-millimeter arms. The troops were assigned to this police force until December 31, 1999 (*El Diario de Yucatán*, September 20, 1999 [www.yucatan.com.mx]).

41 "Intensa labor del ejército con énfasis en las drogas," *El Diario de Yucatán*, November 2, 1999 [www.sureste.com].

assignments and, more importantly, their visibility. Government officials and conservative commentators argue that conditions in Mexico require the military's involvement, at least temporarily (see, for example, Pazos 1999).

The second consequence is that this increase in nontraditional missions has tarnished the military's institutional image. Because the military has not succeeded in reducing either crime or drug-related activity – even as it has been implicated in several scandals involving drug-related corruption within its organizational structure – its prestige as a public institution and a political actor has suffered.

The third contextual condition that has pushed the military into the national spotlight since 1994 is the Zapatista rebellion and the emergence of the People's Revolutionary Army.[43] Some observers have suggested that as many as 70,000 troops have been assigned to missions to contain or combat the EZLN and ERP.[44] In these missions, the military has continued to use techniques traditional to its anti-guerrilla activities, involving it directly in human rights violations. Indeed, since 1995 the military has ranked as the foremost abuser of individual rights in Mexico.[45]

The human rights issue has brought the armed forces into conflict with three important actors in Mexico – the media, the Catholic Church, and human rights organizations, along with their influential sister organizations in the United States and England. In the last several years, the Mexican media have begun taking a more aggressive posture toward the military in their reporting on its anti-guerrilla activities, especially when those activities produce alleged or confirmed human rights violations. The Catholic Church, the most respected institutional voice in Mexico, has taken a very strong, unified posture on human rights, placing it at loggerheads with the armed forces. Moreover, the influential role of Bishop Samuel Ruiz as a defender of the indigenous population in Chiapas during the late 1990s made the military more suspicious of the Church, even though the military has traditionally viewed it as promoting stability.[46]

Finally, the rapid political pluralization of Mexican society has penetrated the armed forces leadership as well, especially younger officers graduating from the Advanced War College and the National Defense College. Increased professionalization

---

42 See, for example, various articles in *El Universal* and *La Jornada*, July 6, 1999.

43 Another clandestine group in Guerrero announced in 1999 that it would initiate attacks against the army. See *El Diario de Yucatán* 1999.

44 Strangely, the public attributes the failure to resolve the Chiapas situation to the presidency and the Ministry of the Interior, not to the armed forces.

45 In its June 1999 report, for example, the Miguel Agustín Pro Juárez Human Rights Center cited the military and paramilitary groups as the number one source of human rights violations for the first third of 1999. Other national and international agencies produced similar figures.

46 According to a recent Advanced War College graduate, the military is strongly opposed to evangelical groups (who are also deeply involved in the Chiapas situation) because many of them will not salute the Mexican flag, an anathema to the military.

within the military – both organizationally and in its training – complements the changing patterns in society as a whole. As suggested above, perhaps the most important impact of domestic and foreign professional influences is the seed of a changing mind-set that considers broader alternatives to how the officer corps view society, the armed forces themselves, and their mission. This shift will definitely have an impact upon civil-military relations, but the direction of change is still difficult, if not impossible, to discern.

References

Aguayo Quezada, Sergio. 1999. "Las fuerzas armadas y la alianza," *Diario de Yucatán*, August 3 [www.sureste.com].

Amos, H., et al. 1979. *U.S. Training of Foreign Military Personnel.* McLean, Vir.: General Research Corporation.

Barajas, Esperanza. 1999. "Señalan que ejército carece de recursos," *Reforma*, May 16.

Beltrán del Río, Pascal. 1999. "Ahora acusado, Gutiérrez Oropeza recibió el apapacho del sistema al que sirvió," *Proceso*, July 4 [www.proceso.mx.com].

Camp, Roderic Ai. 1995. *Mexican Political Biographies, 1935–1993.* Austin: University of Texas Press.

———. 1998. "The Educating and Training of the Mexican Officer Corps." In *Forging the Sword: Selecting, Educating, and Training Cadets and Junior Officers in the Modern World*, vol. 5, edited by Elliott V. Converse. Military History Symposium Series. Chicago, Ill.: United States Air Force Academy.

———. 1999. "Militarizing Mexico: Where Is the Officer Corps Going?" Policy Paper on the Americas. Washington, D.C.: Center for Strategic and International Studies.

Cope, John A. 1995. *International Military Education and Training: An Assessment.* Washington, D.C.: Institute for National Strategic Studies.

———. 1996. "In Search of Convergence: U.S.–Mexican Military Relations into the Twenty-first Century." In *Strategy and Security in U.S.–Mexican Relations beyond the Cold War*, edited by John Bailey and Sergio Aguayo Quezada. La Jolla: Center for U.S.–Mexican Studies, University of California, San Diego.

Diario de Yucatán. 1999. "Un grupo armado de Guerrero anuncia que iniciará ataques contra el ejército," August 19 [www.sureste.com].

Dillon, Sam. 1998. "Court Files Say Drug Baron Used Mexican Military," *New York Times*, May 23.

———. 1999. "General Illuminates '68 Massacre in Mexico," *New York Times*, June 29 [www.nytimes.com].

Fishel, John T., and Kimbra L. Fishel. 1997. "The Impact of an Educational Institution on Host Nation Militaries: The U.S. Army School of the Americas as an Effective Instrument of Policy or Merely a Scapegoat." Paper presented at the international congress of the Latin American Studies Association, Guadalajara, Mexico, April.

Fitch, Samuel J. 1979. "The Political Consequences of U.S. Military Aid to Latin America: Institutional and Individual Effects," *Armed Forces and Society* 5 (3): 360–86.

———. 1993. "The Decline of U.S. Military Influence on Latin America," *Journal of Inter-American Studies and World Affairs* 35 (Summer): 1–49.

Grayson, George W. 1999. *Mexico's Armed Forces: A Factbook.* Washington, D.C.: Mexico Project, Center for Strategic and International Studies.

"Inter-American Defense College." 1970. *Military Review* 50 (April): 21–23.

Latin American Working Group. 1998. *Just the Facts: A Civilian's Guide to U.S. Defense and Security Assistance to Latin America and the Caribbean.* Washington, D.C.

Lefever, Ernest W. 1976. "The Military Assistance Training Program," *Annals of the American Academy of Political and Social Science* 424 (March): 85–95.

Martínez McNaught, Hugo. 1998. "Pedirán explicar el gasto militar," *Reforma*, November 20.

Meisler, Stanley. 1998. "U.S. Bolstering Mexican Military, Report Says," *Los Angeles Times*, July 15.

Pazos, Luis. 1999. "La función del ejército, ¿sólo para la guerra?," *Diario de Yucatán*, August 1 [www.sureste.com].

Piñyero, José. 1989. "The Modernization of the Mexican Armed Forces." In *Democracy under Siege: New Military Power in Latin America*, edited by Augusto Varas. Westport, Conn.: Greenwood.

Poder Ejecutivo Federal. 1997. *Tercer informe de gobierno: anexo.* Mexico City: Presidencia de la República.

———. 1998. *Cuarto informe de gobierno: anexo.* Mexico City: Presidencia de la República.

Ramsey, Russell W. 1993. "U.S. Military Courses for Latin America Are a Low Budget Strategic Success," *North-South, the Magazine of the Americas* 2 (February–March): 39.

———. 1994. "U.S. Strategy for Latin America," *Parameters: U.S. Army War College Quarterly* 29 (3): 74–78.

———. 1995. "Forty Years of Human Rights Training," *Journal of Low Intensity Conflict and Law Enforcement* 4 (2): 254–70.

Reforma. 1999. "El ejército y el EMP," July 5.

Scherer García, Julio, and Carlos Monsiváis. 1999. *Parte de guerra.* Mexico City: Aguilar.

Taw, Jennifer M. 1993. "The Effectiveness of Training International Military Students in Internal Defense and Development." Santa Monica, Calif.: RAND Corporation.

"U.S. Army School of the Americas." 1970. *Military Review* 50 (April).

Williams, Edward J. 1984 "The Mexican Military and Foreign Policy: The Evolution of Influence." In *The Modern Mexican Military: A Reassessment*, edited by David Ronfeldt. La Jolla: Center for U.S.–Mexican Studies, University of California, San Diego.

12

Building the Fourth Estate: Media Opening and Democratization in Mexico

Chappell H. Lawson

In April 1997, media magnate Emilio Azcárraga Milmo – known as "El Tigre" (The Tiger) – died of cancer on his yacht off the coast of Miami (Puig 1997a). His demise provoked a predictable range of reactions across the Mexican political spectrum. Executives and financiers paid tribute to one of the country's richest men, someone who had presided over the spectacular development of Mexico's television industry (Fernández and Paxman 2000).[2] Politicians from the ruling Institutional Revolutionary Party (PRI) lamented the passing of a longtime ally. And civic groups expressed the hope that Azcárraga's demise would stimulate further openness in Televisa, the multibillion-dollar media conglomerate he controlled (*Proceso*, April 20, 1997: 6–16). In all, it was a fittingly mixed tribute for a person who was simultaneously "visionary and authoritarian, magnanimous and dictatorial, ubiquitous and reserved ... a living symbol of the mix of modern high technology and the archaic concentration of power and ownership in a single man" (Monsiváis 1997).

With the Tiger's death, control of Televisa passed to his 29-year-old son, Emilio Azcárraga Jean, and a crew of predominantly younger executives (Marín 1997; Puig 1997b; Fernández and Paxman 2000). Open and informal, Azcárraga Jean presented a stark contrast to his father (who never granted interviews). Optimists predicted at the time that the changing of the guard represented a crucial stage in Televisa's painfully slow evolution toward greater independence.

This chapter draws upon materials presented in the author's *Building the Fourth Estate: Democratization and the Rise of a Free Press in Mexico* (Berkeley: University of California Press, 2002), which contains further detail on all of the points covered here. The author thanks Kevin Middlebrook for valuable comments on earlier drafts of this chapter. He also wishes to express his gratitude to Televisa for the use its extensive video archives for content analysis, and to the Mexican Academy of Human Rights (AMDH) for access to recordings of the news programs used to analyze coverage of the 2000 presidential campaign. Mariana Sanz performed the bulk of the coding for that analysis.

1 In 1994, *Forbes* magazine listed Azcárraga as one of Mexico's wealthiest individuals, with a family net worth of US$5.4 billion. In 1995, following the sudden devaluation of the Mexican peso and ensuing economic crisis, *Forbes* estimated the family's assets at US$1.6 billion; *Forbes*, July 18, 1994, p. 194, and July 17, 1995, p. 194. See also Forbes's on-line list of billionaires [www.forbes.com/2002/02/28/billionaires.html].

The Tiger's passing symbolically marked the end of the collusion and censorship that had long governed Mexico's media. Over the previous decade, halting political reform had rendered the use of certain coercive mechanisms – direct censorship and physical repression, among others – more problematic. At the same time, market competition between different media outlets had increased their responsiveness to audiences' tastes. Meanwhile, in the print media, changes in journalistic norms had discouraged the acceptance of bribes and given rise to a range of independent publications. Despite official harassment, the financial success of these publications had earned them a great deal of autonomy. Mexico's media thus grew quite free and pluralistic during the 1990s, and they continued to do so after the PRI lost control of the presidency in 2000.

Media opening – the growth of independence and pluralism in Mexico's press – began with the emergence of independent publications during the late 1970s and early 1980s. Animated by a new, professional ethic and supported by a growing readership base, these periodicals carved out an autonomous sphere of journalism outside of the old system of media corruption and control. Several of them managed to survive various episodes of government harassment and abuse, becoming well established by the 1994 presidential elections. Over the next decade independent print journalism flourished in Mexico, eventually dominating every major media market.

By comparison to the print media, the evolution of Mexican broadcasting was a protracted and constrained process. Private cartels and official control of broadcast concessions retarded the creation of a true Fourth Estate. Beginning with the devastating Mexico City earthquakes of 1985, however, radio and television programs showed signs of independence. These changes were most rapid and pronounced in radio, as feisty talk programs came to dominate the airwaves in major cities. Television – then dominated by the notoriously pro-government media empire known as Televisa – proved more resistant to change. Nevertheless, competition from a new commercial network created in 1992–1993, as well as leadership changes in 1997, ultimately led the network to alter its coverage. By the pivotal midterm elections of 1997, Mexican broadcasting had become dramatically more independent and pluralistic. Despite the fact that television remains dominated by two private networks with links to the PRI, commercial and civic pressures have pushed television even further toward openness.

These changes in the mass media – themselves partly a result of political liberalization – rippled back across Mexican politics. Increasing coverage of Mexican civil society legitimized political activity outside the regime and promoted collaboration among opposition groups. More aggressive investigation of official misconduct discredited Mexico's authoritarian institutions and created a new context for elite decision-making. Finally, greater balance in campaign coverage – especially on television – transformed the nature of electoral competition in Mexico. Whereas Mexico's traditional media establishment lent support to authoritarian institutions and practices, its new Fourth Estate helped to dismantle the old regime and construct more democratic institutions.

The first section of this chapter describes the old system of corruption and censorship that governed Mexico's media. The second discusses the consequences of this system for press coverage. The third part traces the process of opening in Mexico's print media and broadcasting. The concluding section discusses the main political consequences of changing media coverage in Mexico: increased social mobilization, repeated political scandals, and more equitable electoral competition. It then considers the media's role in Mexican political life and the prospects for future reform.

Media Control under the Old Regime

> A despot doesn't fear eloquent writers preaching freedom – he fears a drunken poet who may crack a joke that will take hold. – *E. B. White*

For much of the period from the 1940s to the 1990s, Mexico's authoritarian regime co-opted and constrained most of the country's media. Lucrative broadcasting concessions were doled out to regime supporters with the dual purpose of bene- fiting political insiders and ensuring favorable coverage. At the same time, different factions of the political elite founded or purchased their own newspapers to advance personal and policy agendas, supporting them through an array of govern- ment subsidies. In this environment, a wide range of ideological rhetoric and a certain amount of criticism "within the system" were tolerated, even encouraged (Adler 1993a). However, core features of the political regime – presidential authority, official corruption, electoral fraud, and so forth – remained decidedly off-limits to the press. Mexico's media thus mirrored the PRI's amorphous political coalition, covering a broad ideological spectrum without questioning the fundamentals of the regime.

As with other institutions in Mexico, the regime achieved control over the press mainly through co-optation. Although Mexico's political leadership sometimes employed more direct instruments of censorship and repression, it used these instruments with greater reticence than do most autocratic regimes. As one analyst put it:

> Like most institutions in the country, the Mexican news media is nominally regu- lated by legal tenets, but it functions within a system of ill-defined practices. Such a system creates an inconsistent environment of informal rules whose net result is the promotion of self-censorship. This atmosphere is fed by a mixture of negative practices such as stringent regulations, threats against journalists, and occasional physical intervention in news organizations. More often, however, persuasion hinges on positive incentives, including subsidies and economic rewards to journalists and media owners in exchange for favorable coverage of government policies and actions (Gamboa 1995: 14).

Although relatively mild, these forms of media control proved remarkably effective. As a senior editor at Mexico's principal newsmagazine, *Proceso*, put it in 1987, "The government is like a defender in a soccer game. He stays on the man with the ball all the time, making sure he never scores a goal. It's not necessarily a dramatic thing, but it's constant" (*Los Angeles Times*, March 4, 1987).

For the most part, a confluence of interests between media owners and the political elite ensured favorable coverage. Media owners wanted, above all, a hospitable business environment in which they could prosper financially and protect their status as members of the country's elite. In order to do well economically, they needed the state to provide them with broadcasting concessions, subsidized inputs, government advertising, protection from competition, and lucrative business opportunities (including opportunities outside the media). To safeguard a system that met these requirements, and to protect their own position within it, they were willing to serve as the regime's chief informational vehicle.

Some of Mexico's leading establishment papers (such as *Excélsior* and *El Universal*) were founded at the end of the revolutionary period and traditionally maintained close ties to the PRI. Others were intertwined with the regime since their inception, or their subsequent re-purchase by members of the political elite.[2] For instance, Gabriel Alarcón's conservative *El Heraldo de México* was born *oficialista*: its first issue featured official praise for the new paper and displayed an oversized picture of then-President Gustavo Díaz Ordaz (1964–1970) on the front page (Rodríguez Castañeda 1993: 101).

Collusion between media owners and the PRI was especially pronounced in broadcasting, where concessions could be divvied up among political allies and sympathizers. When television emerged in the early 1950s, President Miguel Alemán (1946–1952) and several of his associates obtained the original licenses (Mejía Barquera and Trejo Delarbre 1985; Ramírez 1996). Ultimately these holdings were merged into Telesistema Mexicano. With the absorption of another television channel owned by a group of Monterrey-based industrialists in 1972, the group ultimately became Televisa.[3]

Televisa flourished under authoritarianism. Until government-owned channels were privatized in 1992–1993, the company claimed over 80 percent of television audiences and advertising revenues. Successive concessions helped Televisa reinforce its hegemony in television and establish a secure position in related industries (Toussaint 1995: 22–23, Fernández and Paxman 2000). In 1974 the government awarded the company Mexico's first cable television licenses, a technology it continues to dominate through its subsidiary Cablevisión. In 1980–1982, Televisa secured control of 158 government-built satellite signal-capturing stations, as well as access to the government's Morelos satellite, launched in 1985. In December

---

2 Examples in the latter category include the *El Sol* chain, which Mario Vázquez Raña purchased in 1976, and *Unomásuno*, purchased by government supporters in 1989.

3 That same year, the administration of President Luis Echeverría (1970–1976) took over Channel 13, placing Televisa (allied with the conservative wing of the PRI) and the government network (then presided over by the leftist wing of the PRI) in control of virtually all of Mexican television.

1992, the government awarded Televisa 62 vacant television frequencies without a competitive tender, allowing the network to complete a second national network (IPI 1993: 40; Toussaint 1997; Fernández Christlieb 1997). And in 1994 Televisa received two channels for high-definition television (HDTV) in Mexico (Toussaint 1997).[4] Critics referred to the corporation as a private "Ministry of Education," "Ministry of Information," or even "Ministry of Truth."[5]

To be sure, Televisa's relationship with the Mexican government was sometimes stormy. Closely aligned with the conservative wing of the ruling party, Televisa came into conflict with the government whenever the PRI's left wing controlled the presidency. During the administrations of President Luis Echeverría (1970–1976) and, to a lesser extent, President José López Portillo (1976–1982), Televisa had to fend off various government threats to tax, regulate, and even nationalize the television industry. However, these disputes are best viewed as the product of ongoing rivalry between competing factions of Mexico's ruling elite, rather than as conflict between regime opponents and supporters or between the private sector and the state. As such, they were normally resolved through collusive bargains between the rival factions. In the 1970s and 1980s, for example, conflict over television did not end in nationalization, stricter state regulation, or a greater public orientation in Mexican broadcasting. Indeed, it led to an arrangement in which Mexico's dominant private network (Televisa) agreed to provide the regime with 12.5 percent of all airtime in exchange for a tax exemption. Thus Televisa and the PRI continued to be deeply intertwined, with the network dependent upon the government for concessions and for infrastructure development, and the regime relying upon Televisa for political marketing.

Links between Televisa and the ruling party became particularly blatant during the administration of President Carlos Salinas de Gortari (1988–1994). Televisa launched an all-out defense of Salinas during his contested 1988 presidential bid, and it relentlessly supported his administration's modernizing, pro-business policies. At a fund-raising dinner in February 1993, when several leading Mexican businessmen were asked to donate US$25 million each to the PRI's 1994 presidential campaign, Emilio Azcárraga Milmo responded that he had made so much money during Salinas's term that he was prepared to contribute even more (Oppenheimer 1996: 119).[6] With public statements like "I am the number two *priísta* [PRI supporter] in the country," "we are obviously soldiers of the President," and "Televisa considers itself part of the government system," the Tiger personified

---

4 The corporation did not always get its way. For instance, Televisa failed to obtain concessions for cellular phone communications and ultra-high frequency (UHF) television. It also failed in its bid to purchase the government-owned television network in 1992–1993 (De la Vega 1997).

5 Author's interview with Amalia García, Party of the Democratic Revolution, Mexico City, August 1995; *Wall Street Journal*, May 30, 1986, pp. 1, 14.

6 Andrés Oppenheimer (1996) argued that this sum was US$70 million. Others (Ambriz 1996) have reported that Azcárraga contributed only US$30 million.

collusion between media owners and the regime (De la Vega 1997; *Proceso* May 17, 1982, p. 23; Toussaint 1995; Fernández and Paxman 2000).[7]

In addition to structuring the media market so as to benefit pro-government owners, the regime also channeled funds to communications media in exchange for favorable coverage. One of the most important ways it did so was through the selective allocation of government advertising. Official publicity was the mainstay of most pro-government periodicals throughout the 1960s and 1970s, and despite the Mexican state's perennial fiscal crisis, official publicity remained substantial in the 1980s and 1990s. The government provided about half of all advertising revenue in the print media – whether through parastatal companies, PRI–affiliated unions, the ruling party, or federal, state, and local government agencies.[8] In the broadcast media, the PRI and a series of state agencies traditionally ranked among the top advertisers in the country (Toussaint 1995: 23). Furthermore, because Mexico's largest private companies were semi-monopolistic enterprises whose competitive position depended in large measure upon government policies, a portion of purely private-sector advertising remained susceptible to political manipulation. Leading Mexican banks and firms (including Televisa itself) were major advertisers in pro-government newspapers and magazines, including publications whose limited circulations would hardly have recommended them as marketing vehicles. The party-state thus retained broad direct and indirect control over advertising revenues.

Government advertising in the print media often involved the publication of official announcements. Many times, however, newspapers printed paid inserts prepared by government ministries and disguised as bona fide newspaper articles. These *gacetillas* varied in cost, depending upon the importance of the medium in which they were published, the extent to which they were disguised, and the importance of the political moment at which they appeared. In the 1990s, for instance, a *gacetilla* might have cost US$2,000 for a quarter-page in the political section of a midsize capital daily; an equivalent spot on the front page would have cost approximately four times as much.[9] Coupled with other forms of official subsidy, these sums provided substantial rewards for publications that maintained a pro-establishment line.

. Government largesse meant that a plethora of pro-regime newspapers could operate without serious concerns regarding circulation, commercial advertising, or other normal requisites of financial viability.[10] Not surprisingly, most newspapers'

---

7 See also Aranda Luna 1986: 19; Marín 1986: 6–8; and Rivera and Hiriart 1988: 16.

8 Estimates of official advertising as a proportion of total newspaper advertising revenue have ranged from around 20 to 30 percent in 1964 to between 35 and 80 percent in the mid-1990s (Cole 1972: 79; Virtue 1995: 9; Banks 1995: 576; *Business Week*, December 20, 1993).

9 Author's interviews with various Mexican journalists, publishers, and government officials.

10 As Alejandro Ramos, editor of *El Financiero* put it, the only thing one needed to open a newspaper was five well-placed friends in the government who could secure advertising revenues from the Mexican Petroleum Company (PEMEX), the Mexican Telephone Company (TELMEX), and other state-run enterprises (Virtue 1995).

dependence upon official advertising rendered them vulnerable to government pressures, and the government frequently used its ample advertising budget to castigate independent publications or reward sympathetic ones. One of the most celebrated episodes occurred in June 1982, when President López Portillo announced that the government would no longer advertise in periodicals deemed hostile to the regime. The boycott succeeded in suffocating some smaller publications, but it failed to destroy its principal target, *Proceso* magazine, which learned to survive without government support. Subsequent administrations typically relied upon more selective boycotts of particular periodicals (Heuvel and Dennis 1995: 30–31).[11]

For pliant periodicals, the regime often supplemented government advertising with other enticements. Tax forgiveness, subsidized utilities, free service from the government-owned Notimex news agency, bulk purchases by government agencies, and credit at below-market rates were all rewards for suitably *oficialista* periodicals.[12] Perhaps the most familiar – though certainly not the most important – example was the provision of subsidized newsprint through the government-owned monopoly, Newsprint Producer and Importer, Inc. (PIPSA). As with official advertising, these subsidies could serve as both carrot and stick.

One corollary to buying off media owners was buying off their staff. Just as most publishers received ample subsidies that aligned their interests with those of the regime, so, too, most reporters accepted official bribes and favors. Print reporters, for example, traditionally depended upon three sources of income. First, and usually least important, journalists received a base salary from the medium at which they worked. These salaries were low for most reporters and abysmally low for correspondents outside their firm's home base. One reporter formerly employed by a leading Mexico City daily newspaper described his salary there as a sort of stipend that served more to indicate institutional affiliation and gain him access to other sources of remuneration than it did to provide a living.[13] The second source of income consisted of commissions (typically ranging between 8 and 15 percent) from advertising revenues that the reporter procured. Journalists in the print media were thus encouraged to regard their beat as a vehicle for soliciting advertising (including the lucrative *gacetillas*) and to treat their sources as potential customers (Riva Palacio 1995). The third source of income was even more compromising: the vast majority of Mexican journalists also accepted regular cash payments from the government agencies they covered. Until the 1990s, officials at the agencies that journalists covered passed these payments (known as *embutes, chayotes,* or simply *chayos*) directly to journalists once a month in plain, white envelopes. *Chayotes*

11 Author's interview with Alfonso Sotelo Valdés, chief financial officer of *La Jornada*, Mexico City, August 1995; author's interviews with other Mexican journalists and publishers, 1995–1996.

12 Author's interviews with various Mexican journalists and publishers.

13 Author's interview with a former reporter for *La Jornada*, Mexico City, March 1996. Salaries have increased somewhat since then.

ranged from US$75 to $1,500 per month, but they normally totaled a few hundred dollars (more than the average reporter's salary).[14]

As with official advertising, outright bribery was often accompanied by a range of favors, blandishments, or privileges. Lavish Christmas baskets, plane tickets, electronic appliances allegedly related to journalistic work, and other items often complemented *chayotes*. So did the provision of scarce government services, including medical procedures for family members, scholarships, public housing, and the like.[15] In March 1996, for example, the independent daily *Reforma* published a list of reporters and columnists who enjoyed personal police protection, a prized commodity in light of Mexico City's high crime rate. Few of those on the list had received the sort of threats that might merit such special attention (Granados Chapa 1996).

The Changing Nature of Media Control

Most of the time, corruption proved highly effective in controlling the media. Problems arose, however, when independent-minded media proved capable of surviving without government assistance. To control these renegade elements of the press, the political elite often resorted to tougher methods.

From the 1970s until 1996, two government directorates carried out official monitoring and disciplining of the media at the federal level. One was the Ministry of the Interior's (Secretaría de Gobernación) office of social communications; the other was the Office of the President.[16] Because these two entities had parallel structures and shared similar objectives, the organizational boundaries between them were not always clear.[17] In general terms, however, the Ministry of the Interior was in charge of identifying potential problems and trouble-shooting, while the presidential staff handled relations with media owners. Particularly intractable or nettlesome issues were thus passed from the Ministry of the Interior to the Office of the President.[18]

Government monitors paid close attention to the "spin" on a story, and they were not reluctant to eliminate potentially damaging stories outright. One notorious incident occurred as *Proceso* magazine was preparing to publish a report that lambasted then-Minister of the Interior Manuel Bartlett for alleged abuse of

14 Author's interviews with various Mexican journalists, editors, and publishers, 1995–1996. For further details, see Rodríguez Castañeda 1993: 229–30, 291–92, 338–40, 346–48; *Proceso*, May 23, 1983; Scherer García 1995: 46–47; Morrison 1994; Cole 1972: 87.

15 Author's interview with a Ministry of the Interior official, Mexico City, March 1996; author's interviews with various publishers, editors, and journalists, 1995–1996.

16 In 1996, the Office of the President ceded much of the direct responsibility for media management to the Ministry of the Interior, leaving the president's staff focused upon image management and other tasks associated with press relations in more democratic political systems.

17 Both groups were organized by region (Mexico City media, provincial media, and foreign media). Each regional subdirectorate was divided into print and broadcast media.

18 Author's interview with Ministry of the Interior officials, Mexico City, April 1996.

authority.[19] *Proceso* editors Julio Scherer García and Vicente Leñero received a visit from José Antonio Zorrilla Pérez, then head of Mexico's Federal Police. Zorrilla placed a bottle on the edge of the table and told them, "*Proceso* is here. Do you want it to fall off?" *Proceso* opted not to run the story.[20]

Phone calls and summons after the fact were more worrisome and normally indicated intense official displeasure. In such cases, the most common outcome was for media owners to offer – or government officials to demand – the dismissal of an offending journalist or editor. Most senior journalists (even those regarded as sympathetic to the regime) were fired at some point in their careers, and many were fired more than once. The capricious environment in which journalists operated thus encouraged circumspection and self-censorship – which was, of course, the ultimate goal.

If a media outlet failed to respond to these "gentle" tactics, the government typically stepped up harassment. In broadcasting, its ability to withdraw operating licenses hung like the sword of Damocles over radio and television owners. Given the byzantine legal structure that governed Mexico's electronic media, the government could readily find a pretext for withdrawing the license of an unruly radio or television station. Rules governing advertising, educational programming, or the percentage of content imported from abroad, for instance, could be dredged up to justify government intervention.[21] Consequently, the mere threat of withdrawing a station's concession was extremely successful in inducing broad self-censorship in most of the broadcast media.

Harassment, threats, and similar measures were usually sufficient to drive independent media into compliance or out of business. As a consequence, organized official repression against the media was seldom necessary. Nevertheless, what Mexicans call *la mano dura* – the iron fist of the state – remained available should other tactics fail. Perhaps sixty Mexican journalists were murdered between 1980 and 1996, a striking figure even if many of the murders were not related to the journalists' work.[22] The intense repression of the 1980s coincided not only with the

19 The article in question recounted how Bartlett had used his position to arrange for the rescue (or kidnapping, depending upon whose account one believes) of two younger relatives from a religious cult in Venezuela.

20 Author's interview with Carlos Marín, Mexico City, March 1996. Zorrilla was later arrested (in June 1989) for the murder of Mexico City political columnist Manuel Buendía.

21 Comparable tactics in the print media included capricious enforcement of industrial relations laws and building codes, indirect pressure through private advertisers, manipulation of the PRI–affiliated newspaper distribution network (the Mexican Union of Newspaper Sellers and Hawkers), and so forth.

22 In 1986 Mexico had the highest rate of journalists murdered of any country in the world, and until 1988 Mexico was surpassed only by such paragons of press freedom as El Salvador, the Philippines, and Nigeria (Rodríguez Castañeda 1993: 279; IPI 1994: 52–53; Article 19 1989: appendix 1; Alter 1986). According to a report published in *La Jornada* (August 3, 1992), some 52 journalists were murdered between 1982 and 1992. According to the Committee to Protect Journalists (1997), 20 reporters were murdered as a result of their work between 1985 and 1995.

emergence of independent newspapers but also with the deep penetration of drug-related corruption into Mexico's political establishment. Because revelations about drug-related corruption were particularly damaging, threats of exposure often drew especially vicious responses.

For the most part, politically motivated murders of journalists were the work of vindictive mid-level government officials, rather than any premeditated strategy by the federal government. Journalists in Mexico City in the mid-1990s rarely mentioned physical threats as a serious concern, and even provincial reporters placed much greater emphasis upon other forms of state control. One editor of a prominent provincial daily explained that his fears centered on the misguided "loyal friend" of a high-ranking official or the overzealous "subordinate with initiative," whose actions would rarely be endorsed by higher authorities.[23] In this sense, the most worrisome issue for Mexican journalists was a climate of impunity that permitted violent retaliation against the media. Although physical assaults upon journalists were not a standard element of official policy, they clearly had a chilling effect – especially because not all such crimes were solved and assailants were rarely brought to justice.

To summarize, Mexico's old system of press control relied mainly upon pervasive corruption of the media (in all its forms). As a result, there was little overt pressure from the traditional media to investigate controversial topics and publish sensitive information. Most Mexican publishers, broadcasters, editors, reporters, and distributors were part of the old system of rent seeking that benefited both them and the country's political leadership. Given the scope of positive incentives, the overt and brutal methods of media control found in most autocratic political systems were largely redundant. These were normally reserved for independent media that chose to reject the beneficence of the state and consequently might be tempted to disseminate damaging information. However, as Mexico's press became more assertive and less corrupt, overt repression increased.

The Limits of Media Control

Media control in Mexico was quite thorough. Nevertheless, the relatively mild nature of most instruments of control, as well as their somewhat selective application, permitted Mexico's press a modicum of openness even during the heyday of the old regime. The government traditionally tolerated certain types of diversity. First, the PRI's politically amorphous nature allowed an impressive degree of ideological diversity within the media. Leftist-nationalist newspapers like *El Día* coexisted with right-wing dailies like *El Heraldo de México*. The rhetorical range of opinion in the media thus reflected the breadth of the PRI's sprawling political coalition.

Second, intergovernmental, regional, and personalistic divisions within the PRI also encouraged official toleration. For example, the government-owned newspaper *El Nacional* enjoyed periods of slightly greater autonomy when its bureaucratic principals (the Ministry of the Interior, the Office of the President, the PRI, and so

---

23 Author's interview with Jorge Zepeda, editor-in-chief of *Siglo 21*, Guadalajara, April 1996.

on) disagreed.[24] Similarly, some periodicals were able to preserve a measure of independence by playing upon Mexico's federal-state cleavage. The Mérida-based daily *El Diario de Yucatán*, for instance, survived conflicts with local bosses because it rarely came into conflict with federal-level authorities. Conversely, *Proceso* magazine enjoyed good relations with certain PRI figures at the state level, even though it remained locked in perpetual conflict with the national political establishment.

Third, the government showed great sensitivity to the style and timing of critical reporting. Ritual laments (such as leftist condemnations of economic inequality and rightist complaints about official hostility toward the Roman Catholic Church) were more acceptable than focused assaults upon subjects such as official corruption or electoral fraud. Reasoned, erudite critiques couched in respectful tones met with greater tolerance than bawdy or humorous denunciations that might have mass appeal. Personalized barbs lobbed at particular officials were endured (especially when these *ad hominem* attacks represented part of the cyclical jockeying for power among rival cliques within the elite), while incisive criticism of the system as a whole was not. As Ilya Adler pointed out in his analysis of media criticism of the Mexican government during the 1980s:

> Apparent criticism by the press is the vehicle that allows competing factions within the system to carry out their political struggles.... Therefore, criticism in the press serves a central function for the PRI, a party that has to maintain a system of representation of many factions and diverse ideologies under a single body of politics by maintaining a system of negotiation in a public arena (1993a: 16).

Fourth, for government officials, the medium mattered as much as the message. Compared to radio and television, for instance, the government accorded print media greater maneuvering room – both because state intervention was easier to conceal in broadcasting and because print media, with their rather limited circulation, were deemed less threatening. Within the print media themselves, back-page articles were accorded substantially more leeway than front-page headlines, photographs, political cartoons, or editorial columns.[25] And within all types of media, minor reports had more leeway than did lead stories. Publishers and broadcasters thus confronted a hierarchy of official shibboleths, while audiences savvy enough to read between the lines could sometimes obtain a reasonably accurate understanding of events.

---

24 Author's interview with Raúl Trejo Delarbre, Mexico City, September 1995. In absolute terms, of course, *El Nacional* was never very independent. Trejo Delarbre himself resigned his position at the paper in October 1992 after a column he wrote was rejected; a number of other people associated with the paper also left soon thereafter. Author's correspondence with Trejo Delarbre, July 2002.

25 According to Jorge Zepeda, editor-in-chief of *Siglo 21*, the government cared most about front-page articles, followed by photographs, political cartoons, opinion pieces, and back-page news, in that order. Author's interview, Guadalajara, April 1996. Official sources confirmed this basic hierarchy.

The Consequences of Media Control

> I do not ask for silence. Silence is the ally of all that is negative. I simply ask that attention be paid to what is positive ... Let's not hear more about chaos and crimes ... Let's hear about the brilliant successes, the accomplishments, the steps we have taken on the road to progress. – *President Gustavo Díaz Ordaz, in a speech on Freedom of the Press Day, June 7, 1968 (quoted in Rodríguez Castañeda 1993: 119)*

In general, Mexico's system of media control proved effective in producing a relatively docile and domesticated press. Mexico's media were much more varied and independent than media in many autocratic regimes, but they were nevertheless manipulated and controlled through an array of subtle – and sometimes not so subtle – mechanisms. These mechanisms helped guarantee official control of the public agenda, selective silence on issues where the government was particularly vulnerable, and partisan media bias in favor of the PRI.

Official Control of the Agenda

Mexican officials have long been preoccupied with "governability" – that is, the need to convince an allegedly benighted population to endorse official points of view. To achieve this end, Mexico's political leadership needed to determine which issues and policies were viewed as important. Consequently, during the PRI's reign government officials sought to assure regular media coverage of high-ranking members of the party-state and their proposals. For officials in the Office of the President and the Ministry of the Interior, maintaining this sort of agenda control was at least as important as restricting criticism of the political establishment.[26]

Corruption and manipulation of access were highly effective in producing a captive media that faithfully reported what government officials said and did. Newspapers were overwhelmingly dependent upon officialdom for source material, and many headlines consisted of nothing more than assertions by prominent members of the political elite. In television, anchors often read official press releases word for word as the text appeared on the screen. And in both print and broadcast media, each presidential activity and new government initiatives were reported with appropriate deference and fanfare. Even supposedly nonpolitical broadcasts, like soap operas, were occasionally enlisted to support government initiatives on such matters as birth control, literacy, and women's education, thus contributing to the PRI–inspired myth of affirmative state action (Alisky 1981: 57–63; Bernal Sahagún and Torreblanca Jacques 1988).

Televisa's news coverage was particularly *oficialista* in the agenda-setting sense. Instead of reporting rallies, strikes, or demonstrations, Televisa tended to focus upon reports by commissions of "leading citizens" and comments from pro-government experts or politicians. Press releases and official declarations received prominent attention, but representatives of Mexican civil society rarely figured in

26 Author's interviews with Ministry of the Interior officials, Mexico City, April 1996.

news reports. For example, a lengthy story on satellite television education in 1994 did not include a single interview with a teacher, student, or parent, nor a single image of a classroom. It did, however, feature several self-congratulatory statements by government officials, as well as commentary upon Televisa's own role in the expansion of educational television (*24 Horas*, March 7, 1994). The net effect of such coverage was that Mexico's public agenda was set in government offices and disseminated downward by a captive press.

Equally crucial to maintaining control of the public agenda was ensuring the right spin on political coverage. Thus not only were government officials the main subjects of most reports, but they were also the main sources. This helped ensure that events were framed in ways that reflected ruling party paradigms. Articles on drug trafficking, for instance, featured Mexican "successes" in interdiction, along with ritual denunciations of U.S. international counter-narcotics policy. Stories about the Mexican military focused upon relief and rescue operations, ceremonial events, and patriotic paeans to the national army. Coverage invariably presented the political system overall as a democracy – albeit a special brand of democracy that made it uniquely suited to Mexican reality. And it portrayed society as divided mainly along economic lines, typically in a way that mapped neatly to the PRI's state-corporatist sectors. The media systematically avoided alternative political viewpoints, such as those that presented political contestation as a struggle between organized groups in civil society and an entrenched authoritarian regime.

Selective Silence

With their silence about the massacre of student demonstrators in Mexico City's Tlatelolco Plaza in 1968, Mexico's traditional media earned a well-deserved reputation for avoiding sensitive issues.[27] According to one maxim, there were traditionally three "untouchables" in Mexico: the president, the national army, and the Virgin of Guadalupe, Mexico's patron saint. As far as the government was concerned, however, unmentionable issues extended to topics that exposed the true workings of Mexico's postrevolutionary political regime. Consequently, the media ignored or downplayed stories on official corruption, drug trafficking, electoral fraud, opposition protest, political repression, and the activities of the Mexican military, in favor of collusion or strategic avoidance. In certain cases, media silence reached absurd proportions. For example, during a particularly bad economic period in the 1980s the National Autonomous University of Mexico's radio station in Mexico City (Radio UNAM) was forbidden to use the word "inflation."[28]

---

27 The media's reaction (or lack thereof) to the massacre figures prominently in various accounts of the tragedy and in the memorial that now stands in Tlatelolco Plaza.

28 Author's interview with Juan Luis Concheiro, editor of *Motivos*, Mexico City, August 1995. However, others familiar with Radio UNAM have argued that it enjoyed substantial freedom (on both economic matters and student activism) during most of the 1980s. Author's correspondence with Raúl Trejo Delarbre, July 2000.

As opposition leaders were quick tos point out, Mexican television coverage was particularly Orwellian.[29] According to one observer:

> Regular viewers of Televisa are more likely to know about unrest in Madrid, Bogotá, or Chicago than about domestic problems. The picture of Mexico normally presented on its main news program is that of a calm, democratic nation where bullfights are about all that ever turns bloody (DePalma 1994: 4).

Until the mid-1990s, sensitive topics simply were not part of television news. Street demonstrations, for example, typically surfaced in the news only in the context of the traffic congestion they provoked. Coverage of the economy tended to be very positive, even during bad times, and electoral irregularities were studiously ignored.[30] Equally telling was Televisa's avoidance of leading members of the political opposition. Televisa traditionally maintained a list of two to three dozen "vetoed" persons, mainly leftist opposition figures, whom reporters were not allowed to interview. During the Salinas administration, for instance, this list included Cuauhtémoc Cárdenas, leader of the Party of the Democratic Revolution (PRD); deposed petroleum workers' leader Joaquín ("La Quina") Hernández Galicia; former Mexico City mayor Manuel Camacho (after his defection from the PRI in 1994); and human rights activist Rosario Ibarra.[31]

The emergence of independent sources of information during the 1980s and 1990s – and the continual operation of a popular rumor mill – sometimes made complete silence about particular issues or events an untenable strategy. In such circumstances, one familiar pattern for dealing with damaging material was to report official responses to the events in question without providing any orienting context. Consequently, passionate denials of official wrongdoing would appear out of nowhere in the political sections of major Mexico City papers, as if the charges that provoked them had previously been reported. The announcement of new anticorruption initiatives, for example, gently alluded to spectacular episodes of graft, and coverage of stolen elections typically consisted of official retorts, asseverations, and pledges of clean elections in the future. Establishment media also adopted this approach with a number of other salient but delicate subjects: allegations that President Miguel de la Madrid (1982–1988) had deposited approximately US$162 million in foreign bank accounts in 1984, the 1991 ambush (by elements of the Mexican army) of federal police agents pursuing drug traffickers in Veracruz, and electoral fraud in Chihuahua in 1986.

Televisa's handling of the PRI's secret fund-raising banquet (at which Televisa owner Emilio Azcárraga Milmo pledged more than US$25 million to the party's 1994 campaign) was a classic example of such selective coverage. Not only did

29 Author's interview with Amalia García, Party of the Democratic Revolution, August 1995.
30 Author's content analysis of *24 Horas* (then Televisa's main nightly news program) during the first two weeks of March in 1986, 1988, 1990, 1992, 1993, 1994, 1995, and 1996.
31 Author's interview with a former reporter for Televisa, Mexico City, March 1996; author's interview with Gina Batista, reporter at Channel 40, Mexico City, March 1997.

Televisa's principal news program, *24 Horas*, never mention the dinner itself, but it also devoted three days of sustained coverage to spinning the ensuing scandal. The network broadcast a lengthy story comparing the fund-raising activities of different political parties around the world, followed by a brief "investigative" report revealing that the Mexican Communist Party (PCM) had previously received money from the Soviet Union. Additional coverage reported campaign finance reforms proposed by an embarrassed Salinas administration in the wake of the scandal (*24 Horas*, March 1–4, 1993).

The net effect was that potentially shocking events were reported without much in the way of attention, analysis, or follow-up. Consequently, such incidents tended to surface fleetingly and then to disappear, rather than snowballing into scandal. After a day or two in the back pages, the real story would simply fade away amidst a cacophony of conflicting claims and explanations, never having reached the electronic media or the front pages of traditional newspapers.

Electoral Bias

Selective media silence and disproportionate attention to official voices went hand in hand with blatant partiality toward the ruling party during electoral campaigns. Over the course of Mexico's 1994 presidential election, for example, the PRI received approximately 51 percent of television coverage, 89 percent of advertisements, 50 percent of front-page newspaper space, and 66 percent of newspaper photographs (Alianza Cívica 1994; Acosta Valverde and Parra Rosales 1995). These figures represented only a limited improvement over Mexico's 1988 elections, in which coverage of the PRI exceeded 80 percent of total campaign coverage in most media (Adler 1993b; Arredondo Ramírez, Fregoso Peralta, and Trejo Delarbre 1991; Morrison 1994). Bias was even was more flagrant in earlier contests, in which opposition parties' shares of campaign airtime were essentially rounding error on the PRI's percentage.

The tone of coverage also varied dramatically across parties and candidates. In the 1988 campaign, broadcasters reading news about the ruling party tended to be enthusiastic and respectful; footage featured large crowds and patriotic symbols. In contrast, they read news about the opposition in a flat or sarcastic tone, with few favorable supporting images (Adler 1993b: 155). One particularly striking example came during the campaign's closing period. Jacobo Zabludovsky, anchor of Televisa's principal nightly news broadcast, described a rally in Veracruz in favor of PRI candidate Carlos Salinas as "more than a traditional political act ... [It was] an artistic spectacle, full of color, human warmth, and spontaneity" (*24 Horas*, March 8, 1988). The rally in question was certainly colorful, featuring local folk dances and related pageantry. And Salinas's reception was noticeably warmer than at his previous tepid campaign appearances. But it is difficult to imagine a more carefully scripted and *less* spontaneous event than a PRI rally at the close of a presidential campaign.

Not only did Televisa accord strikingly sympathetic coverage to the PRI, but it also played a crucial role in facilitating more sophisticated PRI electoral strategies. Until the late 1990s, Televisa gave disproportionate coverage to minor political parties at the expense of both the center-right National Action Party (PAN) and the Cardenist left. Such coverage reinforced the notion that the PRI confronted a fragmented opposition of fringe political groupings. Moreover, because many smaller parties were actually PRI satellites whose representatives voted consistently with the government once they were in office, coverage of these parties aided the PRI in its strategy of political brand proliferation.

One intriguing example of more subtle media bias occurred during the 1994 presidential election, which took place in an atmosphere of increasing political instability.[32] Throughout the campaign, Televisa gave copious coverage to instances of violence in other countries (including Guatemala, which borders the turbulent Mexican state of Chiapas).[33] Subsequent studies have lent credence to the notion that fear of violence was a crucial factor in generating support for the PRI, long viewed as a guarantor of political stability (Cinta 1999; Poiré 1999). In other words, by selectively accentuating the threat of upheaval and implicitly framing the election in terms of "stability" versus "instability," Televisa helped generate electoral support for the ruling party. Such framing played especially well against the Left, which Mexican television and official propaganda had attempted to associate in the public mind with polarization and violence.

Another notorious example of framing was economic reporting during the Salinas presidency. Together with expert image management on the part of the president's staff, careful media framing of key events conveyed the impression of rapid social and economic progress. These media campaigns contributed to a sweeping PRI victory in the 1991 legislative by-elections and a solid PRI win in the 1994 presidential contest.

However, the media's role in the electoral process went beyond acting as cheer-leader and strategist for the incumbent party. The press was a crucial participant in the rituals of power that legitimized the PRI's hegemonic rule. Unlike many autocracies, the Mexican political system during the PRI's reign did not derive its legitimacy from a single dominant set of norms or institutions. Its claim to political authority rested upon a peculiar combination of revolutionary heritage, state-corporatist intermediation, electoral victory, economic stewardship, and simple tradition. At least until the 1990s, therefore, elections in Mexico served a different function from the competition and choice associated with established democracies. They formed part of a complex political pageantry that simultaneously invoked several of the PRI's claims to legitimacy.

---

32 Worrisome events included the January 1994 uprising by the Zapatista Army of National Liberation (EZLN) in Chiapas and the March 1994 assassination of PRI presidential candidate Luis Donaldo Colosio.

33 Author's content analysis of Televisa news coverage during the 1994 campaign; author's interview with Miguel Acosta, director of media monitoring at the Mexican Academy of Human Rights, Mexico City, April 1996; author's interview with a senior official in the Office of the President, Mexico City, March 1996.

As Ilya Adler argued in his penetrating analysis of the 1988 presidential election, the media helped generate an aura of suspense, drama, and vicarious participation around the unveiling of the PRI's chosen presidential candidate (1993b). During this pre-election period, the media provided a forum for contending factions within the ruling party – technocrats and politicians, rightists and leftists, peasants and laborers – to advance their positions and mobilize support for their favored contenders (known as "pre-candidates"). Once the outgoing president chose the official PRI candidate, the media scrupulously prepared the rest of the country for his ultimate ascension to power. The establishment print media acted as a sort of royal scribe, accompanying the "official" candidate on his campaign tour and chronicling the activities of his court (Adler 1993b). At the same time, saturation coverage in the broadcast media built the candidate up from a mere political operator to an individual of national and historic stature, worthy of being invested with the vast power of a modern Mexican president.

Even in the 1990s, traditional elements of the media continued to play this sort of role. Daniel Hallin's analysis of campaign coverage during the 1994 presidential election revealed that, in addition to favoritism for the PRI, Televisa's reporting nurtured existing authoritarian paradigms. Televised images of future president Ernesto Zedillo (1994–2000) typically portrayed him distributing land titles and similar patronage to duly submissive groups of peasants or poor urban dwellers. Such images tended to reinforce a traditional notion of political participation in which "citizenship" consisted of waiting passively for clientelistic benefits handed down by a paternalistic state (Hallin 1995: 14). In other words, television coverage attempted to legitimate key elements of a system that many of its own supporters viewed as anachronistic.

Media Opening in Mexico

You ask me what relationship we have with the authorities. I don't know. But I do know one thing: if I pay my taxes, if I pay for my newsprint, if I have no outstanding debts to the government, no one can tell me how to run my newspaper. – *Carlos Payán,* La Jornada *(author interview, Mexico City, August 1995)*

The old rules don't operate. We are prevailing over a political system, and suddenly there are those who want it to work according to the old rules, but these no longer count.... We don't dwell on the previous control of the press through newsprint quotas from PIPSA; it's something that is no longer debated. I believe that soon we will no longer remember discussing whether censorship rules apply.... We are in a process of modernization, and I don't believe anyone can stop us – from inside or outside. There is freedom in the print media, in radio. And now we are starting to see it in television.... We don't worry about what the government will think of what we're doing. – *Javier Moreno Valle, Channel 40 (in Corro 1996)*

Mexico's old system of media control began to break down with the emergence of major independent publications beginning in the late 1970s. Reporters and publishers with different professional visions challenged the traditional style of journalism and, with it, Mexico's broader political regime. A more demanding public embraced this new journalism, providing a stable financial base and encouraging other publications to experiment with more independent coverage. Although Mexico's emerging Fourth Estate had to overcome a host of obstacles erected by the government, the independent media's financial success and journalists' desire to practice a new style of reporting sustained them. Ultimately, Mexico's halting process of political liberalization removed the most overt threats to the survival of independent publications. By the mid-1990s, these magazines and newspapers were well ensconced in Mexico, and Mexico's political establishment appeared resigned to their existence.

Meanwhile, Mexico's electronic media were also evolving. Starting with the 1985 earthquakes in Mexico City, a series of dramatic events highlighted how out of step most electronic media were with their audiences. Assertive talk-radio shows that understood the potential rewards of independence captured a large audience, bringing them higher ratings and advertising revenues. Competitive pressures soon encouraged other broadcasters to introduce changes, and independent programming came to dominate Mexican radio news.

By the mid-1990s, even Mexican television – long the bastion of support for the one-party regime – was showing signs of openness. Pressure from opposition parties and civic groups encouraged the country's principal private network, Televisa, to experiment with more critical coverage. These public pressures became financial imperatives after the 1992–1993 privatization of government-run channels, Televisa's loss of market share to its newly created rival (Televisión Azteca), and the 1994–1995 economic crisis. Although Televisión Azteca, like Televisa, was linked to politicians from the old regime, commercial pressures led it to experiment with more independent coverage, and the subsequent battle for market share prompted Televisa to follow suit.[34] Changes at Televisa accelerated after the death of Emilio Azcárraga Milmo in April 1997 and the accession of his son, Emilio Azcárraga Jean. As Azcárraga Jean described his philosophy:

> I'm not a politician … Furthermore, I don't believe that having a good relationship with political figures will benefit us in terms of what matters. I believe in the ratings. I don't think that having a good or bad relationship with the minister of the interior is going to change my ratings, which in the end is what I care about – getting the best ratings possible.… I don't mix ideology with programming (Puig 1997c).

---

34 In 1996, it was revealed that Raúl Salinas, elder brother of President Carlos Salinas, had manipulated the process in favor of Televisión Azteca owner Ricardo Salinas Pliego, and that Salinas Pliego had agreed to invest some US$29 million for Raúl on the eve of the privatization. Televisa originally aired the charges on July 7; newscaster Ricardo Rocha followed up in his weekly television program *Detrás de la Noticia* on October 27, 1996. Several other media outlets, especially *Proceso* magazine, subsequently covered the story (Delgado 1996, Galarza 1996).

By the July 1997 midterm elections, then, Mexican television had been transformed from a private "Ministry of Truth" into a semi-competitive, commercially oriented medium.

A more detailed account of the transformation of Mexico's press is beyond the scope of this chapter.[35] It should be noted, however, that this transformation was not primarily a product of the liberalization of Mexico's political system or the increasing competitiveness of Mexican elections. Rather, it was a bottom-up process driven largely by journalistic norms (in the case of nontraditional print media) and market competition (in the case of both print and broadcast media). As a result, changes in the media exercised an important independent influence upon political developments in Mexico.

With the benefit of hindsight, the evolution of Mexico's print media is perhaps best divided into two periods. The first, from 1976 to 1993, was characterized by the founding of a number of independent publications, all of which came into repeated conflict with the government. Independent publications struggled to carve out a niche for themselves while simultaneously stealing market share from more traditional, pro-government periodicals. Ultimately, many of them succeeded. This phase culminated with the launching of the country's leading newspaper, *Reforma*, in 1993.

During the second, post-1993 period, independent media spread across Mexico. New publications, often founded by publishers of already established independent newspapers, sprouted up across the country. In addition, previously pro-government newspapers (such as *El Universal*) began to reorient editorial policies and upgrade their facilities in order to survive. Despite occasional acts of resistance from members of the political elite (especially outside the Mexico City area), independent publications blossomed.

As with print media, it is also possible to distinguish between "emergence" and "consolidation" in the evolution of Mexican broadcasting. The first phase began in 1985 with the Mexico City earthquakes and culminated in 1997 with the death of Emilio Azcárraga Milmo. During this period, market competition forced both radio and television stations to experiment with more independent coverage. Because there were many more radio stations than television broadcasters in each media market, competition was more pronounced – and reorientation in reporting more rapid – in radio. However, with the privatization of government-owned television stations and the incipient penetration of new communications technologies, Mexican television also began to feel the pinch of market competition. Although official resistance was sometimes effective in restraining media opening, it could not fully hold back the tide.

Since 1997 the trend toward openness has become even more pronounced. Televisa has completed its transition to an essentially commercial network, governed more by the demands of the market than by those of the Ministry of the Interior.

35 For further details, see Lawson 2002.

At the same time, new media concessions in major Mexican cities (including Mexico City, Monterrey, Guadalajara, and Chihuahua) and the spread of new information technologies (such as direct broadcasts from satellites) have spawned alternative sources of programming. The mass media's transition to more open coverage remains incomplete, but tectonic shifts in the Mexican press have occurred – with pivotal consequences for Mexican politics.

The Consequences of Media Opening

> Massacres in Guerrero are not new. What is new is that they are broadcast on television. – *Roberto Zamarripa (1996)*

Under the old regime of press control, media coverage was marked by selective silence on issues of official sensitivity, official dominance of public discourse, and electoral bias in favor of the PRI. Together, these three elements helped legitimize and sustain Mexico's one-party system. Not surprisingly, the transformation of Mexico's media undercut each of these traditional forms of coverage. Press-release journalism was displaced by coverage of Mexico's burgeoning civil society; selective silence gave way to vigorous investigation of potential scandals; and electoral bias succumbed to relatively balanced reporting on rival parties and candidates. Collectively, these changes helped undermine the old regime and promoted democratic transition.

The Efflorescence of Civil Society

A central feature of news coverage under Mexico's old media regime was official dominance of the public agenda. Not only did the president and other officials garner the lion's share of news coverage, but they also served as the primary sources for news reports. Consequently, establishment figures were permitted to interpret and frame virtually all newsworthy events. The discourse presented in the news media was thus the discourse of Mexican officialdom. News coverage of everything from natural disasters to political protest reflected the government's language and spin.

One consequential shift in media coverage since the mid-1980s concerns the space awarded to civil society. Content analysis of Televisa programming indicates that the time devoted to the activities and pronouncements of government officials dropped from about 60 percent of evening news coverage in the late 1980s to less than 40 percent in the mid-1990s.[36] Changes in radio have been even more significant, and those in the print media, more dramatic still.

It is difficult to document with precision the impact of changes in press coverage upon Mexican civil society in the second half of the 1980s and in the 1990s. Most

---

36 Data are based on the author's content analysis of the Televisa news show *24 Horas* during the first two weeks of March in 1986 (63 percent), 1988 (61 percent), 1990 (64 percent), 1992 (62 percent), 1993 (41 percent), 1994 (41 percent), and 1995 (37 percent).

likely, the emergence of independent periodicals both reflected and encouraged the new social movements that emerged in Mexico during this period (Aguayo Quezada and Parra Rosales 1997). An increasingly vibrant civil society provided the readership base for independent publications, but independent publications also helped new social movements gain recognition and shaped their identity and strategies. In this sense, Mexico's nascent Fourth Estate played a decisive role in creating an autonomous public sphere in which intellectuals, activists, and representatives of the political opposition could debate political and social issues. The ultimate result of this interaction was a new civic discourse in the print media that eventually pervaded the rest of the political establishment.

One element of this discourse was a nuanced view of what democracy really means in practice – not a panacea for all social ills nor simply the holding of elections, but a constellation of political institutions designed to ensure rulers' accountability to the ruled. In the mid-1990s, as Mexico's political transition progressed, independent publications began explicitly to target specific institutions of the old order.[38] These included not only electoral rules, but also a range of long-standing norms and practices (hyper-presidentialism, endemic corruption, judicial subordination, and so on) that must change for Mexico to complete its democratic transition. The result was a sweeping, clear, and (at least among the reading public) widely shared agenda for political reform and institutional renovation in Mexico.

Another element of the new discourse in Mexico's independent print media was the reframing of political contestation. In the early 1980s, most of the press adhered to what might be termed an "old regime" framing of politics. From this perspective, the political system represented a unique variety of democracy that best suited postrevolutionary Mexican society. As such, Mexico's political system was the only legitimate form of government for Mexicans, and the "official" party was the only valid representative of the Mexican population as a whole. Thus press coverage naturally focused upon government officials and PRI–affiliated associations, while it largely ignored independent civic organizations. When these organizations were discussed at all, they were often presented as isolated pressure groups with rather parochial agendas.

Of the few journalists who offered different perspectives, most invoked Marxist framings of politics. Although they might not have accepted all elements of the Marxist credo (such as communist teleology or the necessity of violent revolution), they tended to analyze politics in terms of class conflict. Of course, this framing of political contestation had the automatic effect of marginalizing the people who adopted it. Because the PRI already occupied the social reformist position on the ideological spectrum, it was easy for the ruling party to paint opponents on the left as irresponsible, extremist, or simply out of touch with the majority of the population. In addition, ideological framings of politics conferred little legitimacy upon

37 Author's interview with Miguel Acosta, Mexican Academy of Human Rights, Mexico City, April 1996.

civic groups that did not endorse leftist political goals, including organizations aimed at promoting electoral integrity, democracy, or human rights.

In the 1980s, however, independent journalists reporting on Mexico's emerging civic movements began to look at politics and society from a different perspective. A new political framing emerged from their reports and commentaries, one quite distinct from both the old-regime and leftist-ideological framings in traditional media coverage. This way of presenting politics described organized groups of citizens less in terms of PRI sectors or social classes and more in terms of "civil society." Political contestation ceased to be a battle between the Mexican Revolution and the reactionaries, or even between the rich and the poor. Instead, independent media portrayed a struggle between Mexico's emerging civic groups and Mexican officialdom, the latter represented by the state and the PRI. By 1988 such civic interpretations of politics were common at independent publications like *Proceso* and *La Jornada*.

This sort of coverage by Mexico's independent press played a crucial role in the strengthening of civil society. As two noted human rights activists have argued, it was especially important for organizations such as human rights and electoral observation groups that focused explicitly on the issue of regime change:

> Important [for the emergence of civic groups] was the simultaneous emergence of other organizations, among them, independent communications media. In the field of human rights and nongovernmental organizations, the appearance of *Proceso* magazine and *La Jornada* newspaper was crucial. These media took as one of their editorial lines the defense and promotion of human rights, and from the beginning they granted legitimacy to nongovernmental organizations … [The result was a] symbiosis between certain sectors of society and those media (Aguayo Quezada and Parra Rosales 1997: 29).

In other words, social mobilization gave independent media something to write about, and this coverage in turn contributed to the persistence and growth of popular organizing. Independent journalists who traced their own journalistic vision to the "then-incipient expressions of civil society" of the early 1980s sought to reinforce these expressions in their reporting (editorial, *La Jornada*, September 19, 1994). Their reports conferred upon civic activists a measure of prestige they would not otherwise have had, gave them a broader sense of mission, and enhanced the legitimacy of their claims against the state. Press coverage thus increased the perceived benefits of organizing and lowered the perceived risks of getting involved, encouraging the sort of political mobilization that was already under way in Mexico. By the mid-1990s, Mexico's ruling party confronted both an increasingly independent press and an increasingly vocal, well-organized civil society.

Changes in press coverage did not single-handedly propel political organization in Mexico, unify the opposition, or force the government to reach an accommodation with its opponents in civil society. Media opening did, however, make these outcomes more likely. In other words, the development of a new civic discourse did not reshape Mexico's political landscape, but it did provide actors with a new map of that landscape – one that altered their perceptions of routes, distances, and obstacles on the road to democratization.

The New Politics of Scandal

Perhaps the most dramatic consequence of the transformation of Mexico's media has been increasingly assertive coverage of previously "closed" subjects. Stories about drug trafficking, official corruption, electoral fraud, and government repression now appear regularly in publications, radio shows, and even television programs. Practices that were once reliably concealed are now exposed to the harsh light of public scrutiny. One predictable result of such assertiveness has been the efflorescence of political scandal in Mexico.

It is difficult to overstate the impact of these changes in coverage upon Mexican political life. In the second half of the 1990s, revelations by independent media played a crucial role in bringing down at least three hard-line PRI governors (Rubén Figueroa in Guerrero, Sócrates Rizzo in Nuevo León, and Jorge Carrillo Olea in Morelos), as well as a number of other prominent figures. In the case of Figueroa, media coverage culminated in the broadcast on national television of a videotape showing the massacre of unarmed peasant activists by Guerrero state police, which compelled a reluctant President Zedillo to force Figueroa's resignation.

During the 1990s, scandals provoked a series of physical assaults against the press by corrupt officials fearing exposure. Indeed, as Mexico's press became more assertive and less corrupt, overt repression increased. However, these attacks had little impact upon the independent media's willingness to pursue investigations of scandalous activity. Consequently, politicians had to adjust to the new, media-created political context. One classic example occurred in early 1995, when *Reforma* and *La Jornada* newspapers reported that newly appointed education minister Fausto Alzati had never received the Harvard doctorate he claimed on his curriculum vitae. As the scandal was breaking, *Reforma* received a flurry of letters from other government officials who had recently discovered "typographical errors" in their own résumés.

Even when scandals did not lead to prosecutions or resignations, they still played a key role in discrediting authoritarian institutions and practices in the public eye. For instance, by revealing the pervasive corruption that characterized one-party dominance in Mexico, scandals did to the PRI what reporting on Argentina's "dirty war" during the mid-1980s did to that country's military establishment (Bailey and Valenzuela 1997). The web-like interconnectedness of many scandals in the mid-1990s – especially those involving drug trafficking, the Salinas family, or both – only accentuated this effect (Morris 1999).

Survey data from the late 1990s bear out the finding that many Mexicans perceived their government to be more corrupt than ever before, despite the fact that graft was certainly less extreme under President Zedillo than under some previous administrations. These same data also suggest a strong connection between media consumption, perceptions of corruption, and antipathy toward the PRI (Lawson

2002: 151–54). In other words, media-induced scandals played an important longer-term role in delegitimizing Mexico's old regime and generating public support for political change.

Electoral Coverage

One salient feature of media bias under the old regime was favoritism for the "official" party during electoral campaigns. Opposition candidates were presented in an unflattering light (if they were presented at all), and PRI contenders typically received a much greater share of media coverage than of the popular vote. These biases were particularly pronounced on television, which was by far the most important source of most voters' political information.[38] Consequently, Mexican viewing audiences received a homogenous media message designed to generate support for the ruling party, discredit regime opponents, and fragment the partisan opposition.

In the 1990s, however, television coverage began to shift substantially. Although the PRI received as much as 80 percent of television airtime in 1988, its 1994 share approximated its proportion of the national vote (around 50 percent). By 1997, the PRI received only about 34 percent of campaign-related coverage devoted to the main parties – far less than in previous elections and less than the 39 percent of the national vote that it received (Lawson 2002: 159–61).

These changes in the volume of coverage were marked by an equally dramatic shift in tone. In 1988, television reports depicted the PRI as Mexico's only real political party, opposed by a motley assortment of fringe groups. Even in 1994 the PRI could count upon special treatment, ranging from receiving favorable visual treatment to appearing first whenever coverage of the presidential candidates was aired. By 1997, however, televised reporting treated opposition candidates as serious contenders and portrayed opposition parties as responsible political actors with reasonable social agendas (Lawson 2002: 52–55).[39] Even issue-related coverage was not particularly favorable to the PRI because it focused upon the lingering economic effects of the 1994–1995 crisis and a series of recent scandals. The net effect of these changes was to present Mexican audiences with a vastly different set of political cues than they were accustomed to receiving. As one might expect, survey data from the 1997 campaign have since demonstrated that changes in news coverage had a powerful impact upon voters' choices – perhaps sufficient to determine the electoral outcome (Lawson 2002: 160–70).

Survey data from the 2000 presidential race confirm both the balanced nature of television coverage and the potent influence this coverage can have upon public opinion. Despite some mild biases in the tone of coverage, especially against leftist

38 Polls suggest that between two-thirds and three-quarters of Mexicans rely upon television primarily or exclusively for their information about politics and current events.

39 The 1997 campaign included not only legislative races but also the first election since the 1920s for the mayor of Mexico City. Because the latter post was so important, and because all three major-party candidates were of national stature, the race received saturation coverage on nightly news programs broadcast across the country.

opposition candidate Cuauhtémoc Cárdenas, reporting on the 2000 campaign was remarkably equitable. All three major candidates (Vicente Fox, Francisco Labastida, and Cárdenas) received roughly the same amount of coverage on Mexico's two main nightly news programs.[40] Moreover, despite criticism from certain opposition activists, rigorous and systematic analysis of the quality of images indicates that the tone of reporting was quite balanced.[41] As in 1997, survey data support the notion that more even-handed coverage did have a significant effect upon perceptions of the major parties and candidates, an effect that generally worked to Fox's advantage (Lawson and McCann 2001).

Conclusion

The changes in Mexican media coverage over the course of the 1980s and 1990s were nothing short of dramatic: attention to the perspectives of civil society replaced official dominance of the public agenda; selective silence gave way to vigorous investigation of previously "closed" topics; and balanced coverage of opposition parties replaced electoral bias in favor of the PRI. The result of these transformations was a new political context in which civic mobilization increased, scandals became commonplace, and opposition parties faced a more level electoral playing field. These changes in Mexico's communications media, and their impact upon political life, are summarized in table 12.1.

Neither the changes in Mexico's media nor the impact of these changes upon Mexican political life have been total. Concentration of ownership, corruption, and other legacies of authoritarian rule continue to limit the media's ability to reinforce democratic norms and institutions. Furthermore, the mass media themselves have hardly been the only actor in Mexico's political transition. Political parties, governmental elites, grassroots organizations, armed guerrillas, and other groups all played – and continue to play – a role in shaping the country's political trajectory. Nevertheless, the emergence of independent media has exercised a profound influence upon Mexican politics.

In the wake of democratization, this influence will only be more pronounced. Mexico's "scandal machinery" – that nexus of executive-branch leakers, congressional

---

40 Data from the Federal Electoral Institute (IFE) indicate that between January 19 and June 30, 2000, the PRI received 34 percent of television coverage devoted to the three main presidential candidates on Mexico's two principal nightly news programs; the "Alliance for Change" (led by Vicente Fox) received 39 percent of coverage; and the "Alliance for Mexico" (led by Cuauhtémoc Cárdenas) received 28 percent. *Reforma*'s monitoring of all shows broadcast on the two main networks found that Labastida received approximately 34 percent of all coverage devoted to the three major candidates, compared to about 36 percent for Fox and 29 percent for Cárdenas.

41 Author's content analysis of a random sample of Mexico's two main nightly news programs from February 15, 2000 through June 28, 2000. Altogether, the analysis included 57 different indicators of the tone of coverage. For further details, see Lawson and McCann 2001.

Table 12.1: **Changes in Media Coverage in Mexico and Their Political Consequences**

Coverage under the Old System	Coverage by Mexico's Emerging Fourth Estate	Political Consequences of Changes in Coverage
Selective silence	Investigation of closed topics	Scandals and old regime delegitimation
Official agenda control	Attention to civil society	Social mobilization and new civic discourse
Electoral bias	More balanced campaign coverage	Increased support for opposition parties

investigators, nosey journalists, and commercially oriented broadcasters – has now become a key fact of political life. Beyond the question of scandals, the intensity of media scrutiny of governmental decision making is striking, and it is likely to become even more intense following the passage in 2002 of the Law on Transparency and Access to Public Governmental Information (Mexico's equivalent of the U.S. Freedom of Information Act). Government officials are keenly aware of the need to "sell" their policies through the media. Likewise, most civic activists seem to understand that calling attention to their causes through the media is one of the best ways to influence officials and effect change. And during the ever-more-present election season, Mexico's mass media remain the overwhelmingly dominant vehicle through which candidates and parties make their case to the electorate. In short, the mass media have a crucial role to play in shaping democratic politics in Mexico, as they did in shaping the country's democratic transition.

To be sure, significant obstacles remain to the construction of a true Fourth Estate in Mexico. Most important among them is the fact that the ownership of Mexico's dominant medium, broadcast television, remains concentrated in the hands of private companies with their own financial agendas. Along with ensuring the effective implementation of freedom-of-information legislation, the biggest remaining item on the media reform agenda is establishing an equitable and transparent system for allocating (and revoking) broadcasting concessions so as to ensure pluralism and competition. Such a measure is conceivable under the Fox administration (2000–2006), and it would go a long way toward completing the remarkable transition in Mexico's mass media.

References

Acosta Valverde, Miguel, and Luz Paula Parra Rosales. 1995. *Los procesos electorales en medios de comunicación*. Mexico City: Academia Mexicana de Derechos Humanos / Universidad Iberoamericana.

Adler, Ilya. 1993a. "Press-Government Relations in Mexico: A Study of Freedom of the Mexican Press and Press Criticism of Government Institutions," *Studies in Latin American Popular Culture* 12: 1–30.

——. 1993b. "The Mexican Case: The Media in the 1988 Presidential Election." In *Television, Politics, and the Transition to Democracy in Latin America*, edited by Thomas E. Skidmore. Baltimore, Md. and Washington D.C.: Johns Hopkins University Press / Woodrow Wilson Center Press.

Aguayo Quezada, Sergio, and Luz Paula Parra Rosales. 1997. *Las organizaciones no-gubernamentales de derechos humanos en México: entre la democracia participativa y la electoral.* Mexico City: Academia Mexicana de Derechos Humanos.

Alianza Cívica. 1994. "The Media and the 1994 Federal Elections in Mexico: A Content Analysis of Television News Coverage of the Political Parties and Presidential Candidates." May.

Alisky, Marvin. 1981. *Latin American Media: Guidance and Censorship.* Ames: Iowa State University Press.

Alter, Jonathan. 1986. "Reporters under the Gun," *Newsweek*, December 17.

Ambriz, Agustín. 1996. "Ante la Suprema Corte, la petición de Azcárraga y Cañedo White para no pagar impuestos por sus Mercedes Benz blindados," *Proceso*, March 25.

Aranda Luna, Javier. 1986. "'Se la refanfinflan' los problemas a México: Félix Cortés Camarillo," *La Jornada*, June 10.

Arredondo Ramírez, Pablo, Gilberto Fregoso Peralta, and Raúl Trejo Delarbre. 1991. *Así se calló el sistema: comunicación y elecciones en 1988.* Guadalajara, Mexico: Universidad de Guadalajara.

Article 19. 1989. *In the Shadow of Buendía: The Mass Media and Censorship in Mexico.* London: Article 19.

Bailey, John, and Arturo Valenzuela. 1997. "Mexico's New Politics: The Shape of the Future," *Journal of Democracy* 8 (4): 43–57.

Banks, Arthur S. 1995. *Political Handbook of the World, 1994–1995.* Binghamton, N.Y.: CSA Publications.

Bernal Sahagún, Víctor Manuel, and Eduardo Torreblanca Jacques. 1988. *Espacios de silencio.* Mexico City: Nuestro Tiempo.

Cinta, Alberto. 1999. "Uncertainty and Electoral Behavior in Mexico in the 1997 Congressional Elections." In *Toward Mexico's Democratization: Parties, Campaigns, Elections, and Public Opinion*, edited by Jorge I. Domínguez and Alejandro Poiré. New York: Routledge.

Cole, Richard Ray. 1972. "The Mass Media of Mexico: Ownership and Control." Ph.D. diss., University of Minnesota.

Committee to Protect Journalists. 1997. *Attacks on the Press in 1996: A Worldwide Survey by the Committee to Protect Journalists.* New York: Committee to Protect Journalists.

Corro, Salvador. 1996. "En televisión ya podemos hacer todo y decir todo; 'no creo que haya alguien que pueda pararnos': Moreno Valle, de Canal 40," *Proceso*, March 25.

De la Vega, Miguel. 1997. "Azcárraga fue un socio a veces áspero, pero incondicional al gobierno: Trejo Delarbre," *Proceso*, April 20.

Delgado, Álvaro. 1996. "Nuevos episodios de la guerra por el 'rating': el 'descontón' de Rocha y la paz unilateral de Azcárraga," *Proceso*, November 3.

DePalma, Anthony. 1994. "Mexican Press Docile on Revolt," *New York Times*, May 6.

Fernández Christlieb, Fátima. 1997. "Los oficios políticos de la dinastía Azcárraga," *Proceso*, April 20.

Fernández, Claudia, and Andrew Paxman. 2000. *El Tigre: Emilio Azcárraga y su imperio.* Mexico City: Grijalbo.

Galarza, Gerardo. 1996. "Salinas Pliego: presentaré una demanda contra Ricardo Rocha por sus calumnias e infamias," *Proceso*, November 3.

Gamboa, Juan Carlos. 1995. "Media, Public Opinion Polls, and the 1994 Mexican Presidential Election." Paper presented at the international congress of the Latin American Studies Association, Washington D.C., September.

Granados Chapa, Miguel Ángel. 1996. "Personajes protegidos," *Reforma*, March 7.

Hallin, Daniel C. 1995. *"Dos instituciones, un camino:* Television and the State in the 1994 Mexican Election." Paper presented at the international congress of the Latin American Studies Association, Washington, D.C., September.

Heuvel, Jon Vanden, and Everette Dennis. 1995. *Changing Patterns: Latin America's Vital Media.* New York: Freedom Forum Studies Center, Columbia University.

IPI (International Press Institute). 1993. *IPI Report.* December.

——. 1994. *IPI Report.* December.

Lawson, Chappell. 2002. *Building the Fourth Estate: Democratization and the Rise of a Free Press in Mexico.* Berkeley: University of California Press.

Lawson, Chappell and James A. McCann. 2001. "Television Coverage, Media Effects, and Mexico's 2000 Elections." Paper presented at the annual meeting of the American Political Science Association, August-September 2001, San Francisco.

Marín, Carlos. 1986. "Alemán reconoce que en información Televisa se autocensura," *Proceso,* September 15.

——. 1997. "Disputa familiar por el legado de 'El Tigre': un emporio de 1,600 millones de dólares," *Proceso,* July 20.

Mejía Barquera, Fernando, and Raúl Trejo Delarbre. 1985. *Televisa: el quinto poder.* Mexico City: Claves Latinoamericanos.

Monsiváis, Carlos. 1997. "Azcárraga Milmo y la 'filosofía de Televisa,'" *Proceso,* April 20.

Morris, Stephen D. 1999. "Corruption and the Mexican Political System: Continuity and Change," *Third World Quarterly* 20 (3): 623–43.

Morrison, Scott. 1994. "Read All About It! Local News Media Show a Pro-government Bias," *Maclean's,* August 15.

Oppenheimer, Andrés. 1996. *México: en la frontera del caos; la crisis de los noventa y la esperanza del nuevo milenio.* Mexico City: Javier Vergara.

Poiré, Alejandro. 1999. "Retrospective Voting, Partisanship, and Loyalty in Presidential Elections: 1994." In *Toward Mexico's Democratization: Parties, Campaigns, Elections, and Public Opinion,* edited by Jorge I. Domínguez and Alejandro Poiré. New York: Routledge.

Puig, Carlos. 1997a. "La historia de Televisa: el aplauso sumiso al gobierno en turno," *Proceso,* April 20.

——. 1997b. "La pugna llega a los noticiarios: cómo humilló Ricardo Rocha a Zabludovsky el 6 de julio," *Proceso,* July 20.

——. 1997c. "Azcárraga Jean: 'Yo soy empresario...'" *Proceso,* March 16.

Ramírez, Carlos. 1996. "Indicador político," *El Universal,* July 1.

Riva Palacio, Raymundo. 1995. *Más allá de los límites: ensayos para el nuevo periodismo.* Mexico City: Fundación Manuel Buendía / Gobierno Estatal de Colima.

Rivera, Miguel Ángel, and Pablo Hiriart. 1988. "Insiste Azcárraga en la privatización de empresas," *La Jornada,* January 16.

Rodríguez Castañeda, Rafael. 1993. *Prensa vendida.* Mexico City: Grijalbo.

Scherer García, Julio. 1995. *Estos años.* Mexico City: Océano.

Toussaint, Florence. 1997. "La simbiosis entre el estado y Televisa," *Proceso,* April 20.

Toussaint, Florence, ed. 1995. *Democracia y los medios: un binomio inexplorado.* Mexico City: La Jornada Ediciones / Centro de Investigaciones Interdisciplinarias en Ciencias y Humanidades, Universidad Nacional Autónoma de México.

Virtue, John. 1995. "La prensa mexicana se aprieta el cinturón ... y la conciencia," *Pulso* 23 (July–September): 9.

Zamarripa, Roberto. 1996. "Guerrero: una mirada especial," *Reforma,* March 17.

PART IV
Challenges of Rights and Representation

13

Civil Society in Mexico at Century's End

Alberto J. Olvera

Civil society contributes in four main ways to the construction of an authentically democratic public life. First, civil society helps create, stabilize, and expand the rule of law. Second, a vibrant civil society forms the different public spaces through which social actors communicate with each other and with political actors. Third, civil society develops a dense network of associations, thereby strengthening the social fabric. And fourth, civil society helps build and generalize a culture of mutual tolerance and respect. The realization of these potentials is a long-term process.

Civil society in Mexico is still weak in all four of the areas outlined above, mainly because of the legacies of postrevolutionary authoritarian rule. Notwithstanding the institutionalization of transparent electoral processes that permitted opposition forces to defeat the long-ruling Institutional Revolutionary Party (PRI) in the 2000 presidential election, democratization is an incomplete process at the state and local levels in at least half of the country. Partial democratization coexists with a generalized lack of respect for labor rights or, particularly in rural areas, even basic civil and human rights. Civil society (especially its popular components) still lacks operative rights.

Tensions between the growth and consolidation of civil society and the expansion of the public sphere, on the one hand, and the increased social anxiety arising from the economic problems facing the majority of the population and prolonged transition under the uncertain rule of President Vicente Fox Quesada (2000–2006), on the other, reveal the dangers inherent in Mexico's conjuncture. A new cycle of democratic deepening – one that extends democracy into all aspects of public life – will be necessary if Mexico's still-young civil society is to develop further and mature. This new cycle will, in turn, require profound institutional and legal reforms, more extensive citizen participation in public life, additional public spaces, and the improvement of basic living conditions for large segments of the population. Only an active civil society can push forward such a program.

This chapter analyzes the historical development of Mexican civil society and the current challenges facing it. It begins with a discussion of the concept of civil society because theoretical clarification is badly needed in an area often rife with confusion. The second section examines the formation of civil society, a process that analysts of Mexican politics and society often ignore. The third part of the essay then assesses the form and content of contemporary Mexican civil society and the structural weaknesses that must be overcome in order to realize an authentic democratization of public life.

The Concept of Civil Society

How can civil society intervene in the construction of democracy in ways that go beyond mobilization, the role that most theorists assign to it? The mere presence of autonomous social movements does not ensure that they will endure or become institutionalized. Indeed, the unstable character of a civil society composed of social movements that lack functioning civil, political, and social rights limits that civil society's democratizing potential. The paths that Mexican civil society follows – toward growth, institutionalization, and permanence – will define the scope and form of the country's process of democratization.

Two difficulties arise regarding the relationship between democratization and the development of civil society in Latin America. First, theories of democratic transition have focused upon political negotiations between power holders and democratic actors, ignoring the learning processes that democratization entails and the emergence of social actors whose development is the only guarantee of long-term, substantive democratization (Avritzer and Olvera 1992, Avritzer 1995). Second, recent theories about civil society (which assume rights and institutions already consolidated in Western countries) lack conceptual strategies for analyzing nations where profound sociocultural cleavages cut across the social fabric and perpetuate personal and collective dependence (Olvera 1995).

Civil society became very fashionable during the 1990s. International agencies, political leaders and parties, and the media adopted this category as a catchall. In consequence, the concept has become almost meaningless, simultaneously referring to everything and to nothing. The situation has been exacerbated by the spread of analogous categories – such as "social capital" (Putnam 1993) and "third sector" (Salomon and Anheir 1999) – that allude to similar social processes. In Mexico, the notion of "citizen participation" has gained currency as well.[1] Such confusion begs for conceptual clarification.

Two interpretations dominate in the literature on civil society. The first, the liberal interpretation, originated with the Scottish philosophers who developed the concept of civil society.[2] Víctor Pérez Díaz (1993, 1997) is a leading proponent of this perspective in the Spanish-speaking world; his definition of civil society encompasses the market, the rule of law, a dense network of associations, public space, and a tolerant and plural political culture – virtually everything except the state.

---

1 For a critical analysis of citizen participation, see Rivera 1998a, 1998b. For a critique of the use of the concepts of civil society and social capital by international development agencies, see Olvera 1998 and Rabotnikof 1999.

2 See Seligman 1992 and Taylor 1990.

However, the very breadth of Pérez Díaz's definition hinders the identification of the particular type of social action that characterizes civil society. Activities in the market are strategic and oriented toward the search for profits, and the rules of the market are impersonal and not subject to criticism. In contrast, activities in the public sphere and in civil associations are communicative by nature, open to criticism, and not strategic in principle. It is one thing to accept the market as a precondition for civil society (following G. W. F. Hegel), yet quite another to view it as its main institution. To Pérez Díaz's credit, he stresses civil society's "civilization-building" capacity, its pluralistic and tolerant culture-generating capacity. In this sense, civil society becomes a product of modernity, a set of beliefs and principles embedded in the cultural substratum of modern collective life.

Jeffrey Alexander (1993, 1994) shares this notion, arguing that the foundation of civil society is the structure of values and beliefs that directs social action, especially those that promote civil associationism, tolerance, and respect for the law. Evoking the sociologist Talcott Parsons, Alexander defines civil society as "a sphere of universal social solidarity" (1994: 18), overlooking civil society's moral, cultural, and material conflicts. What especially differentiates civil society from political and economic systems is that, in principle, conflicts are discussed in the public sphere and tolerated as a part of public life.

The second concept prevailing in the literature reduces civil society to the sphere of civil associationism. This interpretation dominates in Mexico, where non-governmental organizations (NGOs) and some social movements see themselves as *the* civil society. This reading has been reinforced by such international NGO networks as CIVICUS (De Oliveira and Tandon 1994) and international development agencies.[3] The problem with this interpretation is that it limits civil society to NGOs, overlooking the fact that civil society comprises both a complex set of social actors and a set of institutions. This is, moreover, a highly ideological operation because the field of the "social" is reduced to very specific social practices that cannot explain the vast world of conflict and plurality that defines social reality.

Jean L. Cohen and Andrew Arato (1992) offer a broader definition, heavily influenced by Jürgen Habermas's theory of communicative action. They define civil society as "the institutional framework of a modern lifeworld stabilized by fundamental rights, which will include within their scope the spheres of the public and the private (from a lifeworld point of view)" (p. 492). The public sphere, the terrain of normative learning processes, refers to a set of arenas and sites where free (from systemic constraints) communicative interaction can be approximated in social praxis. The private is the terrain of familial and interpersonal relations (Habermas 1989, Calhoun 1992).

This institutional definition of civil society follows Habermas's theoretical-historical claim of the primacy of lifeworld over system (Habermas 1987).[4] It establishes

---

3 See Rabotnikof 1999 for an excellent critical analysis.
4 See Habermas 1998 for a restatement of the theory and its connection to the law and civil society.

civil society's sociological terrain and agents, and it allows for an interpretation of their democratizing potential that overcomes the "institutional deficit" encumbering many new social movement theories.[5] However, it also shares with Habermas's theory a historically specific character. Only in the West have fundamental rights been effectively institutionalized and extended in successive waves of lawmaking to the fields of political, social, and economic freedoms and entitlements. In the rest of the world, Western institutions were often formally adopted but then frequently ignored – or even utilized as a new instrument of domination.

For this reason, a second dimension of the concept of civil society may be better suited to countries where rights are insufficiently institutionalized. Cohen and Arato (1992) consider social movements to be the active, constructive part of modern civil societies insofar as they push forward new values, identities, and cultural paradigms. In the West, social movements profit from established rights while departing from normalized institutions to introduce new "codes" that challenge the dominant self-interpretations of society (Melucci 1989, 1994, 1996a, 1996b).

Yet a corrective is needed to Western understandings of civil society. Elsewhere, social movements follow one of two main trends. The first is class-based or group-based social movements (such as working-class, peasant, and urban resident movements). In the industrialized world, these movements spearheaded the universal extension of civil and political rights and the institutionalization and universalization of social rights. The absence (or segmentation, partiality, or conditioning) of these rights in the developing world makes class-based social movements important agents of democratization.[6] In historical-comparative terms, however, these movements have been culturally less influential, politically less autonomous, and socially less representative in the developing world than in the West. This weakness partially explains the lack of universal rights and elementary social justice in developing countries. In the absence of autonomous, empowered class-based movements, rights cannot be fixed and made permanent, even under democratic governments.[7]

The second social movement trend is the "new" sociocultural one. Yet outside the West, such movements operate without benefit of democracy, social justice,

---

5 Cohen's (1985) dictum alludes to the fact that social movement theories do not include the legal-institutional dimension in their analysis. It seems that institutions do not matter in the origin, development, and outcomes of social movements. Habermas's theory allows for the correction of this bias.

6 For an analogous argument, see Rueschemeyer, Stephens, and Stephens 1992.
   This is a historically valid argument. Nevertheless, each country can have a very different historical pattern and hence a different likelihood of projecting this trend.

7 There is a difference between this argument and the one most class theories entail. Here we are speaking of a historical need. Class associations can exert pressure over the political system to actualize the rule of law. No substantive mission is ascribed here to the working class, except the social responsibility of acting as a social movement to bring about actual and general rights.

and the rule of law. Without these preconditions, aspirations for alternative universal values, lifestyles, and concepts of progress carry little social, political, and cultural weight. The politics of influence – Western social movements' privileged mechanism – requires a public sphere within which to publicize new societal claims, modern parties receptive to such demands, social spaces and fields in which to experiment with different lifestyles, and a pluralistic culture open to change and able to incorporate what is becoming socially and morally acceptable (Cohen and Arato 1992). These factors barely exist in Latin America; they are operative for small elites only and are generally dissociated from the majority population. For this reason, most cultural movements in Latin America direct their attention to the basics – rights, justice, and democracy.

Civil society as a movement, then, has two main forms: (1) "popular civil society," which comprises class-based social movements (Lynch 1991, Oxhorn 1995), and (2) a set of sociocultural movements that combine "postmaterialist" values with a concern about the undelivered promises of modernity. In Latin America, these two forms not only address the same problems (albeit for different reasons and with different methods), but they also face the same instability caused by the absence of rights and democratic institutions. Thus the greatest challenge for civil society as a movement is its institutionalization – that is, the operationalization and universalization of rights.

It is through this process that civil society's cultural dimension, highlighted by Pérez Díaz (1993) and Alexander (1993), could be constructed. Respect for the law and for others is certainly a symbolic component of contemporary struggles for democracy.

The Latin American experience demonstrates that in situations of extreme economic and social inequality, old political practices and traditions based on links of personal or collective dependence (clientelism, corporatism, patrimonialism) can coexist with formally democratic regimes. Because structural inequality implies enormous problems of social integration, democracy cannot stabilize itself in such conditions despite institutional engineering by elites. Thus the risks of political instrumentalization of social action are enormous, insofar as political actors have a high degree of structural autonomy from society.[8] Therefore, the first dilemma of substantive democratization is how to slow social polarization and the marginalization of a growing share of the population. All these factors, linked by communication problems arising from diffuse local cultures and forms of knowledge, must be analyzed in order to assess the potential for, and problems of, the institutionalization of civil society.[9]

---

8 "Instrumentalization" means here political parties' strategic use of social action. Instead of receiving actual support, social movements are frequently colonized by political activists whose main concern is to channel protest toward electoral, insurrectional, or confrontational aims.

9 For a creative and useful conceptualization of "local" cultures and various forms of cultural institutionalization in regional settings, see Lomnitz-Adler 1992.

The Idea of Civil Society in Mexico

The recovery of the concept of civil society in Mexico had an identity-building aspect. It provided a symbolic means to differentiate society from the state,[10] and this differentiation served as a symbolic response to the authoritarian regime's denial of political rights, its de facto retreat (especially from 1982 onward) from past social justice commitments, and its abandonment of the historical project that had been its main source of legitimation.

This does not mean that the notion of civil society has been absent from political discourse or academic analysis in Mexico.[11] Nevertheless, prior to 1985 collective action was still interpreted in terms of other paradigms. Within the Left, collective action was considered no more than an expression of social and structural contradictions. Social action had to be politically directed toward revolutionary change. At the same time, the established regime did not tolerate autonomous movements because they questioned the regime's monopoly of politics and, by definition, its monopoly of the public sphere. The Right, especially the National Action Party (PAN), had traditionally defended the importance of "intermediary bodies" as autonomous entities of citizen organization. However, as the PAN rediscovered the value of the individual vote during the electoral insurrection in northern Mexico in the 1980s, this party adopted an almost dogmatic vision of political parties as the only acceptable channel for intermediation between citizens and the state.

Anti-authoritarian understandings of the notion of civil society had encountered a difficulty: homogenization of the diverse – that is, of society itself. In some cases this reductionism led to interpretations of civil society as a collective being

---

10 Norbert Lechner (1995) notes that the contemporary recovery of the idea of civil society has the main function of creating a basic antinomy: civil society against the authoritarian state. In this way, the denial of political rights and the abuse of human rights can be criticized and a new aspiration to the rebuilding of social spaces can be expressed.

11 During the 1970s, the Left's interest in the work of Antonio Gramsci led some analysts to postulate an opposition between civil society and political society, with the former being the locus of consent and the latter the space of coercion. However, at the time the category of civil society was not interpreted as the autonomous space of the social, but as a field of cultural struggle where the revolutionary party had to operate.

Carlos Pereyra (1990), recovering the Gramscian tradition, identified civil society with society per se, which can only exist in social practice through organizations. Thus Pereyra identified civil society as "the organized part of society," including as principal representatives the "official" corporatist organizations. Moreover, he considered political parties as part of civil society. Some confusion evidently existed in this regard given that corporatist organizations and Mexico's "official" party were part of the state machinery and, as such, forms of "fusion" between state and society. Pereyra, then, missed the point: civil society has to be defined by its autonomy vis-à-vis the state and the political system. In this case, Pereyra misleadingly mingled form and content, and the formal function of some organizations with their real practice.

with a popular character, a "macrosubject." In fact, the national political culture (which is highly prone to the rescue of populist traditions) encouraged the Left to use civil society as a modern and acceptable substitute for the concept of *lo popular*, excluding both the bourgeoisie and conservative associations.[12] For its part, the Right (especially the PAN) distrusted civil society in the mid-1990s because PAN leaders thought that the civil associations using the concept were allies of the Left. The PAN always preferred the concept of "intermediary bodies."[13]

In the midst of these various interpretations, "civil society" underwent a symbolic redefinition in public opinion. It was being restricted to nongovernmental organizations and pro-democracy civil groups,[14] a form of appropriation that underscored society's autonomy vis-à-vis the political system. This meaning served to legitimate these groups' public and political practices.[15] Although NGOs and citizens' associations are part of civil society, such a restriction of the concept of civil society excludes other kinds of associations – professional, religious, cultural, and "popular" – that also constitute the field of civil society. This effort at conceptual restriction reflected the central place that civic associationism acquired in Mexico's public sphere in the 1990s (Olvera 1999). Indeed, factors such as the gradual liberalization of the media, the state's relative withdrawal from social policy, and increasing external financial support allowed NGOs to expand their public influence.

However, a full understanding of contemporary Mexican civil society requires a long-term analysis. The remaining sections of this chapter adopt a historical perspective in order to demonstrate that Mexican civil society's current form and content suffer from a structural weakness that must be overcome if there is to be an authentic democratization of public life.

12 The radical expression of this inclination was articulated by Subcomandante Marcos, the principal public spokesperson for the Zapatista Army of National Liberation (EZLN): "Civil society must rule" (see Hernández Navarro 1995). Marcos definitively held that "we" – meaning all supporters of the Zapatista movement and all participants in a "progressive" front – are civil society. Such a notion not only breaks with the principle of plurality implicit in the idea of civil society, but it is also a theoretical error. If civil society rules, it would no longer be civil society; rather, it would be political society – and even the state.

13 Carlos Castillo Peraza, president of the National Action Party (PAN) from 1993 to 1996, considered civil society a subterfuge that the Left used in the public sphere, without recognizing its political nature. However, the PAN is (contradictorily) a party with deep roots in civil society. Indeed, its main social base comes from some conservative Catholic associations and business organizations.

14 See, for example, the first issues of *Sociedad Civil*, a journal edited by a group of NGOs, and Canto 1998. For a critique, see Olvera 1998.

15 Lechner (1995) called this process "the questioning of the new social actors," in which actors formerly absent from the public arena came to claim recognition.

The Historical Origins of Mexico's Postrevolutionary Authoritarian Regime and Its Impacts on National Political Culture

The magnitude of the difficulties that an emerging civil society has had to overcome in contemporary Mexico can only be understood by tracing the history of liberalism's defeat in Mexican political culture and institutions.[16] Paradoxically, Mexico rejected its liberal legacy in practice at the same time that it institutionalized its formal democratic principles in constitutional form.[17] This contradiction between the formal legalization of democracy and the de facto institution of authoritarian rule defined the essence of politics in Mexico during much of the twentieth century.

The regime that was established in the aftermath of the 1910–1920 Mexican Revolution initiated two major projects: an anti-liberal program of social and political inclusion that made the state itself the nexus of social integration, and an anti-liberal program of national development in which the state guided and implemented the country's economic modernization (Córdova 1976). The regime's rejection of liberalism amounted to a "fusing" of state and society, on the one hand, and state and economy, on the other.[18] The intermediate spheres of economic and political society virtually disappeared in the concomitant absence of operative legal institutions (Olvera 1995).

The elements of the developmental-authoritarian state that contributed most significantly to the over-politicization and manipulation of collective identities, the closure of spaces for normative political discussion, and the segmented institutionalization of rights were the following:

- Revolutionary legitimacy as the political foundation of a neopatrimonial regime in which legality was bypassed or ignored;
- A corporatist model for integrating society into the state, which promoted particularism, clientelism, and segmentation in the application of rights;
- A contradiction between the state's neopatrimonial character (guaranteed by an extreme form of presidentialism) and the formal democracy prescribed in the

16 See Reyes Heroles 1966 and Guerra 1989.

17 Indeed, after independence in 1821, Mexico followed the very common developing-country practice of institutional imitation. The Constitutions of 1824 and 1857 were remarkably liberal, democratic, federal, and republican manifestos whose relationship with actual political practice was nil. On the "imaginary" character of citizenship in nineteenth-century Mexico, see Escalante 1992. On the contradiction between liberalism and patrimonial rulership, see Guerra 1989, Guerra and Lempériere 1998, Knight 1986, and Sábato 1999.

18 The idea of fusion between the state, society, and the economy may seem exaggerated for the case of Mexico. However, the essence of the historical project of the Mexican Revolution was precisely to integrate the country by means of the state. The state's centrality in Mexican public life from the 1930s to the 1960s was so overwhelming that the allusion to fusion is justified. For a different interpretation, based on the concept of coalition building, see Middlebrook 1995 and Maxfield 1990.

Constitution of 1917, leading to systematic electoral fraud and thus to a rupture between legality and legitimacy;

- A linkage between substantive justice and the state's promotion of economic modernization, encouraging massive state intervention in the economy and official patronage of the bourgeoisie;
- State monopoly over the public sphere and the embedding of official ideology in the educational system, in cultural production, and in forms of national identity creation.

The law essentially became the means to guarantee state sovereignty over social and economic actors, both national and foreign. The market was understood not as an autonomous sphere with independent forms of coordination, but as a way to pursue modernization. Rights were applied in a segmented and selective fashion, undercutting their potential to constitute a form of defense or demarcation of society.

The strategic assimilation of traditional forms of state-society mediation (such as clientelism and patrimonialism) reinforced the institutions and conventions that isolated politics from modern forms of popular participation. The resulting institutional and ideological framework severely limited in practice the scope of "legitimate and valid" social action. Limited spaces of action, narrowly construed definitions of valid action, and monopolization of public life hindered the stabilization of modern lifeworld institutions throughout the rise and consolidation of the developmental-authoritarian state.

Social actors sometimes resisted (and sometimes adapted to) the institutions of the postrevolutionary regime. Unlike some socialist regimes, the Mexican regime proved flexible enough to open multiple spaces of participation and negotiation. By ably combining the politics of repression with the co-optation and integration of social movements, the regime was able to avoid a generalized legitimacy crisis until the late 1980s. Periodic renovations of the political elite helped to avoid open internal conflicts, and the opposition had just enough room to survive but not enough to prosper (Loaeza 1989). Only the Roman Catholic Church persisted (unsuccessfully) in its opposition to the regime's monopoly over the public sphere and the organization of society.[19]

19 Historically, the idea of urban cultural groups working outside the state's framework was launched by the only actor whose institutionality and resources permitted the existence of a small but autonomous sphere of action: the Catholic Church. By the mid-1960s, the church's Pastoral Social (Social Ministry, a specialized church office responsible for promoting social policies) was the driving force behind the formation of several specialized associations: Promoción del Desarrollo Popular (Support for Popular Development); Centro Operacional de Vivienda y Poblamiento (Operational Center for Housing and Population); and the Fundación para el Desarrollo Rural (Rural Development Foundation). These associations were meant to address, with the church's financial assistance, specific development problems at the micro level. The Unión Social de Empresarios Mexicanos (Social Union of Mexican Entrepreneurs) and the Authentic Labor Front (FAT) were class associations whose function

The Emergence and Collapse of a Popular Civil Society and the Turn toward Electoral Politics, 1982–1988

Economic development brought extensive social change to Mexico and gradually undermined the regime's foundations.[20] This regime crisis, whose origins date from 1968, reflected two key factors. The first was the exhaustion of Mexico's post-1940 economic model, characterized by indiscriminate protectionism and a lack of societal control over state investments. In other words, the developmental capacity of the fusion between state and economy had reached its limit. The second was the emergence of new social actors that could not be co-opted through traditional means, making it impossible to maintain the fusion between state and society. Mexico's prolonged regime crisis arose mainly from an ongoing differentiation of the economy, state, and society, ultimately leading to a legitimacy crisis (Olvera 1995).

The emergence of a sense of social autonomy preceded the economic crisis of the 1980s. The regime's inability to tolerate autonomous actors and political plurality alienated broad segments of the increasingly important urban middle classes. One consequence was the 1968 student movement, which radicalized a generation of young professionals. The formation of relatively independent workers' unions and peasant organizations in the early 1970s reflected both the new population of radical activists and President Luis Echeverría's (1970–1976) attempts to weaken the regime's old corporatist pillars so that they would accept a relative political liberalization.

Echeverría's administration marked the beginning of a new wave of social movements in Mexico and the emergence of a tradition of autonomous association. Movements of workers, urban residents, peasants, students, and members of the middle class sprang up throughout the country; entrepreneurs began to create

---

was to introduce social-Catholic values into labor-business relations (Reygadas 1998, Canto 1998). These associations were meant to enhance the Catholic Church's influence in society. Even though their role was limited by the state's omnipresence, all these associations are still operating or have provided the basis for new ones.

20 Economic development meant rapid industrialization and urbanization, concentrated above all in Mexico City and in several other large and midsize cities. During the 1940–1980 period, the Mexican economy grew at an average annual rate of 6.8 percent. Population increased at a median annual rate of 3.1 percent, from roughly 16 million in 1940 to 35 million in 1960 – when, for the first time, the urban and rural populations reached equilibrium. There were 67 million inhabitants in 1980 (65.8 percent of whom were urban) and 82 million in 1990 (79.1 percent urban). The indigenous population diminished from 19.5 percent to 5.1 percent of the total population during the same time span (Aguilar Camín 1988, Cansino, 2000).

Class composition changed as well. Peasants fell from 73.9 percent of the workforce in 1940 to 27.2 percent in 1980. The working class increased from 18.4 percent of the workforce to 25.3 percent over this same period, which meant the creation of almost 3 million new industrial jobs. The remaining workers were incorporated into the service sector, commerce, and the informal urban economy (Aguilar Camín 1988, Cansino 2000).

autonomous associations; and an overall liberalization permitted relative freedom of association, of expression, and of the press.[21] However, it was not until 1977, at the beginning of President José López Portillo's term (1976–1982), that the regime initiated the first significant political reform in its history.[22] The fact that Echeverría combined relative liberalization in the popular sphere with electoral closure demonstrated that his goal was to modernize Mexico's corporatist arrangements, not to achieve a true democratization of politics.

The development of Mexican civil society in the 1970s consisted basically of the appearance of class-associative movements that differentiated themselves from state and market institutions at the national level. Two factors limited the transformative potential of these associations and ultimately demonstrated that they were a weak version of civil society. First, structural changes did not lead to new forms of collective action. The regime's revolutionary origins, its inclusive character, and its ability to negotiate with, absorb, or repress social movements led to a tradition of mass mobilization and radical language in the public sphere. Second, the professional militants of the Left who led many social movements embraced the regime's ideological claim that principles of primary justice had precedence over formal democratic institutions and laws. As a consequence, the Left could only criticize the regime for its shortcomings, not for its authoritarian essence. It was a counterfactual critique, not the positing of an alternative political principle.

A second form of civil society appeared during the 1970s, alongside popular social movements. The spread of liberation theology helped to generalize the formation of Christian base communities (CBCs) in Mexico (though they were less successful than their Brazilian counterparts). With minimal support from the Catholic Church hierarchy, these groups concentrated on "consciousness raising." In other words, the poor should discover their own situation of oppression and find a path to liberation.[23] Apart from this highly abstract discourse, there were few ways to anchor the search for liberation in actual social practice. However, CBCs gave the Mexican people a place for discussion – often the only public space available to peasants and urban settlers – and, in the process, formed a generation of potential social leaders.

Mexico's 1982 economic crisis took all social actors by surprise.[24] After five years

---

21 On workers' movements during this period, see Middlebrook 1995: chap. 6, and Bizberg 1990; for peasant movements, see Olvera 1997; for urban movements, see Núñez González 1990 and Farrera 1994; and for entrepreneurs' associations, see Luna 1992.

22 This reform legally recognized leftist opposition parties (including the Mexican Communist Party, PCM) and established a system of proportional representation in federal elections.

23 On the experience of the Catholic Church in Latin America during this period, see Casanova 1994. On the church in Mexico, see Blancarte 1995 and Muro 1994.

24 Gross domestic product (GDP) fell by 4.5 percent in two years of the decade (1983 and 1986) and on average showed zero growth between 1983 and 1988 (Cansino 2000). Real wages dropped by an average of 35.3 percent over the same period, and labor's share of total national income plummeted from 46.5 percent to 30.2 percent. Public investment in education and

of rapid economic growth and a most impressive expansion of state economic intervention, the country found that it had depleted its financial reserves. It could not service its external debt, and inflation rates rose exponentially. Mexico awakened from its oil-boom dream to a decade of wrenching economic crisis.[25]

The prolonged economic crisis differentially altered the conditions affecting Mexico's developing social movements. Opportunities for clientelistic bargaining in unions and urban associations diminished along with the state's capacity to co-opt popular movements. Independent unions were especially unprepared for the economic crisis. When firms began laying off workers and real wages went into free fall, virtually all independent industrial unions collapsed, defenseless in the face of the loss of internal credibility and legitimacy (De la Garza 1994).

In rural areas, at least three problems plagued the development of civil society. First, social movements were dispersed in time and space. They therefore lacked local or regional webs of political support, means to influence public opinion, and sufficient power to gain local relevance over traditional actors. Second, their main arena – the creation of "self-managed" peasant economic organizations – was highly unstable, depending as it did upon government economic support and occupying a weak position in the marketplace. Their other locus of development – consumer associations organized around the state system of goods distribution – also depended upon public resources and was severely restricted in its activities (Gordillo 1988). Third, these associations' economic character gave them a trade-union profile and forced them to develop technical, administrative, and political capacities rarely found among peasants. Technicians, professional activists, members of NGOs, and peasants with professional backgrounds took over the organizations and dominated their daily operations.[26]

In contrast, urban popular movements consolidated and expanded their sphere of action. Leftist groups had a ready urban clientele as Mexicans continued to migrate from rural areas to cities and the problem of urban land ownership became increasingly urgent. The oldest urban groups opened a second front (a process they called "urban reorganization") following the 1985 Mexico City earthquakes. At the same time, the upper middle classes initiated some self-management experiments in high-income neighborhoods to ensure security services and acceptable public maintenance of urban facilities. The "new" social movements (human rights, environmental, and feminist movements) were, however, in their initial phases of development and still had limited influence (Monsiváis 1987).

---

health suffered a 45.2 percent decrease in real terms. The decline in living standards was Mexico's worst since the 1910–1920 revolution. See Maxfield 1990.

25 Indeed, the crisis meant the end of Mexico's import-substitution industrialization model. Over the course of the 1980s, the government prepared the way for a shift to a neoliberal economic model.

26 Most of these associations were viewed by their rank-and-file members as a kind of state agency in terms of both their functions and the virtual impossibility of controlling the activities of their leader-administrators. See Olvera and Millán 1994: 53–69.

Entrepreneurs and conservative middle-class groups rebelled in their own way. The controversial nationalization of the banking system in 1982 alienated some sectors of the bourgeoisie, and the devastating effects of periodic peso devaluations sparked mobilizations of the middle classes and owners of small and midsize businesses in northern Mexico, where many costs are pegged to the U.S. dollar. When devaluation, inflation, and state intervention severely undermined their living standards (and sometimes even threatened their survival) in the mid-1980s, they turned to electoral politics as a way to escape what they perceived as the regime's impotence and abuse. Existing links between the PAN and some conservative middle-class groups made affiliation with the PAN appear to be an acceptable alternative.

The justification offered publicly for this political activism was the search for the rule of law. For the first time since the administration of President Lázaro Cárdenas (1934–1940), the rupture between legality and legitimacy became the axis of public political action, and (at least for citizens in northern Mexico) democracy became the main aspiration. In response to societal pressures, in 1983 the administration of President Miguel de la Madrid (1982–1988) allowed more or less free municipal elections in several states as a kind of experiment. However, when the PAN won control of almost all the key municipal offices at stake in Chihuahua and important offices in other northern states, the federal government retrenched and returned to its normal practice of electoral fraud.

This reversal on the part of the government radicalized broad sectors of the middle class, and the PAN became an authentic democratic opposition (Loaeza 1989). Participation in the PAN became the way for the conservative middle classes to "do politics," the way to establish relationships with the people. Given the dearth of credible alternatives on the left, some workers and peasants also supported the PAN. As for the rest of Mexico, the reality of systematic fraud was a convincing reason to avoid electoral participation, and most popular social movements maintained their "anti-political" stance.

A new wave of associationism also emerged in the 1980s (Aguayo Quezada and Tarrés 1995). Human rights groups began to appear in 1984, initially as a response to violations of Central American immigrants' human rights and later to human rights violations in Mexico. More than one hundred human rights-related NGOs appeared in the 1980s (Aguayo Quezada and Parra 1995), along with the first professionally staffed NGOs focused upon specific development services.[27]

Most of these NGOs were influenced or promoted by specific Catholic religious orders, though not by the church hierarchy in Mexico. The contradiction between the Catholic hierarchy's conservative character and the leading role that the Jesuits

27 Autonomy, Decentralization, and Management (ANADEGES), established in 1986, was the first network of developmental NGOs staffed by professionals. The network linked more than twenty organizations, all of which worked in very specific, local projects. Similarly, Promoting Health Care and Popular Education (PRODUSSEP), also created in 1986, was a church-related NGO network oriented toward basic services.

and other religious orders played in the NGOs' formation reflected the political plurality in the Catholic Church following the Second Vatican Council of 1962–1965 (Casanova 1994). The growth of Christian base communities from 1970 to 1978 had created a radical tradition among Catholic laypeople; this tradition, in turn, helped establish independent civil organizations.

Neoliberalism, Legitimacy Crisis, and a Modern Civil Society

Three fundamental changes took place in Mexico between 1988 and 1994. First, the turn toward neoliberalism radically altered the economy and drove the constitutional reforms that legalized the state's retreat from its established role in the economy and in social reproduction. These phenomena deepened the differentiation among state, economy, and society, and they also exacerbated the regime's ongoing legitimacy crisis. Second, for the first time since the end of the Mexican Revolution, political parties and elections emerged as potential means of regime change. Third, civic-cultural movements established a civil society centered upon the struggle for political rights, democracy, and the rule of law. In combination, these factors created an opening for democratic transition and the stabilization of a modern civil society. Nevertheless, even at this stage, political society was unable to anchor its action in civil society, leading to a weak and unstable party system.

Mexico's neoliberal departure opened the door to three great transformations: integrating the national economy into world markets (which implied integration with the U.S. economy, with Mexico as a subordinate partner),[28] privatizing government-owned enterprises and state withdrawal from the economy, and lifting constitutional limitations on capital mobility.[29] All three changes were accomplished during President Carlos Salinas de Gortari's administration (1988–1994), building upon far-reaching economic adjustments carried out beginning in 1983.

The symbolic and legal effects of declaring an end to Mexico's agrarian reform program and privatizing public enterprises were enormous. The state was, in effect, rescinding its pact with Mexico's peasants and relinquishing its guiding role in the market – the two principles underlying the state's revolutionary project and its anti-liberal tenor. Their abandonment was a tacit recognition of the collapse of the regime's ideological foundations and the ascendance of classical liberalism.

The depth and pace of neoliberal economic change were not matched, however, in the political arena. On the contrary, democratization was deliberately postponed so as to forestall its inevitable attendants: political limitations on the sovereign state and citizen oversight of economic policy.

---

28 Negotiation of the North American Free Trade Agreement (NAFTA) signaled that rules defining a clear role for private enterprise would remain unchanged in the long term, regardless of any possible political shifts in Mexico. Because national sovereignty had always been understood in Mexico as autonomy vis-à-vis the United States, the NAFTA represented the breakdown of traditional concepts of sovereignty.

From 1989 to 1993, Mexico's states and municipalities became arenas of post-electoral struggle. The federal government continued to deny opposition victories at will, and because the "official" PRI controlled virtually all campaign resources, races were openly unequal. Some opposition victories were recognized, but only after long and complicated negotiations. Such negotiations enabled the PAN to win official recognition of three governorships and dozens of mayoralties, but the center-left Party of the Democratic Revolution (PRD) had to stage huge popular mobilizations to defend its municipal-level electoral victories.

The government refused to recognize PRD wins primarily because President Salinas viewed the PRD as an enemy of modernization. The PRD took shape in mid-1989 through a strategic alliance of communists, radical nationalists, old-style populists, social democrats, and social movement activists, all under the charismatic leadership of Cuauhtémoc Cárdenas. Cárdenas (the son of President Lázaro Cárdenas, one of the creators of the modern Mexican state) came within a hair of defeating Salinas in the 1988 presidential election, and his leadership seemed to offer a means of recovering old political identities deconstructed by neoliberal policies. However, the PRD's call to rebuild the nexus between morality (understood as fidelity to the "revolutionary project") and legitimacy proved unattractive to most people, and its politics of confrontation failed to win over the urban electorate.

In contrast, the PAN was more pragmatic, openly seeking an alliance with President Salinas. Indeed, it backed all of Salinas's major constitutional reforms, most of which had originally been proposed by the PAN itself. *Panistas* undertook this alliance with a view to their long-term objective: PAN control over state and municipal governments. The alliance produced some positive results, but it also compromised the PAN's efforts to highlight the contradiction between legality and legitimacy.

The weight of political tradition and entrenched interests within the regime posed a significant barrier to all reforms initiated from above. Salinas endeavored, therefore, to fashion a parallel political apparatus through a new social-clientelistic initiative named the National Solidarity Program (PRONASOL). Its aim was to involve the poor in designing and controlling public works through organized local committees. The intention was to open a direct negotiating channel between the state and established social organizations, or to offer favorable conditions to create such organizations where they did not exist.

The Salinas administration acted in the belief that a wide gap divided the emerging civil society from the regime's traditional popular constituencies, and it chose to concentrate on the latter, refurbishing its legitimacy by modernizing clientelism among Mexico's popular sectors. These forces were still sufficiently large to guarantee an electoral majority for the "modern" PRI if it could secure their loyalty. In fact, the PRONASOL experience revealed that all levels of government bureaucracy employed old clientelistic strategies that tied access to state favors directly to loyalty to the PRI (Cook, Middlebrook, and Molinar Horcasitas 1994), exposing paternalism's and clientelism's deep roots in Mexican political culture.

Modernizing the old fusion of state, economy, and society provoked a dual crisis – a moral crisis as the regime's foundational myth of the search for social justice crumbled, and a legal crisis over the unacceptability of electoral fraud in normal politics. The Salinas administration's attempt to revive populism by establishing direct relations between government welfare agencies and organized local groups failed when the government was unable to guarantee these groups' institutionalization and permanence. On the political left, the regime's perpetuation of corporatist traditions encouraged the PRD to form clientelistic links with Mexico's social movements. However, most new social movements rejected such continuity with the clientelist past and strove for autonomy from political society. For its part, the political Right considered civil society an unpredictable mass of movements susceptible to political exploitation and antithetical to the modern citizen for whom the PAN had tailored its message.

Nevertheless, the PRD and the PAN began to consolidate themselves as viable alternatives to the PRI. The fact that the PRI–led government was unable to maintain its monopoly hold on politics, or to adapt to increasingly active (though irregular) citizen participation, led opposition parties and most political analysts to view Mexico's transition to democracy as an autonomous process with no intrinsic connections to other societal elements. Taking democratic transition theories at face value, both politicians and intellectuals regarded democracy as the outcome of elite bargaining, with no concern for the empowerment of civil society or the resolution of the representational problems that weak political parties still faced.

It was during this period that a different civil society emerged in the form of NGO networks and pro-democracy social movements. The increasing number of NGOs in all areas of action, and the perceived threats from the government in the early 1990s,[30] led most NGOs to organize collectively in networks, grouped by both thematic interest and political affinity. Three important networks of nongovernmental organizations emerged in Mexico during this period:

- The Forum for Mutual Support (FAM) was established in 1992 with approximately 250 affiliates. It listed its aims as the professionalization and public promotion of NGOs and participation in public policy making.[31]

29 Between 1988 and 1994, the administration of President Carlos Salinas enacted 54 constitutional amendments and 225 amendments to secondary or regulatory laws. The amendments to Article 27 of the Mexican Constitution allowed privatization of some core public enterprises and part of the banking system. Some of these changes led to the end of the agrarian reform program and, after January 1993, the beginning of the privatization of *ejidos* (a collective form of land tenure that had been a principal vehicle for postrevolutionary land distribution). In practice, these amendments virtually remade the Constitution, insofar as the main provisions defining the anti-liberal character of the Mexican regime were lifted.

30 In 1990 the government began for the first time to tax nongovernmental organizations' income, including donations from international foundations.

31 In 2000 the FAM de facto dismantled itself because of administrative irregularities and a loss of confidence in one of its key officials.

- The Convergence of Civic Organizations for Democracy (COCD, or simply Convergencia) was founded in 1990 with some 140 affiliates. Its objectives included protection against taxation, participation in public policy making, and electoral observation.
- The Mexican Action Network Against Free Trade (RMALC) was established in 1991 with approximately 80 collective members, including NGOs, popular social movements, and individual citizens (Chalmers 1995). The group formed in response to negotiation of the North American Free Trade Agreement (NAFTA), an accord that implied the overhaul of national economic policy and long-term commitments to new rules on trade, investment, labor, and the environment.

The creation of the RMALC was especially significant because developmental NGOs, some unions and small business associations, intellectuals, and journalists were forced for the first time to systematize their proposals in the social policy arena. They advocated including a "social agenda" in the NAFTA that would commit Canada, Mexico, and the United States to harmonizing their welfare conditions and labor and environmental policies over the long term.[32]

Pro-democracy movements also emerged during this period. Citizens' groups formed by leading political and cultural figures were the first civic response to massive electoral fraud in the 1988 general elections.[33] At the same time, human rights groups were undergoing a learning process, with most concluding that the absence of rule of law in Mexico was due to authoritarianism. In effect, the government could not be held accountable for its actions.[34] As a logical consequence, the notion of human rights was expanded to include political rights.

A Time of Paradox: Growth and Uncertainty in Civil Society during the Zedillo Administration

The inadequacy of Salinas's neoliberal responses to profound problems of regime legitimization and reproduction came to the fore in 1994 and 1995, when the economic and political foundations of the neoliberal project seemed to collapse. The illusions that Salinas had created vanished in 1994 under the weight of growing divisions within the governing elite, the insurrection by the Zapatista Army of National Liberation (EZLN) in Chiapas, and renewed economic crisis. As a consequence, Salinas and his group lost all credibility and the incoming administration

---

32 Author's interview with Manuel García Urrutia, a representative of the Authentic Labor Front and a founding member of the RMALC, April 1993, Jalapa, Veracruz.

33 The Association for Democracy and Effective Suffrage (ADESE) was created in late 1988, and the Consejo para la Democracia (Council for Democracy) was established in 1990. Both were small groups of former mid-level politicians.

34 Therefore, the only way to ensure the generalization of basic individual rights was to struggle for a democratic regime. See Aguayo Quezada and Parra 1995 and Reygadas 1998.

of President Ernesto Zedillo (1994–2000) was severely weakened. [35] At the same time, the attempts at internal regime transformation halted, causing a political stalemate and exacerbating Zedillo's inability to control the PRI. The government was unable to establish any coherent political strategy during 1995 and 1996, and the political process was left to the rules of the political marketplace (elections) and to chaotic bargaining in the federal Chamber of Deputies. Yet despite a sensation of breakdown, the opposition was unable to gain any lasting benefit, and there were no broad negotiations among political actors. [36]

President Zedillo was eventually able to build a new coalition that acknowledged the power of regional PRI leaders and governors. However, this coalition was clearly unstable, as evidenced by the PRI's inability to avoid internal divisions in at least four states (Baja California Sur, Tlaxcala, and Zacatecas in 1998 and Nayarit in 1999). The PRD, which supported the rebellious local PRI leaders in these four cases, won control of all four states in subsequent elections.

Mexican voters took their first opportunity to show that they were deeply affected by the economic crisis [37] and that they wanted a political change. In the July 1997 midterm elections, opposition parties won a majority in the federal Chamber of Deputies for the first time since the formation of an "official" postrevolutionary party in 1929. Cuauhtémoc Cárdenas, the moral leader of the center-left PRD, became the first elected mayor of Mexico City since the 1920s. The center-right PAN won governorships in three more states. This radically altered political context drove hopes for a rapid end to the authoritarian PRI regime, with public

35 The sudden devaluation of the peso in December 1994 occurred only three weeks after Zedillo had taken the oath of office. This event, for which the government was totally unprepared, was followed by an almost unbelievable chain of economic policy blunders, which culminated in the emergency financial intervention of the International Monetary Fund and the U.S. government. Mexico lost its sovereignty in economic policy making, but the government managed to limit the visible effects of the crisis to 1995. Mexico achieved modest economic growth from 1996 through 2000.

Political divisions within the regime and Zedillo's manifest political weakness led to an open confrontation with former President Salinas and the resignation of three key cabinet members within the first five months of the Zedillo administration.

36 The only effort at such negotiations occurred in early February 1995, when President Zedillo opened a "roundtable" with opposition parties in order to forge a consensus for overcoming the economic crisis and promoting further political reform. However, the government's surprise military offensive against the Zapatista rebels later that same month led to the collapse of negotiations.

37 Agriculture fell into deep recession, provoking the massive out-migration of peasants to urban areas in Mexico and to the United States. The crisis coincided with a reduction in public investment in the agricultural sector and the government's withdrawal from its former role regulating the price of basic foodstuffs.

Real wages in Mexico in the late 1990s were 20 to 30 percent lower than in 1994 (*El Financiero*, August 31, 1998, p.17; *Reforma*, November 3, 1999). Formal-sector employment did not regain its 1994 level until 1999. As a result, income distribution became more unequal than at any point in Mexico's modern history (*La Jornada*, April 30, 1999, p. 26).

attention focused upon the struggles in Congress and the performance of the new Mexico City government.

Nevertheless, the Zedillo administration managed to avoid a terminal political crisis, thanks in large part to four processes. First, opposition parties were unable to create a stable alliance in the federal Chamber of Deputies that might have blocked the government's bailout of private banks.[38] Instead of forging a common political front, PRD and PAN deputies followed different tracks. The PRD tried to gain popular support by denouncing the "massive fraud against the nation" that the bailout represented (López Obrador 1999), a tactic that proved to be a miscalculation. In contrast, the PAN endorsed the government's policy – though it never managed to win any political advantage from its support. The end result was that the banking crisis faded from public view and the government scored an important political triumph.

Second, the PRD government in the Federal District was so uninspired that citizens soon became disenchanted with the leftist political alternative. Constructive interactions had taken place previously between NGOs and municipal governments, and the magnitude of the political change implied by Cárdenas's 1997 victory in the Federal District seemingly presented a new range of opportunities for collaboration. However, realizing these potential opportunities proved much more difficult than anticipated.[39] The new government lacked experience and a clear alternative project; the number, strength, and variety of interest groups in Mexico City made it very difficult to undertake substantial reforms; and the distribution of the Federal District budget was already set by law, severely limiting the resources available for political innovation. Moreover, Mexico City's high rates of crime, pollution, and urban congestion had produced a virtual collapse of urban life.

The PRD government was also disappointing from a civil society perspective. The Cárdenas administration did work to enhance citizen participation by enacting a citizen participation law that created directly elected neighborhood representatives. However, because these representatives only had symbolic powers (and no executive or monitoring functions), most Mexico City residents saw this election exercise as futile. Similarly, although the new government sought direct collaboration with NGOs and civic organizations in developing and implementing public policies by establishing the Platform of Civic Organizations for Democracy, the successes were limited to just a few small-scale projects.[40] More generally, NGO

---

38 The government agreed to make huge investments over twenty years in order to rescue the country's commercial banks. This implied reallocating resources away from much-needed social projects and to the benefit of private business. The moral damage this process should have provoked was limited by the fact that much of the public was not fully apprised of the government's actions.

39 The Cárdenas administration's problems were exacerbated by obvious divisions within the PRD, especially during the election of the party's president in early 1999.

40 A lack of funding severely constrained the Cárdenas administration's efforts to design a new housing policy for the Federal District, decentralize health care services, and increase access to civic centers and sports and cultural activities.

experiences with the PRD administration also underscored some of the risks of collaborating with government: the loss of experienced leaders who take up governmental positions, a diminished capacity to criticize an administration in which former NGO cadres are employed, and problems of organizational identity and declining public credibility if NGOs are perceived to have lost their autonomy vis-à-vis government.[41]

Third, President Zedillo avoided economic collapse through a fortuitous combination of external and internal factors. Very favorable external conditions (including rapid growth in the U.S. economy) facilitated strong exports and brought foreign investment to Mexico's capital markets. At home, neoliberal economic policies produced macroeconomic stability and modest growth, even at the cost of continued depressed wages and increasing rural poverty.

Fourth, the PRI overcame the risk of a damaging internal split over the selection of its 2000 presidential candidate. Roberto Madrazo, governor of the state of Tabasco, challenged the president's customary right to designate his successor, and two more internal candidates emerged as well. The PRI avoided a crisis by conducting an unprecedented primary election to select its candidate. Francisco Labastida won the primary (with the help of the state apparatus), and Madrazo, forced to accept defeat, resumed his governorship. The success of this process helped unify the PRI at the outset of a hotly contested presidential race.

Nevertheless, against all odds, the charismatic presidential candidate of the National Action Party, Vicente Fox, won an unexpected victory in the 2000 presidential election. Had the PRI forecast this outcome, perhaps Mexico's old political guard would have been tempted to organize some sort of electoral fraud. In the event, however, Fox achieved what Cárdenas had in the 1997 elections in the Federal District: he attracted the support of the vast majority of disenchanted voters. He did so by demonstrating his willingness to forge a broad political coalition and by his mastery of the media-led electoral campaign. At the same time, Fox clearly benefited from the institutional conditions created by the politically, administratively, and financially autonomous Federal Electoral Institute (IFE), which organized the electoral process so as to guarantee its fairness and legitimacy.

The results of the 2000 elections in the Congress were more problematic. No single party gained control of either the Chamber of Deputies or the Senate. In overall terms, the PRI remained the country's most important political force, followed by the PAN and the PRD. Moreover, because he was an outsider in his own party, Fox had little control over the PAN and its congressional delegation. At least in the short term, the result was political stalemate as major actors failed to reach agreement on key public policy issues. Mexico's democratic transition, then, was not characterized by an overarching pact or consensus regarding the nature of the new regime.

---

41 On these difficulties, see Alianza Cívica 1999.

New Forms of Civil Society Development

The relative normalization of electoral politics after 1997 ended post-election struggles as a principal form of collective action in Mexico, and the 1996 electoral reform institutionalized "citizen counselors" as key societal representatives before the political system. The results of federal and state elections in 1997 and state elections in 1998 (in which the PRD won three new governorships), as well as the outcome of the 2000 presidential election, suggested to some observers that Mexico's specific form of democratic transition – via a prolonged process of electoral reform – had reached its conclusion.[42]

From a civil society perspective, the 1990s were a time of increasing visibility and recognition, but this was also a period of growing weakness as civil society lost the capacity to influence public policies and the political elite acted with relative autonomy. In this context, parties and elections assumed an even more central place in the public sphere as the only means of articulating political action. In contrast, civic actors could only attract public and media attention if they staged demonstrations of such magnitude that the media were forced to give them priority coverage. This was the context surrounding Mexico's five most important civil-society developments during the late 1990s: the Zapatista movement; the El Barzón debtors' movement; the consolidation of NGO networks; the formation and persistence of pro-democracy social movements; and civic organizations' turn toward a politics of collaboration and articulation with government.

The Zapatista Movement

The Zedillo administration launched a military offensive against the EZLN in February 1995 and attempted to apprehend its leaders. The violence of the government's initiative sparked immediate popular opposition, and the government soon retreated.[43] The Zapatistas, having learned from their earlier missteps, moderated their radical discourse and stressed their movement's indigenous composition and their commitment to democracy. At this point, the peace negotiations with the government recommenced, and the EZLN's standing rose in public opinion.

---

42 This conclusion was premature. The perpetuation of clientelistic practices (including vote buying) in electoral processes represents an intolerable violation of citizens' political rights.

43 In order to find a way out of the legal and political impasse in which the government had placed itself, President Zedillo invited Congress to intervene in the conflict. A national mediation commission already existed, having been created at the time of the first round of government-EZLN peace talks in 1994. The commission was comprised of national civic leaders and headed by Samuel Ruiz, the Catholic bishop of San Cristóbal, Chiapas. In 1995, the government's strategy was to recruit help from a plural congressional commission to draft a law aimed at circumventing the arrest warrant a judge had issued for EZLN leaders. Such a law was drafted and adopted (Law for Dialogue, Conciliation, and a Dignified Peace in Chiapas), and negotiations resumed soon thereafter – this time with the participation of all major political parties. The failure of the Zedillo government's offensive against the Zapatistas increased its unpopularity.

The Zapatistas scored a major success in the 1995 negotiations when the Zedillo administration agreed to an indigenous "bill of rights." However, in 1996 the government retreated from its position, tried to renegotiate the agreements it had previously reached with the EZLN (the so-called San Andrés Accords), and boycotted all discussions on social policy, justice, and democracy. In late 1996, the Zapatistas decided to abandon their negotiations with the government, stating that they would return to the negotiating table only if the San Andrés Accords on indigenous rights were enacted into law. The massacre of indigenous peasants by paramilitary forces at Acteal, Chiapas in December 1997 marked the low point in relations between the EZLN and the national government, after which the Zedillo administration persevered in its political offensive against the Zapatistas.

The main form of civic mobilization in Mexico during this period was solidarity with the EZLN. There were massive spontaneous mobilizations in 1994, 1995, and 1999, and in March 2001 the Zapatistas led a march from Chiapas to Mexico City that passed through several states with large indigenous populations. The "consultations" that the Zapatistas convoked in 1995[44] and 1999[45] were (alongside Civic Alliance's election monitoring efforts in 1994) among the first civic initiatives of national scope. The April 1999 consultation mobilized thousands of citizens throughout the country, demonstrating a widespread consensus that Mexican society had long neglected Indian rights and the time had come to recognize indigenous communities in law and in fact.

Ironically, the fact that these mobilizations were highly spontaneous undercut their political effectiveness. They were clearly relevant in symbolic terms, but they were not sustained by a coherent political strategy that could take full advantage of popular solidarity. The lack of political direction, from both the Zapatista movement and civil actors, was striking.

Indeed, after the Zapatistas abandoned peace negotiations in 1996, their relationship with supportive intellectuals and politicians began to deteriorate. The EZLN suspected its urban allies of using ties with indigenous groups to promote their own political careers. Moreover, given that EZLN leaders were geographically constrained in their movements, the only way to promote a truly national indigenous movement was to permit urban actors and movements to establish the necessary networks. The Zapatistas, reluctant to open such a window, "retired" their counselors.

---

44 More than one million people participated in the 1995 National Consultation for Peace and Democracy, "voting" at the more than 8,000 polling stations set up by Civic Alliance (AC), which organized the referendum. The two key issues under consideration were whether people wanted peace in Chiapas, and whether they felt the EZLN should become a political movement. Most citizens backed the EZLN's demands.

45 In 1999 the Zapatistas dispatched almost 5,000 members of indigenous communities from throughout Mexico to organize the consultation. Human rights networks, members of Civic Alliance, NGO activists, and PRD militants helped the Zapatistas set up voting booths to measure public opinion regarding implementation of the San Andrés Accords.

In September 1997 the EZLN launched a new political initiative – the Zapatista Front for National Liberation (FZLN), a civil-political movement that was to support the EZLN. Unfortunately, the FZLN lacked political direction and leadership. Wanting to maintain political control over the organization, the EZLN excluded its former intellectual and political allies. These urban cadres were prone to internal dissension, and the Zapatistas did not want to become embroiled in the Mexican Left's tradition of factionalism. However, excluding old allies also denied the FZLN the leadership and political and social networks it needed in order to become an effective national political movement.

The EZLN's attempt to retake the political initiative by establishing the FZLN failed. In the absence of a professional, charismatic, and pluralist leadership, constructing a civic-political space proved to be too difficult. In 1994 and 1995, urban Mexicans had demonstrated their strong support for the Zapatistas and indigenous rights, as well their vigorous opposition to civil war and the military repression of Mexico's indigenous population. They were not, however, eager to see the Zapatistas become a quasi-political movement. In addition, the conditions that had favored the creation of a social movement in Chiapas were absent in other indigenous regions,[46] leaving the Zapatistas politically isolated.[47]

This experience demonstrated that civic campaigns are symbolically important and were capable of blocking massive government repression as a solution to the "Indian problem." However, civic campaigns cannot realize their full potential in terms of rights and institutions unless political actors accept input from society and create a consensus with the government. This connection failed to materialize in 2001 when all political parties approved an indigenous rights bill (the Law on Indigenous Rights and Culture) without consultation with the indigenous movement. Civic politics is, then, the politics of influence, not the politics of decision making.

The Case of El Barzón

The only exception to the crisis of class-associative civil society actors after 1994 was El Barzón, a massive debtors' relief movement comprised of small and midsize farmers, urban mortgage holders, and credit cardholders. Mexico's middle classes, victimized by rapidly rising bank interest rates after 1993, were devastated by the 1995 economic collapse. Debtors responded to banks' excessive rates with massive

46 One of the main facilitating conditions in Chiapas was social activism by the Catholic Church. Bishop Samuel Ruiz had developed an impressive network of religious-civic activists, politically radicalized by the teachings of liberation theology. Without this network, the Zapatistas would have been unable to create their own movement.

47 The Zapatistas' political isolation temporarily revived a close relationship between them and the National Indigenous Congress (CNI) in 2001, when movements for indigenous rights reached their peak. However, this relationship ended when the Zapatistas suddenly and incomprehensively left Mexico City for Chiapas just before the federal Chamber of Deputies approved on April 29, 2001 a (limited) indigenous rights bill.

mobilization, first in rural Zacatecas and Jalisco and eventually in nearly all Mexican states. El Barzón mobilized a sector of rural society that had been passive for almost sixty years. When the movement spread to urban areas, it created the possibility of building an alliance between middle classes from the countryside and the city.

El Barzón was characterized by its imagination and innovation in developing collective actions, which combined political pressure with all available legal means to block bank actions against debtors (Torres and Rodríguez 1994). However, the countertendency was the reproduction of old political practices. Various political and personalist tendencies struggled to dominate the movement, ultimately fracturing it as each tendency formed its own grouping. Factionalism limited the movement's political efficacy and muddied its image in public opinion.

El Barzón's core leaders soon turned to participation in political parties, following social movements' national tradition of politicizing social action. Although El Barzón sought relief for indebted Mexicans, it also criticized the Zedillo administration's economic policy as a whole. On this front, it sought alliances with unions and peasant movements in order to force the government to abandon the neoliberal economic model. El Barzón joined RMALC in its effort to open up new spaces for collaboration with other social actors. *Barzonistas* were relatively successful in protecting their constituency from the abuses of commercial banks, but they lacked sufficient political strength to create a true national campaign against neoliberalism.[48]

Similar consumer protests were staged in several states against the Mexican Telephone Company (TELMEX, the private telephone monopoly) and against the Federal Electrical Commission. The most important movements took place in Yucatán against the Federal Electrical Commission in 1988–1989 and against TELMEX in 1992–1993,[49] and in Chihuahua against TELMEX in 1996–1998.[50] Consumer movements of lesser duration and intensity occurred in Baja California, Nuevo León, Sonora, and Veracruz. Even though collective actions such as these had taken place around the country since 1990, these local struggles did not lead to the formation of national movements because they were hampered by differences in timing and the lack of a legitimate, nationally recognized leadership.

Nongovernmental Organizations: A New Form of Associationism?
Mexican NGOs have increased dramatically in number and variety since the mid-1980s. Unfortunately, there is very little accurate information concerning the distribution of these organizations. Most civic groups have no legal recognition, and there is no centralized information on those that do. In the case of so-called civil associations – a form of legal recognition that civic groups (including most

48 See Torres 1999 for an overall evaluation.
49 This discussion is based upon information drawn from newspaper archives held by the Frente Cívico Familiar (Family Civic Front) in Mérida, Yucatán.
50 This discussion is based upon information drawn from newspaper archives held by the Frente Cívico de Chihuahua (Chihuahua Civic Front) in Chihuahua, Chihuahua.

NGOs and all recreational, social, cultural, and even religious associations) often use because it is not under state control – the only office that gathers relevant information is the Ministry of Foreign Relations (SRE), which is not subject to external scrutiny. The SRE has no control over civil associations; it merely maintains a roster of their names and addresses and the objectives listed at the time of their constitution. The SRE guarantees that associations' names are not repeated, but if an association is dissolved for any reason, the Ministry's records will not show this.

Given the lack of reliable statistical information, the only way to gauge the density of associationism in Mexico is through surveys. The best survey, conducted in 1996 by the newspaper *Reforma* (July 15, pp. 8–9), found that 28 percent of Mexico's urban adult population participated in religious groups; 24 percent in recreational or sports clubs; 11 percent in professional associations (including unions); 14 percent in cultural or educational groups; 13 percent in organizations that promoted citizen participation; 8 percent in groups devoted to assisting the poor; and 5 percent each in environmental and human rights associations. Even acknowledging the likelihood of overlapping organizational memberships, it is reasonable to conclude that about 15 percent of adult Mexicans living in urban areas in the late 1990s considered themselves participants in civil associations (excluding religious and recreational groups, which operate in the private realm). This is a surprisingly high proportion for a country without a civic tradition. One would expect that the figure for "professional associations" would be high in the countryside, where there is a long tradition of (merely symbolic) membership in peasant organizations. But in terms of modern civic groups, the figure would have been much lower in the countryside than in the cities.

There are no past surveys with which to compare the *Reforma* data. However, expanding civic participation is clearly a recent phenomenon in Mexico, occurring simultaneously with the regime's legitimacy crisis and the slow but steady process of political liberalization. Although NGOs are just one form that civic participation can take, they were certainly the most visible form of civic associations in Mexico at the end of the twentieth century (see table 13.1).

Almost half of the NGOs operating in Mexico in the late 1990s were located in Mexico City, a concentration that exceeded the proportion of the national population living in the capital.[51] Another quarter of these organizations were found in Guadalajara, Jalisco; Oaxaca, Oaxaca; Saltillo, Coahuila; and Tijuana, Baja California. They are clearly, then, an urban phenomenon – the product of the actions of relatively privileged (culturally and economically) groups. Indeed, NGOs are comprised mainly of professionals and other educated people active in nonprofit activities or supported by wealthy individuals committed to promoting public welfare.

In the late 1990s there were twelve thematic NGO networks in Mexico, the most important of which were engaged with human rights, health-related issues, women's rights, and food provision services (see table 13.2). In addition, there were at least five territorial networks based in the states of Baja California, Guanajuato, Jalisco, Oaxaca, and Veracruz (García 1997) (see table 13.3).

Table 13.1: **Nongovernmental Organizations in Mexico, 1996**

Type	Number of NGOs	Source of Information
Environment	1,027	CEMEFI, 1996
Women's rights	437	FAM, 1996
Human rights	376	CNDH, 1996
Services to indigenous communities	270	FAM, 1996
Rural development	200	FAM, 1996
Multi-purpose activities (but oriented to human rights)	576	CNDH, 1996
Welfare assistance	1,883	CEMEFI, 1996
Arts, science, and culture	248	CEMEFI, 1996
Total	5,017	

Note: See the List of Acronyms for individual organization names.

Table 13.2: **Thematic Networks of Nongovernmental Organizations in Mexico, 1990s**

Network	Focus	Number of Organizational Affiliates	Number of States	Year Founded
Habitat	Housing	30	5	1976
PRODUSSEP	Health	40	21	1984
Network against Extreme Poverty	Socioeconomic development	28	15	1990
Mexican Social Projects Network	Social development	30	10	1990
All Rights for All	Human rights	46	23	1991
Mexican Coordinating Committee in Support of Children	Children	8	1	1992
Front for the Right to Proper Nutrition	Nutrition	130	20	1994
Council for a Sustainable Silviculture	Rural development	7	6	1994
Radio Spaces of Mexican Women	Communications, women's rights	17	11	1995
Action for Youth	Youth services	21	8	1994
Women's Network	Women's rights	12	4	1995
Feminist Millennium	Women's rights	250	30	1996

Source: García 1997.
Note: See the List of Acronyms for the name of individual organizations.

Table 13.3: **Territorial Networks of Nongovernmental Organizations in Mexico, 1990s**

Network	State	Year Founded	Number of Organizational Affiliates
AUDAS	Baja California	1993	16
FOCIV	Jalisco	1995	60
Organized Civil Society	Guanajuato	1995	27
FOCO	Oaxaca	1995	59
ROCVER	Veracruz	1998	45

Source: García 1997.
Note: See the List of Acronyms for the name of individual organizations.

NGOs can be very different kinds of organizations. Some are highly professional; others include family businesses. Some are institutions linked to the Catholic Church; others are closely associated with political parties or conservative social groups.[52] It would be a mistake to draw general conclusions for the sector as a whole. Nevertheless, one can state with certainty that this is the most visible part of civil society in Mexico, the one most directly oriented toward intervention on public issues, and the one that is most actively engaged in development-related activities. Even so, the sector's size and influence are rather limited considering Mexico's large population.[53]

Pro-Democracy Movements

In mid-1991, Dr. Salvador Nava, a renowned opposition figure from the state of San Luis Potosí, achieved what had theretofore seemed impossible: a broad opposition front that brought together the PAN and the PRD, along with the Potosino Civic Front. This broad civic-political alliance attracted the attention of both academic institutions and human rights groups. For example, the Mexican Academy of Human Rights (AMDH) observed the gubernatorial election in San Luis Potosí in which this opposition front challenged the PRI,[54] an action that spurred other groups' interest in election monitoring for the 1991 midterm federal elections.

51 In 2000 the Mexico City metropolitan area accounted for about 20 percent of the national population (nearly 20 million inhabitants).

52 This is the case of the Junta de Asistencia Privada (Private Welfare Board) in Mexico City, an institution that controls social welfare associations and whose former leader is closely linked to the Catholic hierarchy. See San Juan 2001.

53 Brazil has at least five times as many NGOs as does Mexico. Research on the "third sector" (Salomon and Anheir 1999) has shown that Mexico has a very low level of civic organization.

54 Dr. Nava lost the election due to fraud, but a massive post-election struggle forced the "elected" PRI governor to step down after two weeks in office. Dr. Nava, Mexico's strongest voice for a united opposition front to defeat the authoritarian PRI regime, died before a new election could be held.

Such experiences created a collective focus upon elections as a key component of democratic transition. Convergencia formed the Commission on Civic Education and Electoral Processes to observe local and national elections, joining efforts with other academic and civic institutions. This undertaking involved only about 350 observers in each local election. Nevertheless, these experiences helped affirm the principles of political pluralism, professional objectivity, and autonomy from political society and the state.

Prior to Mexico's 1994 presidential election, over four hundred civic groups and NGO networks drew upon the experience they had gained in monitoring state elections[55] and joined forces to create the Civic Alliance in order to monitor the federal electoral process. Civic Alliance soon had local chapters in 29 of Mexico's 31 states.[56]

From May through July 1994, nearly 40,000 citizens throughout Mexico monitored approximately 2,000 polling stations; tracked each party's television coverage (both news reporting and paid advertising); scrutinized the actions of electoral institutions and officials at the district, state, and federal levels; and informed thousands of citizens of their basic political rights. This massive citizen participation was predicated upon the shared conviction that free and fair elections would produce an opposition victory in 1994. This did not prove to be the case, however; the presidency went to Ernesto Zedillo Ponce de León, candidate of the "official" PRI. Nonetheless, participants in the monitoring effort were not diverted from their objective. They determined to remain organized nationally in a loose network of local groups under the Civic Alliance name.

The organization's main objective after the 1994 election was to continue monitoring municipal, state, and federal elections, with the goal of thereby forcing the government to respect electoral rules and guarantee fair elections. But Civic Alliance was soon called upon to perform new functions, as well. For example, the Zapatistas asked it to organize a National Consultation for Peace and Democracy in August 1995 in order to demonstrate public support for indigenous rights and clarify public expectations about the Zapatistas' future role in Chiapas. Over 1,088,000 participants responded to the consultation's questionnaire concerning attitudes toward expanding indigenous rights.[57]

In another instance, a national grouping of economic organizations asked Civic Alliance to convoke a consultation on economic justice. The group also helped organize, though with less success, a referendum on an alternative national economic policy (for which it gathered only 428,345 signatures). These consultations, as well as others carried out in 1996, created an alternative public space in which topics that constituted severe criticisms of the Zedillo administration's political and economic policies were brought to national attention.

55 Monitors had overseen state elections in Yucatán in 1990 and 1993, San Luis Potosí in 1991, and Michoacán in 1992.
56 The states without local branches were Campeche and Durango. For details on the Civic Alliance, see Aguayo Quezada 1998 and Olvera 2001.
57 On the activities and development of the Civic Alliance, see Olvera 2001 and McConnell 1996.

The Civic Alliance also strove to create precedents of government account-ability. Efforts in this area ranged from a legal suit to force the president to release information about his and his staff's salaries to the monitoring of Tabasco's state budget. Initiatives of this kind were generally unsuccessful, however, because they were effectively blocked by a judicial branch that remained strongly dominated by the executive (Olvera 2001).

Besides bringing civil society into the electoral process (albeit only symbol-ically), Civic Alliance introduced another very important innovation: plurality in its membership. It was the first Mexican social movement that was not politically or ideologically homogeneous (although all of its members shared a concern for democracy). Many of the organization's leaders had a common background in NGO activity, but variety was the rule at the grassroots level, making Civic Alliance a very different organization from one state to another. These differences, combined with enormous variation in local political conditions, produced some highly creative and influential experiences – as well as some unexpected failures.

The most successful of the Civic Alliance's chapters were those in areas where strong local social groups were already active in highly authoritarian settings. In these situations, the newly created Alliances strengthened preexisting local groups, which had gained legitimacy through past struggles against other kinds of rights violations. The result was an increase in the local chapters' public influence and their emergence as a common reference point for other collective actions. This was the case in Coahuila, Sonora, and Yucatán, where the Civic Alliance helped promote change in state-society relations.

In contrast, the Civic Alliance did not prosper in areas with an established tradi-tion of civic activism and plentiful nongovernmental organizations. These cases included Mexico City, Guadalajara, and, to a lesser extent, the state of Veracruz. In these places, civic groups had already created their own public spaces, and they did not need the Alliance. Indeed, in some cases the Civic Alliance represented compe-tition. Other factors limiting the Alliance's impact in these areas were internal factionalism, a lack of motivation on the part of some affiliates, and comparatively low visibility in a public space already populated by several civic organizations. The relative weakness of the Civic Alliance in Mexico's less authoritarian regions revealed how preexisting NGOs opted first to preserve their own spaces of action and only secondarily cooperated with the national movement for democracy (Olvera 2001).

In the year 2000, the Civic Alliance again coordinated an impressive operation to monitor the presidential election. The fact that this historic election was won by an opposition candidate, Vicente Fox, made the Alliance's efforts almost invisible. Nevertheless, it continued to detect electoral fraud – especially vote buying, various efforts to exert political or personal pressure upon voters, and attempts to use government programs to influence voters' choices. Problems such as these still limit the full exercise of political rights in Mexico.

The fact that Mexico has achieved a democratic transition in electoral terms represents a success for the Civic Alliance and similar groups. In fact, at least a third of the "citizen officials" responsible for organizing and overseeing the 2000 national elections were at the time current or past members of Civic Alliance affiliates. In a way, however, the fulfillment of the Alliance's national electoral mission may mean a decline in its political influence. In an effort to maintain its position, the Alliance has turned its attention to such challenges as monitoring public finances, and it has initiated a civic education campaign focused upon youth.

Struggling for Visibility and Action in Civil Society

Leaders of NGO networks and pro-democracy movements followed a variety of strategies when attempting to intervene in the political arena. Their core goal was to interlink the diverse networks in order to raise the visibility of their demands and to enhance their public influence. In mid-1995, virtually all NGO networks and pro-democracy social movements in Mexico organized a National Encounter of Civic Organizations (ENOC) to define a national "citizens' agenda" on democratization; the rights of women, minorities, and indigenous peoples; environmental and economic rights; justice and human rights; labor rights and institutions; agrarian laws and institutions; and new local-level government institutions. This consensus agenda, based upon both classic and "third-generation" rights and their institutionalization, was a noteworthy political achievement. It marked the first time that the most active elements in Mexican civil society had agreed upon a rights agenda – and designed a national campaign to force the government to commit itself to recognizing and protecting these rights (San Juan 1999).

Unfortunately, this outstanding programmatic achievement lacked a corresponding political agreement. Tensions soon appeared among the leaders of this initiative. Proponents of activities directed toward party politics or "upward articulation" clashed with leaders who favored "horizontal articulation" and were disinclined toward engagement with political parties. Furthermore, the organizational need to create both a central coordinating body and parallel structures in each state provoked rivalries for these posts among leaders of various NGOs. Thus modern urban civil society showed that it is not free from age-old problems of factionalism, the quest for personal power, and struggles to determine who is the legitimate representative of civil society.

It is not possible to represent a politically plural set of small organizations, most with very specific (even micro-sociological or sectoral) agendas and practices, as if it were a homogenous social or interest group. The only realistic means of creating overarching linkages among such organizations is to emphasize very directed, time-specific campaigns in which most participating organizations concur on the broad issues involved. Any attempt at monopoly representation is doomed to fail because of the very nature of civil society, as the ENOC case clearly demonstrated. But even more important is the fact that civil society politics can only be a politics of influence. Civil society organizations seek to influence the political system through the public sphere and by means of moral and symbolic agreements. The politics of civil society cannot be the politics of sectoral representation in the traditional corporatist style. Nevertheless, the two are often (mistakenly) conflated in Mexico.

After the failure of the ENOC initiative, some of its leaders opted for more direct participation in politics. Several agreed to run as opposition candidates for seats in the federal Chamber of Deputies, ultimately becoming members of their sponsoring party.[58] Others supported the establishment of national political groupings (APNs), a new form of association introduced in the 1996 reform of the federal election law.[59] In effect, the APN classification became a means of legally recognizing proto-political parties[60] and a way for old, delegitimized political elites to survive after losing their formal party registration.[61]

Civic actors did not understand the true nature of the APN classification. Some tried to use this new legal category to win formal recognition for pro-democracy civic organizations. For example, the Civic Alliance opted for this form of legal registration – a controversial decision that generated internal problems and a public image crisis. The Alliance's intention was to use this new classification to force national election authorities to give legal recognition to pro-democracy citizen politics and to its organizations. However, some Alliance members decided not to participate in this venture, and several political analysts noted that the Civic Alliance had finally (and appropriately) determined to become a proto-political party. These analysts saw citizen politics as a false politics, a mere disguise for partisan public practices.

Paradoxically, the Civic Alliance remains a social movement that is profoundly opposed to party politics. Although it sees its role as facilitating democracy, the majority of its members are very critical of parties. When the Federal Electoral Institute made the Alliance's legal registration conditional upon the removal from its statutes of certain articles regarding electoral observation, the Alliance's members felt that the IFE had betrayed them. And when the Electoral Tribunal of the Federal Judicial Branch (TEPJF) rejected the Alliance's protest of the IFE's decision, not only did the Alliance not receive legal recognition, but it also suffered an internal crisis and a loss of public prestige (Olvera 2001).

The Civic Alliance example illustrates the difficulties that NGOs have encountered in their efforts since the mid-1990s to institutionalize their space of action by gaining legal recognition. As long as NGOs remain civil associations, they cannot receive public financial support and they cannot be recognized as "public interest" organizations. In fact, the quest for legislation regulating civic organizations is one

---

58 This occurred in the cases of Demetrio Sodi and Julio Faesler, for example.

59 One such APN was Causa Ciudadana (Citizen Cause), whose aim was to help civic leaders open a space for party politics.

60 Examples included Sociedad Nacionalista (Nationalist Society), Party of the Democratic Center (PCD), and Convergencia, among others.

61 This was the case with the Authentic Party of the Mexican Revolution (PARM) and the ultraconservative Sinarquist movement.

of the few issues on which NGOs are truly united.[62] The PRI government, viewing NGOs as proxies for opposition parties, denied that there was any need to recognize civic organizations legally. The PRD and the PAN offered NGOs their support in this regard, but during his term as governor of the Federal District (1997–1999) Cuauhtémoc Cárdenas was unable to win approval for a civil organizations law because the PAN's delegation in the Federal District legislative assembly refused to support the final draft.

The July 2000 presidential election placed civic organizations in a new predicament by concentrating public attention upon the electoral process and (at least temporarily) pushing civil society issues to the sidelines. Reacting to this situation, a group of civic organizations began promoting horizontal articulation among NGOs in order to define a national civil society agenda and then win candidate and party commitments to that agenda. This campaign, known as "Citizen Action for Democracy and Life," had as its motto "power is the people" ("*el poder es la gente*"). It bore a strong resemblance to the ENOC initiative in 1995, but there was less pluralism among the groups involved. Only relatively leftist organizations – including the Civic Alliance, Citizen Cause, Convergence of Civic Organizations for Democracy, the RMALC, and Movimiento Ciudadano por la Democracia (Citizens' Movement for Democracy) – were engaged in the campaign. The FAM, CEMEFI, and VERTEBRA (a grouping of conservative civic organizations) were not called upon to co-organize the effort. Even more noteworthy, Citizen Action included almost no social organizations. Indeed, the absence of direct participation by labor unions, peasant groups, urban residents' organizations, or student and professional associations once again left the organized NGO networks and pro-democracy movements assuming the role of representatives for society at large. Given Citizen Action's particular composition, it is unlikely that the PAN or the PRI would accept in its entirety any agenda that this organization developed.

Conclusion: Changes in Mexican Civil Society and the Transition to Democracy

Developing a strong civil society is a long-term process, and Mexico's civil society is still weak. This weakness is rooted in the historical legacies of Mexico's post-revolutionary authoritarian regime. The corporatist system was enormously successful at integrating popular and class-based actors into the regime. Collective action was action within and toward the state, and all aspirations toward autonomy were repressed. The fact that the state was the main economic force led to the political

---

62 In the late 1990s, the coalition lobbying political parties, the federal Chamber of Deputies, and the media on this bill included representatives of the Forum for Mutual Support, the Mexican Center for Philanthropy, the Miguel Alemán Foundation, Convergencia, and even the Universidad Iberoamericana. Yet despite strong and widespread civil society support for this legal initiative, it did not meet with success.

subordination of the bourgeoisie as well. The rule of law was ignored, public space was monopolized by the state, and tolerance was relative.

As the corporatist system eroded between the early 1970s and the late 1980s, new social actors – independent labor unions, an opposition peasant movement, student organizations, and alternative business associations – began to appear. Popular mobilizations became the main form of collective action, along with national coordinating networks (*coordinadoras*) of unions, peasant organizations, and urban neighborhood groups. These movements (especially independent unionism) expanded as political liberalization increased. However, the prolonged economic crisis of the 1980s and these movements' own inability to counter the "low-intensity war" that quasi-official corporatist organizations waged against them edged them into decline. Moreover, many peasant organizations and urban dwellers were either co-opted by the government or gravitated to opposition political parties.

The impossibility of achieving true freedom of association forced social actors to channel their efforts into the electoral arena as early as 1988. Class conflicts became less visible and more and more local in character. Although social conflict was probably as intense and widespread as before, factionalism within the PRI government – along with the regime's declining capacity to absorb or repress autonomous actors at will – multiplied the number of political arenas open to social actors.

New kinds of social movements appeared in the late 1980s and early 1990s, most of them directing their activities toward defending human rights or promoting local social and economic development. Over time, these urban-cultural movements formed networks and alliances that helped publicize and extend their activities. These groupings were new insofar as they exposed the regime's authoritarian nature, heralded democratic values as something unprecedented in Mexican political culture, and transcended local and economic goals. They were pluralistic actors organized as loose networks with no formal institutionalization.

These movements offered telling criticisms of the established regime. Not only did they point out the contradiction between legitimacy and legality, but they also broke the regime's moral and practical monopoly over social policy. By proposing and even implementing innovative ways of resolving social problems via direct popular participation, Mexican NGOs demonstrated that there are alternatives to populist and clientelist social policies. Nevertheless, most of these new forms of collective action produced limited results. Nongovernmental organizations typically work in local settings with small groups, and they generally lack the economic, organizational, and professional resources to extend their reach beyond the micro level.

Pro-democracy movements were more successful. They created alternative public spaces, placed respect for political rights at the top of the national agenda, and contributed decisively to the design, creation, and operation of reformed election laws and new institutions that now promote electoral democracy in Mexico. Moreover, as the case of Civic Alliance demonstrates, pro-democracy movements introduced the principle of citizen monitoring of government, and they developed "public consultations" to place important issues on the national agenda. But in this instance, too, practices such as these have still had only limited political impact, and Civic Alliance's successes have had more symbolic than legal or institutional significance.

The fact that Mexico has completed a formal transition to democracy limits the impact of social mobilization in the electoral arena and pushes pro-democracy forces toward professionalization and specialization. A social movement per se cannot carry out citizen monitoring of government. Such tasks require technical, legal, and organizational capacities that depend upon institutionalization and per-manence – in this case, involving the formation of specialized NGOs. For the Civic Alliance, this tension between social movement and institutionalized organization eventually meant organizational paralysis, lack of direction, and loss of public presence.

Few popular movements achieved national significance in Mexico during the 1990s. The EZLN–led uprising in Chiapas highlighted the marginalization suffered by indigenous peoples, and the EZLN helped create a broad national consensus on indigenous rights issues. However, it could not create a nationwide indigenous movement or convert the pro-EZLN urban solidarity movement into a political force, leaving in place a political stalemate between the government and the EZLN. Similarly, El Barzón marked the awakening of traditionally invisible social groups, but the movement's diversity from state to state (even from city to city) allowed it to become a kind of clientelistic association, with competing leaders turned pro-fessional politicians.

Mexican civil society's central achievement during the 1990s was the progressive institutionalization of electoral democracy and increasing respect for political rights. Yet Mexico's transition to electoral democracy has not signified an epochal change in the relationship between government and civil society. The absence of a coherent project to reform the state, political stalemate between the executive and the Congress on important public policy issues, and continued problems of deep economic and social inequality are all factors that constrain prospects for the substantive democratization of public life. In such circumstances, one of the greatest threats to the future of Mexican democracy is the emergence of an antipolitical public mood that might (as has happened in several South American countries) delegitimate party politics.

References

Aguayo Quezada, Sergio. 1998. "Electoral Observation and Democracy in Mexico." In *Electoral Observation and Democratic Transitions in Latin America*, edited by Kevin J. Middlebrook. La Jolla: Center for U.S.–Mexican Studies, University of California, San Diego.

Aguayo Quezada, Sergio, and Luz Parra. 1995. "Los organismos no-gubernamentales de derechos humanos en México." Mimeo.

Aguayo Quezada, Sergio, and María Luisa Tarrés. 1995. "Las organizaciones no-gubernamentales y la democracia en México." Mimeo.

Aguilar Camín, Héctor. 1988. *Después del milagro*. Mexico City: Cal y Arena.

Alexander, Jeffrey. 1993. "The Return to Civil Society," *Contemporary Sociology* 22 (6): 44–76.

———. 1994. "The Paradoxes of Civil Society." SSRC Occasional Paper, no. 16. New York: Social Science Research Council.

Alianza Cívica. 1999. *Conclusiones de los foros sobre participación política de la sociedad civil*. Mexico City: Alianza Cívica.

Avritzer, Leonardo. 1995. "Transition to Democracy and Political Culture: An Analysis of the Conflict between Civil and Political Society in Post-Authoritarian Brazil," *Constellations* 2 (2): 242–67.

Avritzer, Leonardo, and Alberto J. Olvera. 1992. "El concepto de sociedad civil en el estudio de la transición democrática," *Revista Mexicana de Sociología* 54 (4): 227–48.

Bizberg, Ilán. 1990. *Estado y sindicalismo en México*. Mexico City: El Colegio de México.

Blancarte, Roberto, ed. 1995. *Religión, iglesias y democracia*. Mexico City: La Jornada Ediciones / Centro de Investigaciones Interdisciplinarias en Ciencias y Humanidades, Universidad Nacional Autónoma de México.

Calhoun, Craig. 1992. *Habermas and the Public Sphere*. Cambridge, Mass.: MIT Press.

Cansino, César. 2000. *La transición mexicana, 1997–2000*. Mexico City: Centro de Estudios de Política Comparada.

Canto, Manuel. 1998. "La discusión sobre la participación de las organizaciones civiles en las políticas públicas." In *De lo cívico a lo público: una discusión sobre las organizaciones civiles*. Mexico City: Red Mexicana de Investigadores sobre Organizaciones Civiles.

Casanova, José. 1994. *Public Religions in the Modern World*. Chicago, Ill.: University of Chicago Press.

Chalmers, Douglas, 1995. "Mexican NGO Networks and Popular Participation." Papers on Latin America, no. 39. New York: Institute of Latin American and Iberian Studies, Columbia University.

Cohen, Jean L. 1985. "Strategy or Identity: New Theoretical Paradigms and Contemporary Social Movements," *Social Research* 52 (4): 663–715.

Cohen, Jean L., and Andrew Arato. 1992. *Civil Society and Political Theory*. Cambridge, Mass.: MIT Press.

Cook, Maria Lorena, Kevin J. Middlebrook, and Juan Molinar Horcasitas. 1994. "The Politics of Economic Restructuring in Mexico: Actors, Sequencing, and Coalition Change." In *The Politics of Economic Restructuring: State-Society Relations and Regime Change in Mexico*, edited by Maria Lorena Cook, Kevin J. Middlebrook, and Juan Molinar Horcasitas. La Jolla: Center for U.S.–Mexican Studies, University of California, San Diego.

Córdova, Arnaldo. 1976. *La ideología de la revolución mexicana*. Mexico City: Era.

De la Garza, Enrique. 1994. "Los sindicatos en América Latina frente a la reestructuración productiva y los ajustes neoliberales," *El Cotidiano* 64: 24–32.

De Oliveira, Miguel, and Rajesh Tandon. 1994. *Ciudadanos en construcción de la sociedad civil mundial*. Mexico City: CIVICUS (Alianza Mundial para la Participación Ciudadana).

Escalante, Fernando. 1992. *Ciudadanos imaginarios*. Mexico City: El Colegio de México.

Farrera, Javier. 1994. "El movimiento urbano-popular, la organización de pobladores y la transición política en México." In *La construcción de la democracia en México*, edited by Víctor Manuel Durand Ponte. Mexico City: Siglo Veintiuno.

García, Sergio, ed. 1997. *Organizaciones no-gubernamentales: definición, presencia y perspectivas*. Mexico City: Demos / Foro de Apoyo Mutuo.

Gordillo, Gustavo. 1988. *Movimientos campesinos y política agraria en México*. Mexico City: Siglo Veintiuno.

Guerra, François-Xavier. 1989. *México: del antiguo régimen a la revolución*. Mexico City: Fondo de Cultura Económica.

Guerra, François-Xavier and Lempériere, Annick. 1998. *Los espacios públicos en Iberoamérica: ambigüedades y problemas. Siglos XVIII–XIX.* Mexico City: Centro Francés de Estudios Mexicanos y Centroamericanos / Fondo de Cultura Económica.

Habermas, Jürgen. 1987. *Teoría de la acción comunicativa.* Madrid: Piados.

———. 1989. *The Structural Transformation of the Public Sphere.* Cambridge, Mass.: MIT Press.

———. 1998. *Facticidad y validez: sobre el derecho del estado democrático del derecho en términos de teoría del discurso.* Madrid: Trotta.

Hernández Navarro, Luis. 1995. *Chiapas: la guerra y la paz.* Mexico City: ADN Editores.

Knight, Alan. 1986. *The Mexican Revolution.* 2 vols. Lincoln: University of Nebraska Press.

Lechner, Norbert. 1995. "La(s) invocacion(es) de la sociedad civil en América Latina." In *Partidos políticos y sociedad civil.* Mexico City: Congreso de la Unión.

Loaeza, Soledad. 1989. *El llamado de las urnas.* Mexico City: Cal y Arena.

Lomnitz-Adler, Claudio. 1992. *Exits from the Labyrinth.* Berkeley: University of California Press.

López Obrador, Andrés. 1999. *Mitos y realidades del Fobaproa.* Mexico City: Océano.

Luna, Matilde. 1992. *Los empresarios y el cambio político.* Mexico City: Instituto de Investigaciones Sociales, Universidad Nacional Autónoma de México / Era.

Lynch, Nicolás. 1991. "Social Movements and Transition to Democracy in Peru." Ph.D. diss., New School for Social Research.

Maxfield, Sylvia. 1990. *Governing Capital: International Finance and Mexican Politics.* Ithaca, N.Y.: Cornell University Press.

McConnell, Sharon Lean. 1996. "Alianza Cívica: un nuevo actor no gubernamental en el ámbito político mexicano." Master's thesis. Facultad Latinoamericana de Ciencias Sociales–México.

Melucci, Alberto. 1989. *Nomads of the Present: Social Movements and Individual Needs in Contemporary Society.* Philadelphia, Penn.: Temple University Press.

———. 1994. "A Strange Kind of Newness: What's 'New' in New Social Movements?" In *New Social Movements: From Ideology to Identity,* edited by Enrique Larana, Hank Johnston, and Joseph R. Gusfield. Philadelphia, Penn.: Temple University.

———. 1996a. *The Playing Self: Person and Meaning in the Planetary Society.* Cambridge: Cambridge University Press.

———. 1996b. *Challenging Codes: Collective Action in the Information Age.* Cambridge: Cambridge University Press.

Middlebrook, Kevin J. 1995. *The Paradox of Revolution: Labor, the State, and Authoritarianism in Mexico..* Baltimore, Md.: Johns Hopkins University Press.

Monsiváis, Carlos. 1987. *Entrada libre: crónicas de una sociedad que se organiza.* Mexico City: Era.

Muro, Víctor Gabriel. 1994. *Iglesia y movimientos sociales.* Mexico City: Red Nacional de Investigación Urbana / El Colegio de Michoacán.

Núñez González, Óscar. 1990. *Innovaciones democrático-culturales en el movimiento urbano popular.* Mexico City: Universidad Autónoma Metropolitana–Azcapotzalco.

Olvera, Alberto J. 1995. "Regime Transition, Democratization, and Civil Society in Mexico." Ph.D. diss., New School for Social Research.

———. 1997. "Transformaciones económicas, cambios políticos y movimientos sociales en el campo: los obstáculos a la democracia en el mundo rural." In *La democracia de los de abajo en México,* edited by Jorge Alonso and Juan Manuel Ramírez Saiz. Mexico City: La Jornada Ediciones.

———. 1998. "Problemas conceptuales en el estudio de las organizaciones civiles: de la sociedad civil al tercer sector." In *De lo cívico a lo público: una discusión de las organizaciones civiles,* edited by Manuel Canto. Mexico City: Red Mexicana de Investigadores sobre Organizaciones Civiles.

——. 1999. "Introducción." In *La sociedad civil: de la teoría a la realidad*, edited by Alberto J. Olvera. Mexico City: El Colegio de México.

——. 2001. *Movimientos sociales prodemocráticos, democratización y esfera pública en México: el caso de la Alianza Cívica*. Cuadernos de la Sociedad Civil, no. 6. Jalapa, Mexico: Universidad Veracruzana.

Olvera, Alberto J., and Cristina Millán. 1994. "Neocorporativismo y democracia en la transformación institucional de la cafeticultura," *Cuadernos Agrarios* 10: 53–72.

Oxhorn, Philip. 1995. *Organizing Civil Society: The Popular Sectors and the Struggle for Democracy in Chile*. University Park: Pennsylvania State University Press.

Pereyra, Carlos. 1990. *Sobre la democracia*. Mexico City: Cal y Arena.

Pérez-Díaz, Víctor. 1993. *La primacía de la sociedad civil*. Madrid: Alianza.

——. 1997. *La esfera pública y la sociedad civil*. Madrid: Taurus.

Putnam, Robert D. 1993. *Making Democracy Work: Civic Traditions in Modern Italy*. Princeton, N.J.: Princeton University Press.

Rabotnikof, Nora. 1999. "La caracterización de la sociedad civil en la perspectiva del BID y del BM," *Perfiles Latinoamericanos* 15 (December): 27–46 .

Reyes Heroles, Jesús. 1966. *El liberalismo mexicano*. Mexico City: Fondo de Cultura Económica.

Reygadas, Rafael. 1998. *Abriendo veredas: iniciativas públicas y sociales de las redes de organizaciones civiles*. Mexico City: Universidad Autónoma Metropolitana–Xochimilco.

Rivera, Liliana. 1998a. *Dinámica sociopolítica local: entre redes y actores. El caso de Xico, Veracruz*. Jalapa, Mexico: Universidad Veracruzana.

——. 1998b. "El discurso de la participación en las propuestas de desarrollo social. ¿Qué significa participar?" *Sociedad Civil: Análisis y Debates* 7 (3): 9–50.

Rueschemeyer, Dietrich, Evelyne Huber Stephens, and John D. Stephens. 1992. *Capitalist Development and Democracy*. Chicago, Ill.: University of Chicago Press.

Sábato, Hilda. 1999. *Ciudadanía política y formación de las naciones: perspectivas históricas de América Latina*. Mexico City: El Colegio de México / Fondo de Cultura Económica.

Salomon, Lester, and Helmut Anheir. 1999. *Nuevo estudio del sector emergente (resumen)*. Baltimore, Md.: Center for Civil Society Studies, Johns Hopkins University.

San Juan, Carlos. 1999. "Tendencias de la sociedad civil: la puja de la sociedad y el estado a fin de siglo." In *La sociedad civil: de la teoría a la realidad*, edited by Alberto J. Olvera. Mexico City: El Colegio de México.

——. 2001. *Ciudad de México: experiencias de una ciudad en transición*. Cuadernos de la Sociedad Civil, no. 4. Jalapa, Mexico: Universidad Veracruzana.

Seligman, Adam. 1992. *The Idea of Civil Society*. Princeton, N.J.: Princeton University Press.

Taylor, Charles. 1990. "Modes of Civil Society," *Public Culture* 3 (1): 96–118.

Torres, Gabriel. 1999. "The El Barzón Debtors' Movement: From the Local to the National in Protest Politics." In *Subnational Politics and Democratization in Mexico*, edited by Wayne A. Cornelius, Todd A. Eisenstadt, and Jane Hindley. La Jolla: Center for U.S.–Mexican Studies, University of California, San Diego.

Torres, Gabriel, and Guadalupe Rodríguez. 1994. "El Barzón: un nuevo movimiento social," *Cuadernos Agrarios* 10: 74–95.

14

Indigenous Rights: The Battle for Constitutional Reform in Mexico

Luis Hernández Navarro and Laura Carlsen

This chapter analyzes the past and present legal status of Mexico's indigenous peoples,[1] focusing especially upon two alternative versions of constitutional reform on indigenous rights. The first initiative was drafted by the multiparty congressional Commission on Concordance and Pacification (COCOPA) and presented to the federal government and the Zapatista Army of National Liberation (EZLN) in November 1996. The COCOPA developed its proposal in compliance with the terms for implementing the San Andrés Accords on Indigenous Rights and Culture, signed by the EZLN and the Mexican government on February 16, 1996.[2] Although both the EZLN and the National Indigenous Congress (CNI) accepted the COCOPA initiative, President Ernesto Zedillo (1994–2000) rejected it. The second initiative was drawn up by a legislative commission and enacted into law by the Mexican Congress in May 2001. It was subsequently challenged in the courts.

These alternative proposals carried substantially different legal and political implications. The COCOPA proposal extended individual and collective rights to indigenous peoples and laid the groundwork for a pluriethnic Mexican nation. The 2001 law left many aspects of the legal structure fundamentally unchanged, and even the limited rights it proffered are severely constrained in practice.

Rarely in Mexico's history has a proposal for constitutional reform sparked such controversy. A number of factors have complicated the debate. The COCOPA initiative was the result of negotiations with an insurrectionary army, and its implementation would alter the nature of the Mexican state. The broad national

---

1 The authors have chosen to use the term "indigenous peoples" in this analysis, although they are aware of the debate that exists on this issue. "People," the term for which the U.S. government has stated its preference in the United Nations, fails to recognize the specificity of the thousands of indigenous groups in the world. Moreover, it refers to a number of persons rather than a culturally homogenous and historically specific group. "Ethnic groups" applies to all racial minorities within a state and ignores the aspect of pre-colonial insertion central to Mexico's definition of indigenous peoples. The term "indigenous peoples" was agreed upon as the basis for the International Labour Office (ILO) Convention 169 and the San Andrés Accords on Indigenous Rights and Culture.

2 For the complete text and analyses of the San Andrés Accords and the COCOPA initiative, see Hernández Navarro and Vera Herrera 1998; for a summary in English, see *Cultural Survival Quarterly* 23 (1): 33.

indigenous movement supporting the COCOPA proposal has demanded rights, not palliatives, as the solution to its social marginality. Moreover, the debate has taken place within a general climate of political transformation. Many Mexicans perceive collective rights as a threat to their individual rights. And finally, the lack of constitutional jurisprudence regarding indigenous rights – coupled with the absence of normal judicial practice in most indigenous zones – has created a legal vacuum and little experience of constructive precedents for legislating reforms.

Indians in the Mexican Constitution: Invisibility, Assimilation, and Ambiguity

Although Mexico has been pluriethnic and pluricultural since its founding, none of its constitutions has reflected that reality. Ruling elites, obsessed with erasing the "Indian" from the national geography, pressured indigenous groups to abandon their Indian identity beginning in the colonial era and continuing through Independence. Under Spanish colonialism, the enslaved Indian peoples saw their populations decimated by war and disease. Nevertheless, under the royal Laws of the Indies, they retained a certain degree of collective autonomy and property rights within their communities, and they were able to develop social and political subsystems that combined elements of preconquest self-government with obligations to the Spanish crown.[3]

The post-Independence constitutions, drawn up between the declaration of independence from Spain in 1810 and the end of the reform wars in 1857, sought to bind a fractured land by dismantling its colonial heritage. The needs to protect against foreign invasions, combat the power of the Roman Catholic Church and the military, and modernize the country led to a vision of national unity that precluded cultural differences.[4] Although Mexico's policies did not share the brutality of the United States' extermination of native peoples, the country's founding fathers asserted that to be Mexican meant to surrender one's Indian identity and, in the process, accept a de facto second-class citizenship. Although the 1814 and 1824 constitutions subsumed Indians within an image of a homogenous citizenry, in practice, Indian peoples continued to live semi-autonomously in surviving republics and under prehispanic forms of government.[5]

The 1857 constitution explicitly sought to outlaw the extensive landholdings of the Catholic Church and Indian communities. In his introduction to this constitution, Manuel Suárez Muñoz analyzed the consequences of the relevant

3 For a brief history, see Cordero Avendaño 1996: 250.

4 For example, in 1864 Francisco Pimentel wrote: "It should be proclaimed that the Indians forget their customs and even their language, if possible. Only in this way will they lose their concerns and form with whites a homogenous mass, a true nation" (in Monsiváis 1996: 56).

5 Such was the case, for example, in Oaxaca (Velásquez 2000), the Valley of Mexico (Medina 1995), and some Nahuatl lands (Lockhart 1992).

clause – "No civil or ecclesiastical corporation … shall have the legal capacity to acquire property or administer real estate" – for Mexico's indigenous population as follows: "The Indians, who as communal landholders lived in what amounted to almost an economic autarchy, became day laborers, rural proletariats at the service of wealthy new owners. The reform thus laid the foundation for the consolidation and expansion of the hacienda at the end of the nineteenth century" (in Benítez et al. 1996: 36). Indian communities were left without a legal framework for their political and land claims.

The revolutionary constitution of 1917 did little to correct the faults and omissions of its predecessors. The Mexican Revolution of 1910–1920 owed much to Indian peoples, who formed the rank and file of the revolutionary armies and produced its most emblematic national hero, Emiliano Zapata, the Nahuatl-speaking, mustachioed leader of Indian peasants from the state of Morelos.[6] Yet when the winning factions drew up the 1917 constitution, indigenous peoples gained little. The constitution enshrined the principles of social rights and collective subjects, but it did not specifically recognize indigenous peoples. Thus, although it gave indigenous communities a legal foothold by re-legalizing communal landholding, its failure to include specific legal and judicial recognition, in combination with the blatant assimilationist policies applied by a succession of postrevolutionary governments, maintained a regimen of exclusion toward Indian peoples.

Resistance and Perseverance: Legal Recourse and the Fight for Autonomy

Indigenous peoples were thus battered by a succession of laws that effectively prevented them from becoming full citizens on their own lands. However, Mexico's 56 ethnic groups were not passive victims. Alongside their many armed rebellions and insurrections, Mexico's indigenous groups also launched a sustained campaign of legal resistance (León Portilla 1996). From the Aztec scribes who petitioned Spanish monarchs to today's indigenous communities trying to protect their resources, Indian leaders have protested injustice, taken advantage of legal ambiguities, and proposed legal reforms.

Indian communities have also fought to conserve their evolving forms of self-government. In colonial Mexico, Indian republics were formally recognized in law, and they carried on their own affairs with remarkable autonomy. The *altepetl*, the Nahuatl prehispanic form of government, endured in its basic characteristics centuries after the Spanish conquest (Lockhart 1992). During Mexico's revolutionary period, agrarian reform laws gave indigenous groups a new platform on which to legally reconstitute communal landholdings, and some of the institutions designed to manage Indian affairs provided trenches from which to fight.

---

6 For an in-depth biography of Zapata, see Womack 1969.

Many indigenous communities in Mexico still select their local officials, church leaders, and land officers in general assemblies according to the customs of the cargo system.[7] Practices of autonomy – indigenous systems of political representation and decision making, and common-law judicial norms – constitute everyday life in many indigenous regions. These norms knit community, resolve conflicts, reinforce identity, and fill important gaps in a national justice system that often fails indigenous people (Sierra 1997). Conflict arises from the fact that the common-law norms and practices that function within the community are neither respected nor understood in state tribunals and, in the absence of any harmonization mechanisms, often clash with Mexican positivist law.[8]

In this context, the demand for autonomy has become the cornerstone of indigenous groups' efforts to reconstitute their peoples. Autonomy, defined by Guatemalan legal expert and Indian rights defender Augusto Willemsen Díaz (1991) as "the internal form of the exercise of self-determination of peoples," reflects the reality that Mexico contains within its boundaries peoples who have long lived with a sense of their own identity and a consciousness of difference. These peoples are direct descendants of the region's original populations. They conserve many of their institutions, cultures, and languages, and they are demanding that these be legally recognized. The Indian rights movement views autonomy as a guarantee and seeks to achieve full equality under the law through the recognition of differences. For indigenous peoples, the conquest of specific rights (not privileges) will end their status as permanent minorities and make them majorities in their own lands. Putting an end to unequal negotiations that pit indigenous groups against national political institutions will allow Mexico's Indians to commence the rebuilding of their peoples – culturally, economically, and politically.

For its part, the Mexican government has sought to portray Indian demands for autonomy as the result of non-Indian intellectuals' manipulation of indigenous peoples. Government spokespersons emphasize, for example, that Subcomandante Marcos of the EZLN is non-Indian and that his movement has the support of many prominent Mexican intellectuals, also non-Indian.[9] Yet nearly all indigenous groups practice elements of de facto autonomy. Although many Indian languages have no word for autonomy, Indian peoples have defended their customs for years using terms such as "our path." Moreover, indigenous autonomy is now part of Mexican law, pursuant to the country's signing of international treaties that recognize the primacy of the right to self-determination and that define autonomy as its legitimate and necessary practice.[10]

---

7 The cargo system is a socio-religious hierarchy of rotating posts recognized as the predominant form of local government in many Mexican indigenous regions. It has continued to evolve from its prehispanic and colonial roots. For details, see Medina 1995, among others.

8 On indigenous normative systems and the reconstitution of indigenous peoples, see Regino 1999.

9 This argument can be found in Tello Díaz 1995.

10 The United Nations' International Covenant on Civil and Political Rights and International

The Demand for Constitutional Reform

Historical efforts to forge an idealized, homogenous modern state out of the Mexican cultural mosaic – played out against the constant resistance of those who would be Mexicanized – led to today's legal and social contradictions. Although indigenous peoples have (albeit with varying degrees of success) been able to conserve their identity and much of their institutional life and culture, the ideal of assimilation and the consequent lack of a specific legal framework for indigenous peoples have generated complex structures of exclusion, discrimination, marginality, oppression, and exploitation.

With the reform of Article 4 of the Constitution in 1992, Mexico for the first time formally recognized the presence of its Indian peoples. The amended text stated: "The Mexican nation has a pluricultural composition based originally on its indigenous peoples." The article further stipulated that enabling legislation would guarantee the promotion and protection of indigenous languages, cultures, customs, and resources. Yet the would-be beneficiaries of this reform remained in legal limbo because the enabling legislation was never enacted. The revised Article 4 itself failed to specify the principles, relationships, and institutions whereby indigenous rights would be exercised. Instead, in the absence of new laws, the terms of implementation were presumably relegated to existing, often contradictory, laws (Gómez 1997). The constitutional reform thus fell far short of meeting indigenous peoples' minimum demands for recognition of their rights. Indeed, it did not even address their basic demand for autonomy as the exercise of self-determination.

The reform to Article 4 was largely a response to two events. The first was the worldwide attention focused upon Mexico during the quincentennial of Columbus's arrival in the Americas. The second was a related revitalization of the Mexican Indian movement. Several forums on indigenous rights focused national attention upon conditions in indigenous regions. One such forum (in Matías Romero, Oaxaca in 1989) gathered testimonies from indigenous peoples from throughout Mexico and began the process of formulating a consensus on demands for reforms to Article 4 (Carlsen 1989).

The increasing articulation of the Indian movement's various legal demands has produced an overwhelming consensus that the definition of Mexico as a pluricultural nation and the legal recognition of Indian peoples should stand alongside the basic principles of judicial equality and civil liberties that presumably now govern in Mexico. From this perspective, compliance with the present constitution

---

Covenant on Economic, Social, and Cultural Rights begin (article 1) with the statement: "All peoples have the right to self-determination. In virtue of this right, they establish freely their political condition and likewise provide for their economic, social, and cultural development." ILO Convention 169 was approved by the Mexican Senate and published in the *Diario Oficial de la Federación* on January 24, 1991. According to Article 133 of the Mexican Constitution, it therefore now forms part of the nation's legal framework.

is insufficient to do justice to the original peoples of Mexico. Major reforms are essential. Even if enabling legislation were implemented, it could not fill the lacunas in Mexican law as it applies to its Indian citizens.

The swelling call for comprehensive constitutional reform also recognizes that the isolated implementation of existing measures, however well intentioned they may be, cannot assure the full exercise of indigenous rights or the proper administration of justice in indigenous regions. According to Jorge Madrazo, former president of Mexico's National Human Rights Commission (CNDH) and federal attorney general,

> For years I thought that the country's ordinary tribunals would be able to administer justice for Mexico's ten million indigenous people. But the day-to-day facts have disabused me of that illusion. Today, for example, the procedural reforms mandated by the National Human Rights Commission [that require] translators, interpreters, and local judges well versed in indigenous common-law rights cannot be complied with, even on a modest scale (1996: 367).

Throughout the reform process, the new Indian movement – the subject and object of the proposed reforms – has been a central actor in the battle for its own rights. This loose coalition of regional and local groups has steadily gained visibility and leadership and developed its own spokespersons and positions. The movement's effervescence and the government's attempts to head off its popular initiatives have contributed to a virtual epidemic of state-level legislation on indigenous rights.

The first wave of reforms to state constitutions and the related implementing legislation took place while the reform to Article 4 of the federal constitution was still under debate (1989–1992). During this period, Campeche, Chiapas, Chihuahua, Durango, Guerrero, Hidalgo, Jalisco, the State of México, Nayarit, Oaxaca, Querétaro, Quintana Roo, San Luis Potosí, Sonora, and Veracruz all modified those parts of their constitutions that addressed Indian rights. However, the results were mixed.[11] With a few notable exceptions (Campeche, Chihuahua, Oaxaca, and Quintana Roo), the changes were rarely substantive and were not effective in promoting the full exercise of indigenous rights. Indeed, most of these constitutional modifications were, like the 1992 reforms to the national constitution, hollow rhetoric.

Whereas this first wave sought to apply federal reforms at the state level, the next wave of state-level constitutional change aimed to undermine the argument for

---

11 For example, Quintana Roo's Law on Indigenous Justice recognized traditional judges and created a Council of the Judicature on Indigenous Justice. In contrast, the constitutional reform in San Luis Potosí constituted a setback for indigenous rights because it attempted to incorporate Indian peoples into the state apparatus through Indigenous Councils similar to the corporatist structures imposed upon indigenous peoples in the 1970s.

For the complete collection of legal reforms on indigenous rights up to 1997, see Sirvent 1997.

further federal reform.[12] In the second legislative wave, five states (Chiapas, Michoacán, Nayarit, Oaxaca, and Veracruz) further revised their constitutions in ways that represented both advances and setbacks. However, rather than adjusting state laws to indigenous reality, these legislative changes primarily aimed to dilute the national character and urgency of the San Andrés Accords by making more superficial and less expansive reforms at the state level. State legislators from the "official" Institutional Revolutionary Party (PRI) received their instructions on this issue in the form of a Ministry of the Interior policy directive issued to state governments on August 18, 1998. In it, the ministry "suggested" active promotion of state constitutional reforms on indigenous rights, using as a point of reference the constitutional reform initiative that President Ernesto Zedillo had sent to the Senate in March 1998.

Mixtec lawyer and scholar Francisco López Bárcenas noted (1998) that the content of the state reforms corresponded almost exactly to the Ministry of the Interior's model. They include a declaration of Mexico's pluricultural character, followed by a recognition of Indian peoples' right to self-determination, expressed in their communities' autonomy to decide upon internal forms of regulating public life and organizing social, economic, and cultural norms. Whatever small gains these new laws may contain are rendered moot, however, because under Mexico's legal system most are overruled by the primacy of the federal Constitution. Moreover, in the majority of cases, these state-level reforms were enacted or attempted without input from those who are directly affected by them. State governors and local legislators have reduced Indian peoples to passive spectators in the design of state-level initiatives.

Oaxaca: Dilemmas of Indigenous Law

Oaxaca has provided the one bright spot on the horizon. Oaxacan Indian leaders' direct participation in their state's legislative reforms[13] contributed greatly to the San Andrés negotiations. At the end of the 1990s, Oaxaca was the state with the most advanced legal framework for the protection and exercise of indigenous rights. In fact, it has been a pioneer in recognizing Indian rights since 1986, when an organic law created and regulated the Attorney General's Office on Indigenous Defense.

On June 4, 1998, the Congress of the State of Oaxaca approved a constitutional reform that opened the way for a law on the rights of indigenous peoples and

---

12 Ironically, the main catalyst for much of this new legislation – the negotiations on indigenous rights and culture held in San Andrés Larráinzar, Chiapas, between the EZLN and the federal government in 1994–1996 – still awaits incorporation into law.

13 See especially the reforms to Book IV, Title I and Article 136 (paragraph 1) of Oaxaca's Code on Political Institutions and Electoral Procedures. For an analysis of the political process and the law itself, see Hernández Navarro 1999a.

communities.[14] The Law on the Rights of Indigenous Peoples and Communities follows the state's well-documented tradition of advanced legal reforms on indigenous issues by recognizing substantive rights for indigenous peoples and their communities. However, the law has not found unconditional support among the state's grassroots organizations and political parties. One current of the state's indigenous movement – including the Union of Indigenous Communities of the Northern Isthmus (UCIZONI) and the Indian Organization for Human Rights in Oaxaca (OIDHO) – has asserted that widespread human rights violations and the use of illegal means to maintain social control in the state invalidate the legal initiative. Another current of the indigenous movement – including Services to the Mixe People (SER) and the Statewide Coordinating Network of Coffee Producers of Oaxaca (CEPCO) – has, while voicing some criticisms, generally supported the law.

These various organizations have identified a series of shortcomings in the legislation. First, several of its articles violate citizens' right of free association. Second, the law does not stipulate the need to redraw municipal boundaries within the state to better reflect the actual distribution of indigenous peoples (an urgent task in areas such as the Triqui region). Third, it does not provide for the reform of specific state institutions. Fourth, it fails to address the problem of Indian representation in the state congress. And fifth, the law won the support of organizations belonging to the PRI–affiliated National Peasants' Confederation (CNC) and the Indigenous Councils only because these groups, traditionally identified with the government, were willing to give their unconditional support to any and all official actions.

The positions taken by the center-left Party of the Democratic Revolution (PRD) and the center-right National Action Party (PAN) demonstrated that, despite their efforts to democratize the state in other areas, their understanding of the Indian world is extremely limited. The PRD launched a last-minute effort to limit the scope and impact of the indigenous rights law by subordinating it to debate on a broader reform of state institutions (a reform that, it is worth noting, never materialized). Issues of public security, justice, and electoral reform are certainly important, as the PRD underscored. Yet in a state where at least half of the population is indigenous, strengthening indigenous rights is a crucial element in building democracy. Moreover, subordinating indigenous reform to the enactment of a broader democratizing agenda seriously underestimated the urgency of the ethnic struggle.

At the other end of the political spectrum, a statement from PAN deputy Jorge Isaac Jiménez confirmed that his party includes some of the most intransigent and reactionary elements of the Right:

14 The constitutional reform debate was heated. The leader of the National Action Party (PAN) deputies, Jorge Isaac Velazco, walked out of the chamber; Institutional Revolutionary Party (PRI) deputy Teódulo Domínguez argued that the initiative could not be approved before President Zedillo's proposal had been approved at the federal level; and deputies from the Party of the Democratic Revolution (PRD) were divided on the vote.

For an excellent review of the Oaxaca law, see López Bárcenas 1997.

> Three hundred years of conquest were insufficient to finish the mix between Spanish and Indians and that's why there are still eight million Mexicans in self-absorbed isolation and who have not enjoyed the advances of western Christian civilization (in Hernández Navarro 1999b: 85).

Jiménez proceeded to lambast the proposed legislation: "the legal initiative reads like a copy of Subcomandante Marcos's guerrilla plan," and "recognition of autonomy ... would destroy municipal government." Jiménez concluded on a paternalistic note: "more than a government law, what is needed is an effort to incorporate them [indigenous peoples] into civilized life" (in Hernández Navarro 1999b: 85).

Oaxaca's indigenous rights law has two major limitations. First, its recognition of indigenous jurisprudence and the validity of indigenous normative systems is extremely restricted and applies only in relatively minor cases. Second, the reforms it contains are overruled whenever state law conflicts with federal law.

In fact, conflict arises frequently between state law and the federal Constitution. Oaxaca's constitutional amendment permits the 417 Indian townships to bypass the system of political parties and select their local officials through *usos y costumbres* (customary practices). Many of these communities formerly lived under a dual political system, half real and half sham. They first elected their leaders in community assemblies; political parties (usually the PRI) then registered these winners as their own candidates. On election day, long after the real decision had been made, the government set up polling places and a fraction of the population "voted" for the candidates who already had been chosen. The entire process reflected the Indians' second-class status: "You can do it your way as long as you pretend to do it our way" – and as long as power formally remained in the hands of the PRI.

From the moment it was first considered in 1995, Oaxaca's constitutional reform generated conflict between the right of political parties to name candidates and the right of Indian communities to select officials through customary practices. The compromise solution outlined in the state law allows Indian communities to select officials in assemblies, without party affiliation, but it then obliges them to ratify their officials on election day. It also permits political parties to present parallel candidates.

The fragile nature of the Oaxacan compromise indicates the pitfalls of piecemeal legislation on indigenous issues. Similarly, in the state of Chihuahua in northern Mexico, attempts to implement indigenous rights reforms in 1993 ran up against charges of unconstitutionality because federal legislation lagged far behind the state initiative. Both examples demonstrate that, until the federal constitution contains an adequately clear vision of indigenous rights, indigenous electoral participation remains vulnerable to manipulation by established political parties.

The COCOPA Reforms

The Mexican federal government and the EZLN signed the Accords on Indigenous Rights and Culture in San Andrés Larráinzar on February 16, 1996. Over two hundred members of civil society – indigenous and nonindigenous, intellectuals, anthropologists, politicians, and leaders of nongovernmental organizations (NGOs) – had participated in developing and debating proposals for negotiation. The Accords, which were approved by the Zapatista rank and file and by base communities and the National Indigenous Congress, promised, if not an answer to all indigenous demands, at least a legal platform upon which to build a new relationship between Mexico's indigenous population and the government and society at large. The signing also augured a dignified peace between the Mexican army and the EZLN. But most of all, the Accords gave Indian communities a chance to break the stranglehold of rural caciques and local politicos, guide themselves according to their own ways, and become full citizens of a proudly pluriethnic nation. The negotiations had navigated a complex course and weathered many crises, and at last it seemed that real change was at hand.

Nine months later, those hopes lay dashed. In November 1996, the multiparty congressional Commission on Concordance and Pacification presented its legal initiative based on the Accords for an up-or-down decision. The Zapatistas accepted. Initially, the federal government accepted the COCOPA's proposal as well, but President Zedillo then stalled, asking for time to consult legal experts. On December 19, 1996, Zedillo presented his counterproposal, which bore little resemblance to the COCOPA document or to the San Andrés Accords. In January 1997, the Zapatistas rejected the presidential document, spinning the EZLN–government dialogue into a continuing crisis.

The groundbreaking feature of the San Andrés Accords and the COCOPA proposal is their recognition of indigenous peoples as social and historical subjects. The implications of this recognition are profound because it involves modifying the Mexican Constitution to recognize not only individual citizens but also indigenous peoples. Autonomy for Indian peoples further implies the real transfer of faculties, functions, and jurisdictions that currently fall to government agencies. These include political representation within the community and the municipality, autonomy of the local justice system, control over administrative affairs, and control over land and natural resources.

Internal political representation would allow indigenous peoples to bypass the realm of regular electoral participation and the political party system and name their own community and municipal authorities through the cargo system, community assemblies, and elders' councils. Political representation at the state and national levels would be assured through the creation of new electoral districts and special mechanisms to facilitate indigenous participation in elections as voters and as candidates.

The immediate and explicit transfer of judicial authority to autonomous indigenous communities would empower them to apply indigenous normative systems to regulate and solve internal conflicts. The sphere of implementation includes the community, the municipality, and associations of these, when appropriate.

Because this point has been a key issue of debate, it is important to note that these normative systems are generally well institutionalized. Judgments are transmitted orally, validated in a general assembly, and applied by groups of community members.[15] Moreover, there is broad social consensus regarding the content and functioning of these normative systems; they are neither discretionary nor ephemeral, nor are they the product of authoritarian whim. Instead, they are cohesive, based upon historical and cultural existence, and vital for ordering community life in penal, civil, and administrative areas. Through the application of these norms, indigenous communities resolve conflicts between individuals and also regulate the day-to-day operations of indigenous society around commonly held values. Not only have these systems long functioned with remarkable efficiency and legitimacy within Indian communities, but they also tend to compensate for deficiencies of the national justice system in indigenous zones.[16]

In the area of administrative affairs, public funds assigned to indigenous communities would be transferred to them in a gradual, orderly fashion. The realm of administrative jurisdiction includes the community or municipality (or associations of these), which would work directly with state and federal agencies while administering assigned funds within their own communities and municipalities.

Indigenous peoples would have collective use of natural resources on their lands and territories – their "habitat."[17] The COCOPA reform does not state that territories inhabited by indigenous peoples would cease to form part of the nation, but the peoples *would* be given decision-making power in resource management, environmental conservation, and land use. This process would be closely linked to institutional reforms of state agencies that work with Indian peoples to assure a higher degree of Indian participation in regional planning and other resource decisions. Subsoil resources would remain under national domain.

Dormant Negotiations and a Counterreform

A year-long impasse followed Zedillo's rejection of the COCOPA proposals. Then, in December 1997, Chiapas recaptured public attention when PRI–affiliated paramilitary forces massacred 45 men, women, and children in the highland hamlet of Acteal. Worldwide outrage forced the federal government to redefine its Chiapas strategy and compelled Governor Eduardo Robledo and Minister of the Interior Emilio Chuayffet to resign. Sidestepping the entire question of responsibility for the Acteal murders, the new minister of the interior, Francisco Labastida, announced that the federal government had reduced to four its objections to the COCOPA text and would forward its "observations" to the EZLN for discussion. In fact, the government's four observations were just a regrouping of its original objections. Although the EZLN rejected the government's new counterproposal,

15 In other words, a municipal president never judges alone.
16 According to legal anthropologist Teresa Sierra (1997), "The force of the normative systems has served to channel internal tensions and manage links with the outside, thereby reinforcing a national justice system incapable by itself of attending to affairs in the communities."
17 Habitat is defined as the area occupied and used by indigenous peoples, as specified in ILO Convention 169.

on March 15, 1998, President Zedillo presented his reform initiative on indigenous rights and culture to the federal Senate. Although the president's proposal claimed to be true to the COCOPA document and the San Andrés Accords, a detailed analysis showed substantial differences between the versions.[18]

There matters rested until after the July 2, 2000, elections, in which the Mexican electorate broke the PRI's seventy-one-year control over the presidency and carried PAN candidate Vicente Fox Quesada into office. One of Fox's campaign pledges had been to present the COCOPA initiative to the Congress, and shortly after taking office on December 1, he complied with that promise. Then, on March 25, 2001, a delegation of EZLN members culminated a twelve-state caravan from Chiapas to Mexico City with an unprecedented appearance on the floor of the federal Chamber of Deputies, where Comandante Esther and members of the National Indigenous Congress argued in favor of the COCOPA proposals. Nevertheless, despite broad public support for the EZLN caravan and its agenda, in April both chambers of Congress approved a constitutional reform on indigenous rights and culture that bore little resemblance to the COCOPA document.

The reform that was adopted (the Law on Indigenous Rights and Culture) eliminated or distorted many of the guarantees encompassed in the San Andrés Accords. For example, whereas the COCOPA initiative defined indigenous communities as "subjects of public rights," the so-called Fernández de Cevallos-Bartlett-Ortega law (named after the PAN, PRI, and PRD congressional leaders who agreed on it) used the term "subjects of public interest." This formulation was crucially important because it failed to include Indian peoples as part of the state structure, with collective rights and defined areas of jurisdiction.

Traditional forms of self-government were also severely constrained under the counterreform. Indigenous common law based upon communal norms differs substantially from Western law based upon concepts of individual rights and responsibilities, yet the 2001 reform limited the exercise of autonomy and self-government to the community level and required local decisions to be validated by the regular courts. Moreover, the measure remitted the creation of specific norms for the exercise of autonomy to the states, where the power of rural bosses historically opposed to indigenous rights is often notorious. The provision not only contradicted the purpose of establishing national norms through constitutional reform, but it virtually guaranteeds that the terms under which indigenous peoples exercise even limited autonomy will vary from state to state. Indeed, it subordinated indigenous peoples' normative systems even within their own territories.[19]

The most important departure from the COCOPA proposal concerned the specific mechanisms and jurisdictions for self-determination. The actual exercise of

18 See *Ce-Acatl: Revista de la Cultura de Anáhuac* (Centro de Estudios Antropológicos Científicos, Artísticos, Tradicionales y Lingüísticos "Ce-Acatl") 86 (May 1997).

19 Government officials in the state of Oaxaca have expressed concern that the 2001 constitutional reform actually struck down some of the indigenous rights advances contained in state laws. For a comparative analysis of the Mexican constitutional reform, see Carlsen 2002.

autonomy requires detailed norms and an area of legal jurisdiction in which to put it into practice. The 2001 reform purposefully omitted any such legal definitions. For example, the COCOPA initiative recognized indigenous communities' right to "accede in a collective manner to the use and enjoyment of the natural resources of their lands and territories – understood as the totality of the habitat that indigenous peoples use and occupy – with the exception of those whose direct dominion corresponds to the nation." In contrast, the Fernández de Cevallos-Bartlett-Ortega law merely granted indigenous peoples the possibility to "accede to the preferential use and enjoyment of natural resources in the places the communities inhabit and occupy." Legal analysts have pointed out that "preferential use" is not a guaranteed right, and that what this provision of the law recognized is essentially a privilege that any civil entity already enjoyed under Mexican law.

Finally, the 2001 measure did not include specific obligations for government agencies to consult with indigenous peoples concerning development projects, resource use, or changes in land use in the territories they occupy. In fact, it stated that existing constitutional provisions concerning land tenure and land-use decisions remained unchanged. This statement was important because reforms adopted in 1992 embedded in the Constitution the neoliberal objectives of breaking down precolonial and postrevolutionary collective ownership structures and privatizing rural holdings. Specifically, Article 27 was modified to permit the privatization of *ejido* lands, which constitute some 61 percent of the land in heavily indigenous communities (Procuraduría Agraria 2000).[20]

Legal and Political Objections to the San Andrés Accords and the COCOPA Initiative

From its inception, the COCOPA initiative produced vigorous legal and political debate. For example, one Zedillo administration official stated that the COCOPA's proposal "divides the country by positing territorial autonomy and special privileges for indigenous persons, which threatens national sovereignty over subsoil resources and involves establishing a fourth level of government" (*Proceso*, August 27, 2000).[21] Although the COCOPA proposal clearly exempted subsoil resources and made no mention of a fourth level of government, many legal experts upheld the government's refusal to endorse the initiative.

Constitutional scholar Ignacio Burgoa has insisted that the San Andrés Accords were not legal and that the way to guarantee indigenous rights in Mexico is to draw

20 The *ejido*, a collective form of land ownership, was a principal vehicle for the distribution of land during Mexico's postrevolutionary agrarian reform.

21 The possibility of creating a fourth level of government that would elevate indigenous regions to a legal status comparable to the municipal, state, and federal levels was in fact discussed during the San Andrés negotiations. The creation of legally recognized autonomous regions is a fundamental demand of the Plural Indigenous National Assembly on Autonomy (ANIPA). However, this formulation was not included in the San Andrés Accords.

up implementing legislation for Article 4: "The autonomy that indigenous peoples demand is recognized in Article 4 of the Constitution.... [T]his right, respect for cultures and customs, is included in this article" (*Proceso*, August 27, 2000, p. 44). However, Burgoa's equation of "respect for cultures and customs" with autonomy does not concur with the conception developed by indigenous rights experts.

Furthermore, Burgoa has affirmed that the San Andrés Accords could have no legal existence: "These were not accords or conventions, because ... [government representatives] negotiated a presumed pact with masked and disguised persons, which makes it legally non-binding." In his view, the Zapatistas were guilty of "the crime of rebellion" under Article 132 of the Federal Penal Code, making it impossible to conduct legal negotiations with them.

Other analysts have also suggested that the proposed COCOPA reforms were "unconstitutional." However, the Constitution itself outlines the procedures that would confer constitutionality upon them. Adelfo Regino, a Mixe lawyer and Indian rights activist, has noted: "Can the Constitution remain unchanged in the face of changing and bitter realities? For us, it is the Constitution and the laws that must adapt to indigenous reality, not the other way around" (1999).

In the debates preceding the 2001 constitutional reform, the most vociferous opposition to the COCOPA's proposal came from the business sector and President Vicente Fox's (2000–2006) own party, the PAN. Conservative legislators set out to strike from the proposal all clauses that seemed to threaten business interests, and leaders of the Mexican private sector issued outraged declarations to the press that expressed a mixture of racist fears and self-interest. The law on "indigenous rights" that was eventually adopted – devoid of practicable collective rights, meaningful autonomy, secure forms of collective land tenure, or decision-making power over land and resource use – left the private sector satisfied that it had overcome a serious threat to private property.

Congress's legalistic objections to the Fox/COCOPA proposal began with the definition of terms. Its advisers maintained that the COCOPA's definition of "peoples" – "those who descend from populations that inhabited the country when colonization began and before the establishment of the boundaries of the United Mexican States" – was ambiguous. The COCOPA's definition was, however, borrowed directly from ILO Convention 169. In it, "colonization" clearly refers to the Spanish colonization that began in 1521 and gave rise to the colonial regime (and not to subsequent migrations of foreigners).

Opponents also claimed that the COCOPA proposal sought special privileges and would inevitably have led to the "balkanization" of Mexico. Yet the risk of balkanization (or, as some observers see it, the establishment of U.S.–style Indian reservations) is a political assessment that has no legal basis. At no time in the past five hundred years have indigenous institutions presented a threat to Mexico's national unity. The COCOPA initiative did not propose any change in forms of property ownership beyond recognizing indigenous peoples' right "to use collectively and enjoy the natural resources of their lands and territories." As for the claim that the COCOPA initiative would have produced U.S.–style reservations, a review of the vast differences between the COCOPA initiative and the laws that created the U.S. reservations suffices to prove that this argument has no merit.[22]

Nor has de facto autonomy proved to be a source of privilege and exemptions for Indian peoples in Mexico. In the areas where indigenous normative systems are strongest, indices of social and economic well-being tend to be lowest. No evidence has been offered suggesting that legal recognition of indigenous peoples' autonomy would produce mini-nations within the nation, fragment Mexico, or afford special treatment to nonindigenous residents of indigenous regions. In fact, the San Andrés Accords' language regarding respect for human rights, especially women's rights, aimed at eliminating the discriminatory treatment that presently exists in indigenous areas.

Nevertheless, some important questions have been raised about the legal institutionalization of indigenous autonomy and normative systems, as well as the perceived conflict between collective and individual rights. Magdalena Gómez refers to this contradiction as "the false dichotomy" and describes the basis of legal criticisms as follows:

> To ask for recognition of different rights is to question the principle of universality, to create unacceptable regimes of exception and special rights, to establish positive discrimination and, taken to the extreme, to place at risk the pillars of the judicial order.

Gómez then rebuts these criticisms by making a distinction between the concept of rights as belonging to persons and the collective rights of peoples as a "new legal subject":

> All this would be valid if recognition of rights referred to indigenous peoples as persons. However, the demand is for constitutional recognition of a social reality that has been conserved despite the efforts at homogeneity and equality. Indigenous peoples persist and have practiced, and practice, their forms of social and political organization, and they have different cultures that make up part of our roots as a nation (1997: 285–86).

A thorough examination of these issues exceeds the scope of this chapter, but specific points illustrate the clash between Western concepts – devoid of principles of collective rights – and indigenous norms. For example, from a strictly positivist perspective, community labor (*tequio*) seemingly violates the right to one's own labor; voting by a show of hands and decision making by consensus contrast with the principle of a secret, universal vote; and systems of trial and punishment for deviations from social norms seem to violate due process. Yet from an indigenous perspective, these norms form the basis for social cohesion and harmony,[23] and an

---

22 See Hernández Navarro 1999b. For an excellent description of the legal status of U.S. Indian reservations, see Deloria and Lytle 1983.

23 Harvey argues that the Catholic Church has also played a role in the development of these concepts: "The meaning of citizenship was constructed through religious rather than secular,

overwhelming majority of community members not only accept their traditional ways but defend and perpetuate them.

Two areas in which guarantees of individual rights have clashed with the collective right to maintain traditional customs in indigenous communities' day-to-day life are religious freedom and women's rights. Nevertheless, as the following discussion illustrates, these are problems that can and should be resolved within the context of legalized indigenous normative systems.

The fusion of a religious cosmology with political and judicial norms lies at the heart of Indian self-government. This presents a source of mounting friction between spreading Protestantism and resurgent traditional customs. In Oaxaca, the only state with partially legalized Indian norms, traditional governments have expelled or punished members of non-Catholic religions. Although these cases have been used to showcase "Indian intolerance" in the media, defenders of indigenous norms argue that the root cause of such conflicts is often not religious but a violation of community social norms. Moreover, legalization of indigenous systems would lead to legal mechanisms for "harmonizing" Indian law with Western protection of religious freedom, rather than institutionalizing intolerance. Indeed, most of these conflicts have been resolved through agreements in which the traditional municipal government pledges to allow religious freedom and members of the Protestant sect agree to participate in community labor and *cargos* of a nonreligious nature.

Women's rights are a concern to opponents of indigenous normative systems and to indigenous women themselves. In some communities, women cannot vote in assemblies or hold cargos. However, since passage of the Zapatista Law on Women in 1994, all major Indian forums have given their support to granting full rights to women, although there has been a lag in putting this into practice (Carlsen 1999). Opponents of legalizing indigenous normative systems argue that Indian women fare better under the Western legal system of individual rights, but prominent women leaders of the Indian movement insist that indigenous autonomy strengthens, rather than weakens, their cause. For example, Tomasa Sandoval, a Purhépecha from Michoacán and a member of the Organización Nación Purhépecha Zapatista (Zapatista Purhépecha-Nation Organization), voiced the prevailing view at the second conference of the National Coalition of Indigenous Women:

> A woman's right to autonomy cannot exist without the guarantee of autonomy for indigenous peoples. The individual right and the collective right do not contradict one another; they are complementary.... We insist that both individual and collective autonomy be strengthened. This will require creativity and initiative because it is a very difficult task (in Blackwell 2000).

The final declaration of this conference read: "We believe that the autonomy of our peoples includes all areas of our lives – home, family, community, and region –

---

liberal discourses ... Citizenship is understood as the collective enjoyment of social justice rather than the embodiment of individual rights and obligations before a liberal state" (1998: 27).

and that it has to do with respect and recognition of our culture, our territories, our traditional medicine. For us, autonomy means parity, democracy, and equity between men and women, between indigenous and nonindigenous, between all human beings, and, above all, that our rights be recognized as the original peoples we are" (in Blackwell 2000). The conference also called for immediate compliance with the San Andrés Accords.

The COCOPA proposals have met with vehement resistance in part because of racism. Racism has always existed in indigenous regions, but this fact was never fully recognized in the rest of Mexico. As Indian demands became proposals for concrete political reforms, racism triggered an avalanche of opinions that combined ignorance and intolerance of indigenous peoples. The media have generally depicted indigenous normative systems as equivalent to elements of vigilante justice – lynchings, human rights violations, and arbitrary punitive measures. Likewise, they have presented indigenous political institutions and procedures for selecting traditional authorities as antidemocratic, authoritarian, and discretionary.

Critics of the COCOPA initiative – apparently unable to accept that Mexican society includes the largest indigenous population in Latin America and, worse, that these indigenous peoples are rebelling against their exclusion and repression – have tended to repeat common misconceptions and racist stereotypes. Many of the arguments against the proposed reforms have served as a smokescreen for a broader aim – to eliminate the EZLN and stifle Indian rights initiatives at a moment that is crucially important for the consolidation of the federal government's economic integration project, particularly the implementation of the Puebla-Panama Plan in Southeastern Mexico and promotion of the Free Trade Area of the Americas. Although years have passed since Mexico signed ILO Convention 169 on indigenous rights (1991), Article 4 was reformed (1992), and the Zapatista uprising began (1994), the treatment of indigenous peoples under the Mexican Constitution remains largely unchanged.

As the debate has become increasingly polarized, the stakes have risen. Mexico's indigenous population lives in untenable conditions: nearly half of all indigenous people are illiterate, the majority live in "extreme poverty," and malnutrition is a leading cause of death. As Mexico becomes more closely integrated into the global economy, "the economic costs of ethnicity" rise higher and higher (Psacharopoulos and Patrinos 1994). As indigenous zones become increasingly militarized, violent confrontations occur with alarming regularity. These are among the root causes of the Zapatista insurrection, and the negotiation of a lasting peace was predicated upon their eradication.

Broken Promise: Noncompliance with the San Andrés Accords

The story of how the multiparty COCOPA proposal ran up against rival initiatives and ended up as a counterreform is one of pure politics.

Had the Zedillo administration respected the February 1996 San Andrés Accords and reformed the Constitution along the lines agreed with the EZLN, the Zapatistas would have become a legitimate political actor beyond the PRI's control. With the 1997 midterm elections approaching, the federal government wanted to force the EZLN into the mountains and out of the national arena, where the Zapatistas might potentially have influenced the elections' outcome. The government bet on its military might to ensure that it could breach the peace accords with minimal repercussions. As the government saw the situation, the stakes – the PRI's survival as a hegemonic party – were extraordinarily high.

However, resistance to the San Andrés Accords within Zedillo's cabinet went beyond electoral concerns. Influential ministers feared that the accords could provide a framework for indigenous peoples to organize and develop outside the constraints of corporatist government controls. The reforms embodied in the agreement might become a legal instrument with which indigenous communities could resist the government's economic project, the linchpin of the Zedillo presidency.[24] Although government officials insisted that the president's counterproposal followed the mandates of the San Andrés Accords and the Chiapas peace process, the last official negotiator, Emilio Rabasa, unilaterally called for major changes in the Law for Dialogue, Conciliation, and a Dignified Peace, which had sustained the truce with the EZLN since 1995. The Zedillo administration forced the resignation of the National Intermediation Commission in 1998, eliminating its last channel for dialogue, crippling the COCOPA, and putting the Commission on Follow-up and Verification of the Peace Accords out of business because there was no progress toward peace to verify.[25]

When Zedillo presented his indigenous rights initiative to the federal Senate in March 1998, the Mexican public was well aware that the EZLN – far from being contained – had actually expanded its influence, organizing autonomous townships from the Chiapas highlands to the state's southern border. The EZLN's strategy of creating and consolidating autonomous townships was a nonviolent means of implementing the San Andrés Accords and realizing campesinos' and indigenous communities' long-held aspirations for self-government. It also responded to the need to redraw Chiapas's municipal districts.[26]

---

24 As noted above, the 1992 reform of constitutional Article 27 legalized the privatization of ejido lands and the private use of Indian communal lands, and it laid the groundwork for releasing natural resources on indigenous lands to the international market. In addition, the reform permitted private investors to develop export enclaves in indigenous regions, including large-scale monoculture, livestock raising, or massive tourist developments. The authors of this legislation took for granted that indigenous populations would submit to the huge convulsions that such transformations would imply.

25 For a chronology of the San Andrés negotiations and the COCOPA's role, see Bernal Gutiérrez and Romero Miranda 1999.

26 Subcomandante Marcos, in a taped response to questions from International Civil Observers, December 1996, San Cristóbal de las Casas, Chiapas.

The government tried to recover the initiative by sending army and state troops to dismantle three autonomous townships established by Zapatista communities. In the process, the military took over three hundred indigenous leaders and supporters into custody, some on charges of sedition and in many cases without due process. The governor of Chiapas, Roberto Albores Guillén, implemented his own plan to redraw municipalities in the conflict zone, but – in violation of the political agreements reached in San Andrés – he did so without consulting the EZLN or the indigenous communities involved.

The federal government's strategy of low-intensity warfare deepened after 1996. The military and police presence in Chiapas grew to over 50,000. Regional paramilitary groups tightened their grip of terror in zones of Zapatista influence, operating not only with impunity but, in many cases, with government and army support as well (Hernández Navarro 1999c). Thousands of Zapatista sympathizers, forced from their communities, fled into the mountains or congregated in squalid refugee camps.

On March 21, 1999, the EZLN conducted a massive grassroots consultation, in which over 5,000 Zapatista delegates visited the most remote corners of Mexico to promote participation and answer questions about the Chiapas situation. Nearly three million people responded, a record for participation in an initiative of this kind in Mexico. Despite the media's near-boycott of the event, the consultation returned the debate about indigenous rights to center stage. The vast majority of voters who participated in the consultation – from indigenous peoples in Chiapas to Mexican migrants in California – endorsed the COCOPA initiative to legislate the San Andrés Accords.

Other events also helped redefine the political terrain surrounding the Chiapas conflict and the constitutional reform debate. For instance, in the August 2000 state-level elections in Chiapas, the PRI's gubernatorial candidate lost to coalition candidate Pablo Salazar Mendiguchía, a former participant in the San Andrés negotiations and a supporter of the COCOPA initiative.

Nevertheless, these circumstances were insufficient to ensure the adoption of the COCOPA proposal. President Fox adopted an ambivalent position on the COCOPA initiative after submitting it to Congress, and he failed to lobby seriously for its passage. All three of Mexico's largest political parties (the PRI, PAN, and PRD) voted in favor of the Fernández de Cevallos-Bartlett-Ortega counter-reform in the federal Senate, and only the PRD voted against it in the federal Chamber of Deputies. In response, more than 300 indigenous municipalities throughout the country challenged the legislation in the courts. They argued that the procedures under which the requisite two-thirds of Mexico's state legislatures ratified the constitutional amendment were illegal because many states did not carry out mandated consultations with indigenous populations.

Meanwhile, the military, police, and paramilitary groups maintained a strong presence in Chiapas. Violence continued unchecked. For its part, the EZLN remained silent after the passage of the counterreform. Without a change in the military situation – in Chiapas and in other heavily indigenous regions, including parts of Guerrero, Oaxaca, and the Huasteca (the mountainous area where the states of Hidalgo, San Luis Potosí, and Veracruz intersect) – and without progress in resolving the demand for fundamental constitutional reform, Mexico risks becoming a textbook case on how the denial of indigenous rights can lead to conflict and division.

Extending Rights

The federal government's efforts to limit the indigenous rights negotiated in San Andrés Larráinzar came at the same time that indigenous organizations were both influencing and gaining strength from several important trends in law and human rights. Due in large part to the activities of indigenous organizations throughout the Americas, international law has begun to recognize Indian rights as specific and different. Ironically, Mexico was one of the first signatories to ILO Convention 169.[27] Mexico also signed the International Convention on Treaties, which establishes that countries should abide by the international treaties they have signed and that no nation may invoke internal rights to evade compliance. The San Andrés Accords closely followed definitions and rights as presented in ILO Convention 169, causing one to wonder why the Mexican government did not object to these same points when they appeared in the ILO Convention.[28]

International organizations and agencies are struggling to define terms and establish criteria for the equitable treatment of Indian peoples who have been denied justice since the colonial period and its ethic of "might makes right." Two key indigenous demands in particular have fired legal debates throughout the Western Hemisphere: the right to recognize *difference* in the fight for equal rights, and the *collective rights* of peoples.

On face value, "difference in equal rights" may appear to be a contradiction in terms. However, the failure to take into account the fact that indigenous peoples have suffered greatly under equal justice (Gómez 1997: 273) has prolonged discrimination, leading Indian rights activists to embrace the right to a different exercise of rights as fundamental to citizenship. Charles Taylor (1992) has noted that although ethnic identity is not in itself a political category, historical factors and other considerations make ethnic differences subject to relations of power that usually result in demands upon the state. In demanding different citizenship, the Indian movement seeks the *different exercise of rights* in order to ensure access to *universal rights* within a global community, not the defense of a cultural relativism that would exempt them from other legal and moral standards (Laclau 1996: 63).

27 Mexico signed Convention 169 in September 1990. It was published in the *Diario Oficial de la Federación*, and hence became law, on January 24, 1991.

28 This occurred in Guatemala, where the effort to ratify ILO Convention 169 provoked heated controversy. The army, the business sector, and significant elements in the government refused to ratify the convention, even though indigenous peoples mobilized in its favor. See Ordóñez Cifuentes 1994.

Specific laws recognizing and respecting difference as crucial to the exercise of self-determination, religious freedom, and civil liberties have existed in many countries for years. Will Kymlicka (1995) cites three forms of specific rights pertaining to groups: the right to self-government, polyethnic rights (education, promotion of religious and cultural practices), and special rights to representation. Although judges, legal experts, and the public have accepted the legal recognition of differences in the cultural arena, differences in the areas of political and judicial practice have sparked national furors.

Many of the newly recognized rights are of a collective nature. Rights to conserve customs and language and rights to self-determination and self-government are clearly not practicable on the individual level. According to Magdalena Gómez, former director of the legal department of the National Indigenous Institute: "Not one of the so-called individual guarantees can be adapted to these collective rights … The rights of peoples emerge as a new juridical subject … According to classic doctrine, each individual right corresponds to an individual action, and the person entitled to the right is also entitled to the action. In this case, entitlement to rights is diffuse because it cannot be individualized" (1997).

In *third-generation rights* indigenous leaders have found a compelling argument for their demand for a pluriethnic state that guarantees autonomy for indigenous peoples. In the history of constructing a concept and practice of human rights, third-generation rights represent the latest and most crucial stage of development. First-generation human rights played a major role in nineteenth-century efforts to protect individuals from oppressive state actions, serving as "a kind of additional law, an exceptional right for those who had nothing better to lean on" (Hannah Arendt, in Lafer 1991: 146). Second-generation rights were born out of the demands of the least privileged to participate in social welfare. While first-generation rights established limits to state power in the lives of individuals, second-generation rights sought to guide state action to guarantee to all individuals – but especially the most vulnerable groups – the minimum requirements necessary to satisfy economic, social, and cultural needs for the development of a dignified life. In this context, the rights holder is the individual with specific rights (not privileges) based upon essential needs, although the individual may be identified as a member of a vulnerable group that has common demands and needs.

Under third-generation rights, an entirely new subject emerges. The rights holder is not the individual but human groups themselves, and the right is the right of a people to self-determination. The need to define this type of rights arose out of the experience of totalitarian repression. While first-generation rights sought to protect the individual from an infringing state, third-generation rights seek to limit state action regarding culturally homogeneous groups. These rights are collectively, not individually, held.

Forging a New Social Pact

Efforts to broaden indigenous rights vis-à-vis the state form part of a larger effort to achieve social justice, which has increasingly become equated with the protection of rights (Rawls 1971). Two goals characterize this struggle: to rebuild indigenous peoples, and to attain full citizenship.

The definition and defense of indigenous rights also lie at the crux of managing conflict in changing nation-states. In a recent study of the United Nations Research Institute for Social Development's experience with ethnic conflict, Rodolfo Stavenhagen pointed out that even cases that may appear to be inter-ethnic conflicts are in fact conflicts between politically mobilized ethnic groups and an existing state. "The majority of independent states existing today are composed of more than one ethnic group, and this diversity poses challenges to governance and to the prevailing concept of the nation-state itself. One of the problems is that numerous states do not legally recognize the ethnic pluralism existing within their borders, and those that do are still struggling with ways to deal with diversity constructively" (Stavenhagen 1996: 1).

Even though the Mexican government during the 1990s sought to downplay the ethnic aspects of the Zapatista uprising by claiming that it was led by foreigners and manipulated by outsiders, demands for recognition of a pluriethnic, pluricultural state lie at the core of badly needed state reforms. The PRI's electoral defeats during the 1997–2000 period opened up a new phase in Mexico's transition to democracy, a phase that is full of uncertainty. The Zapatista uprising demonstrated that government inaction on issues of poverty, marginality, and multiethnic justice can lead to civil war. In contrast, including indigenous peoples through explicit recognition and exercise of their rights ensures more complete democratic participation. Moreover, it also establishes the historical and theoretical foundations for real democracy. According to Pablo González Casanova, a member of the Commission on Follow-up and Verification of the Peace Accords:

> The Latin American state cannot be conceived of without a multiethnic society, nor can the construction of national people's democracy fail to represent and express that society. To be authentic, democratic and representative participation in Latin America must include the ancient populations of colonial and neocolonial origins as autonomous and full citizens (1996: 35).

Constitutional reforms are a crucial part of defining a new social pact between Indians and the nation and advancing a democratic transition. The armed insurrection in Chiapas and the rise of a peaceful civil movement for Indian rights in nearly all of Mexico's indigenous regions demonstrate that a new relationship will require profound transformations. Militarization is neither a just solution nor an effective one.

The San Andrés Accords, along with ongoing dialogue with indigenous organizations and their leaders, represent the raw material for forging this new pact. This was reiterated by Adelfo Regino: "The San Andrés Accords are a consensus between the federal government, the EZLN, and the rest of society. They form the basis for a new relationship between indigenous peoples and the Mexican state" (in Molina 2000). President Fox's model of handpicking indigenous experts and activists to serve on a policy advisory council ignores the force of the indigenous movement, and it is likely to create divisions and patronizing policies reminiscent of the old *indigenismo*. Any new pact must be founded upon, and upheld by, major constitutional reforms supported by Indian peoples themselves.

Indigenous Rights and Civil Rights

The legislative battle over constitutional reforms on indigenous rights and culture holds enormous repercussions for Mexico's future. Its outcome will affect both the tenuous truce in Chiapas and the redefinition of relations between indigenous peoples and the state.

The president and political parties have the right to present constitutional reform initiatives; Congress has the power to legislate; and the 57th Congress (1997–2000), which came to office in the least-questioned elections in Mexico's modern history, was the most plural and balanced in decades. Why, then, has there been such opposition to the constitutional reform on indigenous rights that emanated from this body?

The reasons are many. First, the reform failed to reflect faithfully the San Andrés Accords, and as such it cannot resolve the Chiapas conflict. The creation of a new legal framework for Indian peoples is inextricably linked to the peace process in Chiapas. "Without recognized and protected human rights, there is no democracy; without democracy, the minimum conditions for the resolution of conflicts do not exist" (Bobbio 1996: 14). The counterreform adopted in 2001 made peace in Chiapas even more difficult to attain than before.

The federal legislature does not have the moral authority to impose a resolution of these issues that does not have the support of indigenous communities. Majority approval of a legislative norm does not justify its content, much less assure its efficacy. Indigenous issues were largely ignored during the year 2000 general elections, and the 58th Legislature (2000–2003), though the most diverse in Mexico's history, had only a handful of Indian representatives.

The 2001 counterreform, which was developed without the participation of the EZLN and the major participants in Mexico's new Indian movement, lacked validity because of its failure to include the subjects of the law. In political terms, the initiative violated the common sense dictum that both parties in a conflict must participate in its resolution. In legal terms, it violated the procedures set forth in the Law for Conciliation, Pacification, and a Dignified Peace and in the San Andrés Accords. Initiatives on indigenous rights cannot be justified by their motives alone. They must also be judged by their consequences, and the consequences of the counterreform were a rupture in the dialogue with the EZLN and a tangible increase in tensions not only in Chiapas but in indigenous zones throughout the country.

Second, the principle of popular sovereignty is expressed both from within and outside of formal representative bodies. Many vital political proposals emerge from civil society – that is, from outside the legislature and the party system. The broad participation achieved in the San Andrés negotiations was a paradigmatic case in this regard. The outcome displayed the power of those who have no formal power, and in San Andrés one heard the voices of those who have no other space in which to speak. By unilaterally rejecting critical aspects of the San Andrés Accords in the 2001 indigenous rights legislation, Congress ignored this form of popular sovereignty. As a consequence, even though the counterreform may have been legal, it will never be legitimate.

In any society, a legislator has the right to legislate. But a citizen also claims the right to be governed wisely and by just laws – and to disobey laws that are unjust. "To take rights seriously means to preserve them in all cases and in spite of any collective objective of the majority. What's more, disobedience of the law is not an autonomous right, but constitutes a characteristic of any genuine fundamental right; to disobey the norm that threatens our rights is to manifest ourselves as the holders of those rights" (Dworkin 1977).

References

Benítez, Fernando, et al. 1996. *Cultura y derechos de los pueblos indígenas de México.* Mexico City: Archivo General de la Nación / Fondo de Cultura Económica.

Bernal Gutiérrez, Marco Antonio, and Miguel Ángel Romero Miranda. 1999. *Chiapas: crónica de una negociación.* Mexico City: Rayuela.

Blackwell, Maylei. 2000. Summary notes from the conference of the National Coalition of Indigenous Women. Unpublished.

Bobbio, Norberto. 1996. *El tiempo de los derechos.* Madrid: Sistema.

Carlsen, Laura. 1989. "12 de octubre: día de la dignidad y desistencia india. Foro internacional sobre derechos humanos de los pueblos indios," *Revista PUEBLO* (December): 34–37.

———. 1999. "Las mujeres indígenas en el movimiento social," *Chiapas* (Instituto de Investigaciones Económicas, Universidad Nacional Autónoma de México) 8: 27–66.

———. 2002. "Self-Determination and Autonomy in Latin America: One Step Forward, Two Steps Back," *Foreign Policy in Focus* [www.selfdetermine.org/regions/indigrights.html]

Cordero Avendaño, Carmen. 1996. "El derecho de la costumbre." In *Cultura y derechos de los pueblos indígenas de México,* by Fernando Benítez et al. Mexico City: Archivo General de la Nación / Fondo de Cultura Económica.

Deloria, Vine, Jr., and Clifford M. Lytle. 1983. *American Indians, American Justice.* Austin: University of Texas Press.

Dworkin, Ronald. 1977. *Taking Rights Seriously.* Cambridge, Mass.: Harvard University Press.

Gómez, Magdalena. 1997. "Derecho indígena y constitucionalidad: el caso mexicano." In *Derecho indígena,* edited by Magdalena Gómez. Mexico City: Instituto Nacional Indígena / Asociación Mexicana para las Naciones Unidas, A.C.

González Casanova, Pablo. 1996. "Las etnias coloniales y el Estado multiétnico." In *Democracia y Estado multiétnico en América Latina,* edited by Pablo González Casanova and Marcos Roitman Rosenmann. Mexico City: Universidad Nacional Autónoma de México / Demos.

Harvey, Neil. 1998. *The Chiapas Rebellion: The Struggle for Land and Democracy.* Durham, N.C.: Duke University Press.

Hernández Navarro, Luis. 1999a. "Reaffirming Ethnic Identity and Reconstituting Politics in Oaxaca." In *Subnational Politics and Democratization in Mexico,* edited by Wayne A. Cornelius, Todd A. Eisenstadt, and Jane Hindley. La Jolla: Center for U.S.–Mexican Studies, University of California, San Diego.

———. 1999b. "El laberinto de los equívocos: San Andrés y la lucha indígena," *Chiapas* (Instituto de Investigaciones Económicas, Universidad Nacional Autónoma de México) 7: 71–91.

———. 1999c. "Mexico's Secret War," *NACLA Report on the Americas* 32 (6): 6–10.

Hernández Navarro, Luis, and Ramón Vera Herrera, eds. 1998. *Los acuerdos de San Andrés.* Mexico City: Era.

Kymlicka, Will. 1995. *Multicultural Citizenship: A Liberal Theory of Minority Rights.* Oxford: Clarendon.

Laclau, Ernesto. 1996. *Emancipación y diferencia.* Buenos Aires: Ariel.

Lafer, Celso. 1991. *La reconstrucción de los derechos humanos: un diálogo con el pensamiento de Hannah Arendt.* Mexico City: Fondo de Cultura Económica.

León Portilla, Miguel. 1996. "La antigua y la nueva palabra de los pueblos indígenas." In *Cultura y derechos de los pueblos indígenas de México,* by Fernando Benítez et al. Mexico City: Archivo General de la Nación / Fondo de Cultura Económica.

Lockhart, James. 1992. *The Nahuas after the Conquest: A Social and Cultural History of the Indians of Central Mexico, XVI through XVIII Centuries.* Stanford, Calif.: Stanford University Press.

López Bárcenas, Francisco. 1997. "La diversidad mutilada," *Ce-Acatl: Revista de la Cultura de Anáhuac* (Centro de Estudios Antropológicos Científicos, Artísticos, Tradicionales y Lingüísticos "Ce-Acatl").88 (October): 3–41.

———. 1998. "Cerco jurídico a los pueblos indígenas," *La Jornada,* February 5–6.

Madrazo, Jorge. 1996. "Perspectiva de la Comisión Nacional de Derechos Humanos." In *Cultura y derechos de los pueblos indígenas de México,* by Fernando Benítez et al. Mexico City: Archivo General de la Nación / Fondo de Cultura Económica.

Medina, Andrés. 1995. "Los sistemas de cargo en la Cuenca de México: una primera aproximación a su trasfondo histórico," *Revista Alteridades* (Universidad Autónoma Metropolitana–Iztapalapa) 5 (9).

Molina, Tania. 2000. "La encrucijada del movimiento indígena," *Masiosare* (supplement to *La Jornada*), September 3.

Monsiváis, Carlos. 1996. "Versiones nacionales de lo indígena." In *Cultura y derechos de los pueblos indígenas de México,* by Fernando Benítez et al. Mexico City: Archivo General de la Nación / Fondo de Cultura Económica.

Ordóñez Cifuentes, José Emilio. 1994. "A propósito del debate sobre el Convenio Número 169 del OIT en Guatemala." In *Derechos indígenas en la actualidad,* by José Emilio Ordóñez Cifuentes. Mexico City: Instituto de Investigaciones Jurídicas, Universidad Nacional Autónoma de México.

Procuraduría Agraria. 2000. "Propiedad de la tierra y población indígena," *Estudios Agrarios* 14 (January-April): 123–47.

Psacharopoulos, George, and Harry Anthony Patrinos. 1994. *Indigenous People and Poverty in Latin America: An Empirical Analysis.* Washington D.C.: World Bank.

Rawls, John. 1971. *A Theory of Justice.* Cambridge, Mass.: Belknap.

Regino, Adelfo. 1999. "Los pueblos indígenas: diversidad negada," *Chiapas* (Instituto de Investigaciones Económicas, Universidad Nacional Autónoma de México) 7: 21–44.

Sierra, Teresa. 1997. "Esencialismo y autonomía: paradojas de las reivindicaciones indígenas." *Revista Alteridades* (Universidad Autónoma Metropolitana–Iztapalapa) 7 (14): 131–43.

Sirvent, Carlos, ed. 1997. *Reformas jurídicas en las entidades federativas en materia de derechos indígenas*. Chiapas: Oficina de Seguimiento y Verificación para la Paz Digna en Chiapas.

Stavenhagen, Rodolfo. 1996. *Ethnic Conflicts and the Nation-State*. New York: United Nations Research Institute for Social Development.

Taylor, Charles. 1992. *Multiculturalism and "The Politics of Recognition": An Essay*. Princeton, N.J.: Princeton University Press.

Tello Díaz, Carlos. 1995. *La rebelión de las cañadas*. Mexico City: Cal y Arena.

Velásquez, María Cristina. 2000. *El nombramiento: las elecciones por usos y costumbres en Oaxaca*. Oaxaca: Instituto Estatal Electoral de Oaxaca.

Willemsen Díaz, Augusto. 1991. "Ámbito y ejercicio de la autonomía interna y el autogobierno para los pueblos indígenas." In Proceedings of the "Reunión de expertos encargada de examinar la experiencia de los países en la esfera de la aplicación de planes de autonomía interna a favor de las poblaciones indígenas," Nuuk, Greenland, September.

Womack, John, Jr. 1969. *Zapata and the Mexican Revolution*. New York: Knopf.

15

Assessing Binational Civil Society Coalitions: Lessons from the Mexico–U.S. Experience

Jonathan Fox

I s globalization producing a transnational civil society? Are the transnational economic, social, and cultural forces that are ostensibly weakening nation-states also empowering civic and social movements that come together across borders? If there is more to this trend than internationalist dreams, then clear evidence should be emerging from the accelerating process of Mexico–U.S. integration. This binational relationship is the broadest and deepest example of global integration between North and South, and therefore it offers a clear "paradigm case" for assessing the dynamics and impact of cross-border civil society interaction. Assessments of impact are especially important if one is to avoid assuming that when international actors get involved, their role automatically becomes determinative.

The transnational civil society hypothesis can be framed in hard or soft terms, each with quite different political implications. In the hard version, international economic integration is generating qualitative changes in the balance of power between nation-states and private capital because of the latter's increased mobility. On the civil society side, some analysts suggest that, due to increasingly accepted international political norms and greater ease of communications and travel, public interest advocacy networking has advanced to such a degree that a "transnational civil society" is emerging. Some use the even more ambitious terms "global social movements" or "global civil society." In the soft version, the international economy has always reconfigured itself, and the current phase is not unprecedented. Most industrial activity remains national, and nation-states retain significant policy levers. From this perspective, "fully" transnational social or civic movements

This study draws upon papers presented at a conference that was held at the University of California, Santa Cruz in July 1998, with the support of a timely grant from the John D. and Catherine T. MacArthur Foundation (see Brooks and Fox 2002). The chapter was made possible by a decade of conversations and collaboration with David Brooks, director of the Mexico–U.S. Diálogos Project and U.S. correspondent for *La Jornada*. The study also benefited enormously from conversations with Luis Hernández Navarro, also of *La Jornada*. In addition, the author thanks Tani Adams, Sonia Álvarez, Maylei Blackwell, Jennifer Johnson, Margaret Keck, Kevin J. Middlebrook, Debra Rose, and Heather Williams for very useful comments on earlier drafts. Earlier versions of this essay appeared as Fox 2000a and (in Spanish) 2001.

are still few and far between, with very limited capacity to go beyond inter-nationalist discourse to influence state or corporate action in practice.

The U.S.–Mexico relationship offers a vast array of experiences with which to assess the "hard" versus the "soft" way of framing the globalization process.[1] This chapter supports the soft rather than the hard version, finding that most Mexico–U.S. civil society relationships involve networking between fundamentally *national* social and civic organizations. Moreover, relatively few networks have consolidated into dense, balanced partnerships.

Assessments of transnational linkages between social and civic actors require clearly defined criteria. Measuring the density and impact of political linkages implies specifying a standard for comparison (dense compared to what? influential compared to what?).[2] Compared to where U.S.–Mexico civil society relations stood in the early 1990s, there is no question that a wide range of networks, coalitions, and alliances has emerged that would once have been hard to imagine. However, compared to the pace of binational integration among *other* actors – including automobile manufacturers, investment bankers, toxic waste producers, drug dealers, television magnates, immigrant families, and national policy makers – both the degree and the impact of binational civil society collaboration have been quite limited (with the notable exception of partnerships actually *on* the border).

Cross-border conversations between national civil society actors have certainly multiplied enormously, encouraging much deeper mutual understanding. But mutual understanding between civil society counterparts does not necessarily lead to actual collaboration. For example, sympathetic journalistic coverage very often

1 Keck and Sikkink (1998) and Tarrow (1998, 2000) are among the analysts who clearly distin-guish between these two approaches. For stronger versions of the transnational social movements approach, see, among others, Brecher, Costello, and Smith 2000; R. Cohen and Rai 2000; J. Smith, Chatfield, and Pagnucco 1997; and Wapner 1996. Keck and Sikkink (1998), like Hanagan (1998), discuss transnational societal linkages in long-term historical context. For a recent overview of the literature, see Florini 2000. For recent conference papers that specifically examine the local impacts of transnational civil society networks, see www2.ucsc.edu/cgirs/conferences/humanrights.

2 In response to the assertion that labor unions need to "catch up" in the integration process, senior American Federation of Labor–Congress of Industrial Organizations (AFL–CIO) strategist Ron Blackwell pointed out at a July 1998 conference at the University of California, Santa Cruz : "Why are we lagging behind [corporations and states]? They make the rules. Not only is it their game, and not only do they take an aggressive posture towards the rest of us, but their activities in organizing people are also self-financing. Business is a masterful and massive organizer of people. So are governments. We don't have that advantage. Moreover, our interests are social interests; they are particular among us, and it takes a while to find each other ... Workers have differences of interest. They often overlap, but they are not identical and they do contradict each other in some areas. The whole project of building a union, of building any organization, is to be able to map the areas of overlapping interests, and to be able to build a working relationship or the capacity for collective action based on what we share."

features headlines like "budding cross-border resistance" (see, for instance, Rosen 1999), yet we have been reading similar headlines about relations between social movements in Mexico and the United States for more than a decade. For reasons not yet fully understood, these "buds" have had considerable difficulty flowering.[3] Consolidating cross-border partnerships turns out to be easier said than done. Their impact, moreover, has often been overestimated. The involvement of international actors in the national arena does not in itself demonstrate that they exercise substantial influence in that arena. There is, for example, a widespread tendency to assume that the international concern provoked by the rebellion led by the Zapatista Army of National Liberation (EZLN) translated into significant international civil society impact upon the course of events in the southern Mexican state of Chiapas. Yet an alternative hypothesis is quite plausible: in practice, international civil society actors engaged in the Chiapas conflict may have been marginal to what has been primarily a nationally determined political process.

This chapter is comprised of four sections. The first part frames society-to-society relationships in terms of the broader U.S.–Mexico context, which involves state and elite actors as well. The second part makes conceptual distinctions among transnational networks, coalitions, and movements, and it then assesses in those terms varying degrees of density of key U.S.–Mexico civil society partnerships. This section synthesizes the patterns in specific sectors, including labor rights, environmental concerns, trade policy advocacy, democracy and human rights, women's rights, and immigrant rights. The third part of the chapter turns from coalition dynamics to impact, building upon Keck and Sikkink's (1998) framework for assessing the impact of transnational advocacy networks. This section focuses upon binational societal partnerships in three sectors: environment, labor, and human rights.[4] The conclusion includes a synthesis of the main analytic findings, presented in terms of a series of propositions for discussion.

---

3 On the late 1980s and early 1990s period of cross-border organizing, see Brooks 1992; Barry, Browne, and Sims 1994; Fox 1989, 1992; Thorup 1991; Heredia and Hernández 1995; and Torres 1997. For comprehensive listings of the organizations involved, see Hernández and Sánchez 1992 and Browne 1996a, 1996b.

4 Keck and Sikkink's book presents an overview of the different kinds of political tools and strategies that transnational civil society advocacy networks use: "(1) *information politics*, or the ability to quickly and credibly generate politically usable information and move it to where it will have the most impact; (2) *symbolic politics*, or the ability to call upon symbols, actions or stories that make sense of a situation for an audience that is frequently far away; (3) *leverage politics*, or the ability to call upon powerful actors to affect a situation where weaker members of a network are unlikely to have an influence; and (4) *accountability politics*, or the effort to hold powerful actors to their previously stated policies or principles" (1998: 16).

Keck and Sikkink's agenda-setting study goes on to evaluate transnational networks in terms of various "stages" of impact: agenda setting, encouraging discursive policy commitments from states and other actors, causing international or national procedural change, affecting policy, and influencing actual behavioral change in target actors (p. 201).

Situating Society-to-Society Relationships

The full array of binational social, civic, and political coalitions involves a wide range of state and social actors. This chapter focuses primarily upon civil society-to-civil society relationships, concentrating in turn upon those actors that pursue broader social participation and public accountability in each country. However, these relations should be understood in the broader context of the many *other* partnerships that link states and societies in Mexico and the United States (not to mention the two countries' private sectors, which have been studied extensively elsewhere). One can situate society-to-society relationships in terms of one of four quadrants in a simple two-by-two table that depicts the U.S. state and civil society on one side, and the Mexican state and civil society on the other. Table 15.1 illustrates the wide array of state-to-state coalitions that exist, ranging from those focusing upon keeping Mexico safe for U.S. investors (such as the financial rescue package that the U.S. government provided to help resolve Mexico's 1994–1995 economic crisis), to the increasing degree of military and anti-drug cooperation, to regular, institutionalized exchanges between federal cabinet officials and governors of border states.

State-to-State links

The wide range of state-to-state links between the United States and Mexico is well known and need not be detailed here. These partnerships reach across the many sectoral agencies in both federal governments, as well as from congress to congress. Subnational governments are also increasingly relating to one another – most notably in the case of regular meetings among the governors of border states, but also including frequent visits from state governors to regions linked by migration across the border. Although some of these cross-border relationships are largely ceremonial, others are quite substantial (as in the U.S. Treasury and White House role in the 1995 financial rescue package for Mexico, and in the increasing levels of cooperation between the two countries' armed forces).[5] Castañeda (1996) highlighted the political implications of these state-to-state partnerships when he argued that the U.S. government's repeated financial bailouts bolstered the Mexican regime and postponed national democratization.

Links between the U.S. State and Mexican Civil Society

Linkages between the U.S. state and Mexican civil society are relatively recent. U.S. development assistance to private Mexican organizations historically focused upon family planning, health, and scientific, agricultural, and educational cooperation, rather than upon civil society capacity-building (even in the aforementioned sectors). Since the late 1980s, however, the U.S. Agency for International Development

5 The United States also played an important role in encouraging the multilateral development banks to invest heavily in Mexico, especially during the debate over the North American Free Trade Agreement (NAFTA) (Fox 2000b).

Table 15.1: **Examples of Mexico–U.S. Partnerships**

	U.S. State	U.S. Civil Society

Mexican State	Treasury ministries
	National cabinet meetings
	Border governors' conferences
	Anti-narcotics aid
	NAFTA trinational institutions
	Military sales and training
	U.S. support for Mexico from
	   multilateral development banks
	Exchanges between judicial
	   authorities
		Policy think tanks
		Private lobbyists
		Universities
		Latino NGOs
		Conservation NGOs
		Elite cultural institutions
		   (museums, for example)
		Mexican immigrant civil
		   society in the United States
		   (hometown clubs and
		   federations)

Mexican
Civil Society
	USAID (and its U.S. contractors)
	National Endowment for
	   Democracy
	Inter-American Foundation
		Religious institutions
		Private foundations
		Media elites
		Environmental coalitions
		Trade union coalitions
		Democracy networks
		Human rights networks
		Women's rights networks
		Migrant voting rights advocacy
		   networks
		Indigenous peoples networks
		Small farmer networks

(USAID) has invested heavily in Mexican conservation organizations, aiming to bolster their capacity to protect biodiversity and, in some cases, to improve the management of what USAID called Mexico's "paper parks." By the late 1990s, environmental projects constituted the largest category of USAID funding to Mexico.[6] Some fraction of this conservation funding probably reached Mexican environmental nongovernmental organizations (NGOs). USAID has also funded the Mexican Red Cross in times of disaster.

When analysts think of U.S. policy toward civil society in other countries, much of the discussion focuses upon so-called democracy promotion. Yet a recent comprehensive overview of the 1980–1995 period found that democracy promotion was never a major U.S. policy goal in Mexico (Mazza 2001). With very few exceptions, the U.S. executive and legislative branches both sustained a strong consensus to leave that issue off the bilateral agenda. By the late 1990s, however, the democracy issue had inched up the agenda. USAID's donations under its category of "more democratic processes" included US$3.725 million for several Mexican civic organizations in fiscal year 2000, complementing the support provided by the

National Endowment for Democracy (NED). Some of this USAID funding was for judicial education, municipal development, and legislative institution-building, and it therefore belongs in the state-to-state category. Nevertheless, USAID's democracy funding also reached the Citizens' Movement for Democracy, the Mexican Center for Victims of Crimes, and the Mexican Society for Women's Rights. The US$1.2 million that USAID proposed for fiscal year 2000 to deal with HIV/AIDS was also mainly targeted to NGOs (international, national, and local).[7]

The National Endowment for Democracy has played a more prominent role in grant-making to Mexican civic and human rights organizations.[8] In the 1997 election year, NED granted approximately US$1.1 million to Mexican civic institutions and democratic processes, including $371,000 to Civic Alliance (AC); $278,000 through the American Federation of Labor–Congress of Industrial Organizations' (AFL–CIO) refurbished international arm; and $274,000 via NED's Republican Party affiliate to the Centro Cívico (Civic Center) and its women's organization.[9] Even though these funding levels were significant from the recipient organizations' point of view, Mexico was not an especially high priority within NED's portfolio, especially during the early 1990s when civic funding might have made more of a difference.

The Inter-American Foundation (IAF), a small federal agency responsible to the U.S. Congress and mandated to be independent of short-term U.S. foreign policy goals, has maintained a long-term, low-profile, but public involvement with Mexican civil society organizations. The IAF has provided grant funding to a wide range of Mexican NGOs, and in the late 1980s it shifted to more direct funding for community-based rural social organizations, including many autonomous indigenous producer groups.[10] The IAF's levels of funding to Mexico were higher than the NED's, averaging approximately US$2.3 million per year over the 1990s.[11]

---

6 This category accounted for US$6 million (the majority of proposed USAID funding) during fiscal year 2000. See www.info.usaid.gov/pubs/cp2000/lac/mexico.html and, for details, USAID/Mexico 1999.

7 There has been very little informed public discussion of USAID's Mexico program in either the United States or Mexico. This absence is both cause and effect of the lack of independent assessments of the program.

8 On the Mexican debate over the implications of National Endowment for Democracy (NED) funding of Mexican pro-democracy organizations, see Aguayo Quezada 2001 and P. Rodríguez 2001. For context, see Dresser 1996, Mazza 2001, and Sabatini 2002.

9 By 1999 funding for Mexico had dropped below US$300,000. See the annual reports at www.ned.org for public data that are more detailed and precise than USAID's information.

10 Since the late 1980s, the Inter-American Foundation (IAF) has made extensive, strategic grant contributions to numerous regional peasant and indigenous movement organizations and networks, including the sustainable coffee and community-based forestry movements.

11 Author's communication with David Bray, the IAF's former Mexico representative, September 1999.

The Mexican State's Ties to Civil Society in the United States

The political opposition's surprisingly vigorous electoral challenge to the legitimacy of the established Mexican regime in 1988 spilled over into the United States,
including open campaigning by the leftist opposition among Mexicans in the
United States. The possibility of change in Mexico resonated with Mexicans in the
United States to an unexpected degree, even though most of the migrant population lacked political rights in both the U.S. and Mexican political systems. In the
aftermath of Mexico's fraud-riddled 1988 presidential vote, post-electoral mobilizations by Mexican immigrants in the United States probably exceeded in size those
staged during the campaign.[12]

In response, the Mexican state launched a multi-pronged strategy to reach out
to Mexican civil society in the United States.[13] The term "civil society in the United
States" (rather than "U.S. civil society") is employed here in order to include the
Mexican state's strategy for reincorporating Mexican nationals. One could argue
that this is only formally a cross-border relationship, given that the state's outreach
to the national diaspora is a cross-border extension of its national efforts to organize
and reincorporate Mexican civil society actors more generally. However, the task of
outreach to emigrants falls to Mexico's Ministry of Foreign Relations (SRE) and its
network of consulates; by definition, therefore, it is a cross-border relationship.
Some state governments have also developed their own outreach strategies, most
notably in the case of Guanajuato.[14] Moreover, one could argue that the Televisa
broadcast network's long-standing dominance over U.S. Spanish-language television
also constituted a prominent example of the (de facto) Mexican state's linkage to
Latino civil society in the United States (A. Rodríguez 1999).[15]

Most instances of Mexican migrant organization in the United States can be
understood as either state-led or migrant-led, with Mexican state actors playing an
especially prominent role in inducing the formation of hometown clubs and their
statewide federations (Goldring 1998, 2002).[16] In the process, the Mexican state

---

12 These protests reverberated within the Mexican state. Dresser (1993: 94) quotes José Ángel
   Pescador, then Mexican consul in Los Angeles: "One of the greatest protest marches against
   the outcome of the elections took place in Los Angeles.... The Mexican government realized
   that there are many anti-PRI Mexicans living in California who return periodically to their
   communities and have influence in Mexico."

13 For details, see Dresser 1991a, 1993; González Gutiérrez 1993, 1997; De la Garza et al. 1998;
   Leiken 2000; and Martínez and Ross 2002.

14 More than thirty Casas Guanajuato are organized into a national network. Author's communication with Laura González, University of Texas at Dallas, August 1999.

15 Televisa was for many years closely aligned politically with the long-ruling Institutional Revolutionary Party (PRI). Its hegemony in the Spanish-language market in the United States was
   particularly notable in televised news, an area in which it lost its lead position in the late 1990s.

16 Research, primarily by sociologists, is beginning to catch up with the 1990s wave of Mexican
   immigrant social and civic organization. See Espinosa 1999; Goldring 1998, 2002; Rivera
   Salgado 1999a, 1999b, 2002; R. Smith 1999; and Zabin and Escala Rabadán 1998. For conceptual context, see M. Smith and Guarnizo 1998.

sought to keep most organized emigrants in the civic, rather than the political, arena. At the same time, a new civic network of emigrant voting-rights advocates began to lobby the Mexican state and the country's major political parties for the first time (Martínez and Ross 2002, Ross 1999). Only in the late 1990s did Mexican immigrants, their leaders, and their organizations begin to influence national politics and gain a voice in the national media. This process is, however, best understood as a relationship within Mexican civil society (see below).

Although the Mexican state's efforts to reach out to its diaspora have been largely invisible outside the Mexican community, its partnerships with more established U.S. civil society actors have received extensive attention.[17] The Mexican state's attempts to woo U.S. opinion makers reached unprecedented levels during the administration of President Carlos Salinas de Gortari (1988–1994), and a wide range of U.S. civic and political elites responded eagerly. The most influential U.S. private universities, think tanks, and large, moderate environmental organizations rushed to see which one could offer Salinas their most public platform and their most distinguished honors. The Mexican state made significant financial as well as political investments in efforts to influence U.S. public opinion through think tanks and lobbyists (Dresser 1991a, 1996; Eisenstadt 1997; Velasco 1997). Mexican American civil rights and business organizations also received significant official attention.[18] Mexican government strategists realized that influencing the U.S. government required influencing U.S. civil society, especially because the North American Free Trade Agreement (NAFTA) overflowed the usual narrow boundaries of conventional bilateral policy making. In the 1990s, then, both the U.S. and Mexican governments increased their efforts to use non-state actors in the other country to influence the other state.

Civil Society-to-Civil Society Links

The importance and density of binational societal relationships ebbed and flowed throughout the twentieth century, as Knight (1997) has suggested. Some of that history continues to resonate. Ricardo Flores Magón remains a hero to radical democratic movements in both societies, especially among Chicanos and southern

17 This was not the first wave of Mexican state–U.S. civil society relationships. For an overview of Mexican relations with the U.S. political system early in this century, see Knight's comprehensive discussion (1997). On U.S. civil society's cultural engagements with Mexico during this period, see Delpar 1992. On the Mexican state's efforts to work with U.S. authorities to repress exiled Mexican radicals (as well as their alliances with the U.S. Left), see MacLachlan 1991. In the past, some ties in this category also involved Mexican government invitations to U.S. nongovernmental organizations to engage with Mexico. Examples include the Rockefeller Foundation's public health (1930s) and agricultural research work (1940s) and the Summer Institute of Linguistics, which was invited by President Lázaro Cárdenas (1934–1940) to promote literacy in indigenous regions in the 1930s.

18 The Mexican state used elite cultural outreach in an attempt to improve Mexico's image in the eyes of U.S. opinion makers with the 1991 "The Splendor of Thirty Centuries" art exhibit in New York, San Antonio, and Los Angeles.

Mexican indigenous movements. John Reed continues to inspire contemporary alternative journalists in the United States.[19] In contrast, other chapters in this history have been largely forgotten, including the mutual identification between the two national labor movements in the late 1930s (Paterson 1998). The oldest sustained binational collaborative effort for social justice and mutual understanding dates back to that period.[20]

This study deals with one subset of the larger universe of civil society actors. The focus is on binational relationships between nongovernmental actors in each country that see themselves as promoting social equality and more accountable public and private institutions. Delimiting the specific set of actors in this way underscores the fact that many groups within both civil societies act primarily to *reinforce* institutional arrangements that limit public accountability and reproduce elitist political-cultural legacies. This characterization would apply, for example, to the dominant broadcast media in both societies, as well as to the dominant tendencies within some religious hierarchies or the Red Cross.[21] Moreover, there are in both societies elements that *oppose* the extension or consolidation of rights won by other social movements, most notably women's rights. Looking at civil society in this broad sense, including its powerful pro-status quo elements, reminds us that civil society is a force of inertia as well as a force for change. This study's focus, however, is on those actors within civil society that share some degree of commitment to democratization and social change.[22]

Disentangling Binational Networks, Coalitions, and Movements

The 1990s witnessed an upsurge of binational civil society discussion in Mexico and the United States, beginning before the NAFTA debate but then rapidly expanding. These interactions often took the form of exchanges of information, practical experiences, and expressions of solidarity. Sometimes exchanges generated *networks* of ongoing relationships; at other times they produced the shared goals, mutual trust, and understanding needed to form *coalitions* that could collaborate

19 See, for example, John Ross's regular email news bulletin "Mexico Bárbaro" at wnu@igc. apc.org.

20 Since 1939 the Quaker-inspired American Friends Service Committee (AFSC) has organized annual summer community development programs in Mexico to bring together youth from both countries. AFSC's main Mexican partner organization is Servicio, Desarrollo y Paz (Service, Development, and Peace, SEDEPAZ).

21 For example, the U.S. Red Cross has been governed by conservative Republican political leaders such as Elizabeth Dole. In contrast, the Mexican Red Cross is corrupt and ineffective at providing disaster relief; it had to return a US$300,000 Hurricane Paulina donation from the U.S. Agency for International Development (Zúñiga and Olayo 1999). In Chiapas, moreover, pro-Zapatista indigenous communities identified the Mexican Red Cross with the Mexican government.

22 The concept of *counterparts* is also relevant here, a notion that does not imply similarity or agreement but rather suggests analogous roles in their respective societies (Brooks 1992).

on specific campaigns. Networks do not necessarily coordinate their actions or come to agreement on specific joint actions (as implied by the concept of coalition). In contrast, "coalitions are networks in action mode."[23] Neither networks nor coalitions necessarily imply significant horizontal exchanges among participants. Indeed, many rely upon a handful of interlocutors to manage relationships between broad-based social organizations that have relatively little awareness of the nature and actions of their counterparts. However, the concept of transnational social *movement* organizations implies a much higher degree of density and much more cohesion than in either networks or coalitions (see table 15.2). The term "transnational movement organizations" suggests a social subject that is present in more than one country, as in the paradigmatic case of the Binational Indigenous Oaxacan Front (FIOB) and other indigenous organizations that literally cross the Mexico–U.S. border (Rivera Salgado 1999a, 1999b, 2002).

The terms "network," "coalition," and "movement" are often used interchangeably in practice. However, for the sake of developing tools for a more precise assessment of the nature of binational relationships, these three concepts will be treated here as analytically distinct, and then applied to a series of cross-border relationships between social and civic actors. In short, transnational civil society exchanges *can* produce networks, which *can* produce coalitions, which *can* produce movements.[24] Note that underscoring these distinctions does not imply any judgment that more cooperation is necessarily better. On the contrary, realistic expectations about what is possible are critical to sustaining any kind of collective action. Indeed, one of the main conclusions of the cross-sectoral comparative analysis that follows is that cross-border cooperation involves significant costs and risks that must be taken into account, depends heavily upon finding appropriate counterparts with whom to cooperate, and needs shared targets to inspire joint action.

It is relevant to bear in mind that, independent of the recent pace of binational integration, numerous civil society actors in Mexico and the United States – including diverse currents within religious, environmental, feminist, human rights, and trade union communities – have long considered themselves to be internationalist. Although many local and national groups see themselves as part of a global movement (for feminism, for human rights, in defense of the environment, and so forth), this chapter focuses upon *sustained cross-border relationships between organized constituencies* (as distinct from groups that share broad goals). As a result, this study employs the relatively tangible category of transnational movement *organization* (as distinct from the more amorphous concept of global civil society, for example).[25]

Distinguishing among networks, coalitions, and movements helps avoid blurring political differences and imbalances *within* what may appear from the outside

---

23 Author's communication with Margaret Keck, Johns Hopkins University, March 2000.
24 The use of the term "transnational" rather than "binational" suggests that this framework can be applied more broadly.
25 The author is grateful to Sonia Álvarez for highlighting this distinction.

Table 15.2: **Transnational Networks, Coalitions, and Movements**

Shared characteristics	Transnational networks	Transnational coalitions	Transnational movement organizations
Exchange of information and experiences	Yes	Yes	Yes
Organized social base	Sometimes more, sometimes less or none	Sometimes more, sometimes less or none	Yes
Mutual support	Sometimes from afar, and possibly strictly discursive	Yes	Yes
Joint actions and campaigns	Sometimes loose coordination	Yes, based upon mutually agreed minimum goals that are often short-term and tactical	Yes, based upon long-term strategy
Shared ideologies	Not necessarily	Not necessarily	Generally yes
Shared political cultures	Often not	Often not	Shared political values, styles, and identities

Note: The ordering of transnational networks, coalitions, and movement organizations (from left to right) reflects the progressively greater density and cohesion of these relationships.

to be "transnational movements."[26] As Keck and Sikkink's pioneering study notes, transnational networks face the hard challenge of developing a common frame of meaning despite cross-cultural differences (1998: 7). In practice, such shared meanings are socially constructed through joint action rather than shared intentions. Political differences within transnational networks are also not to be underestimated, in spite of ostensibly shared goals. Even those transnational networks that *appear* to share basic political-cultural values (including environmental, feminist, or human rights movements) often consist of actors that have very different, nationally distinct political visions, goals, and styles.[27] As Keck and Sikkink point out, "transnational advocacy networks must also be understood as political spaces, in which

26 For a parallel approach to distinguishing among networks, coalitions, and movements, see Khagram, Riker, and Sikkink 2002.

27 National borders may not be the most important ones in this context. For example, ecologists or feminists from different countries who share systematic critiques may have more in common with their cross-border counterparts than they do with the more moderate wings of their respective national movements.

differently situated actors negotiate – formally or informally – the social, cultural, and political meanings of their joint enterprise" (1998: 3).

This essay builds upon Keck and Sikkink's work by exploring the dynamics of these political spaces. However, because the U.S.–Mexico transnational political sphere includes broad-based social organizations as well as nongovernmental organizations, this analysis covers a broader array of transnational actors than does Keck and Sikkink's study.[28] Keck and Sikkink focus upon the subset of civil society actors that are motivated by what they call "principled ideas or values," in contrast to those transnational actors driven mainly by "instrumental goals" (such as corporations) or "shared causal ideas" (such as scientists) (1998: 1, 30). This definition fits many classic transnational advocacy campaigns quite well, but when broad-based social constituencies became involved in transnational campaigns, shared normative values are not the only motivation. Both material interests and shared causal ideas also become very relevant. For example, the U.S. trade unionists and Mexican human rights campaigners who collaborated in a coalition to criticize the NAFTA shared a limited political goal, but they did not necessarily share political values. Because the U.S.–Mexico relationship is characterized precisely by the unusual degree to which "foreign" concerns become "local," with the integration process directly affecting people organized around *interests* as well as values, this chapter employs a definition of "network" that differs from Keck and Sikkink's. The approach used here defines network participants in terms of their actions, not their motivations and values.[29] Keck and Sikkink's reliance upon political values as a *defining* characteristic of transnational advocacy networks is unable to account for the involvement of broad-based membership organizations that perceive their material interests to be directly affected by transnational processes.

Relationships between Social/Civic Counterparts

The following section assesses the degree of density and cohesion among a diverse set of binational society-to-society relationships. Sectors reviewed include labor unions, environmentalists, trade policy advocacy groups, democracy and human rights activists, women's rights activists, and Latino immigrant and civil rights organizations.

28 On the related notion of "transnational public spheres," see Yúdice 1998 and Guidry, Kennedy, and Zald 2000.

29 Keck and Sikkink's (1998) use of the term "network" encompasses both "network" and "coalition" as these terms are employed here. In this study's framework, when networks engage in joint campaigns, they are considered to be coalitions – taking into account that ostensibly transnational networks may well carry out campaigns that are not jointly determined. In instances in which balanced relationships with partners on the ground are lacking, they are more appropriately viewed as international rather than transnational campaigns.

Labor Unions

Mexico–U.S. labor partnerships have been among the most difficult cross-border relationships to construct. There are for four main reasons for this.[30] First, the political cultures of the two countries' labor movements are dominated by powerful nationalist ideological legacies. Second, sometimes workers in certain sectors – especially in industries characterized by high degrees of North American production sharing, such as automobiles, textiles, and garments – have directly conflicting short-term interests. Third, counterpart productive sectors often have very different union structures. Specific industries may be unionized in one country but not in the other, or unions may be centralized in one country but decentralized in the other, creating asymmetries that make it difficult to identify appropriate counterparts.[31] Fourth, some unions have preferred the diplomatic stability of working with politically compatible counterparts and have been unwilling to explore relationships with a broader range of potential partners. Until the late 1990s, the dominant pattern of binational relations between union leaders was to avoid conflict by limiting their diplomatic ties to official counterparts.[32] This sometimes made direct ties between Mexican and U.S. unions difficult, especially in sectors (such as the automotive and textile industries) in which forms of representation differed between the two countries.

A very limited number of cross-border solidarity efforts involving workers predate the NAFTA debate of the early 1990s. One pioneering case involved the American Friends Service Committee's efforts along the Texas border to support discreet community-based organizing of workers in *maquiladora* (in-bond processing) plants, leading to the formation of the now broad-based Border Committee of

---

30 For background on the international politics of U.S. labor unions, see Sims 1992, Shorrock 1999, and McGinn and Moody 1992. On the history of U.S. economic nationalism and unions, see Frank 1999. On variations in trade union responses to the NAFTA in the United States and Canada, see Dreiling and Robinson 1998. On U.S.–Mexican union relations, see Armbruster 1998; Babson 2000; Bandy 1998, 2000; Brooks 1992; Carr 1996, 1998; Cook 1997; García Urrutia 2002; Hathaway 2000a; Kidder and McGinn 1995; La Botz 1992; E. Williams 1997; and H. Williams 1999, 2002. On union relations with immigrants, see Milkman 2000, among others.

31 Such asymmetries are particularly notable in the automotive sector.

32 For example, in the early 1990s the United Auto Workers (UAW) did not pursue relationships with union democracy movements in Mexico (such as the Ford-Cuautitlán movement) in order to avoid alienating PRI union bosses. This permitted a rank-and-file dissident movement within the UAW – New Directions – to gain the moral high ground by leading U.S. solidarity efforts with Mexican Ford workers (La Botz 1992: 148–59, Armbruster 1998). When thugs from the government-aligned Confederation of Mexican Workers (CTM) killed a worker at the Cuautitlán plant, thousands of New Directions UAW workers in the Midwest wore black armbands. Yet that solidarity breakthrough may also have been a weakness, given that associations with New Directions probably made the Ford-Cuautitlán rank-and-file movement anathema to the UAW national leadership.

Women Workers (CFO).[33] Another early effort was Mujer a Mujer (Woman to Woman), which led feminist support for the independent "19th of September" Seamstresses' Union following the 1985 earthquakes in Mexico City.[34] In the first binational U.S.–Mexican union-to-union effort since the beginning of the Cold War, the midwestern Farm Labor Organizing Committee (FLOC) coordinated in the late 1980s with an agricultural workers' union in Sinaloa (an affiliate of the "official" Confederation of Mexican Workers, CTM) to counter Campbell Soup Company's efforts to divide and conquer unions in the United States and Mexico (Neuman 1993, Barger and Reza 1994).

The multisectoral Coalition for Justice in the Maquiladoras (CJM) was founded in 1989, before the NAFTA debate began. It brought together religious, environmental, labor, community, and women's rights organizers who had been working on binational integration issues.[35] Initially led by U.S. religious activists based on the border, over the years the CJM has become increasingly trinational, with Canadian, Mexican, and U.S. members. In fact, in 1996 it began to require 50 percent Mexican representation on its board of directors.

Williams's comprehensive comparative examination of a decade of diverse CJM campaigns found that transborder labor-centered initiatives can generate pressure upon both governments and private-sector interests to reform practices and uphold laws in a manner that they otherwise would not do (Williams 1999, 2002). The CJM has taken up the long-term challenge of bringing labor unions together with community-based worker organizations and NGOs. This is especially important in the maquiladora sector, where many Mexican workers do not see formal unions as organizations that will represent their interests. After all, through "protection contracts" signed without rank-and-file involvement, many of these workers are already nominally members of unions – albeit corrupt and largely invisible ones. Williams's systematic comparison of a large number of solidarity actions shows that the more cross-border they were, the more impact they had on their targets. This suggests that the logic of binational approaches to workers' rights campaigns is driven by its greater practical impact, not simply by ideology.

However, some kinds of cross-border actions create tensions between U.S. and

---

33 See Kamel and Hoffman 1999. The Border Committee of Women Workers is reportedly active in Ciudad Victoria, Río Bravo, Piedras Negras, Ciudad Acuña, and Agua Prieta.

34 See Carrillo 1990 and 1998 on efforts to build cross-border solidarity with the "19th of September" Seamstresses' Union. In the late 1980s, these ties included contacts with the major U.S. counterpart unions, as well as a relationship with Texas-based Fuerza Unida (United Force). International support for the "19th of September" Seamstresses' Union waned following a disputed leadership transition in 1988. See also Mujer a Mujer's (Woman to Woman) innovative binational bulletin "Correspondencia," which linked supporters of female labor organizing in both countries from 1984 to 1992. For further discussion of Mujer a Mujer, see Waterman 1998: 168–72, and Carrillo 1998.

35 For further discussion, see Kamel 1988, 1989; Kamel and Hoffman 1999; Peña 1997; and Ruiz and Tiano 1987.

Mexican labor organizers. According to Martha Ojeda, a former maquiladora worker and now executive director of the CJM, most Mexican maquiladora organizers concentrate upon long-term shop floor and community-based organizing rather than upon U.S.–focused political and corporate campaigns.[36] U.S. initiatives often give priority to short-term media impact, especially during key national political moments such as trade policy debates in Congress. The emphasis upon media impact sometimes conflicts with more subtle shop floor organizing. Mexican maquiladora organizers report cases in which U.S. union delegations standing outside the factory gates televised their denunciations of the factory's terrible conditions, and workers who were organizing on the inside were fired as a result.[37]

Until the late 1990s, Mexican maquiladora organizers had been quite isolated from one another. It was only after several years of participating jointly in cross-border coalitions (such as the Southwest Network for Economic and Environmental Justice and the CJM) that Mexican organizers convened their first border-wide networking meetings in late 1998 in Tijuana. Although U.S.–led cross-border initiatives encouraged networking among Mexican organizers, some Mexican activists grew wary of importing the internal rivalries that existed within U.S. organizations. The second worker-organizing meeting was, therefore, pointedly called "Maquiladora Organizing In and From Mexico."[38] This broad-based gathering sought to further borderwide coalition-building within Mexico by airing concerns, forging shared political goals, and elaborating a series of "ethical principles," point 9 of which read:

> I will accept no support, national or international, that is conditional, that foments divisions and competition among Mexican worker organizations, that subordinates my organization to outside interests, or that undervalues, endangers, or negatively affects Mexican workers.[39]

By the late 1990s, Mexican organizers had begun to speak for the first time of an incipient *movement* of maquiladora workers – a result of both cross-border efforts

---

36 Discussant's remarks at the conference "Lessons from Mexico–U.S. Binational Civil Society Coalitions," University of California, Santa Cruz, July 1998.

37 Author's interview with Carmen Valadez, Casa de la Mujer: Factor X, September 1999, Santa Cruz, California. Note, for example, the case of Custom Trim in Matamoros, where leaders of the visiting delegation reportedly ignored warnings that organizers would likely be fired.

38 It was held in Ciudad Juárez, Chihuahua on August 20–21, 1999; about one hundred organizers (mostly women) participated. Of 65 participants who registered, 23 were active workers and 15 were recently fired workers, a much higher proportion than in any other border network. Of the Mexican organizations that signed the final political declaration, 11 were affiliated with the Coalition for Justice in the Maquiladoras, 6 with Southwest Network for Economic and Environmental Justice, 2 with both, and 3 with neither cross-border network (author's interview with Carmen Valadez, Casa de la Mujer: Factor X, September 1999, Santa Cruz, California).

39 "Principios éticos," August 20–21, 1999, Ciudad Juárez, Chihuahua; distributed by electronic mail.

and organizing initiatives undertaken within Mexico. By this time, increased Mexican (and Canadian) participation in the CJM had transformed the coalition into a much more balanced venue for forging joint strategies and processing very different campaign styles. Most notably, the relationship within the CJM between the AFL–CIO and autonomous Mexican worker-organizing initiatives had become a persistent source of internal debate. Thus, in terms of the conceptual framework presented in this study, the CJM is indeed aptly named – a *coalition*, more coordinated than a network but less unified than a movement.

One very high-profile maquiladora organizing experience involved Tijuana's Han Young automotive component factory. The Han Young union worked very closely with the San Diego Workers' Support Committee. Through its influential labor and political allies, the San Diego Workers' Support Committee generated widespread U.S. union and congressional concern about the blatant violations of freedom of association at the Han Young plant. Within Mexico, the Han Young union had affiliated with the national Authentic Labor Front (FAT) in order to gain sufficient political leverage to demand an open union election. However, it later left the FAT, giving priority to cross-border solidarity over Mexican coalition partners.[40] The cross-border Han Young campaign won important court and media victories, but the factory's workers lost on the ground. Their victories in court were ignored by government authorities in Baja California, and all the pro-union workers were permanently replaced.

The Han Young case tested the limits of cross-border leverage. In this stance at least, U.S. media coverage, plus access to Representative Richard Gephardt and then Vice President Al Gore, seem to have had little effect upon the defense of Mexican workers' rights.[41] The Han Young case led to a claim filed through the U.S. National Administrative Office (one of the national offices established under the NAFTA's so-called labor side agreement to investigate worker rights grievances), but the main outcome was a farcical public hearing on freedom of association in which dissident workers were publicly beaten in a Tijuana hotel (Bacon 2000). The Han Young experience is, then, a cautionary tale that warns against assuming that broad-based, high-level, and high-profile international pressure will be sufficient to influence political decisions within Mexico.

More generally, U.S. and Mexican labor unions have held numerous discussions, exchanges, and conferences, which have yielded frequent internationalist proclamations but relatively few consolidated partnerships. Some important U.S. unions have been divided over whether to pursue nationalist versus internationalist strategies. This was, for example, the case with the International Brotherhood of Teamsters,

40 Han Young organizers did not participate in the new Mexican maquiladora organizing network.

41 For details on the Han Young campaign, see H. Williams 2000; Hathaway 2000a, 2000b; and the "Coalition for Labor Rights" (www.summersault.com/`agj/clr/) and the "Working Together" and "Mexican Labor News and Analysis" bulletins (www.igc.apc.org/unitedelect/ alert.html). For overviews of border labor politics, see Bandy 1998, 2000.

which ended up undertaking both strategies at once during their mid-1990s period of reform leadership. The Teamsters' high-profile campaign against the implementation of the NAFTA's cross-border trucking provisions was remarkably successful; indeed, it was the only case in which a bottom-up U.S. protest blocked implementation of a NAFTA article. Working together with leading politicians from U.S. border states (including Texas Attorney General Dan Morales), the Teamsters managed to frame the issue in terms of public safety and the threat of illegal drug trafficking (rather than the promotion of the union's special interests). In the process, they used media campaigns that many Mexican critics of free trade considered to be anti-Mexican in tone.[42] Yet at the same time, the Teamsters' internationalist wing pursued an organizing campaign in the state of Washington's apple industry that was sensitive to the concerns of Mexican immigrants, coordinated with the United Farm Workers (UFW), and eventually involved Mexican unions.[43] Although seemingly contradictory, these two approaches reflect both the political diversity that exists within the largest U.S. union and the pragmatic, short-term political calculations made by anti-NAFTA forces in the United States more generally.

The most notable binational union partnerships have been between relatively small, progressive unions, including alliances between the United Electrical, Radio, and Machine Workers of America (UE) and the FAT and between the Communications Workers of America (CWA) and the Mexican Telephone Workers' Union (STRM).[44] The FAT–UE alliance was sustained by shared ideological commitments to internationalism and worker empowerment. This partnership helped to launch perhaps the most ambitious trinational North American union coalition so far, the Dana Workers' Alliance, which brought together many industrial unions to defend freedom of association in a Mexican auto parts plant. However, as the case slowly wended its way through the NAFTA labor grievance procedures, the two U.S. unions most involved withdrew from leadership of the initiative. The UE-represented auto parts factory was closed, and the Teamsters' reform leadership lost power.[45]

42 Author's interviews and plenary discussion at the conference "Trinational Exchange: Popular Perspectives on Mexico–U.S.–Canada Relations," Cuernavaca, Mexico, February 1996. For a recent U.S. critique of opening cross-border truck transportation, see Public Citizen 2001. Kourous (2001) argues convincingly that the U.S. groups opposed to the North American Free Trade Agreement's trucking provisions continue to reflect nationalist biases.

43 In contrast to the Farm Labor Organizing Committee, as of the year 2000 the United Farm Workers (UFW) had not ventured beyond tentative gestures toward potential Mexican counterparts. According to local observers, the absence of a binational approach contributed to the failure of the UFW's three-year campaign to organize Mexican strawberry workers in the Pajaro Valley of Central California.

44 See Alexander 1998, Alexander and Gilmore 1994, L. Cohen and Early 1999, García Urrutia 2002, Rosen 1999, and Sepúlveda 1998.

45 Author's communication with United Electrical, Radio, and Machine Workers of America (UE) representative Robin Alexander, September 1999.

The STRM–CWA alliance was especially significant because the unions came together to seek common ground despite their different positions regarding the NAFTA. They formed a coalition to meet long-term challenges, while "agreeing to disagree" over various short-term political questions. The STRM–CWA partnership initiated two cases under NAFTA labor grievance procedures alleging violations of the right to freedom of association. In the first case, the STRM filed a complaint on behalf of U.S. workers – Latina employees at a Sprint telecommunications facility who were fired for union organizing.[46]

Remarkably few organizations have followed the example set by the Farm Labor Organizing Committee when it pioneered the strategy of bringing together unions representing workers employed by the same company in Mexico and the United States. One important exception involved the airline industry, which is increasingly binationally integrated. Delta Airlines and Aeroméxico have one of the most extensive corporate partnerships in the sector; in response, the pilots' organizations representing both companies formed an alliance "to protect wage structures and work distribution ... the first of its kind in Latin America" (Millman 2000).

In summary, cross-border union collaboration has brought to public attention some blatant violations of freedom of association – but thus far without any tangible effect in terms of practical developments in the workplace. Indeed, some U.S. workers who supported their Mexican counterparts saw their own plant shut down, allegedly in retaliation for their solidarity actions (Bacon 1998). Perhaps the most interesting departure is for Mexican unions to pursue trinational claims involving violations of freedom of association of workers (often Mexico-origin workers, as in the cases of Sprint and Washington apple growers) in the United States. These efforts have contributed to more balanced coalitions by showing that the right to freedom of association is also systematically violated in the United States, not just in Mexico.[47]

The national administrative offices created under the North American Agreement

---

46 Communications Workers of America (CWA) leaders note that the second case, involving the border maquiladora Maxi Switch, led to "more success working together," including active rank-and-file participation at the border (especially by the CWA's Tucson local). Nevertheless, U.S. union support was still not sufficient to protect Mexican organizers from being assaulted by factory supervisors (L. Cohen and Early 1999: 158–59).

47 The Sprint grievance led to public hearings and extensive studies on the subject (McKennirey et al. 1997). CWA leaders claimed that the official Commission on North American Labor Cooperation study of threats of plant closings as a violation of freedom of association was first delayed and then watered down (L. Cohen and Early 1999). They further charged that the final study downplayed the findings of one of the project's key researchers, Kate Bronfenbrenner of Cornell University, who found that "plant closing threats and plant closings have become an integral part of employer anti-union strategies" and that the rate of plant closings after U.S. union foundation elections "has more than doubled in the years since NAFTA was ratified" (L. Cohen and Early 1999: 157). Bronfenbrenner's surveys report that U.S. "managers at 70 percent of factories involved in organizing drives threaten to close if workers decide to unionize" (Greenhouse 2001: A10).

on Labor Cooperation have been one of the most tangible institutional results of binational NAFTA union campaigning, and coordinated grievance initiation has constituted one of the most important ways in which unions have sought to sustain and deepen their cross-border coalitions. Having a shared institutional target clearly helped to focus coalition-building efforts. Nevertheless, in the 23 complaints initiated over the 1994–2001 period, the labor side agreement produced very few tangible results in terms of influencing either government policies or private employers, and there were many more complete defeats than partial victories (Human Rights Watch 2001). More generally, the dominant pattern is that the right to organize remains tenuous in both countries, and cross-national ties have been unable to offset labor's weak bargaining power within national political institutions.[48]

Environmentalists

As in the case of organized labor, binational environmental networking and advocacy have been marked by very significant differences within, as well as between, the Mexican and U.S. movements. Both national environmental movements are characterized by high levels of internal diversity, including both groups that see corporate-led economic growth as the answer to meeting environmental needs and elements that view unregulated economic growth as the problem (Hogenboom 1998, Bejarano 2002). Moreover, in both countries the experiences and priorities of groups working directly on the Mexico–U.S. border are often quite distinct from the larger national environmental organizations that have more ample access to the media and policy makers.

There have also been important differences over time in networking effectiveness. The high-profile pre-NAFTA debate was more the exception than the rule in binational environmental politics. Indeed, despite the central role that U.S. environmental organizations played on both sides of the pre-NAFTA debate, none of the major national environmental organizations in the United States devoted serious sustained attention to Mexico or to potential Mexican partners *after* the

---

48 In Mexico, workers seeking independent representation at the huge Duro Bag factory in Tamaulipas found that the secret ballot remains an elusive goal, despite support from the National Union of Workers (UNT) in Mexico City and from the CJM. After watching automatic weapons being brought into the factory, workers were forced by federal arbitration board officials to declare their votes in front of company foremen and PRI–affiliated union leaders. This decision by Carlos Abascal, minister of labor and social welfare in the administration of President Vicente Fox (2000–2006), violated an agreement negotiated between his predecessor and then-U.S. labor secretary Alexis Herman, an agreement that grew out of the Han Young and ITAPSA cases filed under the NAFTA labor side agreement (Bacon 2001). For Abascal, U.S. union support for Mexican labor groups was officially to be considered a threat to national security (Aponte and Pérez Silva 2001). Meanwhile, north of the border, Human Rights Watch (2000) has also recognized that systematic violations of U.S. workers' freedom of association violate international human rights standards.

vote on the NAFTA in the U.S. Congress.[49] This generalization holds true for the Sierra Club, Friends of the Earth, and Greenpeace, which were the only large membership-based U.S. environmental organization to oppose NAFTA. When Washington's short-term agenda moved away from Mexico, so did theirs.[50]

It is not surprising that the major U.S. conservation organizations chose to follow the official logic that Mexico needed trade-led economic growth to generate the resources needed for (hypothetical) environmental investments. These U.S. organizations espoused "free-market environmentalism," and the boards of directors of the most powerful pro-NAFTA U.S. conservation organizations included several prominent corporate representatives, some of whom were simultaneously active within the pro-NAFTA corporate lobby (Dreiling 1997, 2001). Beginning also in the early 1990s, some large U.S. conservation organizations received major grants from the U.S. government to promote the park approach to biodiversity conservation in Mexico.[51]

Despite the high public profile of the biodiversity issue, rare indeed are binational partnerships with established Mexican social counterparts involved in rural natural resource management (with, for example, the vast community forestry movement or the densely organized smallholder coffee cooperative movement, both of which are primarily indigenous). One network began to emerge when the Natural Resources Defense Council, together with the Smithsonian Institution's Center for Migratory Birds, convened a major conference on sustainable coffee in 1996 (Rice, Harris, and MacLean 1997). Since then, however, the U.S. promoters of "bird-friendly" coffee have yet to form many close partnerships with the "fair trade" coffee traders, who focus more on balanced coalitions with Mexican

---

49 The exception was the pro-whale campaign against Mitsubishi Corporation's salt works in Baja California, as discussed below.

50 One important exception to this trend emerged in the late 1990s when the Sierra Club began to take up issues of environmental human rights, including a Guerrero case involving a peasant anti-corporate logging activist (www.sierraclub.org/human-rights/Mexico; Eaton 1999). This campaign contributed to the peasant winning the high-profile Goldman award for environmental activism (Dillon 2000).

   In contrast, the Sierra Club's 1998 internal referendum over whether to consider immigration to be an environmental problem attracted high levels of public attention (Clifford 1998). Although the membership decisively defeated the proposition, neither the internal nor the public debate had any immigrant or binational participation.

51 These organizations included the Nature Conservancy, World Wildlife Fund, and Conservation International. Independent evaluations are lacking of the degree to which these large U.S. conservation organizations have forged balanced partnerships with the communities residing in protected areas. One case worthy of further examination is Conservation International's operation of the Montes Azules Biosphere Reserve, which began in the early 1990s with USAID funds. According to one biologist from Chiapas with extensive field experience in the region, the reserve was managed without community-based civil society partners and to little tangible environmental effect (author's interview, September 1999, Santa Cruz, California).

grassroots coffee producers.[52] The sustainable coffee campaign has had some success at penetrating the U.S. media, but coverage often focuses upon protecting birds rather than forest dwellers' livelihoods, organizations, or human rights. Moreover, the supply of fair-trade and sustainable coffee continues to be much larger than the demand from "conscious" consumers. One common U.S. subtext is occasionally made explicit: the assumption that birds that migrate between the two countries are "American" – as though birds have national identities (Silver 1999).[53] Overall, the alternative coffee issue has produced many meetings and networks but few coalitions.

Greenpeace, with its broad ecological critique, developed one of the very few binational partnerships among the large international environmental membership organizations. In principle, this organization would appear to be a case of a transnational social movement organization, but in practice the "fit" with this concept has been uneven. As part of Greenpeace's effort in the early 1990s to seek greater internal North-South balance, its international leadership sided with its Latin American branches on the controversial tuna-dolphin issue, on the grounds that the Mexican tuna fishing industry had reportedly changed its practices in order to protect dolphins.[54] Southern environmentalists perceived Greenpeace's heterodox stance as a blow against eco-imperialism, but nationalist U.S. ecological groups such as the Earth Island Institute (which lacked strong Mexican partnerships) responded vigorously. Earth Island – a Greenpeace competitor in the direct-mail fund-raising market – seized the opportunity to denounce its rival as anti-dolphin. Greenpeace-International had long been divided over whether to pursue more North-South balance within the organization, and by the mid-1990s the pro-Southern faction within Greenpeace had been defeated.[55] One lesson here is that balanced transnational partnerships can be politically charged when charismatic mega-fauna are involved.[56]

Middle-of-the-road U.S. environmental NGOs appear to have bolstered the Mexican environment ministry's prestige and budgetary resources for dealing with biodiversity protection, but they have had less influence upon border politics. In

---

52 In one notable fair-trade partnership, Equal Exchange and Cultural Survival both launched a support campaign for the Majomut organic coffee cooperative, which had been hit hard by the December 1997 massacre of peasant families in Acteal, Chiapas (see www.equalexchange.org and www.cs.org).

53 For a comprehensive and insightful analysis of sustainable coffee marketing issues, see Rice, Harris, and MacLean 1997. This report provides extraordinary insight into the obstacles that have slowed the emergence of credible coffee labeling and consumer education efforts in the United States, but it does not highlight the role of independent producer organizations as actors. See also Bray 1999.

54 On the tuna conflict, see Bonanno and Constance 1996, Rose 1993, Restrepo 1995, BRIDGES 2000, and Wright 2000.

55 Author's interview with former Greenpeace International leader, December 1998, Santa Cruz, California.

56 Tani Adams (1999) has developed this last point.

contrast, the border's transnational public sphere has been occupied by a civil society that has been gradually thickening from below. Notable NGO coalitions that predated the NAFTA debate include the Environmental Health Coalition (Tijuana–San Diego), the International Sonoran Desert Alliance and other binational tribal initiatives, the CJM's anti-toxics efforts, the Border Ecology Project, and the successful partnership between Chihuahua's Commission for Solidarity and Defense of Human Rights and the Texas Center for Policy Studies to stop a World Bank logging loan in the Sierra Madre's indigenous territories in 1991–1992.[57] Subsequent initiatives have included a broad-based binational coalition bringing together environmentalists throughout the Rio Grande/Río Bravo basin, among others.[58]

Not only have the pace and intensity of binational civil society collaboration on the border increased significantly since NAFTA, but they have also had some very tangible successes. Border environmental coalitions have blocked several controversial proposed projects, including the Tamaulipas canal waterway and, most notably, the Sierra Blanca nuclear waste dump in Texas.[59] Ironically, the fact that the proposed Sierra Blanca dump was designed to receive waste generated at the United States' *northern* border, in New York and Vermont, bolstered critics' charges of environmental racism.

The Sierra Blanca anti-dump campaign was followed by the defeat of the proposed joint venture between Mitsubishi Corporation and the Mexican government to expand an industrial salt works in Baja California. The project threatened to affect the breeding grounds of the California gray whales that migrate between Mexico's coastal waters and the Bering Straits, past the United States. In this case, binational pressure forced project proponents to meet unusually rigorous environmental assessment standards, and both mainstream and radical U.S. environmental organizations engaged in successful mass media campaigns that raised the project's political cost to both the Mexican government and Mitsubishi.[60]

Both the Sierra Blanca and Baja California projects had unusually media-worthy protagonists – nuclear waste in one case, charismatic mega-mammals in the

57 On the Environmental Health Coalition, see www.environmentalhealth.org. On the pathbreaking cross-border campaign against the World Bank forestry project, see Lowerre 1994.

58 The Rio Grande/Río Bravo Basin Coalition, for example, includes more than fifty organizations and defines itself as "a multi-national, multi-cultural organization with leadership from the United States, Mexico, and the Pueblo nations whose purpose is to help local communities restore and sustain the environment, economies, and social well-being of the Rio Grande/Río Bravo Basin" (see www.rioweb.org). Note that not all cross-border environmental collaboration is sustained over time. The Red Fronteriza de Salud y Medio Ambiente (Border Network for Health and the Environment), for example, did not consolidate ongoing cross-border partnerships.

59 On the Sierra Blanca campaign, see Abraham and Cone 1999, LaFranchi 1998, Paterson 1999, Robbins 2000, and Walker 1998. On the Tamaulipas canal project, see Texas Center for Policy Studies 1994.

60 See Preston 2000, Dedina 2000, and www.wavebajawhales.com.

other – that enhanced the campaigners' leverage. These two campaigns show that, given sufficient lead time, environmental NGOs can influence or block *new*, high-profile, high-risk policy decisions. Both initiatives involved balanced coalitions with clear, tangible, shared goals. One could argue, however, that these goals were relatively "winnable" because they did not challenge the dominant pattern of maquiladora industrialization. In contrast, it is difficult to find significant victories in the area of toxic industrial waste disposal despite the issue's high public profile.[61]

In addition to defeating specific proposed projects, border environmental campaigns have also set precedents for constructive public participation in local and binational policy processes. Mainstream U.S. national environmental organizations played a central role in extracting promises of limited procedural reforms for dealing with border environmental threats (Audley 1997, Hogenboom 1998). These concessions – made by the U.S. government and imposed upon Mexico – provided middle-of-the-road environmental NGOs with the political cover they needed to avoid conflict with the administration of President Bill Clinton, which they supported on other, often higher priority, issues. Following the NAFTA vote in 1993, when U.S. national environmental NGO agendas moved on to other topics, it fell primarily to border groups to encourage the Border Environment Cooperation Commission (BECC) and the North American Development Bank (NADBank) to fulfill their mandates (BIOS Action Kit 1999, Mumme 1999). Most independent environmental policy observers see the BECC and NADBank as setting higher standards for public participation in the policy process, even though they have yet to produce significant tangible impacts upon the border environment.[62]

The sensitivity of many border environmental organizations to interlocking human health and natural resource concerns facilitated cross-border coalition-building. U.S. and Mexican border groups also share their distance – and, to some degree, alienation – from their respective national elites. Moreover, border groups have been willing to take on the difficult challenge of recognizing and overcoming cultural differences (Kelly 2002). This commitment is crucial because, as the history of the border shows, proximity does not necessarily generate mutual understanding.

Trade Advocacy Networks

In the United States, the NAFTA debate of the early 1990s focused upon the domestic implications of the North-South relationship – especially upon the nature of U.S. relations with the developing world in general and with Mexico in particular. In Mexico, early opposition to the NAFTA was more limited than in

---

61 For comprehensive overviews of border toxic waste issues, see, for example, Red Mexicana de Acción Frente al Libre Comercio et al. 2000 [http://www.texascenter.org/pubs/pubs.htm] and Varady, Romero Lankao, and Hawkins 2001. The most recent data from the National Institute for Statistics, Geography, and Informatics (INEGI) indicate that, of the estimated 8 million tons of toxic waste generated annually, only 12 percent receive some kind of treatment (Enciso 2001).

62 See diverse critiques in "Borderlines Updater" and Public Citizen 1997, among others.

the United States, but there, too, it generated a very wide-ranging debate about relations with "the North."

The trade debates in both countries had transnational and multisectoral dimensions. Domestic constituency organizations met with their counterparts in the other country (often for the first time) in order to understand each other's perspective and, in some instances, to engage in joint activities and contribute to each other's efforts. At the same time, because diverse actors perceived that their interests were directly affected by the NAFTA, unusual "citizen" coalitions brought together local, regional, and national organizations representing organized workers, farmers, environmentalists, and consumer, immigrant, Latino, and human rights activists. Many of these organizations had never worked together, and some of them had long histories of mistrust, if not outright antipathy.[63] Suddenly, social constituency organizations that once considered themselves as solely "domestic" and conceptually remote from international economic policy entered the transnational arena as they responded to the NAFTA proposal.

In the United States, the NAFTA opposition became a movement with somewhat disjointed nationalist and internationalist wings (Cavanagh, Anderson, and Hansen-Kuhn 2002). Some of the anti-NAFTA forces perceived economic integration as a process that threatened U.S. sovereignty. Ralph Nader's Public Citizen organization stressed this nationalist approach, as did those environmentalists and trade unionists who argued that the NAFTA would supersede the authority of local and national labor, consumer, and environmental laws and standards (Nader et al. 1993). These leftist populists were joined, and then overshadowed, by conservative nationalist populists led by Ross Perot, Jr. and Patrick J. Buchanan.

The NAFTA's proponents were caught off guard by the broad public challenge, and they became increasingly alarmed as the popular debate came to threaten the legislative survival of their project. The U.S. opposition was strong enough to oblige then-presidential candidate Bill Clinton to acknowledge, for the first time in U.S. history, the legitimacy of embedding labor and environmental standards in trade policy. The so-called environmental and labor side agreements designed by the Clinton administration managed to divide the major environmental organizations and provided some political cover for labor leaders, who differed privately over how intensely to oppose their ostensible ally Clinton on the NAFTA (Mayer 1998, Audley 1997, Dreiling 1997). At the same time, an unusual Latino advocacy-environmentalist coalition also led to the creation of new binational institutions (the BECC and the NADBank) to buffer the NAFTA's environmental and social costs on the Mexico–U.S. border (Hinojosa-Ojeda 2002).

The common campaign practice of building broad, often contradictory short-term coalitions around specific legislative conflicts dominated the U.S. process. U.S.–based critics of the NAFTA found relatively few like-minded counterparts in

---

63 See Lehman 2002 and Hernández Navarro 2002 on the many binational exchanges between farmers and campesino organizations.

Mexico, where unilateral trade opening had already occurred and even NAFTA critics limited their political investment because closer economic integration between Mexico and the United States was perceived as inevitable. The nationalist wing of the U.S. NAFTA opposition also used insensitive rhetoric that discouraged binational collaboration. Nationalist U.S. critics of the NAFTA found that their message of "Blame the foreigners" was well received by important mass publics. Economic restructuring had generated widespread insecurity among industrial workers, and many U.S. employers systematically used the threat of flight abroad to weaken union organizing efforts and undermine workers' position in their efforts to negotiate contracts (Greenhouse 2001, Human Rights Watch 2000, McKennirey et al. 1997). Some U.S. environmental and food safety campaigns also sought to play upon images of Mexico as a foreign threat, resonating with inherited popular cultural stereotypes of "dirty Mexicans" – even though the most dangerous food safety threat to U.S. public health is clearly the domestic meatpacking industry (Perl 2000).

The internationalist wing of the U.S. NAFTA opposition recognized that some kind of economic integration was inevitable. Nevertheless, by the time of the NAFTA vote in the Congress, its first slogan, "Not this NAFTA," had been replaced by "No to NAFTA." Although U.S. internationalists worked closely with their Mexican counterparts and with anti-racist social movements in the United States, their ambitious goal of mass economic literacy required sustained political invest-ments, whereas the legislative campaign momentum imposed a short-term political logic that privileged nationalist discourses.

Mexican critics coalesced around the Free Trade Action Network, led by the FAT, human rights groups, environmentalists, and other NGOs (Arroyo and Monroy 1996, Luján 2002, Peñaloza Méndez and Arroyo Picard 1997, RMALC 1994). Despite significant domestic political constraints, this activist network obliged senior governmental officials and even cabinet ministers to engage in an ongoing dialogue with them during the NAFTA negotiation process, a previously unimagin-able possibility.

The Mexican Action Network Against Free Trade (RMALC) was bolstered by its partnerships with the Action Canada Network and, in the United States, the Alliance for Responsible Trade.[64] In spite of the pressures created by the final "yes or no" NAFTA vote, these national networks tried to change the terms of the debate by engaging in an unusual process of trilateral civil society negotiations to produce a shared alternative policy stance. The most important proposal of this kind, "A Just and Sustainable Trade and Development Initiative for North America," was developed by three NGO trade coalitions: Alliance for Responsible Trade (ART), RMALC, and a group within Action Canada Network. This initiative was overshadowed publicly by the highly polarized final phase of the NAFTA debate in the United States, but its innovative trinational consensus-building approach set a historic precedent (ART/CTC/RMALC 1994; Cavanagh, Anderson,

---

64 See Ayres 1998 on the Canadian trade movement.

and Hansen-Kuhn 2001). Even the more nationalist U.S. network eventually supported it. The networks worked from drafts that bracketed their points of difference, in conscious imitation of the treaty negotiation process itself. One of the most important points of contention was the issue of whether (implicitly Mexican) failure to meet minimum environmental and social standards should provoke trade sanctions.

The overall pattern that emerged from a decade of trade policy debate was not a secular trend of ever-increasing levels of binational partnership and coalition-building. Instead, there were ebbs and flows in which both nationalist and internationalist trade advocacy efforts peaked during the debate preceding the NAFTA vote. The NAFTA again appeared on the U.S. policy agenda because of Mexico's December 1994 financial crisis, when U.S. advocacy groups took a distinctively nationalist position. One noted left-liberal advocacy economist even compared the United States' subsequent financial rescue of Mexico to its involvement in the Vietnam war, suggesting that the United States was entering a dangerous quagmire and thereby reinforcing the "Mexico as threat" NAFTA critique (Faux 1995). Similarly, domestic opposition to the 1997 renewal of so-called fast-track U.S. trade legislation involved much less coordination with Mexican counterparts than existed during the NAFTA debate. Sustained U.S. labor and consumer opposition to the implementation of the NAFTA's cross-border trucking provisions also relied upon nationalist approaches. Meanwhile, RMALC continued to monitor the NAFTA's effects, but it focused its advocacy work upon Mexico's free-trade agreement with the European Union, managing to incorporate a significant democracy clause into the agreement (Arroyo and Peñaloza 2000). In short, balanced cross-border civil society coordination is far from an inevitable dimension of increasing international concern about economic globalization.

Democracy and Human Rights

If one had looked ahead from 1988 or 1994, it would have been difficult to predict that the U.S. presidential race of 2000 would suffer from much more serious procedural flaws than the Mexican presidential election held earlier that same year. During the most contested phase of Mexico's transition to electoral democracy, the main pattern of U.S.–Mexico societal relations involving democracy and human rights issues took the form of networks. As Dresser (1996) has shown, Mexico's "democracy network" provides an excellent illustration of the concept of transnational advocacy networks.[65] In terms of the framework proposed in this study, a few organizations went further to sustain coalitions, involving coordinated agreements to pursue joint campaigns.

65 Dresser (1996: 325) notes that "The Mexican democracy network includes domestic and international electoral observer organizations, international NGOs, private foundations, groups of scholars, international secretariats of political parties, and some sectors of the national and international media ... Mexican prodemocracy social movements are key parts of this nascent network."

U.S. civil society organizations concerned with democracy and human rights abroad were slow to focus upon Mexico. Though influential international human rights reports began to appear in the mid-1980s, even Mexico's 1988 electoral conflict did not lead to a sustained strategy of binational pro-democracy or human rights coalition-building.[66] The NAFTA debate created a major opportunity to strengthen these civil society ties, but it was constrained by the narrow confines of the official policy agenda. Although most Mexican civil society organizations were wary of imposing direct pro-democracy or human rights conditionality upon the trade agreement,[67] the NAFTA debate made these issues more visible in the United States. However, with the exception of those organizations involved with election monitoring, this political moment did not produce a major convergence between U.S. and Mexican human rights groups.

Although human rights groups were important actors in the Mexican coalitions dealing with trade issues, democracy and human rights had little relevance for most U.S. trade advocacy groups. According to one of Mexico's leading human rights activists, the issue was a low priority within the trinational coalition-building process (Acosta 2002). Moreover, human rights groups in Canada, Mexico, and the United States had different views about the relationships among economic, social, and political rights.[68] Independently of the trade debate, Mexican national human rights organizations also pursued claims through multilateral legal channels, such as the Inter-American Human Rights Commission. They were successful insofar as the Mexican government was issued several critical decisions, but only in one case did the government actually respond by complying with international law.[69]

It took the 1994 Chiapas rebellion to make human rights in Mexico a priority on the binational civil society agenda. A wide range of U.S. groups responded quickly, contributing to the international pressure for a political solution to the conflict. By 1999, four different national U.S. organizations and networks, as well as many smaller local groups, had made Chiapas a priority (Stephen 2002). Lack of coordination among indigenous rights support groups within the United States reflected

66 Amnesty International published the first significant report (1986). The timing of its release coincided with the peak of Republican political criticism of Mexico from Washington, D.C. This association significantly undermined the report's political impact because the Mexican government could write it off as foreign intervention in the country's internal affairs.

67 For one exception (a Mexican effort to create a link in the U.S. debate over the NAFTA between the trade agreement and democratization in Mexico), see Castañeda and Heredia 1993. For a trinational overview, see MacDonald 1999.

68 Note the thematic change in the more recent reports from Human Rights Watch (1990, 1991a, 1991b, 1993, 1994a, 1994b, 1995, 1996b, 1997, 1998a, 1998b, 1999, 2000a). Over time, the scope of the organization's definition of human rights broadened, eventually including gendered human rights among maquiladora workers.

69 Author's interview with Emma Maza Calviño, international relations director of the Centro de Derechos Humanos Miguel Agustín Pro Juárez, April 2001, Mexico City. For details on Mexico's international human rights legal decisions, see Centro de Derechos Humanos 2000.

different political cultures and constituencies, as well as different approaches among Mexican counterpart groups. Most U.S. support initiatives drew heavily upon the legacy of Central American peace movements in the 1980s, including both faith-based and secular leftist political cultures and strategies (Gosse 1988, 1995; C. Smith 1996). This legacy bolstered Chiapas solidarity work in the short term, but it carried medium-term weaknesses (including the strategic limitations associated with interpreting Mexico through a Central American lens). This pattern began to change with the founding of the Mexico Solidarity Network in 1999. Some 75 organizations participate in this group, which has organized several labor and human rights delegations to Mexico.[70]

Many observers have pointed to the increased volume and velocity of the international information flow from Chiapas as strong evidence of "globalization from below" and an indication of the power of international solidarity. The flow of information to international sympathizers has irritated Mexican government officials, who have referred disparagingly to the Chiapas conflict as a (mere) "war of ink and Internet."[71] However, the conflict on the ground has remained stalemated for years, information flow and international solidarity notwithstanding. Thus the degree to which the Zapatista supporters' able use of the Internet has contributed to their cause remains an open question. Stephen (2002), for example, aptly questions the widespread assumption that more and faster activist access to information *necessarily* leads to greater policy impact.[72] According to one key U.S. strategist (Lewis 2002), solidarity groups' focus upon Chiapas to the exclusion of other militarized regions and national-level democratization in Mexico has also limited the impact of U.S. peace support efforts. Although U.S. civil society efforts to achieve peace in Chiapas gained widespread legitimacy in the United States, they did not penetrate and mobilize major U.S. civil society institutions. This outcome contrasts with what was achieved by the movement against U.S. intervention in Central America in the 1980s, which generated broad-based mainstream participation in religious, civic, and trade union arenas, leading to significant influence in the U.S. Congress. In the 1980s, Central American opposition and peace movements themselves made winning U.S. civil society allies a strategic priority, whereas neither the EZLN nor the National Indigenous Congress (CNI) has given primacy to network-building.[73]

---

70 See www.mexicosolidarity.org.

71 See Ronfeldt and Arquilla 1998 for a U.S. military-sponsored analysis of this issue.

72 The widely assumed direct Internet linkage between the EZLN and the outside world has been overdrawn. In the early years, the principal communication process involved two stages – first between the EZLN and *La Jornada*, and then between *La Jornada*'s website and the rest of the world. For subsequent debate over the role of international solidarity with Chiapas, see Hellman 2000 and Cleaver 2000.

73 For an analysis of why certain radical movements gain international visibility and others do not, including a comparison of the EZLN and the Popular Revolutionary Army (ERP), see Bob 2000.

The Chiapas rebellion focused the attention of U.S. pro-democracy groups – and the U.S. government – upon Mexico's 1994 presidential election. This was the high point of U.S. civil society interest in working with Mexican election observers, although some groups (including Global Exchange and the Washington Office on Latin America) continued to work closely with Mexico's Civic Alliance in their efforts to monitor controversial state-level elections.[74] Mexican independent election observer efforts only began in 1991 (Aguayo Quezada 1998, Álvarez Icaza 2002, McConnell 1996). U.S. observer groups (including participants from traditional human rights organizations, universities, peace groups, Latino rights advocacy groups, and trade unions) became involved in 1994 and together accounted for a large fraction of international observers. However, the entire international contingent during the peak period of foreign concern numbered only about 500 individuals, compared to as many as 25,000 Mexican observers (Álvarez Icaza 2002). In contrast, U.S. citizens' organizations alone sent 700 official representatives to observe El Salvador's 1994 elections (Gosse 1995).

The largest single U.S. citizen contingent in 1994 was organized by Global Exchange, an NGO whose numerous "reality tours" to Chiapas later provoked Mexican government hostility.[75] Unlike most international observers, Global Exchange delegates traveled to remote rural hotspots where electoral violations were most probable. On the night of the 1994 election, however, under media pressure to make a public statement, the logic of the organization's mission led its representatives to take a position even before its Mexican host, Civic Alliance, had decided how to respond to the exclusionary practices that surfaced during the election (practices that were as unexpected as they were difficult to document).[76] At that moment, Global Exchange's exercise of its autonomy caused tension within the binational partnership, reinforcing an image of the organization as a reckless seeker of media attention. Global Exchange subsequently made a long-term, sustained political investment in working with its Mexican partners, and it has since been one of the Mexican pro-democracy movement's most consistent U.S. civil society allies. For example, Global Exchange (in partnership with regional human rights organizations) subsequently organized experienced U.S. observer

---

74 See WOLA 1993, 1994a, 1994b, 1994c, 1995a, 1995b, 1997. For additional information, see www.wola.org.

75 Paraphrasing Dresser (1991b), one might call this a "neo-nationalist reaction to a neoliberal problem."

 The Central American movement experience suggests that internationalist visits to conflict zones can be crucially important for turning sympathy into activist commitment. As many as several thousand U.S. citizens may have visited Chiapas since 1994 (Ross 1999, Sandoval 1999, Stephen 2002).

76 Author's observation and interviews, August 1994, Mexico City. After processing their data for several weeks, Civic Alliance came to the conclusion that, in effect, two different elections had taken place – one relatively clean, the other marked by systematic pressures upon voters and violations of ballot secrecy. For a discussion of the data, see Fox 1996.

delegations for relatively less fashionable missions such as observation of Guerrero's municipal elections.[77]

Several human rights organizations and Chiapas support initiatives formed sustained networks, and some of the campaigns with an on-the-ground presence could clearly be considered coalitions (including, for example, International Service for Peace in Chiapas and the Schools for Chiapas project). The Global Exchange–Civic Alliance partnership was the clearest instance of a sustained pro-democracy coalition that addressed issues beyond Chiapas. Aside from these few cases, however, one could argue that both U.S. and Mexican pro-democracy actors have lacked a sustained strategy for building partnerships that reach deeply into their respective civil societies.

Women's Rights Networks

Binational women's rights networks have been extensive, but they generally have had a lower profile than networks in other sectors because activists have brought gender perspectives to other social movements – most notably supporting the empowerment of women workers and indigenous women. Mujer a Mujer and the American Friends Service Committee's maquiladora support program both played pioneering roles. Sometimes the links between women's rights concerns and binational integration reached deeply into U.S. civil society. For example, the United Methodist Women, a progressive membership organization with more than one million members, was the first women's organization publicly to oppose the NAFTA (Dougherty 1999).

Many experiences of the binational women's movement are remarkably similar to those in other sectors in terms of the distinction between mutual learning and exchanges, on the one hand, and sustaining coalitions and campaigns, on the other. As Carrillo (1998: 394) observed in relation to Mexicana/Chicana movement relations, "the majority of contacts across the border have not yet reached a point of collaborative action, remaining instead in a beginning step of establishing contact and discussing common ground." Carrillo further noted that lack of resources is not the only obstacle to binational coalition-building. "Differences in central focus and agenda" are also important; "Chicanas and Latinas in the United States have focused on questions of race and ethnicity, while Mexicanas have focused on class issues and survival." After reviewing a wide range of cross-border initiatives dating from the mid-1980s, Carrillo concluded that:

> Time and again women showed a strong interest in making connections and taking a more active role in establishing the rules and regulations of the process of regional integration. The frustration voiced by both Chicana/Latina and Mexicana women was that no one knew exactly how to take the next step in transnational network building after establishing initial contact. Women's movements lack a unifying focus or initiative around which groups can find a common ground and take collaborative action. On every front, the move from communication and contact to collaborative action was not clearly defined (1998: 407).

77 For more on Global Exchange's Mexico work, see Lewis 2002 and www.globalexchange.org. On the Civic Alliance, see www.laneta.apc.org/alianza/.

U.S. and Mexican women's rights activists have also worked together to reframe policy discourse for women's organizing in terms of the broader concept of human rights. According to Maylei Blackwell, an analyst of U.S.–Mexican women's movement relations, because of the United Nations conferences on women, "human rights discourse has replaced discrimination as the principal coalition-building element in international women's politics.... For the fiftieth anniversary of the U.N. Declaration of Human Rights, there was a major campaign in Mexico called "Sin mujeres, los derechos no son humanos" ("Without women, rights are not human").[78]

Two converging trends made reproductive rights the highest-impact area of binational women's movement collaboration. First, feminist activists in the United States expanded the framework for understanding reproductive rights to the broader concept of access to reproductive health rights more generally, a shift driven largely by the mobilization of U.S. women of color.[79] Second, several large private U.S. foundations involved in Mexico became increasingly sensitive to feminist approaches to reproductive issues. As a result, since the 1980s U.S. foundations involved in reproductive issues in Mexico have invested millions of dollars to bolster the capacities of civil society organizations that defend women's health rights, contributing significantly to the infrastructure of the Mexican women's movement more generally.

One of the most important instances of binational feminist coalition-building has emerged from the reproductive rights movement. It involves the very close relationship forged between the U.S. and Mexican branches of Católicas por el Derecho a Decidir (Catholics for a Free Choice).[80] Though each is an independent NGO, each also sees itself as the voice of a very large, underrepresented constituency. Both branches of the organization emerged from, and are extensively linked to, diverse feminist movements in their respective country. The Mexican branch is also deeply involved in national movements for human rights, Chiapas solidarity, and liberation theology. The U.S. and Mexican groups share a common mission and values, and both view themselves as part of a larger pro-choice Catholic movement. Both combine policy advocacy with efforts to influence broader public opinion. Finally, they have worked together in joint campaigns, including an initiative to persuade the United Nations to withdraw the Vatican's nation-state status in the interest of separating church and state and efforts to insert pro-choice Catholic perspectives into the ongoing international debates on population and

78 Author's communication with Blackwell, February 2000. See also Blackwell 2000.
   U.S. rights advocates also increasingly recognize gender-specific human rights violations; see, for example, Human Rights Watch 1996a, 1998a, 1998b.
79 The author thanks Maylei Blackwell for relating this observation.
80 This paragraph is based upon the author's interview (March 2000, Santa Cruz, California) with Kathy Toner, an activist with several years' experience working with the Mexican chapter of U.S. Catholics for a Free Choice. The origins of the Latin American branches of this organization can be traced back to the late 1980s, when the founding U.S. organization set up a regional office in Uruguay. Sister organizations are currently active in Argentina, Bolivia, Brazil, Chile, Colombia, Mexico, and Peru. The Latin American partner NGOs have their own autonomous regional boards.

development.

U.S. and Mexican pro-choice Catholic groups clearly constitute a binational coalition. They also share many of the characteristics of a transnational movement – including, notably, a perception of themselves as constituting a movement.[81] As with many other cross-border partnerships, the density of this coalition rests upon the combination of a deeply shared ideology (feminism within the Catholic faith) and a strongly shared campaign target (the Catholic Church itself, perhaps the transnational civil society institution par excellence).

Chicano/Latino Civil and Immigrant Rights

Chicano/Latino leaders and activists have played crucial roles in several cross-border movements discussed under other "sector" rubrics, most notably those promoting labor rights and women's rights.[82] This section, however, focuses specifically upon relationships between civil and immigrant rights movements in the United States and Mexico.

Since the 1980s, domestic U.S. public interest organizations have built broad and deep advocacy institutions and coalitions to defend immigrant rights in the United States. For many years, however, these efforts developed largely without sustained exchange or collaboration with Mexican counterparts. Even some of the most consolidated, regionally based and nationally networked immigrant rights coalitions had relatively little contact with either organized migrants or Mexico. Indeed, in the early 1990s some major national immigrant rights advocacy leaders, after years of being on the defensive, pursued a "pragmatic" strategy of attempting to "de-mexicanize" the U.S. policy debate.[83] Joint U.S.–Mexican efforts to develop binational civil society approaches to immigration issues came together organizationally only in the late 1990s, with the formation of the broad-based Mexico–U.S. Advocates Network (Gzesh 2002).

Binational constituency-based organizing among immigrants, often marked by the difficult choice of whether to participate primarily in the United States or in the Mexican arena, has followed diverse paths. Since the late 1990s, however, organized immigrants have transcended this dichotomy by participating simultaneously in social and political movements in both countries. There is evidence that many Mexican citizens in the United States remain engaged with Mexican civic life. Despite immigrants' lack of voting rights, Mexican political candidates

81 The case of U.S. and Mexican pro-choice Catholic groups thus raises questions about this chapter's effort to distinguish between binational coalitions and movements.

82 For example, the AFL–CIO leadership's decision in the late 1990s to support amnesty for undocumented workers was not simply structurally determined by a tight labor market and the need to organize immigrants; it was also the result of Chicano and Latino trade unionists' years of political work with the AFL–CIO.

83 This conclusion is based upon statements by Washington, D.C.-based immigrant rights advocacy groups at the "Mexico–U.S. Advocates Network Seminar," Carnegie Endowment for International Peace, Washington, D.C., February 1999.

have since the late 1980s carried out open electoral campaigns in the United States (Dresser 1991a, 1993, 1996). In contrast to the expectations created by the wave of immigrant sympathy for opposition presidential candidate Cuauhtémoc Cárdenas in 1988, Mexican opposition political parties did not sink deep roots into immigrant communities in the United States. Nevertheless, many immigrants remain engaged with Mexican politics from afar.[84]

In response, the Mexican government has paid a great deal of attention to Mexican immigrant associations, using its extensive network of consular offices to create semi-official channels for growing cross-border participation (González Gutiérrez 1993, 1997, 1999). Some immigrant organizations have responded enthusiastically to opportunities to collaborate with Mexican governmental authorities, while some have preferred to follow more autonomous paths (Goldring 1998, 2002; Fitzgerald 2000; Leiken 2000; Rivera Salgado 1999a, 1999b, 2002; R. Smith 1999). Most so-called hometown associations engage in "translocal" Mexican politics but remain relatively disengaged from U.S. politics – even during major moments of public debate, such as the furor surrounding California's anti-immigrant Proposition 187 in 1994 (Zabin and Escala Rabadán 1998).

Among U.S. citizens, Mexican American organizations have long grappled with the dilemma of how to gain full and equal rights while defending their right to ethnic self-expression.[85] Because of persistent U.S. perceptions of "foreign-ness," Latinos' struggles to be perceived as legitimate actors in the process of formulating U.S. foreign policy have been especially challenging.[86] Latino civil rights leaders are divided over the implications of Mexican electoral politics in the United States.[87] As Latino civil rights activists continue to debate whether and how immigrants and

---

84 An independent Mexican commission convened to inform the national policy debate over the absentee ballot issue found that an estimated 83 percent of Mexican citizens in the United States would have liked to vote in the 2000 elections if they could have done so from the United States. The commission also estimated that between 1.3 and 1.5 million emigrants in the United States already held valid Mexican electoral registration cards (IFE 1998).

85 There is a rich, diverse literature on relations between Mexican immigrants and Mexican Americans. See, for example, Flores and Benmayor 1997; García Acevedo 1996; Gómez Quiñones 1990; D. Gutiérrez 1995, 1996; Maciel and Herrera-Sobek 1998; Santamaría Gómez 1988; Sierra 1999; Vila 2000; and Weber 1998.

86 On Latinos and U.S. foreign policy, see De la Garza et al. 1998, González 1999, and Public Agenda/Tomás Rivera Policy Institute 1998.

87 For example, influential University of Texas political scientist Rodolfo O. de la Garza has expressed concern about the threat that Mexican absentee voting might pose to Mexican Americans: "An extended display of Mexican politicking on U.S. soil would provoke a nativist fury in the United States directed not only at migrants but also at Mexican-Americans" (Dillon 1998). However, leading voting rights activist Antonio González, director of the William Velásquez Research Institute, has stated that he "just [did not] see any kind of competition or negative effect in terms of U.S. Latino political empowerment, versus Mexican political empowerment. They're complementary" (remarks at the conference "Lessons from Binational Civil Society Coalitions," University of California, Santa Cruz, July 1998).

U.S. Latinos should forge coalitions for social change, increasing Latino political empowerment in the United States has created new political space for cross-border coalitions.[88]

The effects of the dramatic increase in immigrant participation in U.S. politics are only beginning to be understood. In 1996 more than two-thirds of Mexicans in the United States were potentially eligible for U.S. citizenship, yet less than 7 percent had become U.S. citizens (Mexico–United States Binational Commission 1997). Since then, Mexico-born immigrants have become U.S. citizens at much higher rates, and on average these newly naturalized citizens vote at higher rates than U.S.–born Latinos.[89] At the same timse, many Mexicans in the United States continue to identify more with Mexican than with U.S. politics. U.S. immigration reforms of the late 1980s legalized millions of Mexicans, who were then able to reinforce their home ties via more frequent back-and-forth travel than had been possible as long as they lived in the United States in undocumented status (Espinosa 1999).[90]

In 1996 the Mexican Congress granted Mexican citizens abroad the right to vote – in principle. Since then, Mexicans residing legally in the United States have mobilized new advocacy networks to encourage the Mexican government to comply with its commitment. In the process, they have constituted the first transnational advocacy network organized by immigrants to influence Mexican government policy toward them (Ross 1999; Martínez and Ross 2002; Santamaría Gómez 2001).[91] The emigrant advocacy network has found relatively few allies within the Mexican political system; all the major parties have been internally divided on the issue.[92] In 1999 the key voting rights reform provision passed Mexico's federal Chamber of Deputies before stalling in the Senate. Nevertheless, the fact that Mexicans abroad won their political rights, even if only in principle, has permanently redrawn the boundaries of the Mexican immigrant civic arena, with quite open-ended consequences.

The emigrant transnational advocacy network has had its greatest impact at the

88 This change was quite visible in 1999 when Antonio Villaraigosa, then speaker of the California General Assembly, visited Mexico, where he promoted U.S. support for Mexican immigrant-led community development initiatives as an alternative to Proposition 187–style policies (Romney 1999). As an indicator of the "localization" of transnational politics, the *Los Angeles Times* placed this article about a major state political leader's international visit in the metropolitan news section. See also Villaraigosa and Hinojosa-Ojeda 1999.

89 On naturalization and political attitudes, see Pachon and DeSipio 1994 and DeSipio and De la Garza 1998. On Latino voter turnout, see DeSipio 1996 and Arvizu and García 1996.

90 The many immigrants who remain undocumented are not eligible for naturalization in the United States.

91 The Mexican state's strategy, in contrast, has been to encourage emigrants to become U.S. citizens and participate in U.S. politics, rather than to extend the boundaries of the polity to include the entire national diaspora.

92 Author's interview with Raúl Ross, American Friends Service Committee, May 1999, Chicago, Illinois.

level of the public agenda and the ways in which issues are framed. At the very least, immigrant civic leaders now have access for the first time to the national media in Mexico. A March 1999 nongovernmental referendum in Mexico provided a revealing illustration of the resulting shifts in the terrain of political culture. The EZLN called the referendum as part of its effort to break the political stalemate that followed the Mexican government's withdrawal from the San Andrés agreements for peace in Chiapas. One of the leaders of the principal emigrant advocacy network, the "Coalition of Mexicans Abroad – Our Vote in 2000," took advantage of his new access to the national press to appeal directly to EZLN leader Subcomandante Marcos, noting parallels in the ways in which both emigrants and indigenous peoples are excluded from full citizenship rights (Martínez Saldaña 1999). Apparently in response, the EZLN called for a fifth question (on the emigrant voting rights issue) to be added to the referendum at U.S. polling places, where approximately 50,000 votes were tallied.[93] At least 8,000 of these votes came from the Binational Indigenous Oaxacan Front in the Fresno area. The FIOB is one of the few binational social organizations that can be considered a fully transnational social *movement*; its participants are part of a cohesive social subject – politicized paisanos – whether they are in the Mixteca (Northwest Oaxaca), Baja California, Los Angeles, or the central valleys of California (Rivera Salgado 1999a, 1999b, 2002).[94]

Late 1999 witnessed the most tangible evidence thus far of organized emigrants' growing political influence. In its effort to protect the "national" (U.S.–dominated) automobile production industry, Mexico's Ministry of Finance and Public Credit (SHCP) unilaterally decided to crack down upon emigrants' widespread practice of returning to Mexico with used cars, which are much less expensive than automobiles produced by trade-protected Mexico-based manufacturers. To discourage the importation of what are officially illegal vehicles, the ministry announced that all drivers entering Mexico – tourists and returning migrants alike – would be required to leave a substantial financial deposit for each vehicle they brought with them (the deposit would be returned when the vehicle exited the country). The policy – which was to have been implemented shortly before the Christmas holidays, when millions of emigrants would be returning home – provoked a broad wave of protests by the increasingly politicized Mexican community in the United States. Emigrant leaders convinced the Mexican Senate to pass a resolution, supported by both the political opposition and the leaders of the then-ruling Institutional Revolutionary Party (PRI), to end the program after only two days in operation. Even the Ministry of Foreign Relations was reportedly critical of the program; ministry personnel apparently were not consulted in advance, yet they had to bear the brunt of emigrant protests.

---

93 More than two million people voted in Mexico on the original four questions.
94 On the FIOB, see www.laneta.apc.org/fiob/. See Nagengast and Kearney 1990 on the interaction between the immigration process and ethnic identity formation.

The vehicle deposit controversy revealed the extraordinary separation between the worldviews of economic policy makers in Mexico City and the binational reality of as many as one in ten Mexican families. As the *New York Times* observed, "The plan apparently arose from some confusion within the government when officials failed to calculate the impact on Mexicans living north of the border. As many as two million are expected to come home for the holidays, many in their own cars" (Preston 1999). Even though the deposit was to be returned to vehicle owners upon their departure from Mexico, SHCP officials clearly overestimated the credibility of the official promise to refund the money.

The media and legislative lobbying campaign victory against the vehicle deposit is the most clear-cut success to date in binational immigrant organizing.[95] It appears to have built directly upon the previous unsuccessful effort to gain the right for emigrants to vote in Mexico's 2000 elections.[96] As the president of the Concilio Hispano (Hispanic Council), a Mexican group based in Chicago put it, "This is the first time the Mexican community here managed to bring this kind of pressure on Mexico. It shows that we can use our power and make changes" (Preston 1999).

The issue of immigrant rights has catalyzed the formation of several binational networks and coalitions. Some have cross-border targets, as in the cases of the vehicle deposit, absentee voting rights, and immigrant rights policy advocacy issues. Other partnerships have cross-border constituencies, as in the case of immigrant hometown associations. Among hometown associations, the degree to which these U.S.-based groups have actual hometown partner organizations varies significantly. In terms of the distinctions among networks, coalitions, and movements, different

95 Another binational immigrant organizing campaign involved the mobilization of thousands of elderly former participants in the Bracero Program (the Mexico–U.S. contract labor program in effect between 1942 and 1964) now living in Mexico. Immigrant rights activists discovered through archival research that the Mexican government received from the U.S. government and then retained 10 percent of Bracero workers' wages, ostensibly as a contribution to a domestic crop loan program. This program was conceived as an innovative cross-border community investment program, but the government apparently simply kept the money. The organizations involved included the 20,000–member International Network for the Defense of the Full Rights of Migrant Workers and their Families, the Mexican Emigrant and Peasant Union, and the Union Without Borders. For details, see Salinas 1999.

96 This campaign also led the opposition Party of the Democratic Revolution (PRD) to nominate a Mexican immigrant voting rights activist (Raúl Ross) to its proportional representation list of congressional candidates. This nomination was not, however, an unequivocal reflection of a new awareness within the PRD of immigrants as participants with political rights as Mexicans. First, the decision was internally controversial. Ross appears to have been included as PRD founder Cuauhtémoc Cárdenas's only personal nomination (Cárdenas's son coordinated PRD liaison in the United States). Second, it is very revealing that when he reported this decision, national PRD leader Jesús Ortega referred to Ross as the "*compañero chicano*" (Cano and Aguirre 2000). Ross is from Veracruz and emigrated to the United States as an adult. For Ortega to refer to him as a Chicano – an identification that implies having been raised in the United States – underscores the degree to which even leftist Mexico City politicians see emigrants as "not quite Mexican" once they cross the border.

hometown associations would range across the spectrum, with the FIOB being the most clear-cut instance of a transnational social movement organization.

Assessing the Impact of Binational Networks and Coalitions

This section returns to Keck and Sikkink's conceptual framework, applying their categories for assessing different kinds of network impact to three of the most active binational sectors. This process involves addressing in combination two distinct questions. First, was there some kind of civil society impact in these different cases? Second, was that impact due largely to the specifically binational dimensions of each civil society?

Keck and Sikkink's impact categories start with "issue creation and agenda setting," followed by "influence on official discourse (of states and international organizations)," "influence on national and international institutions and pro-cedures," "influence on policy change in 'target actors,' which can be public or private," and finally "impact on state behavior" (1998: 25, 201ff). These authors argue that the different kinds of impact actually constitute stages of impact, because establishing discursive legitimacy and benchmark standards can bolster leverage in the future.[97] It is also possible, however, that in some instances discursive reforms and weak institutional commitments serve to divide or distract civil society actors, weakening pressures for accountability (which, critics might argue, was what happened with the NAFTA environmental side agreement). To "give a centavo [cent] to keep a peso" is an old story in Mexico. The propositions to be presented here constitute, then, a preliminary empirical test of this part of Keck and Sikkink's hypothesis about NGO impact – with the proviso that this study of Mexico–U.S. cases includes organized social constituencies as well as NGOs.

Table 15.3 assesses of the impact of binational civil society networks in the Mexico–U.S. context, framing this issue in terms of Keck and Sikkink's categories and focusing upon the environment, labor rights, and human rights issue areas. The table not only synthesizes this chapter's empirical findings in terms of Keck and Sikkink's different dimensions of potential network impact, but it also summarizes the author's analytic assessment of the degree to which binational politics contributed to observed change in distinct issue areas (judged in terms of low, medium, and high impact). These causal assessments are subject to the usual caveats in terms of the difficulty of making counterfactual claims (for instance, how much policy change would one have found in the absence of cross-border campaigning?). It should also be noted that, because impact is defined here in terms of such categories as influence upon official discourse and policy, this exercise does not consider the consequences of binational networks for civil society actors themselves or for political cultures (see Brooks and Fox 2002).

97 See Fox and Brown 1998 for a comparative study of transnational advocacy network efforts to reform the World Bank – leading to the setting of new environmental and social standards, followed by further campaigns to meet those benchmarks.

In the three issue areas considered here, cross-border civil society activism has had the highest degree of impact upon environmental policy. It was especially consequential in Mexico, and it held the potential to block approval of the NAFTA in the United States. The Mexican state responded to cross-border initiatives by making major, sustained policy and discursive commitments, including the creation of Mexico's first environmental policy ministry (led by a credible, nonpartisan expert). The power of U.S. and Mexican environmental NGOs clearly led to the adoption of the NAFTA side agreement on environmental issues and to the creation of new border investment institutions. Although the side agreement has had little impact in practice, and even though the U.S. and Mexican policy makers who have directed the NADBank so far have not fully pursued its potential of innovation (Boudreau and Hinojosa-Ojeda 1998, Kourous 2000), by the late 1990s the BECC and the NADBank had begun to increase their levels of activity.

Mexico–U.S. NGO partnerships have had notable impacts upon biodiversity-related projects and policies in Mexico, ranging from removing the threat to whales in the San Ignacio Biosphere to sustained support for increased funding and improved management for protected natural areas. In contrast, cross-border campaigns against the industrial pollution associated with the maquiladora industry have had little impact. Moreover, free trade has posed major challenges for Mexico's most consolidated sustainable rural development initiatives (the organic coffee and community forestry movements), where strong cross-border partnerships have been lacking. In summary, cross-border environmental coalitions have produced some of the most dramatic breakthroughs in terms of civil society leverage, but also some of the most clear-cut defeats.

In the area of labor rights, there has been a more consistent pattern of failure. Labor rights briefly gained public prominence as an issue during the NAFTA debate, although it never had as much legitimacy or held as much attention as the environment. The most significant examples of labor's political leverage were the 1997 defeat of U.S. fast-track authority for approving trade agreements (Shoch 2000) and President Bill Clinton's (1992–1996, 1996–2000) electorally driven discursive support for labor rights during the 1999 World Trade Organization (WTO) meeting in Seattle. Neither case, however, involved significant cross-border partnerships. Mexican organized labor continues to lose ground, and it has yet to win a significant foothold in the maquiladora industry. The Han Young campaign – a clear test of the limits of cross-border leverage – revealed that solidarity from the highest levels of the U.S. political system could not compel Mexican authorities to enforce basic court decisions. The enforcement of Mexican labor law continues to be determined almost exclusively by local and national politics.[98]

Many analysts assume that international human rights campaigns have an impact. Keck and Sikkink, for example, claim that "from 1988 to 1994, the international

---

98 One exception was the student anti-sweatshop campaign for workers' rights at Nike's Puebla subcontractor, Kukdong (Campaign for Labor Rights 2001).

network in collaboration with recently formed domestic human rights groups
provoked a *relatively rapid and forceful* response from the Mexican government,
contributing to a *decline* in human rights violations and a strengthening of democratic institutions" (1998: 116, emphasis added). Yet in reality, the human rights
record in Mexico is actually quite mixed.

Sustaining the case for international impact upon the human rights situation in
Mexico requires stronger evidence in two areas. First, it is far from clear that
human rights violations dropped during the period Keck and Sikkink discuss, and
their indicators of change are very limited. Even though a lack of consistent
baseline data makes systematic analysis of change over time difficult, the opposition Party of the Democratic Revolution (PRD) alleged that more than 600 of its
activists were assassinated during this same period.[99] Second, Keck and Sikkink's
conclusion assumes that international factors were of primary importance in
shaping the government's (largely symbolic) response. This may hold for the
creation of the official National Human Rights Commission (CNDH), which
Keck and Sikkink offer as a principal indicator of impact.[100] But whether the
CNDH made a significant contribution to the prevention of human rights abuses
is widely questioned. The clearest way to assess its impact is to review government
responses to its official recommendations (that is, official CNDH findings that
government agencies violated human rights). Here, according to a top CNDH
appointee, the general pattern was one of impunity (Ballinas 2001); government
agencies nominally accepted CNDH recommendations but then did little in
practice to prevent future human rights violations. Even in the very clear-cut case
of peasant-ecologist political prisoners in the state of Guerrero, strong national and
international campaigns (led by Amnesty International and the Sierra Club) did
not prevent the Mexican legal system from sentencing individuals to long jail terms
on trumped-up charges. They were finally released well into the presidency of
Vicente Fox – and only after their lawyer was killed in her downtown Mexico City
office.[101]

99 The situation appeared to improve somewhat in the late 1990s, although whether that was
    because of international pressure or a post-1994 decline in the electoral threat from the Left
    was not clear. What is clear is that serious and systematic human rights violations persisted –
    and not only in Chiapas. On the case of Guerrero, see M. Gutiérrez 1998. During the 1996–
    1998 period alone, the Centro de Derechos Humanos Miguel Agustín Pro Juárez documented
    115 disappearances (Centro de Derechos Humanos 1999).
100 Not all Mexican human rights analysts agree on this point. For example, the analysis of the
    CNDH's creation in Sierra Guzmán, Ruiz Harrell, and Barragán 1992 barely refers to inter-
    national factors.
101 This case is very revealing of how the "boomerang effect" described in Keck and Sikkink (1998)
    operates in practice. The two political prisoners, Rodolfo Montiel and Teodoro Cabrera, were
    first arrested in May 1999. In August 1999, a local human rights organization in Guerrero,
    The Voice of the Voiceless, brought their case to a major national human rights NGO, the
    Centro de Derechos Humanos Miguel Agustín Pro Juárez (author's interview with Emma
    Maza Calviño, international relations director of the Centro de Derechos Humanos Miguel

The impact of cross-border civil society partnerships upon Mexico's gradual democratization process is also easily overstated. Mexico's pro-democracy movement received remarkably little international support, and there is scant evidence that such support made a qualitative difference (for example, in ensuring that the 1994 elections were as clean as they were). The turning point in favor of electoral reform was a January 1994 agreement among Mexico's major political parties, and many Mexican observers concur that the government was pushed to the bargaining table by the delegitimizing effect of the Chiapas rebellion.

The Chiapas rebellion itself is probably the clearest example of the importance of international factors, which contributed directly to blocking a full-scale military response to the EZLN in mid-January 1994. For the U.S. mass media, hitherto entranced by President Carlos Salinas de Gortari (1988–1994), the rebellion revealed that the "emperor had no clothes" and led to the immediate rejection of Salinas's claim that the rebels were illegitimate and foreign-inspired. International human rights protests certainly helped, although they were effective largely because both the U.S. government and the U.S. private sector were unenthusiastic about the prospect of their new NAFTA partner becoming engaged in a televised bloodbath. In this regard, the NAFTA had contradictory effects in January 1994 – contributing to the outbreak of the Chiapas rebellion, and then helping to stay Salinas's initial military response.

National factors are often downplayed in discussions of the Chiapas conflict. Yet Mexican civil society mobilized very quickly for peace, and key national political elites – most notably, then-foreign minister and one-time presidential "pre-candidate" Manuel Camacho Solís – threatened to break with Salinas if the government did not cease fire in January 1994. Disentangling the relative weights of national and international factors is always a challenge, but many analysts simply assume that the international (and, specifically, civil society) factors were primary, rather than consider them in national context.

Among the various international factors surrounding the Chiapas conflict, it is also important to consider the growing weight of European civil society and government human rights protests. The Zapatista support movement appears to be significantly broader and deeper in Europe than in the United States. President Ernesto Zedillo (1994–2000) signed the San Andrés peace accords in 1996, just before he was about to travel to Europe to promote Mexico's free-trade agreement

Agustín Pro Juárez, April 2001, Mexico City). The Center, in turn, took the case to Amnesty International, which in March 2000 finally decided to consider Montiel and Cabrera prisoners of conscience. The international campaign began there, leading to strong Sierra Club support, the Goldman Prize, and high-profile endorsements from Ethel Kennedy and Hilary Clinton. However, even after the inauguration of President Vicente Fox Quesada (2000–2006) the prisoners remained in jail (along with 67 other political prisoners remaining in Guerrero). See www.sierraclub.org/human-rights/ and www.sjsocial.org/PRODH/.

with the European Union. European concerns did not, however, prevent him from later backing out of the peace agreement. This sequence of events reflects a more general pattern in which international protests about human rights violations in Mexico are sufficient to prompt partial and symbolic concessions, but not enough to break the political stalemate on indigenous rights and peace in Chiapas.

Concluding Propositions

This final section steps back from the specific cases examined in the course of this chapter to draw out several propositions for discussion, involving both the dynamics of networks and coalitions and their impact. As noted in the introduction, these propositions refer only to the subset of civil society actors that seek increased participation and public accountability.

- *Networks often need shared targets to become coalitions.* Mutual sympathy or shared concerns are usually not enough for networks to become coalitions, in the sense of agreeing to sustain joint campaigns. Jointly held political ideologies help, but they are not necessary; if they were, the list of binational coalitions would be much shorter. Shared targets can certainly be politically constructed, but it helps to have some tangible political opportunity structure that can make collective action seem potentially effective. Shared targets include: policy makers poised to make policy decisions that affect both Mexico and the United States (such as congressional trade votes); transnational corporations operating in both countries (such as Campbells Soup Company and Delta Airlines/Aeroméxico); entire economic sectors (maquiladoras); specific products (organic coffee, for example); shared watersheds (the Rio Grande/Río Bravo); migrating whales, butterflies, or birds; and international institutions such as the BECC, NADBank, the trilateral labor or environmental commissions, the World Bank, or even the Catholic Church.

- *National and Mexico–U.S. border trends in binational relations have followed two different paths since 1994.* Binational networks and coalitions have not followed any one single trend over the past decade. Rather, border and national trends appear to have diverged along two different paths. Environmental and labor coalitions grouped along the Mexico–U.S. border have gradually increased their density as. In contrast, national-level networks and coalitions have displayed less consistent patterns. In the case of some environmental, human rights, and labor organizations, the pace of non-border binational social and civic relationship-building slowed after 1994. The 1997 fast-track debate over U.S. trade policy revealed significant backsliding compared to the 1994 high point. In retrospect, the NAFTA vote and the initial phase of the Chiapas rebellion sparked upsurges of binational political action and created a certain sense of a "war of movement," producing the hope that binational coalition-building might be broadened and deepened. Instead, the handful of binational coalitions that have managed to sustain coordinated relationships have pursued more of a "war of position." Perhaps this should not be surprising given the extensive investments in within-organization and general public education that balanced binational coalitions require.

- *Broad-based organizations that have sustained cohesive partnerships tend to "think locally to act binationally."* The classic formulation of global environmental philosophy ("think globally, act locally") does not help to explain why relatively few broad-based social organizations sustain cohesive binational partnerships. Accountability may be more important than ideology in this regard. Mass-based social organizations governed by their members are under more pressure than NGOs to be accountable to organized constituencies. They must allocate resources based upon perceived tangible benefits for their members. To justify investing resources in binational coalition-building, social organizations usually need to be able to demonstrate that these initiatives have local results. For example, the International Brotherhood of Teamsters reached out to Mexican immigrants and worked with Mexican unions to protect the rights of workers in the state of Washington's apple industry because such efforts promised to increase the union's bargaining power. Mexican trade-advocacy networks tolerated a degree of nationalist rhetoric on the part of U.S. NAFTA critics because those relationships increased their leverage. Similarly, the U.S. and Mexican telephone workers' unions joined forces in 1992 (despite deep differences over the upcoming NAFTA vote) because they perceived that such an exchange would reinforce their bargaining power over the longer term, with or without the NAFTA. In the same way, both U.S. and Mexican environmental organizations on the border appear willing to make serious investments in the difficult process of overcoming cultural differences because they increasingly share the view that the local is binational, and vice versa. Binational ideological convergence, though rare, can help sustain "think locally, act binationally" perspectives because it establishes a longer time horizon for assessing local benefits. Shared ideological visions can also sustain long-term alliances (such as that between the United Electrical, Radio, and Machine Workers of America and the Authentic Labor Front) whose tangible victories so far have been limited.
- *Binational networks and coalitions have had significant impact upon official policy discourse, but they have only rarely won tangible increases in public or private accountability.* The experiences of human rights, labor, and environmental coalitions suggest that there is a very large gap between their influence upon public discourse and more tangible kinds of impact. Assessing impact is often method-ologically problematic, especially when some of the most important forms of impact involve counterfactual assumptions ("the situation would be even worse if not for..."). One might plausibly argue that binational networks and coalitions have indeed been important in some such circumstances (helping to prevent a full-scale military assault in Chiapas or the downfall of Mexico's reformist environmental policy makers). But even in counterfactual scenarios

Table 15.3: **Assessing the Impact of Mexico–U.S. Civil Society Networks and Coalitions**

Impact	Environmental standards	Labor rights	Human rights
Issue creation and agenda setting	High This became a key public issue in the NAFTA debate. It remains on the binational public agenda and receives regular media attention.	Medium This became a key public issue in the NAFTA debate. It occasionally returns to the binational agenda, and it influenced the defeat of fast-track U.S. trade legislation in 1997. Binational coalitions engendered incipient Mexican-side *maquiladora* organizing network.	Low-Medium This became a secondary issue in the NAFTA debate, but it then fell from the U.S. public agenda (except) for the 1994–1995 Chiapas period).
Influence upon official discourse (states and international organizations)	High Both states and the NAFTA institutions continue to make strong discursive commitments to environmental concerns.	Low-Medium Both states continue to recognize some labor rights, but both also ignore systematic violations of the right to organize. Trinational NAFTA labor institutions occasionally raise the issue, but with little impact upon broader public discourse.	Medium Both governments are obliged to recognize and condemn violations when the media and binational coalitions make them difficult to ignore. U.S. Department of State reports and incipient congressional resolutions raise human rights concerns. The Mexican state expresses concern over migrant rights.
Influence upon national and international institutional procedures	Medium The trinational NAFTA side agreement remains weak, but the binational BECC and and NADBank created new practices and standards for public participation on the border. Lack of progress institutional-izing and broadening	Low The NAFTA labor side agreement is extremely weak, with a very limited mandate and no authority over violations of the right to organize. However, public hearings and ministerial-level consultations have been held.	Medium The NAFTA debate contributed to the launching of the National Human Rights Commission. Mexican human rights organiza-tions have prioritized multilateral (United Nations, Organization of American States) over binational fora.

NADBank contributed to the 1997 defeat of fast-track trade legislation in the United States.

Influence upon policy change in target actors, public or private	*Medium* There has been increased external funding for Mexican environmental protection from the World Bank, USAID, U.S. private foundations, and the U.S. Environmental Protection Agency. Binational environmental coalitions have successfully blocked large, controversial projects in both countries.	*Low* Despite the labor side agreement's limitations, several coalitions have tried to use its procedures – though so far with no policy impact. The main labor union impact upon integration policy (the U.S. Teamsters' trucking campaign) was not binational. However, several binational *maquiladora* worker-defense campaigns have led to modest, plant-specific concessions.	*Low-Medium* To the degree that Mexican laws and institutions have recognized human rights since the NAFTA debate, there is little evidence that binational coalitions were important. International concern did contribute to the government's decision to pursue a combination of negotiations and low-intensity conflict in Chiapas (rather than a full military assault), but it has been too weak to break the national stalemate.
Influence upon the behavior of target actors	*Low-Medium* Mexican environmental reform authorities have had uneven effectiveness, but at least they remain in power, indirectly bolstered by persistent international (mainly U.S.) concerns. Environmental policymakers' room for maneuver, however, has been economically and politically limited. Basic environmental laws continue to be violated often and with impunity.	*None* There is no evidence of tangible progress in terms of the right to organize, wages, or working conditions in either country (especially in the *maquiladoras*). The Han Young case showed that even a binational campaign that generated extensive, high-level U.S. concern had little or no effect upon Mexican legal processes and respect for labor rights in practice.	*Unclear* Because of the lack of consistent, independent, nationwide data, changes in levels of impunity over time are difficult to assess. Even if improvements were documented, the role of binational civil society remains uncertain. The clearest impact has been in Chiapas, where the military usually limits easily televisable abuses. Binational coalitions may have contributed to limited prosecutions of the perpetrators of the 1997 Acteal massacre.

such as these, it is difficult to establish conclusively that transnational factors or binational relationships were of primary importance. In terms of bolstering more reformist policies or inducing qualitative changes in actual state behavior (for example, increased authority for Mexican environmental reformers, significantly greater opportunities for Mexican and U.S. unions to organize, or indigenous rights reforms that could begin to resolve the Chiapas conflict), binational partnerships have not had much impact thus far. The NAFTA–origin border environmental institutions are the main exception to this generalization, and their impact so far has been quite limited compared to their mandate. The environmental campaign defeats of the Sierra Blanca and Mitsubishi projects were significant, but each had unusual features (they involved, respectively, nuclear waste and whales) that limit their generalizability. In summary, binational networks appear to have much more influence over public agendas and official discourse than on what their target actors actually do in practice.[102] This should not be surprising; where the main points of leverage used against them are informational and symbolic politics, targeted actors can respond with symbolic concessions and arrangements such as a trinational commission that produces information.

- *Binational coalitions are long-term investments with uncertain payoffs.* Networks that do more than exchange information from afar require human and material resources. Coalitions, because they involve higher levels of coordination, require even more resources to endure. Although some organizations can afford to invest such resources without short-to-medium-term payoffs, organizations that are less well endowed must carefully weigh the tradeoffs involved. Transportation costs and other financial considerations aside, every week that an activist spends in another country is a week not spent organizing on home ground. Moreover, coalitions can involve certain risks, insofar as one set of partners may or may not consult before making decisions that could be politically costly for the other. On the positive side, investments in networks and coalitions often generate social capital (understood as resources for collective action embodied in horizontal relationships), and social capital can produce often unpredictable multiplier effects. But precisely because the empowering effects are difficult to assess, political investments in coalitions compete with much more pressing demands and with alternative investments that promise more immediate results.[103]

102 This hypothesis resonates with the World Bank campaign experience. In that case, transnational networks were a crucial reason why the World Bank decided to make environmental and social reform commitments, but national factors primarily determined the degree to which states met those commitments in practice (Fox and Brown 1998).

103 For many organizations, networks – with their lower levels of commitment – may make much more sense than coalitions. Relatively few binational interlocutors can draw "strength from weak ties" (Granovetter 1973), serving as resources when their organizations need them. In this scenario, relatively low-cost binational networks can exercise leverage at key turning points, as long as they link organizations that have some degree of influence in their respective societies. For an application of this argument to transnational advocacy networks, see Fox and Brown 1998.

In sum, binational civil society networks and coalitions have had much more impact upon *themselves* than on the broader processes and targets that provoked their emergence.[104] Organized constituencies in each civil society have become better acquainted with their counterparts. Greater mutual understanding is likely to have empowering effects, at least in the long term. Broad-based actors in both civil societies are qualitatively more open to, and experienced with, binational cooperation than ever before. This accumulated social capital constitutes a potential political resource for the future. Whether and how national civil society actors will choose to draw upon it remains to be seen.

References

Abraham, Lotti, with Kathy Cone. 1999. "Cross-Cultural Organizing: How It Stopped a Nuclear Waste Dump," *The Workbook* (Spring): 4–11.

Acosta, Mariclaire. 2002. "Lessons Learned from the Bilateral Relations between Mexican and U.S. Human Rights Organizations." In *Cross-Border Dialogues: U.S.–Mexico Social Movement Networking*, edited by David Brooks and Jonathan Fox. La Jolla: Center for U.S.–Mexican Studies, University of California, San Diego.

Adams, Tani. 1999. "Whose Environment Are We Trying to Save Here? The Consequences of 'Occidental' Notions of Civilization and Nature in International Environmentalism." Paper presented at the conference "Transnational Organizing in the Americas," Chicano/Latino Research Center and Latin American and Latino Studies, University of California, Santa Cruz, December.

Aguayo Quezada, Sergio. 1998. "Electoral Observation and Democracy in Mexico." In *Electoral Observation and Democratic Transitions in Latin America*, edited by Kevin J. Middlebrook. La Jolla: Center for U.S.–Mexican Studies, University of California, San Diego.

———. 2001. "El financiamiento extranjero y la transición democrática mexicana: el caso de Alianza Cívica." Paper presented at Casa Lamm, Mexico City, August [www.alianzacivica. org.mx/Conferencia%20%20Sergio.htm].

Alexander, Robin. 1998. "The UE–FAT Strategic Organizing Alliance." In *Enfrentando el cambio: obreros del automóvil y producción esbelta en América del Norte/Confronting Change: Auto Labor and Lean Production in North America*, edited by Huberto Juárez Núñez and Steve Babson. Puebla, Mexico: Benemérita Autónoma Universidad de Puebla / Wayne State University.

Alexander, Robin, and Peter Gilmore. 1994. "The Emergence of Cross-Border Labor Solidarity," *NACLA Report on the Americas* 28 (1): 42–48.

Álvarez, Sonia. 1997. "Reweaving the Fabric of Collective Action: Social Movements and Challenges of 'Actually Existing Democracy' in Brazil." In *Between Resistance and Revolution: Cultural Politics and Social Protest*, edited by Richard Fox and Orin Starn. New Brunswick, N.J.: Rutgers University Press.

Álvarez Icaza, Emilio. 2002. "Mexico–U.S. Collaboration with Alianza Cívica." In *Cross-Border Dialogues: U.S.–Mexico Social Movement Networking*, edited by David Brooks and Jonathan Fox. La Jolla: Center for U.S.–Mexican Studies, University of California, San Diego.

---

104 For a related effort to broaden the criteria and scope for assessing social movement impact, see Álvarez 1997.

Amnesty International. 1986. *Mexico – Human Rights in Rural Areas*. London: Amnesty International.

Aponte, David, and Ciro Pérez Silva. 2001. "Sindicalistas de EU pretenden *desestabilizar* en Mexico: Abascal," *La Jornada*, February 23.

Armbruster, Ralph. 1998. "Cross-Border Labor Organizing in the Garment and Automobile Industries: The Phillips Van-Heusen and Ford Cuautitlán Cases," *Journal of World-Systems Research* 4 (1) [www.csf.colorado.edu/wsystems/jwsr.html].

Arroyo, Alberto, and Mario Monroy. 1996. *Red Mexicana de Acción frente al Libre Comercio: 5 años de lucha (1991–1996)*. Mexico City: Red Mexicana de Acción frente al Libre Comercio.

Arroyo, Alberto, and Andrés Peñaloza, eds. 2000. *Derechos humanos y Tratado de Libre Comercio México–Unión Europea*. Mexico City: Red Mexicana de Acción frente al Libre Comercio.

ART/CTC/RMALC (Alliance for Responsible Trade / Citizen Trade Campaign / Red Mexicana de Acción frente al Libre Comercio). 1994. "A Just and Sustainable Trade and Development Initiative for the Western Hemisphere." Washington, D.C., December.

Arvizu, John R., and Chris F. García. 1996. "Latino Voting Participation: Explaining and Differentiating Latino Voting Turnout," *Hispanic Journal of Behavioral Sciences* 18 (2): 104–29.

Audley, John J. 1997. *Green Politics and Global Trade: NAFTA and the Future of Environmental Politics*. Washington, D.C.: Georgetown University Press.

Ayres, Jeffrey M. 1998. *Defying Conventional Wisdom: Political Movements and Popular Contention against North American Free Trade*. Toronto: University of Toronto Press.

Babson, Steve. 2000. "Cross-Border Trade with Mexico and the Prospects for Worker Solidarity: The Case of Mexico," *Critical Sociology* 26 (1/2): 13–35.

Bacon, David. 1998. "A Plant Closes in Revenge for Cross-Border Organizing," *Mexican Labor News and Analysis*, 3 (22), December 16 [www.igc.apc.org/unitedelect/vol3no22.html].

———. 2000. "Tijuana Troubles," *In These Times*, August 21.

———. 2001. "Secret Ballot Denied in Mexican Factory Vote," Internet Bulletin, March 12 [www.igc.org/igc/gateway/pnindex.html].

Ballinas, Víctor. 2001. "Impunidad, sello en 10 años de labor de la CNDH: visitadores," *La Jornada*, March 19.

Bandy, Joe. 1998. "Border Crossings: Transnational Movements for Alternative Development and Radical Democracy in the U.S.–Mexico Border Region." Ph.D. diss., University of California, Santa Barbara.

———. 2000. "Border the Future: Resisting Neoliberalism in the Borderlands," *Critical Sociology* 26 (3): 232–67.

Barger, W.K., and Ernesto M. Reza. 1994. *The Farm Labor Movement in the Midwest: Social Change and Adaptation among Migrant Farmworkers*. Austin: University of Texas Press.

Barry, Tom, Harry Browne, and Beth Sims. 1994. *The Great Divide: The Challenge of U.S.–Mexico Relations in the 1990s*. New York: Grove / Interhemispheric Resource Center.

Bejarano, Fernando. 2002. "Mexico–U.S. Environmental Partnerships." In *Cross-Border Dialogues: U.S.–Mexico Social Movement Networking*, edited by David Brooks and Jonathan Fox. La Jolla: Center for U.S.–Mexican Studies, University of California, San Diego.

BIOS Action Kit. 1999. "Effectiveness of NAFTA Side Accords," *Borderlines* 7 (9), October [www.irc-online.org/bios/].

Blackwell, Maylei. 2000. "Geographies of Difference: Mapping Multiple Feminist Insurgencies and Transnational Public Cultures in the Americas." Ph.D. diss., University of California, Santa Cruz.

Bob, Clifford. 2000. "The Marketing of Rebellion: Insurgent Groups, Global Media, and the Growth of International Support." Manuscript.

Bonanno, Alessandro, and Douglas Constance. 1996. *Caught in the Net: The Global Tuna Industry, Environmentalism, and the State.* Lawrence: University of Kansas Press.

Boudreau, Julie-Anne, and Raúl Hinojosa-Ojeda, eds. 1998. "Las nuevas instituciones del Tratado de Libre Comercio de América del Norte: integración económica regional y cooperación. Procedimientos de una conferencia, 19–20 junio 1998." Los Angeles: UCLA North American Integration and Development Center / U.S. Department of Labor.

Bray, David. 1999. "Coffee That Eases the Conscience," *New York Times*, July 5.

Brecher, Jeremy, Tim Costello, and Brendan Smith. 2000. *Globalization from Below: The Power of Solidarity.* Boston: South End Press.

BRIDGES. 2000. "The Battle between Environmental Co-operation and Trade Embargoes Flares Up with Possibility of Tuna Dolphin III," *BRIDGES between Trade and Sustainable Development*, July–August [www.ictsd.org/html/arct_sd.htm#Bridges].

Brooks, David. 1992. "The Search for Counterparts," *Labor Research Review* 19 (Fall): 83–96.

Brooks, David, and Jonathan Fox, eds. 2002. *Cross-Border Dialogues: U.S.–Mexico Social Movement Networking.* La Jolla: Center for U.S.–Mexican Studies, University of California, San Diego.

Browne, Harry, ed. 1996a. *Cross-Border Links: A Directory of Organizations in Canada, Mexico, and the United States – 1997 Labor Directory.* Silver City, N.M.: Interhemispheric Resource Center.

———. 1996b. *Cross-Border Links: A Directory of Organizations in Canada, Mexico, and the United States – 1997 Environmental Directory.* Silver City, N.M.: Interhemispheric Resource Center.

Campaign for Labor Rights. 2001. "Update on Kuk Dong Struggle, Mexico," *Campaign for Labor Rights' Labor Alert*, June 20 [www.summersault.com/~agj/clr].

Cano, Arturo, and Alberto Aguirre. 2000. "Los enredos de las listas," *Masiosare* (supplement to *La Jornada*), April 2.

Carr, Barry. 1996. "Crossing Borders: Labor Internationalism in the Era of NAFTA." In *Neoliberalism Revisited: Economic Restructuring and Mexico's Political Future*, edited by Gerardo Otero. Boulder, Colo.: Westview.

———. 1998. "Globalisation from Below? Reflections on the Experience of Labor Internationalism under NAFTA, 1994–1998." Paper presented at the international congress of the Latin American Studies Association, Chicago, September.

Carrillo, Teresa. 1990. "Women and Independent Unionism in the Garment Industry." In *Popular Movements and Political Change in Mexico*, edited by Joe Foweraker and Ann L. Craig. Boulder, Colo.: Lynne Rienner.

———. 1998. "Cross-Border Talk: Transnational Perspectives on Labor, Race, and Sexuality." In *Talking Visions: Multicultural Feminism in a Transnational Age*, edited by Ella Shohat. Cambridge, Mass.: MIT Press.

Castañeda, Jorge G. 1996. "Mexico's Circle of Misery," *Foreign Affairs* 75 (4): 92–105.

Castañeda, Jorge G., and Carlos Heredia. 1993. "Another NAFTA: What a Good Agreement Should Offer." In *The Case Against "Free Trade,"* edited by Ralph Nader et al. San Francisco: Earth Island Press.

Cavanagh, John, Sarah Anderson, and Karen Hansen-Kuhn. 2001. "Crossborder Organizing Around Alternatives to Free Trade: Lessons from the NAFTA-FTAA Experience." In *Global Citizen Action*, edited by Michael Edwards and John Gaventa. Boulder, Colo.: Lynne Rienner.

———. 2002. "Trinational Organizing for Just and Sustainable Trade and Development." In *Cross-Border Dialogues: U.S.–Mexico Social Movement Networking*, edited by David Brooks and Jonathan Fox. La Jolla: Center for U.S.–Mexican Studies, University of California, San Diego.

Centro de Derechos Humanos Miguel Agustín Pro Juárez. 1999. *Images of Repression: A Critical Time for Human Rights in Mexico, 1996–1998.* Mexico City: Centro de Derechos Humanos Miguel Agustín Pro Juárez.

——. 2000. *Recomendaciones sobre derechos humanos al gobierno mexicano, 1997–2000.* Mexico City: Centro de Derechos Humanos Miguel Agustín Pro Juárez.

Cleaver, Harry. 2000. "The Virtual and Real Chiapas Support Network: A Review and Critique of Judith Adler Hellman's 'Real and Virtual Chiapas: Magical Realism and the Left,' *Socialist Register, 2000*," July [www.eco.utexas.edu/faculty/Cleaver/anti-hellman.html].

Clifford, Frank. 1998. "Immigration Vote Divides Sierra Club," *Los Angeles Times*, March 16.

Cohen, Larry, and Steve Early. 1999. "Defending Workers' Rights in the Global Economy: The CWA Experience." In *Which Direction for Organized Labor? Essays on Organizing, Outreach, and Internal Transformations*, edited by Bruce Nissen. Detroit, Mich.: Wayne State University Press.

Cohen, Robin, and Shirin M. Rai, eds. 2000. *Global Social Movements.* London: Athlone.

Cook, Maria Lorena. 1997. "Regional Integration and Transnational Politics: Popular Sector Strategies in the NAFTA Era." In *The New Politics of Inequality in Latin America*, edited by Douglas A. Chalmers et al. New York: Oxford University Press.

De la Garza, Rodolfo O., et al. 1998. "Family Ties and Ethnic Lobbies: Latino Relations with Latin America." Policy Brief. Claremont, Calif.: Tomás Rivera Policy Institute.

Dedina, Serge. 2000. *Saving the Grey Whale.* Tucson: University of Arizona Press.

Delpar, Helen. 1992. *The Enormous Vogue of Things Mexican: Cultural Relations between the United States and Mexico, 1920–1935.* Tuscaloosa: University of Alabama Press.

DeSipio, Louis. 1996. *Counting on the Latino Vote: Latinos as a New Electorate.* Charlottesville: University of Virginia Press.

DeSipio, Louis, and Rodolfo O. de la Garza. 1998. *Making Americans, Remaking America: Immigration and Immigrant Policy.* Boulder. Colo.: Westview.

Dillon, Sam. 1998. "Mexico Weighs Voting by Its Emigrants in U.S.," *New York Times*, December 7.

——. 2000. "Jailed Mexican Wins Environmental Prize," *New York Times*, April 5.

Dougherty, Laurie. 1999. "Active Culture: Profile – The Methodist Women's Active Faith," *Dollars and Sense* 223 (May–June): 6.

Dreiling, Michael. 1997. "Remapping North American Environmentalism: Contending Visions and Divergent Practices in the Fight over NAFTA," *Capitalism, Nature, and Socialism* 8 (4): 65–98.

——. 2001. *Solidarity and Contention: The Politics of Security and Sustainability in the NAFTA Conflict.* New York: Garland.

Dreiling, Michael, and Ian Robinson. 1998. "Union Responses to NAFTA in the U.S. and Canada: Explaining Intra- and International Variation," *Mobilization* 3 (2): 163–84.

Dresser, Denise. 1991a. "La nueva política mexicana en Estados Unidos," *Estados Unidos: Informe Trimestral* 1 (4): 15–31.

——. 1991b. *Neopopulist Solutions to Neoliberal Problems: Mexico's National Solidarity Program.* Current Issue Briefs, no. 3. La Jolla: Center for U.S.–Mexican Studies, University of California, San Diego.

——. 1993. "Exporting Conflict: Transboundary Consequences of Mexican Politics." In *The California-Mexico Connection*, edited by Abraham F. Lowenthal and Katrina Burgess. Stanford, Calif.: Stanford University Press.

——. 1996. "Treading Lightly and Without a Stick: International Actors and the Promotion of Democracy in Mexico." In *Beyond Sovereignty: Collectively Defending Democracy in the Americas*, edited by Tom Farer. Baltimore, Md.: Johns Hopkins University Press.

Eaton, Tracy. 1999. "Jailed Timber-Cutting Foe Seen as Guerrilla by Mexican Officials," *Dallas Morning News*, August 27.

Eisenstadt, Todd. 1997. "The Rise of the Mexico Lobby in Washington: Even Further from God, and Even Closer to the United States." In *Bridging the Border: Transforming Mexico–U.S. Relations*, edited by Rodolfo O. de la Garza and Jesús Velasco. Lanham, Md.: Rowman and Littlefield.

Enciso, Angélica. 2001. "Sólo 12% de los residuos peligrosos que generan industrias reciben tratamiento," *La Jornada*, March 26.

Espinosa, Víctor. 1999. *The Illinois Federation of Michoacán Clubs: The Chicago-Michoacán Project Report*. Chicago, Ill.: Heartland Alliance for Human Needs and Human Rights.

Faux, Jeff. 1995. "Mexico and Vietnam," *Dissent* 42 (2): 169–74.

Fitzgerald, David. 2000. *Negotiating Extra-Territorial Citizenship: Mexican Migration and the Transnational Politics of Community*. Monograph Series, no. 1. La Jolla: Center for Comparative Immigration Studies, University of California, San Diego.

Flores, William, and Rina Benmayor, eds. 1997. *Latino Cultural Citizenship: Claiming Identity, Space, and Rights*. Boston, Mass.: Beacon.

Florini, Ann, ed. 2000. *The Third Force: The Rise of Transnational Civil Society*. Washington, D.C. and Tokyo: Carnegie Endowment for International Peace / Japan Center for International Exchange.

Fox, Jonathan. 1989. "Time to Cross the Border: Paying Attention to Mexico," *Radical America* 22 (4): 53–62.

——. 1992. "Agriculture and the Politics of the North American Trade Debate," *LASA Forum* 23 (1): 3–9.

——. 1996. "National Electoral Choices in Rural Mexico." In *Reforming Mexico's Agrarian Reform*, edited by Laura Randall. Armonk, N.Y.: M.E. Sharpe.

——. 2000a. "Assessing Binational Civil Society Coalitions: Lessons from the Mexico–U.S. Experience," Working Paper no. 26, Chicano-Latino Research Center, University of California, Santa Cruz, April [www.irc-online.org/bios/pdf/index_docs.html].

——. 2000b. "Los flujos y reflujos de préstamos sociales y ambientales del Banco Mundial en México." In *Las nuevas fronteras del Siglo XXI: dimensiones culturales, políticas y socioeconómicas de las relaciones México–Estados Unidos*, edited by Norma Klahn, Pedro Castillo, Alejandro Álvarez, and Federico Manchón. Mexico City: La Jornada Ediciones / Universidad Nacional Autónoma de México / Chicano-Latino Research Center / Universidad Autónoma Metropolitana.

——. 2001. "Evaluación de las coaliciones binacionales de la sociedad civil a partir de la experiencia México–Estados Unidos," *Revista Mexicana de Sociología* 63 (3): 211–68.

Fox, Jonathan, and L. David Brown, eds. 1998. *The Struggle for Accountability: The World Bank, NGOs, and Grassroots Movements*. Cambridge, Mass.: MIT Press.

Frank, Dana. 1999. *Buy American*. Boston, Mass.: Beacon Press.

García Acevedo, María Rosa. 1996. "Return to Aztlán: Mexico's Policies towards Chicano/as." In *Chicanas/Chicanos at the Crossroads: Social, Economic, and Political Change*, edited by David Maciel and Isidro D. Ortiz. Tucson: University of Arizona Press.

García Urrutia, Manuel. 2002. "The Authentic Labor Front in the Process of Regional Integration in the NAFTA Era." In *Cross-Border Dialogues: U.S.–Mexico Social Movement Networking*, edited by David Brooks and Jonathan Fox. La Jolla: Center for U.S.–Mexican Studies, University of California, San Diego.

Goldring, Luin. 1998. "From Market Membership to Transnational Citizenship? The Changing Politicization of Transnational Social Spaces," *L'Ordinaire Latino-Americaine* 173–174 (July–December): 167–72.

——. 2002. "The Mexican State and Transmigrant Organizations: Negotiating the Boundaries of Membership and Participation," *Latin American Research Review* 37 (3): 55–99.

Gómez Quiñones, Juan. 1990. *Chicano Politics: Reality and Promise, 1940–1990.* Albuquerque: University of New Mexico Press.

González, Antonio. 1999. "Chicano Politics and U.S. Policy in Central America." In *Chicano Politics and Society in the Late Twentieth Century,* edited by David Montejano. Austin: University of Texas Press.

González Gutiérrez, Carlos. 1993. "The Mexican Diaspora in California: The Limits and Possibilities of the Mexican Government." In *The California–Mexico Connection,* edited by Abraham F. Lowenthal and Katrina Burgess. Stanford, Calif.: Stanford University Press.

———. 1997. "Decentralized Diplomacy: The Role of Consular Offices in Mexico's Relations with its Diaspora." In *Bridging the Border: Transforming Mexico–U.S. Relations,* edited by Rodolfo O. de la Garza and Jesús Velascos. Lanham, Md.: Rowman and Littlefield.

———. 1999. "Fostering Identities: Mexico's Relations with its Diaspora," *Journal of American History* 86 (2): 545–67.

Gosse, Van. 1988. "'The North American Front': Central American Solidarity in the Reagan Era." In *Reshaping the U.S. Left: Popular Struggles of the 1980s,* edited by Mike Davis and Michael Sprinker. London: Verso.

———. 1995. "Active Engagement: The Legacy of Central America Solidarity," *NACLA Report on the Americas* 28 (5): 22–30.

Granovetter, Mark S. 1973. "The Strength of Weak Ties," *American Journal of Sociology* 78 (6): 1360–80.

Greenhouse, Steven. 2001. "Labor Leader Sounds Do-or-Die Warning," *New York Times,* February 19

Guidry, Jon, Michael Kennedy, and Mayer Zald, eds. 2000. *Globalizations and Social Movements: Culture, Power, and the Transnational Public Sphere.* Ann Arbor: University of Michigan Press.

Gutiérrez, David. 1995. *Walls and Mirrors: Mexican Americans, Mexican Immigrants, and the Politics of Ethnicity.* Berkeley: University of California Press.

Gutiérrez, David, ed. 1996. *Between Two Worlds: Mexican Immigrants in the United States.* Wilmington, Del: Scholarly Resources.

Gutiérrez, Maribel. 1998. *Violencia en Guerrero.* Mexico City: La Jornada Ediciones.

Gzesh, Susan. 2002. "Mexico–U.S. Immigration and Cross-Border Organizing." In *Cross-Border Dialogues: U.S.–Mexico Social Movement Networking,* edited by David Brooks and Jonathan Fox. La Jolla: Center for U.S.–Mexican Studies, University of California, San Diego.

Hanagan, Michael. 1998. "Irish Transnational Social Movements, Deterritorialized Migrants, and the State System: The Last One Hundred and Forty Years," *Mobilization* 3 (1): 107–26.

Hathaway, Dale. 2000a. *Allies across the Border: Mexico's "Authentic Labor Front" and Global Solidarity.* Boston, Mass.: South End Press.

———. 2000b. "Transnational Support of Labor Organizing in Mexico: Comparative Cases." Paper presented at the international congress of the Latin American Studies Association, March.

Hellman, Judith Adler. 2000. "Real and Virtual Chiapas: Magical Realism and the Left." In *Socialist Register, 2000,* edited by Leo Panitch. New York: Monthly Review Press [www.yorku.ca/socreg/].

Heredia, Carlos, and Ricardo Hernández. 1995. *Citizen Diplomacy in the Age of Globalization: The Case of Mexico.* Mexico City: Equipo Pueblo.

Hernández, Ricardo, and Edith Sánchez, eds. 1992. *Cross-Border Links: A Directory of Organizations in Canada, Mexico, and the United States.* Albuquerque, N.M.: Interhemispheric Resource Center.

Hernández Navarro, Luis. 2002. "Globalization and Transnational Coalitions in the Rural Sector." In *Cross-Border Dialogues: U.S.–Mexico Social Movement Networking,* edited by David

Brooks and Jonathan Fox. La Jolla: Center for U.S.–Mexican Studies, University of California, San Diego.

Hinojosa-Ojeda, Raúl. 2002. "North American Integration Policy Formation from the Grassroots Up: Transnational Implications of Latino, Labor, and Environmental NGO Strategies." In *Cross-Border Dialogues: U.S.–Mexico Social Movement Networking*, edited by David Brooks and Jonathan Fox. La Jolla: Center for U.S.–Mexican Studies, University of California, San Diego.

Hogenboom, Barbara. 1998. *Mexico and the NAFTA Environmental Debate*. Utrecht, The Netherlands: International Books.

Human Rights Watch. 1990. *Human Rights In Mexico: A Policy of Impunity*. New York: Human Rights Watch.

——. 1991a. "Prison Conditions in Mexico." New York: Human Rights Watch.

——. 1991b. "Unceasing Abuses – Human Rights in Mexico One Year after the Introduction of Reform." New York: Human Rights Watch.

——. 1993. "Human Rights Watch Writes to President Clinton Urging NAFTA Summit on Human Rights." New York: Human Rights Watch.

——. 1994a. "The New Year's Rebellion: Violations of Human Rights and Humanitarian Law during the Armed Revolt in Chiapas, Mexico." New York: Human Rights Watch.

——. 1994b. "Mexico at the Crossroads: Political Rights and the 1994 Presidential and Congressional Elections." New York: Human Rights Watch.

——. 1995. "Army Officer 'Held Responsible' for Chiapas Massacre." New York: Human Rights Watch.

——. 1996a. "No Guarantees – Sex Discrimination in Mexico's Maquiladora Sector." New York: Human Rights Watch.

——. 1996b. "Torture and Other Abuses during the 1995 Crackdown on Alleged Zapatistas." New York: Human Rights Watch.

——. 1997. "Implausible Deniability: State Responsibility for Rural Violence in Mexico." Washington, D.C.: Human Rights Watch.

——. 1998a. "Mexico – A Job or Your Rights: Continued Sex Discrimination in Mexico's Maquiladora Sector." New York: Human Rights Watch.

——. 1998b. "Discrimination in Mexico's Maquiladora Sector." New York: Human Rights Watch.

——. 1999. "Systemic Injustice: Torture, 'Disappearance,' and Extrajudicial Execution in Mexico." New York: Human Rights Watch.

——. 2000. "Unfair Advantage: Workers' Freedom of Association in the United States under International Human Rights Standards." New York: Human Rights Watch [www.hrw.org/reports/2000/uslabor/].

——. 2001. "Trading Away Rights: The Unfulfilled Promise of NAFTA's Labor Side Agreement" [www.hrw.org/press/2001/nafta0416/html].

IFE (Instituto Federal Electoral). 1998. "Informe final que presenta la comisión de especialistas que estudia las modalidades del voto do los mexicanos residentes en el extranjero," *Perfil de la Jornada*, November 16.

Kamel, Rachel. 1988. "'This Is How It Starts': Women Maquila Workers in Mexico," *Labor Research Review* 7 (1): 15–26.

——. 1989. *The Global Factory: An Organizing Guide for a New Economic Era*. Philadelphia, Penn.: American Friends Service Committee.

Kamel, Rachel, and Anya Hoffman, eds. 1999. *The Maquiladora Reader: Cross-Border Organizing since NAFTA*. Philadelphia, Penn.: American Friends Service Committee.

Keck, Margaret E., and Kathryn Sikkink. 1998. *Activists beyond Borders: Advocacy Networks in International Politics*. Ithaca, N.Y.: Cornell University Press.

Kelly, Mary. 2002. "Cross-Border Work on the Environment: Evolution, Success, Problems, and Future Outlook." In *Cross-Border Dialogues: U.S.–Mexico Social Movement Networking*, edited by David Brooks and Jonathan Fox. La Jolla: Center for U.S.–Mexican Studies, University of California, San Diego.

Khagram, Sanjeev, James V. Riker, and Kathryn Sikkink, eds. 2002. *Restructuring World Politics: Transnational Social Movements, Networks, and Norms.* Minneapolis: University of Minnesota Press.

Kidder, Thalia, and Mary McGinn. 1995. "In the Wake of NAFTA: Transnational Workers' Networks," *Social Policy* 25 (4): 14–21.

Knight, Alan. 1997. "Dealing with the American Political System: An Historical Overview." In *Bridging the Border: Transforming Mexico–U.S. Relations*, edited by Rodolfo O. de la Garza and Jesús Velasco. Lanham, Md.: Rowman and Littlefield.

Kourous, George. 2000. "The Great NADBank Debate," *Borderlines Updater*, September 1 [www.irc-online.org/bios/].

——. 2001. "NAFTA Trucking Dispute: Still Talking Trash," *Borderlines Updater*, February 12 [www.irc-online.org/bios/].

La Botz, Dan. 1992. *Mask of Democracy: Labor Suppression in Mexico Today.* Boston, Mass.: South End Press / International Labor Rights and Education Research Fund.

LaFranchi, Howard. 1998. "Mexico on Nuclear Dump: Not on Our Border," *Christian Science Monitor*, June 18.

Lehman, Karen. 2002. "Farmers and Regional Integration in North America." In *Cross-Border Dialogues: U.S.–Mexico Social Movement Networking*, edited by David Brooks and Jonathan Fox. La Jolla: Center for U.S.–Mexican Studies, University of California, San Diego.

Leiken, Robert S. 2000. *The Melting Border: Mexico and Mexican Communities in the United States.* Washington, D.C.: Center for Equal Opportunity.

Lewis, Ted. 2002. "U.S.–Mexico Grassroots Challenges: Looking for a Winning Strategy." In *Cross-Border Dialogues: U.S.–Mexico Social Movement Networking*, edited by David Brooks and Jonathan Fox. La Jolla: Center for U.S.–Mexican Studies, University of California, San Diego.

Lowerre, Richard. 1994. "Update on World Bank Forestry Loan to Mexico." Austin: Texas Center for Policy Studies.

Luján, Bertha. 2002. "Citizen Network Action in the NAFTA Region." In *Cross-Border Dialogues: U.S.–Mexico Social Movement Networking*, edited by David Brooks and Jonathan Fox. La Jolla: Center for U.S.–Mexican Studies, University of California, San Diego.

MacDonald. Laura. 1999. "Democracy, Human Rights, and the Transformation of Civil Society: The Case of the New North America." In *Racing to Regionalize*, edited by Kenneth P. Thomas and Mary Ann Tétreault. Boulder, Colo.: Lynne Rienner.

Maciel, David, and María Herrera-Sobek, eds. 1998. *Culture across Borders: Mexican Immigration and Popular Culture.* Tucson: University of Arizona Press.

MacLachlan, Colin. 1991. *Anarchism and the Mexican Revolution: The Political Trials of Ricardo Flores Magón in the United States.* Berkeley: University of California Press.

Martínez, Jesús, and Raúl Ross. 2002. "Suffrage for Mexicans Residing Abroad." In *Cross-Border Dialogues: U.S.–Mexico Social Movement Networking*, edited by David Brooks and Jonathan Fox. La Jolla: Center for U.S.–Mexican Studies, University of California, San Diego.

Martínez Saldaña, Jesús. 1999. "Propuesta a Marcos," *La Jornada*, January 23.

Mayer, Frederick. 1998. *Interpreting NAFTA: The Science and Art of Political Analysis.* New York: Columbia University Press.

Mazza, Jacqueline. 2001. *Don't Disturb the Neighbors: The United States and Democracy in Mexico, 1980–1995.* New York: Routledge.

McConnell, Sharon Lean. 1996. "Alianza Cívica: un nuevo actor no-gubernamental en el ámbito político mexicano." Master's thesis, Facultad Latinoamericana de Ciencias Sociales–México.

McGinn, Mary, and Kim Moody. 1992. *Unions and Free Trade: Solidarity vs. Competition*. Detroit, Mich.: Labor Notes.

McKennirey, John, Lance Compa, Leoncio Lara, and Eric Griego. 1997. *Plant Closings and Labor Rights: A Report to the Council of Ministers by the Secretariat of the Commission for Labor Cooperation on the Effects of Sudden Plant Closings on Freedom of Association and the Right to Organize in Canada, Mexico, and the United States*. Dallas, Tex.: Bernan Press / North American Commission for Labor Cooperation.

Mexico–United States Binational Commission. 1997. *Mexico–U.S. Binational Study on Migration*. Mexico City: Commission on Immigration Reform / Secretaría de Relaciones Exteriores.

Milkman, Ruth, ed. 2000. *Organizing Immigrants: The Challenge for Unions in Contemporary California*. Ithaca, N.Y.: Cornell University Press.

Millman, Joel. 1999. "U.S. Airlines Expand Service to Destinations within Mexico," *Wall St. Journal*, December 20.

———. 2000. "Aeroméxico Union Forges Alliance with Delta Pilots," *Wall St. Journal*, February 28.

Mumme, Stephen. 1999. "NAFTA's Environmental Side Agreement: Almost Green?" *Borderlines* 7 (9) [www.irc-online.org/bios/pdf/index_docs.html].

Nader, Ralph, et al. 1993. *The Case against "Free Trade:" GATT, NAFTA, and the Globalization of Corporate Power*. San Francisco: Earth Island Press.

Nagengast, Carole, and Michael Kearney. 1990. "Mixtec Ethnicity: Social Identity, Political Consciousness, and Political Activism," *Latin American Research Review* 25 (2): 61–91.

Neuman, Talli. 1993. "Labor Solidarity Crosses the Border," *El Financiero International*, August 9–15.

Pachon, Harry, and Louis DeSipio. 1994. *New Americans by Choice: Political Perspectives of Latin Immigrants*. Boulder, Colo.: Westview.

Paterson, Kent. 1998. "Sierra Blanca Protests Sweep Both Sides of the Border: TNRCC Decision Set for October 22," *Borderlines Updater*, October 20 [www.irc-online.org/bios/].

———. 1999. "Indigenous and Environmental Groups Unite to Stop Ward Valley Dump," *Borderlines Updater*, February 3 [www.irc-online.org/bios/].

Peña, Devon Gerardo. 1997. *The Terror of the Machine: Technology, Work, Gender, and Ecology on the U.S.–Mexico Border*. Austin: Center for Mexican American Studies, University of Texas at Austin.

Peñaloza Méndez, Andrés, and Alberto Arroyo Picard. 1997. *Espejismo y realidad: el TLCAN tres años después – análisis y propuesta desde la sociedad civil*. Mexico City: Red Mexicana de Acción frente al Libre Comercio.

Perl, Peter. 2000. "Packaged Poison," *Washington Post*, National Weekly Edition, January 24.

Preston, Julia. 1999. "Mexico Suspends Plan for Hefty Deposit on Cars," *New York Times*, December 4.

———. 2000. "In Mexico, Nature Lovers Merit a Kiss from a Whale," *New York Times*, March 5.

Public Agenda / Tomás Rivera Policy Institute. 1998. "Here to Stay: The Domestic and International Priorities of Latino Leaders." Claremont, Calif.: Tomás Rivera Policy Institute.

Public Citizen. 1997. "Deals for NAFTA Votes II: Bait and Switch 97." Washington, D.C.: Public Citizen / Global Trade Watch [www.tradewatch.org/nafta/reports/baitnswt.html].

———. 2001. "The Coming NAFTA Crash: The Deadly Impact of a Secret NAFTA Tribunal's Decision to Open U.S. Highways to Unsafe Mexican Trucks." Washington, D.C.: Public Citizen / Global Trade Watch, February 6 [www.tradewatch.org].

Restrepo, Iván. 1995. "Salvar a los delfines o los intereses de EU?" *La Jornada*, October 9.

Rice, Robert, Ashley Harris, and Jennifer MacLean, eds. 1997. *Proceedings: First Sustainable Coffee Congress, September 1996*. Washington, D.C.: Smithsonian Institution Migratory Bird Center.

Rivera Salgado, Gaspar. 1999a. "Migration and Political Activism: Mexican Transnational Indigenous Communities in a Comparative Perspective." Ph.D. diss., University of California, Santa Cruz.

———. 1999b. "Welcome to Oaxacalifornia," *Cultural Survival Quarterly* 32 (1): 59–61.

———. 2002. "Binational Grassroots Organizations and the Experience of Indigenous Migrants." In *Cross-Border Dialogues: U.S.–Mexico Social Movement Networking*, edited by David Brooks and Jonathan Fox. La Jolla: Center for U.S.–Mexican Studies, University of California, San Diego.

RMALC (Red Mexicana de Acción frente al Libro Comercio). 1994. "Memoria del Encuentro Nacional: 'Integración, Democracia y Desarrollo.' Hacia una agenda social continental." Mexico City: RMALC.

Robbins, Carla Anne. 2000. "Border Lines: How Would Bush Fare with Foreign Policy? Check Out Mexico," *Wall St. Journal*, February 29.

Rodríguez, América. 1999. *Making Latino News*. Thousand Oaks, Calif.: Sage.

Rodríguez, Primitivo. 2001. "La conexión ONG mexicanas-EU," *Masiosare* (supplement to *La Jornada*), May 1.

Romney, Lee. 1999. "Fledgling Programs Used to Create Economic Opportunities Back Home Could Stem the Migration to California," *Los Angeles Times*, August 6.

Ronfeldt, David, and John Arquilla. 1998. *The Zapatista Social Netwar in Mexico*. Santa Monica, Calif.: RAND Arroyo Center.

Rose, Debra. 1993. "The Politics of Mexican Wildlife: Conservation, Development, and the International System." Ph.D. diss., University of Florida.

Rosen, Fred. 1999. "The Underside of NAFTA: A Budding Cross-Border Resistance," *NACLA Report on the Americas* 32 (4): 37–39.

Ross, Raúl. 1999. *Los mexicanos y el voto sin fronteras*. Chicago, Ill.: Salsedo Press / Universidad Autónoma de Sinaloa / Centro de Estudios del Movimiento Obrero y Socialista.

Ruiz, Vicki, and Susan Tiano, eds. 1987. *Women on the U.S.–Mexico Border: Responses to Change*. Boston, Mass.: Allen and Unwin.

Sabatini, Chris. 2002. "Whom Do International Donors Support in the Name of Civil Society?" *Development in Practice* [www.developmentinpractice.org].

Salinas, Eleázar. 1999 "Detectan fondos 'perdidos' de los braceros; son millones de dólares descontados de sus salarios," *El Rincón Latino* (Long Beach), December.

Sandoval, Ricardo. 1999. "Sightseers Amid the Struggle," *San Jose Mercury News*, June 24.

Santamaría Gómez, Arturo. 1988. *La izquierda norteamericana y los trabajadores indocumentados*. Culiacán, Mexico: Universidad Autónoma de Sinaloa.

Santamaría Gómez, Arturo, with Nayamín Martínez Cossío, Alejandra Castañeda Gómez, and José Jaime Saínz Santamaría. 2001. *Mexicanos en Estados Unidos: la nación, la política y el voto sin fronteras*. Culiacán, Mexico: Universidad Autónoma de Sinaloa / Partido de la Revolución Democrática.

Sepúlveda, Alicia. 1998. "El caso de SPRINT y el estudio sobre el cierre repentino de empresas y la libertad de asociación." Paper presented at the conference "Las nuevas instituciones del Tratado de Libre Comercio de América del Norte: integración económica regional y cooperación," North American Integration and Development Center, University of California, Los Angeles, May.

Shoch, James. 2000. "Contesting Globalization: Organized Labor, NAFTA, and the 1997 and 1998 Fast Track Fights," *Politics and Society* 28 (1): 119–50.

Shorrock, Tim. 1999. "Creating a New Internationalism for Labor," *Dollars and Sense* 225 (September–October): 36–40.

Sierra, Christine Marie. 1999. "In Search of National Power: Chicanos Working the System on

Immigration Reform, 1976–1986." In *Chicano Politics and Society in the Late Twentieth Century*, edited by David Montejano. Austin: University of Texas Press.

Sierra Guzmán, Jorge Luis, Rafael Ruiz Harrell, and José Barragán. 1992. *La Comisión Nacional de Derechos Humanos: una visión no gubernamental*. Mexico City: Comisión Mexicana de Promoción y Defensa de los Derechos Humanos.

Silver, Sara. 1999. "Made in the Shade: Environmentalists Tout New Breed of 'Bird Friendly' Coffee Plants," *Santa Cruz Sentinel*, December 27.

Sims, Beth. 1992. *Workers of the World Undermined: American Labor's Role in U.S. Foreign Policy*. Albuquerque, N.M.: Interhemispheric Resource Center.

Smith, Christian. 1996. *Resisting Reagan: The U.S.–Central American Peace Movement*. Chicago: University of Chicago Press.

Smith, Jackie, Charles Chatfield, and Ron Pagnucco, eds. 1997. *Transnational Social Movements and Global Politics: Solidarity beyond the State*. Syracuse, N.Y.: Syracuse University Press.

Smith, Michael Peter, and Luis Eduardo Guarnizo, eds. 1998. *Transnationalism From Below*. New Brunswick: Transaction.

Smith, Robert. 1999. "Migrant Membership as an Instituted Process: Transnationalization, the State, and the Extra-Territorial Conduct of Mexican Politics." Manuscript.

Stephen, Lynn. 2002. "In the Wake of the Zapatistas: U.S. Solidarity Work Focused on Militarization, Human Rights, and Democratization in Chiapas." In *Cross-Border Dialogues: U.S.–Mexico Social Movement Networking*, edited by David Brooks and Jonathan Fox. La Jolla: Center for U.S.–Mexican Studies, University of California, San Diego.

Tarrow, Sidney. 1998. *Power in Movement: Social Movements and Contentious Politics*. 2d ed. Cambridge: Cambridge University Press.

———. 2000. "Beyond Globalization: Why Creating Transnational Social Movements Is So Hard and When It Is Most Likely to Happen," posted at Global Solidarity Dialogue [www.antenna.nl/~waterman/tarrow.html].

Texas Center for Policy Studies. 1994. "Preliminary Report on the Proposed Extension of the Gulf Intracoastal Waterway and the Laguna Madre." Austin: Texas Center for Policy Studies.

Thorup, Cathryn L. 1991. "The Politics of Free Trade and the Dynamics of Cross-Border Coalitions in U.S.–Mexico Relations," *Columbia Journal of World Business* 26 (2): 12–27.

Torres, Blanca. 1997. "La participación de actores nuevos y tradicionales en las relaciones internacionales de México." In *La política exterior de México: enfoques para su análisis*. Mexico City: El Colegio de México / Secretaría de Relaciones Exteriores.

USAID (U.S. Agency for International Development)/Mexico. 1999. "FY 2001 Results Review and Resource Request." Arlington, Va.: USAID, May.

Varady, Robert, Patricia Romero Lankao, and Katherine Hawkins. 2001. "Managing Hazardous Material along the U.S.–Mexican Border," *Environment* 43 (10): 22–36.

Velasco, Jesús. 1997. "Selling Ideas, Buying Influence: Mexico and American Think Tanks in the Promotion of NAFTA." In *Bridging the Border: Transforming Mexico–U.S. Relations*, edited by Rodolfo O. de la Garza and Jesús Velasco. Lanham, Md.: Rowman and Littlefield.

Vila, Pablo. 2000. *Crossing Borders, Reinforcing Borders: Social Categories, Metaphors, and Narrative Identities on the U.S.–Mexico Frontier*. Austin: University of Texas Press.

Villaraigosa, Antonio, and Raúl Hinojosa-Ojeda. 1999. "Oportunidad para estrechar lazos," *Perfil de La Jornada*, May 18.

Walker, Tony. 1998. "Sierra Blanca (population 700) Goes Ballistic over Plans for Big Nuclear Waste Dump Site: Texas Community Is Environmental Battleground Whose Ripples Could Spread to the Presidential Campaign," *Financial Times*, August 4.

Wapner, Paul Kevin. 1996. *Environmental Activism and World Civic Politics*. Albany: State University of New York Press.

Waterman, Peter. 1998. *Globalization, Social Movements, and the New Internationalism.* Washington, D.C.: Mansell.

Weber, Devra. 1998. "Historical Perspectives on Transnational Mexican Workers in California." In *Border Crossings: Mexican and Mexican-American Workers,* edited by John Mason Hart. Wilmington, Del.: Scholarly Resources.

Williams, Edward J. 1997. "Discord in U.S.–Mexican Labor Relations and the North American Agreement on Labor Cooperation." In *Bridging the Border: Transforming Mexican–U.S. Relations,* edited by Rodolfo O. de la Garza and Jesús Velasco. Lanham, Md.: Rowman and Littlefield.

Williams, Heather. 1999. "Mobile Capital and Transborder Labor Rights Mobilization," *Politics and Society* 27 (1): 139–66.

———. 2000. "Of Labor Tragedy and Legal Farce: The Han Young Factory Struggle in Tijuana, Mexico." Paper presented at the conference "Human Rights and Globalization: When Transnational Civil Society Networks Hit the Ground," Center for Global, International, and Regional Studies, University of California, Santa Cruz, December [www2.ucsc.edu/cgirs/conferences/humanrights/index.html].

———. 2002. "Lessons from the Labor Front: The Coalition for Justice in the Maquiladoras." In *Cross-Border Dialogues: U.S.–Mexico Social Movement Networking,* edited by David Brooks and Jonathan Fox. La Jolla: Center for U.S.–Mexican Studies, University of California, San Diego.

WOLA (Washington Office on Latin America). 1993. "The Elections in Yucatán, Mexico: Summary and Conclusions of Citizen Observers." Washington, D.C.: WOLA.

———. 1994a. "The Media and the 1994 Federal Election in Mexico: A Content Analysis of Television Coverage of the Political Parties and Presidential Candidates." Washington, D.C.: WOLA / Mexican Academy of Human Rights, in collaboration with Civic Alliance / Observation 94.

———. 1994b. "The 1994 Mexican Election: A Question of Credibility." Washington, D.C.: WOLA / Academia Mexicana de Derechos Humanos.

———. 1994c. "The Clinton Administration and the Mexican Elections." Washington, D.C.: WOLA / Interhemispheric Resource Center Press.

———. 1995a. "Peace and Democratization in Mexico: Challenges Facing the Zedillo Government." Washington, D.C.: WOLA.

———. 1995b. "Mexican Insights: Mexican Civil Society Speaks to the United States." Washington, D.C.: WOLA.

———. 1997. "So Close and Yet So Far: Mexico's Mid-Term Elections and the Struggle for Democracy." Washington, D.C.: WOLA.

Wright, Brian. 2000. "Environmental NGOs and the Dolphin-Tuna Case," *Environmental Politics* 9 (4): 82–103.

Yúdice, George. 1998. "The Globalization of Culture and the New Civil Society." In *Cultures of Politics, Politics of Cultures: Re-visioning Latin American Social Movements,* edited by Sonia E. Álvarez, Evelina Dagnino, and Arturo Escobar. Boulder, Colo.: Westview.

Zabin, Carol, and Luis Escala Rabadán. 1998. "Mexican Hometown Associations and Mexican Immigrant Political Empowerment in Los Angeles." Aspen Institute Working Paper Series. Aspen, Colo.: Aspen Institute.

Zúñiga, Juan Antonio, and Ricardo Olayo. 1999. "Con Barroso, desfalco por $7.5 millones a Cruz Roja," *La Jornada,* September 11.

16

"For 118 Million Mexicans": Emigrants and Chicanos in Mexican Politics

David Fitzgerald

When Vicente Fox Quesada won the Mexican presidency in July 2000, he pledged to govern on behalf of "118 million Mexicans," including the 18 million people of Mexican origin living in the United States (J. Smith 2000).[1] His expanded constituency included the new leader of El Granjenal, a village in the Mexican state of Michoacán, who shortly after his election flew north to his construction job in Santa Ana, California. His deputy stayed behind to attend to village affairs. Every few months, the leader returns and the deputy migrates, as they take turns governing El Granjenal on behalf of a community whose members mostly live in Santa Ana (Fitzgerald 2000). Yet the participation of Mexican emigrants in Mexican politics remains contested, as Andrés Bermudez found when he was elected mayor of Jerez, Zacatecas in 2001 – twenty-eight years after leaving Zacatecas to make his fortune in tomato farming in California. Bermudez's election was later overturned because of his California residency (Garrison 2002).

These vignettes illustrate the ways that relations between the U.S.–resident population of Mexican origin and political institutions in Mexico are enacted on multiple levels. Boundaries of national and hometown communities – and the rights of members absent from these communities – are subject to negotiation. This chapter discusses various aspects of such transborder politics, including Mexican hometown associations and their relationship with Mexican federal, state, and local governments; negotiations of dual nationality; the right to vote abroad; the proposed creation of an extra-territorial electoral district in the Mexican Congress; and U.S.–resident Mexicans' and Chicanos' interest in participating in Mexican politics.

The author is grateful to Wayne Cornelius, James Holston, David López, and Kevin J. Middlebrook for their comments and suggestions.

1 Fox was not the first opposition presidential candidate to campaign among the Mexican population in the United States, but he was the first to win.

A Brief History of Transborder Politics

Mexicans have been engaged in cross-border politics as long as there has been a border.[2] "Juárez Clubs" formed throughout the American Southwest in the 1860s to support exiled president Benito Juárez by raising funds, procuring weapons, and recruiting volunteers for military action in Mexico. In what must be one of the earliest attempts to form a "Mexico lobby," Juárez Clubs supported Republican candidates in U.S. elections because Republicans were considered to be more favorable to Juárez (Gómez-Quiñones 1983: 421–22).

Cross-border political activity continued in the early twentieth century as Ricardo Flores Magón attracted workers in both Mexico and the United States to his revolutionary Mexican Liberal Party (PLM) and Mexican émigrés formed "Constitutionalist Clubs" during the 1910–1920 revolution to support the government of Venustiano Carranza (Gómez-Quiñones 1973, Santamaría Gómez 1994, Weber 1998).[3] In 1928, Mexican presidential candidate José Vasconcelos campaigned in the Southwest and in Chicago against the "official" candidate, Pascual Ortiz Rubio. Ortiz Rubio received support from clubs in California organized by the Revolutionary National Party (PNR), precursor to the long-ruling Institutional Revolutionary Party (PRI) (Zazueta 1983, Santamaría Gómez 1994).

Mexican consulates organized unions and social assistance among the Mexican and Chicano populations during the 1920s and 1930s (Balderrama 1982), but Gilbert González argues that "no other activity occupied as much time and effort as that of fomenting and orchestrating loyalty to the Mexican government and adherence to its politics" (1999: 37).[4] The consulates made little distinction between Mexican citizens (including children born abroad to Mexican parents) and Chicanos until the 1940s (A. Gutiérrez 1986: 47). Because most of the Mexican-origin population consisted of first- or second-generation immigrants, the consulates assumed they were all Mexican nationals. Second-generation immigrants were de facto dual

2 An estimated 75,000 to 100,000 Mexicans lived in the territory seized by the United States in 1848 (D. Gutiérrez 1995). For a brief history of Mexican migration since then, see Massey et al. 1987.

   The historical literature on U.S.–resident Mexicans' participation in Mexican politics often does not distinguish among émigré elites, U.S.–born Chicanos, and Mexican migrants. "Mexican" is used here to mean a Mexican citizen, while Chicano and Mexican American are used interchangeably to mean a U.S. citizen of Mexican origin or ancestry. The term "migrant" is not intended to imply constant movement, nor does "immigrant/emigrant" imply permanent settlement/departure.

3 In an instance of early ethnic lobbying, a newspaper financed by the Mexican consul in San Diego urged Constitutionalist Clubs to petition President Woodrow Wilson to recognize the government of President Venustiano Carranza (1917–1920) (Santamaría Gómez 1994).

4 In the early 1930s, Mexicans in Los Angeles demonstrated outside the consulate to protest the Mexican government's suppression of leftist labor unions in Mexico. U.S.–resident Mexicans also publicly denounced the suppression of the Roman Catholic Church (González 1999; Sánchez 1993).

nationals, although neither the U.S. nor the Mexican government recognized dual nationality (Zazueta 1983: 458).

One of the consulates' main projects during the Great Depression of the 1930s was to support U.S. authorities in the repatriation of Mexicans to Mexico. Nationalists in Mexico had long viewed mass emigration as an affront to their nation-building project. According to this view, "emigrants were opportunists who went to the U.S. to cash in on the available opportunities there, while leaving others in the country behind to solve the problems posed by the Revolution" (quoted in Zazueta 1983). Officials hoped that migrants would return with valuable skills that were lacking in Mexico (Sánchez 1993). The government did not, however, always anticipate the political consequences of mass repatriation. Returnees led miners' strikes in Sonora and were accused of being agents of Bolshevism through-out the country (Weber 1998: 228). In conducting oral histories among *ejidatarios* in Los Altos de Jalisco, Ann Craig found that "the single most distinctive characteristic shared by the majority of the first *agraristas* is that they had worked in the United States before becoming ejidatarios, usually even before joining the agrarian reform" (1983: 178).[5]

There was little political contact between U.S.–resident Mexicans and the Mexican government in the 1950s and early 1960s (Bustamante 1986). Interactions increased in the 1960s when Chicano activists began seeking the support of the Mexican government to promote Mexican-American socioeconomic and political advancement within the United States (De la Garza and Vargas 1992). There was a tension within the Chicano movement between establishing a relationship with the Mexican government and promoting a sense of the "nation" of Aztlán distinct from Mexico. "Having attempted to redefine the Chicano community by rejecting the assimilationist model and emphasizing the central importance of Mexican culture, history, and language to contemporary Chicano society, Chicano activists had raised some complex questions as to the boundaries of their community" (D. Gutiérrez 1995: 190).

President Luis Echeverría (1970–1976) saw Chicanos as a potential ethnic lobby in the United States and met with Chicano leaders. However, cross-border contacts were not institutionalized until the administration of José López Portillo (1976–1982), when the Mexican president and leaders of Chicano organizations like the Mexican American Legal Defense and Educational Fund (MALDEF) formed the Hispanic Commission (Santamaría Gómez 1994).

Jorge Bustamante, a strong proponent of contacts between the Mexican government and Chicano groups, has argued against the "false politicization" of cultural contacts, which would raise the specter of intervention in the sovereign affairs of

---

5 *Ejidatarios* are members of *ejidos*, a collective form of land tenure that was a principal means of distributing land during Mexico's postrevolutionary agrarian reform.

A similar concentration of former migrants among the first *agraristas* has been noted in various sending communities in Michoacán (Alarcón 1986, Fonseca 1988, Gledhill 1993, Weber 1998).

Mexico (1986). Yet even the selection of participants in high-level "cultural" meetings between Chicano groups and the Mexican government is subject to political negoti-ation. During the period when the Institutional Revolutionary Party held national power, some Chicano leaders criticized colleagues who pursued relations with the Mexican government for legitimating authoritarian policies. There is credible evidence that, under the PRI, the Mexican government sought to exclude Chicano critics from cross-border meetings (De la Garza 1986, Santamaría Gómez 1994).

The Opposition Challenge and State Response

Relations between Mexican political actors and the Mexican-origin population in the United States changed substantially in the aftermath of the 1988 Mexican presidential election. Cuauhtémoc Cárdenas, the center-left opposition candidate for president in 1988 who later founded the Party of the Democratic Revolution (PRD), drew large crowds of Mexican migrants while campaigning in California and in Chicago. Cárdenas appealed to Mexican citizens to influence the vote of their family members in Mexico and promised emigrants dual nationality and the right to vote from abroad (Jones-Correa 2000). His policies attracted many U.S.–resident Mexicans who had "voted with their feet" by leaving a Mexico beset with economic and political troubles, problems that migrants often blamed upon PRI–led governments (Dresser 1993).

Since the 1988 election, Mexicans in California have helped the PRD by raising funds for campaign events in California, sending pro-PRD pamphlets to Mexico, and – according to the PRI – illegally raising money for PRD candidates in Mexico (Pérez Godoy 1998). Local PRD committees from migrant sending communities also raise funds in the United States, which they claim they send to their home communities for nonelection expenses.[6] Supporters of Cuauhtémoc Cárdenas formed a number of U.S.–based organizations such as the Mexican Unity Group and the Organization of Mexicans for Democracy (OMD). At the PRD's first national congress in Mexico City in 1990, the leader of the OMD and two Southern California *cardenistas* were appointed as California delegates to the PRD's national assembly (Martínez Saldaña 1993).

A former Mexican consul in Los Angeles acknowledged that the 1988 Cárdenas campaign in the United States and subsequent protests against electoral fraud in the presidential race demonstrated migrants' transborder influence and encouraged the Mexican government to reformulate its policy toward Mexicans abroad (Dresser 1993: 94). Prior to 1988, the network of Mexican consulates executed most govern-ment programs directed at emigrants. In the early 1990s, however, the PRI created a separate system of Compatriot Aid Committees in U.S. cities to support the party in open ways that consular agents could not (Dresser 1993, García-Acevedo 1996). These new policies aimed to circumvent the opposition's organizations among

6 Author's interview with PRD activists in Anaheim, California, June 2000.

emigrants, promote a Mexico lobby, encourage remittances, and protect the civil rights of Mexicans both in the United States and upon their return to Mexico.

Mexican political leaders from Echeverría to President Ernesto Zedillo (1994–2000) have intermittently attempted to create a "Mexican American lobby," often explicitly modeled on the American Jewish or Cuban lobbies (Santamaría Gómez 1994, De la Garza 1997). President Carlos Salinas de Gortari (1988–1994), for example, took concrete steps to promote a specific policy concern among Chicanos when he urged them to promote the North American Free Trade Agreement (NAFTA). Galavisión, the Spanish-language television affiliate of Televisa, broadcast commercials urging Mexicans in the United States to call their U.S. congressional representatives and express their support for the NAFTA (Martínez and Ross 2002). Nevertheless, despite the support for the NAFTA among Mexican Americans in Congress and some Chicano organizations, "there is no evidence ... that Mexican American members of Congress voted for NAFTA because of Mexican lobbying or because they supported Mexican interests" (De la Garza 1997).

The Mexican government's courtship of migrants also serves to encourage migrant remittances to Mexico. Even state-sponsored projects that are putatively nonpolitical and noneconomic (cultural exchanges, for example) encourage thicker social ties to Mexico that may promote increased remittances. Most remittances are made at the household level, yet they are one of the country's leading sources of foreign exchange (Lozano Ascencio 1993). In April 2000, the Banco de México estimated that annual remittances rose from US$3.7 billion in 1995 to almost $6 billion in 1999. However, a report released in March 2000 by Mexico's National Population Council (CONAPO) estimated that only three-fourths of the remittance flow was captured by the Banco de México study, suggesting that annual remittances of US$8 billion were of essential economic support to 1.1 million households in Mexico (*SourceMex* 2000). In areas of Mexico with extremely high emigration rates, remittances support entire local economies (Massey et al. 1987).

Among the most important Mexican government initiatives to institutionalize relations with emigrants is the Program for Mexican Communities Abroad (PCME), created under the jurisdiction of the Ministry of Foreign Relations in 1990. Diplomatic elites have historically tended to denigrate both working-class migrants and Chicanos, categorizing the latter as *pochos*[7] (A. Gutiérrez 1986). Yet the PCME targets working-class Mexican emigrants as well as Chicanos. Under its auspices, the Mexican government has founded cultural institutes in U.S. cities with large Mexican-origin populations and encouraged the formation of hometown associations (González Gutiérrez 1997).[8] In 1992, President Salinas created Solidarity

---

7 *Pocho* literally means "overripe." It is used as a pejorative term to describe people of Mexican origin who imitate Americans (González Gutiérrez 1998).

8 The PCME was preceded by the Program for Enhanced Relations between the Mexican Government and the U.S. Mexican American Community, established in 1987. The latter was inactive until the administration of Carlos Salinas de Gortari (1988–1994). See García-Acevedo 1996.

International, the branch of his National Solidarity Program (PRONASOL) that was charged with soliciting financial contributions from Mexicans abroad for infrastructure development projects in their places of origin. Salinas hoped that a decentralized development program that involved community leaders in the planning process would be less corrupt and more likely to address local needs, while simultaneously generating support for the federal government (Salinas de Gortari 1982: 39–42). In the form in which they were implemented, however, the international activities of PRONASOL and the PCME excluded migrants from the decision-making process (Martínez Saldaña 1993: 15). The programs acknowledged migrants' economic rights in their sending country but continued to restrict their political rights (Pérez Godoy 1998).

More generally, Mexican consulates have sought to protect their citizens' civil rights in the face of U.S. border enforcement strategies that indirectly caused the deaths of approximately 1,700 migrants attempting to cross the border illegally from 1994 to mid-2001 (Cornelius 2001). The Salinas administration also created the Paisano Program in 1989 to protect migrants returning to Mexico from extortion by Mexican police (González Gutiérrez 1998), and successive administrations have continued it. One of Vicente Fox's first acts as president was to tour Mexico's northern border cities in December 2000 to "monitor" returning migrants, whom he called "heroes" (*New York Times* 2000).

Hometown Actors and the State

Migrant cross-border activities frequently are oriented toward narrowly defined *hometown* communities rather than the national "imagined community" of the *homeland* (B. Anderson 1991, R. Smith 1998a). Even migrants from towns that are practically contiguous may have completely separate projects and no institutional interaction (Fitzgerald 2000: 70–71). The Mexican government has encouraged hometown connections by attempting to institutionalize hometown networks through the consular apparatus. A state discourse outlining an expanded Mexican nation encourages substantive practices, like remittances, at the hometown level.

PRONASOL is no longer active, but hometown associations (HTAs) continue to raise funds for hometown public works and charity projects. More than five hundred HTAs were registered with the PCME as of 1998.[9] Most of these groups have formed since the mid-1980s, although some date back as far as 1958. The HTAs from the state of Zacatecas have been most effective in developing sustained

9 The *Los Angeles Times* reported that there were some 1,500 HTAs in the United States in 2000, although it did not cite a source for this figure (Kraul 2000). The number and proportion of Mexican emigrants who participate in HTAs are unknown. The 1988 National Latino Immigrant Survey found that 10 percent of adult Mexican immigrants were members of social clubs, although it is not clear how many of those clubs were HTAs (NALEO 1990). It is important to note that this survey was conducted before the explosion of HTAs in the 1990s.

projects. Zacatecan HTAs around the United States are organized into five federations of Zacatecan Clubs – in California, Chicago, Houston, Georgia, and Colorado. The federation in California, which includes 51 clubs in the Los Angeles area alone, has worked closely with the Zacatecan state government since 1985, when the state government began matching funds raised by HTAs to finance projects in their communities of origin (R. Smith 1998b: 34). This relationship was strengthened by the "2 for 1" program, whereby federal and state governments each provided a matching dollar for every dollar that the federation raised for public works projects. Since 1992, about 350 projects have been completed, including street paving; water, electrification, and lighting projects; and the construction of sports facilities (Kraul 2000, Félix 1999). The federation's entire contribution to Zacatecas's development, including matching funds, was US$2 million in 1994 alone. In many communities, "2 for 1" funding was several times higher than regular government investment in public projects (Goldring 1999a: 9).

In 1997 the Mexican consulate in Los Angeles attempted to gain control of the Zacatecan HTAs by forming a single confederation of all five Zacatecan federations in the United States. The new organization was to be led by a president imposed by the consulate. However, migrant delegates altered the charter that the consulate proposed and formally limited the influence of the consulate, the PCME, and federal and state governments in Mexico. Rather than accepting a clientelistic relationship with the Los Angeles consulate, confederation members engaged in a democratic process of debating a founding charter and freely electing their leaders (R. Smith 1998b: 41). As this example illustrates, migrants' ability to operate outside the boundaries of the state sometimes enables them to resist government co-optation (Goldring 1999b).[10]

Migrants have also become involved in Zacatecan electoral politics. Ricardo Monreal, a PRI defector who won the governorship of Zacatecas on the PRD ticket in 1998, made three trips to California during his campaign. He ran radio ads in California urging migrants to call their relatives in Zacatecas and encourage them to vote for him. Some Zacatecans in California supported Monreal by sending money to their families in Zacatecas, who in turn contributed to the campaign (Sheridan 1998). Monreal reciprocated by building ties to Zacatecans in the United States. For example, he proposed that Zacatecans in Los Angeles elect two deputies to serve in the Zacatecas state legislature (Félix 1999), an arrangement similar to the proposal for an extra-territorial district in the federal Congress. A migrant who is a cabinet-level representative of the governor attends meetings of the Zacatecan

10 Transborder activities do not always encourage democratic accountability. Robert Smith describes a case of migrants from Ticuani, Puebla, living in New York City who financed a potable water system for their home community. A committee in New York controlled the Ticuani water supply. Although the New York committee saw itself as more democratic than the clientelistic municipal government of Ticuani, Ticuani residents in effect depended upon a group of unelected migrants thousands of miles away for basic municipal services (R. Smith 1998a).

federation, and during his term in office the governor regularly visited the Zacatecan federation in Los Angeles.

Moreover, Monreal implemented a new program providing matching dollars for federation projects, and he agreed to migrant demands that funds be deposited in locally controlled accounts rather than in the state treasury (Goldring 1999b). In all of these matching programs, clientelistic control of the funds has been a major issue (R. Smith 1998b). HTAs cannot force sending-area governments to become more accountable for all government spending, but HTAs *can* create incentives for greater government accountability through their ability to direct or restrict resources to public projects.

Municipal presidents, congressional representatives, and state governors from migrant sending areas routinely visit their satellite communities in the United States to solicit financing for public works projects or emigrant investment in their home communities. For example, the governors of Jalisco, Sinaloa, Aguascalientes, Nayarit, and Guanajuato encouraged the creation in Los Angeles of federations grouping HTAs from their respective states, and the governor of Michoacán worked with HTAs in Chicago to develop a federation there (González Gutiérrez 1995, Espinosa 1999). During his term as governor of Guanajuato (1995–1999), Vicente Fox was particularly active in soliciting emigrant investment for *maquiladora* (in-bond processing) plants and creating a mechanism for family remittances through which a small percentage of remittances would finance public projects in the state (De la Garza 1997, Sheridan 1998). Part of the motivation was probably political; the independent links that National Action Party (PAN) municipal and local officials established with emigrants could strengthen a PAN–controlled area economically. "To the extent that [such efforts were] successful it may further entrench PAN in that state, and potentially strengthen it elsewhere in the country" (De la Garza 1997).

Many HTAs and other cross-border groups are divided internally over the politicization of their activities. They often represent themselves as apolitical or even anti-political groupings (Zabin and Escala Rabadán 1998, author's interviews 1999). During the period of PRI control over the federal government, some HTA members viewed Mexican consulates as an extension of the PRI's political apparatus and were reticent to cooperate with them even though consular officials can help HTAs develop networks within the Mexican population abroad and with government agencies in Mexico. There are, moreover, informal migrant cross-border networks that are not associated with Mexican consulates or other state agencies. Their narrowly defined interests and lack of institutionalization suggest that they will not become major collective actors capable of influencing Mexican politics at the national level, but they can have profound impacts in sending communities (Fitzgerald 2000: 96–100).

Members of formal and informal transborder networks are divided regarding the degree to which they should orient their activities toward life in the United States, Mexico, or both (Zabin and Escala Rabadán 1998). Some clubs, including a number whose primary goal is to develop projects in sending communities, encourage their members to become U.S. citizens, even though HTAs historically have avoided participation in U.S. politics (Zabin and Escala Rabadán 1998). Nevertheless, in June 2000, Los Angeles-based HTA club presidents from Guanajuato, Jalisco, Oaxaca, Sinaloa, and Zacatecas called for an amnesty for undocumented immigrants (Cleeland 2000). Some hometown associations also have arranged "sister-city" agreements between the local governments of Mexican sending communities and U.S. destination communities (Fitzgerald 2000: 91–96).

Redefining Nation and Citizen: Dual Nationality and the Vote Abroad

Reconceptualizing the Mexican Nation

In his 1995–2000 National Development Plan, President Ernesto Zedillo declared that "the Mexican nation extends beyond the territory contained within its borders" (González Gutiérrez 1997). Zedillo's redefinition of "the Mexican nation" went beyond earlier references to emigrants as "*el México de afuera*" ("Mexico outside Mexico"), as part of the Mexican "people." It is difficult to differentiate conceptually between "peoplehood" and "nationhood," but nationalism implies a form of politics (Breuilly 1994). Portraying Mexicans in the United States in explicitly national terms creates an opening for their participation in the Mexican polity. Zedillo's rhetoric and the legal reforms detailed below suggest a conceptualization of Mexican nationhood that places more emphasis on descent.[11] Carlos González Gutiérrez, one of the architects of the PCME, has written that the Mexican state will be able to "better the living standards of the communities abroad" and "generate support in its diaspora for development of the homeland" when "people of Mexican descent [feel] they belong to the Mexican nation" (1998: 5). "To support immigrants' ethnic mobilization in terms of lines of origin and 'compatriotism' is one of the most powerful resources available to the Mexican government to defend and stimulate the *mexicanidad* of its absent sons" (González Gutiérrez 1995: 89).

Emigrants and activists seeking the vote abroad also have phrased their demands in explicitly nationalist terms, noting not only economic contributions to "our co-nationals" but also "ties of belonging and national identity" (Ross Pineda 1999: 195). Hometown ties that are the basis of remittances and social networks serve to legitimate emigrant inclusion at the transnational level. Responding to demands from emigrant organizations dating from the 1988 Cárdenas campaign, President Zedillo and the PRI–controlled Congress amended the Constitution in 1996 to allow Mexicans to maintain their Mexican nationality even when they become naturalized citizens of another country. Former Mexican nationals can "recover" their Mexican

11 Neither the nation nor the state has been "deterritorialized," according to the formulation by Basch, Glick Schiller, and Szanton Blanc (1994). Rather, territory has become a *less important* component of nationality than descent.

nationality, and children born abroad to Mexican nationals also are eligible for dual nationality (R. Smith 1998a).[12] By October 2000, about 30,000 U.S. citizens had been "renationalized" as Mexicans (Valdez 2000). Nevertheless, dual nationality is not dual citizenship.[13] Dual nationals have property rights in Mexico and other privileges denied to foreigners, but they do not have the right to vote (R. Smith 1998a).

Territory is still an important component of Mexican nationality because only the first generation born abroad is attributed Mexican nationality by virtue of *jus sanguinis* (the principle of blood).[14] Territoriality and ethnicity are not, however, mutually exclusive principles of nationality. The territorial principle is horizontally bounded, legalistic, and emphasizes citizenship, while the ethnic principle emphasizes descent ties. "Nations" are conceived in terms of both territorial and ethnic principles, although "given nations will exhibit ethnic and territorial components in varying proportions at particular moments of their history" (A. Smith 1986: 149).

The state-sponsored nationalist project in Mexico historically has faced the challenge of creating a sense of collectivity in a highly heterogenous (European, indigenous, and mestizo) population (Valenzuela Arce 1999). Mexican elites typically viewed ethnicity as a barrier to nation building because it accentuated the division between indigenous and nonindigenous populations. Yet when Fox spoke of eighteen million Mexicans in the United States, he referred to a population in an ethnically plural society that for many has become ethnicized as one "group" through practices of self-identification and U.S. government categories like those in the census. Nevertheless, Mexican Americans and U.S.–resident Mexicans may not share a sense of ethnic identity. Some of the migrants most active in transborder politics are indigenous Oaxacans, who often identify themselves in more distinctly ethnic terms in the United States than they did in Mexico. Migrant organizations like the 2,000–member Binational Indigenous Oaxacan Front (FIOB) have created a sustained, binational movement in Oaxaca, Baja California, and California, calling upon the Mexican government to recognize special rights for indigenous peoples – demands that redefine Mexican nationhood in more ethnically plural terms (Rivera Salgado 1999).

President Vicente Fox (2000–2006) has extended Zedillo's *völkisch* conceptualization of "the Mexican nation" to assert not only that such a nation exists but also that members of that nation outside Mexico should be full participants in

12 Mexican nationality also remains available via naturalization to immigrants to Mexico from Europe, China, and the Middle East who do not make claims to Mexican descent (González Navarro 1994). González Navarro notes a "certain Mexican attitude that seems to want the children of immigrants [to Mexico] immediately to be 'pure Mexicans,' and, on the other hand, the children of Mexicans born abroad always to be Mexicans" (p. 191).

13 According to anecdotal evidence from sending communities in Michoacán, some children become de facto dual citizens, although neither the U.S. nor the Mexican government recognizes that status. A child born in the United States automatically becomes a U.S. citizen. Some parents fraudulently register the child's birth in Mexico so that he or she can have Mexican citizenship as well.

14 Thus Mexican nationality is not attributed to U.S.–born grandchildren of Mexican nationals.

national life. In a speech in Los Angeles in November 2000, Fox called for "the active participation of the entire Mexican nation, defined in the broadest sense of the word.... Mine will be the first Mexican administration to honor sincerely the ties that bind people of Mexican descent to the United States. I will hear the needs and respect the dreams of all those who share our Mexican heritage, here in Los Angeles and in Mexico" (McDonnell 2000).

The inclusion of U.S.–resident Mexicans in the framing of nationhood is indicative of the dramatic shift in Mexico's foreign policy toward the United States since the late 1980s. Given the United States' conquest of Mexican territory in 1848 and a history of U.S. interventionism, modern Mexican political identity has been defined largely in opposition to the United States. Yet, "by the early 1990s, nationalism and sovereignty were redefined so that the United States became an ally rather than the enemy" (De la Garza 1997: 70–71). The Mexican state extended its contacts with U.S. residents of Mexican descent with little fear of creating a precedent for the violation of state sovereignty that could later justify U.S. intervention.

The post-1988 period of more intensive cross-border Mexican politics, initiated by opposition parties and then reinforced by the Mexican state, has historical precedent in the early twentieth century. What appears to be novel is the Mexican government's promotion of *dual nationalism*, in which Mexican migrants are encouraged to become Americans while maintaining their *mexicanidad*.[15] González Gutiérrez argues that "for Mexico, the ultimate goal in approaching the Mexican community abroad must not be that of stopping the process of acculturalization of Mexican Americans nor of aspiring to create a situation whereby, like in other countries, emotional attachment to the homeland takes precedence over strategic rational calculations and the self-interest of different sectors of the diaspora" (1998: 5). From this perspective, nationhood is not necessarily based upon culture; the "acculturalization" of Mexicans into something other than exclusively "Mexican" does not strip them of their Mexicanness. Fox, for example, has encouraged U.S.–resident Mexicans to become U.S. citizens and integrate themselves into the life of

15 "Transnationalism" in the migration literature often conflates "state" and "national" borders. Akzin (1966) notes a similar definitional problem with "international," which in most uses would be better phrased as "inter-state." Modern states are a set of administrative institutions exercising control over a bordered territory. Borders of "nation" may be more ambiguous because they include mobile persons as well as an element of ethnoculture that is difficult to delimit sharply. *Transborder nationalism* involves the crossing of a *state*, rather than a *national*, border.

This chapter distinguishes between two different forms of nationalism that are conflated as "transnationalism." The first is *transborder nationalism* among diasporic groups or states claiming to represent "their" ethno-national kin who are residents of other states (B. Anderson 1998, Brubaker 1998). The second is *dual nationalism*, in which persons identify with two distinct "nations." Transborder and dual nationalism are complementary in some circumstances, but they are analytically distinct and one does not necessarily imply the other.

For a useful classification scheme of transborder political activities between the United States and Mexico in the broadest sense, see J. Fox 2000.

the United States. In his November 2000 speech in Los Angeles, Fox told an audience comprised largely of Mexicans that immigrants "want their children to learn English, they want to graduate from college, they want to live in integrated neighborhoods, they want to dream the American dream and wake up as citizens … I share those hopes …We have no desire to interfere in the powerful processes that tie Mexican immigrants to this country" (McDonnell 2000).

The Mexican government may stress that it is not interfering in processes of integration or naturalization in part as a rhetorical maneuver to protect itself against charges of violating U.S. sovereignty. Nevertheless, nationalism is a discursive formation (Calhoun 1997), and state-sponsored changes in public discourse alter the form of nationalism.[16] In the national formulations that Fox and González Gutiérrez expressed, the interests of the Mexican state are best served by allowing Mexicans in the United States to adopt not only the legal category of dual nationality, but also the concomitant practical and identificational aspects of dual nationalism.

Mexicans Abroad and the Right to Vote

State-sponsored dual nationalism carries political risks. It is difficult to execute a policy that encourages emigrants to integrate into U.S. life to a sufficient degree to make them an effective force in U.S. politics while simultaneously maintaining or developing interests, contacts, and investments in Mexico. Furthermore, many migrants believe that the Mexican government is inconsistent in its recognition of dual nationality but not dual citizenship.

Even Mexican citizens do not have the full rights of citizenship when they are outside Mexican territory – including, most conspicuously, the right to vote. PRD legislators have argued that Mexicans residing abroad are entitled to vote because they are affected by Mexican government policies. They maintain, for example, that migrants should be able to demand that the Mexican government respond to U.S. immigration policies. According to this argument, migrants can protect themselves from abuses in the United States by engaging in politics in Mexico. Many U.S.–based migrant groups that promote the vote abroad, such as the Mexican Assembly for Effective Suffrage, have aligned closely with the PRD.[17] Other organizations, such as the Binational Alliance for the Vote Without Borders, present themselves as nonpartisan (Martínez and Ross 2002). Historically, the PAN has offered only tepid support for the right to vote abroad (Pérez Godoy 1998), although President Fox has publicly supported this right (McDonnell 2000).

16 There is no single phenomenon that can be called "Mexican nationalism," but the forms discussed here are particularly salient in the discourse of government, civil society, and the mass media.

17 As early as 1929, *La Opinión* in Los Angeles called upon the Mexican president to give Mexicans in the United States the right to vote (Valenzuela Arce 1999: 283). For an insider's perspective on emigrant organizations seeking the vote abroad, see Ross Pineda 1999 and Martínez and Ross 2002.

The PRI purports to accept extending suffrage rights to Mexicans abroad, but it has not supported this position in practice. In July 1996, the PRI–dominated Congress amended the Constitution to allow Mexicans to vote for president outside their respective district of residence.[18] The amendment would allow Mexican citizens to vote from abroad, but only if enabling legislation is passed directing the Federal Electoral Institute (IFE) to organize elections outside Mexico (Molinar Horcasitas 1999). The opposition-controlled federal Chamber of Deputies passed the implementing law in July 1999, but the PRI–controlled Senate killed the measure (*La Jornada* 1999). Most commentators – and evidently the PRI as well, at least at the time – believe that migrant voters would favor the PRD or the PAN. The PRI historically discouraged democratic participation from citizens within Mexico, and during the late 1990s it did not perceive any self-interest in encouraging electoral participation from citizens abroad (Martínez and Ross 2002).

Mexican citizens voting from abroad could have a significant impact upon electoral politics. In 1998, the IFE projected that on election day 2000 there would be a universe of almost 10 million potential Mexican voters living abroad, including 6.1 million migrants who had not acquired a foreign nationality, approximately 1 million migrants who had acquired another nationality by naturalization, and 2.7 million persons born abroad to at least one Mexican parent. The population of potential citizens living abroad (over 98 percent of whom were in the United States) would represent 14 percent of the total Mexican adult population (IFE 1998).[19] A further 857,000 Mexican residents would be abroad temporarily on election day.

If citizenship were interpreted broadly and a large proportion of absentees voted, Mexicans abroad could exercise tremendous influence. However, if only those voters abroad with a current IFE credential (about 1.5 million individuals) were allowed to participate, actual electoral participation would likely be a few hundred thousand people, just a small fraction of the 37.6 million ballots cast for president in July 2000 (see www.ife.org.mx).

There are difficult logistical problems associated with implementing the right to vote abroad, such as how voters would be registered, where polling sites would be located, and what kind of voting credential would be acceptable (Molinar Horcasitas 1999). Some of the mechanisms to ensure electoral transparency that opposition parties negotiated with the PRI after years of political struggle would be difficult to implement abroad. Ironically, the high potential for fraud has been a main PRI argument against expanding the right to vote abroad. Opponents of the vote abroad have also raised concerns about the expense of extra-territorial elections, the potential influence of the U.S. government and media, and the specter of U.S. Immigration and Naturalization Service raids on polling sites.

18 See Martínez and Ross 2002 on the history of changes in constitutional and election law relating to citizens abroad.

19 The total Mexico-born population in the United States rose from 5.3 percent of Mexico's total population in 1990 to 7.7 percent in 1994 (De la Garza et al. 2000: 53).

Beyond technical objections and party interests, there is a tension between the theoretical principles of citizenship that are at stake in the right to vote abroad. Voting from abroad is an exercise of extra-territorial citizenship through which migrants claim citizenship in their country and community of origin even when they are physically absent (Fitzgerald 2000). As in ancient Rome, citizens "own" their right of citizenship, regardless of their place of residence. Citizenship can, however, be differentiated by multiple levels of simultaneous membership in different polities. Those who object to the right to vote abroad apply the model of ancient Greece, where citizenship was territorially bounded, duties were empha- sized as well as rights, and citizenship was based upon daily participation in the public life of the community (Pocock 1998, Oldfield 1998). Migrants who reside outside the polity cannot fulfill their obligations in a Greek model, and therefore they do not deserve the full rights of citizenship.

Over forty countries (including the United States) grant their citizens the right to vote abroad (Martínez and Ross 2002). However, the concepts of dual nation- ality and voting from abroad have strong ideological critics in both Mexico and in the United States. For example, note the reaction of newspaper columnist Juan Antonio Guerrero, writing from an area of Michoacán with historically high levels of emigration:

> Some unhappy person, who was possibly brainwashed in a Yankee university, had the bad idea that Mexicans who renounce their fatherland and swear loyalty to the flag of the stars and stripes should not lose their Mexican nationality for this felony, but rather should keep intact the rights of citizenship (Guerrero 1998).

Guerrero concluded that dual nationals were not really Mexicans and would be a tool of the United States to "screw over" Mexico. Opponents of the right to vote abroad claim that migrants "live a different reality" and therefore do not deserve inclusion in Mexican affairs.[20] Negative attitudes toward Mexicans who have emigrated to the United States and toward their U.S.–born descendants are common in Mexico. In a 1997 survey of Mexico City residents, 47 percent of respondents said they had a "negative or very negative" impression of Mexicans who go to work in the United States (in González Gutiérrez 1998).[21]

In the United States, analysts who oppose immigration raise the specter of "balkanization" and the end of "national unity" (Brimelow 1995, Geyer 2000). Some commentators are concerned that migrant voting in Mexican elections will further suppress the already low rates of naturalization and voting among Mexican

---

20 Author's interviews with local political leaders in migrant sending communities in Michoa- cán, 1999–2000.

21 A survey in an area of Mexico with higher emigration rates might find different attitudes. Mexico City historically has not been a major sending area, although migrants are increas- ingly likely to originate there (Marcelli and Cornelius 2001). "Emigrants have less of an overall impact on national life than would otherwise be expected," given that Mexico City domi- nates Mexico to such a large degree (De la Garza et al. 2000: 68).

immigrants, politically divide the Mexican and Mexican-origin population, and provide a target for nativists who question immigrants' loyalty to the United States (Ayón 1996).

Both Cuauhtémoc Cárdenas and Vicente Fox campaigned in the United States in May 2000 and urged their followers either to return to Mexico and vote or to influence their family members by phone or mail (J. Anderson 2000). In the absence of the right to vote abroad, some U.S.–resident Mexican citizens returned to Mexico individually and in small caravans to cast ballots in the 2000 general elections. The IFE established 64 special polling sites in the six Mexican states that border the United States.[22] Each site had only 750 ballots, for a total of 48,000 ballots. This supply was quickly exhausted, and many returnees could not vote. Because Mexico-resident citizens in transit voted at the same special polling sites (and outnumbered emigrants in some places; B. Fox 2000), the emigrant share of these 48,000 ballots cannot be determined. It was, however, clearly a mere fraction of the 37.6 million ballots cast for president nationwide.[23] Even assuming that some emigrants voted in their districts of residence or at scattered special sites in the interior of Mexico, the emigrant vote had little direct impact upon the 2000 election.

For most migrants, returning to Mexico to vote requires a major commitment of time and money. Undocumented migrants are unlikely to return home specifically to vote because of the great expense and physical risk involved in reentering the United States illegally. Moreover, most Mexicans in the United States do not have valid voting credentials. To obtain such a credential, migrants must return to their hometowns, apply at the local IFE office, and then wait four to six weeks for the credential. Most migrants return to the United States before their credentials are ready; they then have two years in which to return to collect the credential in person.[24] Thus a U.S.–resident Mexican who wishes to vote must make a series of well-planned trips to Mexico to apply for the credential, collect it, and cast a ballot. Considering all these obstacles, it is not surprising that so few Mexican emigrants voted in 2000.

It is difficult to judge emigrants' indirect influence upon family members in sending communities. In the 2000 elections in at least one PAN stronghold in Michoacán where emigration rates are extremely high, migrants generally supported Fox. For the most part, however, emigrants did not appear to make strong

22 In the 2000 elections there were a limited number of special voting sites throughout Mexico to accommodate citizens in transit. At regular polling sites, poll workers and party representatives match voters' credentials with copies of the credentials of all registered voters in each precinct. Special sites do not have these controls. Opposition parties like the Party of the Democratic Revolution (PRD) and the National Action Party (PAN), which likely would have benefited most from increased numbers of special ballots along the border, had been wary of allowing too many special ballots for fear of fraud.

23 See www.ife.org.mx.

24 Author's interview with a Federal Electoral Institute (IFE) official in Jiquilpan, Michoacán, July 2000.

partisan appeals to family members or return to Mexico to vote in the 2000 elections (Fitzgerald 2000).

Several Mexican citizens who were at least part-time residents of the United States ran for seats in the Mexican Congress in 2000. The three PRD candidates – who lived in Chicago, Arizona, and Los Angeles – lost (Claiborne 2000, Steller 2000). However, Eddie Varón Levy, a 42-year-old legal consultant in Los Angeles who had lived in the United States for over twenty years, won a PRI congressional seat in a district in the greater Mexico City area. Varón Levy was the first Mexican living abroad to win congressional office, but his election (based upon a party list rather than the direct popular vote) was due more to his political ties in Mexico than to a base of support among U.S.–resident Mexicans. Varón Levy, who supported extending suffrage to Mexicans abroad, stated that he would represent Mexicans in both the United States and the Mexico City area (Olivo and Kraul 2000).

Mexican leaders in Los Angeles have proposed the creation of an extra-territorial district to represent Mexicans abroad in the Mexican Congress. The PRD and some sectors of the PAN have responded favorably to this idea. In 2000, PAN legislators introduced a bill to allocate ten seats in the 500–seat federal Chamber of Deputies to U.S.–resident Mexican citizens. In a postelection meeting with Mexican community leaders in Los Angeles, Fox promised to consider the creation of such a district, although the breadth and depth of PAN support for the measure was questionable (McDonnell 2000, Sheridan 2000). The PRD chapter in Los Angeles, citing the example of a global extra-territorial congressional district that Colombia created in 1991,[25] called for the election of congressional representatives from abroad in the 2003 midterm elections.[26] However, the requisite legislation was not passed in time.

Who Cares about Mexican Politics?

Studies of transborder nationalism, like studies of nationalism more generally (Brubaker 1998), tend to emphasize the nationalist activities and discourses of political elites or activists without adequately addressing the resonance of nationalism in daily life. Political entrepreneurs can identify and negotiate the boundaries of a national community, but whether ascribed members will self-identify as members – and the degree of their identification – remains uncertain.

Existing survey data only measure transborder nationalist attitudes indirectly. The two most important surveys predate the recent wave of intensive transborder activity on the part of both U.S.–resident Mexicans and the Mexican government (De la Garza and DeSipio 1998). Attitudes are also fluid. A longitudinal study of

25 Despite the existence of the special district and the right to vote abroad, only a small percentage of Colombian immigrants residing in the United States have participated in Colombian congressional or presidential elections (Jones-Correa 2000).

26 Author's interview with PRD activists in Anaheim, California, June 2000.

over 700 second-generation Mexican adolescents found in 1992 that only 17 percent identified themselves as "Mexican," while 80 percent self-identified as "American" or "Hispanic." Four years later, following backlashes against immigrants, bilingual education, and affirmative action, over 40 percent of the respondents had shifted to identify themselves as "Mexican" (Portes 1999). However, these data do not reveal respondents' understandings of "Mexican" or the extent to which (or in what ways) self-identified Mexicans might relate to Mexico.

In the 1988 National Latino Immigrant Survey, 98 percent of adult Mexican immigrants either eligible for naturalization or already naturalized said they planned to live permanently in the United States. Fifty-eight percent said their "primary national identification" was with Mexico, although that identification decreased with length of residence in the United States (De la Garza and DeSipio 1998). The survey excluded Mexican immigrants ineligible for U.S. citizenship, a population that is likely to have stronger ties with Mexico. The 1989–1990 Latino National Political Survey found that, among respondents of Mexican origin, "2 percent of citizens and 20 percent of noncitizens say they are more concerned with Mexican politics than with U.S. politics, while 90 percent of citizens and 38 percent of noncitizens say they are more concerned with U.S. politics than with Mexican politics." The survey data also suggested that Mexicans and Mexican Americans had negative views of the Mexican government and Mexican elections. "Although they have positive feelings for Mexico as a nation, their feelings toward the United States are much stronger" (De la Garza and DeSipio 1998).

Survey data indicate that, at the aggregate level, identification with Mexico decreases with length of residence in the United States. However, most HTAs are led by immigrant men who have lived in the United States for many years and have achieved financial security (Zabin and Escala Rabadán 1998). Transborder activities and attitudes can be sustained or stimulated over time, particularly among a core of activists.

There is also a gendered aspect to this process. Michael Jones-Correa (1998) found that Latino immigrant men in New York City are more likely than women to become involved in transborder politics. In part this may be because men are more likely to suffer a loss of social status when they emigrate. Status can be (re)attained through transborder action or by returning to the home country. Immigrant women are more likely to gain status in the United States and become familiar with institutions like schools and government social services, and they are more likely than men to want to settle in the United States. Ethnographic evidence from California supports these findings (Hondagneu-Sotelo 1994).

Since anti-immigrant politics crystallized in 1994 with the debate over California's Proposition 187 (a legislative initiative that sought to restrict undocumented immigrants' access to education and public services), there has been a wave of defensive naturalizations among Mexicans, who historically have one of the lowest naturalization rates. However, naturalization does not necessarily suggest a shift in identification to another country. It may, for example, be part of a strategy to elect politicians less hostile to immigrants or Latinos in general, or to maintain access to social rights that were further restricted to citizens in the 1996 federal welfare law (González Baker et al. 1998). Adopting U.S. citizenship could allow Mexican-origin residents to become a more effective lobby in the United States, but it might also mark a step away from political engagement with Mexico.

Jorge Bustamante has argued that Mexico's dual nationality law was intended to encourage Mexican nationals to become U.S. citizens in order to vote against anti-immigrant politicians like former California governor Pete Wilson, who endorsed Proposition 187 (in Martínez and Ross 2002). The Mexican-origin population in the United States and the Mexican government might tend to view politicians like Wilson as a common enemy, but that does not make Chicanos a lobby for the Mexican government's efforts to ease U.S. immigration restrictions. According to the Latino National Political Survey, more than 75 percent of Mexican American citizens feel that there are "too many immigrants in the United States." This is virtually the same proportion found among Anglos and non-U.S. citizen Mexicans (De la Garza and DeSipio 1998). The overwhelming Latino vote against Proposition 187 apparently reflected these voters' perception of an attack on Latinos in general rather than their support for increased immigration (Uhlaner 1996). History offers little evidence that Mexican Americans will be a strong ally for promoting Mexico's policy interests in Washington, even if there are areas of common interest (De la Garza et al. 2000).

Although the attitudinal and historical data suggest that most Mexican Americans are unlikely to participate in Mexican politics either as an ethnic lobby in the United States or in some other fashion, U.S.–resident Mexican citizens express interest in Mexican politics. A 1982 survey of Mexican citizens in Los Angeles, Chicago, and San Antonio, Texas, found that 77 percent of the respondents supported the right to vote abroad in Mexican elections (Bustamante 1982). In a 1998 IFE study of naturalized and unnaturalized Mexicans living in the United States, 65 percent said they knew there would be a presidential election in Mexico in 2000, and 83 percent said they would like to vote in that election if they were able to do so from the United States. Fifty-five percent of those who expressed an interest in voting said they would vote if the process took less than an hour, and 21 percent said they would spend a day or more of their time to vote (IFE 1998). Not surprisingly, Mexico-born immigrants appear much more likely than Chicanos to engage in Mexican politics. González Gutiérrez (1995) has noted that the Mexican government should act quickly to build ties with the Mexican-origin population before Mexico-born immigrants decline as a share of the total Mexican-origin population.[27]

---

27 In 1996 Mexico-born immigrants made up 38 percent of the total Mexican-origin population in the United States. See González Baker et al. 1998.

Looking Forward

During the 1990s, emigrant organizations and Mexico's opposition parties sought to redefine Mexican nationhood to include emigrants in the political community. The Zedillo administration responded by promoting an expansive redefinition of Mexican nationhood in an attempt to promote the influence of the PRI and the domestic and international power of the Mexican state. Paradoxically, the government sought to expand state power by defining nationality in less state-centered terms to include Mexicans outside the country's territorial boundaries. In doing so, however, it only acknowledged a truncated form of citizenship for extra-territorial nationals.

The PAN's presidential victory in July 2000 opened the way to important changes in state-emigrant relations. Fox's migration policy focused principally upon an attempt to negotiate a legalization and guest worker agreement with the United States. Migrant activists and Latino political organizations supported the legalization program, although its prospects remained uncertain in the wake of significant U.S. congressional opposition and the political climate following the September 11, 2001 attacks in the United States (*Migration News* 2002).

It remains to be seen whether President Fox will comply with his promise to extend the right to vote abroad, how much political capital he is prepared to expend in that effort, and what the eventual outcome will be. The PAN and the PRD had the capacity to form an ad hoc coalition to pass the necessary legislation in both houses of Congress. If Fox were to orchestrate the enabling legislation, emigrant voters in the 2006 presidential election would likely reward his party. Yet many *panistas* offer only tepid support for the measure, and some strongly oppose it.[28]

What are the likely political consequences if Fox does not follow through with a good-faith effort to extend suffrage abroad? The vote-abroad movement in the United States can apply moral suasion and indirect pressure, but to pass the required legislation it must rely upon political allies within Mexico. Its main ally, the PRD, was severely weakened in the 2000 elections, with PRD representation in the federal Chamber of Deputies dropping from 125 to 53 seats (Urrutia 2000).[29] Most emigrant organizations have limited political leverage outside their sending communities, and there is no effective umbrella organization of emigrant groups.[30]

Organizations such as the recently formed coalition of HTAs in Los Angeles could become more important actors in this arena. In 1999 a coalition based upon

---

28 Other measures – such as allowing Mexicans to obtain voting credentials at Mexican consulates and increasing the number of special border polling places and ballots – would encourage higher emigrant electoral participation without allowing Mexicans to vote abroad.

29 The PRD recouped some (but not all) of these losses in the 2003 midterm elections.

30 The International Coalition of Mexicans Abroad formed in 2000, but it quickly collapsed as a result of internal partisan divisions (Notimex 2001).

the vote-abroad movement forced the Mexican government to withdraw its plan to require anyone bringing a U.S.–made vehicle into Mexico to leave a sizable sum of money on deposit until the vehicle exited the country (J. Fox 2000). Emigrant organizations could, moreover, refuse to cooperate with the Mexican government on joint public works or investment projects, even though these projects have represented only a small fraction of total remittances (Lozano Ascencio 1993). Most remittances are made at the household level and are not subject to political bargaining.

However, the high-profile attention that President Fox has shown to emigrants, as well as their mutual interests on questions of efficient remittance mechanisms, investment, public works projects, and immigration policy, suggest that a more cooperative relationship between emigrants and the Fox administration is likely. One of his first acts as president was to meet with hundreds of emigrants and Chicanos in Mexico City (J. Smith 2000). Fox appointed Juan Hernández, a U.S. citizen raised in Guanajuato, as the first director of a new cabinet-level office of migrant affairs. Hernández regularly visited Mexican populations in the United States seeking support for a new *padrino* (godfather) program in which emigrants and Mexican Americans would "sponsor" a sending community in Mexico by investing in employment-creating enterprises. But the program yielded few projects (*Migration News* 2002), and in mid-2002 the office was closed.

If Fox's emigrant policies appear excessively partisan, he runs the risk of appearing to be little different from PRI politicians, toward whom emigrants and Chicanos have been critical. Many Mexican emigrants have been reticent to participate in consular-sponsored activities because they view the consular network as a partisan tool (González Gutiérrez 1995, Fitzgerald 2000). If consular officials appear to be acting as *panista* partisans, emigrant participation is likely to be suppressed. In contrast, a perceived depoliticization of Mexican consulates would probably strengthen programs like the PCME and mechanisms for emigrant investment. A PAN government's success in promoting substantial emigrant investment would not only improve emigrants' perceptions of the PAN, but it would also provide them with strong incentives to participate actively in the Mexican political process in order to protect their material interests.

Some commentators have assumed that binationally active or returned migrants will have a democratizing influence upon Mexico because of their exposure to the competitive party politics and democratic milieu of the United States (Gamio 1969, Castañeda 1993). There is, however, little evidence to support this assumption. Dresser argued that the PRD party organization in California mistakenly assumed that all Mexicans in the state shared the PRD's interest in a more democratic Mexican government, whereas many U.S.–resident Mexicans have narrow interests organized around their particular migration circuit (1993: 102). Nor do many HTA leaders have experience in U.S. politics (González Gutiérrez 1995). The impacts of transborder political action are, then, still largely unknown.

Although cross-border politics raises important normative questions about the nature of citizenship and the absentees' accountability to residents affected by their actions, greater political expression for extra-territorial nationals would likely encourage the decentralization and democratization of Mexican politics. The most significant forms of cross-border activity are oriented toward a distant locality. The federal government sometimes participates in cross-border activities that take place at the hometown and home state levels through matching-fund programs and consular activities, but localist actors have a significant degree of autonomy. As a larger percentage of migrants come from source communities outside the historical emigration zone of west-central Mexico (Marcelli and Cornelius 2001), emigrants may expand their influence geographically and further decentralize their own economic and political power. Decentralization, however, is no guarantee of democratization. Illiberal politics has thrived in some subnational contexts even as national politics has become more democratic (Cornelius 1999), and clientelism remains a feature of many transborder networks. Nevertheless, greater inclusion of emigrants would strengthen government accountability.

Over six million Mexicans living in the United States in 2000 were not U.S. citizens. These millions are effectively disenfranchised – or have disenfranchised themselves – in both countries. Although Mexican migrants increasingly settle in the United States (Marcelli and Cornelius 2001) and express less interest in Mexican politics over lengthy periods of residence and several generations, many first-generation migrants will continue to seek a greater political voice in Mexico. They are unlikely to be satisfied having a Mexican president speak on their behalf until they have the right to participate in the presidential selection process.

References

Akzin, Benjamin. 1966. *States and Nations*. Garden City, N.Y.: Anchor.

Alarcón, Rafael. 1986. "Los primeros norteños de Chavinda," *Relaciones* 3: 163–86.

Anderson, Benedict. 1991. *Imagined Communities: Reflections on the Origin and Spread of Nationalism*. New York: Verso.

——. 1998. *The Spectre of Comparisons: Nationalism, Southeast Asia, and the World*. London: Verso.

Anderson, John Ward. 2000. "Politicians without Borders: Mexico's Candidates Court Support of Migrants in U.S.," *Washington Post*, May 9.

Ayón, David R. 1996. "Democratization Imperils U.S. Latino Empowerment," *Los Angeles Times*, May 26.

Balderrama, Francisco. 1982. *In Defense of La Raza: The Los Angeles Mexican Consulate and the Mexican Community, 1929 to 1936*. Tucson: University of Arizona Press.

Basch, Linda, Nina Glick Schiller, and Cristina Szanton Blanc. 1994. *Nations Unbound: Transnational Projects, Postcolonial Predicaments, and Deterritorialized Nation-States*. Langhorne, Penn.: Gordon and Breach.

Breuilly, John. 1994. *Nationalism and the State*. 2d ed. Chicago, Ill.: University of Chicago Press.

Brimelow, Peter. 1995. *Alien Nation: Common Sense about America's Immigration Disaster*. New York: Random House.

Brubaker, Rogers. 1998. "Myths and Misconceptions in the Study of Nationalism." In *The State of the Nation: Ernest Gellner and the Theory of Nationalism*, edited by John Hall. Cambridge: Cambridge University Press.

Bustamante, Jorge A. 1982. "Mexicanos residentes en Estados Unidos." Tijuana, Mexico: Centro de Estudios Fronterizos del Norte de Mexico.

———. 1986. "Chicano-Mexicano Relations from Practice to Theory." In *Chicano-Mexicano Relations*, edited by Tatcho Mindiola, Jr., and Max Martinez. Mexican American Studies Monographs, no. 4. Houston, Tex.: Mexican American Studies Program, University of Houston, University Park.

Calhoun, Craig. 1987. *Nationalism*. Minneapolis: University of Minnesota Press.

Castañeda, Jorge G. 1993. "Mexico and California: The Paradox of Tolerance and Dedemocratization." In *The California-Mexico Connection*, edited by Abraham F. Lowenthal and Katrina Burgess. Stanford, Calif.: Stanford University Press.

Claiborne, William. 2000. "3 Expatriates Appear to Lose Congress Bids," *Washington Post*, July 4.

Cleeland, Nancy. 2000. "Mexican "Hometown Clubs' Turn Activist," *Los Angeles Times*, June 8.

Cornelius, Wayne A. 1999. "Subnational Politics and Democratization: Tensions between Center and Periphery in the Mexican Political System." In *Subnational Politics and Democratization in Mexico*, edited by Wayne A. Cornelius, Todd A. Eisenstadt, and Jane Hindley. La Jolla: Center for U.S.–Mexican Studies, University of California, San Diego.

———. 2001. "Death at the Border: The Efficacy and Unintended Consequences of U.S. Immigration Control Policy," *Population and Development Review* 27 (4): 661–85.

Craig, Ann L. 1983. *The First Agraristas: An Oral History of a Mexican Agrarian Reform Movement*. Berkeley: University of California Press.

De la Garza, Rodolfo O. 1986. "Chicanos as an Ethnic Lobby: Limits and Possibilities." In *Chicano-Mexicano Relations*, edited by Tatcho Mindiola, Jr., and Max Martinez. Mexican American Studies Monographs, no. 4. Houston, Tex.: Mexican American Studies Program, University of Houston, University Park.

———. 1997. "Foreign Policy Comes Home: The Domestic Consequences of the Program for Mexican Communities Living in Foreign Countries." In *Bridging the Border: Transforming Mexico–U.S. Relations*, edited by Rodolfo O. de la Garza and Jesús Velasco. Lanham, Md.: Rowman and Littlefield.

De la Garza, Rodolfo O., Harry P. Pachon, Manuel Orozco, and Adrián D. Pantoja. 2000. "Family Ties and Ethnic Lobbies." In *Latinos and U.S. Foreign Policy: Representing the "Homeland"?* edited by Rodolfo O. de la Garza and Harry P. Pachon. Lanham, Md.: Rowman and Littlefield.

De la Garza, Rodolfo O., and Louis DeSipio. 1998. "Interests Not Passions: Mexican-American Attitudes toward Mexico, Immigration from Mexico, and Other Issues Shaping U.S.–Mexico Relations," *International Migration Review* 32: 401–22.

De la Garza, Rodolfo O., and Claudio Vargas. 1992. "The Mexican-Origin Population of the United States as a Political Force in the Borderlands: From Paisanos to Pochos to Potential Political Allies." In *Changing Boundaries in the Americas: New Perspectives on the U.S.–Mexican, Central American, and South American Borders*, edited by Lawrence A. Herzog. La Jolla: Center for U.S.–Mexican Studies, University of California, San Diego.

Dresser, Denise. 1993. "Exporting Conflict: Transboundary Consequences of Mexican Politics." In *The California-Mexico Connection*, edited by Abraham F. Lowenthal and Katrina Burgess. Stanford, Calif.: Stanford University Press.

Espinosa, Víctor. 1999. "La Federación de Clubes Michoacanos en Illinois: construyendo puentes entre Chicago y Michoacán." Chicago, Ill.: Heartland Alliance for Human Needs and Human Rights.

Félix, Edgar. 1999. "La suave patria y Estados Unidos," *El Financiero*, January 13.

Fitzgerald, David. 2000. *Negotiating Extra-Territorial Citizenship: Mexican Migration and the Transnational Politics of Community*. Monograph Series, no. 2. La Jolla: Center for Comparative Immigration Studies, University of California, San Diego.

Fonseca, Omar. 1988. "De Jaripo a Stockton, California: un caso de migración en Michoacán." In *Movimientos de población en el occidente de México*, edited by Thomas Calvo and Gustavo López. Zamora, Mexico: El Colegio de Michoacán.

Fox, Ben. 2000. "Mexicans Head South To Cast Ballots," Associated Press, July 3.

Fox, Jonathan. 2000. "Assessing Binational Civil Society Coalitions: Lessons from the Mexico–U.S. Experience." Paper presented at the international congress of the Latin American Studies Association, Miami, March.

Gamio, Manuel. [1930] 1969. *Mexican Immigration to the United States: A Study of Human Migration and Adjustment*. New York: Arno.

García-Acevedo, María Rosa. 1996. "Return to Aztlán: Mexico's Policies towards Chicanas/os." In *Chicanas/Chicanos at the Crossroads*, edited by David R. Maciel and Isidro O. Ortiz. Tucson: University of Arizona Press.

Garrison, Jessica. 2002. "Farmer Gives Up Mexican Mayoralty," *Los Angeles Times*, January 28.

Geyer, Georgie Anne. 2000. "Mexican Leaders Encourage Split Loyalties," *The American Enterprise*, December.

Gledhill, John. 1993. *Casi nada: capitalismo, estado y los campesinos de Guaracha*. Zamora, Mexico: El Colegio de Michoacán.

Goldring, Luin. 1999a. "El Estado mexicano y las organizaciones transmigrantes: ¿reconfigurando la nación y las relaciones entre Estado y sociedad civil?" In *Fronteras fragmentadas*, edited by Gail Mummert. Zamora, Mexico: El Colegio de Michoacán.

———. 1999b. "From Market Membership to Transnational Citizenship? The Changing Politization of Transnational Social Spaces." Chicano-Latino Research Center Working Paper. Santa Cruz: University of California, Santa Cruz.

Gómez-Quiñones, Juan. 1973. "Piedras contra la luna. México en Aztlán y Aztlán en México: Chicano-Mexicano Relations and the Mexican Consulates, 1900–1920, An Extended Research Note." Paper presented at the International Congress of Mexican Studies, Santa Monica, California, October.

———. 1983. "Notes on an Interpretation of the Relations between the Mexican Community in the United States and Mexico." In *Mexican–U.S. Relations: Conflict and Convergence*, edited by Carlos Vásquez and Manuel García y Griego. Los Angeles: Chicano Studies Research Center, University of California, Los Angeles.

González, Gilbert G. 1999. *Mexican Consuls and Labor Organizing: Imperial Politics in the American Southwest*. Austin: University of Texas Press.

González Baker, Susan, Frank D. Bean, Agustín Escobar Latapí, and Sidney Weintraub. 1998. "U.S. Immigration Policies and Trends: The Growing Importance of Migration from Mexico." In *Crossings: Mexican Immigration in Interdisciplinary Perspective*, edited by Marcelo M. Suárez-Orozco. Cambridge, Mass.: David Rockefeller Center for Latin American Studies, Harvard University.

González Gutiérrez, Carlos. 1995. "La organización de los inmigrantes mexicanos en Los Angeles: la lealtad de los oriundos," *Revista Mexicana de Política Exterior* 46: 59–101.

———. 1997. "Decentralized Diplomacy: The Role of Consular Offices in Mexico's Relations with Its Diaspora." In *Bridging the Border: Transforming Mexico–U.S. Relations*, edited by Rodolfo O. de la Garza and Jesús Velasco. Lanham, Md.: Rowman and Littlefield.

———. 1998. "Mexicans in the United States: An Incipient Diaspora." Paper presented at the workshop "Advancing the International Interests of African-Americans, Asian-Americans, and Latinos," Pacific Council on International Policy, Los Angeles, California, March.

González Navarro, Moisés. 1994. *Los extranjeros en México y los mexicanos en el extranjero, 1821–1970.* Vol. 3. Mexico City: El Colegio de México.

Guerrero, Juan Antonio. 1998. "Chicanos y mecsicanos," *Guía,* April 19.

Gutiérrez, Armando. 1986. "The Chicano Elite in Chicano-Mexicano Relations." In *Chicano-Mexicano Relations,* edited by Tatcho Mindiola, Jr., and Max Martinez. Mexican American Studies Monographs, no. 4. Houston, Tex.: Mexican American Studies Program, University of Houston, University Park.

Gutiérrez, David G. 1995. *Walls and Mirrors: Mexican Americans, Mexican Immigrants, and the Politics of Ethnicity.* Berkeley: University of California Press.

Hondagneu-Sotelo, Pierrette. 1994. *Gendered Transitions: Mexican Experiences of Immigration.* Berkeley: University of California Press.

IFE (Instituto Federal Electoral). 1998. "Informe final que presenta la comisión de especialistas que estudia las modalidades del voto de los mexicanos residentes en el extranjero," *Perfil de La Jornada,* November 16.

Jones-Correa, Michael. 1998. *Between Two Nations: The Political Predicament of Latinos in New York City.* Ithaca, N.Y.: Cornell University Press.

———. 2000. "Under Two Flags: Dual Nationality in Latin America and Its Consequences for the United States." Working Papers on Latin America, no. 99/00–3. Cambridge, Mass.: David Rockefeller Center for Latin American Studies, Harvard University.

La Jornada. 1999. "México: PRI boicotea debate de reforma electoral en el Senado," July 1.

Lozano Ascencio, Fernando. 1993. *Bringing It Back Home: Remittances to Mexico from Migrant Workers in the United States.* Monograph Series, no. 37. La Jolla: Center for U.S.–Mexican Studies, University of California, San Diego.

Kraul, Chris. 2000. "Tapping Generosity of Emigrants," *Los Angeles Times,* June 8.

Marcelli, Enrico A. and Wayne A. Cornelius. 2001. "The Changing Profile of Mexican Migrants to the United States: New Evidence from California and Mexico," *Latin American Research Review* 36 (3): 105–31.

Martínez, Jesús, and Raúl Ross. 2002. "Suffrage for Mexicans Residing Abroad." In *Cross-Border Dialogues: U.S.–Mexico Social Movement Networking,* edited by David Brooks and Jonathan Fox. La Jolla: Center for U.S.–Mexican Studies, University of California, San Diego.

Martínez Saldaña, Jesús. 1993. "At the Periphery of Democracy: The Binational Politics of Mexican Immigrants in Silicon Valley." Ph.D. diss., University of California, Berkeley.

Massey, Douglas S., Rafael Alarcón, Jorge Durand, and Humberto González. 1987. *Return to Aztlán: The Social Process of International Migration from Western Mexico.* Berkeley: University of California Press.

McDonnell, Patrick J. 2000. "Fox Vows Better Ties with Mexican Immigrants in U.S.," *Los Angeles Times,* November 11.

Migration News. 2002. "Mexico: Legalization, Returns, Economy," 9 (2), February [http://migration.ucdavis.edu/mn/archive_mn/feb_2002–04mn.html].

Molinar Horcasitas, Juan. 1999. "Una aproximación al caso de México." Paper presented at the University of California Comparative Immigration and Integration Program Research Workshop, Center for U.S.–Mexican Studies, University of California, San Diego, February.

NALEO (National Association of Latino Elected Officials). 1990. *The National Latino Immigrant Survey.* Los Angeles: NALEO Educational Fund.

New York Times. 2000. "Mexican President Praises Migrant 'Heroes,'" December 12.

Notimex. 2001. "A punto de expirar organización mexicana," *Excélsior* (Santa Ana, Calif.), January 12.

Oldfield, Adrian. 1998. "Citizenship and Community: Civic Republicanism and the Modern World." In *The Citizenship Debates,* edited by Gershon Shafir. Minneapolis: University of Minnesota Press.

Olivo, Antonio, and Chris Kraul. 2000. "L.A. Man Shows Clout of Mexican Expatriates," *Los Angeles Times*, July 10.

Pérez Godoy, Mara S. 1998. "Social Movements and International Migration: The Mexican Diaspora Seeks Inclusion in Mexico's Political Affairs, 1968–1998." Ph.D. diss., University of Chicago.

Pocock, J. G. A. 1998. "The Ideal of Citizenship since Classical Times." In *The Citizenship Debates*, edited by Gershon Shafir. Minneapolis: University of Minnesota Press.

Portes, Alejandro. 1999. "Conclusion: Towards a New World: The Origins and Effects of Transnational Activities," *Ethnic and Racial Studies* [Special Issue: *Transnational Communities*, edited by Alejandro Portes, Luis E. Guarnizo, and Patricia Landolt] 22 (2): 462–77.

Rivera Salgado, Gaspar. 1999. "Migration and Political Activism: Mexican Transnational Indigenous Communities in a Comparative Perspective." Ph.D. diss., University of California, Santa Cruz.

Ross Pineda, Raúl. 1999. *Los mexicanos y el voto sin fronteras*. Chicago, Ill.: Salsedo Press / Centro de Estudios del Movimiento Obrero y Socialista, Universidad Autónoma de Sinaloa.

Salinas de Gortari, Carlos. 1982. *Political Participation, Public Investment, and Support for the System: A Comparative Study of Rural Communities in Mexico*. Research Report Series, no. 35. La Jolla: Center for U.S.–Mexican Studies, University of California, San Diego.

Sánchez, George J. 1993. *Becoming Mexican American: Ethnicity, Culture, and Identity in Chicano Los Angeles, 1900–1945*. New York: Oxford University Press.

Santamaría Gómez, Arturo. 1994. *La política entre México y Aztlán*. Culiacán, Mexico: Universidad Autónoma de Sinaloa.

Sheridan, Mary Beth. 1998. "Candidates from Mexico go Stumping in Southland," *Los Angeles Times*, July 31.

———. 2000. "Mexican Candidates Look to the U.S. for Swing Votes," *Los Angeles Times*, May 5.

Smith, Anthony. 1986. *The Ethnic Origins of Nations*. Oxford: Blackwell.

Smith, James F. 2000. "Fox Embraces Mexicans Living in U.S.," *Los Angeles Times*, December 4.

Smith, Robert Courtney. 1998a. "Transnational Localities: Community, Technology, and the Politics of Membership within the Context of Mexico and U.S. Migration." In *Transnationalism from Below*, edited by Michael Peter Smith and Luis Eduardo Guarnizo. New Brunswick, N.J.: Transaction.

———. 1998b. "Thick and Thin Membership within a Transnational Public Sphere: Diasporic Politics at Home, Domestic Politics Abroad, and the Program for Mexican Communities Abroad." Paper presented at the Willen Seminar, Barnard College, October.

SourceMex. 2000. "Expatriates Sent US$5.9 Billion in Remittances to Mexico in 1999," 11 (14), April 12.

Steller, Tim. 2000. "Part-time Tucsonan Loses Race for Mexican Congress," *Arizona Daily Star*, July 6.

Uhlaner, Carole J. 1996. "Latinos and Ethnic Politics in California: Participation and Preference." In *Latino Politics in California*, edited by Aníbal Yáñez-Chávez. La Jolla: Center for U.S.–Mexican Studies, University of California, San Diego.

Urrutia, Alonso. 2000. "Diputados del PRD culpan a su directiva del fracaso del 2 de julio," *La Jornada*, July 12.

Valdez, Diana Washington. 2000. "El Pasoans Pursue Mexican Nationality," *El Paso Times*, October 5.

Valenzuela Arce, José Manuel. 1999. "Diáspora social y doble nacionalidad." In *La identidad nacional mexicana como problema político y cultural*, edited by Raúl Bejar and Héctor Rosales. Mexico City: Siglo Veintiuno.

Weber, Devra. 1998. "Historical Perspectives on Transnational Mexican Workers in California."

In *Border Crossings: Mexican and Mexican-American Workers*, edited by John M. Hart. Wilmington, Del.: Scholarly Resources.

Zabin, Carol, and Luis Escala Rabadán. 1998. "Mexican Hometown Associations and Mexican Immigrant Political Empowerment in Los Angeles." Nonprofit Sector Research Fund Working Paper Series. Washington, D.C.: Aspen Institute.

Zazueta, Carlos H. 1983. "Mexican Political Actors in the United States and Mexico: Historical and Political Contexts of a Dialogue Renewed." In *Mexican–U.S. Relations: Conflict and Convergence*, edited by Carlos Vásquez and Manuel García y Griego. Los Angeles: Chicano Studies Research Center, University of California, Los Angeles.

Contributors

GRACIELA BENSUSÁN is Research Professor at the Universidad Autónoma Metropolitana-Xochimilco in Mexico City. She also teaches at the Facultad Latinoamericana de Ciencias Sociales (FLACSO)-México. Her research focuses primarily upon labor organizations and labor policies and institutions in Mexico. Professor Bensusán is author of, among other works, *Estándares laborales después del Tratado de Libre Comercio con América del Norte* (FLACSO-México / Friedrich Ebert Stiftung / Plaza y Valdés, 1999) and *El modelo mexicano de regulación laboral* (Friedrich Ebert Stiftung / Plaza y Valdés / FLACSO / Universidad Autónoma Metropolitana-Xochimilco, 2000) and coauthor of *Relaciones laborales en las pequeñas y medianas empresas de México* (Friedrich Ebert Stiftung and Juan Pablos Editor, 1996). She is also coeditor of *Negociación y conflicto laboral en México* (Friedrich Ebert Stiftung and FLACSO-México, 1991) and *Trabajo y trabajadores en el México contemporáneo* (Porrúa, 2000), which in 2001 received the book prize awarded by the Labor Studies Section of the Latin American Studies Association.

JORGE BUENDÍA LAREDO is Associate Professor of Political Science at the Instituto Tecnológico Autónomo de México in Mexico City. During 1996–1997 he was a Visiting Research Fellow at the Center for U.S.–Mexican Studies. He has published extensively on electoral behavior and public opinion in Mexico, including articles in *Comparative Political Studies*, *Desarrollo Económico*, and *Política y Gobierno*.

RODERIC CAMP is McKenna Professor of the Pacific Rim in the Department of Government at Claremont McKenna College (Claremont, California). He previously taught at Tulane University and Central College (Pella, Iowa). Professor Camp's research interests include Mexican politics and the comparative study of elites, political recruitment, church-state relations, and civil-military affairs. He is the author of many books and articles on Mexico, including *Mexico's Leaders: Their Education and Recruitment* (University of Arizona Press, 1980), *Entrepreneurs and Politics in Twentieth-Century Mexico* (Oxford University Press, 1985), *Intellectuals and the State in Twentieth-Century Mexico* (University of Texas Press, 1985), *Generals in the Palacio: The Military in Modern Mexico* (Oxford University Press, 1992), *Political Recruitment Across Two Centuries: Mexico* (University of Texas

Press, 1995), *Crossing Swords: Politics and Religion in Mexico* (Oxford University Press, 1997), *Mexico's Mandarins: Crafting a Power Elite for the Twenty-First Century* (University of California Press, 2002), and *Politics in Mexico: The Democratic Transformation* (Oxford University Press, 2003). Professor Camp also directed the Hewlett Foundation-supported project "Democracy Through Latin American Lenses."

LAURA CARLSEN is a writer and development policy analyst based in Mexico City. She holds a master's degree in Latin American Studies from Stanford University. Between 1988 and 1992 she served as staff writer and coeditor for such publications as *The Other Side of Mexico, PUEBLO, Mexico Update,* and *Business Mexico.* She is author of a book manuscript titled "When Stones Speak: Mexico's New Indigenous Movement" and coeditor of *Enfrentando la globalización: respuestas sociales a la integración económica en México* (Miguel Ángel Porrua, 2002) and *Fair Trade and Equity for Peasant Coffee Producers in Mexico* (Oxfam-Great Britain, 2002).

JOSÉ ANTONIO CRESPO is Research Professor at the Centro de Investigación y Docencia Económicas (CIDE) in Mexico City. During 1992–1993 he was a Visiting Research Fellow at the Center for U.S.–Mexican Studies. His many publications on political parties and elections include *Urnas de Pandora: partidos políticos y elecciones en el gobierno de Salinas* (Espasa Calpe / CIDE, 1995), *Jaque al rey: hacia un nuevo presidencialismo en México* (Joaquín Mortiz, 1996), *Votar en los estados: análisis comparado de las legislaciones electorales estatales en México* (Miguel Ángel Porrua / Fundación Naumann / CIDE, 1996), *¿Tiene futuro el PRI? Entre la supervivencia democrática y la desintegración total* (Grijalbo / Raya en el Agua, 1998), *Fronteras democráticas en México: retos, peculiaridades y comparaciones* (Océano / CIDE, 1999), *Los riesgos de la sucesión presidencial: actores e instituciones rumbo al 2000* (Centro de Estudios de Política Comparada, 1999), *PRI: de la hegemonía a la oposición; un estudio comparado, 1994–2001* (Centro de Estudios de Política Comparada, 1999), and *Fundamentos políticos de la rendición de cuentas* (Congreso de la Unión, 2002).

ALBERTO DÍAZ-CAYEROS is Assistant Professor of Political Science at Stanford University. He was previously an Associate Researcher at the Centro de Investigación para el Desarrollo, A.C. in Mexico City and Assistant Professor of Political Science at the University of California, Los Angeles. His research focuses principally upon federalism and the political economy of Mexican development. Professor Díaz-Cayeros is the author of *Desarrollo económico e inequidad regional: hacia un nuevo pacto federal en México* (Centro de Investigación para el Desarrollo, A.C. / Miguel Ángel Porrua / Fundación Naumann, 1995) and coeditor of *Memoria del Congreso Nacional de Ciencia Política: federalismo* (Congreso Nacional de Ciencia Política y Administración Pública, 1996) and *Dentro de México: estudios comparativos de gobierno local* (Miguel Ángel Porrua, 2003).

DAVID FITZGERALD is a Mellon Foundation Fellow in Latin American Sociology at the Department of Sociology, University of California, Los Angeles. He is the author of *Negotiating Extra-Territorial Citizenship: Mexican Migration and the Transnational Politics of Community* (Center for Comparative Immigration Studies, University of California, San Diego, 2000). His research focuses upon the relationship between international migration and nation-state building in migrant sending and receiving countries.

JONATHAN FOX is Professor of Social Sciences and Chair of the Department of Latin American and Latino Studies at the University of California, Santa Cruz. He has held postdoctoral fellowships from the Center for U.S.–Mexican Studies and the Council on Foreign Relations. Professor Fox is author of *The Politics of Food in Mexico: State Power and Social Mobilization* (Cornell University Press, 1993), co-author of *Decentralization and Rural Development in Mexico: Community Participation in Oaxaca's Municipal Funds Program* (Center for U.S.–Mexican Studies, University of California, San Diego, 1996), and editor or coeditor of *The Challenge of Rural Democratization: Perspectives from Latin America and the Philippines* (Frank Cass, 1990), *The Struggle for Accountability: The World Bank, NGOs, and Grassroots Movements* (MIT Press, 1998), and *Cross-Border Dialogues: Mexico-U.S. Social Movement Networking* (Center for U.S.–Mexican Studies, 2002).

SILVIA GÓMEZ TAGLE is Research Professor at the Center for Sociological Studies at El Colegio de México in Mexico City. She is also editor of *Revista Nueva Antropología* and a columnist for *La Jornada*, a leading Mexico City newspaper. Professor Gómez Tagle is author of, among other works, *De la alquimia al fraude en las elecciones mexicanas* (Plaza y Valdés Editores, 1994) and *La transición inconclusa: treinta años de elecciones en México* (El Colegio de México, 1997), as well as editor or coeditor of *Las elecciones federales de 1991: la recuperación oficial* (La Jornada Ediciones, 1993), *1994: elecciones en los estados* (La Jornada Ediciones / Centro de Investigaciones Interdisciplinarias en Ciencias y Humanidades, Universidad Nacional Autónoma de México, 1997), and *La geografía del poder y las elecciones en México* (Instituto Federal Electoral / Plaza y Valdés Editores, 2000). She was a member of the United Nations Electoral Observation Advisory Committee for Mexico's 2000 elections.

LUIS HERNÁNDEZ NAVARRO is Opinion Page Editor and a columnist at the national daily newspaper *La Jornada* in Mexico City. For many years he has worked as an adviser to diverse peasant and labor organizations, and he participated actively in the Chiapas peace negotiations, including serving as Technical Secretary on the Commission on Follow-up and Verification of the Peace Accords. Mtro. Hernández is the author of *Chiapas: la guerra y la paz* (Mexico City: ADN Editores, 1995) and *Chiapas: la nueva lucha india* (Madrid: Talasa, 1998), as well as coeditor of *Autonomía y nuevos sujetos sociales de desarrollo rural* (Mexico City: Siglo

Veintiuno, 1992) and *Los Acuerdos de San Andrés* (Mexico City: Era, 1998). His analyses of social movements in Mexico and anti-globalization movements since Seattle have appeared in academic and popular journals in Latin America, the United States, and Europe.

J. CHAPPELL H. LAWSON is Associate Professor of Political Science at the Massachusetts Institute of Technology, where he holds the Class of 1954 Career Development Chair. He has held postdoctoral fellowships at the Center for U.S.–Mexican Studies at the University of California, San Diego and at the Hoover Institution on War, Revolution, and Peace at Stanford University. Professor Lawson is the author of *Building the Fourth Estate: Democratization and the Rise of a Free Press in Mexico* (University of California Press, 2002) and numerous articles on Mexican media and public opinion.

MATILDE LUNA is Research Professor at the Institute of Social Research at the Universidad Nacional Autónoma de México (UNAM). Her work focuses principally upon business and politics and the generation and diffusion of knowledge in Mexico. She is the author of, among other works, *Los empresarios y el cambio político: México, 1970–1987* (Ediciones Era / UNAM, 1992) and editor or coeditor of *Relaciones corporativas en un periodo de transición* (UNAM, 1992), *El gobierno, la academia y los empresarios en México* (Plaza y Valdés Editores / UNAM, 1997), and *Itinearios del conocimiento: formas, dinámicas y contenido. Un enfoque de redes* (Instituto de Investigaciones Sociales, UNAM, 2003).

HORACIO MACKINLAY is Research Professor in the Department of Sociology at the Universidad Autónoma Metropolitana-Iztapalapa in Mexico City. During 1998–1999 he was a Visiting Research Fellow at the Center for U.S.–Mexican Studies. His research and publications have focused principally upon the impact that the privatization of state-owned firms has had on small agricultural producers in Mexico.

BEATRIZ MAGALONI is Assistant Professor of Political Science at Stanford University. She previously taught in the departments of political science at the Instituto Tecnológico Autónomo de México in Mexico City and the University of California, Los Angeles. Her research has focused upon political economy, democratization, and political institutions.

KEVIN J. MIDDLEBROOK is Reader in Latin American Politics at the Institute of Latin American Studies, University of London. Between 1995 and 2001 he was director of the Center for U.S.–Mexican Studies at the University of California, San Diego. He is the author of *The Paradox of Revolution: Labor, the State, and Authoritarianism in Mexico* (Johns Hopkins University Press, 1995) and editor or coeditor of, among other works, *The United States and Latin America in the 1980s: Contending Perspectives on a Decade of Crisis* (University of Pittsburgh Press, 1986),

The Politics of Economic Restructuring: State-Society Relations and Regime Change in Mexico (Center for U.S.–Mexican Studies, University of California, San Diego, 1994), *Electoral Observation and Democratic Transitions in Latin America* (Center for U.S.–Mexican Studies, 1998), *Conservative Parties, the Right, and Democracy in Latin America* (Johns Hopkins University Press, 2000), *Party Politics and the Struggle for Democracy in Mexico: National and State-Level Analyses of the Partido Acción Nacional* (Center for U.S.–Mexican Studies, 2001), and *Confronting Development: Assessing Mexico's Economic and Social Policy Challenges* (Stanford University Press and Center for U.S.–Mexican Studies, 2003).

ALBERTO J. OLVERA is Director of the Institute of Historical and Social Research at the Universidad Veracruzana in Jalapa, Veracruz. He has held teaching positions at the Universidade Federal de Minas Gerais in Brazil and the Universidad Nacional de Colombia, and in 2002 he was a Visiting Research Fellow at the Center for U.S.–Mexican Studies at the University of California, San Diego. Professor Olvera is author of *Movimientos sociales pro-democráticos, democratización y esfera pública en México: el caso de la Alianza Cívica* and editor of *La sociedad civil: de la teoría a la realidad* (El Colegio de México, 1999) and *Sociedad civil, espacios públicos y democratización en América Latina* (Fondo de Cultura Económica and Universidad Veracruzana, 2002), as well as several essays on civil society and democratization in Mexico.

JEFFREY A. WELDON is Professor of Political Science at the Instituto Tecnológico Autónomo de México in Mexico City. His publications on legislative politics and electoral systems in Mexico include articles in *Estudios Sociológicos, Nexos, Perfiles Latinoamericanos*, and *Revista Mexicana de Sociología*, as well as numerous chapters in edited books.

GUILLERMO ZEPEDA is Research Analyst at the Centro de Investigación para el Desarrollo, A.C. (CIDAC) in Mexico City. An attorney by training, he previously taught legal sociology at the Universidad de Guadalajara. His research focuses upon rule-of-law issues (judicial reform, penal justice, and legal culture), crime, and human rights in Mexico. He is the author of *La procuración de justicia penal en México* (Instituto de Investigaciones Jurídicas, Universidad Nacional Autónoma de México / CIDAC, 2003).

Index